INTERVENTION
INTO THE 1990s

INTERVENTION INTO THE 1990s

U.S. Foreign Policy in the Third World

———— Second Edition ————

edited by

Peter J. Schraeder

Lynne Rienner Publishers • Boulder & London

Published in the United States of America in 1992 by
Lynne Rienner Publishers, Inc.
1800 30th Street, Boulder, Colorado 80301

and in the United Kingdom by
Lynne Rienner Publishers, Inc.
3 Henrietta Street, Covent Garden, London WC2E 8LU

Library of Congress Cataloging-in-Publication Data
Intervention into the 1990s : U.S. foreign policy in the Third World /
    edited by Peter J. Schraeder.
    Rev. ed. of: Intervention in the 1980s. c1989.
    Includes bibliographical references and index.
    ISBN 1-55587-292-1
    1. Developing countries—Foreign relations—United States.
    2. United States—Foreign relations—Developing countries.
    3. United States—Foreign relations administration. 4. United
    States—Foreign relations—1989– 5. Intervention (International
    law) I. Schraeder, Peter J. II. Intervention in the 1980s.
    D888.U615   1992
    327.730172'4—dc20   92-5190
                                                                  CIP

British Cataloguing in Publication Data
A Cataloguing in Publication record for this book
is available from the British Library.

Printed and bound in the United States of America

The paper used in this publication meets the requirements
of the American National Standard for Permanence of
Paper for Printed Library Materials Z39.48-1984.

To Tom, Laura, and Tommy Montbriand

Contents

Tables

Preface

The genesis of the first edition of this book, *Intervention in the 1980s: U.S. Foreign Policy in the Third World* (1989), was a shared desire of the contributors to write a systematic analysis of U.S. interventionist practices in the Third World. Since the appearance of that volume, a radical realtering of the international system—most notably marked by the fragmentation of the Soviet Union and its replacement by several independent and noncommunist countries—has challenged many of the assumptions shared by policymakers, the informed public, and scholars and policy analysts such as ourselves. And, as evident from the unfolding of Operation Desert Storm, the largest U.S. military operation in the post-Vietnam era, this realtering of the international system seemingly has had a dramatic effect on U.S. interventionist practices in the Third World. For example, it is difficult to imagine the landing of over 400,000 troops in a region considered to be so strategically important to the former Soviet Union during either the height of the Cold War or even as late as the mid-1980s. Moreover, this operation was carried out against a close Soviet ally that had been a major recipient of economic and military aid. As a result, we believe the time is ripe to reassess the findings of our initial volume in order to contribute to the growing debate over the proper role of the United States in the emerging post–Cold War era. Specifically, *Intervention into the 1990s: U.S. Foreign Policy in the Third World* offers a comprehensive overview of the origins, tools, and constraints of U.S. intervention in the Third World during the post–World War II era, with special attention devoted to the impact of the end of the Cold War on these interventionist practices.

*   *   *

As editor of this volume, I have the distinct pleasure of acknowledging those who contributed to its successful completion. I gladly take full responsibility for any remaining deficiencies. First and foremost, I wish to thank the authors, who cheerfully revised their original submissions. As readers of the first edition will remark, three new case studies of U.S. intervention have also been added to the current volume: the Persian Gulf (Chapter 18), Panama (Chapter 19), and the Arab-Israeli conflict

xi

(Chapter 20). To our great sadness, one of the coauthors of the South Africa chapter, Gwendolen M. Carter, died in February 1991 after a long illness. The current coauthors are deeply indebted to Gwen for the understanding and insights she provided on South African politics over her long career as an Africanist scholar. The chapter on South Africa is dedicated to her memory.

All eighteen of us enjoyed the support of numerous individuals— administrative staff, colleagues, family members, research assistants, and students—who were crucial in contributing to the final product but whose numbers preclude personal recognition. At the very least, it is important to recognize the efforts of Bonnie Juettner and Mike Walsh, my two graduate research assistants, and Miegen Lesher, a secretary in the Department of Political Science, who carried out many tasks associated with the completion of the manuscript. It is also important to thank for their efforts Peter Papadopoulas, Debbie Giuliano, and Sabina Paredes, three employees at Loyola's Computer Center, whose skills averted a computer crisis just days before the manuscript was to be submitted! And, at Lynne Rienner Publishers a highly skilled and supportive staff enhanced the readability and coherence of the ideas presented. To all these individuals, we extend a heartfelt thank you.

Peter J. Schraeder
Loyola University
of Chicago

◼ Part 1
INTRODUCTION

■ 1

Studying U.S. Intervention in the Third World

Peter J. Schraeder

A series of dramatic international events at the beginning of the 1990s seriously called into question the ways in which scholars, policymakers, and individual citizens perceived the world. Among the most significant of these was the decline of Communist party rule in the Soviet Union, a process that led not only to the overthrow of similar single-party regimes in Eastern Europe and the various regions of the Third World but also to the fragmentation of the Soviet Union itself into a host of smaller independent and noncommunist countries. Other aspects of the rapidly changing international environment at the beginning of the 1990s included the reunification of Germany and its assumption of a dominant role in Central Europe; the rising strength of an increasingly integrated European Community (EC); the spread of democratization movements in Africa and other regions of the world; and the rising influence of Japan as an economic superpower with an increasingly prevalent political agenda. Although this critical turning point in world history offers tremendous opportunities, particularly the possibility of replacing Cold War confrontation with a greater sensitivity to a host of development problems in the Third World, it is also ushering in an emerging post–Cold War era replete with problems as old as history itself, such as rising ethnic conflict, religious fundamentalism, and economic nationalism. To these one can add a variety of more recent but equally threatening problems: nuclear proliferation, chemical weapons production, and the spread of international drug cartels.

As policymakers prepare to guide the United States into the twenty-first century, the time seems ripe for a critical examination of over fifty years of U.S. interventionist practices in the Third World during the post–World War II era. The primary purpose of this book is to assess the shortcomings of these policies in the hope that an understanding of past mistakes may provide the basis for a more enlightened foreign policy of the future. This is no mere academic exercise. Ill-conceived policies have had severe consequences for

1

U.S. society as a whole, the most notable example being U.S. involvement in the Vietnam War. More recently, the Iran-contra affair led to an exceptionally vociferous public debate in which the Reagan White House found itself accused of covertly trading arms for U.S. hostages held in Iran—a significant reversal for an administration that claimed it would never "deal" with terrorists.

An equally important purpose of this book is to contribute to the ongoing debate in official policymaking circles and academia and among the general public as to what should constitute a proper U.S. foreign policy in the Third World during the post–Cold War era. It is only by reasoned debate that a policy consensus—the basis for an effective foreign policy in a democracy—can be achieved.

This chapter is devoted to answering three basic questions frequently asked by those interested in learning more about U.S. interventionist practices in the Third World: What are the meanings of "intervention" and "Third World"? Why study about U.S. intervention in the Third World? What are the themes that guide this study? A final section offers an overview of the chapters that follow.

■ WHAT ARE THE MEANINGS OF "INTERVENTION" AND "THIRD WORLD"?

Any discussion of U.S. intervention in the Third World first requires a brief explanation of what is meant by "intervention" and "Third World." Both concepts are widely used and are potentially confusing, meaning many different things to many different people.

"Intervention" is most commonly understood to mean the use of military force by one country to interfere in the internal affairs of another country. A classic example would be the Bush administration's invasion of Panama in 1989 to remove the unpopular military government of Panamanian dictator Manuel Antonio Noriega. This narrow definition may be expanded to include the use of economic force, such as the U.S. adoption of economic sanctions in 1990 to pressure Iraq to end its illegal occupation of Kuwait, an act that served as a prelude to direct U.S. military intervention in 1991. In an even broader sense, intervention may be defined as any form of interference with the domestic policies of a country. It has been argued, for example, that President Jimmy Carter's mere declaration in 1979 of his administration's support for the presidential aspirations of South Korea's Lieutenant Colonel Chun Doo Hwan actually prompted Chun to assume the presidency by military force.[1] In the extreme, the definition of intervention could even include the absence of foreign policy behavior in some situations. For example, if Israel were subjected to an extended military conflict with all of its Arab neighbors, complete U.S. neutrality most likely would ensure Israeli defeat. Although the United States would not have physically intervened, its inaction—contrary to Israeli expectations—would be crucial in determining the outcome of the conflict.

For the purposes of this book, intervention is defined in a broad sense as the calculated use of political, economic, and military instruments by one country to influence the domestic or the foreign policies of another country. Four important aspects of this definition stand out. First, intervention is seen as purposeful, underscoring the intentional nature of the act. Second, intervention entails a wide choice of instruments ranging from the extension of economic and military aid to economic sanctions, covert action, paramilitary interference, and, finally, direct application of military force. Third, attempts to influence a country's domestic or foreign policies need not be restricted to efforts to change those policies but may also support a given regime in order to insulate it from change. Finally, intervention is not limited to affecting the domestic politics of a given country but can be undertaken to affect that country's foreign policy as well. This broad definition of intervention is adopted to capture the richness of U.S. actions in the Third World.

"Third World" is a popular label for the majority of the world's countries in Africa, Asia, Latin America, and the Middle East that historically belonged neither to the "First World" (the United States and other industrialized capitalist nations, including Australia, Canada, Japan, and Western Europe) nor the "Second World" (the former communist countries of the Soviet Union and Eastern Europe). The concept of a Third World arose from these countries' wish to pursue a third, "nonaligned" path of development during the Cold War period, independent of the political-military wishes of either the Soviet Union or the United States. Implicit in this approach was a desire to draw attention to the economic inequalities between the industrialized North (including both the First and Second Worlds) and the developing South (the Third World) and to the need for a restructuring of North-South economic relations through plans like the New International Economic Order (NIEO).[2]

Several characteristics further distinguish the Third World from the industrialized North.[3] Typically former colonies, Third World countries exhibit low levels of industrialization, lack well-developed infrastructures in terms of transportation, energy, education, and social services, and exhibit large inequities in the distribution of wealth and resources. Moreover, they often are saddled by high rates of population growth, are unable to bring the majority of their populations into the formal economy, and rely on a single agricultural or mineral export to sustain their economies. Most important, the combination of these factors contributes to the economic and political fragility of Third World regimes, making their systems highly vulnerable to intervention. This state of affairs has been described as one of "dependency" in which the northern industrialized countries not only control the destinies of their neighbors to the south, but have contributed to the "underde-velopment" of their economies and political systems.[4]

Despite the common label and shared characteristics of dependency, the Third World is not a homogeneous group of countries with identical interests. Rather, it constitutes a highly heterogeneous set of countries divided along numerous lines—ideological, ethnic, religious, and economic.[5] Ideology, or the principles and assumptions that guide the formation of a nation's domestic and foreign policies, has served as a tremendous barrier to effective Third World cooperation. In the case of Central America, for example, Marxism served as the inspiration for the Faribundo Martí Front for National Liberation (FMLN), a guerrilla group that sought to overthrow the ruling government of El Salvador. The actions of this group contributed to an intense ideological conflict between El Salvador and Nicaragua, with the El Salvadoran leadership accusing the Nicaraguans of supporting the FMLN. Similarly, the Marxist-inspired policies of the former Sandinista government of Nicaragua made that country a flash point of Cold War conflict between the United States and the Soviet bloc during the 1980s. One outcome of this conflict was the polarization of Central America along ideological lines.

Ethnic differences constitute an equally important point of division both within and between Third World countries. In the case of Africa, arbitrarily drawn colonial boundaries formalized during the independence period of the 1960s often did not coincide with the wishes of the local peoples. As a result, almost every African country comprises numerous ethnic groups that, at best, had never sought significant relations and, at worst, were historical rivals. In the case of Nigeria, composed of three major (Yoruba, Ibo, and Hausa-Fulani) and literally hundreds of minor ethnic groups, the result was a brutal civil war in the late 1960s in which the Ibos unsuccessfully sought to secede from the union. At the other extreme are African countries, such as Somalia, that comprise only one ethnic group (Somalis) and have resorted to war (the 1977–1978 Ogaden war with Ethiopia) to reunify peoples of that group who were incorporated into neighboring territories during the colonial period.

Third World countries are also distinguished by religious differences, such as those between Jewish Israel and its Muslim neighbors in the Middle East. As clearly demonstrated by Iraq's unprovoked Scud missile attacks against Israel during the 1991 Persian Gulf war, these religious differences are often manipulated by leaders for national gain. In fact, deep divisions within major religions have sometimes exacerbated historical rivalries. Among the factors that contributed to the bloody Iran-Iraq War of the 1980s was the animosity between the dominant Sunni Muslim regime in Iraq and its Shia counterpart in Iran.

Economic factors, particularly levels of economic development, also divide Third World countries. Within Asia, some countries (such as Indonesia) may be members of the oil-rich Organization of Petroleum

Exporting Countries (OPEC) or be one of the Newly Industrializing Countries (NICs), such as the four so-called Asian tigers: Hong Kong, Singapore, South Korea, and Taiwan. And, countries such as Bangladesh belong to what the World Bank has termed the "Fourth World," or the "poorest of the world's poor."

The often dramatic similarities and differences among the southern developing countries lie at the heart of an ongoing debate over the relevance of even using the "Third World" label. As demonstrated by a series of articles published in *Third World Quarterly,* such as a 1987 contribution titled "Why 'Third World'?: Origin, Definition and Usage," the debate over usage of this term most assuredly will continue.[6] Indeed, with the collapse of communism and the fragmentation of the Soviet Union into several smaller republics, the Second World seemingly no longer exists (although some argue that this label should be retained to distinguish the former communist bloc countries that are industrialized). Moreover, despite levels of industrialization that perhaps require inclusion of these countries under the First World label, other characteristics, such as growing ethnic turmoil and dependence on the West, favor their inclusion in the Third World category. Although for the purposes of this book the term "Third World"—referring to the lesser-developed regions of Africa, Asia, Latin America, and the Middle East—is retained as a useful distinction for an analysis of U.S. intervention, one should not lose sight of the characteristics that divide the countries included in this grouping.

■ **WHY STUDY U.S. INTERVENTION IN THE THIRD WORLD?**

U.S. scholars and policymakers traditionally have paid greater attention to U.S. foreign policy toward the industrialized countries of Western Europe and the West, as well as toward the former communist bloc countries of the Soviet Union and Eastern Europe, to the detriment of the study of U.S. interventionist practices in the Third World. This Europe-centric tendency was reinforced in the 1990s by three important events: the reunification of Germany, the growing integration of Western Europe, and the fragmentation of the Soviet Union. Yet the study of U.S. interventionist practices in the Third World has become increasingly important during the post–World War II era for five reasons:

☐ *The Third World Constitutes an Increasingly Important Focal Point for U.S. Trade and Investment*

According to the U.S. Department of Commerce, imports from Third World countries in 1988 totaled $164.2 billion, or 37.2 percent of the $441.3

billion in total U.S. imports. Similarly, U.S. exports to the Third World in 1988 totaled $114.5 billion, or 35.7 percent of the $320.4 billion in total U.S. exports. Moreover, U.S. direct private investment in the Third World during 1988 exceeded $78 billion, or 23.9 percent of total U.S. private investment in the world, earning nearly $7 billion for U.S. private industry (nearly 32 percent of all U.S. profits earned from overseas private investment).[7] This trend was not unique to the United States, but was indicative of the Third World's rising fortunes throughout the 1980s. According to a United Nations (UN) study published in 1991, foreign direct investment in the Third World rose 22 percent annually from 1985 to 1989, a significant increase in the 3 percent annual growth rate for the years 1980–1984. According to this report, the five largest targets of foreign direct investment in 1989 were Singapore, the PRC (People's Republic of China), Brazil, Mexico, and Hong Kong.[8]

This gradual shift in U.S. financial interests is perhaps best reflected by the changes in the extension of U.S. government foreign grants and credits overseas since the end of World War II. From 1945 to 1955, the lion's share of U.S. grants and credits were targeted toward the reconstruction and economic rehabilitation of war-torn Western Europe. Delivered under the sponsorship of the Marshall Plan, over 63 percent (nearly $34 billion) of U.S. government grants and credits went to Western Europe. By the late 1980s, however, Western Europe was receiving a mere 1.8 percent of these resources, whereas the various regions of the Third World were the recipients of nearly 90 percent. Although northern industrialized countries remain the premier economic partners of the United States—indeed, the collapse of communism in the former Soviet Union and Eastern Europe has led to a dramatic rise in investment capital flowing to these regions—there can be no doubt that the Third World will become increasingly important in the economic calculations of U.S. policymakers.

☐ *The Third World Is a Theater for*
   Conflict of Increasing Scope and Intensity

Prior to 1945, the center of conflict in the world was Europe—two world wars were fought there in the first half of the twentieth century. In the second half of this century, however, the major portion of conflict moved to the Third World. As the 1980s drew to a close, a cursory overview of Third World conflict turned up wars between Cambodia and Vietnam, Iran and Iraq, and Libya and Chad; domestic uprisings in the search for national self-determination by black nationalists in South Africa, Palestinian nationalists in the Middle East, and Tamil separatists in Sri Lanka; and civil wars in Afghanistan, Angola, El Salvador, Ethiopia, Nicaragua, and the Philippines. Although U.S.-Soviet competition during the Cold War period was a major element behind the growing intensity of these conflicts, increasingly significant for the post–Cold War era of the 1990s is the rise of regional powers attempting to pursue strategies of regional hegemony (i.e., domination), often through the use of military force. Among the most noted examples of such aspirations at the beginning of the 1990s was Iraq's 1990 invasion of Kuwait. Other examples of potential regional hegemonic powers include Brazil (South America), Nigeria (West Africa), South Africa (southern Africa), India (South Asia), Vietnam (Southeast Asia), and Saudi Arabia (Middle East). This trend toward the diffusion of power within the international system has been complemented by the growing salience of nationalism, ethnic strife, and religion in contributing to regional conflict in the Third World.

A number of global military trends—what one author has called the "deadly convergence"—at the end of the 1980s clearly demonstrate why the Third World undoubtedly will be the theater for conflict of increasing scope and intensity, especially in a post–Cold War era.[9] First, the conventional arms trade greatly expanded as Third World countries imported record numbers ($381 billion) of increasingly sophisticated weaponry between 1981 and 1988).[10] A second, more deadly trend was the increased proliferation of nuclear weapons technology. In addition to the five declared nuclear powers of the 1960s (Britain, France, the PRC, the Soviet Union, and the United States), during the 1970s and the 1980s four countries (Israel, India, Pakistan, and South Africa) developed de facto nuclear weapons capabilities, while several others (Argentina, Brazil, Iran, Iraq, Libya, Taiwan, and North and South Korea) launched programs clearly designed to develop a nuclear weapons capability.[11] The obvious threat posed by nuclear proliferation, enhanced even more so by the breakup of the massive Soviet nuclear arsenal among several independent republics at the beginning of the 1990s, was matched by a third trend: the spread of chemical weapons technology. And, the acquisition and development of sophisticated missiles and aircraft provided Third World countries with a greater capability to deliver these conventional, chemical, and nuclear weapons systems over longer distances.[12] As demonstrated by the 1991 Persian Gulf war against Iraq—a formerly rising regional hegemonic power embodying all four of these trends—the origins and theater of any future world war involving the United States very likely could be in the Third World.

□ *U.S. Strategic Planning Is Being*
   Reoriented Toward the Third World

U.S. strategic thinking in the 1980s began to question the traditional emphasis on preparing for a conventional, full-scale military conflict in Western Europe and focused more on the rise of "low-intensity conflict"

(LIC) in the Third World. As a result, U.S. military strategists began to emphasize the need for the United States to reorient its military capabilities to deal with this "unconventional" threat. Secretary of Defense Caspar Weinberger captured this growing sentiment within the military establishment in his 1987 annual report to Congress:

> Today there seems no shortage of adversaries who seek to undermine our security by persistently nibbling away at our interests through these shadow wars carried on by guerrillas, assassins, terrorists, and subversives in the hope that they have found a weak point in our defenses . . . these forms of aggression will remain the most likely and the most enduring threats to our security.[13]

This type of thinking obviously received a major boost in the 1990s as the fragmentation of the Soviet Union removed the greatest perceived threat to the national security of the United States. Clearly unwilling to accept quietly the inevitable budget cuts destined to accompany the end of the Cold War, those seeking to maintain a strong defense establishment pushed the threats posed by LIC and radical Third World leaders to the forefront of a rising domestic debate. In this regard, the 1991 Persian Gulf war against Iraqi leader Saddam Hussein, described by administration officials as the "Hitler" of the 1990s, was successfully used by these same officials to partially stem rising domestic calls for dramatic cuts in military budget outlays.

The net result of this shift in the policy debate at the beginning of the 1990s was the continued development of LIC doctrine and the expansion of "projection forces" (such as the army's Green Berets and the navy's SEALs, or sea-air-land commandos) especially designed to take part in a host of military operations within the Third World. Divided into eight major categories that are discussed at length in Chapter 3, these operations include counterinsurgency (aid to an allied government to defeat a guerrilla insurgency); proinsurgency (aid designed to foster a guerrilla insurgency against a foreign government); peacetime contingency operations (such as short-term rescue missions); terrorism counteraction; antidrug operations; pacification or control of ethnic conflicts; humanitarian assistance; and military civic action. Two fundamental assumptions lie at the heart of this rising strategic emphasis within the U.S. policymaking establishment: (1) Vital U.S. interests are threatened by radical and revolutionary violence in the Third World; and (2) the United States must be prepared to use military force to protect these interests. As Michael T. Klare argues in Chapter 3, just as a growing emphasis on counterinsurgency during the 1960s led to increasing U.S. involvement in Vietnam, so the current evolution in strategic thinking ensures that LIC "will be an increasing U.S. strategic concern of the 1990s, potentially leading to ever-increasing U.S. involvement in regional conflicts."

☐   *Official Recognition of Strategic Interests in the Third*
     World Provides the Basis for Increased U.S. Intervention

The designation of individual Third World countries or regions as "vital" to U.S. strategic interests continues to provide the basis for U.S. intervention to safeguard these interests. The Carter Doctrine, for example, identified the continued flow of oil from the Persian Gulf as one of the paramount strategic interests of the United States, to be defended with U.S. military force if necessary. This doctrine served as the basis for the 1987 Reagan administration policy of reflagging Kuwaiti oil tankers in the Persian Gulf, as well as U.S. involvement in the 1991 Persian Gulf war against Iraq, a conflict that led to the deployment of over 400,000 U.S. troops and the most massive intervention abroad since the Vietnam War. Among the other examples of perceived strategic interests that have led to U.S. intervention in the Third World throughout the post–World War II period are the critical importance of maintaining stability in the U.S. "backyard" (the Caribbean and Central America), a factor that led to the 1983 military invasion of Grenada and the promotion of the contra war against the Sandinista government of Nicaragua during the 1980s; the maintenance of a free and open Panama Canal, one of the many rationales offered for the 1989 military invasion of Panama; continued Western access to strategic minerals in southern Africa, the basis for close U.S. relations with the apartheid regime of South Africa from the 1940s to the 1980s until Congress (over executive-branch objections) passed sanctions in 1986 in the form of the Comprehensive Anti-Apartheid Act; and the maintenance of Western control over strategic maritime "choke points" (such as the Straits of Bab el Mandeb in northeastern Africa), an interest that partially underscored U.S. rationales for providing nearly $800 million in economic and military assistance to Somali dictator Siyaad Barre before his overthrow at the beginning of 1991.

Although individuals from all points of the ideological spectrum agree that the United States has strategic interests worth defending in the Third World, differences arise over where they are, their relative level of importance, and the proper means of maintaining their integrity. For example, although the conservative Committee on the Present Danger considers the Persian Gulf to be a region of vital strategic importance to the United States and favored the Bush administration's 1991 war against Iraq, policy analysts from the libertarian Cato Institute questioned both the strategic value of the Persian Gulf to the United States and the war itself. Even when these two schools of thought have agreed upon a region of vital strategic importance to the United States (such as Central America), policy prescriptions greatly differed. Whereas the Committee on the Present Danger favored expanding U.S. support for the contras to overthrow the Sandinista regime in Nicaragua, the Cato Institute viewed such a policy as counterproductive to long-term U.S. foreign policy interests in the region.[14]

Despite these differences, the fact remains that the official designation of areas of vital strategic importance provides the basis for increased U.S. intervention in the Third World.

☐ *U.S. Intervention in the Third World Has Had a Spillover Effect into U.S. Society*

Perhaps the most important reason for studying U.S. intervention in the Third World is to understand the effects it has had on U.S. institutions and society. In the case of the Vietnam War, for example, the wiretaps initiated to uncover who had leaked highly sensitive information pertaining to secret U.S. B-52 bombing raids into Cambodia gradually mushroomed into the Watergate scandal, which drove Richard Nixon from the presidency.[15] The Iranian hostage crisis revealed the seeming impotence of the Carter administration in protecting U.S. citizens abroad, contributing to President Carter's ultimate defeat and the subsequent election of Ronald Reagan in the 1980 presidential elections. U.S. intervention in Nicaragua under the Reagan administration led to the Iran-contra affair, which led to further straining of relations between the executive branch and Congress over the proper role each should play in the foreign-policymaking process. And, the Bush administration found itself attacked by both liberals and conservatives during the 1992 election campaign for his administration's failure during the Persian Gulf war to remove Saddam Hussein from power and, subsequently, protect Iraq's Kurdish minority when they unsuccessfully rebelled against the Iraqi regime. In short, U.S. intervention in the Third World has contributed to U.S. domestic crises of legitimacy.

Moreover, the study of U.S. foreign policy in the Third World will aid in clarifying and understanding past U.S. failures and in providing the basis for formulating future policy prescriptions. The most destructive of these failures was U.S. involvement in the Vietnam War: Social costs included over 350,000 U.S. casualties (including approximately 58,000 dead) and the erosion of the social fabric of U.S. society; experts have estimated that the cumulative economic costs of carrying out the war exceeded $220 billion.[16] Vietnam was not unique, but rather is indicative of a foreign policy whereby the United States has intervened in numerous Third World civil wars during the post–World War II period.[17]

Foreign policy failures are not endemic to a particular president or political party but may be found throughout the post–World War II era: Presidents Dwight D. Eisenhower and John F. Kennedy organized and carried out the unsuccessful Bay of Pigs invasion of Cuba in 1961; Lyndon B. Johnson became increasingly mired in a losing war in Vietnam; Nixon expanded the Vietnam War to Cambodian territory, prompting ever greater unrest in the United States; Gerald R. Ford involved the United States in a losing civil war in Angola; Carter continued a faulty policy toward Iran and the shah that ended in disaster; Reagan suffered a major policy defeat in Lebanon when terrorists killed several hundred U.S. Marines with a truck bomb; and Bush, despite initial public support for his handling of the Persian Gulf war, found his administration increasingly criticized for its failure to remove Saddam Hussein from power. Only by understanding the past—while recognizing that no two case studies are exactly alike—can one look to the future.

■ WHAT ARE THE THEMES THAT GUIDE THIS STUDY?

Five themes serve as the intellectual guidepoints of the twenty-one chapters of this book:

□ *Overemphasis in U.S. Foreign Policy on What Has Been Titled the Globalist Perspective*

The globalist vision, which dominated U.S. foreign policy in the Third World during the post–World War II period, stressed the central importance of East-West confrontation at all levels of the international system, relegating Third World countries to the role of pawns in the greater East-West conflict. According to proponents of this viewpoint, oppressive social conditions, such as the lack of land reform or government indifference to human welfare, were not the primary causes of revolution and other forms of social conflict in Third World countries from the 1940s to the 1980s. Rather, revolution and social conflict were primarily caused by communist aggression led by the Soviet Union.

This globalist logic assumed that radical revolutionary regimes (for example, Nicaragua), along with the Soviet Union, could successfully export revolution to other areas of the Third World and conjured up visions of falling dominoes once a radical regime had established itself in any given region. In the case of Central America and the Caribbean, for example, the revolutionary government of Fidel Castro was perceived as facilitating the creation in 1979 of a communist "beachhead" (the Sandinista government in Nicaragua) in Central America. This development, unless vigorously countered by Washington, was perceived as leading to the downfall of U.S. allies in neighboring countries (El Salvador, Guatemala, and Costa Rica) and their replacement with communist regimes. In the extreme, the metaphor of falling dominoes ultimately was perceived as leading to communist rule throughout Central and South America and, possibly, even in the United States itself. Typical of this type of thinking was President Reagan's characterization of revolutionary conflict in the early years of his administration: "Let us not delude ourselves. The Soviet Union underlies all the unrest that is going on. If they weren't involved in this game of dominoes, there wouldn't be any hotspots in the world."[18]

But history does not support this proposition. Successful revolutionary movements usually fight at first with weapons acquired locally, often from opposing forces; external arms generally do not arrive until the guerrillas have proven themselves on the battlefield.[19] For example, Fidel Castro received Soviet military support only after the Cuban revolution was won, and Vietnam's Ho Chi Minh initially armed his forces with Japanese and French arsenals captured during World War II. In fact, when Castro attempted to export revolution to Central America during the 1960s, he met with failure: The guerrilla forces were easily defeated because of their inability to attract a major following. The example of the Sandinista-led revolution in Nicaragua during the 1960s is especially instructive. Although the Sandinista National Liberation Front (FSLN) received Cuban arms during the 1960s, this aid was discontinued in the early 1970s and did not begin again until the insurrection against Somoza was already well under way.[20]

This is not to say, however, that external powers—whether a communist Soviet Union of the 1980s, a noncommunist Russia of the 1990s, or a radical Third World leader, such as Libya's Muammar Qaddafi—cannot exacerbate or profit from revolutionary upheaval within a given Third World country. Rather, this evidence underscores the misplaced emphasis on these external powers as the causes for regional turmoil, once the social, economic, and political conditions for revolution are ripe. As distinguished specialists on Central America have noted,

> . . . those who point to external assistance as responsible for exploiting internal problems often miss the depth of these internal problems. It is not poverty and inequality that suddenly get ignited by outside arms and ideas; it is the brutal suppression of attempts at nonviolent reform by oligarchs and officers that moves numbers of people to pick up arms and risk their lives to make revolutions. By pointing to insurgents who seek outside arms, policymakers in Washington mistake symptoms for causes and justify aid for the very military and security forces whose opposition to reform generated armed insurgency in the first place.[21]

□ Desirability of a U.S. Foreign Policy that Emphasizes a Regionalist Perspective

Rather than placing undue emphasis on external forces as the chief provocateurs of conflict and instability in the Third World, the regionalist approach emphasizes the internal economic, cultural, political, and historical roots of these upheavals. According to proponents of the regionalist approach, several internal conditions have led to the downfall of numerous Third World regimes: increasing income gaps between rich and poor; accumulation of vast wealth by the ruling family through personal control of major aspects of the economy; accentuated mass poverty (from already low levels) in the rural areas and urban shantytowns; limited access to basic social services; lack of meaningful political participation for the majority of the population; exclusion of the rising middle class from sharing in the political and economic benefits enjoyed by the ruling class; lack of equitable land reform; and government suppression of peaceful attempts at reform.[22]

Focus on the internal causes of a particular conflict lends importance to that conflict in its own right and renders it amenable to resolution based on internal political and economic reforms. For example, in the case of mounting guerrilla insurgency in Rhodesia (now Zimbabwe) during the late 1970s, the Carter administration supported Great Britain's initiatives in pressuring the white minority regime of Ian Smith to accept universal suffrage and transition to black majority rule—even though this ensured a regime dominated by the Patriotic Front, a coalition of two guerrilla groups led by avowed Marxists and supplied by the Soviet Union and the PRC. By avoiding the traditional U.S. reflex to attribute the growing guerrilla conflict to Soviet-Cuban interference and to back the beleaguered government, the United States correctly perceived that resolution of the conflict depended on internal political and economic reforms and that its influence could aid in bringing such a settlement about. The United States was rewarded for pursuing this policy. Despite the Marxist rhetoric of Zimbabwe's Prime Minister Robert Mugabe, he has clearly followed a pragmatic policy of socioeconomic reform and maintained extensive links with the West.[23]

The regionalist logic may be applied to many other examples. In El Salvador, as has been argued persuasively, guerrilla insurgency was fueled by lack of agrarian reform and by political repression.[24] In the Horn of Africa, the arbitrary colonial drawing of boundaries significantly contributed to the Somali-Ethiopian conflict over the Ogaden region. In the Middle East, conflict between Iran and Iraq during the 1980s was fueled, in part, by opposing and hostile interpretations of Islam (Shia for the former and Sunni for the latter). In short, the primary theme of the regionalist approach is that although it is important to understand the nature of external involvement within a particular conflict, this dimension should be deemphasized in favor of its internal dimension. Local issues and concerns, not adherence to the ideology of some foreign power, are the primary reasons for conflict and revolution. As a result, correctly argues the regionalist, one must focus primarily on the local level for both the causes and, ultimately, the resolution of any given conflict.[25]

□   *Increasing Nonviability of Military Force in Achieving*
    Long-Term U.S. Foreign Policy Goals in the Third World

The international system and the role of direct military intervention therein by the major powers has changed substantially since the end of World War II. First, one is struck by the way unwritten norms governing the use of military force have been altered in the post–World War II period. For example, when the government of Nicaragua did not pay its debts in the 1930s, the United States sent in its marines to force payment. Yet, it is extremely difficult to conceive of Washington in 1992 dispatching the marines should either Mexico or Brazil decide to default on its substantial loan repayments to the United States. As the interdependence theorists correctly have noted, although military force is "ultimately necessary to guarantee [national] survival" and is therefore a "central component of national power," it is "often not an appropriate way of achieving other goals (such as economic and ecological welfare) that are becoming more important."[26]

A more important constraint is found in the evolution of the Third World itself, whereby former colonial empires have evolved into a system of independent states of widely varying and increasing levels of power. Although the major powers of the colonial era, including the United States, still predominate militarily within the international system, there can be no doubt of the increasing diffusion of power within the system as individual Third World countries acquire more sophisticated weapons systems. As one author has noted:

> Compared to the situation that the colonial powers found in the heydays of imperialism, when a small flotilla of gunboats could manhandle an ancient civilization or conquer disorganized territories, many of today's Third World states wield much more formidable degrees of organized power. . . . While most Third World states may not yet be powerful enough to guarantee their own sovereignty, it has certainly become more problematical for foreign powers arbitrarily to impose their will upon them.[27]

U.S. involvement in the Vietnam War is especially instructive. Whatever lessons may be drawn from U.S. intervention in Vietnam—indeed, there are as many conflicting interpretations as there are days in a month[28]— two themes in particular stand out: (1) Even the most sophisticated levels of military technology make victory against popular revolutionary nationalism, at the least, highly unlikely and, at the most, prohibitively costly; and (2) the U.S. people are not willing to support protracted, direct U.S. military intervention in the Third World. Although the latter condition could potentially change sometime in the future, the former is likely to persist.

□ *U.S. Inability to Control Third World Nationalism*

U.S. intervention against revolutionary nationalism in the Third World during the post–World War II period was based upon the assumption that revolutionary elites were extremely vulnerable to the political wishes of a dominant external power (such as the Soviet Union) in the sense of becoming a "tool" for international communism. *The Pentagon Papers,* for example, dismissed the possibility that Ho Chi Minh or Mao Zedong could be both nationalists and communists.[29] Despite the more sophisticated view of the fragmented nature of international communism that existed in Washington in the 1980s—a result primarily of U.S. recognition of the enduring Sino-Soviet split—U.S. policymakers still viewed with suspicion Third World leaders seeking close relationships with the Soviet Union. This "tool-for-communism" thesis was dubious at best. Although Soviet allies such as Cuba surely followed the Soviet lead when such a course was viewed in Cuba's own national interests, these common interests should not have been construed as Soviet control or ability to dictate policy. History is replete with examples of former so-called Soviet client states—including China, Egypt, Ghana, Indonesia, Somalia, and Sudan—that have expelled the Soviets when the Soviet presence became inimical to the client states' foreign policy interests. In Third World politics, self-interest and nationalism remain stronger than ideological affinity.

The importance of nationalism and self-interested elites in stemming Soviet influence in the Third World from the 1950s to the 1980s is also relevant to U.S. special relationships with various Third World regimes. As was suggested by Panamanian General Manuel Noriega's purported sharing of U.S. military secrets with Cuba, his involvement in the international drug trade, and his clear defiance of U.S. demands in 1988 that he step down, U.S. client states may act against the wishes of Washington. Some authors have argued that, in fact, a case of "reverse dependency" often exists in which the United States falls prey to the demands or interests of the client state.[30] Indeed, a more apt description of Third World elites is that they are relatively independent actors who may act contrary to the wishes of any of the major powers, including the United States.

The failure of U.S. policymakers to comprehend their limited power in controlling Third World nationalism has been especially acute concerning its populist revolutionary variant. Despite Castro's political and economic excesses by Western standards, there should have been little doubt in Washington in 1959 that his revolution generated mass support and ignited Cuban nationalism. Rather than accept the legitimacy of Castro's revolution, the United States attempted to isolate the regime diplomatically, initiated a trade embargo, authorized assassination attempts, and ultimately managed the unsuccessful Bay of Pigs invasion of the island in 1961 by CIA (Central Intelligence Agency)-trained exiles. Rather than overthrow Castro, these actions served as focal points whereby Castro strengthened his position on the island by whipping up "anti-Yankee" nationalism and painting those elements still opposed to his rule as mere lackeys of U.S. imperialism. The lesson to draw from this—which should become the guiding principle for U.S. relations with revolutionary nationalism—is simple: "When a regime has any large degree of popular support and legitimacy, a foreign state's force, pressure, and propaganda directed against the country may only cause the people to rally around their government."[31]

☐ *Need for Greater U.S. Tolerance of Social Change in the Third World, Regardless of Ideology*

Despite the heritage of the United States as a revolutionary nation that fought against oppression and external control, U.S. policymakers have consistently failed to understand the growth of this phenomenon in the Third World. Although the original intent of the Monroe Doctrine, as enunciated in 1823, was to protect Central American revolutions from external influence, these revolutions, and the economic and political instability that accompanied them, were increasingly viewed by U.S. policymakers as injurious to U.S. interests.[32] This regional antirevolutionary propensity became globalized and fused with a virulent anticommunism as the United States embarked on an ideological competition with the Soviet Union at the end of World War II. The net result is that all U.S. administrations in the post–World War II period have been hostile in varying degrees to revolutionary change in the Third World, combining antagonism toward radical regimes with support for traditional authoritarian allies, often with dire consequences for U.S. foreign policy.

The key to U.S. tolerance of social change is recognition that opposing ideologies should not automatically preclude mutually beneficial relationships and that similar ideologies should not automatically provide the basis for strong U.S. support. Indeed, growing U.S. ties with Marxist Mozambique during the latter half of the 1980s, despite U.S. conservative calls to support a noncommunist guerrilla insurgency titled the Mozambique National Resistance (RENAMO),[33] demonstrated that fruitful relationships could be sought with revolutionary communist regimes. To the contrary, the downfall of Fulgencio Batista's Cuban regime and the fallout then experienced by the United States underscored the dangers of supporting a traditional dictator who, although joining the United States in its anti-communist crusade, rules through a repressive regime marked by immense social inequality.

■ **OVERVIEW**

This book is divided into five major sections. The first three analyze the origins, tools, and constraints on U.S. intervention in the Third World, and the final two comprise the case studies and a concluding essay.

Part 2, "Origins of Intervention," begins with Lloyd C. Gardner's chapter on the evolution of the interventionist impulse. Gardner shows how the American revolutionary spirit of 1776 and U.S. expansion throughout the

North American continent under the guise of Manifest Destiny spawned a mythic belief in the universalism and innocence of the U.S. cause. According to Gardner, these beliefs led to U.S. expansion beyond the North American continent in the early part of the twentieth century and the globalization of U.S. intervention in the Third World in the immediate post–World War II period. Michael T. Klare, in Chapter 3, continues this historical perspective, tracing the origins and evolution during the post–World War II period of the military doctrine of low-intensity conflict (LIC). Klare also examines the application of LIC doctrine to direct and indirect U.S. military involvement during the 1980s and beyond in eight types of operations in the Third World: counterinsurgency, proinsurgency, peacetime contingency operations, terrorism counteraction, antidrug operations, pacification or control of ethnic conflicts, humanitarian assistance, and military civic action. In Chapter 4, Charles F. Doran examines the nature of the globalist-regionalist debate surrounding the proper role of U.S. intervention in the Third World. Whereas globalists historically stressed "the primacy of East-West confrontation at all levels of international political behavior, in all parts of the international system," regionalists continue to emphasize "the dilemmas of North-South relations, the idiosyncrasies of politics and culture within the various geographic regions, and the comparative autonomy of the struggles that go on within and between the states inside each of these regions." The differences between these divergent perspectives are discussed within three broad categories: the origins of change and stability; foreign policy purpose; and foreign policy strategy and means.

Part 3 centers on the different instruments of intervention that the United States has employed in the pursuit of foreign policy goals in the Third World. Each author explores how Washington's use of a particular instrument has changed or evolved during the post–World War II period, presents the field of case studies in which it has been employed, and asks why it has been successful or unsuccessful. In Chapter 5, Doug Bandow examines Washington's use of official economic and military aid to Third World governments. Kimberly A. Elliott, in Chapter 6, reviews fifty-eight cases of U.S. implementation of economic sanctions. In Chapter 7, Harry Howe Ransom examines U.S. covert intervention in the Third World, including assassination plots, coups d'état, election intervention, and propaganda or psychological warfare. In Chapter 8, Peter J. Schraeder examines Washington's use of paramilitary intervention, or external economic and military aid to guerrilla forces intent on overthrowing a government deemed counter to U.S. foreign policy interests. Ted Galen Carpenter, in Chapter 9, reviews Washington's use of the ultimate interventionist tool: direct military force.

Part 4 consists of four chapters centering on the domestic and international constraints inhibiting successful U.S. intervention in the Third World. In Chapter 10, Jerel A. Rosati presents an analysis of the U.S.

domestic environment, exploring how a domestic consensus built upon the twin themes of anticommunism and containment of the Soviet Union favored an interventionist Third World policy led by the executive branch during much of the post–World War II period. U.S. involvement in Vietnam shattered this consensus, however, making it increasingly difficult for presidents to continue implementing interventionist policies and leading "to such crises of leadership and legitimacy as Watergate, the Iran hostage crisis, and the Iran-contra scandal." In Chapter 11, Stephen Daggett analyzes significant barriers to the effective application of force that persist in the U.S. government—especially within the military establishment—despite recent efforts by some elements of the political leadership and by parts of the military to prepare for armed responses to conflict in the Third World. Among those factors discussed are the interplay between bureaucracy and ideology, priority of large-war planning in the military establishment, bureaucratic politics, and interservice rivalries. In Chapter 12, Harry Piotrowski argues that the evolving structure of the international system increasingly inhibits successful U.S. intervention in the Third World. He focuses on resurgent nationalism and anticolonialism, indigenous applications of Marxism-Leninism, communist polycentrism, proliferation of both conventional and nuclear weapons, the rise of regional powers, and the relative decline of U.S. economic and military power. In Chapter 13, Christopher C. Joyner examines the role of international law and of the internationally accepted norms of intervention and nonintervention. Joyner argues that U.S. policymakers have adopted "convenient legal license to interpret international law such that it serves their own interests as a supportive foreign policy instrument rather than as a force of restraint conducive to a greater public world order."

The case studies presented in Part 5 provide an overview of U.S. interventionist practices in seven Third World countries and regions. Each case study includes a description of the historical nature and evolution of the particular area's relationship with the United States, the instruments that the United States has adopted in pursuit of specific foreign policy goals, why these have been successful or unsuccessful, and general lessons that may be drawn from U.S. involvement. In Chapter 14, R. Hunt Davis, Jr., and Peter J. Schraeder examine U.S. policy toward the apartheid regime of South Africa, particularly focusing on the evolution of the sanctions debate and the viability of economic sanctions in forcing the Afrikaner elite to change their domestic system of governance. In Chapter 15, Richard J. Kessler focuses on the evolution of the U.S.-Philippine relationship as it evolved through successive stages of direct colonial rule, the creation of a patron-client relationship with President Ferdinand Marcos, and the democratic revolution led by Corazon Aquino. Peter Kornbluh, in Chapter 16, analyzes the equally extensive U.S.-Nicaraguan relationship, focusing on how the United States has dealt with what it perceived to be a radical revolution led by the

Sandinistas in Washington's backyard. In Chapter 17, Eric Hooglund examines U.S. intervention in Iran ranging from the landing of 30,000 U.S. troops in that country during World War II, to U.S. involvement in the 1953 coup d'état that restored the shah to power, to U.S. relations with the Islamic governments that followed the Iranian revolution of 1978. Hooglund also is the author of Chapter 18, which is devoted to explaining the evolution of U.S. interventionist practices in the Persian Gulf region that culminated in the Persian Gulf war of 1991. In Chapter 19, Margaret E. Scranton discusses the evolution of the U.S.-Panamanian relationship ranging from U.S. involvement in Panama's revolutionary movement to seek independence from Colombia, to the construction of the Panama Canal, to the 1989 U.S. military invasion to remove General Noriega from power. In Chapter 20, Deborah J. Gerner analyzes the evolution of U.S. involvement in the Arab-Israeli conflict, focusing specifically on U.S. relations with a succession of Israeli governments and the delicate question of seeking an independent Palestinian state. In the final chapter, Peter J. Schraeder draws several conclusions about U.S. intervention in the Third World.

■ Part 2

ORIGINS OF INTERVENTION

■ 2

The Evolution of the Interventionist Impulse

Lloyd C. Gardner

From the first stirrings of nationhood in the middle of the eighteenth century, Americans fixed their gaze outward. It could hardly have been otherwise. Born into an empire that had achieved preeminence among world powers by defeating the French in the Great War for Empire, 1754–1763, leaders in the thirteen colonies on the Atlantic coast expectantly looked forward to exploiting that position to add new lands and wealth to British North America. When London blocked westward expansion, the colonial elite transformed themselves into American nationalists and risked a war of independence rather than abandon their pretensions. Even in the darker moments of the American Revolution, visions of a new empire of liberty extending northward to Canada, southward to Central America and the Caribbean, and westward across the continent fired the cause with a belief in what would be called, in the middle of the following century, the United States' Manifest Destiny.[1]

Fervent belief in Manifest Destiny ensured rapid expansion beyond the initial confines of the thirteen colonies as French and Spanish claims were eliminated by the Louisiana Purchase and the 1819 Trans-Continental Treaty, the British relinquished Oregon, the Mexicans were forced to yield up California, and Russia sold Alaska. By 1900, moreover, Manifest Destiny included expansion beyond the North American continent and produced the Monroe Doctrine, Caribbean hegemony, and acquisition of an island chain across the Pacific to outermost Asia. At the end of World War II, what had been foretold by the American Revolution seemed fulfilled. A French diplomat noted dourly, in 1945, that the United States appeared to interest itself "in everything that was taking place" and further stated that at the recent graduating exercises at Annapolis the new naval officers had "dipped their rings in a vase of water from the seven seas, whereas previously the water for this ritual had come from the Atlantic, the Pacific, and the Caribbean."[2]

■ **THE REVOLUTIONARY SPIRIT
AND WESTERN EXPANSIONISM**

Private fortune and public responsibility went hand in hand in early American expansionist visions. And like other challengers to old ways, Americans had a tendency to believe a special virtue accompanied their ambitions. But prospects for the colonies in commerce and westward expansion suddenly dimmed when London made it clear that the mother country had no intention of turning the West over to the colonials to do with as they pleased. Major disputes arose as Britain pursued colonial reorganization in an effort to make the colonies pay the costs of their own defense, including those associated with the recently concluded Great War for Empire and the continuing conflict with native American Indians. This policy gave rise to suspicions that the mother country was even indifferent to the dangers of "creeping Catholicism" from culturally different French Canada.

What had only yesterday seemed a glorious banner—the British Union Jack—now appeared to symbolize repression and corruption. The bolder colonials were soon debating independence in courthouses and taverns. Behind the irksome restrictions London imposed on colonial trade and the mother country's suddenly timid attitude toward the Indians—it was now being said—lurked a calculated effort to deprive the colonies of their future.

Nearly two hundred years later, Secretary of State Dean Acheson explained how the Founding Fathers had arrived at the conclusion that independence was the only solution. "The whole mercantile system was irritating," he noted in a brief lesson for fellow diplomats,

> whereby trade had to go through the center at London and could not take place directly between the colonies and other trading points. . . . At every point they were met by restrictions imposed on the ruling, powerful, directing groups by a government which was far away and, most important of all, had shown its inability to govern. . . . What happens when people who want to resist want support? They generalize their position. They don't ask support to fight against timber restrictions. They talk about taxation without representation, and each generalization leads to broader generalizations. Until finally they get to the broadest generalization; which is that all men are created equal.[3]

So it seemed at the time to Benjamin Franklin. Like the Virginia planter George Washington, Franklin had heavy investments, both material and spiritual, in western lands. The Philadelphia printer, who by 1767 had risen to high office as deputy postmaster for the colonies, and who was regarded on both sides of the Atlantic as perhaps the best thinker the new world had produced, had developed a powerful vision of what settlements in the Illinois country would yield the Americans, with or without their British forebears. Occupation of that territory, he lectured correspondents in the mother country, would allow the holder to raise a force, "which on occasion of a future war, might easily be poured down the Mississippi upon the lower country, and into the Bay of Mexico, to be used against Cuba, or Mexico itself."[4] Even before they called upon the world to bear witness to the justice of their cause, by officially separating the thirteen colonies from British control in the Declaration of Independence on July 4, 1776, colonial leaders had authorized an attack on British Canada, ordering a hastily assembled army to march northwards in 1775 to overthrow British rule.

The Canadian invasion, like the wars resulting from the French and Russian revolutions, was motivated as much by ideological factors as by military questions. And although the American Revolution did not witness the same profound social upheavals as those in France or Russia, the urge to carry forward its ideals on bayonets gradually melted into what in the nineteenth century would come to be known as Manifest Destiny. In that narrow sense, the "revolutionary spirit" lasted longer in the United States than it did after the Napoleonic Wars or after Stalin's consolidation of Bolshevist Russia into socialism in one state.[5]

As ambassador to France, a key post in the Revolutionary War, Benjamin Franklin devoted himself tirelessly to the game of nations in order to achieve both Canada and the Mississippi for an envisioned American empire on the North American continent. During the protracted peace negotiations, he was adamant that the Mississippi be the new country's western boundary. When the treaty was ready, Franklin and the other negotiators bragged that although the new nation's allies, France and Spain, had sought to "coop up" the Americans, the treaty boundaries "appear to leave us little to complain of and not much to desire."[6]

Actually, the Americans desired a lot more. Franklin had even suggested that it would be "advisable" for the British to cede Canada if they wanted to gain the goodwill of the United States. London laughed at such pretensions. When the Americans came to their senses, they would see that their only option would be to buy their way back into the empire, at least economically, with such concessions as king and Parliament might deem proper for the privilege of trading with His Majesty's subjects in the home islands or anywhere else in the empire.

The shock of independence in a world dominated by mercantilist theory and still-powerful empires did, in fact, sober the Americans. Until things were straightened out at home, it was now argued by those who demanded a strong central government, it was necessary to put aside thoughts of Canada, Florida, and the West Indies. Those who met at the Federal Constitutional Convention in Philadelphia in 1787 to remedy the supposed excesses of individual state action, as George Washington would put it, were divided on many questions. But they all saw a new constitution as an absolute necessity for foreign policy. The Founding Fathers granted the executive powers therein that only a few years before would have been unthinkable, as is clearly demonstrated by the weak federal government established under the original Articles of Confederation ratified in 1781.

The controversial "imperial presidency" was not an invention of post–World War II occupants of the White House. The U.S. Constitution, as every president from Washington on understood, gave the executive a decisive edge over Congress in making foreign policy. When he assumed office in 1801, President Thomas Jefferson declared that the nation had escaped tyranny (which he blamed on Federalist excesses) only because of its large territory. Albert Gallitin, Jefferson's secretary of the treasury, who knew a good deal about frontier democracy, agreed absolutely: "If the cause of the happiness of this country was examined into, it would be found to arise as much from the great plenty of land in proportion to the inhabitants . . . as from the wisdom of their political institutions."[7]

In 1803, Jefferson annexed the Louisiana territory to the United States—almost an empire unto itself—and for $15 million provided the nation with unlimited navigation of the Mississippi River, thereby assuring control of the restless westerners and a strategic position for projecting U.S. power and democracy abroad. Jefferson embodied the fervent belief in the U.S. cause: "Our southern defensive force can take the Floridas, volunteers for a Mexican army will flock to our standard, and rich pabulum will be offered to our privateers in the plunder of their commerce and coasts. Probably Cuba would add itself to our confederation."[8]

A chronicler of the westward movement, Patricia Nelson Limerick, noted that although historians have come to terms with the legacy of slavery, they have yet to do so with the legacy of conquest by which Americans moved across the continent:

> To most twentieth-century Americans, the legacy of slavery was serious business, while the legacy of conquest was not. . . . Conquest took another route into national memory. In the popular imagination, the reality of conquest dissolved into stereotypes of noble savages and noble pioneers struggling quaintly in the wilderness. These adventures seemed to have no bearing on the complex realities of twentieth-century America.[9]

The rationales for U.S. expansionism are not unique; similar stereotypes and rationalizations (which Limerick insightfully calls foundations for an "Empire of Innocence") are notable throughout European writings on Africa and Asia. Not uniqueness, but the deceptive ease of conquest sets the U.S. historical tradition apart, providing Americans with both a false sense of security about their past and an illusory notion that all foreign policy questions are somehow capable of being resolved expeditiously—like Jefferson's straightforward solution to the threatened closing of the port of New Orleans: Buy Louisiana.[10] That sense of security and belief in a unique American innocence, exalted by all U.S. presidents, is captured in President Ronald Reagan's second inaugural address in 1985, in which he called upon

Americans to heed the "echoes of our past" to meet the challenges of the future: "The men of the Alamo call out encouragement to each other; a settler pushes west and sings his song, and the song echoes out forever and fills the unknowing air. It is the American sound: It is hopeful, big-hearted, idealistic—daring, decent and fair. That's our heritage, that's our song. We sing it still. For all our problems, our differences, we are together as of old."[11]

After direct conflict between the United States and Great Britain in the War of 1812, which did not exactly conform to these legendary accounts, and which required promoting some rather dubious victories to boost confidence and erase the memory that the British had burned Washington, the United States found itself in the fortunate position of being able to take advantage of revolutions in Central and South America. The successful quest of Latin American nations for independence from Spain and Portugal allowed the United States to detach Florida from Madrid by diplomatic pressure (and less well known military pressure exerted by Andrew Jackson) and then boldly to announce the Monroe Doctrine in 1823. The doctrine declared that henceforth the Western Hemisphere was closed to European colonization and that European states must refrain from intervening in Latin American affairs. Though the Monroe Doctrine was unenforceable without the British fleet standing behind U.S. rhetoric of regional hegemony, the legend grew that the United States had put an end to European intriguing in the Western Hemisphere and had intervened successfully in world politics to protect democracy against repression.

All revolutions spawn a mythic belief in the universality of their cause and the dangerous conviction that the world eagerly awaits an opportunity to participate in its fulfillment. In the case of the French Revolution—and later, the Russian Revolution—this myth was dispelled rather soon. Attempts to universalize those revolutions through territorial expansion, behind the slogans "Liberty, Equality, and Fraternity" and "All Power to the Soviets," met with overpowering resistance at those nations' borders. Not so in the case of the United States. The Mexican War of 1846, even with its vested and ambiguous origins in the slave controversy and its blatantly imperialist character (indeed, an incident was manufactured to bring on the war: U.S. forces occupied Mexican-claimed territories), because of the ease of the U.S. conquest, confirmed basic aspects of the American belief in the nation's Manifest Destiny and in the Empire of Innocence.

The men at the Alamo fit into the legend of an Empire of Innocence, but the reality of the Mexican War a decade later rested upon an opportunistic view that Mexico was about to disintegrate, and the time was right to gain California. According to the last president of the short-lived Texas republic, Anson Jones, war resulted when President James K. Polk decided to "consummate views of conquest which had been entertained probably for years, bringing down an army and a navy upon us, when there was not a hostile foot, either Indian or Mexican, in Texas; not (as afterwards became apparent) to protect Texas . . . but to insure a *collision* with Mexico."[12] In the 1848 Treaty of Guadalupe Hidalgo, which ended the war, Mexico was forced to cede two-fifths of its territory to the United States.

Until the American Civil War in 1861, wrote historian Henry Adams (the first of his illustrious family to find irony history's most compelling lesson), the nation's foreign affairs had encompassed a single general principle: "the steady absorption of all the neighboring territory."[13] The ease of expansion had permitted Americans to carry forward the revolution while maintaining a "loose and separately responsible division of government."[14]

Lincoln preserved the Union, the first truly defensive move of the U.S. empire since the Revolutionary War, only by using every power granted by the Constitution against a "foreign" power. His secretary of state, William H. Seward, declared that a Confederate success would so upset "the equilibrium of the nations, maintained by this republic,"[15] that no one could be sure that mankind would even have another chance. Seward further stated:

> Dissolution would not only arrest but it would extinguish the greatness of our country; it would drop the curtain before all our national heroes. . . . Public prosperity would give place to retrogression, for standing armies would consume our substance; and our liberty, now as wide as our grand territorial dimensions, would be succeeded by the hateful and intolerable espionage of military despotism.[16]

It was Seward, of course, who negotiated in 1867 the Alaska purchase from Russia—nearly 600,000 square miles, the single largest addition to U.S. territory since the Louisiana Purchase. According to Seward, adding Alaska to an expanding United States was necessary for commercial purposes. Time and again he would say that it had become the objective of the United States to contest for "the commerce of the world, which is the empire of the world."[17]

Having purged itself of the debilitating influence of slave power through defeat of the South's attempt at secession from the Union, the United States could go forward with commercial expansion unencumbered politically and uplifted morally by the terrible blood sacrifice of war and martyrdom. Seward had foreseen all this in an 1852 speech on the great commercial future of the United States in Asia:

> Who does not see that this movement must effect our own complete emancipation from what remains of European influence and prejudice, and in turn develop the American opinion and influence which shall remould constitutions, laws, and customs in the land that is first greeted by the rising sun? Sir, although I am no socialist, no dreamer of a suddenly coming millennium, I nevertheless cannot reject the hope that peace is now to have her sway.[18]

■ EXPANSION BEYOND THE NORTH AMERICAN CONTINENT

Seward's purchase of Alaska represented a thrust into Asia that prefigured events of three decades later once considered accidental by-products of the 1898 Spanish-American War. Since the 1850s, U.S. policymakers had wanted to get Spain out of Cuba. Unfortunately for expansionists, the larger aims of diplomacy became enmeshed in the "filibustering" expeditions operating out of New Orleans at midcentury, including the ill-fated and confused attempt of William Walker to conquer Nicaragua for a new slave state and the attempt to purchase Cuba for the same reason.[19]

The time was still not right for such expansion immediately after the Civil War. Political conflicts during Reconstruction (the reorganization and reintegration of the defeated Confederacy with the Union) were a vital factor in curbing the expansionist impulse and prevented President Ulysses S. Grant from achieving his goal of annexing Santo Domingo, a former Spanish colony in the Caribbean. Grant's ambitions were caught in a political cross-fire between conservative and radical views: Whereas conservatives opposed annexation on the grounds that the "colored" peoples of the Caribbean and Central America—unlike the Native Americans of the U.S. West—would not be a "vanishing race," radicals, also opposed to annexation, felt that such efforts would divert the government from its primary task of Reconstruction. In short, both groups had little taste for taking on new racial problems when they could not solve ones closer to home. But when Cuban nationalists rose up against Spain in the 1890s, the situation had changed. Eager for commercial expansion in both the Caribbean and the Pacific, U.S. leaders championed the revolutions against Spanish colonial rule in Cuba and in the Philippines.

War came when the United States demanded revenge for the 1898 sinking of the *U.S.S. Maine* in Havana Harbor, an incident blamed on the Spanish, whose culpability was never proved and was later disputed. The fruits of U.S. victory included Cuba, Guam, the Philippines, and Puerto Rico. The brief "imperialist" debate of 1898–1900, when Americans divided over the question of what to do with Cuba and the Philippines, ended when the administration of William McKinley convinced enough people that its foreign policy objectives—protection of U.S. economic and security interests—did not require extensive additions of territory or the incorporation into the U.S. political system of large numbers of "subject peoples" of "alien race."

The Cuban question, for example, was resolved rather quickly by U.S. adaptation of the European protectorate form of imperialism, though it was never recognized as such. Unlike direct colonial control, protectorate status means that the territory retains nominal sovereignty and its people do not become citizens of the conquering nation. The work of General Leonard S. Wood and the U.S. Army in improving health conditions in the former

Spanish colony eased the minds of those who still felt any qualms about the terms whereby Cuba was granted its semi-independence.

Cuba became the model for a series of U.S. interventions in the Caribbean area in the first two decades of the twentieth century; these interventions were designed to protect the interests of U.S. property holders (actual and projected) and the entrances to a long-planned isthmian canal. "The people ask me what we mean by a stable government in Cuba," General Wood wrote the secretary of war, Elihu Root. "I tell them that when money can be borrowed at a reasonable rate of interest and when capital is willing to invest in the Island, a condition of stability will have been reached."[20] When the nominally independent Cuban government accepted a treaty guaranteeing the United States the right to intervene to restore order, the troops that had been sent to the island to overthrow Spanish misrule came home. But they returned whenever danger threatened. Under the terms of the Platt Amendment as inserted into the American-Cuban Treaty of 1903, the United States retained the right to keep a military base on the island—it is still there (Guantanamo Bay)—and the right to oversee Cuban financial matters, at least in regard to foreign debt. As discussed in Chapter 19, even more extensive interventionist rights were granted in the 1903 Hay–Bunau-Varilla Treaty between the United States and Panama in which the United States gained the right to construct, maintain, and defend the Panama Canal. Similar treaties, establishing "customs house" protectorates, were also sought with Haiti, Nicaragua, and Santo Domingo. When these sometimes failed, as in Haiti in 1915, the U.S. Marines came back—to stay as long as a decade, or more.

President Woodrow Wilson's policies, although paved with good intentions, followed in the interventionist path established by his predecessors. Rejecting crude bids by Haitian politicians to avoid U.S. intervention by awarding economic concessions to selected interests, Secretary of State William Jennings Bryan declared: "While we desire to encourage in every proper way American investments in Haiti, we believe that this can be better done by contributing to stability and order than by favoring special concessions to Americans."[21] Yet, while Wilson waged war against the Central Powers to secure the right of self-determination for small countries under the hegemony of Germany and Austria, U.S. forces intervened throughout the Western Hemisphere to establish reliable governments. Mexico became a test case for Wilson's oft-stated belief that he could teach the Latin Americans to elect good men who would pursue the same goals as elected leaders in advanced industrial societies. But, having sent the marines to Vera Cruz in 1914 and General John Pershing into northern Mexico in 1916, Wilson came to realize that stability usually was not enhanced by foreign bayonets.

World War I gave these hemispheric interventions a strongly strategic cast in much historical writing about the era. But this was often post facto rationalization. Robert Lansing, Bryan's successor, had before the outbreak of the war authored a memorandum on the modern meaning of the Monroe Doctrine, which summed up U.S. concerns about the security of the Western Hemisphere. The presumed right to intervene under the Monroe Doctrine should not be lightly abandoned, said Lansing. "With the present industrial activity, the scramble for markets, and the incessant search for new opportunities to produce wealth, commercial expansion and success are closely interwoven with political domination over the territory."[22]

If Cuba served as the prototype for hemispheric intervention, retaining the Philippines, deemed essential to gaining access to the vast market of China, involved a more complicated procedure. The suppression of Philippine guerrillas under General Emiliano Aguinaldo's leadership proved costly in a number of ways. Defeating Spain had taken three months; establishing U.S. rule took 125,000 soldiers and cost $160 million. In the process 5,000 U.S. soldiers and an estimated 200,000 Filipinos died, some from wounds and most as a result of a war-induced famine.

One of the last barriers to the full realization of the imperialist program—the U.S. Constitution—was removed as an obstacle by a series of rulings between 1901 and 1904: the "insular cases," whereby the U.S. Supreme Court accepted the McKinley administration's arguments that the Constitution did not follow the flag (that is, occupants of conquered territories did not enjoy the rights of U.S. citizens). This issue had been hidden under the surface since the debate over the annexation of Santo Domingo in Grant's day. If, as had been the case in westward expansion, new territories had to become states, all sorts of problems arose to confront the expansionists—the race question, for one. Wide powers to rule newly acquired territories were needed, powers that might deny occupants the rights of U.S. citizens under the Constitution, the attorney general argued, because in the future the United States might need to become involved "in Egypt, the Sudan, Central Africa, or a spot in the Antarctic Circle, or a section of the Chinese Empire."[23]

Expansionist voices drowned out the doubters. Typical of the time was an editorial in the *Army and Navy Journal*, which proclaimed about the Philippine action: "While it is true that a people have a certain right to say what shall be done in a political way on their own soil, it is equally true that a narrow-minded race have not the right to shut out from use by other peoples vast natural resources."[24]

Wilson strove mightily during the peace negotiations at the end of World War I to reinvigorate a "liberal" worldview that would produce agreement among the industrial nations to exercise collective self-restraint in dealing with places like China, thereby removing, he hoped, the basic causes of the tragic cycle of imperial competition, war, and violent revolution. Essential to this world view was recognition of the principle of self-determination and the creation of the League of Nations. These two themes were embodied in the Treaty of Versailles, the most important of five treaties ending World War I.

Wilson believed that once the industrial powers—following his leadership—established the rules of the game, the increasingly dangerous situation between the industrial powers and the rest of the world could be ameliorated. After the war, Wilson told a delegation of Mexican newspaper editors that all nations would be held to strictly accountable standards of behavior, "because so soon as you can admit your own capital and the capital of the world to the free use of the resources of Mexico, it will be one of the most wonderfully rich and prosperous countries in the world."[25]

Wilson's effort to be in the world but not of it produced such paradoxes as U.S. intervention in Mexico before World War I and in Siberia in 1918, as the war came to an end—both in the name of making the world safe for democracy. Having tried out something similar in Mexico, with far less than satisfactory results, U.S. troops were sent to Asian Russia both to check Japanese imperial ambitions and to support spontaneous efforts by local governments to resist revolutionary leader V. I. Lenin's efforts to consolidate the Russian Revolution. Good sense prevailed—especially as the Bolsheviks eliminated their rivals—and U.S. military intervention in Russia came to an end. But a picture of communist intrigues had been established, and, very soon, Washington policymakers were blaming their failures in Mexico and elsewhere on Soviet-inspired communist agents who, it appeared, were capable of influencing the course of political affairs in every far-off place around the globe.

U.S. withdrawal from European political affairs following the failure of the Treaty of Versailles to gain Senate approval signaled a change in approach—but not isolationism, as was once commonly argued.[26] Seeking to untangle centuries of European diplomacy, now overlaid with revolutionary passions, the Wilsonians had lost their way. Not wanting the responsibility for enforcing the peace treaty's punitive clauses against Germany, largely out of fear of destroying the only reliable barrier blocking a perceived expansionist Soviet Union, the United States used its new financial power in an independent attempt to reshape world politics, much as British economic power had been exercised in the aftermath of the French Revolution and the Napoleonic Wars.[27]

The plan to use financial power fell victim to accumulated ills, with the Great Depression and the subsequent collapse of worldwide financial markets applying the coup de grace to a half-realized vision of Wilsonian internationalism. A similar working relationship with the Japanese, an effort to curb competition in the Pacific area, also broke down under the strain of the depression. Of all the policies initiated in the 1920s, only President Herbert Hoover's retreat from overt interventionism in Central America lasted and became the Good Neighbor policy during President Franklin D. Roosevelt's domestic reform program known as the New Deal.

Isolationism is a better description of both the atmosphere and the policy trends of the 1930s than it ever was of the decade following World War I. But

Adolf Hitler's ambitions for domination over Europe finally exceeded what the European democracies could afford to give away simply to keep the peace. With war looming in 1939, Dean Acheson spoke at Yale University on the U.S. predicament. The principal source of trouble, Acheson noted, was Britain's faltering economic power. "We can see that British naval power no longer can establish security of life and investment in distant parts of the world, and a localization of conflict nearer at home."[28]

■ GLOBALIZATION OF INTERVENTION

Ever since the promulgation of the Monroe Doctrine, U.S. policies had been at least partially underwritten by British naval power. World War II put an end to that support. U.S. policymakers, inheriting the fruits of a fallen Europe-centric system that had been dominant in international affairs since the sixteenth century, perceived the Soviet Union as a distinctive challenge to U.S. goals in the postwar world. This perception fueled an intense ideological competition that came to be known as the Cold War. U.S. leaders welcomed the opportunity to take on this challenge. President Harry S Truman reconfirmed that message in the speech he delivered before Congress on March 12, 1947, asking for $500 million to aid Greece and Turkey, the former threatened by a communist insurgency. Truman said that it "must" be U.S. policy to support all nations seeking to resist "attempted subjugation by armed minorities or by outside pressures."[29] The sweeping nature of Truman's new doctrine, both in regard to its extent—apparently global—and in respect to the assumption that it would be possible to determine when "attempted subjugation" was under way (as opposed to indigenous revolutionary tumult), caused some concern even within a Congress that was militantly anticommunist and anti-Soviet.

Dean Acheson tried to reassure the Senate Foreign Relations Committee that the administration was aware of the limits on intervention or, as it would soon be called, "containment," but committee members were not so sure. Senator Alexander Wiley confessed, for example, that he was "in doubt as to which way to go," and Senator Walter F. George pondered the implications of leaving the United Nations on the sidelines in favor of unilateral action:

> I do not see how we are going to escape going into Manchuria, North China, and Korea and doing things in that area of the world. . . . [W]e have got the right to exercise commonsense. But I know that when we make a policy of this kind we are irrevocably committing ourselves to a course of action, and there is no way to get out of it next week or next year. You go down to the end of the road.[30]

George's prescience did not lead the committee to oppose Truman, partly out of concern for the consequences in an unsettled world (even if the Soviets were *not* planning a campaign of subversion, might not a split in the U.S. government be too tempting to resist?); partly because the Cold War had not yet shifted from Europe, with its traditional boundary lines, to the soon-to-be-called Third World; and partly because Americans now had the atom bomb, which added to the frontier-days legend of the ease of conquest.

The Korean War not only proved Senator George right, it also reinforced the Truman Doctrine world view. The invasion of South Korea by the "communist" North, like the Chinese Revolution of 1949, was interpreted, wrongly and tragically, as an extension of Soviet power across the Eurasian landmass. Americans were predisposed to see in both events the Kremlin's dark hand, stretching out to take into the Soviet domain not only the Chinese but, beyond those vast borders, the industrial workshops of Asia, Japan, and the raw materials areas of former European colonies.

The interventionist impulse, as it developed in the 1950s and 1960s, also worked from the premise of "nation-building." U.S. leaders, from the end of World War II to the fall of Saigon in 1975, justified intervention in the Third World as defense against communist expansion and convinced themselves that they best understood the needs of newly emerging areas. After all, the world system they had created to replace the worn-out prewar structure that collapsed before the Japanese onslaught at Singapore in 1942 had originated in the first successful example of revolutionary nationalism: the American Revolution of 1776.

Presidents Harry S Truman, Dwight D. Eisenhower, and John F. Kennedy celebrated U.S. exceptionalism without embarrassment as well as with a good deal of pride. Theirs was a nation with a privileged history: a history that had seen the United States progress across the North American continent largely uncontested, brushing aside overextended European empires, opening up the prairies and interning the remnants of Indian nations, and swooping up vast mineral resources as they went along—finally, to make of the nation a land rich beyond previous human experience.

The one era in U.S. history that challenged certain of these assumptions, the Great Depression and New Deal years, was only a bad memory. After the almost traumatic experience of the limited experiment in self-containment during the early New Deal, U.S. policymakers, from the time of World War II to the 1990s, vowed never to return to isolationism, economic or political. Blocking Soviet expansionist thrusts was crucial, but U.S. leaders also undertook to restructure the world capitalist system on stronger foundations. The United States, said Dean Acheson around the time the Truman Doctrine was formulated, now found itself "far more dependent upon exports than before the war to maintain levels of business activity to which our economy has become accustomed." The nation's aid programs would have to be concentrated "in areas where it will be most effective in building world political and economic stability, in promoting human freedom and democratic institutions, in fostering liberal trading policies, and in strengthening the authority of the United Nations."[31]

If U.S. economic aid was to be concentrated in certain areas, the scope of interventionist operations to protect the security of this "free world" system could not be so restricted. The basic charter for U.S. covert operations around the world may be found in a policy paper prepared for the National Security Council (NSC) in early 1950. This famous paper (NSC-68) was drafted in the wake of the Soviet atom bomb, which signaled the end of the U.S. nuclear monopoly, and of the Chinese Revolution. Its authors had tried to strike a balance between the limits imposed on the means a free society might use without doing violence to its basic institutions and the requirements of meeting the challenge posed by the USSR's ability to exploit a still-chaotic world situation:

> In a shrinking world, which now faces the threat of atomic warfare, it is not an adequate objective merely to seek to check the Kremlin design, for the absence of order among nations is becoming less and less tolerable. . . . The integrity of our system will not be jeopardized by any measures, covert or overt, violent or non-violent, which serve the purpose of frustrating the Kremlin design, nor does the necessity for conducting ourselves so as to affirm our values in actions as well as words forbid such measures, provided only they are appropriately calculated to that end and are not so excessive or misdirected as to make us enemies of the people instead of the evil men who have enslaved them.[32]

From that paragraph written in 1950 to the oral testimony of Lieutenant Colonel Oliver North in the summer of 1987 in justification of the Iran-contra affair is no great leap, even if it is not exactly a straight line. In certain well-known instances, such as Vietnam in the 1950s and Chile in the 1970s, U.S. actions extended measures permitted under NSC-68 to the prevention of democratically elected regimes. In the case of Vietnam, Secretary of State John Foster Dulles simply ruled out all-Vietnamese elections in 1956 as required under the 1954 Geneva Agreement ending the Vietnamese war against the French. In the case of Chile, Secretary of State Henry Kissinger was reported to have said, "I don't see why we need to stand by and watch a country go communist due to the irresponsibility of its own people."[33]

In a discussion with congressional leaders at the height of the first Vietnam crisis in 1954 (how was the United States to respond to imminent French defeat at Dienbienphu at the hands of the communist insurgents?), President Eisenhower provided an explanation of what the United States sought with these interventions.

> The President said that every individual is the center of the universe so far as that individual is concerned; in the same manner, every nation is

the center of the universe in working out its own problems. Yet, in a general sense. . . it is correct to say that the United States is the central key, the core of democracy, economically, militarily and spiritually. Consequently in simple terms, we are establishing international outposts where people can develop their strength to defend themselves. Here we are sitting in the center, and with high mobility and destructive forces we can swiftly respond when our vital interests are affected. We are trying. . . with these programs to build up for the United States a position in the world of freedom of action. . . . One of our greatest hopes. . . is to get our troops back home. As we get these other countries strengthened economically, to do their part to provide the ground forces to police and hold their own land, we come closer to the realization of our hopes. . . . [W]e cannot publicly call our Allies outposts . . . [but] we are trying to get that result.[34]

Eisenhower always had feared the consequences of a permanently mobilized society. He had sought to prevent that danger and its consequence, the dominance of the military-industrial complex, leading to financial insolvency as well as to political malaise. In the event, the reverse happened. The globalization of the interventionist impulse and its synthesis with an anticommunist ideology presaged not the demobilization of U.S. society during the postwar period, but rather the dominance of a national security culture increasingly committed to intervention abroad. The application of this interventionist ethos in the Third World (most noted by U.S. involvement in the Vietnam War), would, as the following chapters attest, have significant implications for both U.S. foreign policy and the U.S. domestic political system in the postwar period.

3

The Development of Low-Intensity-Conflict Doctrine

Michael T. Klare

The U.S. Commission on Integrated Long-Term Strategy reported in January 1988 that nearly "all the armed conflicts of the past forty years have occurred in what is vaguely called the Third World" and that such conflicts "have had and will have an adverse cumulative effect on U.S. access to critical regions, on American credibility among allies and friends, and on American self-confidence." Because Third World challenges to U.S. interests are multiplying, moreover, "in the coming decades the United States will need to be better prepared to deal with conflicts in the Third World."[1]

The notion that U.S. interests are facing increased pressure in the Third World and that new military initiatives are needed to resist these threats became a prominent theme in U.S. strategic thinking in the late 1980s.[2] With the signing of an accord on the elimination of intermediate-range nuclear forces (the INF Treaty) and the accompanying decline in U.S.-Soviet tensions, many strategists focused their attention on the growing incidence of "low-intensity conflict" (LIC)—that is, conflict falling below the threshold of full-scale combat between modern armies. "Since the end of World War II," Secretary of Defense Frank C. Carlucci wrote in 1988, "ambiguous aggression in the form of low-intensity conflict has become an increasing threat to our interests, as well as those of our allies and friends."[3]

To counter this challenge, Secretary Carlucci recommended an increase in U.S. military and economic aid to threatened allies in the Third World, along with a significant buildup of U.S. "power projection" forces intended for rapid insertion into distant Third World areas. As part of this effort, Carlucci also urged the further expansion of U.S. Special Operations Forces—the army's Green Berets, the navy's SEALs, and similar groups—plus continued U.S. support for anticommunist guerrillas in the Third World. Such measures were essential, he argued, because "LIC is one of the most serious challenges we face today, and our survival and well-being depend on how we comprehend the threat and respond to it."[4]

This focus on Third World military developments continued into the early 1990s and, with the rapid erosion of the Soviet threat, came to dominate the strategic thinking of the Bush administration. "The security challenges we face today do not come from the East alone," President Bush affirmed in his first major address on U.S. security interests. "It is the unfortunate fact that the world faces increasing threat from armed insurgencies, terrorists, and . . . narcotics traffickers." To curb this threat, Bush argued, the United States must strengthen its ability to suppress disorders in the Third World. "We have not yet mastered this complex challenge," he noted, but "we and our allies must construct a common strategy for stability in the developing world."[5]

With the fall of the Berlin Wall and the subsequent liquidation of the Warsaw Pact, conflict in the Third World assumed even more importance in U.S. military thinking. Thus, in his first annual report to Congress, Secretary of Defense Richard Cheney observed that the threat posed by the Soviet bloc had declined, but that "U.S. interests over the coming decades will face a growing number of potentially serious threats from other sources." In particular, the United States must be prepared "for potential Third World conflicts, and for the expansion of threats from insurgencies, terrorism, and narcotics trafficking." This being the case, Cheney argued, the United States must develop strategies "that rely more heavily on mobile, highly ready, well-equipped forces and solid power-projection capabilities."[6] The enhancement of such capabilities became a major Defense Department priority in the spring of 1990, and has dominated Pentagon planning ever since.

The ascendancy of such views in U.S. strategic thinking has been accompanied historically by increased U.S. military involvement in regional Third World conflicts. Because the United States appears to be in the initial stages of such a period today, it is important to examine the evolution of U.S. interventionist policy since World War II and its resurgence—in the form of LIC doctrine during the 1980s and the 1990s.

■ THE TRUMAN DOCTRINE, KOREA, AND VIETNAM

In the years immediately following World War II, U.S. foreign policy was focused largely on the East-West struggle in Europe. Most of the early Cold War crises arose from conflicting U.S. and Soviet positions on the postwar political order in Eastern Europe and on the status of Berlin. And, with the demobilization of the large U.S. armies established in the 1942–1945 period, U.S. strategy came to depend more and more on the use of nuclear weapons to offset the purported Soviet advantage in nonnuclear, "conventional" forces.

But although East-West issues dominated strategic thinking in the late 1940s, North-South concerns were not entirely absent from the political-military landscape. Indeed, two of the earliest crises of the postwar period—the emergence of a Soviet-backed republic in Azerbaijan (a northern province of Iran) and the civil war in Greece—were largely the products of revolutionary and separatist pressures indigenous to the Third World. That such events were generally perceived through the lens of East-West conflict (a recurring pattern throughout the Cold War era) should not prevent us from seeing them as part of a succession of Third World upheavals.

The Greek civil war of 1946–1949 played an especially pivotal role in the evolution of U.S. policy. Although viewed by many historians as a quintessential expression of Cold War hostilities, the Greek conflict actually had much in common with the Vietnam War both in military and political terms. Because the U.S. public was weary of war by 1946, and leery of involvement in what was essentially viewed as an internal Third World conflict, the administration of Harry S Truman encountered considerable domestic resistance to its plans for aiding the conservative forces in Greece. And because this resistance was seen as a significant obstacle to the emerging policy of containment—which envisioned active U.S. military efforts to prevent further communist gains on the Soviet periphery—President Truman was determined to use the Greek affair to mobilize public support for a policy of global interventionism.[7]

To achieve a transformation in public attitudes, Truman sought to portray all conflicts in the world—whatever their origins—as manifestations of a global struggle between light and dark, tyranny and freedom. On March 12, 1947, he articulated this theme in a major speech on U.S. military aid to Greece. Suggesting that the spread of communism to any corner of the globe posed a significant threat to U.S. security, the president affirmed—in what was subsequently dubbed the Truman Doctrine—that "it must be the policy of the United States to support free peoples who are resisting attempted subjugation by armed minorities or by outside pressures." Although this policy was initially to be applied solely to Greece and Turkey, Truman made it clear that it would be extended to other nations when and if he deemed it necessary.[8]

Propelled by the crusading rhetoric of the Truman Doctrine, Congress approved the president's request for substantial military aid to anti-communist forces in Greece. In succeeding years, U.S. policymakers sought to amend the doctrine to allow for the *direct use* of U.S. forces (as distinct from the provision of military aid) in resisting Soviet/communist gains abroad. Such a policy, indeed, was explicitly proposed in National Security Council Memorandum No. 68 (NSC-68), a secret strategy paper drawn up by Paul Nitze of the NSC in 1950. Nonetheless, most Americans continued to oppose the direct use of U.S. troops in Third World conflicts.[9]

With the fall in 1949 of Jiang Kaishek in China, however, the public mood began to change. Angered by heavy-handed Soviet moves in Eastern Europe, and alarmed by the communist victory in China, many public figures began to call for a more vigorous struggle against international communism. Some of this fear and anger also was directed against those Americans who were said to have contributed to the success of communism abroad, either through espionage or by their failure to adopt a more aggressive anticommunist stance. This sort of paranoia, popularly known as McCarthyism (after the most prominent crusader against domestic communists and "fellow travelers," Senator Joseph R. McCarthy of Wisconsin), helped to generate a new mandate for the use of military force in combating future communist advances in the Third World.[10]

This commitment was soon put to the test in Korea. On June 25, 1950, North Korean forces crossed into the South in what appeared to be naked communist aggression against a U.S. ally. Although Korea had not previously been viewed as a major strategic interest of the United States, the president immediately invoked the Truman Doctrine and ordered U.S. forces to resist the North Korean attack. At first, most Americans supported President Truman's action, especially when it appeared that General Douglas MacArthur would succeed in forcibly "liberating" North Korea from communist rule. But when communist China entered the conflict, thereby introducing a significant risk of nuclear confrontation, senior U.S. leaders recoiled from further escalation and chose instead to fight a conventional campaign restricted to the Korean peninsula. This decision, along with the introduction of large numbers of Chinese forces, produced a bloody and frustrating stalemate on the ground—which, in turn, provoked considerable public discontent in the United States.

In the wake of the frustrating Korean conflict, President Eisenhower adopted a new, scaled-down defense posture, which relied to a great extent on the threat of "massive retaliation" (with nuclear weapons) to deter Soviet probes in the Third World. In line with this "New Look" policy, Eisenhower ordered a substantial cut in U.S. conventional capabilities, particularly the army's ground forces and the navy's surface fleets. For the next half-dozen years, East-West issues dominated the strategic landscape, as President Eisenhower presided over a major buildup of nuclear forces; only at the end of his tenure, with the 1958 U.S. landing in Lebanon and the accompanying Eisenhower Doctrine (authorizing U.S. military action to prevent a communist takeover of Middle Eastern countries), did he envision a direct U.S. military role in regional, nonnuclear conflicts.[11]

As the 1950s drew to a close, some U.S. strategists began to question the logic of Eisenhower's New Look posture. These dissidents, led by General Maxwell D. Taylor of the army, charged that massive retaliation was an inappropriate and ineffective response to the many insurgencies and low-level military challenges facing the United States around the world. "While our massive retaliatory strategy may have prevented the Great War," Taylor wrote in *The Uncertain Trumpet*, "it has not maintained the Little Peace: that is, peace from disturbances which are little only in comparison with the disaster of general war."[12] In order to provide a credible, realistic response to such "disturbances," Taylor called for a significant expansion of U.S. nonnuclear forces. Such a buildup, he argued, would permit the president to implement a strategy of "flexible response"—that is, the use of whatever type of forces, nuclear or nonnuclear, would constitute the best response to any given challenge.

Taylor's views were embraced by John F. Kennedy, then a senator, who pledged in the 1960 presidential campaign to mount a more vigorous U.S. military response to communist probes in the Third World. After his election, Kennedy invited General Taylor and like-minded strategists to join his administration and to implement their military ideas. Taylor was named security adviser to the president and, later, chairman of the Joint Chiefs of Staff (JCS), and the strategy of flexible response became the cornerstone of a massive buildup of nuclear and conventional forces. In initiating this buildup, Kennedy placed special emphasis on the development of forces and tactics for "counterinsurgency"—that is, for the defeat of revolutionary guerrilla upheavals (or, as they were known at the time, "wars of national liberation").

The Kennedy approach to counterinsurgency was spelled out in a number of secret NSC documents, including National Security Action Memorandum No. 124 (NSAM 124), dated January 18, 1962, and NSAM 182, dated August 24, 1962. NSAM 124 affirmed that "subversive insurgency . . . is a major form of politico-military conflict equal in importance to conventional warfare," and directed the various agencies of the government (such as the NSC and CIA) to develop coordinated plans for resisting this threat. NSAM 182 provided for the adoption of an Overseas Internal Defense Policy (OIDP) that was to govern U.S. counterinsurgency operations in threatened Third World countries. Drawing on the British counterinsurgency experience in combating communist guerrillas in Malaya from 1948 to 1956 and U.S.-backed operations against the communist Huk guerrillas in the Philippines during the mid-1950s, the OIDP called for coordinated political, economic, and military efforts intended to mobilize popular support for the established government while isolating the guerrillas from the rural populace. Although the brunt of these efforts was to be borne by agencies of the host regime, the OIDP allowed for the direct employment of U.S. military forces at "higher levels of insurgency."[13]

To test the Pentagon's new weapons and tactics, and to demonstrate the effectiveness of counterinsurgency strategy, President Kennedy authorized a substantial increase in the U.S. military presence in South Vietnam. In justifying this move before Congress, General Taylor affirmed in 1963 that "here we have a going laboratory, where we see subversive insurgency, the Ho Chi Minh doctrine, being applied in all its forms." To perfect U.S.

defense against such threats, he noted, "we have recognized the importance of the area as a laboratory [and] have had teams out there looking at the equipment requirements of this kind of guerrilla warfare."[14]

Although perceived initially as a laboratory, Vietnam soon turned into something rather more significant. For, having designated Vietnam as a proving ground for counterinsurgency, it became essential for the United States to avoid defeat lest U.S. failure in Indochina encourage revolutionaries in other countries to undertake guerrilla campaigns of their own. Hence, U.S. counterrevolutionary credibility was put on the line, and it became more and more difficult to contemplate retreat, especially when U.S. counterinsurgency efforts fell apart following the overthrow of Vietnamese President Ngo Dinh Diem in 1963. As suggested by Taylor in 1964,

> . . . the failure of our programs in South Vietnam would have heavy influence on the judgments of Burma, India, Indonesia, Malaysia, Japan, Taiwan, the Republic of Korea, and the Republic of the Philippines with respect to U.S. durability, resolution, and trustworthiness. Finally, this being the first real test of our determination to defeat the communist wars of national liberation formula, it is not unreasonable to conclude that there would be a corresponding unfavorable effect upon our image in Africa and Latin America.[15]

This perception of Vietnam's critical importance created an excruciating dilemma for U.S. officials: Orthodox counterinsurgency doctrine assumed that the host nation would assume primary responsibility for both political and military operations against the guerrilla insurgency, but in Vietnam (as in other Third World countries aided by the United States), the government was so alienated from the general population that it was incapable of sustaining an effective politico-military campaign without substantial outside help. As the United States ultimately discovered in Vietnam, counterinsurgency cannot work when the prevailing regime lacks popular support for the antiguerrilla effort. In such cases, an increasing number of U.S. troops must be substituted for unreliable indigenous forces in order to save the regime from collapse. On this basis, Kennedy and his successor, President Lyndon B. Johnson, deployed more and more troops in Vietnam in what became an ever-expanding (and ultimately futile) test of U.S. military "credibility."[16]

■ THE POST-VIETNAM ERA

In the wake of Vietnam, U.S. citizens and policymakers sought to prevent any repetition of such a fiasco by imposing a number of important restrictions on U.S. military involvement in regional Third World conflicts. These restraints, inspired by the "Vietnam syndrome"—a clear and pervasive reluctance on the part of American citizens to support U.S. intervention in local, Third World conflicts—included the abandonment of conscription, a substantial reduction in U.S. military aid to unstable Third World governments, and, under the War Powers Act of 1973, a legislative ban on the extended deployment (without congressional approval) of U.S. troops abroad.

Recognizing the depth of public opposition to involvement in regional Third World conflicts, U.S. strategists focused most of their attention in the 1970s on defense issues in Europe. Charging that Moscow had used the Vietnam interregnum to build up its nuclear and conventional capabilities in Eastern Europe, Presidents Gerald R. Ford and Jimmy Carter called for a major buildup of U.S. forces in the North Atlantic Treaty Organization (NATO). Significant funding increases were requested for the modernization of U.S. armored forces and for the deployment in Europe of a new generation of "theater" nuclear weapons (the weapons that were later eliminated by the INF Treaty). At the same time, spending on the Special Forces and other Third World–oriented capabilities was reduced.

This European focus was attractive to the military for a variety of reasons: It was easy to sell to Congress (because it had no taint of Vietnam and hinged on opposition to a traditional enemy, the USSR); because U.S. troops could not fight the Soviets in Europe with Vietnam-oriented equipment, it required a vast modernization of U.S. ground and air capabilities (thus producing lucrative contracts for the U.S. defense industry and thereby satisfying important domestic constituencies); it underscored an old-school style of military management (one that favored the tank generals of World War II rather than the counterinsurgency experts of Vietnam fame); and it simplified military recruiting in an all-volunteer setting (Europe being a much more attractive posting than Vietnam). For all these reasons, preparation for a European conflict became the central concern of U.S. defense planning in the mid-1970s.

The existence of the Vietnam syndrome did not, however, entirely discourage those U.S. strategists who sought to enhance U.S. power and influence in the Third World. To get around the impediments described, National Security Adviser (later Secretary of State) Henry Kissinger and his colleagues devised what may be called the "post-Vietnam strategy" of indirect intervention. This strategy eschewed the direct use of U.S. combat forces in regional Third World conflicts but employed other means for exercising U.S. power. In particular, this strategy entailed: (1) the extensive use of arms transfers and military aid to bolster the defense capabilities of friendly Third World countries (the policy known as the Nixon Doctrine); (2) the extensive use of covert operations to manipulate the political environment of selected Third World countries (most evident in the U.S. campaign of 1971–1973 to undermine the Chilean regime of President Salvador Allende); and (3) the cultivation of surrogate gendarmes to guard U.S. interests in critical Third

World areas (the most important such surrogate was Iran under the shah).
Together, these measures constituted the major thrust of U.S. policy toward
the Third World in the immediate post-Vietnam period.[17]

It cannot be said, therefore, that interventionism disappeared entirely
from the repertoire of U.S. policy in the 1970s. But there certainly was a
decreased level of *direct* military involvement in Third World conflicts, as
exemplified by the U.S. failure to directly intervene in the Angolan civil war
of 1975–1976 (in which U.S. involvement was precluded by the Clark
Amendment to the Defense Appropriations Bill for Fiscal Year [FY] 1976),
in Iran during the collapse of the shah in 1978–1979, and in Nicaragua during
the overthrow of Anastacio Somoza in 1979.

Although strongly supported by most Americans, this aversion to direct
intervention in regional Third World conflicts was criticized by some
strategists who viewed it as a retreat from global power and leadership. For
these strategists, U.S. preoccupation with East-West issues in Europe was
distracting Washington from significant military perils arising in other
critical areas. In particular, they warned of mounting threats to Western
control over Third World sources of energy supplies and strategic minerals,
coupled with growing political and social unrest—threats that they believed
required a direct U.S. military response. To overcome the U.S. public's
continuing resistance to such a response, these critics obscured the
indigenous nature of these disputes by painting an alarming picture of
aggressive Soviet expansion in the Third World. "The Soviet Union clearly
created an important new threat to Western interests during the 1970s—a
capability to project military power into areas far from the Soviet Union,"
Admiral Elmo R. Zumwalt warned in 1980. Moreover, "Moscow's
willingness and ability to exploit Third World crises have complicated U.S.
efforts to maintain stability in the Third World."[18]

Despite such warnings, East-West concerns dominated U.S. military
planning for most of the 1970s. In 1979, however, the pendulum began to
swing back to Third World concerns in response to four critical events: (1)
the fall of the shah of Iran, whose departure from the scene eliminated a
crucial pillar of the Nixon Doctrine; (2) the emergence of revolutionary
governments in Nicaragua and Grenada, heralding a new wave of guerrilla
upheavals in Central America and the Caribbean; (3) the Iranian hostage
crisis, which produced an emotional public outcry in the United States and
generated strong demands for U.S. military retaliation against Third World
terrorists; and (4) the Soviet invasion of Afghanistan, which culminated a
series of Soviet and Cuban thrusts into Africa and the Middle East, most
notably in Angola and Ethiopia. In response to these challenges, the Carter
administration undertook a major review of U.S. strategy in the Persian Gulf
and the Third World in general. What emerged from this review was a
consensus that critical U.S. interests in the Third World were at risk and that
the United States should take stronger action to protect these interests. As

suggested by National Security Adviser Zbigniew Brzezinski in April 1979, the United States was recovering from "a very deep philosophical-cultural crisis" induced by the Vietnam War and was now ready to "use force when necessary to protect our important interests."[19]

In June 1979, following a series of secret NSC meetings, the new interventionist consensus was translated into several key presidential decisions: a commitment to the use of U.S. military power to protect key economic resources in the Third World (especially oil); the activation of the Rapid Deployment Force (RDF), an assortment of units from all four military services earmarked for intervention in the Third World; the acquisition of new basing rights in the Indian Ocean area (notably in Oman, Kenya, and Somalia); and the permanent deployment of a carrier battle group in the Indian Ocean.[20] These decisions were made in June 1979—prior to the onset of the Iranian hostage crisis in November of that year and the Soviet invasion of Afghanistan in December—but were not announced to the U.S. public until President Carter's State of the Union Address of January 23, 1980. In this address, Carter affirmed Washington's readiness to use military force in protecting the oil flow from the Persian Gulf. "Let our position be absolutely clear," Carter declared. "An attempt by any outside force to gain control of the Persian Gulf will be regarded as an assault on the vital interests of the United States of America, and such an assault will be repelled by any means necessary, including military force."[21] This announcement, soon dubbed the "Carter Doctrine," continues to govern U.S. military action in the Persian Gulf.

These moves were not, however, sufficient to overcome public dissatisfaction with the president's performance during the Iranian hostage affair and other international crises, and so Carter lost to Ronald Reagan in the 1980 election. President Reagan subsequently moved much further in implementing a policy of resurgent interventionism; it should be noted, however, that much of what he did—especially with respect to the RDF and the expansion of U.S. power projection capabilities—was initiated by President Carter during his last months in office.

Although Reagan certainly owed a debt to the interventionist buildup initiated by Carter, it is undeniable that he placed much more emphasis on the use of force to advance U.S. foreign policy objectives in the Third World. In early policy declarations, Reagan denounced the Vietnam syndrome as "a temporary aberration," and vowed to enhance U.S. capacity for intervention abroad.[22] Moreover, the $2-trillion military buildup launched by the Reagan administration in 1981 gave high priority to the expansion of U.S. power projection capabilities, particularly the army's Special Forces, the navy's carrier and amphibious fleets, and the air force's long-range airlift units.[23] In defending this buildup, Defense Secretary Weinberger declared in 1981 that "we and our allies have come to be critically dependent on places in the world which are subject to great instability," and therefore the United States must "urgently [acquire] a better ability to respond to crises far from our shores, and to stay there as long as necessary."[24]

This buildup was accompanied, moreover, by a conspicuous readiness to use force in overseas conflict situations. "Over the last 18 months," Richard Halloran of the *New York Times* observed in January 1984, "President Reagan has clearly stepped into the front ranks of those American Presidents who, since World War II, have been willing to employ military force as an instrument of national policy." Often disregarding the cautionary advice of his military advisers, Reagan deployed U.S. troops or advisers to Central America, Grenada, and Lebanon, authorized air strikes against Libya, and sent a powerful naval fleet into the Persian Gulf. Such action, Halloran wrote, places Reagan "in a league with President Truman, who sent forces to fight in Korea, and Presidents Kennedy and Johnson, who led the United States into the war in Vietnam."[25]

■ THE EMERGENCE OF LOW-INTENSITY CONFLICT DOCTRINE IN THE 1980s

The revived U.S. commitment to intervention in the Third World during the 1980s was largely encapsulated in the doctrine of low-intensity conflict, or LIC as it is known in military circles. In military terms, LIC connotes the low end of the "spectrum of violence," embracing terrorism, guerrilla warfare, counterinsurgency, ethnic and border conflicts, show-of-force operations, and what the Pentagon deceptively calls "peacetime contingency operations." Furthermore, under Reagan, low-intensity conflict took on broader significance, representing a new policy of military intervention in Third World areas. Indeed, U.S. military strategists began to speak of the "doctrine of low-intensity conflict," and new military manuals, tactics, and forces were created in accordance with this doctrine.[26] The LIC doctrine of the 1980s rested on two fundamental assumptions:

1. *Vital U.S. interests are threatened by radical and revolutionary violence in the Third World.* Perhaps no figure stated this view with greater urgency than Lieutenant Colonel Oliver North, who told the Select Committee on the Iran-Contra Affair in June 1987 that extraordinary measures of the sort he employed were justified because "this nation is at risk in a dangerous world."[27] North was very clearly influenced by other theorists of low-intensity warfare, including Pentagon counterinsurgency expert Neil C. Livingstone. "Unfulfilled expectations and economic mismanagement have turned much of the developing world into a 'hothouse of conflict,' capable of spilling over and engulfing the industrial West," Livingstone told senior officers at the National Defense University (NDU) in 1983. Although the Soviets may not always be directly responsible for this disorder, they

view guerrilla warfare "as a means of undermining the West, wearing it down, nibbling away at its peripheries, denying it the strategic minerals and vital straits critical to its commerce." This being the case, U.S. policymakers must recognize that "what is at stake [in low-intensity conflict] is nothing less than the survival of our own country and way of life."[28]

2. *The United States must be prepared to use military force to protect its vital interests in the Third World.* In the view of the U.S. theorists, the threat posed by LIC was equivalent to an all-out assault by the Soviet Union and its allies and had to be countered, therefore, by vigorous U.S. political and military action. "Police actions, peacekeeping missions, and counterinsurgency . . . are all part of the same long, continuous war," Livingstone argued in 1983, "a war composed of many small, often nameless battles of short duration in dozens of different venues against an unchanging enemy and its proxies and surrogates." Accordingly, "the security of the United States and the rest of the Western World requires a restructuring of our warmaking capability, placing new emphasis on the ability to fight a succession of limited wars and to project power into the Third World."[29]

These assumptions, although not always expressed in such explicit terms, formed the core of U.S. doctrine on LIC in the 1980s. Added together, they provided a potent rationale for intervention. This rationale, moreover, was given formal recognition by the Reagan administration, as indicated by Secretary of State George Shultz's comments to participants in the Pentagon's LIC conference held in 1986:

> We have seen and we will continue to see a wide range of ambiguous threats in the shadow area between major war and millennial peace. Americans must understand . . . that a number of small challenges, year after year, can add up to a more serious challenge to our interests. The time to act, to help our friends by adding our strength to the equation, is not when the threat is at our doorstep, when the stakes are highest and the needed resources enormous. We must be prepared to commit our political, economic. and if necessary, military power when the threat is still manageable and when its prudent use can prevent the threat from growing.[30]

On this basis, the Department of Defense developed an elaborate body of doctrine for low-intensity warfare. This doctrine, as articulated in Pentagon documents of the late 1980s, envisioned direct or indirect U.S. military involvement in five types of operations:

1. *Counterinsurgency,* or U.S.-backed political and military efforts to isolate and suppress revolutionary guerrilla movements in the Third World. (These U.S. efforts are also identified as "foreign internal defense.") In line with the tenets of "classical," 1960s-style counterinsurgency, LIC doctrine stresses the efforts of host-nation military and civilian personnel in "winning

the hearts and minds" of rural peasants. Such operations, generally described in the doctrinal literature as "military civic action" and "psychological operations" (psyops), are intended to convince disaffected peasants that the established government is sensitive to their needs and concerns. Military operations, in such a setting, are aimed at driving the rebels away from populated areas without causing excessive destruction to the civil infrastructure.

As the United States found in Vietnam, however, it is easier to promulgate such policies than to carry them out. Typically, the United States is asked to assist in counterinsurgency operations only in the case of governments that have so abused and exploited the rural peasantry that no amount of good deeds (civic action) and public relations (psyops) will suffice to arouse public support. In such cases, the incumbent regime tends to rely increasingly on military action to crush dissent, and this, in turn, tends to feed the insurgency—thereby increasing the pressure on Washington to step up U.S. involvement. This dynamic appeared well under way during the 1980s in El Salvador and the Philippines, where the United States was supporting major counterinsurgency efforts.[31]

2. *Proinsurgency,* or U.S. paramilitary support for anticommunist guerrillas who seek to overthrow pro-Soviet governments in the Third World (see Chapter 8). Such efforts, which included covert and overt support for the anti-Sandinista contras, fall under the Reagan Doctrine. Other U.S.-backed proinsurgency campaigns were launched in in Afghanistan, Angola, and Cambodia.

3. *Peacetime contingency operations,* or any limited short-term use of military power as an instrument of U.S. foreign policy. Such actions may include the rescue of U.S. citizens caught in overseas war zones; "show-of-force" operations intended to signal U.S. displeasure with the behavior of a particular regime (by threatening direct intervention); "peacekeeping" operations designed to restore order in war-torn countries or to separate two warring parties; and punitive strikes against governments that support terrorism or otherwise threaten U.S. interests. Examples of such U.S. operations include the 1983 invasion of Grenada, the 1983–1984 mission in Beirut, periodic naval exercises in the Gulf of Sidra (claimed by Libya), and the reflagging and protection of Kuwaiti ships during the final years of the Iran-Iraq War.[32]

4. *Terrorism counteraction,* or the use of military force to prevent or deter terrorist attacks on U.S. personnel or facilities abroad. Although the emphasis here is on preventative measures, U.S. policy—as spelled out in National Security Decision Directive No. 138 (NSDD 138) of April 3, 1984—allows for retaliatory strikes against terrorist groups (and their supporters) identified as being responsible for attacks on U.S. citizens and facilities. "The United States . . . will not use force indiscriminately," National Security Adviser Robert C. McFarlane avowed in 1985. "But we

must be free to consider an armed strike against terrorists and those who support them, where elimination or moderation of the threat does not appear to be feasible by other means."[33] Such strikes were conducted on April 14, 1986, against the headquarters of Libyan leader Colonel Muammar Qaddafi.

5. *Antidrug operations,* or the use of military force to interdict the flow of illegal drugs into the United States or to locate and destroy narcotics plantations and laboratories located in other countries. Until fairly recently, U.S. law and policy precluded the use of U.S. military force in law-enforcement functions of this sort; under a presidential directive signed by President Reagan in April 1986, however, the Department of Defense was empowered to play a direct role in antidrug operations. Specifically, the Pentagon was authorized to conduct aerial and naval surveillance of suspected drug traffickers and to plan and support strike operations against drug laboratories and processing facilities in foreign countries. A large-scale action of this sort—Operation Blast Furnace—was conducted in the coca-growing Chapere area of Bolivia in 1986.[34] More recently, U.S. forces have been aiding Peruvian troops in their campaign against Shining Path guerrillas and coca growers in the Upper Huallaga Valley.

■ LOW-INTENSITY-CONFLICT
DOCTRINE IN THE 1990s

When President Bush took office in early 1989, the development of doctrine for low-intensity conflict was already well advanced. As previously noted, Bush placed particular emphasis on the threat posed by regional conflict in the Third World, and this emphasis was reflected in the strategic thinking of the Department of Defense. With the demise of the Soviet threat, regional conflict assumed even greater importance in Pentagon planning, and, by the early 1990s, had become the dominant concern of U.S. military policy.

This concern with regional conflict in the Third World was evident in Secretary of Defense Cheney's first annual report to the Congress (quoted earlier) and in a series of articles and speeches by many of the nation's top military officers. In all of these statements, the Pentagon leadership stressed that Third World conflict was increasing in virulence, and that a vigorous U.S. response was needed in order to protect vital interests. "The underdeveloped world's growing dissatisfaction over the gap between rich and poor nations will create a fertile breeding ground for insurgencies," General A. M. Gray of the Marine Corps observed in May 1990. "These insurgencies have the potential to jeopardize regional stability and our access to vital economic and military resources." This situation would grow increasingly serious as U.S. dependence on imported raw materials grew,

Gray argued, and thus, "If we are to have stability in these regions [and] maintain access to their resources . . . we must maintain within our active force structure a credible military power projection capability with the flexibility to respond to conflict across the spectrum of violence throughout the globe."[35]

Until 1990, such views were usually encapsulated within a Cold War framework. That is, turbulence in the Third World was typically described as a direct product of Soviet (or Soviet-Cuban, or Soviet-Libyan) meddling, or as a problem that required U.S. attention because of a potential for Soviet exploitation. With the collapse of the Soviet threat, however, U.S. strategists began to describe such upheavals as an *autonomous* threat to U.S. interests, quite independent of any Soviet involvement. "For 40 years . . . Third World conflict was seen as superpower conflict in miniature," Steven Metz of the Air War College wrote in 1991. "This image was never fully accurate and now is useless. Today, we simply cannot treat Third World conflict as a reflection of the Cold War but must look for endogenous [internal] causes and effects."[36]

Accompanying this shift in perspective has been a significant change in the relative status accorded such conflict in the hierarchy of perceived threats to U.S. national security: Whereas previously viewed as a secondary, subordinate danger, regional conflict is now seen as a major security challenge, requiring a commensurate allocation of resources and attention. Although the Cold War has diminished in intensity, Secretary Cheney observed in 1991, "we face the sobering truth that local sources of instability and oppression will continue to foster conflicts small and large virtually across the globe." This, in turn, "will require that we be able to respond if necessary, very rapidly, often very far from home, and against hostile forces that are increasingly well armed."[37]

Consistent with this assessment of the burgeoning Third World threat, President Bush has accelerated the actual use of U.S. forces in regional crises and conflicts. Thus, in the first two years of his presidency alone, Bush committed U.S. forces to two major military actions, Operation Just Cause in Panama (see Chapter 19) and Operation Desert Storm in Kuwait and Iraq (see Chapter 18). In addition, he authorized the use of U.S. forces in a number of "humanitarian" or peacekeeping operations with a potential military dimension, including Operation Sharp Edge in Liberia (June–August 1990), Operation Eastern Exit in Somalia (January 1991), and Operation Provide Comfort in northern Iraq (April–July 1991).[38]

Of these operations, Desert Storm naturally received the greatest attention from military analysts and the public. In the wake of the Persian Gulf conflict, the Defense Department and the four military services began to speak of a new type of threat—"mid-intensity conflict" (MIC)— involving combat between heavy U.S. forces and powerful Third World armies.[39] As suggested by Cheney in March 1991, "The Gulf War presaged very much the type of conflict we are most likely to confront again in this new era—major regional contingencies against foes well armed with advanced conventional and unconventional weaponry."[40] As time went on, however, many Pentagon analysts concluded that MIC encounters of the Desert Storm type were likely to be a rare occurrence, and that most Third World threats to U.S. security would probably continue to fall under the LIC heading. "Terrorism, civil wars, and remote insurgencies may not threaten our interests with the same immediacy and clarity as did the Iraqi invasion of Kuwait," Assistant Secretary of Defense James R. Locher III observed in July 1991, "but a succession of unaddressed low-intensity conflict challenges can destabilize the international order that is essential for our security and prosperity."[41]

Thus, with the Cold War over and Operation Desert Storm concluded, LIC emerged early in the 1990s as the major theme in U.S. security planning. Indeed, U.S. strategists began to speak of a post–Cold War era in which "instability itself" represents the greatest threat to world peace.[42] Such instability poses great danger to the "new world order" envisioned by President Bush and thus, according to his worldview, must be curbed or contained by U.S. military action whenever necessary. "The Cold War's end didn't deliver us into an era of perpetual peace," Bush noted on April 13, 1991. "As old threats recede, new threats emerge." Hence, "the quest for the new world order is, in part, a challenge to keep the dangers of disorder at bay."[43]

To keep the dangers of disorder at bay will obviously entail a wide variety of military and paramilitary operations, far exceeding the intended boundaries of LIC activity as perceived by the Reagan administration. Indeed, the very character of the LIC threat has been redefined in light of the Bush administration's new post–Cold War/post–Persian Gulf war assessment of the global security environment. "Numerous phenomena foment instability around the world," explained Assistant Secretary of Defense Locher in 1991. These include "rising nationalism, burgeoning international arms bazaars, increasing ethnic tensions, religious fundamentalism, environmental degradation and disease, economic stagnation coupled with rising expectations, and overpopulation and urbanization." Moreover, "Terrorists, drug traffickers, anti-American insurgents, and other aggressors will seek to capitalize on this instability."[44]

This broadening of the parameters of low-intensity conflict has been accompanied by an increase in the types of military operations that are covered by LIC doctrine in current U.S. military planning. Thus, in addition to the five categories previously described, we should now add three more:

1. *Pacification or control of ethnic conflicts.* As is all too evident in Yugoslavia, Ethiopia, Somalia, India, Sri Lanka, and other war-torn areas,

ethnic and religious conflicts have acquired fresh vigor and intensity over the past few years. Such conflicts may not raise political or strategic issues of direct concern to the United States, but the very proliferation of such disorders poses a significant threat to regional and international security—and thus, under the new Bush policy, could invite U.S. efforts to restore order and separate the combatants. The most significant U.S. effort of this type to date was Operation Provide Comfort of May–July 1991, which entailed the deployment of U.S. forces in northern Iraq to establish a protective screen behind which Kurdish refugees could reoccupy the villages they had fled in March and April following an abortive uprising against Saddam Hussein.[45] Such operations can be carried out by U.S. forces acting unilaterally, or, as in Operation Provide Comfort, may be conducted under UN or multilateral sponsorship of some sort.

2. *Humanitarian assistance.* Several of the operations conducted by U.S. forces under Bush's direction, including Sharp Edge and Eastern Exit, were characterized as "humanitarian" missions, aimed at rescuing foreign nationals from war-torn countries or at providing food and medical care to the victims of war or natural disaster. Such missions are, in fact, seen as a major U.S. military responsibility in the post–Cold War era. Although long considered an ancillary function of U.S. military forces, humanitarian operations of this sort can fall into the LIC category when conducted against a backdrop of ethnic or political conflict, as in Liberia, Somalia, and Iraq. In such cases, U.S. forces risk being caught in the crossfire between hostile parties, or in playing a protective role for one side or another, as occurred in Operation Provide Comfort.[46]

3. *Military civic action.* At a time when the prestige of the militaries of many Third World countries is in decline because of their close association with authoritarian rule and the systematic abuse of human rights, the U.S. military is encouraging its fellow services in Latin America and elsewhere to increase their involvement in military civic action, or the use of military forces in civil development projects that aid the rural population and thereby enhance the popular image of the military. Under current LIC doctrine, U.S. forces are encouraged to support such activities by providing training and material assistance to Third World armies and, in some cases, participate directly. "As part of a program of nation-building," Assistant Secretary of Defense Locher affirmed in 1991, U.S. forces "take part in humanitarian assistance and civic action programs building roads and digging wells in South America." Such activities, he noted, are likely to play an increasing role in the Pentagon's LIC repertoire in the years ahead.[47]

Together with the five categories described earlier, these three additional mission types suggest the range and complexity of low-intensity conflict operations that are currently envisioned by U.S. doctrine. While all-out high-intensity conflict seems less and less likely in the post–Cold War era, and mid-intensity operations of the Desert Storm type are likely to be relatively rare occurrences, LIC is likely to figure more and more prominently in U.S. military policies and practices. And although U.S. officials sometimes speak of the need to develop nonmilitary solutions to regional conflicts, the growing importance accorded LIC doctrine in U.S. strategic thinking suggests a continuing reliance on military intervention as the ultimate U.S. response to such challenges.

■ 4

The Globalist-Regionalist Debate

Charles F. Doran

Much of the debate surrounding U.S. foreign policy in the Third World in the post–World War II period may be subsumed in the dialogue between the globalists and the regionalists. These two perspectives on foreign policy are not mutually exclusive on all points of conduct, legitimacy, and style, nor are they unique to the setting of U.S. foreign policy. To some extent, other governments and societies have also been preoccupied with these questions of priority and emphasis in terms of East-West and North-South. But globalist-regionalist perspectives certainly characterize much of analysis in the 1990s about where U.S. foreign policy ought to head and about how it ought to get there.

Defining such broad persuasions about foreign policy priority is not easy, and such definition should not be undertaken casually. The globalists stressed in the 1980s the primacy of East-West confrontation at all levels of international political behavior, in all parts of the international system. All of international relations was seen through the lens of Soviet-U.S. relations and, indeed, as a virtual outgrowth of bipolar relations. The regionalists emphasize the dilemmas of North-South relations, the idiosyncrasies of politics and culture within the various geographic regions, and the comparative autonomy of the struggles that go on within and between the states of these regions. More than just a divergent interpretation of the nature of the contemporary international system, these two perspectives involve divergent interpretations about the meaning and origin of contemporary international politics, differences that can be separated into three broad categories: (1) the origins of change and stability; (2) foreign policy purpose; and (3) foreign policy strategy and means.

The fragmentation of the Soviet Union into a host of noncommunist independent countries has changed but not shattered the globalist-regionalist dichotomy. First, the historical justification of the globalist position as exposited in the post-1945 period is itself worthy of examination for what it tells the analyst about the sources of U.S. foreign policy in this period. Second, even without the ideological urgency and political rationales that once accompanied the globalist-inspired doctrine of containment of the Soviet

Union, many elements of the globalist perspective will survive, will find adherents, and will continue to shape important aspects of U.S. foreign policy. In a number of ways, the globalist-regionalist debate is enduring.

■ ORIGINS OF CHANGE AND STABILITY

The fundamental difference in perspective between the globalists and the regionalists is in understanding the meaning and origins of social and political change.[1] Other policy distinctions are important but derivative. Although some elements of this difference in social understanding are timeless and universal, other elements are quite parochial in the temporal sense and are an outgrowth of the East-West struggle and contemporary North-South debates.

□ *Order Maintenance from the Top Versus Self-Determination at the Bottom*

A presumption of the globalists is that order starts at the top of the international system.[2] If war breaks out there, it is very likely to become major. Thus, a premium is placed upon effectively "managing" relationships at the top of the systems hierarchy among the leading states. It is further assumed that order-maintenance, especially in a bipolar system (one in which two major powers are dominant), is never easy but is feasible. Because of the relative directness of communication, the continuity of probe and counterprobe, and the high quality of information available to each party, surprise and uncertainty are kept to a minimum. Small crises having their origin at the top of the system are not allowed to get out of hand. This has been the general experience of superpower relations in the post–World War II period, including the Berlin Crisis (1948), the Cuban missile crisis (1962), the October War (1973), and the problems of oil transport through the Persian Gulf (1987–1988).

The globalists, likewise, are troubled about the danger of confrontations among small powers that eventually percolate to the top of the system and become unmanageable.[3] The relationship between Austria-Hungary and Serbia (and, particularly, Germany and Austria-Hungary) in 1913 come to mind, but one could as easily point to the American colonies in the 1760s as a source of problems for France and Britain, to Korea in 1903 for Russia and Japan, or to Vietnam in the post-1945 period for China, the Soviet Union, and the United States. Thus, the inclination of the globalists is to attempt to control local and regional wars or to attempt to defuse the conditions of such wars before they ignite. It is true that these efforts often entangle the United States more deeply in the domestic and external affairs of small allies and client states than is otherwise preferable. But the alternative, according to globalists, is to stand aside, to do nothing, and to see the regional confrontations smolder into wider confrontations that may become even more problematic.

Opposed to this analysis on almost every point is the regionalist interpretation. From the regionalist perspective, a stable world system is best described as a system of interdependence among states with autonomous and unfettered foreign policies. The greatest threat to world order comes from oppression from the top.[4] The aftermath of colonialism (direct external governmental control of the colony's foreign policy) and perhaps imperialism (indirect external cultural, economic, or political influence over states abroad) is held to be proof of the failure of a hierarchical world order. Major states at the top of the system have no greater insight into the maintenance of world order, or any greater capacity to achieve it, than do smaller states. All states are equal in international legal attributes and in membership to bodies like the United Nations. All states have a right to the full expression of their grievances, in international bodies such as the World Court or in regional bodies such as the European Community (EC). Growing interdependence between states assures a more stable international environment in which to carry out individual foreign policy preferences.

Thus, according to the regionalist perspective, suppression of legitimate foreign policy grievances from the top of the global hierarchy is the principal source of extensive (global) warfare.[5] This suppression creates frustration and hostility toward global powers that lead to open military challenge. The United States, it is argued, should understand this message better than most states as it was born during the eighteenth century in rebellion against oppression by a state at the top of the international system. The American colonies revolted against what were seen as the unjust, coercive, and exploitative policies of Great Britain. Whether from a liberal or a Marxist persuasion, these arguments often expressed by regionalists—sometimes favoring a "multipolar" conception of world order (several autonomous, comparatively equal regional centers of power); sometimes supportive of the thesis of growing interdependence among states—often reflect the way governments and opinion elites within regions appear to look at the world system.[6]

In short, the globalists implicitly favor order-maintenance from the top of the international system because they fear the escalation of wars on the periphery to eventual conflagrations at the center. Regionalists implicitly reject this concept of systemic stability, arguing that the greater danger is that a confrontation of major powers at the center is likely to spill war onto the periphery. Causation of extensive, global instability, they argue, moves from center to periphery rather than from the periphery to center. Moreover, regionalists object to efforts to control stability from the top of the system that become oppressive and even exploitative, creating the most dangerous conditions of all for aggravated rebellion and warfare within regions as well as between regional actors and the major states at the top of the system.

□   *Foreign Meddling Versus*
    Indigenous Causes of Conflict

Many contemporary globalists believe that foreign powers are behind most important regional turmoil in the Third World, if not as deus ex machina, then as catalysts once the social, economic, and political conditions for revolution are ripe. During the Cold War era, for example, these writers and analysts focused primarily on the threat posed by the Soviet Union and the perceived desire of its leaders to expand Soviet power into new areas of geostrategic opportunity.[7] Its national capability was rising. Its capacity to project naval power throughout the world had grown significantly since the 1970s. It was the only country that could mortally wound the United States militarily; thus, every Soviet advance and marginal political achievement became a relevant factor in the overall military balance. Despite the possibility of Soviet-U.S. cooperation, the globalist perceived East-West conflict in a bipolar system as essentially zero-sum (that is, a Soviet gain represented a U.S. loss, and vice versa).

According to this version of globalism, a shift in the balance of power between the West and the Soviet Union was likely to have a significant impact upon world order and upon accepted rules of international behavior.[8] Both neutrals and allies were likely to feel this negative change. The Soviets understood coercion and used it skillfully. The quality of the relationship between East Germany or Poland and the Soviet Union was not the same as the relationship between Brazil or Mexico and the United States, for example. The Soviet Union used elite manipulation, party control, direct military intimidation, and economic bribery in a way that was regarded as far more constraining than anything employed by the United States, even assuming that each superpower had an equivalent interest in international political stability. A system in which the Soviet Union was more dominant would be a system, according to the globalists, that allowed for much less freedom— individual freedom within subordinate states, external freedom for the foreign policies of dependent polities.[9]

Regionalists were no more fond of the brand of world order promoted by the Soviets than were globalists, but they see world politics through a more complex political lens. They see the primary source of regional instability as emergent within societies and internal to regions themselves. External catalysts of such instability are regarded as clearly secondary in importance. If access to guns and military hardware were the deciding factor in regional instability, these could be purchased on the black market or taken from government armed forces units. But the deciding factor, as regionalists see the matter of internal stability, is the effort of organized political movements and parties—some of them Marxist-Leninist, some of them not—to cope with governments heavily burdened by maladministration and indifference to human welfare. As population pressures grow and stagnant economies fail to meet the needs of large sectors of society, the conditions for guerrilla activity and other forms of violent opposition to government will increase.[10] Not carried out by illiterate peasants or an unemployed urban proletariat, but led by frustrated, belligerent members of the middle class, either within the army or outside it, most violent political change is perpetrated by individuals who seek to gain power for themselves in the name of transforming oppressive social conditions. Most massive social upheavals, according to the regionalists, are pragmatic and homegrown. Political freedom is often a forgotten variable. So is economic efficiency, as governmental control is substituted for whatever private enterprise may exist. But the response to indigenous problems, in the eyes of most regionalists, should still be indigenous, not imported from abroad.

Regionalists also lament the lack of knowledge globalists portray about the complexity of cultural, social, and political differences within regions.[11] For example, to understand the relationship between Iraq or Syria and the former Soviet Union, one must understand the extent to which domestic communist parties have been subjected to repression and the extent to which governing elites (representing minority communal groups) have been able to stay in power by maintaining an internal equilibrium among offsetting Moslem orthodoxies. Radicalism has many fathers. Shia Moslems may not have as much in common with the Palestine Liberation Organization (PLO) as with Iranian nationalists, and the Kurds (largely nomadic peoples living in sections of Iraq, Iran, and Turkey), for historical as well as ethnolinguistic reasons, may reject both.[12] One of the most telling regionalist challenges to the globalists is that the latter often do not have the facts of social, political, and cultural organization upon which to make sound policy judgments concerning regional politics.

In sum, the regionalists recognize the overwhelming importance of indigenous factors in contributing to internal social and political unrest within regions. For them, the solution to such unrest must take into account internal regional dynamics and cleavages. In this vein, solutions are more likely to come from within regions than be imposed from outside. The Soviet Union was perceived as only one of the many possible stimuli of societal turmoil and rarely the most relevant. Indeed, according to regionalists, unless long-term indigenous factors are addressed, stability will not be possible in many areas of geostrategic interest to the United States.[13] Concentrating upon what the Soviet Union might or might not do was exactly the wrong way to make foreign policy that was regionally sensitive and, therefore, reasonably successful.

In contrast, the globalist is skeptical about many regionalist claims, not on grounds of factual understanding but on grounds of political interpretation.

The globalist sees revolution as quite different from social unrest.[14] Revolution in the international system during the Cold War era was thought likely to be Marxist-Leninist for many reasons, not the least of which was that most of the leaders of significant guerrilla movements received their training either in Moscow or Havana. Even in the aftermath of the Cold War, globalists continue to focus on the threats posed by foreign (albeit noncommunist) powers such as a resurgent Russia and an Islamic fundamentalist Iran.

□ *Change as Orderly Political Process*
   Versus Inevitable Destabilization

Globalist ideas stress the necessity for orderly political change—first, to permit significant economic development; second, to create at least the possibility of the growth of democratic institutions. Globalists tend to see the purpose of economic and military aid, for example, as creating the conditions whereby growth and development become possible.[15] They point out that, even in communist societies, a top priority is placed upon orderly political processes. Why should the allegedly more conservative noncommunist routes to political and social development be less supportive of a stable environment in which to carry out economic enterprise than the communist route?

For the globalist, orderly processes of development are not sufficient, but they are necessary. To use sad examples, Haiti under Papa Doc Duvalier may have been "orderly" in a narrow political sense, just as Albania is "orderly" from another political persuasion. But neither Haiti nor Albania has displayed much economic growth or development. Political order is necessary for economic achievement; indeed, from the viewpoint of liberal economic development theory, it is the most fundamental task of government. In the absence of political order (that is, in the atmosphere of continued social turmoil, civil war, or revolution), little progress can be made toward sustained economic achievement, as most attention is turned toward the struggle to remain in power or the struggle merely to survive.

But political order alone is not enough. As South Korea demonstrates for the globalist camp, substantial economic growth for the individual citizen must be accompanied by increasing access to the wealth produced. Likewise, welfare and social services ought to be provided broadly. Yet, throughout this process efficiency and equity are tradeoffs—a proper balance must be maintained for each step of the development process. Without a modicum of political order, the government will be unable to deliver benefits to the society; without delivering social and economic benefits, maintenance of political order increasingly will have to rely on coercion. For the globalist looking at the problems of economic development in the Third World, it is difficult to ignore the high correlation between cultural cohesion, political order, entrepreneurship, and economic growth among the Newly

Industrializing Countries (NICs), such as Hong Kong, Taiwan, and, despite student unrest, South Korea. Remove political order as a variable from this equation and the record of the NICs would have been far less impressive.

For the regionalist, economic growth and development are inevitably destabilizing, and it is the wise government that prepares for this and allows a certain level of such turmoil to proceed.[16] Governments on the right (such as the former Somoza family regimes in Nicaragua or regimes in Liberia) that place so much emphasis on maintaining order through coercion and neglect to create the proper atmosphere either for economic enterprise or for adequate schooling and governmental services discover they have neither growth nor long-term stability.[17] Similarly, governments on the left, such as China, North Korea, and Vietnam, have discovered that the ideological structures of authoritarian control and central planning have denied the opportunities for growth and economic development. Only room for decentralized enterprise, responsiveness to market signals, and economic entrepreneurship and risk will enable an economy to move forward at its potential, at least beyond the phase of heavy industrialization accompanied by the severest austerity.

The regionalist, likewise, is aware of what empirical research has pointed out concerning the impact of foreign assistance on the recipient polity. The effect of foreign assistance in the short run may be that it is not smoothly or effectively absorbed by the society. As it destroys old practices and allegiances, new ones may not easily be fashioned. Serious political instability may result.[18] For example, a road built deep into the rain forests along Brazil's Amazon River may open up new stresses and strains to development, as villagers are able to migrate to Brasilia and the influences of industrialization are carried to individuals living in the rural areas.[19]

In short, whereas globalists tend to be suspicious of instability of any variety, preferring to believe that modernization can proceed quietly and without confusion, regionalists recognize that modernization and economic development place enormous strains on any society, strains that for the most part are probably unavoidable. Yet, the globalist maintains that instability, however endemic to the development process, is nonetheless antithetical to economic enterprise and growth. Instability may be inevitable, but it is not desirable. Those Third World governments that learn to manage instability, often with initial outside help, while creating the conditions under which both import-competing and export industries can prosper, are the governments that will experience the highest levels of per capita income in the twenty-first century.

■ FOREIGN POLICY PURPOSE

Apart from their opposing understandings of the origins of social and political change, regionalists and globalists differ regarding the values and preferences they would bring to foreign policy conduct. They differ in how they perceive foreign-policy-making priorities and in the scope of the responsibilities to be assumed by good government abroad.

□ *Maintenance of World Order*
  Versus Economic Development

Globalists believe that the maintenance of order and security is the highest priority a government can establish for itself.[20] They also believe that security is a specialized function of government requiring substantial resources and great attention. All the techniques, strategies, and instruments commonly associated with security and order-maintenance, therefore, are given a high priority in relations with Third World countries.

The globalist tends to believe that any government committed to order-maintenance responsibilities probably has its hands full without assuming a variety of other functions better left to other national governments or to business firms or to local communities. Foreign assistance is thus a servant to order-maintenance objectives and is supplied with emphasis placed upon distributing military as opposed to economic aid to ward off problems made evident by crisis. By straying from the primary task of order-maintenance (providing economic assistance to achieve development objectives), government policymakers probably will perform this function less well, according to the globalist, and will end up convincing themselves that they have, in fact, replaced the local government as the primary purveyor of services, leadership, and economic incentive. By restricting assistance to order-maintenance functions and the distribution of military aid, globalists believe they are setting limits upon U.S. commitments and are neither misleading nor over-promising benefits to foreign governments.

In contrast, the regionalist tends to adopt a very different mind-set. The number one problem facing Third World governments is sufficiently rapid economic progress to offset the growth of population and the rise in public expectations.[21] Likewise, the regionalist believes that Americans ought to be concerned both on humanitarian and practical political grounds with the problems of broadly shared economic development.

Because, as the regionalist perceives, the existence of deep social inequality in repressive Third World countries is one of the key contributors to revolution, the United States can only achieve its objective of stability and security through the proper attention to meaningful economic growth and development. In the absence of such meaningful growth and development, revolution and war, slippage toward regimes with an extreme leftist orientation, and political realignment are the evident consequences in polities as diverse as Ethiopia and Nicaragua. Given these negative consequences, the regionalist cannot understand how a rich society with global interests such as the United States would not put a very high priority on assistance for economic growth and development.

To put a finer edge on the argument, the regionalist believes that a preoccupation with local balances of power, alliances, military security, and arms considerations cannot achieve order and security for the United States or for countries within more isolated areas.[22] This approach to foreign policy conduct is narrow-minded and bound to fail in its objectives. The principal analytic problem is that the globalist has misplaced causation. War and revolution spring from deeper economic and social problems within developing societies. Only by addressing these can the security and stability of the United States be obtained.

□ *Containment of Foreign Expansionism Versus Cultivation of Third World Ties*

The regionalist tends to prefer long-term policy elaboration to achieve "positive" goals, such as broadly shared economic development, whereas the globalist takes a foreign policy position that often amounts to crisis management. The globalist, therefore, was more predisposed during the Cold War era to treat East-West questions in which response to problems rather than foreign policy initiation was more fitting, whereas the regionalist continues to be more conditioned to the type of North-South problems in which the solutions are seen as long-term and which require the initiation of foreign policy programs.

Starting from the assumption that the Soviet Union was the principal U.S. rival and security threat, the globalist reasons that this justifies supporting insurgencies against formerly Soviet-backed regimes. The irony here is that this East-West concern quickly could drag the unwary government into a quagmire such as Vietnam. The costs of direct military intervention are replaced by the costs of protracted guerrilla warfare.[23] Conversely, the regionalist may stress improved ties to individual Third World countries based upon a strategy of broadly shared development as a way to build a foundation for avoiding serious security problems (domestic instability and revolution) in the long run. Yet, the regionalist who actually faces foreign policy implementation may discover that many Third World governments are more interested in arms aid and security problems than they are in economic aid and the esoterics of growth and development.[24]

The regionalist criticizes the notion of Soviet containment as not only irrelevant to more important issues but unworkable in practice, as the Soviet Union was in no sense "contained" by U.S. actions in the Third World. Indeed, the regionalist argues that factors indigenous to the Third World, such as nationalism, constrained the Soviets just as effectively as they have constrained the United States. The globalist rejects as empty and moralistic the notion of "improving ties" to the Third World, claiming this amounts to placing foreign policy emphasis where the international political "action" is not, and that there is no way of cementing ties for the future in any consistent, or cost-acceptable manner.

☐ *Defense of Democratic Values Versus*
Evenhandedness in Human Rights

Globalist logic would suggest that democracy is a superior form of government, that true democracies are few in number (and, in some cases, may be on the political endangered-species list), and that alliances among such governments are likely to be necessary for reinforcement. Some globalists with idealist tendencies, however, maintain that democracy and economic development are strongly related and that only poor governments or governments in troubled intervals are likely to be drawn toward totalitarianism.[25]

It is implicit in the globalist outlook that U.S. ties to nondemocratic governments are also mandatory, either to prevent retrenchment in numbers or to assist in the nascent shift toward representative government. Those globalists who do not believe that democracy is inevitable, no matter how virtuous this form of government is, generally lean toward rightist regimes more than leftist ones, rationalizing this behavior under a hundred guises but, in practice, promoting the argument that "once communist, always communist," while also assuming that rightist generals sometimes can be overthrown. Totalitarian (that is, communist) governments are considered immutable; authoritarian governments (that is, traditional dictatorships) are thought to be capable of redemption. The globalist tends to make foreign policy on the basis of conclusions about the form of government, its institutions, and, most of all, its commitments.[26]

By contrast, regionalists, perhaps because they are closer to some of the regimes about which they speculate, perhaps because they are at once more pragmatic and more skeptical than most globalists, tend to dismiss much of the discussion regarding governmental form, constitutions, institutions, and even formal treaty commitments. What regionalists focus on is behavior, the track record of actual performance. For most regionalists, the human rights record is a very meaningful record of behavior, and they tend to follow this record intently, assisted by analyses that they or organizations such as Amnesty International are able to provide.[27] As the record varies across regimes of the same type, and across comparable historical intervals, great familiarity with individual societies is needed for this type of judgment, a situation in which the craft of regional specialization provides obvious rewards.

A further demand made by most regionalists is that the treatment of human rights be evenhanded. Governments that are allies should receive the same scrutiny as those that are not. Governments on the far right should be evaluated just as carefully as those that may be on the far left. Although intellectually honest, such analysis is sometimes revealed to be politically awkward.[28] How does one accuse a favorite uncle of larceny, especially when he may be contributing to the family welfare in terms of security?

But true regionalists, again because of their greater expertise in comparative government and politics than in international relations and foreign policy, tend to insist that no international standard is likely to be effective unless it is evenly applied across polities. Here the globalists, often experts on international relations, disagree, because they would prefer to compare the human rights record not so much across states as across the overall policy record of the individual government, quite a different situation.[29]

■ STRATEGY AND MEANS

A priori, regionalists and globalists may disagree about foreign policy goals without disagreeing about the strategy to implement those goals or about the means employed in the strategy.[30] Observed debate, however, suggests that there is no more agreement about strategy and means than there is about foreign policy objectives.

□ *Intervention Versus
Constructive Nonintervention*

Ever since British Lord Robert Stewart Castlereagh sought to institute a strategy of nonintervention, following the Napoleonic Wars (1801–1814) and the Congress of Vienna (1815), to be abided by all of the major powers in order to prevent France from using intervention as a means of once again threatening the peace of the Central European system, governments periodically have opted for a strategy that sets limits on intervention or outlaws it altogether. Although this strategy in its contemporary U.S. form allegedly has roots in Wilsonian ethics, President Woodrow Wilson in actuality intervened repeatedly in the Caribbean and Central America in an effort to promote political stability. Yet, the principle of nonintervention, akin in some ways to that of the self-determination of peoples, is an idea that tends to divide globalists and regionalists.

Regionalists are very skeptical of great-power intervention. They see all too often a frightening great-power ignorance of the politics and culture—even geography—of the target state. One is reminded of the Kennedy fiasco in the Bay of Pigs, in which the Cuban swamps and mountain ranges had not been properly delineated. More salient than this was the invaders' naive anticipation of rebellion by the populace against Castro. Regionalists also question the significance of external ties to local insurrection, removing one of the substantial globalist justifications for intervention. Regionalists know the negative impact intervention has on regional public and elite opinion and the criticism intervention evokes when outside force is used ostensibly to promote self-determination and representative government.[31] The regionalist also may argue the moral position that one cannot lament Russian intervention in Eastern Europe while practicing intervention in Central America or the Caribbean. Most important, the regionalist believes that indigenous nationalism is stronger than the affinity for foreign ideologies backed by foreign aid and advisers. The Cold War examples of abrupt ruptures of relations with the Soviet Union by Egyptian leader Anwar Sadat and Somalia's Siyaad Barre, despite both leaders' supposed economic and military dependence on the USSR, are cited by regionalists as proof of the resilience of local nationalism and the reversibility of ties once a country has aligned itself with a foreign ideology and, in this case, communism as led by the Soviet Union.

A very telling criticism of intervention from the regional perspective is the nature of politics inside the target state *after* intervention. Although radical revolution may have been deterred, democracy is often nowhere in evidence, social progress is absent, and human rights continue to be trampled. For the most part, the polity is forgotten as long as it is no longer perceived as a threat. Even if foreign assistance is augmented, corruption eats up that assistance in such fashion that the polity is worse off than it was prior to the intervention. Hence, the record of economic and social progress following intervention is scarcely a matter of which the intervening state may be proud, in part because the main objective was military success and not a program of political and economic development founded on a pluralist party structure.

Yet, the globalist will hesitate to reject intervention as a foreign policy instrument.[32] The issue for the globalist is not the type of government a polity freely chooses for itself, but whether it (1) seeks to destabilize the countries around it through exported revolution; and (2) invites a foreign power—whether a communist Soviet Union of the 1980s, a noncommunist Russia of the 1990s, or a radical Third World leader such as Libya's Muammar Qaddafi—to expand its military presence within the region and thus serve as a proxy for foreign intelligence operations and subversion. In terms of contemporary U.S. foreign policy practice, the globalist sees these considerations as central in determining whether intervention is justified or not.[33] Although in some cases agreeing with these conditions, the regionalist may object that the problem is to determine when these conditions prevail in advance of their actual occurrence.

□   *Utility of Force Versus*
    Economic and Cultural Instruments

A closely associated argument involves whether force or noncoercive instruments are the more effective. Without reviewing the lengthy literature on this subject, suffice it to say that the utility of force is more apparent to the globalist than to the regionalist. Perhaps the correct judgment is that the globalist puts too much confidence in the utility of force as both a deterrent and a defense, and the regionalist puts too little.

The globalist is accustomed to thinking in terms of nuclear strategic weaponry and large standing armies. But within Third World regions, domestic stability and external stability are even more intertwined and less separable than among advanced industrial countries because the polity is more fragile and subject to foreign manipulation.[34] Subconventional warfare is more common than conventional. From the regionalist perspective, noncoercive instruments—such as cultural ties, economic assistance, and political cooperation—have a very long reach. The limits of military intervention are apparent both because of the risks of military failure and the political costs of military success. Thus, the regionalist often tends to reject force as the arbiter of regional politics.

The administration of foreign aid is the fulcrum over which this policy debate stretches. The globalist finds domestic political support in Congress for combined packages of military and economic aid awarded during crisis intervals when some form of communist threat seems imminent. The regionalist tends to want to divide economic and military aid and to provide economic aid in peacetime when the capacity to absorb this aid is greatest. Military assistance remains a crisis instrument. The problem for the regionalist is that the votes just have not existed in Congress for the equivalent amount of financial aid in the absence of crisis; nor, however much Third World governments want overall foreign assistance, are they prepared to value economic over military help.[35] Perhaps this is why, in addition to comparative availability, the Soviet Union in the past provided so much military aid to its dependents and so little true economic assistance.

□ *Traditional Alliance Association
Versus Basic Human Needs*

Finally, regionalists and globalists differ on the proper instruments of association and involvement in the Third World. The globalist tends to favor traditional alliance association: hence, the creation of multilateral defense organizations such as the Central Treaty Organization (CENTO) and the Southeast Asian Treaty Organization (SEATO).[36] But these organizations collapsed of their own weight because of internal disputes among the members. Or, more precisely, collapse of these multilateral alliance systems occurred because the external threat they were designed to offset was less compelling to the members than internal political, cultural, communal, and ideological differences within the region. Similarly, the United States has attempted to rely on client governments like the shah of Iran or Ferdinand Marcos of the Philippines, whose rules eventually decayed into corruption and repression that contributed to domestic unpopularity and the regimes' overthrow. Far from acting as regional stabilizers, these regimes ultimately were unable to foster development and to govern effectively. Indeed, as some subsequent regimes (Iran's Khomeini, Nicaragua's Sandinistas, and Libya's Qaddafi) attempted to exploit dissociation with the pro-U.S. policies of preceding governments, disparagement of ties with the United States became the modus vivendi for local rule.

Regionalists, conversely, have been much taken by the campaign to address basic human needs.[37] In terms of foreign policy means, the essence of the needs approach is very simple. The failure of traditional U.S. policy as favored by the globalist has been attributed to working at the wrong level— namely, the systemic or governmental levels. Basic human needs are individual. Thus, the regionalist often urges that U.S. foreign policy focus upon the requirements of the individual citizen regarding nutrition, shelter, health care, and education. The regionalist sometimes recommends that policy should outflank or circumvent often bureaucratically inefficient and corrupt local governments to bring resources directly to the individuals most in need of them.

But to the frustration of the regionalist, the reaction of the polity supposedly benefiting from the basic human needs approach is often starkly negative. Foreign governments are accused of intervention and imperialism.[38] Far from reaching the poorest members of the recipient society, assistance is left to "rot in the sun," as in Ethiopia, or fails to find adequate local transportation. Local citizens are intimidated and fear participation in basic human needs programs.

A reasonable judgment is that the globalist often views relations with Third World countries as too highly institutionalized and subject to management by formal arrangements with governments internal to the region. The globalist response is too political. By contrast, the regionalist response, although correctly targeted in terms of who would benefit, is sometimes rather naive in terms of mechanics of distribution and implementation. The regionalist, thoroughly aware of the shortcomings of local bureaucracy, eventually recognizes that outsiders must work with local governments at the risk of not being able to work at all. But the regionalist approach is sometimes not political enough.

■ GLOBALISM IN THE POST–COLD WAR ERA

Some analysts might assume that the collapse of the globalist posture is an inevitable outcome of the fragmentation of the Soviet Union into a host of noncommunist independent countries. Nothing could be more mistaken. Absent to be sure is the fear of Soviet behavior as a stimulus to globalist thinking. The initial effect of the changed Soviet role is, it is true, quite striking for U.S. foreign policy in the Third World.

As Jorge Castenada has pointed out, the left in the Third World has been denied support, both ideological and material.[39] But not only the political left has been affected. The greatest denial has come to those governments on the right and center that in the past could count on the globalist rivalry to induce assistance, both economic and military, from the United States. Now that strategy has been thwarted by the sudden and unpredicted withdrawal of the Soviet Union from the bipolar competition. Senators currently have a much harder time defending assistance to El Salvador than to Harlem.

But in a longer-term sense, many elements of the globalist outlook will live on. Arguments that world order is a top-down affair and that internal political order is a prerequisite of economic development as well as of global prosperity will continue. These justifications for political intervention, as Charles Maechling, Jr., observes regarding Panama, need not find a principal motivation in anti-Soviet or even in anticommunist rhetoric.[40] World order can be regarded as a seamless web in which rips or tucks need mending.

Indeed, as in the Panama case, the defense of democratic values, though not an international legal argument, can become a potent international political justification, even where its uneven implementation and its challenge to traditional international law in terms of sovereignty are evident. Instead of the threat of communism being used as a defense of intervention, the effort to fight drugs, reinstate democracy, and shore up an ally will find appeal from the globalist perspective, a perspective that after all puts other aspects of foreign policy conduct behind the maintenance of security writ large and the preservation of world order.

A surprising aspect of U.S. interventions is how continuous and similar has been their justification.[41] Much of this justification has come from the globalist outlook. That justification is likely to continue even without the Soviet Union as a real or imagined adversary and perpetrator of unrest. Moreover, intervention is likely to find a vindication from other than the globalist or regionalist perspective as well. As H. W. Brands, Jr., reminds his reader, "The shadow of past failures and present problems elsewhere" may be a sufficient incentive to consider intervention seriously where the political and military costs seem low.[42]

In the future, the focus of the globalist-regionalist debate is likely to shift toward "hegemonic" versus "balance-of-power" initiatives and "internationalist" versus "isolationist" interpretations. Interventionist motivation will be identified with hegemonic or, more positively, with internationalist thinking. Globalists in turn will associate the regionalist outlook with the advocacy of isolationist or, at best, a balance-of-power mentality. Hidden behind this debate is a very real reincarnation of the premises of the old globalist-regionalist debate, cast perhaps now more sharply in terms addressed to a domestic audience.

The analyst should not for a moment think, however, that the new globalist-regionalist debate is less important than the old. Given the present reality of only a single Rankean Great Power (defined by Ranke as a state that can "stand alone"), the problem of choosing between the arguments of the global and regional perspectives will become ever more difficult. Uncertainty contained in the present interval of systems transformation will endow every U.S. foreign policy action with even more visibility and responsiveness from other states. The United States itself will become obliged to select its actions more prudently so as not to elicit a "global" negative response from other governments often in the past experienced only at the regional level by less-than-grateful observers. Regionalism and globalism thus are not concepts limited to a single historical epoch, but are continuing dichotomies that separate foreign policy goals, strategies, and, above all, means.

■ THE DEBATE IN PERSPECTIVE

Although the globalist and the regionalist perspectives are not complete opposites, nor unrelated to other pressing aspects of foreign policy conduct, the assumptions of both schools of thought do underlie much that is profound and even perhaps ambiguous about U.S. foreign policy behavior in the Third World. As an ideal type, neither of these perspectives corresponds perfectly to the outlook of any U.S. administration in the post–World War II period. Yet, administrations may be categorized in terms of their comparative enthusiasm for either interpretation. For example, the policies of both the Truman administration (1945–1953) and the Reagan administration (1981–1989) reflected the globalist interpretation, whereas policies of the early years of the Carter administration (1977–1978) and certain aspects of those of the Kennedy administration (1961–1963) favored a regionalist approach. Differences are even discernible within each administration, as certain officials and policymakers became known for their globalist or regionalist emphasis. In the Carter administration (1977–1981), National Security Adviser Zbigniew Brzezinski favored a globalist orientation, whereas UN Ambassador Andrew Young and Secretary of State Cyrus Vance emphasized regionalist approaches. Over time, administrations have even changed in outlook concerning these perspectives. In general, the Carter administration began with a strong regionalist commitment. But that commitment was supplanted by a globalist outlook as events in Afghanistan, Nicaragua, and the Horn of Africa seemed to involve more and more of an East-West orientation. The strong globalist outlook of the Reagan administration—wholeheartedly supported by the Bush administration, albeit minus the harsh anticommunist rhetoric—was already in the making before the Republicans took office. Perhaps, overall, U.S. foreign policy in the post–World War II period has shown a tendency to be globalist in interpretation. The degree to which these perceptions corresponded to objective evaluation is a function of a great many factors, some of which I have attempted to assess in this chapter.

The tension between globalist and regionalist outlooks is central to any discussion of intervention in the Third World by the great powers, including the United States. Although persons of goodwill and intellectual honesty will differ on the validity of these perspectives, the shortcomings of each and strengths of each are worthy of examination by an informed U.S. public. U.S. foreign policy can only be conducted on the basis of broad consensus. Such consensus can only be formed through reasoned debate about priorities as different as those embodied in the globalist and regionalist outlooks.

■ Part 3

TOOLS OF INTERVENTION

5

Economic and Military Aid

Doug Bandow

Since World War II, the United States has provided $241.3 billion in bilateral (that is, government-to-government) economic assistance. Most of this money officially has been intended to promote economic development in other nations, either by underwriting specific projects or augmenting foreign treasuries. The United States has also extended roughly $145.6 billion in bilateral grants and loans to recognized governments (in contrast to guerrilla movements) for avowed security purposes. The largest program is Military Assistance Grants, which provides cash to other nations to enhance their defense. Moreover, the largest share, 25 percent or more, of the nearly $400 billion worth of multilateral (that is, international organization–to–government) economic assistance during the post–World War II period has come from the United States. Almost 75 percent of that money has gone through the World Bank and its two affiliates, the International Development Association and the International Finance Corporation. Other assistance has been channeled through the three regional development banks, the United Nations Development Program, and other UN agencies.

This flood of cash has thrust the United States into the affairs of virtually every other nation on earth, and, increasingly since the end of World War II, those nations comprising the Third World. In fact, although the United States most directly and effectively asserts its power through military force, foreign assistance has affected far more countries on a more frequent basis. However, the benefits of the roughly $500 billion (about $1.1 trillion in 1992 dollars) spent on foreign aid since World War II are less clear: Many developing states have been moving backward economically; well-subsidized U.S. allies have been overthrown; and funds have continued to flow to nations that regularly oppose U.S. interests abroad.

■ EVOLUTION OF THE FOREIGN AID PROGRAM[1]

The first official U.S. foreign aid bill was passed in May 1812; it provided $150,000 in disaster relief to Venezuela following an earthquake. Although certainly a substantial 7.5 percent of the nation's $20 million budget at the time, it was not until World War II that foreign aid became a significant tool of U.S. intervention in the Third World. As President Harry S Truman's administration demobilized much of the military—which had numbered 12 million—at the end of the war, it turned to foreign assistance to augment the U.S. arsenal for overseas intervention. In the early 1990s, the United States grants and lends roughly $15 billion annually to other nations, both bilaterally and multilaterally.

The U.S. assistance program effectively began at the end of World War II with the Marshall Plan, though a few UN programs for rehabilitation and refugees preceded it. Between 1948 and 1952, the Marshall Plan consumed 15 percent of federal outlays, roughly fifteen times the burden of the much more diverse foreign aid program of the 1990s. The Marshall Plan theoretically was created for humanitarian purposes—to aid in the reconstruction of Europe—but the Truman administration also viewed U.S. assistance as a means to bolster Western Europe against the threat of both domestic communist revolutions and external Soviet invasion. The first official recipients of military aid were Turkey and Greece, and Greece was facing a serious communist insurgency at the time.

The role of foreign aid was greatly enhanced in 1949 when President Truman, in his inaugural address, advocated a much wider distribution of U.S. funds in his Point Four program. Truman proposed to make available to other countries the benefits of U.S. technical knowledge and to foster capital investment in developing countries. Five years later, Congress created the Food for Peace program in an effort to reduce U.S. crop surpluses and feed the hungry in developing nations.

Programs involving security aid were constantly changed, as Congress successively established the Mutual Defense Assistance Program, the Mutual Security Program, Supporting Assistance, and Security Supporting Assistance. The Agency for International Development (AID) was established by presidential executive order in 1961 to administer economic aid programs. In 1973, Congress passed the New Directions legislation, which instructed that economic assistance be used more to meet "basic human needs," through literacy and health-care programs, for example. A few years later, Congress enacted the Economic Support Fund (ESF). Though technically a form of economic aid, ESF in actuality functions as a type of military assistance by subsidizing nations deemed important to U.S. security, either because of the bases they offer (such as Turkey) or their role as regional military surrogates for the United States (such as Israel). The other major defense programs are the Foreign Military Sales Credits Program, the Military Assistance Program Grants, and International Military Education and Training.

The United States has actively promoted multilateral assistance programs as well. The World Bank, established as one of the Bretton-Woods institutions in 1944, theoretically lends for the purposes reflected in its official name: the International Bank for Reconstruction and Development. Over the years, the bank added the International Development Association, which makes essentially interest-free loans to poor states, and the International Finance Corporation, which extends credit to private and public firms in foreign nations. The UN, too, through several different programs, provides funds and technical assistance to underdeveloped states.

Though both economic and military aid have been constants of U.S. policy, the amount, recipients, and form of assistance have varied sharply. As is shown in Table 5.1, though spending has fluctuated over time, ranging between $40.9 billion in 1949 and $12.5 billion in 1976, it has steadily dropped as a percentage of U.S. gross national product (GNP). Aid consumed roughly 2 percent of GNP at the start of the 1950s but only 1 percent a decade later. In the early 1970s, the percentage of GNP devoted to foreign assistance dropped to roughly .7 percent; it was just .28 percent at the beginning of the 1990s.

The beneficiaries of U.S. aid, as portrayed in Table 5.2, have also changed as U.S. strategic interests have evolved. This is just as true of development assistance, designed to promote economic growth, as it is of security aid, for economic assistance generally has been doled out in a manner thought to advance U.S. political and security interests. As a result, during the late 1940s and early 1950s the bulk of U.S. aid went to Europe, which was viewed as the region most vulnerable to communism. Between 1949 and 1952, annual U.S. assistance to Europe ranged between $25 billion and $33 billion. Once the major northern European nations, particularly Great Britain, West Germany, and France, began to recover, aid flows shifted toward poorer Greece and Turkey, which along with Spain and Portugal are the major European beneficiaries of U.S. funds in the late 1980s.

Asia was a distant second on the aid recipient list until Europe began to recover economically and the Korean War highlighted the threat of communist aggression in the Far East. In 1955, assistance to Asia totaled $9.2 billion and surged past that to Europe, $6.1 billion, which further declined in the 1970s. Throughout the mid-1950s and early 1960s, Asian assistance fell below $8.4 billion a year only once; the Vietnam War briefly pushed that figure above $15 billion. Moreover, during the war the United States provided an additional $40 billion—$8.4 billion in 1973 alone— through the Military Assistance Service Fund, which aided Vietnam and the U.S. allies that supplied troops in the conflict. But the collapse of Vietnam and Cambodia in the mid-1970s cut U.S. assistance to that region by more than half in 1974; in the 1980s assistance to Asia fell below $2 billion annually.

Throughout much of the 1960s, Latin America ranked second behind Asia as a recipient of U.S. aid money. There was a sharp but temporary increase—to $4 billion—in assistance during the mid-1960s as part of the Alliance for Progress; but once the specter of more Cuban-style revolutions

TABLE 5.1
U.S. Foreign Aid as a Percentage of Gross National Product, 1946–1991

Year	Aid
1946	1.47
1947	2.88
1948	1.23
1949	3.21
1950	2.08
1951	2.30
1952	1.96
1953	1.36
1954	1.30
1955	1.02
1956	1.15
1957	1.10
1958	.89
1959	1.04
1960	1.03
1961	1.04
1962	1.16
1963	1.07
1964	.83
1965	.78
1966	.91
1967	.79
1968	.77
1969	.70
1970	.66
1971	.73
1972	.76
1973	.71
1974	.59
1975	.45
1976	.52
1977	.41
1978	.42
1979	.57
1980	.37
1981	.36
1982	.40
1983	.41
1984	.43
1985	.43
1986	.39
1987	.35
1988	.29
1989	.29
1990	.29
1991	.28

Source: Data provided by the Congressional Research Service, Washington, D.C.

TABLE 5.2
U.S. Foreign Aid by Major Region, 1946–1986[a]
(2-year averages, in billions of constant 1987 dollars)

Year	Europe	Asia	Middle East	Africa	Latin America	Totals
1946	13.217	2.239	.129	.049	.203	15.837
1947	30.744	6.677	.134	.009	.159	37.723
1948	11.101	4.023	.007	.003	.212	15.346
1949	33.338	6.646		.001	.131	40.116
1950	25.566	3.468	.059	.001	.141	29.235
1951	28.506	5.485	.137	.004	.083	34.215
1952	25.309	4.621	.683	.011	.344	30.968
1953	14.688	5.348	.700	.119	.603	21.458
1954	9.977	8.764	1.006	.144	.309	20.200
1955	6.074	9.185	1.141	.043	.527	16.970
1956	6.499	10.680	.971	.052	1.096	19.298
1957	4.695	10.828	1.394	.107	1.352	18.376
1958	5.105	6.751	2.050	.067	.857	14.830
1959	5.611	8.762	1.804	.299	.901	17.377
1960	5.025	10.430	1.959	.173	.878	18.465
1961	4.817	8.582	2.496	.850	2.010	18.755
1962	3.690	10.798	2.487	1.240	3.753	21.968
1963	3.764	9.722	2.442	1.013	3.559	20.500
1964	2.256	8.351	1.559	.872	3.999	17.037
1965	2.146	8.673	1.675	.784	3.273	16.551
1966	2.319	12.261	2.076	.962	3.540	21.158
1967	1.635	10.623	1.754	.974	2.559	17.545
1968	1.205	13.155	1.360	.679	2.727	19.126
1969	1.271	12.815	1.194	.801	1.494	17.575
1970	1.127	12.240	.549	.623	1.843	16.382
1971	1.180	14.052	2.359	.702	1.502	19.795
1972	1.392	16.508	1.832	.620	1.504	21.856
1973	1.088	15.589	1.681	.572	1.305	20.235
1974	.707	7.412	6.366	.689	1.125	16.299
1975	.531	5.768	2.992	.716	1.224	11.231
1976	.522	2.906	5.903	.552	1.089	10.972
1976[b]	.551	.834	1.912	.194	.262	3.753
1977	1.122	2.299	5.711	.754	.717	10.603
1978	1.532	2.326	5.527	.974	.780	11.139
1979	1.069	1.954	12.281	.883	.744	16.931
1980	1.160	1.723	4.694	1.167	.739	9.483
1981	1.177	1.627	5.353	1.180	.868	10.205
1982	1.599	1.590	5.523	1.286	1.195	11.193
1983	1.816	1.939	6.275	1.196	1.533	12.759
1984	2.192	2.076	6.301	1.355	1.755	13.679
1985	2.170	2.100	6.903	1.670	2.300	15.143
1986	1.853	1.840	6.831	1.119	1.714	13.347
Totals	271.352	293.689	118.228	25.527	56.928	765.724

Source: Data provided by the Congressional Research Service, Washington, D.C.
[a]Figures do not include $120 billion focused on specific regions.
[b]Transition quarter (fiscal year shifted).

receded, interest in the program waned, and a decade later aid to Latin America had fallen below that to Europe. Funding increased again in the 1980s, peaking at $2.3 billion annually in 1985 as a result of the Reagan administration's efforts to bolster the governments of El Salvador and its noncommunist neighbors. But when assistance fell by $600 million in 1986, Latin America fell behind Europe once more. (The administration also launched the Caribbean Basin Initiative to promote regional economic development; the program involved little money, however, and flopped badly when Congress imposed quotas on sugar imports, one of the Caribbean's most important export goods.)

Concern over Israel's security caused the Middle East, which between 1946 and 1973 had never received more than $2.5 billion in a single year, to catapult into the number two aid position, after Asia, in 1974. Two years later, with the end of U.S. aid to Vietnam and Cambodia, the Middle East became the largest regional recipient of aid; in fact, outlays for the Middle East escalated above $5 billion annually by the middle of the decade and spurted to $12.3 billion in 1979, largely as a result of the Camp David accords and the informal U.S. agreement to subsidize Egypt heavily as well as longtime ally Israel.

Aid to Africa has lagged far behind that to other regions. Only in the late 1950s did U.S. assistance rise above minimal levels; aid flows broke the $1 billion level only twice between 1946 and 1979. Even after African aid peaked at $1.7 billion in 1985, that continent was still the smallest regional recipient of U.S. help.

An examination of Table 5.3 shows that foreign aid priorities have also varied sharply over the years. Immediately following World War II, development and economic assistance accounted for the largest share of U.S. aid—$39.4 billion out of a total of $40.9 billion in 1949—though military assistance took first place at $20.2 billion in 1951, as the Marshall Plan was waning. With an occasional exception, including the years 1962–1965, security aid has stayed in the lead position, even after military assistance fell sharply from $13.3 billion in both 1972 and 1973 to $3.9 billion in 1977 after the collapse of Vietnam and Cambodia. The Reagan administration markedly increased military aid, pushing it above the $7-billion mark in 1984, though outlays fell in succeeding years.

Spending on food assistance, which is predominantly economic aid mixed with some humanitarian elements, has ranged from $1.4 billion to $5.5 billion between 1955 and 1987. During a few years, food aid actually exceeded development assistance, though the latter generally has been higher. Finally, aid given through the Economic Support Fund, which essentially provides economic aid based on security criteria, and its predecessor programs actually exceeded development aid in the mid-1950s, when it ran as high as $7 billion. Spending in this category fell throughout the 1960s and early 1970s, hitting a low of $1.4 billion in 1969, but climbed back above the

TABLE 5.3
U.S. Foreign Aid by Major Program, 1946–1986
(2-year averages, in billions of constant 1987 dollars)

Year	Development Assistance	Food Aid	Other Economic Aid	Multilateral Development Banks	Economic Support Fund	Military	Total
1946			16.749	4.357			21.106
1947			37.670			.958	38.628
1948			14.333			1.638	15.971
1949	31.627		7.780			1.516	40.923
1950	18.343		5.657		.003	5.949	29.952
1951	11.896		3.729		.750	20.186	36.561
1952	8.489	.393	1.607		.908	20.844	32.234
1953	6.997	.018	1.350		2.013	12.633	23.011
1954	3.214	.318	.439		7.023	10.835	21.829
1955	2.628	2.421	.070		5.690	7.499	18.308
1956	1.645	3.802	.202		5.053	10.247	20.949
1957	2.223	4.844	.164	.146	4.716	8.209	20.302
1958	3.488	3.188	.091		3.196	6.313	16.276
1959	4.321	3.349	.073		3.382	8.994	20.119
1960	4.178	3.784	.065	.310	3.201	8.707	20.245
1961	4.937	4.419	.055	.282	3.235	8.112	21.040
1962	6.863	5.291	1.042	.647	3.014	7.781	24.638
1963	6.749	5.365	1.090	.450	2.270	7.466	23.390
1964	6.613	5.484	.658	.407	1.702	4.358	19.222
1965	6.061	4.872	.929	1.114	1.757	4.644	19.377
1966	6.156	5.414	.676	1.230	3.143	7.369	23.988
1967	5.529	3.262	.598	1.256	2.595	8.051	21.291
1968	5.108	4.308	.530	1.376	1.952	8.623	21.897
1969	3.839	3.630	.539	1.478	1.363	9.593	20.442
1970	3.997	3.322	.515	1.396	1.464	8.417	19.111
1971	3.560	3.404	.469	.497	1.583	12.154	21.667
1972	3.806	3.205	1.319	.372	1.623	13.313	23.638
1973	3.433	2.791	.556	1.934	1.561	13.371	23.646
1974	2.704	2.252	.717	1.883	1.482	10.655	19.693
1975	2.713	2.787	.580	1.645	2.572	4.214	14.511
1976	2.354	2.527	.429	.046	2.181	4.928	12.465
1976a	.797	.361	.149	.646	1.673	1.262	4.888
1977	2.547	2.149	.519	1.677	3.180	3.944	14.066
1978	3.140	2.067	.407	1.857	3.737	3.960	15.168
1979	2.850	1.993	.547	2.528	3.070	10.463	21.451
1980	2.640	2.046	.848	2.105	3.109	3.058	13.806
1981	2.558	1.997	.735	1.276	2.847	4.232	13.645
1982	2.502	1.585	.680	1.523	3.343	5.239	14.872
1983	2.595	1.588	.614	1.721	3.440	6.518	16.476
1984	2.827	1.487	.563	1.475	3.504	7.285	17.141
1985	3.059	2.330	.651	1.664	5.642	6.408	19.754
1986	2.447	1.810	.564	1.189	5.017	5.811	16.838
Totals	201.449	103.889	106.978	38.501	108.013	315.778	874.608

Source: Data provided by the Congressional Research Service, Washington, D.C.
aTransition quarter (fiscal year shifted).

$5-billion level by 1985, as it was used to pay de facto rent for bases in allied countries, as well as to underwrite the Middle East peace treaty between Egypt and Israel. More recently ESF outlays, too, have fallen.

Grouping foreign aid programs into the categories of economic/developmental and security/military (see Table 5.4) provides another way of viewing U.S. priorities over the years. Between 1946 and 1986, for example, U.S. aid devoted to economic/development priorities declined from 100 percent to 35.7 percent of the U.S. foreign aid budget, with this type of assistance predominating from 1946 to 1950, 1962 to 1966, and in three later isolated years. By the mid-1980s, security/military aid accounted for nearly two-thirds of U.S. foreign aid outlays, though the form of aid was changing sharply. Purely military assistance (that is, aid directly tied to defense uses), which actually accounted for more than half of all aid expenditures during some years in the early 1950s and 1970s, had fallen to about one-third in 1986, whereas the ESF (a more general form of assistance provided to strategic client states) had risen to almost one-third. At the beginning of the 1990s the shares of foreign aid devoted to ESF and security were falling; the share for economic purposes was rising.

Finally, multilateral aid took on increasing importance during the 1960s and the 1970s, as bilateral development assistance levels were falling. However, multilateral assistance, which rose from $310 million in 1960 to $1.4 billion a decade later and $2.1 billion in 1980, never matched bilateral development aid levels. And, under pressure from the Reagan administration, multilateral assistance fell sharply from its $2.5-billion peak in 1980, ending up at just $1.2 billion in 1986. Thus, bilateral programs remained the far more important source of economic aid.

Though foreign assistance has been a traditional political target of conservatives, the Reagan administration, devoted to an interventionist foreign policy, boosted outlays from $13.6 billion in 1981 to $19.8 billion in 1985, a 37 percent real increase. As a share of GNP, foreign aid rose from .36 percent to .43 percent. However, the increase was distributed unevenly between the different programs, for the administration primarily viewed foreign aid as an adjunct of the defense budget. Outlays for bilateral economic/development assistance rose 14.4 percent, whereas security/military aid jumped 70.3 percent. Multilateral assistance increased too, though only after being cut sharply—39.5 percent—in 1981.

Spending rose, despite public dissatisfaction with foreign aid, largely because of congressional and presidential logrolling. The administration was able to garner large hikes in military aid by supporting smaller increases in the development assistance programs favored by liberals in Congress; in effect, the Democrats' price for supporting aid to El Salvador was more money for health projects in Africa. However, this high-budget consensus came to a dramatic end in 1986, after the huge budget deficit and the budget-balancing legislation known as the Gramm-Rudman-Hollings Act created

TABLE 5.4
Distribution of U.S. Foreign Aid by Type, 1946–1991
(percent of total)

Year	Development	ESF & Precursors	Military
1946	100.0		
1947	97.6		2.5
1948	89.7		10.3
1949	96.3		3.7
1950	80.1		19.9
1951	42.7	2.1	55.2
1952	32.5	2.8	64.5
1953	36.4	8.7	54.9
1954	18.2	32.2	49.6
1955	30.0	31.1	41.0
1956	27.0	24.1	48.9
1957	36.3	23.2	40.4
1958	41.6	19.6	38.8
1959	38.5	16.8	44.7
1960	41.2	15.8	43.0
1961	46.1	15.4	38.6
1962	56.2	12.2	31.6
1963	58.4	9.7	31.9
1964	68.5	8.8	22.7
1965	67.0	9.1	24.0
1966	56.2	13.1	30.7
1967	50.0	12.2	37.8
1968	51.7	8.9	39.4
1969	46.4	6.7	46.9
1970	48.3	7.7	44.0
1971	36.6	7.3	56.1
1972	36.8	6.9	56.3
1973	36.8	6.6	56.5
1974	38.4	7.5	54.1
1975	53.2	17.7	29.0
1976	43.0	17.5	39.5
1976[a]	40.0	34.2	25.8
1977	49.2	22.7	28.1
1978	49.2	24.6	26.1
1979	36.9	14.3	48.8
1980	55.3	22.5	22.1
1981	48.1	20.9	31.0
1982	42.3	22.5	35.2
1983	37.5	20.9	39.6
1984	37.1	20.4	42.5
1985	39.0	28.6	32.4
1986	35.7	29.8	34.5
1987	38.8	26.6	34.6
1988	43.0	22.1	34.9
1989	44.0	23.2	32.8
1990	43.4	25.5	31.1
1991	48.8	21.3	29.9

Source: Data provided by the Congressional Research Service, Washington, D.C.
[a]Transition quarter (fiscal year shifted).

strong pressure on Congress to cut outlays. Legislators quickly focused on foreign aid, which has never been popular with voters, as a place to make cuts; as a result, outlays fell 14.7 percent in 1986. Though the cuts were made across the board on economic and military programs, they nonetheless fell disproportionately on different geographic regions. As demonstrated by the top ten recipients of U.S. foreign aid for FY 1992 (listed in Table 5.5), Congress acceded to executive branch requests to insulate traditional U.S. allies in the Middle East (Israel and Egypt), some of the nations with U.S. military bases (Turkey, Greece, Portugal, and the Philippines), and countries which prior to 1992 had been threatened with a leftist insurgency (El Salvador), had aided U.S. paramilitary efforts against leftist regimes (Pakistan), or had replaced a leftist regime with a more democratic system of governance (Nicaragua). The case of Bolivia is unique in that it demonstrates the growing interest of U.S. policymakers during the 1990s in stemming the flow of drugs from Latin America. Nonetheless, in early 1988 the State Department announced that it was ending assistance to a number of countries because of congressional cutbacks. Aid has increased only slowly in subsequent years and has fallen as a percentage of GNP. Given the likelihood of continuing deficits, foreign aid outlays are unlikely to grow much during the 1990s. As a result, the primary political battle is likely to continue to be over distribution of foreign aid resources rather than spending increases.

■ THE EFFICACY OF FOREIGN AID

Does foreign assistance as a tool of intervention achieve its goals? That is a difficult assessment to make, in part because the various aid programs have several divergent objectives and may interact with each other in complicated ways. For example, although economic/development assistance is typically justified as fulfilling two major objectives—alleviation of human suffering in emergencies and disasters, and promotion of economic growth—every president since Dwight D. Eisenhower has also justified this form of assistance as supporting U.S. national security. President Reagan's first AID director, Peter McPherson, explained that the administration was pressing for large transfers to Central America to help "attack political and social unrest at their roots."[2]

Similarly, security/military assistance has two official purposes. The first is to help stabilize allied regimes, especially those facing armed insurgencies. The second is to enhance the military power of friendly states. However, this form of assistance is also thought to be a useful means of buying political favor for the United States.

Thus, the value of foreign aid as an instrument of intervention should be judged by its ability to relieve human suffering (humanitarian), promote economic growth (development), stabilize potentially unsteady societies

TABLE 5.5
Recipients of Largest Amounts of U.S. Bilateral Aid, 1992
(total grants and loans in millions of U.S. dollars)

Country	Amount
Israel	3,000.0
Egypt	2,266.8
Turkey	703.9
Philippines	557.1
Greece	350.5
El Salvador	294.2
Pakistan	267.9
Nicaragua	204.7
Portugal	167.8
Bolivia	138.7

Source: Data provided by the Congressional Research Service, Washington, D.C.

(security), improve the defense capabilities of allied governments (military), and buy influence for Washington (political). It is not surprising that the U.S. foreign policy establishment, which has consistently supported financial transfers abroad, harbors few doubts—publicly, at least—about the efficacy of the half trillion dollars in foreign aid distributed during the post–World War II period. For example, Secretary of State George Shultz in 1983 formed the Commission on Security and Economic Assistance (informally known as the Carlucci Commission) to review "the goals and activities of United States assistance efforts." The commission concluded that "the [foreign aid] program makes an indispensable contribution to achieving foreign policy objectives."[3]

Yet, this conclusion rests on shaky ground. The commission itself admitted that it is not "clear that specific programs have been consistently effective with regard to any one objective"; nevertheless, it argued, "on balance" the programs have been a success.[4] In fact, there is substantial reason to question whether foreign transfers regularly fulfill any of their official ends, and there is substantial evidence that any successes achieved are largely ephemeral. The impact of foreign assistance on humanitarian, development, security, military, and political goals will be reviewed here in turn.

☐ *Humanitarian Goal of*
   Relieving Human Suffering

There will probably never be a lack of need for humanitarian assistance. The Hunger Project, a New York–based organization whose goal is to eradicate world hunger, estimates that 13 to 18 million people die of starvation every year. Another half-billion are thought to be undernourished, and twice that number live in serious poverty. Life expectancies and infant mortality rates, though improving throughout the Third World, still lag significantly behind those in the industrialized West. Citizens of developing countries are also particularly vulnerable to natural and human-made disasters.

There is no doubt that at times foreign aid has helped meet serious humanitarian needs. AID manages a small general disaster assistance program, for example, that provides emergency goods and services. Among the beneficiaries of this disaster relief have been victims of drought in Africa, a cyclone in Bangladesh, fire in Burma, a volcano in Colombia, a cholera epidemic in Mali, an earthquake in Mexico, floods in Mozambique, a landslide in Peru, and civil strife in Sri Lanka. AID also offers predisaster planning and technical/managerial assistance to foreign governments and operates an early warning system that utilizes weather and geologic monitoring and forecasting technology to predict crop failures and potential famine. The application of this technology in the Horn of Africa, for example, was helpful in predicting crop shortages in 1987 and 1988 and in facilitating advance preparations for famine relief. It is hard to criticize short-term relief programs that respond to natural disasters.

Far more significant is the "Food for Peace" program (commonly referred to as P.L. 480), which grew out of a U.S. famine relief program in India in 1951. Created in 1954, Food for Peace has given away and sold, at reduced prices, more than 653 billion pounds of U.S. agricultural products to help feed starving Third World peoples. Despite its humanitarian intentions, however, the primary purpose of the program was (and continues to be) the cultivation of foreign markets to take price-depressing surpluses of agricultural products off the U.S. market (only 14 percent of food aid goes to disaster areas). Moreover, since the crops are sold at artificially low prices, U.S. competitors have charged that the United States is illegally "dumping" its surplus agricultural commodities on the international market. In short, Food for Peace has become a permanent subsidy for U.S. farmers, costing approximately $1.5 billion annually, rather than supplying emergency assistance to needy foreign peoples.

The fundamental problem with the Food for Peace program is that large-scale transfers of cheap U.S. food products make it economically difficult for small producers in recipient countries to compete effectively, often forcing them out of business. As a result, concluded one internal AID audit, "the long-term feeding programs in the same areas for ten years or more have great potential" for creating disincentives to indigenous food production.[5] Similarly, complained one Third World observer, "Food for Peace became a stumbling block to development" as the United States offered and poor states accepted cheap food, despite "its impact on their farmers and on the fate of their agriculture and of their struggling economies."[6]

Specific examples of how well-intentioned projects have gone awry abound. Regular and large shipments of food to India bankrupted local farmers throughout the 1950s and 1960s, while farmers in Haiti do not bring their products to market during periods when Food for Peace food is distributed. In a more detailed example, analysts from the Institute for Food and Development Policy (IFDP) have highlighted the negative effects of extended Food for Peace aid on Colombia's domestic wheat industry:

> Between 1955 and 1971, Colombia imported from the U.S. over one million tons of wheat that could have been produced more cheaply locally. The marketing agency of the Colombian government fixed the price of the imported grain so low that it undercut domestically-produced wheat. This dumping resulted in 50 percent lower prices to Colombian farmers. From 1955 . . . to 1971, Colombia's wheat production dropped by 69 percent while its imports increased 800 percent. By 1971, imports accounted for 90 percent of domestic consumption.[7]

In fact, even well-meaning, short-term, disaster-related assistance may effectively undercut local producers in the recipient country.[8] Following the devastating 1976 earthquake in Guatemala, farmers—who in the previous year had enjoyed exceptionally high yields of corn and other grains—sought to sell their stockpiled grains to earn the cash necessary to rebuild their homes and farms. Yet, according to IFDP analysts, massive relief from the United States "helped to lower the prices for locally grown grain, just when farmers most needed cash for their grain. As a result, food aid *stood in the way* of reconstruction." Although IFDP does not oppose disaster relief, it warns that "even in short-term emergencies, relief food should be purchased, as much as possible, from local and national producers whose families' livelihood depends on their selling grain."[9]

In short, humanitarian aid is very much a double-edged sword: Although it can help relieve human suffering when limited to the short-term alleviation of natural disasters, long-term subsidized transfers of food aid may ultimately cause more harm than good. In this regard, Food for Peace often has been a better deal for U.S. farmers than for foreign recipients.

□ *Developmental Goal of Promoting Economic Growth*

The U.S. government makes bilateral loans and grants and provides technical assistance and advice, through AID, that is officially intended to encourage economic growth—the traditional rationale for most economic aid.[10] Several multilateral agencies, such as the World Bank, International Monetary Fund (IMF), and the United Nations Development Program, are also partially funded by the United States; they provide funds both for individual projects and general financial support.

Although U.S. taxpayers provide billions of dollars annually to poor countries to spur economic growth, there is little evidence that foreign aid has any significant beneficial impact on Third World incomes. Despite large doses of economic assistance, the average increase in the per capita GNP of developing countries fell steadily from 6 percent in the 1960s and 5 percent in the 1970s to 2.5 percent in 1980 and 1 percent in 1983. In 1986, real per capita GNP actually fell; a number of countries, particularly heavily indebted states and sub-Saharan African states, lost ground economically throughout the late 1980s.

The lack of an obvious relationship between foreign assistance and economic growth is even more apparent in a comparison of the growth rates of individual nations with the amounts of aid they have received.[11] For example, of the twenty top recipients of U.S. funds between 1960 and 1985, twelve actually fell behind their neighbors economically during that twenty-five-year period.[12] Nor do overall aid levels correlate with economic growth. The recipients of the greatest amounts of total foreign assistance (from the United States, other individual donor nations, and international organizations) in 1986 were, in descending order, India, Israel, Egypt, Bangladesh, China, the Philippines, Pakistan, and Sudan. In terms of average growth rates between 1965 and 1986, however, these countries ranked far differently: China, Egypt, Israel, Pakistan, the Philippines, India, Bangladesh, and Sudan. The annual average growth rate varied between 5.1 percent and minus .2 percent.

An interesting case study is that of Tanzania, which has received more foreign aid per capita than any other nation. According to one observer, "its output per worker had declined 50 percent over a period of a decade," while "it had turned from an exporter of maize to an importer." Moreover, "nearly half of the more than 300 companies expropriated by the government ('nationalized') were bankrupt by 1975, with many of the remainder operating at a loss."[13] Although obviously an extreme example, this scenario has been repeated in varying degrees throughout much of the Third World.

There are many reasons why aid has so little impact on foreign growth rates. One point is that world economic forces and the openness of foreign markets have a far greater effect on the relatively small economies of developing states. Moreover, capital is not a dominant factor in economic development; more than two decades ago Harvard economist Simon Kuznets estimated that capital accounted for just one-fifth to one-seventh of the per capita income growth in industrialized states, which are more efficient users of capital than developing countries. Furthermore, the Third World, which by 1991 had amassed a $1.4 trillion debt, has had no problem arranging commercial financing for development projects. Indeed, "money—or the lack thereof—is not a significant constraint on development," according to analysts of the Development Group for Alternative Policies, an organization committed to the restructuring of U.S. foreign-aid practices in the Third

World. "All too often, Third World agencies are overloaded with funds that they cannot effectively absorb and utilize."[14]

Of course, "development" requires more than the simple manifestation of a rising per capita GNP. Equally important is the building of a just society in which everyone, including the impoverished rural dwellers who usually make up the majority of Third World populations, has an opportunity to share in the benefits of economic development. Unfortunately, neither the U.S. government nor foreign ruling elites have generally pursued such a strategy, instead utilizing foreign aid to serve their own self-interests.

For example, despite AID's professed commitment to alleviate rural poverty, the reality remains that much U.S. assistance has a very different purpose—namely subsidizing domestic businesses by promoting U.S. trade and investment interests. This emphasis on serving U.S. interests was clearly reflected in a 1987 AID newsletter titled "Foreign Aid: What's in It For You":

> [Foreign aid is] a sound investment that benefits both Americans and the people of developing countries. To make certain this investment pays off, programs are carefully planned and carried out by experts who know what works and what doesn't. Most of the talent and tools needed in an ambitious foreign assistance program come from American business and industry. That's why 70 percent of the money appropriated for direct, or bilateral, U.S. assistance is spent here, not overseas. . . . In addition . . . fully one-half of the U.S. contribution to [multilateral development agencies] is spent on American goods. The benefits from foreign aid are shared throughout the nation. Business, research centers or universities in 49 states received foreign assistance contracts in 1985.[15]

The key to failed development strategies in the Third World is not external aid policies, however, but rather the way this aid is utilized by recipient governments. Indeed, the domestic policies of developing nations are of paramount importance. Although a detailed analysis of these factors is beyond the scope of this chapter, suffice it to say that no amount of assistance can overcome the stifling statism of so many nations—bloated government bureaucracies, money-losing state enterprises, price and production controls, and perverse monetary, fiscal, and credit policies—or force the reform of programs that benefit political and economic elites at the expense of the rest of the population.[16] Countries that, for example, steal from their farmers by requiring peasants to sell their crops at artificially low prices to state marketing boards cannot expect to increase per capita grain production and feed their people, irrespective of the number of irrigation projects being funded by AID and the World Bank.

Zimbabwe provides a notable example, underscoring the importance of sensible domestic policies in promoting agricultural development. Described by the Hunger Project as an "agricultural miracle," Zimbabwe's agricultural program made over 800,000 small-scale black farmers more productive by raising the once confiscatory prices paid by the government for their crops, as well as by extending other services to rural areas. According to one analyst, "These communal farmers, who once produced mainly for subsistence, now account for more than 50 percent of Zimbabwe's grain production, compared with less than 10 percent at independence." Unlike the majority of African countries, which increasingly depend on food imports, Zimbabwe "today is self-sufficient in food and sends excess as famine relief to neighboring states."[17]

☐ *Security Goal of Stabilizing Unsteady Societies*

Virtually all forms of assistance are assumed to promote the stability of allied states, many of which suffer from enormous problems of poverty, social unrest, and guerrilla insurgencies. And in the short term, at least, U.S. aid does advance this objective somewhat. That is, the governments of Egypt, Pakistan, Zaire, and other nations allied to the United States have been strengthened by the receipt of millions or billions of dollars from Washington. Moreover, in some cases, such as El Salvador, which during the 1980s was threatened by a serious communist insurgency, massive aid may play a role in preventing a pro-U.S. government from collapsing.

Foreign aid often appears to do more to undercut than promote U.S. security in the long run by discouraging incumbent regimes from adopting needed reforms, prompting them to cultivate support abroad instead of at home, and tying the United States to unsavory dictatorships. First, by subsidizing what are often authoritarian and corrupt regimes, U.S. assistance makes it easier for leaders to resist popular pressures for reform. President Ferdinand Marcos of the Philippines, for example, looted his country, wrecked the economy, and emasculated the military; yet generous U.S. aid, nearly $600 million between 1983 and 1985 alone, helped prop up his corrupt government (see Chapter 15). Second, U.S. aid encourages foreign leaders to look to Washington rather than to their own polities for legitimacy. Again, as long as Marcos was able to reap the financial benefits of U.S.-leased bases in the Philippines, his general inclination was to suppress increasingly vocal opposition. The result is potentially not only more brutal regimes but also less stable ones. Third, U.S. subsidies act as a public endorsement of brutal regimes that often seem destined to fall: Only the Reagan administration's last-minute abandonment of Marcos saved the U.S. reputation in the Philippines.

Marcos's 1986 overthrow, ultimately supported by the United States, seems to have reduced the likelihood of a communist revolution in the Philippines. By contrast, U.S. policy in Nicaragua, the subject of Chapter 16, proved a far greater disaster. Anastacio Somoza, confident of extensive U.S. economic and political support, created a personal kleptocracy and suppressed moderate democrats, radicalizing the opposition. U.S. aid did nothing to temper Somoza's greed, but it did inextricably link the United States to his venal autocracy; when Somoza was finally overthrown, Washington found itself confronted with a hostile revolutionary regime in his place.

Similarly, strong support for Shah Mohammad Reza Pahlavi of Iran—symbolic as well as financial—tarnished the U.S. reputation without restraining growing Iranian unrest with the shah's autocratic rule (see Chapter 17). U.S. aid may have purchased some temporary stability for what was viewed as a powerful U.S. surrogate in the Middle East, but in the long run U.S. intervention contributed to the creation of the revolutionary state that now threatens to unsettle the entire region.

The United States could face similar problems in Zaire, a longtime U.S. client state ruled by another corrupt autocrat. Although President Mobutu Sese Seko has successfully survived a series of crises, his country is in disastrous economic shape and suffers from serious ethnic and regional divisions. By late 1991, Mobutu seemed to be losing control as Zaire descended into chaos. U.S. aid, $68.3 million in 1989, has helped Mobutu maintain his hold on power, but it has done nothing to relieve the underlying pressures that threaten to tear Zaire apart. If Mobutu should be overthrown, the United States might find itself facing a more unstable and less friendly government.

In fact, by helping authoritarian regimes hang on to power, U.S. foreign aid often conflicts with the United States' professed goal of promoting democracy abroad. Even the Carlucci Commission, which enthusiastically endorsed U.S. aid, acknowledged "the possibility that the assistance supplied will be used to suppress democratic forces."[18] This possibility raises fundamental moral issues that, unfortunately, are rarely seriously considered in the formulation of U.S. foreign policy. And aid to dictatorships has negative practical consequences for the United States as well, as democracies, however volatile, seem likely to be more stable and receptive to basic U.S. freedom values and political interests in the long run, even if they are not necessarily as supportive of the specific policy goals of a particular U.S. administration.

U.S. involvement in El Salvador's guerrilla war underscores the difficulties of achieving the stabilization of a client state through massive amounts of economic and military aid.[19] Despite approximately $3.3 billion in U.S. aid during the eight years of the Reagan administration (more than $1 million a day), El Salvador's guerrilla war intensified as the "politics of polarization" continued to undermine the fragile centrist policies of the ruling Christian Democratic party led by President José Napoleón Duarte. The right-wing Nationalist Republican Alliance (ARENA) won the March 1989 elections, while the leftist Faribundo Martí National Liberation Front (FMLN), stepped up the guerrilla war. In fact, U.S. aid during the 1980s had a destabilizing impact in at least two ways: It strengthened the military vis-à-vis the civilian authorities, and it funded a poorly designed land reform program (that did not vest ownership in the peasant operators) that proved disastrous and was later abandoned.[20]

In any case, U.S. funds could not overcome the most serious problem: that, according to diplomats and Salvadoran officials, Duarte "never had the power to stand up to the Army, the oligarchy, or the U.S. Embassy. He never had the courage to call a halt to corruption. And despite his good intentions, he never addressed the grave social inequities that fuel the conflict."[21] After the defeat of Nicaragua's Sandinistas in 1989, hopes for peace in El Salvador rose. But many obstacles remain.

In short, handing out cash does not automatically promote social, economic, or political stability. On the contrary, U.S. aid often results in long-term instability by insulating ineffective and brutal regimes from serious domestic upheaval, and taints the United States by tying Washington to illegitimate autocrats.

□ *Military Goal of Enhancing the*
   Defense Capabilities of Allied Countries

Although U.S. aid programs may have largely failed in promoting either economic growth or social stability, they have strengthened the defense of some nations.[22] There seems little doubt, for example, that the Foreign Military Sales Credits Program, by subsidizing the purchase of U.S. weapons, has enhanced the military preparedness of countries ranging from Egypt to South Korea. Yet, it is very hard to judge how important those improvements have been to the security of either the recipients or the United States. The Carlucci Commission admitted that "success is largely measured by what does not happen—the attack or insurrection that did not occur or did not succeed."[23]

Proving that U.S. aid prevented a war or insurgency is virtually impossible, especially as U.S. military assistance, aside from the unusually high levels of support for countries such as South Vietnam and El Salvador, has accounted for only a small proportion of recipients' defense spending. In fact, in some cases, U.S. aid probably displaced domestic military spending by the recipient regime rather than increased overall military outlays. South Korea, for example, received hundreds of millions of dollars annually in subsidized credit through 1986, even though its economy was growing faster than any other during the preceding decade. U.S. assistance merely allowed Seoul to devote more of its ample resources to activities other than defense.

Even if U.S. aid prompts the beneficiary to build a stronger military than it otherwise could afford, there may be no practical benefits for the United States. The size of many nations' militaries is irrelevant to U.S. security. Official military assistance has flowed to more than one hundred nations annually, far more than are strategically important in any meaningful sense. Countries such as Fiji faced no serious security threats; Luxembourg plays a minor role in the European military balance; and what justification was there for giving security aid to neutral Austria and communist Yugoslavia?

True, in individual cases—Turkey, which is a member of NATO, but which has a poorly equipped military; El Salvador, which lies in the U.S. backyard and faced a dangerous communist insurgency during the 1980s; and Israel, which is considered by many to be the most valuable U.S. surrogate in the Middle East—military assistance may provide the United States with some security benefits. But, even then the cost may be prohibitive. (Israel, for example, receives $3 billion in U.S. aid annually.) In far too many other cases, however, assistance does not appear to advance its official objectives, let alone do so in a cost-effective manner. Military aid outlays may have more than doubled between 1980 and 1985, but the United States seemed no more secure as a result.

☐ *Political Goal of Buying Government Influence*

The ultimate, but usually unstated, justification for all forms of foreign assistance is to gain political influence for the United States within a particular Third World country. The logic of foreign aid in this context is relatively simple: The greater the amount of U.S. economic and military aid to a Third World country, the greater that nation's willingness to comply with the foreign policy wishes of the United States. Economic and military aid provides "bargaining chips" to be used when discussing issues considered to be of importance to Washington.

Where U.S. assistance is high enough to turn a Third World country into a client state, such as in Vietnam during the 1960s or in El Salvador during the 1980s, the United States may enjoy considerable influence over the political, economic, and military policies of that country. This is not likely to be healthy for the long-term development or stability of that country, of course, but massive amounts of foreign aid will have gained some measure of temporary influence .

Lesser amounts of aid can reap political influence when the topic in question is of little or no importance to a particular Third World government, but assistance usually does not enable the United States to dictate foreign policy compliance when the ruling elite is strongly opposed to U.S. interference or meddling. In August 1988, for example, the Reagan administration pressured Costa Rica, El Salvador, Guatemala, and Honduras to ratify a U.S.-sponsored document denouncing Nicaragua's role in destabilizing the region. El Salvador and Honduras, which receive significant amounts of assistance from the United States and were closely tied to Washington's anti-Sandinista policies, agreed to Washington's demand. However, Costa Rica and Guatemala, which are also aid recipients, refused to make the desired declaration. Whether because of fear of Nicaraguan retaliation or genuine disagreement in approach, they resisted enormous U.S. pressure, including "veiled threats of economic reprisals," according to Guatemalan officials.[24]

There are many other examples of nations that have gone their own way despite generous U.S. assistance. Zimbabwe, for one, was a steady recipient of U.S. aid ($162.8 million between 1983 and 1985) but nevertheless moved toward a one-party socialist state and regularly opposed the United States in international forums (Zimbabwe abstained on the vote condemning the Soviet shoot-down of Korean Airlines Flight 007 and sponsored an anti-U.S. resolution concerning Grenada, for example). The United States eventually slashed its assistance levels after Zimbabwean officials denounced U.S. policy in front of a U.S. delegation that included former President Jimmy Carter. And consider the case of longtime U.S. ally Morocco, which has collected more than $3 billion in U.S. assistance since World War II. King Hassan was long considered to be pro-Western, but he shocked U.S. officials by signing a short-lived Treaty of Arab-African Union with Libya, the Reagan administration's international enemy number one. Similarly, Somalia was the beneficiary of $112 million in U.S. aid between 1987 and 1989. Although the United States was the primary external supporter of Siyaad Barre's regime prior to its overthrow in 1991, the U.S. embassy could not gain permission to evacuate U.S. citizens from the northern portion of the country at the height of hostilities between government troops and guerrilla insurgents.

These examples, far from being "exceptions" to the general rule of the economic dependence–political compliance thesis, illustrate the wide latitude enjoyed by Third World elites despite their acceptance of aid from Washington. Even a State Department spokesman, although referring specifically to the U.S.-Somali incident, acknowledged that "foreign assistance gives very little leverage when you want one-for-one results." Nevertheless, he advocated continued aid: "The sign that you give is that you stick by your friends."[25]

The argument that aid brings with it political influence is called into question by simply reviewing which nations receive foreign aid. In 1988, the Reagan administration proposed giving money to eighty-seven countries that had voted against the United States at least two-thirds of the time in the UN; another thirteen would-be beneficiaries opposed the United States at least half of the time.[26] This may be an imperfect measure of the state of U.S. bilateral relations with other nations, but it nevertheless raises questions regarding the political benefits of U.S. foreign aid.

In reality, the State Department rarely supports a cut in funding because, in its view, either relations with the recipient nation are getting better, or they are getting worse. In either case, the recommended course of action is usually to increase aid in order to ensure the continuation of enhanced ties or to prevent the further slippage of the relationship. As a result, beneficiaries know that while they should let the U.S. ambassador occasionally visit the presidential palace, they can freely ignore U.S. advice.

An even more fundamental objection to the use of aid to gain political influence, however, especially when the recipient is a corrupt autocracy, is that there is no warrant for doing so unless fundamental national interests are at stake. Garnering support on a UN vote, resolving some commercial dispute involving a U.S. firm, and reducing the relative influence of Washington's international adversaries are all potentially worthy goals, but their value is limited: Forcing U.S. taxpayers to underwrite corrupt dictatorships is far too high a price to pay to score minor political points. There is a moral aspect of foreign aid policy that all too often seems to be lost in the rush to implement realpolitik.

Moreover, as discussed earlier, U.S. attempts to buy influence can backfire disastrously where the United States ties itself to a discredited regime that is toppled. The United States presumably had influence with the Somoza regime in Nicaragua, but the value of that access seems small compared to the problems of its relations with the Sandinista regime during the 1980s. Iran provides a similar example; less dramatic cases include Sudan, where U.S. favorite President Gaafar Mohammed Nimeri was overthrown, and the Philippines, where popular pressure appears to have finally forced the closure of U.S. military bases.

■ FOREIGN AID IN PERSPECTIVE

Once the United States decided to try to enforce *pax americana* in the aftermath of World War II, foreign aid became an integral part of U.S. interventionist policies. Although military force was considered to be the ultimate guarantor of U.S. interests, financial and technical assistance was perceived as a less expensive and less intrusive means of reshaping the global order, especially throughout the Third World, in the U.S. image.

Over the years, foreign aid priorities have varied sharply, both in terms of recipients and types of assistance. The consistent theme underlying the program for four decades, though, has been a commitment to promoting U.S. economic, security, and political interests, however these are defined. Foreign aid has often been presented to the U.S. public and advertised to the world as selfless humanitarianism; in reality, nationalistic goals have always been dominant.

Throughout its history, foreign aid has been assumed to achieve its objectives. Indeed, its very name—foreign "aid" or "assistance"—implies that the program's overall results are salutary. Yet, the actual benefits of foreign aid for U.S. foreign policy are debatable. Temporary humanitarian assistance has alleviated some suffering, but aid programs like Food for Peace have often done more harm than good. Financial flows to poorer states have underwritten some good projects but have also left a string of expensive white elephants across Africa and other nations. And although there are a few plausible success stories in which assistance has spurred economic growth, disastrous examples abound in which U.S. and other Western aid has subsidized corrupt, autocratic elites as they destroyed their economies in the pursuit of their narrow self-interests.

Foreign assistance is also viewed as a means of stabilizing Third World states that face social unrest, thereby advancing U.S. security interests. Yet, strengthening incumbent regimes that suppress moderate opposition forces may ultimately be destabilizing. U.S. support for dictatorships in Nicaragua, Iran, Haiti, and the Philippines only seemed to make their rulers more intransigent, thereby hastening their downfall. Some defense goals have been achieved through U.S. assistance, but the programs directed at enhancing the military prowess of other nations have often been devoted to countries that can afford to defend themselves or are of dubious strategic value. Moreover, although an unending stream of foreign aid may buy political influence with other countries, Washington's promiscuous use of assistance has ensured that most states receive funds irrespective of their actions. Most important, access bought today may very well lead to a closed door tomorrow, as revolutionary regimes turn against the United States for helping to keep a prior government in power.

Overall, foreign aid has been successful as an interventionist tool in one sense: It has thrust the United States into the affairs of the majority of other nations around the globe. But whether the impact of that involvement has been beneficial or has achieved official U.S. foreign policy goals is quite another question.

6

Economic Sanctions

Kimberly A. Elliott

Economic sanctions have enjoyed widespread application as an instrument of intervention during the post–World War II period. Such sanctions typically involve reducing or even eliminating the flow of goods and/or money between a *sender* country, the country imposing sanctions, and a *target* country. The first documented use of economic sanctions occurred in 432 BC when Athens, in retaliation for Megara's attempted expropriation of territory and the kidnapping of three women, issued the Megarian Decree—limiting entry of Megara's products into Athenian markets—thereby contributing to the outbreak of the Peloponnesian War between Athens and Sparta.

The United States has been the dominant user of sanctions—defined here as the deliberate government-inspired withdrawal, or threat of withdrawal, of customary (rather than contractual) trade or financial relations between two or more countries—in the twentieth century. As of spring 1992, U.S. economic sanctions were in force against Angola, Burma, Ethiopia, Iran, Iraq, Libya, Pakistan, Somalia, South Africa, and Sudan; in addition, long-standing trade embargoes were in place against Cuba, North Korea, and Vietnam.[1] The United States has taken the lead in imposing sanctions in 77 of 116 episodes occurring between 1914 and 1990 and has targeted Third World countries in 58 of these, successfully 38 percent of the time in those Third World cases. Closer examination of the record, however, reveals that the effectiveness of U.S. sanctions in the Third World declined substantially after 1973, even as the frequency with which sanctions were imposed greatly increased. The 116 cases on which my analysis is based are documented in a study published in 1990.[2] Although reference will be made to the conclusions of that broader study for comparative purposes, I focus in this chapter on the subset of 58 cases specifically pertaining to U.S. sanctions in the Third World.

■ EVOLUTION OF U.S. SANCTIONS IN THE THIRD WORLD

The United States first intervened in the Third World with economic sanctions in 1938 in concert with the United Kingdom. Both financial and trade sanctions were imposed over a period of nine years (1938–1947) to force Mexico to compensate British and U.S. oil companies for property that had been nationalized. Except for this case and another targeting Argentina (1944–1947), the fifty-six remaining cases listed in Table 6.1 (see the following section, "Success and Failure") occurred after the end of World War II, almost 40 percent in the 1970s alone. Nearly half of the cases involved sanctions against Latin America, almost a quarter targeted the Middle East or South Asia, with the rest centering on countries in Africa and East Asia (four cases relate to the war in Vietnam).

In attempting to shape the postwar world to its liking, the United States did not hesitate to use economic leverage to coerce, even destabilize, uncooperative governments. Sanctions efforts in the first twenty-seven years after World War II focused on moderating—or, failing that, overthrowing—nationalist, often left-leaning leaders in newly independent countries. In nearly half of the episodes in this period (nine of twenty-one), the United States sought to destabilize governments led by such leaders. Another third of these cases involved relatively modest goals, including several aimed at settling disputes over expropriated or nationalized property (also a source of conflict in half of the destabilization efforts). Sanctions twice accompanied U.S. military efforts and on one other occasion were used in an attempt to influence a military conflict in which the United States was not directly involved.

One of the earliest cases grew out of U.S. dissatisfaction with Argentina's lack of cooperation in World War II against Germany. It evolved into an effort to destabilize Argentine President Juan Perón, initially because of his Nazi sympathies and, later, because of his nationalist rhetoric and general unwillingness to cooperate with U.S. foreign policy. As the Cold War between East and West replaced the hot war between the Allies and the Axis as the focus of U.S. foreign policy, the United States frequently initiated sanctions efforts against leaders considered too independent and too leftist, such as Prince Souvanna Phouma in Laos, President Rafael Trujillo in the Dominican Republic, and Indonesia's President Achmed Sukarno. Others, such as General Phoumi Nosavan in Laos and Ngo Dinh Diem in Vietnam, were deemed a liability, not for ideological reasons, but because of excessive ambition or corruption, which was perceived in Washington as inhibiting the global fight against communism. And, when that fight erupted into violence in Korea and Vietnam, comprehensive economic sanctions, including trade embargoes and the freezing of financial assets, accompanied the military effort.

In several other destabilization cases, sanctions initially were imposed as a result of the nationalization or the expropriation of private property held by U.S. companies or citizens in those countries. Such actions provided both the justification for intervention and confirmation of suspected anti-Western, anticapitalist tendencies on the part of the leaders of these countries. Sanctions efforts of this sort were directed against Prime Minister Mohammad Mosaddeq of Iran (1951–1953), who made the mistake of impinging on British and U.S. interests when he nationalized the oil industry, and President João Goulart of Brazil (1962–1964), who interfered with International Telephone and Telegraph's (ITT) interests in Brazil, as well as Cuba's Fidel Castro (1960 present) and President Salvador Allende in Chile (1970–1973).

Besides these cases and the case of Mexico, expropriation or nationalization of private property was the source of lesser conflicts in three other instances. The 1956 U.S. sanctions effort against Egypt, following nationalization of the Suez Canal, eventually escalated into military conflict, with Israel, the United Kingdom, and France uniting against Egypt. But the United States was interested primarily in settling the dispute over the canal and, in fact, used economic pressure to force Britain and France to disengage militarily. In the 1960s, U.S. economic leverage was brought to bear against both Ceylon (1961–1965) and Peru (1968–1974), once again to force compensation for the expropriation of assets of U.S. petroleum companies.

In addition to using sanctions to retaliate against perceived anticapitalist policies, the United States also imposed economic sanctions on at least three occasions in the mid-1960s in attempts to encourage the adoption of "appropriate" economic policies. It sought to influence Chile's copper pricing policy (1965–1966), primarily as part of its domestic efforts to fight inflation; manipulated food aid (1965–1967) to encourage India to shift resources to agricultural development; and briefly cut off aid to Peru (1968) because of its planned purchase of French fighter jets, which Congress did not think should be subsidized by U.S. aid dollars.

Since 1973, U.S. objectives in the Third World with respect to sanctions have been relatively more modest than in the earlier post–World War II period. Less than 15 percent of the cases in this period involved destabilization efforts, one-third of the level in the earlier period. President Jimmy Carter's efforts to ease General Anastacio Somoza out of power in Nicaragua (1977–1979) were part of his campaign to improve human rights around the world, and the Reagan-Bush administration's subsequent efforts (1981–1990) to destabilize Somoza's Sandinista successors signaled the chilling of détente, as did the militarily preempted sanctions against Grenada (1983). The Reagan-Bush administration's two other destabilization attempts involving economic sanctions, against Muammar Qaddafi in Libya (1978–present) and against General Manuel Noriega in Panama (1987–1990), reflected growing U.S. concerns with fighting terrorism and drug smuggling. There were two prominent exceptions to this trend: the congressionally mandated expansion of sanctions against South Africa in 1986, and the U.S.-led embargo of Iraq in 1990–present.

With the Cold War easing as a result of détente, the end of direct U.S. military involvement in the conflict in Indochina, and the later rapprochement with China, relatively more modest goals of improving human rights and deterring the proliferation of nuclear weapons dominated much of the 1970s. These issues were only briefly at the forefront of U.S. foreign policy, however, and faded quickly with the inauguration of President Reagan and the chilling of U.S.-Soviet relations in 1981. Although Reagan increased the use of sanctions against industrialized countries in an East-West context, his administration relied relatively more on military force, either direct or through the support of proxy forces, than on any economic lever in the struggle against Soviet influence. In the Third World, he followed the 1970s pattern of employing sanctions for relatively modest objectives, most prominently to deter drug smuggling and terrorism .

Congress initiated the strategy of using U.S. economic sanctions to promote human rights as a goal of U.S. foreign policy several years before President Carter, who is prominently associated with this effort, was elected. In December 1973, Congress amended the Foreign Assistance Act, adding a "sense of Congress" resolution that the president "should deny any . . . military assistance to the government of any foreign country which practices the internment or imprisonment of that country's citizens for political purposes."[3] The following year, Congress attached Section 502(b) to the Foreign Assistance Act, calling on the president to "substantially reduce or terminate" military assistance to any government that "engages in a consistent pattern of gross violations of internationally recognized human rights."[4] Frustrated by the Ford administration's reluctance to use security assistance as a lever to improve human rights, Congress amended the "sense of Congress" language to make it legally binding. Unable to override Ford's veto, Congress and the administration compromised on language whereby Section 502(b) is the "policy" of the United States.[5]

It is ironic that Chile's General Augusto Pinochet was one of Congress's first targets (1973–1990) in the human rights campaign. Sanctions against his government were initiated just months after U.S. covert intervention and economic sanctions (1970–1973) had contributed to overthrowing Chile's left-wing leader President Salvador Allende. Other targets of economic sanctions imposed with the goal of improving human rights were Argentina (1977–1983), Brazil (1977–1984), Bolivia (1979–1982), El Salvador (1977–1981), Ethiopia (also involving an expropriation dispute, (1976–present), Guatemala (1977–1986), Kampuchea (1975–1979), Paraguay (1977–1981), South Korea (1973–1977), and Uruguay (1976–1981). Most of these sanctions were dropped in the late 1970s and early 1980s when several of the targeted countries elected civilian governments for the first time in many years. In the late 1980s, support for human rights—especially the right to vote in open, democratic elections—made a comeback, with sanctions being imposed following military coups in Haiti (1987–1990 and again in 1991), Burma (1988–present), and Sudan (1989–present).

The spread of nuclear weapons to countries that did not already possess them was another major concern, first of Congress and then of the Carter administration. In 1976, at the behest of Democratic Senators Stuart

Symington and John H. Glenn, Congress amended the Foreign Assistance Act to require the suspension of economic and military assistance to countries buying or selling facilities for the enrichment or reprocessing of uranium (either of which could contribute to the development of nuclear weapons) unless the recipient was either a signatory of the Non-Proliferation Treaty (NPT) or had accepted "full scope " safeguards (international inspection procedures designed to prevent nuclear weapons proliferation). In 1978, with the support of President Carter, Congress passed the Nuclear Non-Proliferation Act (NNPA), which required foreign buyers of U.S. nuclear materials or technology to submit to full-scope safeguards and allowed the United States to veto the retransfer or reprocessing of U.S.-supplied fuel. South Africa was the first target (1975–1991) of export controls on nuclear materials, although the sanctions were driven as much by abhorrence of its system of apartheid as by its development of unsafeguarded enrichment facilities.[6] The United States subsequently imposed economic sanctions on Argentina (1978–1982), Brazil (1978–1981), India (1978–1982), Pakistan (1979–present), South Korea (1975–1976), and Taiwan (1976–1977) because they refused to sign the NPT, submit to international inspection, were actively seeking sophisticated nuclear technologies, and/or had an apparent motive for the acquisition of nuclear weapons. Several of these cases also overlapped with those in which sanctions were imposed for human rights reasons.

A major foreign policy concern in the 1980s has been the spread of international terrorism. Although international efforts to combat terrorism were initiated after the 1972 massacre of Israeli athletes at the Munich Summer Olympics, terrorism did not become a frequent subject of economic sanctions campaigns until the late 1970s. In 1979, President Carter signed the Export Administration Act with an amendment proposed by Republican Congresswoman Millicent Fenwick attached. The Fenwick Amendment requires the State Department to identify countries that have "repeatedly provided support for acts of international terrorism" and to notify Congress of proposed exports to those countries that might "enhance the ability of such country to support acts of international terrorism."[7]

In accordance with the Fenwick Amendment, the State Department in 1980 cited Iraq, Libya, South Yemen, and Syria as supporters of terrorism. The Reagan administration State Department deleted Iraq from the list and added Cuba in 1982 and Iran in 1984. North Korea was added in 1987 for its suspected involvement in the downing of a South Korean airliner. Iraq was restored to the list after its invasion of Kuwait in August 1990. Sanctions of varying degrees of severity were imposed against Iran (1984–present), Iraq (1980–present), Libya (1978–present), and Syria (1986–1987). All trade with Cuba and North Korea had already been banned (in 1960 and 1950 respectively) by the time they were listed as supporters of terrorism, and sanctions against South Yemen would have been moot given the insignificance of its trade with the United States.

Discouraging drug smuggling is the most recent objective of economic sanctions and has attained prominence since the Reagan administration imposed sanctions against Panama (1987–1990), especially in light of the indictment of strongman General Noriega on drug smuggling and money-laundering charges in Miami in February 1988. Congress had passed legislation conditioning U.S. economic and military assistance on cooperation with U.S. antidrug efforts in 1986, and, in addition to Panama, there have been rumblings about the alleged lack of cooperation from the Bahamas, Bolivia, Mexico, Paraguay, and Peru.

The two most prominent sanctions efforts in recent years were the passage over a presidential veto of the Comprehensive Anti-Apartheid Act in 1986 and the U.S.-led UN embargo of Iraq after its invasion of Kuwait in August 1990. Both of these cases involved very ambitious and difficult goals, and both were multilateral efforts, though the embargo of Iraq is unprecedented in the level of cooperation attained by the sanctioning parties. The sanctions against South Africa were ad hoc and, though significant, were not mandated by the UN and were not comprehensive, as were the sanctions against Iraq.

The impact of the Iraqi case on the use of sanctions in the future is likely to be long-lasting in at least one area. It raised to a new prominence the decades-old concern about the proliferation of nuclear weapons, adding intensity also to more recent concerns about the spread and use of other "unconventional" weapons—chemical and biological—as well as the proliferation of missile technology for delivering them over long distances. The heightening of these concerns raises the possibility that a new, more formal international system of North-South export controls will evolve to replace current ad hoc arrangements and the system of East-West controls erected at the beginning of the Cold War and now being dismantled.

■ SUCCESS AND FAILURE

Despite the popular wisdom that "sanctions never work," economic coercion has been both a popular and somewhat effective tool of U.S. intervention in the Third World. Sanctions contributed to the advancement of U.S. foreign policy objectives in the Third World in twenty-two of fifty-eight episodes. Foreign policy goals, in this analysis, are changes actually and purportedly sought by the sender state in the political behavior of the target state.[8] Thus, the success of an economic sanctions episode—as viewed from the perspective of the sender country—is judged by two criteria: the extent to which the policy outcome sought by the sender was, in fact, achieved and the contribution to that achievement made by the sanctions (see Table 6.1).

A relatively simple index has been devised, scaled from 1 to 4, for each of these criteria:

Policy result:

    1—*failed outcome,* as in the ongoing U.S. efforts (1960–present) to destabilize Cuba's Fidel Castro;

    2—*unclear but possibly positive outcome,* illustrated by the U.S. effort to improve human rights in South Korea (1973–1977);

    3—*positive outcome,* a somewhat successful result—for example, U.S. efforts (1938–1947) to force Mexico to pay compensation arising out of the nationalization of its oil industry; and

    4—*successful outcome,* illustrated by Ceylon's settlement of expropriation claims by the United States (1961–1965).

Sanctions contribution:

    1—*zero or negative contribution,* illustrated by the U.S. embargo against North Korea since 1950;

    2—*minor contribution,* illustrated by the U.S. effort (1963–1966) to destabilize President Achmed Sukarno in Indonesia;

    3—*modest contribution,* such as U.S. sanctions (1979–1981) against Iran during the hostage crisis; and

    4—*significant contribution,* illustrated by the successful destabilization of President Rafael Trujillo in the Dominican Republic in 1960–1962.

The two indexes are multiplied together to get an overall success score; a rating of 9 or higher constitutes success. Success, by this definition, does not mean that the target country was vanquished by the denial of economic contacts or even that the sanctions decisively influenced the outcome. A score of 9 means that sanctions made a modest contribution to the goal sought by the sender country and that the goal was partially realized; a score of 16 means that sanctions made a significant contribution to a successful outcome. By contrast, a score of 1 indicates that the sender country failed to achieve its goals.

It is clear that economic sanctions cannot force a rival to surrender territory as easily as they can induce a country to pay compensation for expropriated property. Therefore, the cases were analyzed in terms of four categories of objectives: (1) modest goals, (2) destabilizations, (3) disruption of military adventures, and (4) major goals.[9] Although the "destabilization" and "disruption of military adventure" categories are relatively straightforward, "modest" and "major" are relative terms. In this instance, modest goals include settlement of expropriation disputes, deterrence of terrorism, improvement of human rights (including the restoration of democracy), prevention of nuclear proliferation, changes in economic

TABLE 6.1
Cases of U.S. Economic Sanctions in the Third World

Target	Year(s)	Goal	Policy Result	Sanctions Contribution	Success Rating[a]
Mexico (with UK)	1938–1947	Settle expropriation claims	3	3	9
Argentina	1944–1947	Remove Nazi influence; destabilize Perón	2	2	4
North Korea	1950–*	Withdraw attack on South Korea	2	1	2
Iran (with UK)	1951–1953	Reverse nationalization of oil facilities; destabilize Mosaddeq	4	3	12
North Vietnam	1954–*	Impair military potential	1	1	1
Egypt (with UK and France)	1956	Ensure free passage through the Suez Canal; compensate for nationalization	3	3	9
Laos	1956–1962	Destabilize two governments; prevent communist takeover	3	3	9
Cuba	1960–*	Settle expropriation claims; destabilize Castro; disrupt military adventures	1	1	1
Dominican Republic	1960–1962	Cease subversion in Venezuela; destabilize Trujillo	4	4	16
Ceylon	1961–1965	Settle expropriation claims	4	4	16
Brazil	1962–1964	Settle expropriation claims; destabilize Goulart	4	3	12
South Vietnam	1963	Ease repression; remove Nhu; destabilize Diem	4	3	12
Egypt	1963–1965	Deter military adventurism; stop anti-U.S. rhetoric	4	4	16
Indonesia	1963–1966	Cease "crush" Malaysia campaign; destabilize Sukarno	4	2	8
Chile	1965–1966	Reduce copper price	3	4	12
India	1965–1967	Change agricultural policy	4	4	16
Peru	1968	Prevent buying of French jets	1	1	1
Peru	1968–1971	Settle expropriation claims	3	4	12
Chile	1970–1973	Settle expropriation claims; destabilize Allende	4	3	12
India, Pakistan	1971	Stop military conflict	2	1	2

continued

TABLE 6.1 Continued
Cases of U.S. Economic Sanctions in the Third World

Target	Year(s)	Goal	Policy Result	Sanctions Contribution	Success Rating[a]
Uganda (with UK)	1972–1979	Improve human rights; destabilize Amin	4	3	12
Chile	1973–1990	Improve human rights	3	2	6
South Korea	1973–1977	Improve human rights	2	2	4
South Africa	1975–1991	Deter nuclear proliferation	2	2	4
South Korea (with Canada)	1975–1976	Deter nuclear proliferation	4	4	16
Kampuchea	1975–1979	Improve human rights	1	1	1
Ethiopia	1976–*	Settle expropriation claims; improve human rights	2	3	6
Taiwan	1976–1977	Deter nuclear proliferation	4	4	16
Uruguay	1976–1981	Improve human rights	3	2	6
Guatemala	1977–1986	Improve human rights	3	2	6
Nicaragua	1977–1979	Improve human rights; destabilize Somoza	4	3	12
El Salvador	1977–1981	Improve human rights	2	3	6
Paraguay	1977–1981	Improve human rights	2	3	6
Argentina	1977–1983	Improve human rights	3	2	6
Brazil	1977–1984	Improve human rights	3	3	9
Libya	1978–*	End support for terrorism; destabilize Qaddafi	2	2	4
Brazil	1978–1981	Deter nuclear proliferation	2	2	4
India	1978–1982	Deter nuclear proliferation	2	2	4
Argentina	1978–1982	Deter nuclear proliferation	2	2	4
Pakistan	1979–*	Deter nuclear proliferation	1	1	1
Iran	1979–1981	Return hostages	4	3	12
Bolivia	1979–1982	Improve human rights; prevent drug smuggling	2	3	6
Iraq	1980–*	End support for terrorism; renounce chemical, nuclear, and biological weapons	2	2	4
Nicaragua	1981–1990	Destabilize Sandinistas	4	2	8
Suriname (with Netherlands)	1982–1988	Improve human rights; limit Cuban-Soviet influence	3	3	9
Grenada (with OECS)	1983	Destabilize Austin government	4	2	8
Zimbabwe	1983–1988	Stop anti-U.S. rhetoric	2	2	4
Iran	1984–*	End support for terrorism; end war with Iraq	2	3	6

continued

TABLE 6.1 Continued
Cases of U.S. Economic Sanctions in the Third World

Target	Year(s)	Goal	Policy Result	Sanctions Contribution	Success Rating[a]
South Africa	1985–*	End apartheid	2	3	6
Syria (with UK)	1986–*	End support for terrorism	2	3	6
Angola	1986–*	Expel Cuban troops	3	1	3
Haiti	1987–1990	Improve human rights; hold elections	3	3	9
Panama	1987–1990	Stop drug smuggling; destabilize Noriega	4	1	4
El Salvador	1988	Prevent amnesty for killers of U.S. advisers	4	4	16
Burma (with Japan, Germany)	1988–*	Improve human rights; restore democracy	2	3	6
Somalia (with UK)	1988–*	Improve human rights; end civil war	2	2	4
Sudan	1989–*	Improve human rights; restore democracy	1	1	1
Iraq (with UN)	1990–*	Withdraw from Kuwait; release hostages; restore legitimate Kuwaiti government	4	2	8
Haiti (with OAS)[b]	1991–*	Restore Aristide to elected position as president	—	—	—

* = Sanctions are ongoing (even if some portion has been lifted).
[a]The success rating was derived by multiplying the two component indexes together; indexes are explained in the text. For a greater discussion of methodology, see Gary Clyde Hufbauer, Jeffrey Schott, and Kimberly Elliott, *Economic Sanctions Reconsidered*, 2 vols., rev. (Washington: Institute for International Economics, 1990).
[b]Estimates are not given for Haiti because this case arose after the publication of *Economic Sanctions Reconsidered*.

policies, and interruption of drug smuggling. Examples of major goals include U.S. efforts to impair the military potentials of North Korea and North Vietnam and to force the Republic of South Africa to dismantle its racially based system of apartheid.

U.S. goals in 60 percent of the fifty-eight episodes were modest and they succeeded 34 percent of the time. In 24 percent, the United States sought the destabilization of the target country's ruling regime and succeeded 57 percent of the time. Overall, these two categories of objectives accounted for all but one of the successes, a case in the third category (disruption of military adventures) in which the United States interrupted economic and food aid (1963–1965) to pressure Egyptian President Gamal Abdel Nasser to remove troops from Yemen and halt aid to Congolese rebels, as well as to mute his anti-U.S. rhetoric. Efforts to influence the fighting between India and Pakistan in 1971 and halt Vietnamese intervention in Kampuchea failed (two of three such cases), as did the major sanctions campaigns against North Korea, North Vietnam, and South Africa.[10]

Besides the difficulty of the objective sought, a second major factor in success is the political and economic health and stability of the target. Third World target countries were, on average, less stable than target countries in the broader universe of 116 cases. Within the narrower subset, the health and stability of countries successfully targeted was typically lower still than that of countries against which sanctions failed. For example, although destabilization of a government would appear to be a relatively difficult goal to achieve, the success of sanctions in these cases may be explained in large part by the fact that the targeted regimes were often tottering even before the sanctions were imposed—for example, Allende's Chile in the early 1970s. In fact, in all but one of the successes—the replacement of Iranian Prime Minister Mosaddeq with the shah—the target faced substantial economic and political problems.

Several other political and economic factors may be identified that might play a role in the outcome of a sanctions episode: (1) the presence or absence of companion policies, such as covert intervention or military force; (2) cooperation from one's allies; (3) the closeness of relations between sender and target prior to the imposition of sanctions; (4) the extension of offsetting assistance from third countries; (5) the degree of trade linkage between sender and target; (6) the costs to target and sender; and (7) the type of sanction. Each of these factors shall be considered in turn.

The United States applied noneconomic companion measures in addition to economic ones in one-third of the cases. Sanctions were a complement to the use of U.S. military force during the Korean and Vietnam Wars, whereas quasi-military maneuvers (such as moving an aircraft carrier into the Bay of Bengal during the fighting between Pakistan and India in 1970–1971) and covert intervention bolstered economic sanctions in other cases. Such companion policies were most prominent in destabilization efforts, in which they accompanied economic sanctions in eleven of the fourteen cases. However, the presence of such measures is not terribly helpful in distinguishing successes and failures: Companion policies were present in more destabilization failures (83 percent) than successes (75 percent). Economic sanctions contributed to the downfall of Idi Amin in Uganda (1972–1979) and of Anastacio Somoza in Nicaragua (1977–1979) without accompanying measures from the United States, although military pressure from Tanzania and indigenous rebels, respectively, obviously were the key deciding factors. To the contrary, the combination of complete trade embargoes, financial sanctions, and military measures have failed to dislodge popular revolutionary leaders in Cuba (1960–present) and Libya (1978–

present). Furthermore, companion policies also do not appear to have played a significant role in cases other than destabilization efforts.

One caveat is in order, however. Three of the six destabilization cases counted as failures in fact involved policy successes from the perspective of the U.S. government (Nicaragua, 1981–1990; Grenada, 1983; and Panama, 1987–1990). But in all three, the impact of the economic sanctions was either swamped or superseded by military action.

Another common perception seemingly contradicted by the evidence is that cooperation from allies is an essential component of a successful sanctions effort. However, although the case studies revealed a negative correlation between cooperation and success, a more nuanced conclusion is in order. Cooperation typically is sought in major sanctions efforts, although such efforts are unlikely to force fundamental changes in policy even if a relatively high degree of cooperation is attained. Obvious examples include the sanctions campaign against South Africa and the effort to destabilize Castro. When modest objectives were involved, as in most of the cases discussed here, international cooperation usually was not needed and often was not sought by Washington.

The warmth of presanctions relations between target and sender is important, however. First, it might be expected that the trade linkage (as measured by the ratio of target country trade with the sender to its total trade) would be higher between friends than between enemies. Second, it would also be expected that the willingness to change policies to accommodate an ally would certainly be higher than such willingness among countries whose relations are strained. Analyzing the set of cases reveals that in successful cases relations prior to the imposition of sanctions were more likely to be friendly—such as U.S. efforts to discourage the development of a nuclear-weapons capability in Taiwan (1976–1977) and in South Korea (1975–1976). In failed cases, relations had usually been more neutral and occasionally antagonistic, as with Libya even before 1978 .

The sanctions effort may also be undermined if the target can convince a third country to come to its rescue, as even very high economic costs may be offset if another country is willing to step in with countervailing assistance. In the fifty-eight episodes involving U.S. sanctions against Third World countries, offsetting assistance was three times as likely to have been a factor in failed cases as in those that succeeded. These cases usually involved targets in the struggle between the two superpowers, and the offsetting assistance frequently came from the former Soviet Union or its allies, such as in the cases of U.S. sanctions against Cuba, Ethiopia, Nicaragua, North Korea, and Vietnam. With the apparent end of the Cold War, this variable may become less important in the future.

These factors are primarily political in nature; yet, in order to be able to inflict pain, the sender country must control something of value to the target, which in this case is measured by the target's value of trade with the sender as a ratio of the target's total trade. Although the level of trade necessary to bestow coercive power still depends on the importance to the target of the policy change being demanded, a higher trade linkage should, on average, correlate positively with success. For example, 37 percent of Chile's total trade was with the United States in the mid-1960s when U.S. sanctions (1965–1966) were successfully imposed to influence Chile's copper-pricing policy. Conversely, only 10 percent of Uruguay's trade was with the United States when unsuccessful sanctions were imposed (1976–1981) to improve Uruguay's support for human rights. Overall, evidence from the fifty-eight cases shows that the trade linkage in successful cases was 30 percent as compared to 17 percent in failed episodes.

Other factors contributing to effectiveness are the economic costs to the target, as well as those that the sender must bear. There is no magic ratio of costs to target and sender that guarantees success. Rather, each cost variable is important independently. It is the degree of pain inflicted on the target economy balanced against the cost of complying with the demanded policy change that largely determines the effectiveness of the sanctions effort. From the sender's perspective, the higher the self-inflicted cost, the louder the protest from adversely affected domestic interests and the less sustainable the effort is likely to be.

As would be expected, the average cost to the sanctions target in the successful episodes was over 2 percent of GNP, whereas the average cost in failures was half that. For example, the cost to Iran was nearly 4 percent of GNP in the (eventually) successful U.S. effort to get the hostages out of that country. To the contrary, cost was negligible in most of the failed cases of sanctions intended to deter nuclear proliferation, which typically involved fairly narrow export controls on nuclear fuels and technology that often could be obtained elsewhere. The cost to sender was less significant in these cases than in the total universe of 116 cases because the trade affected was usually of far less importance to the United States than to its target.

A final and very important factor contributing to effectiveness is the inclusion of financial sanctions. The economic and political effects of trade sanctions and financial sanctions differ in several ways. Trade controls are usually selective, affecting one or a few goods—for example, U.S. exports of nuclear technology. In such cases, the trade may only be diverted rather than cut off. Whether import (export) prices paid by (received by) the target country increase (decrease) after the sanctions are applied depends on the market in question. Often the price effects are very modest. By contrast, finding alternative financing may be harder and is likely to carry a higher price (in terms of the interest rate) and require greater credit security because of the uncertainties created by sanctions. Official development assistance may be irreplaceable. In addition, financial sanctions, especially involving trade finance, may interrupt a wide range of trade flows even without the imposition of explicit trade sanctions.

The economic effects of financial sanctions also tend to tilt the political balance in a more positive direction, from the perspective of the sender country. The pain from trade sanctions, especially export controls, usually is diffused through the target country's population. Financial sanctions are more likely to hit the pet projects or personal pockets of powerful government officials who are in a position to influence policy. On the sender's side of the equation, an interruption of official aid or credit is unlikely to create the same political backlash from business firms and allies abroad as an interruption of private trade.

The United States interrupted aid or other financial flows to Third World countries in fifty of the fifty-eight cases. Financial sanctions without accompanying trade controls succeeded almost 50 percent of the time, whereas trade controls alone (export controls in six cases) succeeded only once, when they contributed to Taiwan's decision to shut down a nuclear facility in which it was suspected of developing a nuclear reprocessing capability.

■ DECLINING SUCCESS AND SANCTIONS IN PERSPECTIVE

Despite the relative success that economic sanctions have achieved on average since the end of World War II, their effectiveness has declined substantially since the early 1970s. Approximately 67 percent of the episodes involving U.S. sanctions against the Third World between 1938 and 1972 were at least partial successes, compared to only 22 percent during the period 1973–1990. There appear to be four major reasons for this collapse in effectiveness.

The first is the relative decline of the U.S. position in the world economy. Immediately following World War II, the United States was the largest source for development assistance for newly independent Third World countries. Even well into the 1960s, the United States remained the primary source of development assistance and an important market for many developing countries, especially in Latin America. Since then, however, resource constraints in the United States, the recovery in Europe, and the emergence of Japan as a major economic player have made the United States just one aid donor and source of trade and finance among many. Moreover, with economic development has come reduced vulnerability for many potential targets. Perhaps, too, the relative decline of the United States and the post-Vietnam caution of U.S. leaders mean that target countries are less fearful that economic sanctions presage "something worse."[11]

A second reason for the greater success in the earlier period may have been a shift in the objectives that the United States hoped to achieve. Economic sanctions proved more effective in settling expropriation disputes and in campaigns to destabilize "undesirable" governments than in improving human rights, deterring nuclear proliferation, or combating terrorism and drug smuggling. In addition, as 76 percent of the goals in the more recent cases were modest (compared to 33 percent in the earlier period), more important objectives, usually concerns about Soviet influence or strategic position, often superseded them. Moreover, although the goals may have been modest from the perspective of the United States, they were increasingly less so if viewed from the other side.[12] Stifling political opposition or keeping up with a rival thought to be pursuing a nuclear-weapons option were obviously far more important to military leaders in Argentina, Brazil, El Salvador, Pakistan, and elsewhere than continued economic assistance or nuclear technology from the United States.

A third and related trend is the growing assertiveness of Congress in foreign policy since 1973. Although it was the Hickenlooper Amendment, attached to the Foreign Assistance Act in 1962 by Republican Senator Bourke B. Hickenlooper, that provoked administration intervention in many of the expropriation disputes of the 1960s, that was a rare example of congressionally mandated economic sanctions. Increasingly in the 1970s, however, Congress has forced action on foreign policy priorities not shared by the executive branch through legislation constraining the president's discretion and requiring the use of economic sanctions in certain situations. The confused signals sent by administrations reluctantly imposing legislatively mandated sanctions, especially in the human rights and nuclear nonproliferation episodes, may have led target countries to believe (often correctly) that the sanctions would not be sustained.

The fourth major difference between the two periods is the form of sanctions imposed. Financial measures were part of the sanctions package in every episode prior to 1973 but were present in only 78 percent of the cases after that. The type of financial sanction used most frequently changed as well. Economic aid was the dominant choice in the earlier period, whereas military assistance was prominent in the later period, especially in the human rights cases where military governments were often the target. Given that many of these governments depended on force to maintain themselves in power, it is surprising that suspension or termination of military assistance—including training, police gear and other equipment—did not have more impact. As noted, however, these governments obviously perceived internal dissent to be the greater threat to their longevity.

Can the declining utility of economic sanctions be reversed? Although possible, the various factors that contributed to U.S. success in the earlier post–World War II period are continuing to move in a negative direction from the perspective of the U.S. government. The budget deficit will remain large for some time, which means the resource constraints on foreign economic and military aid will get tighter, and reluctance to interfere with trade flows for noncommercial reasons, especially in regard to U.S. exports, will grow.

But even after reaching sustainable fiscal and trade positions, it is highly unlikely that previous levels of U.S. dominance in the global economy can be restored. That dominance was inevitably a temporary phenomenon, the duration of which the U.S. government shortened when it adopted a policy of active reconstruction and development assistance for newly independent nations after World War II. These trends are accelerating. The European Community will be an even stronger economic competitor if it successfully completes the transition to a truly internal market envisioned by the "1992" initiative. Japanese influence, rising out of its strong creditor position, will continue to grow for some time. The PRC is also emerging as a major player in the world economy, and a noncommunist Russia may yet do so if the political and economic reforms espoused by President Boris Yeltsin can be implemented and sustained.

Nor will potential developing-country targets ever again be as vulnerable as they once were. The newly industrializing countries of East Asia—Hong Kong, Singapore, South Korea, and Taiwan—successfully adopted a strategy of export-led growth and have become important trading partners of the United States (as such, they are increasingly subjected to sanctions for economic rather than political reasons), with growth rates that are the envy of the world. Many of the Latin American countries, favorite targets of the past, have also successfully penetrated the U.S. market, while diversifying their sources of supply for goods and finance.

Although the United States rightly recognized that it was in its interest to assist in the reconstruction and further development of the world economy after World War II, it does not seem to have recognized that the subsequent growth of healthy and powerful competitive economies would entail a parallel reduction in its leverage relative to other countries and, thus, in its ability to influence them. The circumstances in which U.S. economic leverage may be effectively applied have narrowed, and success will increasingly depend on the subtlety, skill, and creativity with which it is exercised.

■ 7

Covert Intervention

Harry Howe Ransom

Covert action is, by definition, a foreign policy instrument based upon secrecy and deception. Note the CIA's official definition: "Covert action is a special activity conducted abroad in support of United States foreign policy objectives and executed so that the role of the United States government is not apparent or acknowledged publicly. Covert action is distinct from the intelligence gathering function. Covert action often gives the United States an option between diplomatic and military action."[1]

This one official paragraph captures the essence of and rationale for a policy of maintaining the ability to intervene covertly in the politics of Third World countries. The "special activity" referred to in official documents has included secret propaganda, manipulation of foreign electoral processes, overthrowing of governments, secret financial assistance, paramilitary operations, and assassination of political leaders. The secrecy required for covert action makes it difficult for an outside analyst to describe in authentic detail the past and, in particular, the recent application of this instrument. Often, only the tip of the iceberg is visible. In describing such a variety of supposedly secret activities, one must, therefore, proceed by making inferences from known facts, speculating, or relying on undocumented accounts. At the same time, the pluralism of U.S. institutions and special interests makes secret-keeping a nearly impossible challenge for foreign policy decisionmakers and secret operators. Consequently, many, if not most, of past U.S. major covert operations have not remained secret.

■ EVOLUTION OF COVERT ACTION

The Truman Doctrine as enunciated in 1947 underscored the U.S. intention to contain Soviet communism around the globe and to protect noncommunist governments from communist subversive activities. The public side of this policy was economic and technical assistance, initially to Greece and Turkey, to strengthen capabilities for economic and political independence and self-defense. Yet, heightened U.S. fears in 1948 of an aggressive Soviet Union, fueled by the ruthless Soviet takeover of Czechoslovakia, the perceived communist threat to Italian independence in its 1948 elections, and accession to power of communist governments in Poland, Hungary, and other Eastern European countries, persuaded Truman that containment required an additional, covert side. This included the organization within the CIA of a new unit, titled the Office of Special Operations (OSO), to conduct counterintelligence and espionage programs aimed at the Soviet Union. The initial covert policy of the OSO—which provided the foundation for later covert interventions in the Third World—was aptly described by Harry Rositzke, a CIA official at the time: "The Soviet Union was the enemy, and the 'Soviet target' our intelligence mission. We were professionally and emotionally committed to a single purpose. We felt ourselves as much a part of the American crusade against Stalin as we had against Hitler."[2]

President Truman signed a National Security Council directive (NSC 10/2) that set in motion several secret covert-action programs to contain communist expansion, carried out under the newly created Office of Policy Coordination (OPC). A vigorous internal debate occurred within the highest councils of government about the proper organization and control of covert actions. Despite State Department objections, the CIA, because of its existing capabilities and procedures for espionage through secret congressional funding, was chosen as the agency for covert action. Although such actions were assigned to the CIA, the State Department, Defense Department, and White House staff were expected to play the dominant role in policy controls. The problem of congressional consultation, however, which would come back to haunt the CIA with a vengeance, was ignored.

By the end of the Truman administration in 1952, and under the directorship of General Bedell Smith, the CIA's functions of espionage (OSO) and covert action (OPC) had been consolidated under a "deputy director for plans" (DDP). At this point the clandestine service was unified and began to grow and take on new assignments in the shadowy world of secret intervention. This occurred within the context of a consensus "communist containment" foreign policy for which there was strong bipartisan support. This policy required a major capability for secret intervention, primarily to counter Soviet support of Third World "wars of national liberation" around the globe.

Dwight D. Eisenhower, assuming the presidency in 1953, reaffirmed the need for a major covert-action capability. Eisenhower came into office on a platform of aggressive campaign rhetoric regarding containment—indeed, "rolling back"—of Soviet communism. The new administration was soon mounting covert actions to change the political climate in Iran, Guatemala, and elsewhere in the Third World. The temper of the times is illustrated by the words of a secret report to the president by a special Hoover Commission subcommittee in 1954. The report declared that "hitherto accepted norms of human conduct do not apply . . . to survive, long standing American concepts of 'fair play' must be reconsidered. We must . . . learn to subvert, sabotage and destroy our enemies by more clever, more sophisticated, and more effective methods than those used against us."[3] Hundreds of covert actions were undertaken throughout the Third World, ranging from propaganda through paramilitary actions to attempted assassinations. A national, bipartisan Cold War consensus permitted these activities to go forward with little congressional knowledge or supervision. There was also little media exposure, because journalists and editors, in a spirit of wartime self-censorship, did not aggressively pry into secret operations. They adopted a government-knows-best attitude, in sharp contrast to that prevailing since the mid-1970s, when media passivity ended dramatically with almost constant investigations and disclosures about covert operations.

First came the Rockefeller Commission, an eight-member panel of conservative citizens (chaired by Vice President Nelson Rockefeller) that included Ronald W. Reagan. The commission, which limited its investigations to domestic intelligence activities as opposed to covert action abroad, concluded that the CIA had engaged in activities that were "plainly unlawful and constituted improper invasions upon the rights of Americans."[4] Its report cited such illegal conduct as opening of private mail, maintaining files on 300,000 individuals, infiltration of domestic groups, illegal break-ins, wiretaps, and investigations of tax records.

The Senate Select Committee to Study Government Operations with Respect to Intelligence, known as the Church Committee, was established in January 1975 to evaluate both the foreign and domestic activities of U.S. intelligence agencies. Its final report in April 1976 revealed that the CIA had conducted nearly 900 major and several thousand smaller covert-action projects since 1961, the vast majority taking place in the Third World. Although the report concluded that the impact of covert actions had been costly to U.S. foreign policy interests and reputation, it did not recommend the abolition of the covert action function. Rather, it recommended that covert action be sharply restricted and that Congress assert a more aggressive monitoring of all future activity.[5]

The House Select Committee on Intelligence (Pike Committee) was organized in July 1975 to investigate allegations of illegal or improper intelligence activities by U.S. government agencies. In an unusual action, the full House of Representatives voted to suppress the Pike Committee's final report. The House had become convinced that the committee had acted irresponsibly with regard to some allegedly sensitive information that the president wanted deleted from the final report prior to publication. But the report was leaked to the press in February 1976.

The Pike Committee had analyzed all official covert-action approvals since 1965 and had concluded, contrary to popular beliefs, that the evidence gathered suggested that the CIA had not been a "rogue elephant," operating independently of presidential control or outside the boundaries of established foreign policy but, in fact, was responsive to the instructions of the president and his assistants.[6] The issue of covert intervention became not so much one of executive control as one of legitimacy, efficacy, or morality—in other words, a question of policy. Harry Rositzke, a veteran CIA officer, observed that the CIA had become as much a symbol of U.S. imperialism abroad and of secret government at home as the KGB, the CIA's rough equivalent in the former Soviet Union.[7]

The Rockefeller Commission and Church and Pike Committees signaled the end of the Cold War foreign policy consensus, influenced in part by disillusionment with the Vietnam War, the Watergate scandals, and revelations about U.S. intervention in Chile. In fact, a sign of the times was the 1974 congressional Hughes-Ryan Amendment, which explicitly prohibited use of the CIA for covert action unless the president had specifically certified its vital necessity for national security *and* had duly informed half a dozen congressional committees. This seemed to assure that covert action would rarely be undertaken in the future.

The hastily drawn Hughes-Ryan Amendment remained controversial throughout the administration of Jimmy Carter, as the president oversaw a massive reduction in covert-action budgets and staffs in which the number of covert actions in the Third World presumably were reduced. The Soviet invasion of Afghanistan in 1979, however, prompted renewed use of covert methods. In late 1980, Carter signed legislation, titled the Intelligence Oversight Act, that repealed the Hughes-Ryan Amendment. The act requires that the CIA and other U.S. intelligence agencies keep the two permanent standing intelligence committees of Congress fully and promptly informed of all secret intelligence activities—past, present, and anticipated—including sensitive, covert political interventions. Despite loopholes giving the president some discretion in extraordinary situations, a new national policy on covert action was established that seemed likely to reduce the future use of this secret instrument. Covert action was now to be a shared executive-congressional responsibility.[8]

The administration of President Ronald Reagan departed from the concept of shared responsibility, instead calling for "unleashing the CIA" from such inhibiting restrictions. Indeed, Reagan named William J. Casey, a veteran of the U.S. Office of Strategic Services (OSS) and covert operations in World War II, as director of the CIA and point man in an effort to reestablish covert-action programs on a par with those of the 1950s. A guiding program for the reinvigorated CIA was the Reagan Doctrine and its pledge to aid anticommunist guerrillas, which the administration was fond of calling "freedom fighters."

In the case of Nicaragua, the CIA became the instrument of "overt" covert action. This was because the CIA had become somewhat circumscribed by more aggressive congressional restrictions, such as the Boland Amendment prohibiting government efforts or expenditures to overthrow Nicaragua's government. Thus constrained by attempted congressional oversight, the White House turned to the National Security Council staff for a new and bizarre form of covert action. The actions of Lieutenant Colonel Oliver North and his associates brought upon the presidency a crisis in credibility and legitimacy that remains unresolved as of this writing. Indeed, the Iran arms-for-hostages deals and illegal diversion of funds to the contras placed the question of covert intervention at the center of national attention in 1987 and 1988. Iran-contra investigations continued into the 1990s. Congressional inquiries and efforts of investigative journalists suggest that secret foreign policies conducted by invisible and unaccountable governmental processes became the mode in the mid-1980s.[9] Questions and problems have been brought up regarding the place of covert actions in a constitutional democracy; these will be discussed later.

■ TYPES OF COVERT INTERVENTION

The covert action option for foreign policy implementation exists along a conceptualized "scale of coercion." It is one thing to give a little aid and comfort to U.S. friends in strategic Third World areas. It is quite another to change a regime by the direct action of plotting to overthrow its leader, perhaps by assassination. Indeed, the most extreme (coercive) form of covert action represents a foreign policy instrument just short of war. The four primary types of U.S. covert action to be discussed (in descending order of violence) are assassination plots, coups d'état, election intervention, and propaganda and psychological warfare. Paramilitary warfare, usually carried out covertly, and obviously located at the more coercive end of the spectrum, will be discussed in Chapter 8.

□ *Assassination Plots*

Political assassination of a foreign leader is the most extreme form of covert action and is usually part of a greater goal to change the existing government of the target country. Documented evidence provided by Church Committee investigators brought home the reality that assassinations had been regular instruments of U.S. foreign policy, a fact that came as a shock to many Americans. The finding of the congressional inquiry was that the CIA had been deeply involved in assassination plots during several decades of the Cold War, despite the absence of any clear-cut proof of presidential authorization or concrete evidence that in any case an agent of the CIA "pulled the trigger."[10] It seems clear that a policy of "plausible denial" existed, leaving no paper trail implicating a president and no direct evidence that the CIA was directly involved in political murder.

Little doubt exists, however, that the CIA was to some degree involved in a number of assassination plots, including efforts to murder Fidel Castro in Cuba, Patrice Lumumba in the Congo (now Zaire), and Colonel Abdul

Kassem in Iraq. The CIA also was associated with conspirators who plotted the death of Rafael Trujillo in the Dominican Republic, Ngo Dinh Diem in Vietnam, and General Réné Schneider, army chief of staff, in Chile. The degree of U.S. complicity remains uncertain. Even less certain is whether such plots were authorized at the highest level—by the presidents themselves.

In the case of Castro, the Church Committee reports that the CIA began to plot his "elimination" as early as December 1959.[11] Earlier that year, Castro had turned to the Soviet Union, nationalized U.S. property (offering compensation in the form of 200-year bonds), and began exporting guerrilla teams to other Caribbean nations. By early 1960, Washington perceived Castro as directly challenging U.S. interests in the region, and the NSC's Special Group began discussing contingency plans for the overthrow of his government. It was soon clear that such plans included assassination. By the end of 1960, agents of the CIA had approached U.S. underworld leaders with the idea of placing a death contract on Castro, to be carried out by notorious U.S. mobsters or their agents. Other methods considered for doing away with Castro included various forms of poison from CIA labs, as well as poison pens, exploding seashells, a poison dart gun, and bacterial powder in a scuba-diving suit. Such plans were pursued during the administration of President John F. Kennedy. Obviously, none succeeded.

After the U.S.-supported Bay of Pigs landing in 1961 met with defeat, the president's brother, Robert F. Kennedy, insisted that the CIA continue its efforts to remove Castro from the scene. The renewed effort to kill Castro was directed within the CIA by William Harvey and bore the code name "Operation Mongoose." The Mongoose team, carefully monitored by Robert Kennedy, developed some thirty different plans to dispose of Castro, ranging from economic warfare to outlandish attempts at convincing Cuba's large Catholic population that Christ would return to Cuba in a Second Coming if they would rid themselves of their leader. Eventually it became clear that none of these schemes would work and nothing short of a U.S. military invasion could oust Castro. After the Cuban missile crisis in October 1962, the CIA was ordered to cease all covert operations in Cuba. We cannot know if this order was obeyed.

□ Coups D'État

The United States has been more successful, at least in the short-run, in staging coups d'état against foreign governments deemed inimical to U.S. interests. The first documented example in the post–World War II period was the CIA-directed overthrow in 1953 of Iranian Prime Minister Mohammad Mosaddeq and his replacement by Shah Mohammad Reza Pahlavi. The democratically elected Mosaddeq had nationalized the Anglo-Iranian Oil Company in 1951 and increasingly was perceived in Washington as falling under Soviet influence. Then, as now, the United States was interested in maintaining the flow of oil from the region.

Kermit Roosevelt, the grandson of President Theodore Roosevelt and a member of the CIA's covert operations branch, was put in charge of "Operation Ajax." The plan was to overthrow Mosaddeq by an internal coup d'état, based upon intelligence assumptions that powerful groupings existed in the country that could be aided by the CIA. Within sixty days this was accomplished with the support of the Iranian army, a large segment of public opinion loyal to the shah, and the British intelligence services. The cost was small in both dollars (less than $200,000) and lives (the coup was virtually bloodless).[12] Unfortunately, the political leadership in Washington drew more about the efficacy of covert action than was warranted from this example. The heady wine of success led them to believe that this was a foreign policy tool that could be applied with equal success in other problem areas of the world. More important perhaps, as is discussed in Chapter 17, U.S. intervention in 1953 contributed to the fostering of a virulently anti-U.S. revolutionary regime some twenty-five years later.

A second example of U.S. covert intervention against a democratically elected leftist regime in the name of anticommunism—which, in the long run, would lead to dubious results—is Chile. During the Kennedy administration, the CIA had been very active in Chile, trying to shape favorable political outcomes, with considerable success. Kennedy, noting that Chile was a nation with a democratic tradition that had extended longer than a century (the last military coup d'état had been in 1925), hoped to make the country a model of democracy and capitalism in Latin America.

Under the administration of President Richard M. Nixon, however, Washington became aware that Salvador Allende, the leader of the Chilean left wing, was likely to win that country's 1970 presidential elections. Fearful of the prospect of a Marxist regime in South America, Nixon ordered the CIA to derail Allende's quest for the presidency. A "Track I" plan of covert intervention centered on manipulating the Chilean congressional vote through intense diplomatic and economic pressure, propaganda efforts, and subsidies of political groups opposed to Allende. The more nefarious side of U.S. covert intervention went under the heading of "Track II" and stressed the removal of Allende by a U.S.-induced military coup d'état. In 1973, Allende indeed was killed during a successful military coup d'état. Although the CIA apparently was not directly involved, the efforts of the Track I and II programs from 1970 to 1973 undoubtedly contributed to the outcome.[13] Chile's democratic system was replaced by a right-wing repressive regime.

☐ *Election Intervention*

Assassinations and coups d'état were the exception in the CIA's program of covert action during the Cold War years. Other forms of covert action, such as interference with the electoral processes in areas of perceived strategic importance to the United States, were more common. In addition to the Chilean case, Italy, although not a Third World country, provided the classic *documented* example of U.S. intervention in the electoral process in target lands, and one that would become the blueprint for future U.S. intervention of this type in the Third World. U.S. secret intervention in the 1958 Italian election was, in the words of its director, William Colby, "by far the CIA's largest covert political action program undertaken until then, or indeed, since."[14] CIA political operations chief in Rome in 1953, Colby stated that the Italian political scene was "an unparalleled opportunity to demonstrate that secret aid could help our friends and frustrate our foes without the use of force and violence."[15]

Colby's job was to ensure that NATO's line of defense was not breached by the possibility that a democratically elected Italian government headed by the nation's communist party would take power in 1958. Moscow was reportedly spending some $50 million per year to aid the Italian communists. The U.S. government assigned the CIA the task of secretly intervening in Italy to counter Soviet political action. A multimillion-dollar program was devised with the primary purpose of supporting Italy's center democratic political parties. This support was provided mainly in the form of direct payments for political activities, such as newsletters, leaflets, posters, and other propaganda material; staging congresses and public rallies; and membership drives, voter registration, and related political action. Additional CIA funds were allocated for supporting noncommunist trade unions, consumer and farmer cooperatives, cultural societies, youth groups, veterans' organizations, and a variety of local committees. In other words, CIA funds were used for a total penetration of Italian society in a massive secret effort to manipulate future political outcomes in keeping with the United States' perceived national interest.

The 1958 Italian national elections were a test of the efficacy of U.S. covert intervention. Yet, the results were inconclusive. Colby argued that covert political action in Italy was successful in terms of the long-term strategy of strengthening center democracy, deterring the growth of communist electoral strength, and eliminating the socialist-communist coalition. The Italians would possibly have produced such an outcome without U.S. intervention. In any case, U.S. covert election intervention, documented in an allied nation such as Italy, surely has taken place in Third World countries where possible leftist electoral victories were perceived as threatening U.S. interests. Indeed, one author has described various episodes of U.S. election intervention in countries as diverse as Brazil, British Guiana, the Dominican Republic, Ecuador, Jamaica, Laos, Lebanon, Nicaragua, the Philippines, and Vietnam.[16]

□ *Propaganda and Psychological Warfare*

The least coercive tool of covert action is propaganda/psychological warfare. Since the early 1950s, the United States has maintained a dual track for propaganda overseas: an open program, implemented by the United States Information Agency (USIA), and covert activities, most often performed by the CIA.

Congressional investigators have made public details of some covert propaganda activity. From these one can infer how such secret efforts are applied. For example, the Church Committee documented that U.S. covert action expenditures in Chile from 1963 to 1973 were targeted toward propaganda for elections and material support for political parties ($8,000,000), producing and disseminating propaganda and supporting mass media ($4,300,000), influencing Chilean interest groups (such as students and labor), and supporting private-sector organizations ($900,000).[17] This accounting demonstrates that propaganda efforts were combined with psychological warfare and political action to influence political outcomes believed to be favorable to the United States. Efforts were focused on aiding anticommunist forces within Chile with such programs as simple manipulation of the press, sponsoring of public opinion polls, placement of U.S.-written material in the Chilean media, and direct financial support of publications.

A 1977 survey in the *New York Times*[18] disclosed a number of details about the CIA's propaganda activities in the Third World at large. For example, at the peak of such activities, the CIA "Propaganda Assets Inventory" listed over 800 news and public information organizations and individuals that were on its payroll. Furthermore, the CIA secretly subsidized not only Radio Free Europe and Radio Liberty but also Radio Free Asia and Free Cuba Radio, as well as numerous social democratic magazines throughout the Third World, including *El Mundo Nuevo* in Latin America and *Quiet and Thought* in India. In Saigon, the CIA set up and financed the Vietnam Council on Foreign Relations, an organization designed to influence elite Asian opinions. Finally, the CIA maintained a major book-publishing program, which included the secret financing of over 200 English-language books since the early 1950s. As part of this effort, the CIA supported its own proprietary publishers, such as Allied Pacific Printing in Bombay and the Asia Research Center in Hong Kong.

■ COVERT INTERVENTION IN THE 1980s AND THE 1990s

For examples of covert action in the 1980s and especially the 1990s, the details are more sketchy and the evidence softer. We must rely on the writings of investigative journalists—Bob Woodward of the *Washington*

Post is the outstanding recent example. His book *Veil: The Secret Wars of the CIA, 1981–1987* detailed a variety of covert actions taken by the Reagan administration to influence political events in selected Third World areas.[19] Woodward's work, full of intriguing particulars about secret operations, cites few sources and contains no footnotes. One major source cited is most unexpected and puzzling: William J. Casey, who was the director of the CIA from 1981 to 1987.

Accepting Woodward as a reliable source, one sees the CIA during the 1980s returning to a worldwide program of secret manipulation comparable in scope to activities in the 1950s and 1960s. For example, the Reagan administration attempted to overthrow or weaken the regime of Libya's Muammar Qaddafi. A crucial aspect of this effort was covert assistance to Qaddafi's enemies both within Libya and in neighboring countries. Second, the United States initiated a major covert action in Chad beginning in 1981. The purpose of this program—which included arms, money, technical assistance, and political support—was to support Hissène Habré, Chad's former minister of defense, in his effort to overthrow the existing pro-Libyan government. Finally, in 1982, the CIA, in coordination with Saudi Arabia, sponsored efforts by exiled Yemenis to conduct sabotage activities against the Soviet-dominated state of South Yemen on the Arabian Peninsula. The sabotage team was captured and tortured, ultimately confessing its CIA sponsorship. As stated earlier, these examples represent the tip of the iceberg of covert action, as scores of such activities remain invisible. In general, it is the failed secret operations that receive the most publicity.

One of the priorities of the CIA under the Reagan administration was combating international terrorism. Woodward claimed that the administration attempted to assassinate Lebanon's Sheikh Fadlallah, the fundamentalist Muslim leader of Hizbollah (Party of God), who was believed to be responsible for the three terrorist bombings of U.S. facilities in Beirut. Operations control was given to the Saudis, who, in turn, hired a British Special Air Services commando veteran. He, in turn, recruited members of the Lebanese intelligence service to direct the operation. The net result: an automobile laden with explosives detonated on March 8, 1985, within the vicinity of Fadlallah's high-rise apartment, killing eighty persons and wounding many more (Fadlallah escaped uninjured). After the bombing, Fadlallah's followers hung a "Made in USA" banner on the devastated building. Despite the attempt on his life, Fadlallah remained a problem. Changing course, the Saudis then apparently approached him with a $2-million bribe to cease attacks on Saudi and U.S. facilities. Fadlallah-supported attacks against Americans ceased.[20]

The most prominent aspect of the Reagan administration's covert activities revolved around the Reagan Doctrine and paramilitary support for anticommunist guerrilla insurgencies in Afghanistan, Angola, Cambodia, and Nicaragua. Although these activities are amply discussed in Chapter 8, three examples of direct CIA intervention relating to Nicaragua illustrate the problems that use of this tool have entailed for relations between Congress and the executive branch.[21]

The first example relates to the Reagan administration's decision to put counterrevolutionary pressure on the Sandinista government. The policy was implemented at a time when Congress was seriously divided over the issue. Many saw diplomacy as a better course to follow than aiding the Honduras-based contras, who sought to destroy the government in Managua. Senate and House intelligence committees became very involved in this policy. Not only had the House committee by law prohibited CIA efforts to overthrow the Sandinista government, but in January 1985 it issued a stinging report on other aspects of CIA-directed operations in Central America. The committee singled out for criticism the CIA-sponsored document *Psychological Operations in Guerrilla Warfare,* labeled by the media as the "CIA Manual." After investigating the circumstances of the manual's production, the House Democratic committee majority concluded that the manual (1) violated the Boland Amendment by advocating overthrow of the Sandinistas; (2) violated presidential orders prohibiting assassination; (3) created profound embarrassment for the United States; (4) demonstrated that the CIA did not have effective procedures for controlling its agents; and (5) violated congressional spending guidelines placing a cap on aid to the contras. The report symbolized the new congressional posture of involving itself in CIA management issues.

The second example involves the CIA's direct role in the mining of Nicaraguan harbors. On April 10, 1984, CIA Director Casey was required to report to the full Senate on the harbor-mining project. Consequent to this briefing, the Senate voted eighty-four to twelve to prohibit future funds from being used for mining ports or territorial waters of Nicaragua. Again, Congress was involved in secret operational issues. Shortly thereafter, Casey met with the Senate Intelligence Committee and apologized to members for not keeping them properly informed. On June 6, 1984, Casey—with the president's approval—signed an agreement with the Senate committee pledging to follow precise procedures for fully informing the committee in the future, an agreement he apparently violated later.

The third example centers on the controversy raised in November 1986 by disclosure of arms shipments in 1985–1986 to Iran. This operation, which allegedly went forward under direct White House supervision and control, with CIA participation, was completely unknown to Congress until publicized in late November 1986. More than any other intelligence controversy since the beginning of the CIA, the arms-for-hostages (and diversion of funds to the contras) episode magnifies the national security dilemmas of the United States' constitutionally mandated separation of powers. In this case, the president claimed the right to withhold information, even from the congressional leadership, in the interest of the operation's security. Some congressional leaders have asserted that the president had violated legislative statutes designed to force the chief executive to consult in a timely manner with Congress—at least its leadership—on even the most sensitive of operations. Indeed, executive branch actions were in violation of the spirit if not the letter of the Intelligence Oversight Act of 1980, which required all intelligence agencies to keep the select oversight committees fully and promptly informed of all secret intelligence activities. The controversy produced a crisis for the Reagan presidency, threatening to produce a foreign policy stalemate between Congress and a president unwilling to give up independent, discretionary power in certain covert actions.

U.S. foreign policy confronts a radically changed context in the 1990s. The 1947 Truman Doctrine undergirding covert action lost much of its relevancy as the 1990s began. The fragmentation of the Soviet Union into numerous independent and noncommunist countries created a new context for defining national interests. President George Bush's vague talk of a "new world order" appeared to be based upon radically revised assumptions about communist threats in the Third World. On September 13, 1991, in a strikingly symbolic event indicative of the end of the Cold War, Secretary of State James A. Baker III had a cordial meeting at KGB headquarters in Moscow with KGB chief Vadim V. Bakatin. Reportedly they discussed the need to end covert action, each country's against the other's.

Consequently, this exchange raised the questions of policy, efficacy, and organization regarding the standard tools of covert action applied during the post–World War II period—tools earlier described as ranging from assassination to more benign forms of psychological warfare. By 1991, a perceived monolithic Soviet state, operating a massive secret arm in the form of the KGB, had quickly dissolved into an uncertain confederation of Eastern European nationalities that were struggling to maintain a viable economy and had little apparent thought of foreign adventure. Communist ideology was in disrepute, and the motivation for secret foreign "wars of national liberation" had vanished. What, then, for the future of U.S. covert intervention? Let us consider three major elements.

1. *Assassination.* The deliberate removal by killing of a foreign political leader is the ultimate instrument of foreign policy. Assassination in fact goes beyond war in the sense that it can be said to violate the "rules of war" (Geneva Convention). Yet it is clear that this violent foreign policy tool, although prohibited by presidential executive order since the administration of Gerald Ford, continues to rise to the level of national policy discussion. Such a debate surfaced in late 1989 when the *New York Times* reported that CIA Director William H. Webster suggested that President Bush and Congress give the CIA "greater latitude in supporting potentially violent efforts to overthrow foreign dictators."[22] What the CIA

director was apparently proposing was that prohibitions against assassinations be modified to permit the United States to assist local groups in deposing leaders judged dangerous to U.S. strategic interests. Because of the secrecy in such matters, it is not known if the rules for covert action were in fact made more permissive. What is known is that the United States ultimately took direct military action to depose and arrest Panamanian dictator Manuel Noriega. This may signify that the government had finally learned that covert action is not a reliable instrument. As discussed in Chapter 19, direct, open action in Panama occurred after secret plots had been judged too risky or had failed.

Proposals that strong prohibitions against assassination plots be compromised stirred a short-lived public debate. Leading the opposition to any change in prohibitive assassination rules was Senator Daniel Patrick Moynihan. The senator took an absolutist position: no direct or indirect participation in assassinations. He viewed such an instrument as contrary to international law, the UN Charter, and various treaties. On a more pragmatic note, he argued that assassinations are counterproductive. Fundamentally he argued that assassinations violate the law.[23]

Nonetheless, as this is being written (early 1992), one continues to hear rumblings and rumors that "administration officials" throughout 1991 were discussing and perhaps plotting covert efforts to depose President Saddam Hussein of Iraq. Having defeated Iraq's armies in the Persian Gulf war and driven them out of Kuwait, the Bush administration remained embarrassed by its failure to remove Hussein. Covert action toward this end has remained an option, but no public knowledge has appeared as to its attempted implementation.

2. *Covert-action organization.* In fall 1991, the public was able to observe unprecedented disclosures of the inner workings of the primary agency—the CIA—charged with carrying out covert action. This came about in the Senate Intelligence Committee hearings on the nomination of Robert Gates to head the CIA. Little discussion in open sessions centered on covert action. But it was significant that Gates was the first career analyst to head the CIA. This signified that the covert-operations directorate that had tended to dominate the agency since the early 1950s would decline in influence. Testimony in these hearings revealed that a high degree of tension and distrust existed over the years between the intelligence (analytical) branch and the operation (covert-action) directorate. Patently, the right hand of intelligence (information) gathering and the left hand of covert action were being exercised in isolation, one from the other.

Covert action always has been the major problem area for the CIA. A high agency official was once heard to declare: "Covert action has only about 15 percent of the agency's budget but causes 90 percent of its problems." These problems have been secrecy and accountability, which tend to be mutually exclusive. No other world power experiences the degree of difficulty that exists in the United States when covert action is the policy choice. U.S. political culture is suspicious of government secrecy. Covert action without secrecy is irrational.

3. *Transformation of the KGB.* As earlier indicated, nothing is more striking at the beginning of the last decade of the twentieth century than the dissolution of the Soviet Union. With this has come the dismantling of the Soviet KGB, which temporarily was transformed into an "Inter-Republican Council for Security." The disappearance of the KGB from the international scene is significant because, to some degree, the CIA—in particular its covert-operations directorate—was created in reaction to the perceived threat of KGB agents encircling the globe in pursuit of world communist domination. The KGB, backed by Soviet nuclear power, symbolized the "Soviet threat." The CIA, through its covert-action arm, was part of the deterrence structure created in response. The sharply altered nature of the international balance of power calls into question the need for a CIA in its current form, particularly its covert-action function. Indeed, a presidential executive directive to the U.S. intelligence community succinctly pointed to the changed international environment: "The Soviet Union and Eastern Europe have been transformed, the Warsaw Pact dissolved, and Soviet activism (especially in the Third World) dramatically curtailed. There is growing interest here at home in our intelligence services tackling new issues and problems."[24]

We may be entering the age of overt intervention. As one observer of the CIA succinctly noted in 1991, "The old concept of covert action, which has gotten the agency in such trouble during the past 40 years, may be obsolete."[25] Perhaps today national interests are best served through open intervention in aid of prodemocracy activists abroad. It may be that the 1990s will see a privatization of intervention in which nongovernmental groups such as the Center for Democracy will be doing work abroad in furtherance of democratic values, work once performed in secret by the CIA. Furthermore, private enterprises like the CNN (Cable News Network) will in the future be doing the work previously done by covertly funded agencies like Radio Free Europe and Radio Liberty. Another form of intervention, once covert to some degree, is the oversight of foreign elections by private election-watch groups, which provide intervention aimed at promoting free and honest elections in the Third World. Without doubt, the 1990s will see a transformation of U.S. covert intervention in the Third World.

■ **EFFICACY OF COVERT ACTION**

How should the United States protect its foreign interests in the 1990s and beyond? There is no question that the national interests of the United States are inextricably intertwined with events at the world's four corners. What happens in the geographic areas the authors of the seven case studies of this book address can affect the welfare and security of the United States. Is covert intervention the most reliable instrument to protect these interests?

What have been the arguments for and against covert action? Four basic arguments favoring its use are (1) The United States should have a capability in certain situations that offers a choice between doing nothing and resorting to open military action; (2) the Soviet Union, through its KGB and other secret agencies, was engaged globally in covert action, and the United States had to fight fire with fire; (3) the United States can sometimes assist friends and allies secretly when open assistance would be embarrassing to the recipient; and (4) the United States' complex political structure is an impediment to decisive executive action in a crisis.

Major arguments against covert action include: (1) It is illegal, a violation of the United Nations charter or international law, and, in any case, immoral; (2) the covert act, designed to impose one's will on a foreign nation is, in effect, an act of war; (3) covert action, by definition, requires secrecy, but in an open democratic society, secrecy may be impossible; (4) it puts a severe strain on accountability, a requisite for democratic government; and (5) covert action dangerously distorts the intelligence function, often leaving leaders misinformed on foreign realities.

Covert action's most fundamental problem is its inherent incompatibility with the demands of U.S. constitutional democracy. A strong likelihood exists that a secret instrument of power will ultimately corrupt. The CIA was initially created for foreign information collection, analysis, and estimates—all noncoercive activities that are vital to keeping decisionmakers appraised of important events around the world. However, because some of its information was to be collected by espionage, the agency was clothed in extraordinary secrecy. Covert action required a similar secrecy, so, as a matter of administrative convenience, it too was assigned to the CIA. This unwise combination of the intelligence function with secret foreign policy implementation created enduring problems. On the one hand, U.S. constitutionalism demands policy accountability as a means for evaluating policy application. Yet, covert action requires that Congress and the public must be deceived by the executive branch. Indeed, Congress has accused the presidency of deceiving the public and Congress and of behavior so extreme as to elicit suggestions of impeachment. Members of the executive branch typically respond by accusing Congress of "micro-managing" foreign policy and encroaching on the president's claimed exclusive role in the conduct of foreign policy. Furthermore, executive branch officials constantly contend that Congress is unable to keep state secrets. An executive-congressional stalemate on foreign policy is threatened. Because secrecy and democracy are incompatible, the covert-action instrument of foreign policy has confronted U.S. foreign policy decisionmakers—executive and congressional—with the extremely difficult problem of weighing costs versus benefits in an uncertain world.

This review of the evolution of covert-action policy and organization and the citation of past examples of covert actions leads to certain tentative generalizations. First, covert action must be understood as existing on a scale of coercion that categorizes it penultimately as an activity just short of war. This is because its purpose is secretly to impose the will of one nation upon another. Some covert action is a form of secret aggression—indeed, sometimes terrorism. In particular, however, covert action may be seen as existing along a subscale of coercion, in a category of benign activity that does not represent aggressive, immoral, or illegal activity. In other words, some covert action may be acceptable, discreet behavior—acceptable, at least, in terms of international behavior. Such would be the case when friends of democracy are secretly aided, and no fundamental violence is applied to the principle of self-determination. But its acceptability within the U.S. democratic framework remains a dilemma because of the tension between secrecy and accountability and between the executive branch and Congress.

Second, to foster and strengthen truly democratic forces in a foreign nation with nonviolent assistance presents a different problem from fostering violent anticommunist counterrevolutionary action that leads to nondemocratic consequences or which places the United States in alliance with repressive, authoritarian forces. Too often U.S. covert action has produced such nondemocratic consequences as the early and later Cold War "successes" of Chile, Guatemala, and Iran.

Third, whether or not foreign democracy can be fostered by U.S. covert action, such action has little chance of fulfilling its objective in the absence of a strong bipartisan foreign policy consensus within the United States. The cycles of isolationism-interventionism make this an inherent problem. When strong bipartisan support exists for clear foreign policy ends and means, covert action will be an unlikely choice. Yet, ever since World War II, U.S. presidents have been using covert action to seek foreign policy results they were unwilling—for a variety of reasons—to disclose publicly. Usually the reason for secrecy has been the absence of consensus about foreign policy ends and means within U.S. traditions and the institutional framework. In fact, the secret often has been kept from Congress and the public rather than from the target country or the adversary. Covert activities make extremely difficult the implementation of the design of the constitutional Founding Fathers, who intended that the president and Congress share the burden of foreign policy and its evaluation. When consensus exists, covert action, be it wise or unwise, at least stands a chance of remaining secret in its contemporary context.

Fourth, destabilizing foreign governments by covert action, as a foreign policy goal, is a risky enterprise for U.S. foreign policy, for the outcome usually cannot be accurately predicted or controlled. U.S. experience since

World War II suggests that sending covert operators into action always risks the loss of policy control and guidance of these forces, with unpredictable and often undesirable consequences. For example, the 1983 "CIA Manual" suggested the hiring of professional killers and the selective assassination of Sandinista leaders in rural villages, despite executive orders prohibiting assassinations. Once set in motion, covert action agents operating under deep cover often cannot be effectively controlled by responsible authority. The Iran-contra affair demonstrates how politically accountable officials at home may be kept in the dark about certain secret operations, thus allowing these operations to proceed without executive supervision.

Finally, many years after events, information and judgments about the Iran-contra covert action scandal of 1985–1987 remain incomplete. Criminal indictments against some major White House principals remain. At the very least, however, in the words of the presidentially appointed Tower Commission, "the arms sales in Iran [in 1985–1986] and the NSC support for the Contras demonstrate the risks involved when highly controversial initiatives are pursued covertly [emphasis added]."[26] One of the most serious risks, beyond policy failure, is the fostering of disrespect for the law by those sworn to see that the laws are faithfully executed. The Iran-contra investigations reveal reveal the corruptive impact of secrecy, which invites serious violations of law and moral standards. One can agree with the Senate Select Committee on Intelligence, which recommended in 1976 that covert action should be used sparingly. It should be seen as an "exceptional act" to be undertaken only when national security is in extreme jeopardy. One could go further to stipulate that covert action is an act of war to be used only when vital national interests are directly challenged. If covert action is needed to combat impending terrorist threats or, say, to prevent a nuclear war, then its use may be necessary.

Invisible government, based upon a doctrine of ends justifying means, had become a reality. If the United States is to serve as any kind of model for developing countries in the Third World, the decisionmaking process must be repaired in order to sustain democratic ideals. In the last analysis, covert action represents a cynical view of world politics. Its routine use rejects the ideal of a world of diversity, sustained by the rule of international law and order, based upon the consent of the governed.

8

Paramilitary Intervention

Peter J. Schraeder

Paramilitary intervention is defined as economic and military aid designed to foster an armed insurgency against a foreign government, usually with the intent of overthrowing that government. This type of intervention represents a proxy use of force in situations in which policymakers of a hostile government have decided that direct military intervention would be counterproductive. As a result, the agents of paramilitary wars are usually existing guerrilla insurgencies within the target country or exiled nationals living outside of that country. In short, use of this instrument allows policymakers of a hostile government to carry a war to the territory of another country while at the same time avoiding the most costly aspects of that war: military casualties that ultimately result from direct military intervention.

The paramilitary option was often implemented by the United States during the 1950s and the 1960s against such varied countries as Angola, Cuba, Guatemala, Indonesia, Iraq, and the PRC. In each of these cases, covert operations included the provision of military weaponry through CIA-contracted airlines and the organization and training of insurgents by CIA personnel in allied nations adjacent to the target country. Despite the existence of rationales that usually underscored the Cold War requirements of anticommunism and containment of the Soviet Union, it was not until the 1980s that paramilitary intervention became a comprehensive and coherent instrument of U.S. intervention in the Third World. During its time in office, the Reagan administration committed the United States to supporting guerrilla insurgencies attempting to overthrow self-proclaimed Marxist regimes in Afghanistan, Angola, Cambodia, and Nicaragua, all under the rubric of what became known as the Reagan Doctrine. Each of these paramilitary wars was continued under the Bush administration.

■ THE PARAMILITARY OPTION
FROM THE 1940s TO THE 1970s

In the Cold War atmosphere of the late 1940s, President Harry S Truman authorized a variety of covert operations that served as the precursors of U.S. paramilitary intervention in the Third World. Among these were the creation of covert links with partisan guerrillas in the Soviet Union in a largely unsuccessful effort to obtain military intelligence; cooperation with the British in several unsuccessful attempts at infiltrating emigré Albanians into their homeland to organize guerrilla bands and overthrow the country's communist dictatorship; and the training of Korean commando squads as part of U.S. direct military intervention in the Korean War. It was not until the administration of President Dwight D. Eisenhower, however, that the United States would vigorously pursue the overthrow of Third World governments through paramilitary intervention.

The Eisenhower administration's first paramilitary intervention resulted in the successful overthrow in 1954 of Guatemala's democratically elected and reform-minded Jacobo Arbenz Guzmán, a leader perceived by U.S. policymakers as leading Guatemala on a path toward communism.[1] Arbenz, attempting to promote broadly based development and build on reforms initiated in a 1944 middle-class revolution, formulated a land reform program targeted toward the largely landless rural farmer. The program immediately ran into problems because it included redistribution of 234,000 acres (95,000 hectares) of unused land owned by the United Fruit Company, a U.S. multinational company whose owners loudly protested these actions to the U.S. government. Arbenz also met with disfavor in Washington when he legalized the Guatemalan Communist party and brought a few of its leaders into the government. The Eisenhower administration's response was to formulate a covert psychological destabilization program, which included the creation of a paramilitary invasion force of 170 Guatemalan exiles (aided by air strikes carried out by CIA pilots) and the construction of a radio station to spread anti-Arbenz propaganda. Organized by the CIA at a mere cost of $20 million, the program succeeded in generating popular and military unrest, forcing a panicked Arbenz to flee; he was replaced by a military government led by Castillo Armas.

The inexpensive overthrow of Arbenz undoubtedly gave the Eisenhower administration (and future administrations) a false sense of power and of their ability to control the nature of Third World regimes through the paramilitary option. One must note that the United States was successful because the Arbenz regime represented a fragile democratic coalition with powerful domestic enemies—most notably a disenchanted military—that were all too happy to take control in exchange for U.S. economic and military support. Yet, this short-term "success" proved to be rather disheartening: The next four decades would find Guatemala ruled by a host of repressive military dictatorships that would balk at any measure of social reform and thus fuel growing levels of guerrilla insurgency. Nonetheless, the Guatemalan case provided the model for future paramilitary interventions in the Third World.

A second intervention entailing an expanded version of the Guatemalan model was the CIA-organized paramilitary invasion of Cuba at the Bay of Pigs in 1961, designed to overthrow the revolutionary regime of Fidel Castro.[2] Castro's success in ousting the popularly hated and U.S.-supported regime of Fulgencio Batista in 1959, his clear intent to reform Cuba's economy along socialist lines, and his support for revolutionary movements in the Western Hemisphere quickly incurred the wrath of Washington. Rather than accept the reality of a leftist regime ninety miles from U.S. shores, the United States attempted to overthrow Castro by initiating a trade embargo (which continues in 1992), authorizing assassination attempts, and ultimately training, equipping, and providing logistical support for nearly 1,500 Cuban exiles at bases in Nicaragua for a paramilitary invasion. Initially authorized under the Eisenhower administration, the invasion forces were given the green light by President John F. Kennedy.

Unlike the weak government overthrown in Guatemala, Castro's revolutionary regime enjoyed a large degree of support among the general population and especially within the military. Miscalculation within U.S. intelligence circles over the extent of Castro's popularity was one of the factors contributing to the invasion's failure. (It was felt that if the exiles could maintain an invasion beachhead, popular rebellions, over time, would occur throughout the island).[3] Rather than lead to Castro's overthrow, the attempted invasion merely allowed Castro to whip up nationalist anti-U.S. feelings and strengthen his position on the island—the exact opposite of what the United States was trying to achieve. More important, Castro, who was completely isolated by the United States, had little choice but to turn to the willing embrace of the Soviet Union to ensure the longevity of the Cuban revolution in the face of possible future U.S. intervention. Ridiculing as "stupid" U.S. efforts to "drive Castro to the wall," Soviet Premier Nikita Khrushchev nonetheless relished the expected results: "Castro will have to gravitate to us [Soviet Union] like an iron filing to a magnet."[4]

A third leader targeted by the Eisenhower administration for overthrow through paramilitary means was President Achmed Sukarno of Indonesia.[5] Sukarno met with disfavor in Washington because he accepted communists into his cabinet, announced his intention of adopting one-party rule under "guided democracy," and, most important, was a leader of the nascent Non-Aligned Movement (NAM) in the Third World (hosting its first conference in Bandung, Indonesia, in 1955). As is well known, the Eisenhower administration (and particularly Secretary of State John Foster Dulles) vehemently rejected neutralism: Nations were either pro-Soviet or pro-United States, with nonaligned nations falling in the pro-Soviet category and ultimately being suspected of harboring procommunist tendencies.

Unlike the previous two cases, the vehicle for subverting Sukarno was paramilitary support beginning in 1956 for an existing secessionist movement that incorporated the Indonesian islands of Celebes, Java, and Sumatra. The covert CIA program included transfers of military weapons to the rebel government and CIA-piloted B-26 bombers flying support missions. Yet, when one of the U.S. pilots, Allen Pope, was shot down and captured by the Sukarno government in 1958—clearly establishing the CIA link—Eisenhower ordered the halt of the paramilitary program. Five months later, the rebel government collapsed. Although the withdrawal of U.S. support hastened the defeat of the rebels, the primary reason for the movement's failure was the lack of nationwide support for the secessionist generals and the clear superiority of military forces remaining loyal to President Sukarno.

A final paramilitary operation of the Eisenhower administration involved covert military support for Tibetan guerrillas fighting against communist China's attempts to consolidate control over the formerly independent territory. The case of Tibet is unique in that although Beijing considered it to be an integral part of China—indeed, it was a vassal state of China for centuries—the territory had functioned as an independent state since the beginning of the twentieth century, generating popular pressures for the maintenance of some semblance of autonomy from Beijing. U.S. support for the indigenous guerrilla movement, which lasted from 1956 to 1973, included the training of guerrillas in the United States, India, and Nepal, as well as direct resupply of military materiel into Tibet through CIA air support. Unlike the previous three cases, however, U.S. intervention was just a "holding" exercise against consolidation of rule by communist China, as U.S. policymakers agreed that it was highly unlikely that the Tibetans could achieve independence.[6]

U.S. support for the guerrillas was curtailed significantly in 1960 when Eisenhower ordered the cessation of violations of communist airspace (including the CIA resupply operations into Chinese-controlled Tibet) after the U-2 pilot Francis Powers was shot down over the Soviet Union. The subsequent decline of U.S. support during the 1960s (completely ceasing after the 1973 warming of Sino-American relations), was matched by the increasing inability of the Tibetan guerrilla forces to mount effective campaigns against the superior Chinese military forces. Despite achieving its short-term goal of harassing communist China, the covert program proved to be ultimately counterproductive when future administrations sought to achieve closer relations with the PRC.

In a twist to the paramilitary trend of the 1960s, the United States also became involved in organizing and funding rather substantial guerrilla armies in U.S.-allied Laos and South Vietnam to further the widening counterinsurgency war against communist guerrillas in both nations. In both cases, the CIA and U.S. Defense Department created autonomous guerrilla armies with the acquiescence of the host government, most notably among the Hmong ethnic groups in Laos (1960–1973) and the montagnards of South Vietnam's central highlands (1961–1970). As the creation of these guerrilla armies was part of overt military intervention in allied nations, they differ from the defined subject of this chapter. Yet, it is important to note that both efforts inevitably unraveled once the United States withdrew from Indochina and had, perhaps, all along worked contrary to U.S. regional strategic interests: Support of the ethnically based armies in essence created self-interested "nations within nations," defeating the primary U.S. goal of fostering unified, national governments capable of defeating highly motivated communist guerrilla insurgencies.[7]

Apart from U.S. operations carried out in Laos and South Vietnam, the paramilitary option during the 1950s (including intervention in Cuba in 1961) thus centered around three basic themes. First, the Eisenhower and Kennedy administrations sought the overthrow of leftist governments considered inimical to long-term U.S. foreign policy interests. The demands of the Cold War struggle with the Soviet Union ensured that the paramilitary option would be applied even to democratically elected (although leftist) regimes. Second, it was deemed critical by U.S. policymakers that the role of the United States remain hidden, therefore requiring covert action as carried out by the CIA. Most important, however, is that presidents and their advisers dominated the policymaking process as they formulated covert interventionist policies with little or no oversight from Congress. As Harry Howe Ransom noted in the previous chapter, a "national, bipartisan Cold War consensus permitted these activities to go forward with little congressional knowledge or supervision."

Yet, despite extensive use of the paramilitary option against leftist governments during the 1950s, no new operations were begun in the 1960s after 1961. Two reasons may be posited for this decline: Growing U.S. military involvement in the Vietnam War increasingly focused U.S. attention on Indochina to the detriment of other areas of the world, and the dramatic failure of the Bay of Pigs operation may have made policymakers reluctant to utilize the paramilitary instrument. The United States instead relied on more discreet forms of covert intervention, not resurrecting the paramilitary option until the early 1970s when it was applied against Iraq and Angola.

U.S. paramilitary intervention in Iraq was different from all the previous cases in that it was only an adjunct to (and at the request of) an ally's previously established program. In order to force a settlement in a territorial dispute with Iraq that would be favorable to Iran, Shah Mohammad Reza Pahlavi offered to provide military aid to a Kurdish group seeking to secede from Iraq.[8] Fearful that the shah would drop his military commitment once the border issue was resolved, the Kurdish leadership insisted upon a U.S. guarantee that aid would continue until independence was won. President Richard M. Nixon decided to help the shah and authorized $16 million in covert aid over a three-year period (1972–1975). The intervention was highly successful; in return for the shah's guarantee that no further aid would be furnished to the Kurdish guerrillas (including U.S. aid), Iraq in 1975 recognized Iran's claims in the Persian Gulf and Shatt al-Arab waterway. In the absence of external aid, the guerrillas were decimated by Iraq in the months following the signing of the agreement.

Although in the short run U.S. policymakers could be pleased that such a small investment had substantially helped an ally, the long-term effects were much more dubious in nature; four years later a revolution in Iran created an intensely anti-U.S. regime, and five years later Iraq would go to war in what became a bloody regional conflict in part to regain the Shatt al-Arab. The irony of the paramilitary campaign is that the United States in 1988 was leaning toward Iraq in the Iran-Iraq War (see Chapters 17 and 18).

The second paramilitary program of the 1970s, which served as the precursor of renewed emphasis on use of this tool during the 1980s and 1990s, involved U.S. intervention in Angola's 1975 civil war. Three guerrilla groups had been fighting Portuguese colonialism in Angola since the 1960s: Agostinho Neto's Popular Movement for the Liberation of Angola (MPLA), backed by Cuba and the Soviet Union; Holden Roberto's National Front for the Liberation of Angola (FNLA), backed by the PRC and Zaire; and Jonas Savimbi's National Union for the Total Independence of Angola (UNITA), backed by South Africa and the PRC. (The United States had maintained limited covert links with Roberto since the early 1960s and only began aiding Savimbi in 1975.) In 1974, Portugal announced it was divesting itself of its Angolan colony and convened a conference in Alvor, Portugal, with the heads of the guerrilla groups to work out a transition agreement. The conference was a great success; all three leaders became signatories to the Alvor Agreement, which outlined the nature and timetable for democratic elections and the formation of a tripartite transitional government in which power would be shared.

The administration of President Gerald R. Ford, however, had other plans. It has been asserted that, rather than risk a victory by the Soviet and Cuban-backed MPLA in free elections, the Ford administration provided Roberto's FNLA with over $300,000 in covert aid (funneled through neighboring Zaire), which prompted him to seek control militarily rather than risk defeat in agreed-upon elections.[9] Both South Africa and Zaire sent troops to aid the FNLA. The entire equation changed, however, when Cuba, in response to FNLA attacks and external intervention, introduced 30,000 combat soldiers into the conflict and emerged, along with the MPLA, victorious. In the wake of Vietnam and fearful of growing U.S. involvement that might result in miring U.S. combat troops in another distant guerrilla war, Congress passed the Clark Amendment in 1976 prohibiting any further aid to guerrilla forces in Angola, effectively terminating this paramilitary operation. The net result of the intervention was disturbing; chances for a peaceful transition and future democratic government were lost, and the Soviets and Cubans gained a major ally and foothold on the African continent—the exact opposite of what the Ford administration had been attempting to achieve.[10]

The most significant aspect of the Angola intervention was that it represented congressional assertion of oversight of U.S. foreign policy in general and covert intervention in particular. Harry Howe Ransom, in Chapter 7, has adequately explored the evolution of congressional-executive branch conflict over the covert action function during the post–World War II period. Let it suffice to note here that, from 1976 on, Congress became a force to be reckoned with when the executive branch sought to implement paramilitary strategies in the Third World.

■ THE REAGAN DOCTRINE AND PARAMILITARY INTERVENTION IN THE 1980s AND THE 1990s

The Reagan Doctrine both intensified and departed from past U.S. paramilitary intervention in the Third World. Whereas past administrations sporadically intervened to overthrow or harass leftist regimes, the Reagan Doctrine provided a comprehensive ideologically based program for arming insurgencies intent on overthrowing self-proclaimed communist Third World regimes.[11] In a significant departure from the 1960s and 1970s, when paramilitary operations were to be kept hidden from public view, the doctrine became an openly announced policy of intervention in the name of democracy and anticommunism. As President Reagan proclaimed in his 1985 State of the Union Address: "We must stand by our democratic allies. And we must not break faith with those who are risking their lives—on every continent, from Afghanistan to Nicaragua—to defy Soviet-supported aggression and secure rights which have been ours from birth."[12] In fact, despite serious friction between the executive branch and Congress over aid to the Nicaraguan contras, Congress adopted public resolutions of support for administration policies in Angola, Afghanistan, and Cambodia. For the first time in post–World War II history, the United States publicly adopted and implemented a program that went beyond traditional containment and embraced instead the need to roll back already established communist Third World regimes. It is to the specifics of the four applications of this doctrine that we now turn.

□ *Afghanistan and the Holy War of the Mujahedin*

The Soviet Union invaded the bordering nation of Afghanistan in December 1979 with over 100,000 troops in what was intended to be a short-term exercise to prop up a communist regime threatened by a mounting guerrilla insurgency. Nearly nine years later, approximately 120,000 Soviet troops remained, the insurgency had intensified, and the Soviet-installed leadership of Babrak Karmal, unable to end the guerrilla war of attrition, had been replaced by the Soviet-blessed Najibullah. In an effort to end what he had called a "bleeding wound" costing the Soviets as much as $6 billion a year and over 30,000 casualties (what some U.S. policymakers termed "the USSR's Vietnam"), Soviet President Mikhail Gorbachev announced on February 8, 1988, his determination to seek a negotiated settlement to the Afghan conflict. Moving beyond rhetoric, Afghanistan, Pakistan, the United States, and the Soviet Union signed agreements (known as the Geneva Accords) on April 14, 1988, in which the Soviet Union pledged the complete withdrawal of its troops by February 15, 1989—a deadline that was rigorously observed.

Two factors cast a shadow over the seemingly productive peace process. First, the guerrilla forces opposing the Soviet occupation, popularly referred to as the "mujahedin" (holy warriors), rejected the peace accords, vowing to continue an Islamic "jihad" (holy war) against the departing Soviet troops and the communist Najibullah regime. This stance enjoyed a large degree of regional support, with the mujahedin receiving economic and military aid from such diverse countries as the PRC, Egypt, Iran, and Saudi Arabia. U.S. covert support for the mujahedin, publicly supported by Congress in 1985 and actually begun in 1980 under the Carter administration, was the largest and most expensive paramilitary undertaking in U.S. history; reaching an annual peak of $260 million (totaling $750 million for the 1980–1985 period alone), U.S. paramilitary aid largely was funneled through neighboring Pakistan and, after 1986, included the highly effective U.S. Stinger antiaircraft missile.[13] The overriding goal of this involvement was the overthrow of the pro-Soviet Najibullah regime.

The issue of foreign assistance to groups in Afghanistan constituted a second problem of the Geneva Accords. Although both the United States and the Soviet Union committed themselves to noninterference and nonintervention in Afghanistan, the 1988 agreement allowed for continued U.S. aid to the mujahedin as long as Moscow continued to arm the Kabul government. In essence, the basis was set for a continuing proxy war between the Soviet-sponsored Afghani government and the U.S.-supported mujahedin. As a result, the Soviet Union as late as 1991 was providing approximately $250–$300 million in annual aid to the Najibullah government, a figure matched by comparable amounts of CIA-distributed aid to the mujahedin.

The thorny issue of superpower aid was resolved on September 13, 1991. On that date, Secretary of State James A. Baker III and Soviet Foreign Minister Boris D. Pankin signed an agreement that committed both of their countries to terminating military shipments to all belligerents in Afghanistan by January 1, 1992—another deadline that was rigorously adhered to by both sides.[14] The decline of the Cold War was the obvious factor leading to the resolution of superpower involvement in what constituted one of the bloodiest proxy conflicts (perhaps exceeded only by the Vietnam War) between the United States and the Soviet Union. "We no longer saw Afghanistan as the Soviet thrust for a warm-water port in the Persian Gulf or as a beachhead for a close alliance with Iran," explained a State Department official involved in the negotiating process. "We were playing out an old grudge without really knowing why we got in there in the first place."[15]

The termination of Soviet (and, subsequently, Russian) military support for the Najibullah regime was clearly perceived by U.S. policymakers as a victory for the United States in the rapidly ebbing Cold War. As noted by several of those interviewed who played a role in the paramilitary war, three circumstances legitimized extending U.S. aid to the mujahedin: (1) According to accepted precepts of international law, the Soviet Union illegally invaded and occupied the country; (2) the vast majority of the Afghani people desired a Soviet withdrawal; and (3) the mujahedin continue to enjoy a large degree of regional support and overwhelming international support. The case study of Afghanistan undoubtedly will become one of the "success" stories of those who, in the future, will argue for other applications of the paramilitary option as an instrument of intervention.

Yet those analysts and policymakers less enchanted with the paramilitary war have questioned whether U.S. policy in Afghanistan remains "mired in success"; although the United States achieved its primary goals of fostering a Soviet military withdrawal and a termination of all Soviet aid to the Najibullah regime, the future prospects of Afghanistan's political system and relations with the United States remain unclear.[16] It is important to note, for example, that the 1991 superpower accord—superseded, of course, by the fragmentation of the Soviet Union only months later—only extricated the superpowers from a very bloody internal civil war. Despite Najibullah's attempts during 1991 to cast off his Marxist clothing and seek a government of national unity, the majority of the mujahedin forces opposed to his government refused to accept any sort of power-sharing arrangement that included the former Marxist leader.[17] Moreover, despite the fall of the Najibullah regime and the subsequent occupation of Kabul (the country's capital) by the mujahedin in early 1992, deep divisions within the mujahedin ranks make a government of national unity difficult to achieve. Despite rhetorical support for what has been called the Islamic Unity of Afghan Mujahedin—a loose federation of the major resistance groups (numbering approximately 50,000–100,000 fighters)—the guerrilla forces are fractionalized by religious and political objectives. Among the most serious divisions is that between the Islamic fundamentalists led by Gulbuddin Hekmatyar, the most militant mujahedin leader who refuses to entertain any sort of compromise solution short of an Islamic fundamentalist regime, and those guerrilla factions that espouse a more traditional form of Afghani nationalism (and, thus, are perhaps more inclined to entertain the idea of a more moderate coalition government). As succinctly explained by Hamed Karzai, a foreign policy adviser to the president of the guerrilla coalition, "Afghanistan is so divided and there are still so many hands in the Afghan issue that the country may lose itself to its divisions."[18]

The potential intensification of the Afghani civil war—already exacerbated by billions of dollars in foreign military aid although no longer desired by either Russia or the United States—poses a serious problem for the United States. As policymakers continue to seek stability in the fragile republics that once constituted the Soviet Union, the rising tide of Islamic fundamentalism in Afghanistan threatens the secular nature and, in the eyes of U.S. policymakers, the stability of those republics. One analyst has warned, for example, that several of the Muslim republics, particularly neighboring Tajikistan and Uzbekistan, are fearful that the establishment of an Islamic fundamentalist regime in Afghanistan may threaten the survivability of their own largely secular forms of government.[19] Moreover, Pakistani Prime Minister Nawaz Sharif indicated in January 1992 that his country, once the staging area for the majority of U.S. paramilitary assistance to the mujahedin, was not bound by the 1991 superpower agreement. Fearful that a new Afghani government may look to India for support, both the Pakistani military and intelligence services continue to press for active involvement in determining the nature of the post-Najibullah regime.[20] "As much as, if not more than, the former Soviet Union, Afghanistan is threatened with economic collapse and ethnic and sectarian conflict," explained one analyst underscoring the explosive potential for even greater levels of regional conflict. "Combined with the coming crisis of the international state system in Central Asia and the escalation of tensions between nuclear-armed adversaries on the Indian subcontinent, Afghanistan threatens to become part of a regionwide challenge to world peace."[21]

A further point to consider is that even a negotiated outcome among the various mujahedin factions is unlikely to yield a democratic government in the Western tradition, even though both the Reagan and the Bush administrations portrayed the mujahedin as democratic freedom fighters. The dominant Islamic fundamentalist faction, for example, proclaims the need to create an Islamic republic and, in fact, is ideologically much closer to the teachings of Iran's now deceased leader, Ayatollah Khomeini, than to the democratic vision often portrayed by the White House. In fact, Pakistan's leadership traditionally has supported the radical fundamentalist Hezb-e-Islami guerrilla faction's bid to play a dominant leadership role in a post-Najibullah government.[22] Even if the nationalist faction were to gain power, it too rejects the need for a pluralist-type democracy in the Western sense.

Finally, regardless of whether one approved or disapproved of U.S. intervention in Afghanistan, the paramilitary program was in direct contradiction with another cornerstone of the Bush administration's foreign policy in the Third World: the so-called "war on drugs." In 1989 alone, those areas in Afghanistan controlled by the U.S.-supported mujahedin were responsible for exporting nearly 700 tons of opium, making Afghanistan the world's second largest exporter after Burma. One mujahedin leader, Nasim Akhunzada, was even known as the "heroin king" before his death.[23] As is so often the case in covert activities such as paramilitary wars, the achievement of one objective (building up a guerrilla force to defeat a Soviet occupation force) demands involvement with unsavory individuals (such as drug traffickers) in a foreign policy trade-off having potentially devastating implications for the United States.

☐ *Cambodia and Continuing Conflict in Indochina*

The Vietnamese army invaded Cambodia in December 1978 to overthrow the Khmer Rouge government of Pol Pot. As depicted in the world-renowned movie *The Killing Fields,* the Khmer Rouge headed an internationally denounced communist regime that had slaughtered nearly 1 million of its own people between 1975 and 1978. Originally welcomed by the Cambodian people, the Soviet-backed Vietnamese army installed a government under the leadership of Heng Samrin and, as late as 1989, continued to maintain an occupation force of approximately 70,000 troops on Cambodian soil to combat an antigovernment guerrilla insurgency. By September 1989, however, a variety of factors had led to the removal of all remaining Vietnamese troops (although some elite units were returned in October of that year): the financial drain on an already struggling economy to maintain an occupation force against a growing guerrilla insurgency (as seemed to be the case in the Soviet withdrawal from Afghanistan); pressures by Mikhail Gorbachev (Vietnam's largest financial patron in 1989), who wished to extricate the Soviet Union from regional conflicts; and Vietnamese confidence in the ability of a new Cambodian regime headed by Prime Minister Hun Sen to maintain itself in power.

In events that roughly parallel the Soviet withdrawal from Afghanistan, two factors contributed to an escalating civil conflict in Cambodia even after the Vietnamese troops were withdrawn. First, the array of guerrilla groups opposed to the Vietnamese occupation force formed a loose military coalition titled the Coalition Government of Democratic Kampuchea (CGDK) and vowed to continue fighting until the "puppet" Cambodian regime was overthrown. The three major groups that formed this loose coalition were the Khmer People's National Liberation Front (KPNLF), led by former Prime Minister Son Sann (numbering roughly 8,000 fighters); the Armée Nationale Sihanoukienne (ANS), loyal to Prince Norodom Sihanouk (boasting 18,000 guerrillas); and the feared Khmer Rouge, led by Khieu Samphan (controlling between 40,000 and 50,000 guerrilla troops).

The overall military objective of the CGDK enjoyed a large degree of regional support, with various guerrilla factions receiving economic and military aid from such diverse countries as the PRC (which supports the Khmer Rouge) and Thailand (whose territory borders Cambodia), as well as from regional organizations, such as the Association of Southeast Asian Nations (ASEAN) (which backs the noncommunist factions of the resistance). Compared to the exceptional degree of U.S. involvement in Afghanistan, however, the U.S. commitment to the CGDK was rather limited. The Reagan administration implemented a paramilitary program subsequently continued by the Bush administration that gradually increased the levels of nonlethal aid extended to the noncommunist factions of the CGDK (KPNLF and ANS) from $5 million in 1982 to $12 million in 1985 and nearly $18 million in 1988. This covert aid, largely funneled through neighboring Thailand, was complemented by nearly $3.5 million a year in overt aid as authorized by Congress through the Solarz Amendment in 1985. U.S. military support for the guerrillas was cautious to say the least—obviously because of the still-strong memory of past U.S. intervention in Indochina. And when it became clear that U.S. aid had violated congressional restrictions by contributing to the growing military success of the Khmer Rouge, Congress in April 1991 suspended U.S. aid to all of the guerrilla factions.

A second factor clouding the initially welcomed withdrawal of Vietnamese troops was the continuation of a proxy war—with Cambodia as the battlefield—between a variety of foreign powers. The Soviet Union and Vietnam backed the Hun Sen regime as an ally in their historical competition with China for influence within the region. It is precisely for this historical reason that the PRC backed the pro-Beijing Khmer Rouge, regardless of how murderous its leaders had been when in control of Cambodia before 1978. Similarly, Thailand backed all the guerrilla factions regardless of ideology, perceiving them as effective counterweights to an expansionist Vietnam. ASEAN and the United States backed the noncommunist factions of the CGDK.

The civil war by proxy tentatively came to an end on October 23, 1991, when all four Cambodian belligerents signed a UN-enforced peace treaty brokered by the United States, the Soviet Union, and the PRC. Among the major elements of the treaty already in place by January 1992 were the maintenance of a cease-fire (that took effect the day the treaty was signed); the termination of all foreign arms supplies to military factions within Cambodia; and the creation of a twelve-member Supreme National Council, a national body composed of representatives from each of the four Cambodian military factions that is to serve as a transitional administration until UN-supervised elections are held in 1993.[24] As in the case of Afghanistan, the end of the Cold War was a crucial factor leading to the October 1991 peace accord. A derivative element of this process was a greater willingness on the part of China and Vietnam—the primary military supporters of the Khmer Rouge and the Hun Sen regime, respectively—to place pressure on their clients to negotiate in good faith for a diplomatic resolution of the conflict.[25]

The combination of Vietnam's military withdrawal from Cambodia and subsequent agreement by the Hun Sen regime to allow for UN-supervised elections was clearly perceived as a victory by U.S. policymakers opposed to any form of communist rule—regardless of whether it was pro-Chinese (Khmer Rouge) or pro-Soviet (Hun Sen). As in the case of Afghanistan, several factors seemed to merit U.S. paramilitary aid to the guerrillas: (1) According to international law, the Vietnamese illegally invaded and occupied the country; (2) the Cambodian people desired a Vietnamese withdrawal; and (3) the Vietnamese occupation was denounced both regionally and within the international system. Explained one Defense Department official in 1991: "Despite the fact that we [the United States] played a somewhat minor role in providing covert military aid when compared to others, such as China, who were obviously more concerned with events in their immediate backyard, it was nevertheless the *combination* [emphasis added] of external aid from several quarters which achieved the diplomatic settlement."[26]

Despite the upbeat atmosphere that immediately followed the signing of the 1991 peace accords, two factors clouded the prospects of maintaining internal peace in Cambodia while seeking to carry out UN-supervised elections scheduled for 1993. First, the greatest dilemma for those seeking a noncommunist solution in Cambodia is that the Khmer Rouge constitutes the military backbone of the former three-member guerrilla coalition and is continuing to consolidate its military hold over occupied territory. "As best anyone can tell, the Khmer Rouge are hiding equipment and people wherever they can," explained one Western diplomat who was involved in the peace process. "There's no way to detect a lot of it."[27] It is precisely for this reason that Congress, prior to the signing of the 1991 peace accord, passed legislation prohibiting the provision of any U.S. paramilitary aid to the communist faction (the Khmer Rouge) of the CGDK. As pointed out by critics of any paramilitary aid, however, strengthening two-thirds of the antigovernment guerrilla coalition (the KPNLF and the ANS) inevitably strengthened the other one-third (the Khmer Rouge) that was militarily dominant to begin with. As a result, the Khmer Rouge, rather than being isolated, remained a force to be reckoned with. "Listen, the Khmer Rouge is not made part of this peace agreement out of any belief that Pol Pot [reportedly in retirement] has reformed his ways," explained another Western diplomat. "We involved the Khmer Rouge because they were the most powerful rebel group out there, and they could not be ignored."[28] In short, a major fear of foreign observers, and particularly Cambodians, is that past military aid and current political recognition within the peace process could lead to another government dominated by the Khmer Rouge. This scenario is perhaps the most important reason why, in sharp contrast to its major commitment to the mujahedin in Afghanistan, the United States was hesitant to commit significant sums of paramilitary aid to the guerrilla war in Cambodia.

A related problem with the peace process is the inherent incompatibility of the four Cambodian factions. During the duration of the guerrilla war from 1978 to 1991, one could discern little cooperation among the guerrilla groups either militarily on the battlefield or in the political realm. In fact, in the military realm, the dominant trend was one of growing clashes between the Khmer Rouge and the noncommunist factions of the CGDK. This infighting not only hindered success on the battlefield as well as at the diplomatic bargaining table, it also threatens the current peace process. For example, upon his arrival in Phnom Penh on November 27, 1991, as part of the UN-sponsored peace process, Khmer Rouge leader Khieu Samphan was savagely beaten by Cambodians screaming "murderer!" and "kill the monster!"[29] A legitimate question for Khmer Rouge leaders was whether the attack was spontaneous or part of a government-sponsored event to discredit further the former rulers of Cambodia. Indeed, several days earlier in a surprise announcement, the ruling Hun Sen regime announced the appointment of former enemy Prince Sihanouk as president of Cambodia, underscoring a new alliance apparently designed to isolate the Khmer Rouge.[30] As each of the factions continues to jockey for political position, the ultimate success of the still-fragile peace accord—which, by necessity, requires the full cooperation of the Khmer Rouge—is anything but assured.

☐   *Angola and Paramilitary Aid to Savimbi's UNITA Forces*

The military conflict in Angola was a continuation of the 1975 civil war in which the Soviet- and Cuban-backed MPLA emerged victorious over the FNLA and UNITA guerrilla factions, both of which had been supported by the United States. At the end of 1988, the MPLA government continued to rely on approximately 50,000 Cuban troops and over 1,000 Soviet advisers, in addition to its 50,000-strong army, to maintain the regime against Savimbi's UNITA guerrilla forces and repeated military interventions by the latter's regional patron, South Africa. Although unable to achieve military supremacy on the battlefield, the combined UNITA–South African forces were able to decimate Angola's economy in a guerrilla war that by 1986 reportedly had cost the Angolan government close to $15 billion that otherwise could have been spent on development.[31]

The United States played an extremely important parmilitary role in what became another proxy war within the East-West framework of the Cold War. The Reagan administration, denouncing Angola as a Soviet puppet and portraying Savimbi as a democratic freedom fighter, was handed congressional repeal of the Clark Amendment in 1985, an action that thereby removed a major obstacle to providing military aid to UNITA under the auspices of the Reagan Doctrine. Congress subsequently voted that same year to authorize the president to extend $15 million in covert paramilitary aid on a yearly basis to UNITA, a figure that had grown to approximately $60 million in annual aid under the Bush administration. The paramilitary aid, including Stinger antiaircraft missiles, was funneled to UNITA forces through Zaire and, to a lesser degree, South Africa. The primary goals of U.S. involvement were to achieve the withdrawal of Cuban forces from Angola and pressure the MPLA to accept a power-sharing role with UNITA.

The resolution of South Africa's illegal occupation of Namibia, a former League of Nations Trust Territory that acted as a buffer between southern Angola and northern South Africa, was a critical component of early diplomatic efforts designed to seek the removal of Cuban troops—the most important goal of the Reagan administration. Because South Africa had repeatedly used Namibia to invade Angola, the bargaining position of the MPLA was that Namibia's independence, and therefore a withdrawal of South African troops, would decrease the security threat to Angola and allow the parallel withdrawal of Cuban troops. Yet South Africa traditionally had resisted international pressures to grant Namibia independence, for fear that the Angola-based and Marxist-oriented South West People's Organization (SWAPO) would dominate free elections and pose a direct security threat to South Africa's northern frontier.

The stumbling block of Namibian independence was resolved by diplomatic means in 1988. On July 20 of that year, a U.S.-mediated accord among Angola, Cuba, and South Africa was made public in which all three nations agreed in principle to work toward Namibian independence as the basis for the withdrawal of Cuban troops. This initial step was enhanced by a preliminary peace accord outlined on November 15, 1988, that mapped out a timetable for the simultaneous withdrawal of Cuban and South African troops from Angola and Namibia, respectively, and acceptance of a UN-sponsored plan for Namibian independence. On December 22, 1988, these positions were formalized by the signing of two agreements known as the Namibia and the Angola Accords.[32] Hailed as a success by both critics and supporters of the Reagan administration's policies in southern Africa, these accords led to the independence of Namibia on March 21, 1990, and the removal of all remaining Cuban troops in Angola by June of that year.

The 1988 accords were clouded, however, by the lack of comprehensive negotiations over external aid to UNITA guerrillas or the issue of national reconciliation (i.e., power sharing) between the MPLA and UNITA (the second major goal of U.S. paramilitary support for Savimbi's forces). The Namibia Accord, signed by Angola, Cuba, and South Africa, alluded to the UNITA issue by pledging the signatories to "respect the principle of non-interference in the internal affairs of the states of south-west Africa" and to "insure that their respective territories are not used by any state, organization, or person" in connection with acts of violence against any state of southwestern Africa. Yet, although South Africa, in keeping with the accord, announced its intention to cease aiding UNITA, the Reagan and Bush administrations pledged continued U.S. aid to Savimbi's forces.[33] For its part, the Angolan government incorrectly believed that once Namibia was independent, the question of UNITA would be more easily dealt with militarily than through some type of political compromise that decreased the power of the MPLA. In short, the examples of Afghanistan and Cambodia had another parallel: The withdrawal of foreign forces (in this case Cuban and South African) left in place a continuing civil conflict. At the end of 1990, Moscow was still supporting the MPLA with approximately 1,100 advisers and $800 million in economic and military aid, a figure unmatched by the much smaller amount of $60 million in U.S. covert paramilitary aid to UNITA forces.[34]

The delicate issue of resolving Angola's internal civil war through some sort of power-sharing agreement was tentatively resolved on May 31, 1991, when President José Eduardo dos Santos of Angola and Savimbi signed a peace agreement brokered by Portugal, the former colonial power. Under the terms of the agreement, both sides agreed to (1) abide by an informal military truce that went into effect on May 15; (2) build a unified armed force; and (3) support the creation of a multiparty political system in preparation for UN-monitored free elections in 1992.[35] As in the case of Afghanistan and Cambodia, the end of the Cold War was a crucial factor leading to the May 1991 peace accord. For example, whereas the decline of single-party rule in Eastern Europe and the former Soviet Union led to the dramatic rise in popular pressures for multiparty democracy in Angola and throughout Africa, in essence forcing the MPLA and other African leaders to seek compromise or risk being swept out of office, Savimbi had to confront the growing reality of decreasing funds from the United States as policymakers sought to capitalize on the "peace dividend" associated with the end of the Cold War. Toward this end, the U.S. Congress earmarked only $30 million in aid to UNITA for 1992 with the restriction that it be used only for transforming the guerrilla movement into a political party.[36]

Similar to U.S. pronouncements related to the 1988 peace accord, the 1991 agreement effectively ending Angola's bloody civil war was hailed as a victory for U.S. foreign policy and, implicitly, U.S. financial support for a paramilitary war between 1986 and 1991. "Once adversaries in war, you now stand together as partners in peace," announced an obviously pleased Secretary of State Baker. "You have the opportunity to show the world that a multiparty democracy can be built where before there was only destruction and distrust."[37] As one indication of the likely success of the 1991 accord, State Department officials underscored the incident-free return of Savimbi to Luanda, the capital of Angola, on September 29, 1991 (after sixteen years of self-imposed exile fighting in the countryside), to prepare for presidential elections in 1992.[38]

Although clearly supportive of the 1991 peace accord, critics of U.S. paramilitary involvement in Angola from the 1970s to the 1990s fundamentally questioned the assumed "successes" of administration policies from Nixon to Bush. First, U.S. support for Savimbi was fraught with negatives and contradictions. The major problem tarnishing Savimbi's guerrilla struggle (and U.S. foreign policy by association) was his obvious initial dependence on South Africa. The sensitive nature of the apartheid issue among black African countries originally contributed to regional recognition of the MPLA regime in 1975 and rejection of Savimbi's military struggle because of its association with South Africa.[39] Second, contradictory U.S. policies sent confusing diplomatic signals to both South Africa and black African countries: Whereas adoption of comprehensive economic sanctions in 1986 underscored U.S. opposition to South Africa's system of apartheid, support for UNITA, by association, supported South Africa's regional policies of destabilization.

The greatest irony of U.S. support for the current power-sharing agreement is that the Ford administration, in the hopes of excluding the Marxist MPLA from sharing power in 1975, contributed to the unraveling of the Alvor Agreement and the possibility for peaceful transition to a democratic government. Although one can only speculate as to whether all three factions would have abided by the agreement (indeed, the opposite is just as likely), intervention on the part of the United States and others effectively precluded this possibility. Most important, it was the ensuing civil war that led to the massive introduction and long-term presence of Cuban troops in Angola, the issue of greatest concern to the Reagan administration for its policies in Africa. In short, explain the critics of the Reagan/Bush paramilitary policy in Angola, the 1991 peace accord largely constitutes the implementation of the accord that was shattered in 1975.

☐ *Nicaragua and the Contra War*

Anastacio Somoza—one in a long line of popularly hated and U.S.-supported Nicaraguan dictators—was overthrown in 1979 by a broad-based revolution led by the Sandinistas. Declaring their allegiance to the major cornerstones of Marxism-Leninism, the Sandinistas gradually centralized control over Nicaragua's political system, established close ties with Cuba and the Soviet Union, and began providing assistance to other revolutionary movements in Central America, most notably in El Salvador. Although the Carter administration in its last year in office attempted to construct a productive relationship with the Sandinista regime (with debatable results), the Reagan administration entered office with a negative preconception of the revolution and a determination to prevent "another Cuba" in the Western Hemisphere. Perceiving Nicaragua as a beachhead for Soviet-led communist destabilization throughout Central America, U.S. officials made support for the contras into the showcase for what paramilitary intervention could achieve under the Reagan Doctrine. Although official administration justifications for supporting the contras wavered between interdicting arms being sent to El Salvadoran Marxist guerrillas, forcing the Sandinistas to democratize their system of governance, and limiting Soviet and Cuban influence in the region, the real aim seemed to be to overthrow the Sandinista regime. This policy was continued by the Bush administration after it assumed office in 1989.

The multifaceted low-intensity warfare campaign against the Sandinistas included elements of economic destabilization, military psychological warfare, propaganda warfare, and, most important for this chapter, paramilitary intervention. Because these matters are extensively discussed in Chapter 16, this section is limited to brief highlights of some of the problems faced by the Reagan and Bush administrations in the pursuit of this policy. First, of the four paramilitary wars implemented under the banner of the Reagan Doctrine, U.S. support of the contras fueled the greatest amount of public debate and controversy and contributed to a virtual tug-of-war between the executive branch and Congress. In brief, although originally endorsing military aid in 1982 (only for the purpose of interdicting arms flows into El Salvador), Congress on February 8, 1988, prohibited any future military aid to the contra effort. These congressional cutbacks mirrored international opinion: Not only was the Reagan administration's contra policy declared illegal by the International Court of Justice, it was opposed by the majority of Nicaraguans and disputed by a significant number of nations within Central America as well as within the international system. It was precisely because of the lack of domestic support that the administration pursued what many have agreed was an illegal, covert extension of the contra war that not only contravened the spirit, if not the letter, of laws passed by Congress, but led to a crisis of leadership for the Reagan administration that came to be known as the Iran-contra affair. According to the *Report of the Congressional Committees Investigating the Iran-Contra Affair,* administration actions demonstrated a "disdain for the law" that challenged the basic checks and balances of the U.S. Constitution.

An equally important problem associated with the paramilitary war was that the contras themselves suffered several shortcomings that limited the effectiveness of their organization as a viable alternative to the Sandinista regime: Few, if any, of the contra leaders were respected in Nicaragua; they were unable to enunciate an attractive alternative program of government; and they were discredited by continued atrocities in the rural areas.[40] Nonetheless, the massive destruction wrought by the paramilitary campaign during the 1980s was unquestionably a contributing factor that led to the massive defeat of the Sandinistas in free elections held in Nicaragua on February 25, 1990. However, a critical point of debate between proponents and critics is whether the paramilitary campaign was the *crucial* element leading to the holding of elections and the defeat of the Sandinistas. Although several proponents of the paramilitary war (such as Lt. Col. Oliver North) underscored the electoral victory of President Violeta Chamorro as a vindication of the Reagan administration's efforts, critics can just as easily argue that U.S. paramilitary support for the contras forced the Sandinistas to rely more heavily on Cuban and Soviet support and advisers, the exact opposite of U.S. foreign policy objectives in the region during the 1980s. As a result, these critics could argue, the paramilitary war only delayed what might have been earlier elections and, perhaps, just as resounding of a defeat for the Sandinistas. "In truth," explains Kornbluh (Chapter 16) in a contribution to this debate, "the elections resulted from a Costa Rica–sponsored peace process that Washington repeatedly tried to sabotage, and were scheduled only after Congress finally cut off contra aid over the Reagan administration's bitter objections."

■ PARAMILITARY INTERVENTION IN PERSPECTIVE

Drawing upon the case studies of U.S. paramilitary intervention in the Third World from the Truman to the Bush administrations, one can discuss several tentative conclusions about the efficacy of this interventionist tool. First, it is clear that paramilitary intervention can be highly effective if the goal is to harass or otherwise disrupt the normal political or economic proceedings of a Third World country. For example, there is no doubt that support for UNITA contributed to the severe disruption of Angola's economy and that support for Tibetan guerrillas delayed China's consolidation of control over disputed territory. In fact, the critical premise of paramilitary warfare—inflicting severe casualties on a target country without incurring any of your own—was borne out by the varying impacts of the Reagan Doctrine. In addition to hundreds of thousands killed or wounded in Afghanistan, Cambodia, and Nicaragua during the 1980s, it has been estimated that 341,000 people (mostly civilians) were killed in Angola alone from 1975 to 1991. Sadly, Angola has the macabre distinction of being the "amputee" center of the world (with over 50,000 victims) as a result of the extensive use of land mines during the guerrilla war.[41]

If the goal of paramilitary intervention is to overthrow militarily the government in question, however, the results have been less positive. Only in the case of Guatemala in 1954—a democratic government with powerful domestic enemies, most notably a disenchanted military—did the United States succeed in overthrowing a government considered inimical to U.S. foreign policy interests through paramilitary means. In all other cases, the paramilitary option has fallen short. This especially was the case when the United States attempted to overthrow leftist revolutionary regimes (such as Nicaragua's Sandinistas or Cuba under Castro) that initially enjoyed a large degree of popular support. Rather than overthrowing these types of regimes, U.S. intervention seemingly only served to stiffen their resolve and anti-U.S. rhetoric.

Yet, just as nationalism can be harnessed by revolutionary regimes to avoid defeat by counterrevolutionary paramilitary forces, so too can it be harnessèd when the goal is withdrawal of a foreign occupation army. As evidenced by the Soviet Union's withdrawal of its forces from Afghanistan—regardless of the domestic configuration of a future Afghani regime—the combination of a popular guerrilla struggle with effective regional paramilitary support can make the costs of occupation potentially untenable in the long run. The key to success in Afghanistan, however, was not the level of external aid but rather the widespread support that the guerrilla insurgency enjoyed among the Afghani people. As is shown by the case of the contra war in Nicaragua, large infusions of external aid were insufficient to achieve a military victory when the majority of the population rejected the legitimacy of the paramilitary group.

As demonstrated by the long-term application of the Reagan Doctrine, the time factor and the willingness to maintain high levels of aid played significant roles in bringing an opponent to the bargaining table. For example, the tremendous costs associated with extended paramilitary wars in Angola and Nicaragua inevitably played a part in prompting the MPLA and the Sandinistas to consider some form of power sharing with their opponents. This does not mean, however, that the foreign-sponsored paramilitary wars played the crucial role in the decision to negotiate. Of equal if not greater importance was the decline of a countervailing power (the Soviet Union) willing to provide both regimes with military and economic aid to stem the advances of counterrevolutionary forces.

The potentially contradictory short-term and long-term effects of paramilitary intervention also must be taken into account. In the case of Tibet, for example, although the short-term goal of harassing communist China seemed to be successful, the long-term effect proved ultimately to be counterproductive, as the United States sought to achieve closer relations with the PRC. In the case of Iraq, the coerced border demarcation provided one of the reasons for the bloody Iran-Iraq War. In the cases of Angola, Cuba, and Nicaragua, attempts at isolating these self-proclaimed Marxist regimes offered them little alternative—especially when confronting externally supplied guerrilla forces—than to seek even closer relationships with Eastern bloc countries, the opposite of what Washington was attempting to achieve. The possibility of long-term results contrary to the original foreign policy objectives is not limited to paramilitary intervention but rather may be applied to all types of intervention.

The question of long-term results is especially important as concerns the democratic or undemocratic nature of a successor regime if the U.S.-supported guerrillas achieve their goal and assume power. The Reagan administration, for example, fondly referred to anticommunist guerrillas as democratic freedom fighters. As already stated, the final outcomes of paramilitary struggles in both Afghanistan and Cambodia could entail radical Islamic fundamentalist and pro-Chinese communist governments in those two countries, respectively. In this regard, it is difficult to see how this promotes the cause of democracy or even pro-U.S. regimes. In the case of Guatemala, U.S. paramilitary success led to a litany of corrupt dictatorships and a cycle of guerrilla insurgency that has yet to reach its full conclusion. A democratic outcome in Angola or Nicaragua also was highly unlikely if either the contras or UNITA were to have gained power, although it may be argued that these regimes would at least have been more pro-U.S. than their predecessors.

Finally, the role of regional allies and the risks of escalation must be noted. In all the examined cases of U.S. paramilitary intervention, a regional ally bordering the target nation was imperative for training guerrillas and serving as a conduit for military aid. This situation provides the potential for future escalation, as the target nation, fed up with its neighbor's interference in its domestic affairs, may decide to eliminate guerrilla camps across the border or widen the war by mounting a full-scale invasion. The former scenario has occurred frequently; punitive strikes were carried out by Nicaragua against contra bases in Honduras, by Vietnam against guerrilla camps in Thailand, and by Afghanistan against mujahedin guerrillas in Pakistan. What would or should be the U.S. response if the latter scenario were to take place, and a U.S. ally were invaded by the target of a paramilitary campaign? The invasion of Honduras by Nicaragua, for example, could have provided the basis for direct U.S. military intervention in Central America with potentially disastrous effects. Indeed, the Reagan administration responded positively to a Honduran request for U.S. troops after Sandinista soldiers apparently crossed the Honduran border on March 15, 1988, to attack contra guerrilla bases. Although U.S. troops were sent merely as a show of military muscle, the stage was set for a wider regional conflict that neither Washington nor Managua wanted.

■ 9

Direct Military Intervention

Ted Galen Carpenter

Direct military intervention in the affairs of Third World countries has been a crucial component of U.S. foreign policy throughout the twentieth century. The scope of such coercion is quite significant. Cambodia, Cuba, the Dominican Republic, Haiti, Iran, Korea, Lebanon, Libya, Mexico, Nicaragua, Panama, the Philippines, Vietnam, and—most recently—Iraq have all experienced occupation by U.S. troops or at least significant examples of U.S. military power at various times.

The use of military force has a number of gradations. At the low end of the spectrum are relatively minor measures such as the *Mayaguez* rescue operation in 1975 (which was designed both to rescue U.S. personnel and to "send a message" to the new communist governments of Indochina), the air duels with Libyan aircraft over the Gulf of Sidra in 1981, and the abortive Desert One mission to rescue the Iranian hostages in 1980. Efforts to militarize the drug war by sending U.S. combat trainers and advisers to drug-source countries such as Peru—an important part of President George Bush's "Andean Initiative"—belong in the same category. Indeed, the international phase of the drug war may be serving as a pretext to wage low-intensity conflicts for other objectives. Assistance provided to the military forces of Peru, for example, also helps in Lima's ongoing battle against the Maoist Sendero Luminoso (Shining Path) guerrillas.[1] Selecting arenas for other low-intensity conflict missions represents a growth industry for Pentagon officials who need alternative justifications for large military budgets and force levels now that the Cold War has faded.

At the opposite end of the military intervention spectrum would be such full-scale enterprises as the Korean, Vietnam, and Persian Gulf wars. These three cases all involved the deployment of hundreds of thousands of U.S. troops and massive applications of firepower. The other interventionist episodes examined in this chapter would fall at various points between those two extremes.

■ CONTINUITY AND CHANGE

Certain characteristics of military intervention have remained surprisingly constant during the century, whereas others have changed markedly, especially since the end of World War II. The underlying motives for military intervention have remained fairly consistent. U.S. leaders typically employ force to prevent political instability in important client states, to install or preserve regimes considered friendly to perceived economic and security interests, or to coerce unfriendly regimes. It is somewhat ironic that the United States, a country that once symbolized revolutionary republican values and pursued an aggressive policy of territorial expansion, now seems obsessed with maintaining "stability" in the world. But that is the dominant theme of President Bush's "new world order," as it was the less elegantly titled "containment" policy of the Cold War era. U.S. actions throughout most of the twentieth century, and especially since World War II, have exemplified the objectives of a conservative status quo power. In virtually every case in which Washington has resorted to military force, it has done so to prop up clients (including several highly authoritarian ones), to thwart radical insurgencies, or to stymie "revisionist" regimes. The underlying (although rarely explicit) rationale has been to eliminate challenges to U.S. hegemony from any source, especially in regions such as the Western Hemisphere or the oil-rich Middle East that are deemed crucial to U.S. interests.

The official justifications for various coercive episodes also exhibit fairly constant and predictable features. U.S. leaders habitually stress idealistic and emotionally laden objectives to mobilize and maintain public support for what otherwise might be divisive interventionist initiatives. The strategy contains two elements: an exaggeration of the importance of the conflict (usually describing the adversary as an implacable menace to U.S. security) and an emphasis on the moral imperative of the U.S. reaction. Frequently, those justifications bear little resemblance to the more plausible political, economic, or strategic motives for intervention.

That approach was apparent as early as World War I. President Woodrow Wilson repeatedly described the conflict in millennial terms, insisting that it was a struggle to "make the world safe for democracy," while portraying Wilhelmine Germany as the bloodthirsty "Hun" bent on global domination. U.S. leaders employed similar rhetoric to justify military intervention during the Cold War era. For example, the complex Vietnam struggle was reduced to a simplistic conflict between the forces of freedom and democracy in South Vietnam and a monolithic communist aggressor threatening the security of the entire free world.[2] More recently, President Bush explicitly compared Saddam Hussein to Adolf Hitler and insisted that Iraq's annexation of Kuwait was equivalent to the expansionism of the fascist powers in the 1930s. Such aggression must be confronted immediately and without compromise, the president argued, or the entire fabric of international peace might unravel.[3]

A reliance on moral justifications frequently produces an embarrassing chasm between rhetoric and reality. In the case of the Vietnam War, many Americans were properly skeptical of the arguments put forth by the administrations of presidents John F. Kennedy, Lyndon B. Johnson, and Richard M. Nixon. They were unwilling to believe that if the United States did not fight communists in Southeast Asia it would eventually confront them in San Francisco. Moreover, a parade of corrupt, authoritarian regimes in Saigon thoroughly discredited the moral basis of U.S. policy.

A similar skepticism was warranted regarding the Bush administration's hyperbole concerning the Persian Gulf crisis. The equation of Iraq and Nazi Germany was patently absurd. A country of fewer than 18 million people, Iraq had an economy devastated from the long war against Iran. Iraqi forces, although numerically impressive, were generally ill-trained, ill-equipped, and afflicted by poor morale. Baghdad's military had barely held its own against Iran. Conversely, Nazi Germany was Europe's second most populous country in the 1930s and possessed a world-class economy and military. An aggressively expansionist Germany had posed a threat to world peace—and potentially to U.S. security—that never could have been duplicated by Baghdad. Washington's willingness to leave Saddam in power after the Persian Gulf war suggested that U.S. officials did not believe their own apocalyptic rhetoric. It would have been impossible to imagine the United States allowing Hitler to remain in office.

The administration's moral case was hardly compelling either. President Bush repeatedly contended that the goal of the Persian Gulf war was to restore Kuwait's freedom. He conveniently failed to mention that freedom in Kuwait was in short supply long before Iraq's invasion. The "legitimate" Kuwaiti government that Bush insisted be restored to power was an utterly corrupt autocracy dominated by the Al-Sabah ruling family.

Another consistent feature of U.S. military interventions in the twentieth century is the lack of congressional control or influence. The various coercive missions undertaken against Latin American states during the early decades of the century were all executive branch operations. There were no requests for declarations of war or even limited forms of explicit congressional authorization. Congress acquiesced in these repeated dilutions of its war-power prerogatives with only scattered murmurs of protest.

The pattern of executive dominance became even more apparent with the emergence of the imperial presidency during the Cold War era.[4] President Harry S Truman brazenly bypassed Congress when committing U.S. forces on a massive scale to assist South Korea in 1950. Similarly, President Johnson acted solely on his own authority when he sent troops ashore in the Dominican Republic in 1965. President Ronald Reagan did the same with regard to the 1983 Grenada "rescue mission," the air strikes against Libya in

1986, and the Persian Gulf naval operations in 1987–1988. President Bush continued in that tradition when he ordered the invasion of Panama in December 1989.

On those rare occasions when Congress has provided some policy input, its influence has been decidedly limited. President Dwight D. Eisenhower sent the U.S. Marines to Lebanon in 1958 at least arguably pursuant to the provision of a congressional resolution approved the previous year. But that measure essentially gave the president a blank check to use U.S. forces to defend Middle Eastern nations from "communist-inspired" aggression. The more famous Gulf of Tonkin Resolution that Johnson used as a pretext to escalate U.S. involvement in the Vietnam conflict exhibited a similar vagueness, thereby enabling the chief executive to conduct the war in virtually any manner he chose. It is also pertinent to observe that U.S. military activity in Vietnam was quite substantial long before Congress approved the Gulf of Tonkin Resolution in August 1964.

The approval in early January 1991 of a congressional resolution authorizing President Bush to take military action against Iraq altered that pattern less than it might appear. Congress did not act until the administration requested a supporting resolution on the eve of a deadline for Iraq's withdrawal from Kuwait that had already been adopted by the UN Security Council. More important, Congress played no meaningful role in making the crucial decisions leading up to the January showdown. In the intervening months after Iraq's August 2 invasion, President Bush had led efforts to impose a complete air and naval blockade on Iraq and deployed more than 400,000 U.S. forces in the Persian Gulf region. By the time Congress finally voted on the force-authorization resolution, it was confronted with a virtual fait accompli. Moreover, Bush left few doubts that he would have used military force against Iraq in the absence of a supporting congressional resolution. Indeed, there were strong indications that he would have done so even in the face of a resolution explicitly prohibiting him from using force.[5]

Although the actual motives and official rationales for U.S. interventionist policy as well as for executive branch control of that policy have remained fairly constant throughout the twentieth century, other features have changed in important ways. One discernible change is a decline in the geographic selectivity of U.S. military intervention. During the early years of this century, the United States repeatedly coerced recalcitrant hemispheric neighbors and asserted its dominance in Central America and the Caribbean. Nicaragua experienced the most frequent and prolonged examples of U.S. intervention and was occupied on a nearly continuous basis between 1912 and 1933.[6]

That stifling paternalism in the Western Hemisphere contrasted with a general lack of U.S. military activity elsewhere in the world. Still heavily influenced by a potent isolationist heritage, the United States rarely employed its military power outside the hemisphere until World War II. The Spanish-

American War in 1898, however, was an unpleasant omen of subsequent U.S. meddling throughout the Third World. Although the conflict itself was a brief, comic-opera affair, its consequences were not. At war's end the United States acquired its first overseas colonies, most notably the Philippines. Acquisition of colonies expanded U.S. geopolitical interests—especially in East Asia—and, equally significant, it helped create an imperial mentality among U.S. political leaders.[7]

Isolationist traditions acted as a brake on U.S. imperial impulses outside the Western Hemisphere until World War II, but the disappearance of such inhibitions at the end of that conflict greatly expanded the geographic scope of interventionism. During the Cold War era, U.S. military might was employed in distant regions, with Korea, Lebanon, and Vietnam the most obvious cases. Although the United States remains especially prone to use its armed forces in the Caribbean Basin—as evidenced by the invasions of the Dominican Republic, Grenada, and Panama—other regions now also constitute arenas for the application of U.S. power.

But at the same time that the United States has become geographically less selective in employing military force, it has become somewhat more selective in viewing that tactic as the preferred option. Earlier in the century, U.S. leaders rarely hesitated to "send in the marines" to restore order or implement political and economic objectives. The frequency of intervention throughout the Caribbean before the mid-1930s was ample testimony to the popularity of that approach. Since World War II, however, U.S. officials have preferred to rely on other policy tools whenever possible. More subtle techniques to expand U.S. influence over foreign governments, such as the selective use of economic and military assistance programs and economic sanctions (see Chapters 5 and 6), have come into vogue. When such methods are not sufficient, the CIA is frequently called in to conduct covert operations. As noted in Chapters 7 and 8, covert operations range from propaganda and psychological warfare to election intervention, coups d'état, assassination plots, and paramilitary intervention.

It is not so much that the use of military coercion is considered an option of last resort. The distinction is somewhat more subtle. There has been a greater hesitation to employ military force since World War II than there was before the advent of nuclear weapons. The necessity for caution was especially evident during the Cold War era when direct military intervention by either the United States or the Soviet Union risked a dangerous superpower confrontation. It is difficult to imagine, for example, that the United States would have continued to tolerate a communist regime in Cuba had it not been for the restraint required in a thermonuclear context. In that sense, the waning of the Cold War may produce one unfortunate result: a greater willingness by Washington to use military force against Third World adversaries now that it need not fear a confrontation with Moscow. The aggressive, uncompromising nature of U.S. policy in the first major post–Cold War conflict, the Persian Gulf crisis, seems to confirm that fear.

At the same time, it is important to note that the unsatisfactory outcome of the Vietnam intervention may have created a lasting element of caution in the calculations of U.S. leaders regarding the military option. It became clear in the aftermath of that episode that public support for prolonged interventionist campaigns involving substantial numbers of U.S. troops was problematical at best. Secretary of Defense Caspar Weinberger clearly recognized this reality in a speech at the National Press Club in 1984. Weinberger argued against sending U.S. forces into combat unless the stakes were "vital," and then the troops must be sent "with the clear intention of winning." Those forces should serve "clearly defined political and military objectives" and be limited to the levels needed to achieve those objectives. Finally, there must be "some reasonable assurance" of popular and congressional support, and "the commitment of U.S. forces to combat should be a last resort."[8]

Weinberger's guidelines underscored the principal characteristics of most military interventions during the Reagan years—although the coercive actions were rarely taken only as a last resort or only in cases where vital U.S. interests were threatened. A premium was placed on achieving decisive results in a brief period of time with a minimum commitment of U.S. personnel. The invasion of Grenada and the bombing raids against Libya were the quintessential examples of how such a preference for low-intensity conflicts operated, and the administration was rewarded with widespread public acclaim. When U.S. leaders became more adventurous or had vaguely defined objectives, as in the Lebanon peacekeeping operation of 1982–1983, popular support eroded rapidly, confirming that the American people remained wary of situations that harbored the potential to become Vietnam-style quagmires.

Most of Weinberger's guidelines were followed in the Persian Gulf war as well, especially the determination to avoid the agonizingly slow escalation that marked the Vietnam War. U.S. leaders used massive power to neutralize Iraqi forces and minimize U.S. casualties. Nevertheless, the war against Iraq was on a much larger scale than such operations as the Grenada and Panama invasions or the air assault on Libya, and the Bush administration took a considerable risk that a quick and decisive result might prove elusive. The political consequences of such a miscalculation would have been grave, because a substantial minority of the U.S. population opposed the decision to go to war and would assuredly have turned against the administration if the conflict had not gone smoothly.

Although President Bush proclaimed that the "Vietnam syndrome" had been laid to rest by the military success in the Persian Gulf, several administration actions indicated otherwise. The way the military waged that conflict suggested an acute awareness of the fragility of public support.

Similarly, Washington's determination to avoid getting involved in the postwar struggle between Saddam Hussein's regime and rebel forces, and the speed with which U.S. forces were withdrawn from the region, spoke eloquently of a realization that the popular aversion to Third World military quagmires remained strong.

Perhaps the greatest change has occurred in the style of military intervention. Before World War II, U.S. military initiatives were typically undertaken on a unilateral basis. An isolationist heritage stressed the need to avoid alliances and other foreign entanglements. That tradition made unilateralism mandatory whenever the United States used its armed forces, especially in the Western Hemisphere, a region viewed as constituting a special U.S. sphere of influence.

Virtually the opposite strategy has prevailed since World War II. U.S. officials routinely have portrayed military operations as multilateral enterprises, often going to elaborate lengths to do so. In part, this stratagem is necessary to preserve the impression that military action against another country is consistent with provisions of the UN Charter, which authorizes efforts at regional collective defense. As one of the founders of the UN, the United States wishes to maintain at least the image of compliance with the principles of that organization—hence, the preferred reliance on multilateral rather than unilateral interventions.

The vast U.S.-led alliance system that emerged during the first decade of the Cold War relied heavily on the collective-defense provisions of the UN Charter. Beginning with the Rio Treaty in 1947 and NATO two years later, there was a proliferation of such regional mechanisms. Most U.S. military interventions also have been conducted on a multilateral basis—or, more accurately, with a plausible multilateral cover. In addition to paying official respects to UN principles, this technique has the more practical benefit of diluting accusations of U.S. imperialism or aggression, even though at times the multilateral cover has been rather threadbare. For example, the Korean "police action"—ostensibly a collective peacekeeping operation conducted under the auspices of the UN—was patently a U.S. enterprise.

Most other U.S.-directed interventions have exhibited a similar or even greater degree of U.S. dominance. Yet, with the exceptions of the 1958 occupation of Lebanon, the April 1986 air strikes conducted against Libya, and the December 1989 invasion of Panama, the United States has avoided acting on an explicitly unilateral basis when conducting major military operations. (Hostage-rescue episodes and immediate self-defense cases, such as the 1981 Gulf of Sidra incident, have, of course, been handled unilaterally.) Significant mitigating circumstances accounted for the unilateral actions against Lebanon, Libya, and Panama. In the first two instances, none of the "friendly" regimes in the Middle East felt sufficiently secure to risk domestic turmoil by enlisting in a U.S.-led operation. In the case of the Libyan raids, Washington's principal European allies were also opposed to the strategy. Similarly, opposition from the members of the Organization of American States (OAS) to the Panama invasion was intense.

There appear to be three key factors that determine whether U.S. officials opt for a multilateral facade or blatant unilateralism. The first factor is whether there exists in the affected region a multilateral security organization that could provide at least a minimally credible cover for U.S. actions. The second factor is whether efforts at coalition building would support or undermine Washington's overall policy objectives. The third consideration is whether the crisis is evolving at a speed that would make coalition diplomacy (especially its inherent delays) a dangerous luxury. As a general rule, U.S. officials have tended to favor unilateral actions in the Western Hemisphere (where opposition from other members of the OAS can be anticipated) and in cases where a credible regional security association does not exist or a pliable ad hoc arrangement cannot be created in time. In all other instances, they have preferred to use the multilateral method.

■ EPISODES OF INTERVENTION

Various episodes since World War II illustrate the complex nature of U.S. military intervention in the Third World. The Korean conflict was representative of four features: the employment of military force in a rapidly evolving situation; executive branch dominance; the desire for a multilateral cover; and the gilding of actual motives. Within hours of the June 25 invasion, Truman ordered U.S. air units to assist South Korea and obtained a UN Security Council resolution calling on member nations to help repel North Korean aggression. He then invoked that resolution to justify sending U.S. ground units into Korea. The president took all of these steps without once requesting congressional authorization—an omission that provoked vehement protests from critics such as Republican Senator Robert A. Taft.[9]

Truman's exclusion of Congress from any decisionmaking role was not accidental. He asserted that because the Korean intervention was a UN police action, he needed no congressional declaration of war; because the Senate had ratified the UN Charter, the president was supposedly empowered to act upon the call of the Security Council. Truman explicitly rejected the suggestion of some aides that he seek an authorizing resolution from Congress, fearing that such a step might trigger a divisive debate over Korean policy and lead to undesirable congressional interference.[10] This insistence on exclusive executive branch control over the Korean intervention persisted throughout the conflict, even after the PRC's involvement created a wider, bloodier, and considerably more dangerous war.

The multilateral facade for the operation was also continued. Truman insisted that the United States was acting as an agent of the UN—as merely one member among many responding to the Security Council's call to repel aggression. Military units in Korea were carefully designated "UN forces," and the UN flag flew over their installations. Nevertheless, the assertion that intervention in Korea was a truly multilateral peacekeeping enterprise lacked credibility. The commander of UN forces was always an American, and the United States provided approximately 90 percent of the troops and equipment. Crucial decisions, such as whether to cross the 38th parallel into North Korea, were made in the White House and the Pentagon, not at UN headquarters.[11] It is difficult to escape the conclusion that rhetoric about "collective security" was largely used to disguise a military operation that primarily served U.S. foreign policy objectives.

Just as the administration stressed the supposed multilateral nature of the Korean intervention, it insisted that the United States was helping to preserve freedom and democracy in South Korea, as well as resisting the initial stage of a possible global communist offensive. Although U.S. leaders may have sincerely believed the latter point, they were certainly aware that there was a dearth of South Korean freedom and democracy. President Syngman Rhee was a ruthless autocrat who routinely harassed and jailed political opponents and censored the press.[12] Yet both the Truman and Eisenhower administrations conveniently overlooked that record when justifying the Korean operation to the American people.

The dispatch of U.S. Marines to Lebanon in July 1958 mirrored the Korean intervention in some respects but differed from it in others. As in the Korean episode, the United States responded to rapidly deteriorating events. After a bloody coup d'état in Iraq staged by admirers of Egyptian president Gamal Abdel Nasser, U.S. officials feared for the survival of fragile pro-Western governments in Lebanon and Jordan. Lebanese leader Camille Chamoun had faced significant opposition for several months following his effort to gain an unprecedented second term as president, but opposition forces seemed to acquire added strength after the Iraqi revolution.

In a sense, Eisenhower's decision to send the marines to keep Chamoun in office was not an example of unfettered executive power. Several months earlier, Congress had passed a resolution expressing support if the president decided to use military force to "secure the territorial integrity and political independence" of Middle East nations from "any nation controlled by International Communism." Yet even Eisenhower conceded privately that the Lebanese situation did not really fit the criteria of this "Eisenhower Doctrine," as it involved an internal political struggle, not external aggression.[13] Nor was it all clear that the rebel forces were procommunist, although some elements were emphatically hostile to the United States.

Eisenhower simply chose to ignore such inconvenient matters. In justifying the Lebanese intervention to Congress and the U.S. citizenry, he stressed the danger of a communist takeover of Lebanon.[14] Although the intervention was not on the same scale as Truman's presidential war in Korea (the U.S. occupation force consisted of a division-size unit), Eisenhower's action certainly stretched the intent of the congressional resolution. His explanation for the intervention also replicated the Truman administration's lack of candor. Moreover, the Lebanon incident represented an especially graphic example of U.S. willingness to use force to keep a compliant, pro-U.S. regime in power in a region that was considered strategically and economically important.

Lebanon also showed Washington's willingness to use force unilaterally when a multilateral enterprise could not be arranged. All of the troops involved in the occupation were U.S. forces. The unilateral nature of the intervention occurred more from default than any conscious design. Indeed, there is evidence that Eisenhower originally wanted to pursue a joint operation with British forces but was dissuaded by Secretary of State John Foster Dulles and other advisers who reminded him of Britain's odious imperial reputation throughout the Middle East.[15]

Perhaps even more significant, no multinational mechanism for such a mission existed in that region. The embryonic Baghdad Pact had effectively disintegrated with the overthrow of the pro-Western monarchy in Iraq, and any UN endorsement was out of the question, especially given the Soviet Union's veto power on the Security Council. U.S. officials would face a similar obstacle in 1982 when they had to create a hasty, ad hoc multinational peacekeeping force for Lebanon. The absence of a regional security organization comparable to NATO or the OAS has always posed a problem for U.S. military policy in the Middle East. Washington's ability to assemble a broad coalition against Iraq in 1990–1991 did not really remedy that structural problem. It was no accident that in the months following the end of the Persian Gulf war, Washington repeatedly pressed for the creation of a formal collective-defense arrangement for the Gulf region—including efforts to draw in Egypt and Syria. At least initially, such U.S. prodding failed to overcome the deep-seated political divisions among the various parties.

Sometimes the presence of a regional security organization still could not provide a credible multilateral facade for U.S. actions. Even with the existence of the OAS, the Johnson administration found it difficult to portray the U.S. occupation of the Dominican Republic in 1965 as a bona fide multilateral enterprise. Part of the problem was that Mexico and other key OAS members were bitterly opposed to coercion of a Latin American nation by the "Colossus of the North." An equally important reason was that the Dominican crisis flared so rapidly it became impossible to recruit hemispheric clients for a joint operation.

On April 24, 1965, young army officers still loyal to President Juan Bosch (who had been overthrown in a right-wing coup two years earlier) tried to restore him to office. Disorder rapidly engulfed the capital of Santo Domingo as pro- and anti-Bosch military units—and armed civilian factions—vied for power. Johnson reacted to these developments swiftly and decisively. On April 28, he sent in a contingent of marines, followed a few days later by the army's 82nd Airborne Division. By early May, the occupation force totaled approximately 22,000 personnel, slightly larger than the Lebanese operation seven years earlier. Johnson acted without soliciting OAS participation or even providing advance notification, both because of the perceived need for rapid action and the desire to avoid embarrassing opposition. For essentially the same reasons, he excluded Congress from a decisionmaking role.

Once the situation stabilized, however, the administration sought to give the occupation a multilateral image. In his memoirs, Johnson stated that the United States wanted the other members of the OAS to "share responsibility" for the operation.[16] That goal proved elusive, as Chile, Mexico, Venezuela, and other major OAS members continued to oppose the intervention. Within a few weeks, Washington was able to obtain token military contingents from other nations, thus giving the ongoing occupation at least a plausible multilateral patina. But the political orientation of those partners—Brazil, Honduras, Nicaragua, and Paraguay—was revealing: These were Washington's most authoritarian clients in the Western Hemisphere.

The alleged multilateralism of the Dominican operation was an illusion, and U.S. explanations for the invasion were equally dubious. Johnson initially contended that action was necessary to protect Americans who were caught in a dangerously turbulent political situation—a rationale President Reagan would use with respect to Grenada two decades later. Almost immediately, however, he adopted a different argument, asserting that communists had been gaining control of the insurgency, thereby threatening to transform the Dominican Republic into another Cuba. The U.S. embassy in Santo Domingo subsequently issued a list of fifty-eight "prominent and documented Communist and Castroite leaders" in the rebel forces, a list, it was later revealed, that had been compiled by longtime Dominican dictator Rafael Trujillo in the late 1950s and bore little resemblance to reality.[17]

It is possible that the Johnson administration sincerely, albeit erroneously, believed the communist-takeover thesis. A more likely explanation, however, is that U.S. leaders desperately wanted to thwart the return of Bosch to power. They considered him soft on communism and were hostile because he had previously penalized U.S. business interests on the island. Whatever the reason, the United States had shown a willingness to use military force to keep the Dominican Republic in the pro-U.S. camp.[18]

The invasion of Grenada in October 1983 demonstrated that the United States was equally willing to use its armed forces to oust a regime considered inimical to U.S. interests. Since early 1979, Grenada had been ruled by a radical leftist regime led by Maurice Bishop, who came to power in a coup d'état that ousted the corrupt and erratic Prime Minister Eric Gairy. Although the Reagan administration repeatedly criticized the Bishop regime for its growing ties with Cuba and other members of the Soviet bloc, it was the massacre of Bishop and many of his followers by a rival faction in the ruling

New Jewel Movement (NJM) on October 19, 1983, that triggered the U.S. invasion.

Even though events evolved almost as rapidly as they had in the Dominican Republic, the Reagan administration was able to create a multilateral facade for the Grenada operation. The official rationale for the invasion was that the United States was responding to a "request" from the previously obscure Organization of Eastern Caribbean States (OECS) for action against a threat to the peace of the region.[19] Most members of that group did provide token police and paramilitary forces for the invasion and occupation, although their level of participation could scarcely disguise the fact that it was a U.S. operation.

The rapidity with which the United States organized this supposedly multilateral military campaign (fewer than six days passed between Bishop's assassination and the invasion) strongly suggests that the Reagan administration had prepared the diplomatic groundwork long before. The notion of a spontaneous OECS request is plausible but unlikely. Another portion of the official U.S. justification—that the invasion was primarily a "rescue mission" to protect some 700 American students at St. George's University Medical School—also strains credulity. Despite considerable pressure from U.S. officials, many of the students insisted they had not been in danger. There was certainly no evidence that they were in greater peril on October 25 than during the turmoil immediately following the events of October 19.

Two other elements of the Grenada invasion typified U.S. military interventions in the post–World War II era. First, President Reagan completely excluded Congress from any policymaking role. Much as Truman did in Korea and Johnson had done in the Dominican Republic, he merely informed congressional leaders of a policy that he had already adopted. Moreover, Reagan relayed that information barely hours before the first troops landed in Grenada. This move seemed calculated to neutralize any criticism or opposition—a motive that also may have contributed to the unprecedented decision to prevent the press from covering the invasion.

The other predictable element of the Grenada operation was the heavy emphasis placed by administration officials on an alleged communist threat to the East Caribbean region. They implied that the Soviet Union and Cuba were behind the hard-line Marxist faction that had ousted Bishop—an especially curious assertion given that the Castro government vehemently condemned the coup d'état.[20] U.S. leaders also exaggerated the number of Cubans on the island and insisted these were professional soldiers when most were apparently construction workers employed on the Point Salines airport project. The airport itself was portrayed as a future base for Soviet bombers despite the longstanding contention of the Bishop government that it was needed for jumbo jets to bring tourists to the island. The plausibility of that benign explanation was underscored when the postinvasion, anticommunist

Grenadian government also desired the airport to enhance tourism and successfully solicited U.S. aid to complete the project. In sum, the Reagan administration's contention that the invasion thwarted the creation of a new Soviet puppet in the Western Hemisphere was, at the least, exaggerated.

President Bush's decision to oust the regime of Panamanian dictator Manuel Noriega in December 1989 again demonstrated Washington's low threshold for using military force in the Western Hemisphere. Most of the features of earlier military interventions were replicated in the Panamanian episode. Bush launched the invasion without authorization or even significant input from Congress. In an ostentatious display of contempt, Bush "notified" congressional leaders of the impending invasion just hours before it occurred. The military actions in Lebanon and Grenada had already demonstrated that the White House could successfully defy the War Powers Resolution, which had been enacted in 1973 following the Vietnam debacle to prevent future presidential wars. The Panama invasion showed that Bush viewed that legislative restraint on his power with similar disdain. Once again Congress failed to assert its constitutional authority, and that inaction confirmed the de facto demise of the War Powers Resolution.

Other aspects of the Panama invasion also conformed to a familiar pattern. As Johnson had done in the Dominican Republic and Reagan in Grenada, Bush insisted that the intervention was necessary to protect American lives, seizing on an incident in which Panamanian Defense Forces had beaten and killed a U.S. Marine. Although that was undoubtedly an odious incident, there was no credible evidence that U.S. forces stationed in Panama were about to be subjected to a reign of terror. The swift and devastating nature of the U.S. military response suggested that Washington had planned the invasion long before and was merely waiting for a pretext. That parallel with the Grenada operation was noticeable, as was the administration's determination to keep the news media from covering the military operations except under rigid conditions established by the government.

The rapid ebbing of the Cold War precluded U.S. officials from raising the specter of Noriega somehow serving Soviet interests—although they had earlier cited his cozy relationship with Fidel Castro. Nevertheless, Washington was able to find two moral motives for the invasion: bringing democracy to Panama and striking a blow against one of the post–Cold War bogeymen, the international drug menace.[21] Some U.S. officials apparently viewed the Panama episode as the opening gambit in the effort to involve the military more extensively in antidrug missions throughout the Western Hemisphere.[22]

The gap between the official justifications and the underlying reality was considerable. Noriega was unquestionably a brutal and corrupt dictator who was involved in the drug trade, but a succession of U.S. administrations were aware of those facts and yet continued to deal with him as a valuable ally. It was only when he became greedy and untrustworthy (e.g., by apparently passing intelligence information to Castro) that Washington decided he no longer could be tolerated. As in the case of so many Third World military interventions, the moralistic rhetoric of U.S. leaders concealed far more mundane motives.

The largest and best-known interventionist episode in the Cold War period—Vietnam—exhibited many of the same characteristics of other episodes but also some important differences. The most significant difference was the prolonged, gradual evolution of the U.S. commitment, as opposed to the rapid commitment of forces in the other cases. The massive combat role that dominated the Johnson and Nixon years followed a sizable but relatively restrained program of military aid under Eisenhower and the fateful introduction of hundreds, ultimately several thousands, of combat "advisers" under Kennedy. It was only after it became evident that such measures were insufficient to preserve a pro-U.S. government in Saigon that Washington made the disastrous decision to escalate the military stakes.

The scale of the Vietnam intervention likewise was unique. It substantially surpassed both in size and duration even the Korean episode and utterly dwarfed the operations in Lebanon, the Dominican Republic, and Grenada. At the peak of the conflict in 1968, more than 500,000 U.S. troops were involved—a commitment not equaled in size until the onset of Operation Desert Storm against Iraq. Equally important, the war generated far more domestic opposition than any previous or subsequent intervention.

In other respects, Vietnam corresponded to the pattern of U.S. post–World War II interventionism. The calculated exaggeration of an alleged North Vietnamese threat to U.S. security already has been noted. Manifestations of the imperial presidency were also present. Congress did play a role with the passage of the Gulf of Tonkin Resolution and the continued funding of a military presence in Southeast Asia, but the operation remained predominantly a presidential war. In fact, both Johnson and Nixon insisted that their inherent constitutional powers as commanders in chief authorized them to pursue that conflict even in the absence of the Gulf of Tonkin Resolution or any other congressional authorization.[23] Nixon even expanded military operations into Cambodia and Laos on that basis.

The United States also sought to portray the Vietnam War as a multilateral undertaking. Washington exerted diplomatic pressure to persuade various allies and clients—most notably Australia, New Zealand, and South Korea—to send combat units. Except for South Korea, however, the commitments never surpassed the level of tokenism. Those additional forces served little relevant military purpose, but they did help preserve the fiction that the Vietnam intervention was a collective regional peacekeeping enterprise rather than superpower meddling in the affairs of a small Third World nation. In this case, the attempt at a multilateral cover was even less credible than in the other interventionist campaigns.

The U.S. naval buildup in the Persian Gulf and the subsequent attacks on Iranian targets also generally fit the pattern of post–World War II military interventionism. Washington predictably cajoled its Japanese and Western European allies as well as client states in the region to support U.S. strategy. That campaign to give the operation a multilateral image was only partially successful. Britain and France overcame their initial reluctance and ultimately dispatched modest naval contingents in response to intense U.S. diplomatic pressure, but Japan remained aloof and the Persian Gulf states seemed willing to provide only meager, covert support.

Disingenuous official explanations were prominent throughout the buildup. Despite official rhetoric about protecting U.S.-flagged ships in the Gulf, the Reagan administration's primary motive was to blunt growing Iranian power throughout the region. The naval operations symbolized a clear U.S. tilt toward Iraq in its war with Iran. An important secondary motive was to preempt any move by the Soviet Union to become a major player in that part of the Middle East. It was an omen of the approaching post–Cold War era, however, that in this instance, concern about Islamic fundamentalism seemed to overshadow the usual Cold War obsession with Soviet designs.

The Persian Gulf conflict of 1990–1991 is generally viewed as the first major crisis in the post–Cold War international system. Although that was true in some respects, the U.S.-led military effort against Iraq generally fit the pattern of other interventions orchestrated by Washington since World War II. President Bush responded quickly to Iraq's August 2, 1990, invasion of Kuwait by dispatching air, naval, and ground units to the Persian Gulf region, ostensibly to deter an Iraqi attack on Saudi Arabia. The administration immediately sought and obtained a series of UN Security Council resolutions condemning Baghdad's aggression, demanding the restoration of Kuwait's sovereignty, and imposing a naval and air blockade on Iraq. The buildup of U.S. forces in the region continued, reaching some 200,000 by early November. On November 8—just two days after the midterm congressional elections—the president announced a "second stage" buildup of forces to more than 400,000 for the explicit purpose of giving the U.S.-led coalition "an offensive capability." In the weeks following that announcement, Washington engineered additional Security Council resolutions, including one imposing a January 15 deadline for a complete Iraqi withdrawal from Kuwait and authorizing member states to use force if Baghdad failed to comply.

As previously noted, Bush took all of those actions (which inexorably brought the United States closer to war) without seeking congressional authorization. They were also accompanied by numerous statements stressing the moral basis of U.S. policy: Officials highlighted alleged Iraqi atrocities in Kuwait, invoked the "1930s analogy," and asserted that curbing aggression was a vital feature of a "new world order" based on respect for sovereignty and the rule of international law. But the administration and its supporters had unguarded moments of candor. Senator Robert Dole conceded that the United States was willing to take military action in the Persian Gulf "for one reason, o-i-l." Secretary of State James Baker, apparently frustrated that many Americans were not responding to an idealistic call to arms, offered a far more practical reason. He insisted that Iraq's control of Kuwait's oil would give Baghdad a "stranglehold" on Western economies. "To bring it down to the average American citizen, let me say that means jobs. If you want to sum it [the justification for intervening] up in one word, it's jobs."[24]

Just as Washington tried to give its intervention an idealistic patina, it went to great lengths to portray the response to Iraq as a genuine collective security enterprise. But the Persian Gulf operation was a U.S.-controlled enterprise from the start—almost to the same degree that the Korean intervention had been forty years earlier. The Bush administration was content to work through the UN as long as the other Security Council members endorsed U.S. policy objectives. (Washington had considerable leverage to secure compliance. The PRC, for example, realized that casting its veto would mean the end of most-favored-nation [MFN] trade status and access to the lucrative U.S. market. The Soviet Union understood that a lack of cooperation would doom any hope of aid for its collapsing economy.) Despite the carefully cultivated image of a collective security partnership, the military decisionmaking authority and the composition of the command structure remained under firm U.S. control. Another revealing point was that, of the nations outside the Persian Gulf region, the United States provided approximately three quarters of the military personnel and nearly the same proportion of the ships, planes, tanks, and other military hardware. The parallels with the Korea "police action" were striking in that respect, although Washington was able to cajole its allies into paying most of the financial costs of the Gulf intervention.

The administration managed to avoid extensive scrutiny of its motives and justifications because of the spectacular military success of Operation Desert Storm. Critics might legitimately wonder in retrospect whether the Iraqi military menace was ever as great as Washington had contended. The ease with which the coalition aircraft controlled the skies over Iraq and rained destruction on that country and coalition ground units swept Iraqi forces from Kuwait without serious opposition was inconsistent with the propaganda image of a powerful adversary.[25] One exuberant U.S. military officer who described the operation as "a turkey shoot" was correct—except that more than 100,000 Iraqi soldiers and civilians may have died in that turkey shoot and its aftermath. Most Americans greeted the military victory with an attitude of triumphalism. Concerns about such disturbing developments as the continuing presidential usurpation of the congressional war power, the disingenuous nature of the administration's policy justifications, yet another dangerous precedent of excluding the media from freely covering military operations, and the long-term consequences of the war to Iraq and other nations in the Gulf region were drowned out in a chorus of victory cheers.

■ PITFALLS AND LIMITATIONS OF MILITARY INTERVENTION

The results of decisions to employ direct U.S. military coercion have been decidedly mixed. Vietnam was an obvious failure. Despite a military commitment lasting longer than a decade at a cost of 58,000 American lives and more than $140 billion, communist forces triumphed throughout Indochina. Moreover, subsequent events in the rest of East Asia have demolished the original rationale for U.S. intervention. Contrary to alarmist predictions, the noncommunist nations bordering Indochina did not fall like so many dominoes. Quite the contrary—Malaysia, Singapore, Thailand, and other East Asian countries proceeded to enjoy an unprecedented degree of economic expansion and (with the exception of the Philippines) are less vulnerable to external or internal pressure from communist elements in the 1990s than they were in the 1960s.

Most of the other interventions appeared superficially to be successful— at least from the standpoint of advancing U.S. geopolitical objectives. A more comprehensive examination, though, casts some doubt on that conclusion. The United States did prevent a unification of the Korean peninsula on communist terms, but that effort required a considerable expenditure in lives and national treasure. The situation remains volatile, as heavily armed North and South Korean forces confront each other.

The results of the 1958 Lebanon intervention were ultimately far more disappointing. For several years, it appeared that the U.S. occupation had preserved a pro-Western government, thereby sustaining a useful client in the Middle East. But that illusion was dispelled in the mid-1970s when a chaotic civil war engulfed Lebanon. Eisenhower's intervention did not fundamentally alter the destiny of that unhappy country; it only delayed the inevitable.

Indeed, the "successful" Eisenhower intervention unraveled to the point that a second U.S. effort to maintain a pro-Western Lebanese regime occurred. Seizing an apparent opportunity to rectify unpalatable developments in Lebanon afforded by the Israeli invasion in the summer of 1982, the Reagan administration embarked on another occupation program—this time as the leader of a multinational peacekeeping force. The policy was ill-conceived and ineptly executed. The "government" of Amin Gemayel, which the United States supported, enjoyed the allegiance of only one faction among many in the bitter internecine struggle and was unable to exert control over any sizable portion of the country. The U.S. attempt to restore Lebanon as a client collapsed ignominiously in the rubble of the U.S. Marine barracks when a suicide driver detonated a truck bomb killing 241 marines in October

1983. Both the marines and U.S. policy became victims of political and religious forces Washington could not defeat with conventional military measures nor even comprehend.

The United States apparently has enjoyed somewhat greater success in the Dominican Republic and Grenada. Moreover, the professed commitment to freedom and democracy in those cases was followed by some constructive action, unlike the developments in Lebanon, Vietnam, and—for many years—Korea. The United States presided over elections in the two Caribbean countries that were at least free of obvious fraud or intimidation (the more subtle influence resulting from the presence of U.S. occupation forces and the flow of financial assistance to pro-Western factions is another issue). Happily for U.S. policymakers, candidates acceptable to Washington won the elections. Even in these two countries, however, substantial economic and social problems remain, and the possibility of political instability is an ever-present danger.

The April 1986 air strikes against Libya produced ambiguous results. The prediction of critics that such attacks would merely strengthen and radicalize the Libyan regime of Muammar Qaddafi, leading to increased acts of terrorism, appeared for a time to be unwarranted. The November 1991 indictment of two high-ranking members of Libya's intelligence services for the December 1988 bombing of Pan American flight 103, however, indicates that Qaddafi may have exacted a grisly revenge for the air strikes. Moreover, the United States did not succeed in its larger policy objective—using the raids to pressure dissident military elements to overthrow the mercurial dictator.

The legacy of the December 1989 invasion of Panama is not entirely clear either. Washington did oust a brutal and corrupt autocrat and install the government that apparently had been chosen by the voters in the May elections, before the balloting was nullified by Noriega's armed thugs. Nevertheless, the invasion was hard on the Panamanian population. Hundreds of civilians perished, and nearly 10,000 were made homeless by the fighting. Panama's economy, which had already been severely damaged by the sanctions Washington had imposed in 1988, declined further during the months following the invasion. Democracy has hardly flourished either. It was an inauspicious debut for Guillermo Endara's government when its first edicts were issued from the confines of a U.S. military base, thereby leading to allegations that it was a Yankee puppet. Since Noriega's ouster, the political situation has steadily deteriorated amid mounting accusations against the Endara administration of corruption, nepotism, and harassment of political opponents.[26]

Washington's decision to reflag Kuwaiti ships and engage in protective convoying in 1987–1988 proved to be a dubious enterprise. U.S. naval intervention in the Persian Gulf temporarily diminished Iran's power and influence, although the Islamic fundamentalism symbolized by the Tehran regime remains a potent force. Such a limited short-term gain was completely overshadowed by the subsequent adverse developments. The U.S. tilt toward Iraq helped build up the power of Saddam Hussein, leading to Baghdad's invasion and attempted annexation of Kuwait. In short, Washington's support for Iraq to contain Iranian power helped set the stage for a bloody clash between Baghdad and the U.S.-led anti-Iraq coalition.[27] As in the case of most U.S. interventionist initiatives, the consequences of the Persian Gulf reflagging and convoying episode ultimately proved to be detrimental to U.S. interests.

There are indications that even the overwhelming military success of Operation Desert Storm may not produce lasting geopolitical gains. The destruction of Iraq's military has done little to solve the endemic conflicts of the region or achieve an elusive stability. Indeed, it has unleashed powerful disintegrative trends that could ultimately fragment Iraq and bring about greater instability. The efforts of the Kurdish minority to carve out an autonomous region in northeastern Iraq are viewed with suspicion and apprehension in neighboring Turkey. Turkish leaders understand all too well that an autonomous "Kurdistan" would be a political magnet for the sizable Kurdish population in Turkey, including the guerrilla forces that have long waged a struggle against Ankara's authority.

The weakening of Iraq is also likely to benefit the long-term expansionist aspirations of Iran. Evidence that Tehran has been pursuing a concerted program to develop a nuclear arsenal indicates that the Iranian leadership does not intend to tamely accept U.S. hegemony in the Gulf indefinitely. Fear of Iranian expansionism caused Washington to support Iraq throughout the 1980s, but Iraq is no longer in any condition to counterbalance Iran. Saudi Arabia and the other conservative Persian Gulf powers seem inclined to rely on the United States to rescue them again if aggression occurs rather than build up their own military forces and create a collective-defense arrangement. Nor are the conservative gulf sheikdoms willing to adopt meaningful political reforms to satisfy increasingly restless populations.

A potentially explosive situation exists in the Persian Gulf. Washington has made itself the protector of an assortment of reactionary regimes that show little inclination to provide for their own defense; it has badly disrupted the already fragile political and social fabric of the area; and it has inadvertently strengthened the position of the one country that has the potential to become a regional hegemon. The combination of those factors makes it possible that the United States will eventually be confronted with the necessity to wage "Desert Storm II" to preserve its preeminence in the region.

The pattern of U.S. military intervention in the Third World since World War II suggests that it is a strategy possessing only marginal effectiveness. U.S. leaders understandably seem to prefer using more gradual and less blatant mechanisms, including economic and security assistance programs and the various covert activities of the CIA. When Washington has resorted to force, the emphasis has been upon quick and decisive solutions, in large part because the American people will not tolerate costly, drawn-out crusades. The Korean and Vietnam conflicts demonstrated that quick, decisive outcomes are not always possible, and the Lebanon interventions demonstrated that apparent gains can prove exceedingly ephemeral. The "victories" in Panama and the Persian Gulf may turn out to be equally transitory. Although no great power can eschew the use of military force in all circumstances, the history of U.S. post–World War II interventions illustrates the numerous pitfalls and limitations of that strategy.

Unfortunately, the trend appears to be toward more, not fewer, interventionist episodes. The Bush administration and many of its allies in the foreign policy community seem to regard the Persian Gulf operation as a model for Washington's political and military role in the post–Cold War world. Assertions that the international system is now "unipolar," with the United States as the "sole remaining superpower," are accompanied by calls for an increasingly activist U.S. policy.[28] Under such schemes, the United States would play the role of global policeman, albeit using the UN to implement Washington's policy objectives whenever possible. That is the essence of the new world order with its emphasis on maintaining "stability."

■ Part 4

CONSTRAINTS ON INTERVENTION

◼ 10

The Domestic Environment

Jerel A. Rosati

In order to better understand U.S. interventionist practices in the Third World during the post–World War II period, one must examine the impact of domestic politics as they have evolved during three major historical periods: the Cold War era (1940s–1960s), the post-Vietnam era (1970s–1980s), and the post–Cold War era (1990s–present). Throughout the Cold War era, a domestic consensus supported an active and globally interventionist U.S. foreign policy. Based on the politics of anticommunism, this consensus was reinforced by the growth of a national security state—that is, the growth of institutions in government and throughout society oriented around the president and directed toward the promotion of a policy of global containment of the former Soviet Union. Thus, the beliefs and institutions of U.S. society provided encouragement for the policy of intervening throughout the globe, most notably in the Third World, in order to contain the threat of Soviet communism.

The agonizing U.S. defeat in Vietnam shattered this domestic consensus and modified the national security state that supported the anticommunist impulse to intervene abroad, thus ushering the post-Vietnam era in the politics of U.S. foreign policy. Since Vietnam, U.S. citizens have disagreed over the external threats and the proper foreign policy responses. In addition, Congress, the media, and private interest groups no longer acquiesced to presidential leadership; they became increasingly critical of presidential goals and aspirations while simultaneously seeking independent policy roles. Hence, where presidents once were given wide latitude to intervene abroad in the name of national security and the national interest during the Cold War era, constraints on executive-branch power multiplied significantly after Vietnam. The rise of domestic fragmentation and pluralism in the politics of U.S. foreign policy made it increasingly difficult for presidents to implement interventionist policies in the Third World and led to such crises of leadership and legitimacy as Watergate, the Iran hostage crisis, and the Iran-contra affair.

The end of the Cold War marked by the collapse of communism in Eastern Europe and the fragmentation of the Soviet Union into a host of independent and noncommunist countries has brought the politics of U.S.

foreign policy into a new era. Given these changes, the 1990s may offer new opportunities as well as constraints for U.S. interventionism abroad. Although the ultimate implications will remain unclear until the politics of U.S. foreign policy work themselves out over time, the general patterns that have prevailed since Vietnam are likely to be reinforced into the future. Therefore, a crisis of leadership in the making of U.S. foreign policy and the unpredictable nature of U.S. interventionism may intensify as the United States approaches the twenty-first century.

■ THE COLD WAR YEARS AND THE RISE OF ANTICOMMUNISM

Following the end of World War II, Americans gradually became more and more preoccupied with the potential threat posed by the Soviet Union and communism. Isolationist tendencies associated with the prewar period had been firmly discredited with the Japanese bombing of Pearl Harbor and U.S. entry into the conflict. Most Americans realized that the United States had become too powerful to minimize its global involvement following the war. Therefore, a great debate took place among leaders and intellectuals of U.S. society about the world around them, the nature of the Soviet Union, and the proper foreign policy of the United States.[1]

Some people, like Henry Wallace, Franklin Roosevelt's former vice president and presidential candidate in 1948 on the Progressive party ticket, argued it was important to maintain a cooperative relationship with the Soviet Union and prevent a new conflict from arising, through policies emphasizing spheres of influence and a type of détente. Others, like George Kennan, a Sovietologist and important policymaker in the administration of President Harry S Truman, asserted that the major threat was Soviet expansion in Europe; therefore, the United States needed to contain the Soviet threat in Europe. Still others, like Paul Nitze, another important policymaker in the Truman administration, emphasized that the Soviet Union was a revolutionary state with designs to aggressively export communism throughout the world. Such a threat meant that the United States had no choice but to contain the Soviets militarily throughout the globe.

During the late 1940s, individuals representing the two more pessimistic schools of thought struggled for control of foreign policy within the Truman administration. Truman himself was initially undecided about the nature of the Soviet Union and the appropriate U.S. response. With time, however, he increasingly became skeptical of Soviet intentions. Problems over a divided Germany, the communist coup d'état in Czechoslovakia, the "fall" of China, and the North Korean attack of South Korea eventually convinced most members of the Truman administration, including the president, that the Soviet Union was indeed a revolutionary, communist state attempting to achieve world domination. Therefore, U.S. policymakers concluded that the United States had to assume the role of leader of the "free world" to stop communist aggression.

It is not surprising that Congress and the public initially were reluctant to support such an activist policy abroad so soon after the country had fought a world war. Nonetheless, there was an underlying anticommunist sentiment embedded in U.S. society that could be traced back to the policies of President Woodrow Wilson following the Bolshevik Revolution in 1917. Therefore, when the Truman administration responded to the post–World War II environment with proclamations like the Truman Doctrine, which committed the United States to assist Greece and Turkey in order to contain the communist threat, the result was growing and substantial public support for an overall policy of containment. The paramount lesson of World War II that was conveyed—that the "appeasement" of Adolf Hitler and fascism by England and France at Munich only produced more aggression—was transferred to the situation at hand: The United States must not appease Stalin and communist aggression. Instead, the United States would build up its military and contain communist aggression wherever it occurred.

These same events also propelled another segment of U.S. society to the forefront of politics—people who feared that the United States was losing the Cold War because it was not doing enough to stop and defeat communism. Not only did they perceive that the United States was losing the war *abroad*, especially in Asia; they believed the United States was threatened by subversion from *within*. Therefore, they argued that containment was not enough; a policy of rollback was necessary to stop and defeat communist advances. People who shared this view gained control of Congress during the late 1940s and early 1950s and were prominent within the Republican party—most notable was Senator Joe McCarthy. They attacked the policy of containment, as well as the Truman administration and its supporters, for losing the Cold War.[2]

McCarthyism was not successful in getting either the Truman or the Eisenhower administrations to reorient their foreign policies beyond containment. However, the challenge had two lasting effects. First, it reinforced perceptions held by U.S. policymakers and the public that communism was monolithic—controlled by the Soviet Union—and an ever-present threat. Second, liberals and those of the political left who were critical of the policy of containment and argued for a more cooperative policy (such as Wallace) lost all credibility and legitimacy during the Cold War years.[3]

In short, a consensus had developed within the United States by the 1950s that the world was divided by two hostile forces: communism led by the Soviet Union and democracy led by the United States. Despite disagreements over tactics (how much force? and where?), most Americans agreed on the nature of the threat—communism—and the necessity to use force to forestall its expansion in the Third World. This consensual view fostered the development of certain U.S. institutions to fight communism, thus leading to the rise of the national security state.

■ THE COLD WAR YEARS AND THE RISE OF THE NATIONAL SECURITY STATE

Containment originally was applied to Europe and then to Asia by the Truman administration, then extended throughout the globe during the administrations of Presidents Dwight D. Eisenhower, John F. Kennedy, and Lyndon B. Johnson. The United States relied initially on economic assistance in the form of programs like the Marshall Plan to defeat the threat of communism. However, beginning with the Truman Doctrine, the threat and use of force became the basis of containment—by developing nuclear weapons, expanding and deploying the military throughout the world, creating alliances, providing military assistance, conducting covert operations, and overtly intervening abroad with armed troops. In other words, U.S. foreign policy increasingly became globalized and militarized. To promote and maintain such a policy direction, there was a corresponding growth in the national security apparatus of the United States.

Before World War II, few institutions within the government or throughout U.S. society were oriented toward foreign affairs and national security. The policymaking elite was extremely small and centered within the executive branch in the State Department. World War II changed this dramatically. Overnight, the U.S. government was redirected to devote itself to waging a global war; the military expanded enormously, and civilian agencies grew to assist the president in pursuing the conflict. This governmental effort, in turn, put the economy and the society on a war footing to provide the necessary personnel, equipment, and services to achieve U.S. victory. Therefore, as a result of war, a national security state was formed.

Unlike the situations after previous wars in U.S. history, however, the United States demobilized only for a short time following victory in World War II. With the rise of anticommunism, the United States once more expanded its resources in order to fight a global Cold War. The national security state thus continued to operate and grow during the Cold War years and became a permanent part of the U.S. landscape. The dominant elements of this apparatus consisted of the presidency, the national security bureaucracy, the foreign policy establishment, and a military-industrial-scientific infrastructure throughout the economy and society.

The president was the predominant policymaker in the making of foreign policy.[4] During times of national emergency, power usually flowed to the president, and, especially during war, the president has been able to exert his considerable powers as commander in chief, head of state, chief diplomat, and chief administrator. The 1950s and 1960s were considered by most U.S. citizens to be such a time of national emergency, when the national security of the United States was directly threatened by communism. The United States was preparing to fight World War III directly with the Soviet Union in Europe, while it indirectly fought the Soviet regime for the "hearts and minds" of the people and the elites of the Third World by intervening throughout the globe.

The development of consensus in U.S. society behind the need to contain communism helped make the president dominant on questions of war and peace. As the Cold War escalated, Congress became increasingly acquiescent to presidential initiatives. The president committed troops to foreign lands with little or no input or consultation from Congress. The rise of a bipartisan consensus between Democrats and Republicans that developed by the mid-1950s resulted in the virtual abdication of the congressional constitutional right to declare war. With the rise of presidential power, these decisions now became presidential decisions.

Congressional passage of the National Security Act of 1947 provided the president with a national security bureaucracy to formulate and conduct foreign policy. The act created the National Security Council (NSC), reorganized the military into the Department of Defense, and developed an intelligence community under the Central Intelligence Agency.[5] The NSC was to provide policy advice to the president and be supported by a director and staff. Eventually, the NSC became responsive to presidential needs, serving as the mechanism by which presidents centralized and coordinated foreign policy in the executive branch. This was very important to the president's power in foreign affairs, particularly as the national security bureaucracy grew dramatically in size and scope during the Cold War.

The repercussions of the National Security Act were felt in institutions beyond the White House as well. Prior to 1947, the military was made up of two separate departments—Navy and War. The act created the Department of Defense, which consisted of three branches—Army, Air Force, and Navy; the Joint Chiefs of Staff to promote military coordination; and the Office of the Secretary of Defense to provide civilian leadership and policy advice to the president. The Department of Defense soon became the largest bureaucracy in the U.S. government. With the globalization of containment, it grew to almost 3 million military personnel and 1 million civilians located in hundreds of military bases throughout the United States and the world. The primary mission of the department throughout the Cold War years was to develop and deploy the requisite military forces not only to provide nuclear deterrence and to defend Europe but also to intervene in the Third World if directed by the president.

The National Security Act also produced a large intelligence community to collect and analyze information for policymakers. Numerous agencies were created and grew in importance, including the National Security Agency (NSA), the Defense Intelligence Agency (DIA), and the CIA. The CIA developed two additional functions. First, it coordinated the intelligence analyses of the various organizations; thus, the director of central intelligence (DCI) served as the principal spokesperson to the president. As noted in Chapters 7 and 8, the CIA also developed a covert operations capability—that is, the ability to conduct clandestine activities (such as propaganda campaigns, assassinations, and small paramilitary wars) in support of U.S. foreign policy objectives in the Third World.

Other executive branch organizations also have been involved in foreign affairs, including the State Department, the Agency for International Development, the Arms Control and Disarmament Agency, and the Peace Corps. In the area of international political economy, the Treasury Department, Commerce Department, and Department of Agriculture have been heavily involved, among others. In fact, almost every department of the executive branch developed international divisions in response to the Cold War and U.S. global activism.[6] In sum, following World War II, foreign policy was no longer made principally in the State Department or with much congressional involvement; power moved away from Congress toward the executive branch bureaucracy and to the president.

The Cold War years also saw the rise of a foreign policy establishment that produced much of the personnel and expertise that made up U.S. foreign policy.[7] The war effort forced the government to recruit personnel from all over U.S. society to staff the ever-expanding national security bureaucracy—especially, scientists, academics, lawyers, and businesspeople. For example, such people were brought together to work on the Manhattan Project in order to develop the atom bomb. Similar interactions in other foreign policy areas occurred throughout the government. Thus, as people began to meet each other and work together, a network of individuals from diverse walks of life developed who came to share the assumptions of the anticommunist consensus.

With the rise of the anticommunist consensus and the expansion of the national security bureaucracy following the war, many of the same people who had staffed the government during World War II became involved in the effort to fight the Cold War. These same individuals, and many new recruits, constantly moved back and forth between the government and private world, maintaining their foreign policy ties through membership in a few prominent groups, such as the Council on Foreign Relations. Thus, a foreign policy establishment of prominent individuals was formed, providing a critical bridge between the government, the national security bureaucracy, and key institutions throughout U.S. society.

The development throughout the economy and the society in general of a support infrastructure—including U.S. industry, labor, academia, research institutes, and intellectuals—was the final element contributing to the rise of the national security state.[8] Much of U.S. industry was directly involved in expanding defense efforts in response to the Cold War. This transformation began with U.S. entry into World War II, when the production of materials and services for civilians changed to military production to defeat Germany and Japan. Many of the largest U.S. companies, such as General Motors, Chrysler, McDonnell Douglas, and Boeing, retooled their assembly lines to produce tanks and bombers rather than cars and airplanes. With the rise of the Cold War, these same companies continued to work for the government and, especially, for the Defense Department. Thus was born the permanent Cold War economy.

U.S. banks and companies also increasingly became part of U.S. foreign policy abroad as they multinationalized following World War II, often locating in other countries where there was a strong U.S. governmental presence. U.S. businesses were routinely involved in other ways—such as through subcontracting the building of facilities at a local military base or by building a retail outlet near a base heavily patronized by military personnel. Through these various activities, much of U.S. business became increasingly part of what President Eisenhower called the "military-industrial complex." In addition, U.S. labor also supported the Cold War effort. For example, the American Federation of Labor–Congress for Industrial Organization (AFL-CIO) became a major supporter of free trade and U.S. foreign policy throughout the world. Both organized and unorganized labor—that is, U.S. employees—were bulwarks of the national security state and the anticommunist crusade.

Activity by business and labor was also reinforced by behavior in the scientific, research, and educational community. This class of individuals was important in communicating the need for containment, developing many of the national security ideas and plans (such as deterrence and nation-building), and often served as part of the foreign policy establishment and the government. Research institutes and "think tanks" devoted to national security concerns, such as the RAND Corporation, became a prominent part of the effort to contain communism. The same trend occurred throughout the entire educational system but was most visible at prominent universities such as Harvard, the Massachusetts Institute of Technology, and the University of California at Berkeley. Anticommunism, as well as the need for containment and intervention abroad, was further promoted by the supportive messages communicated to the public by the mass media. Finally, most intellectuals supported the rise of the anticommunist national security state.

Thus, the late 1940s and 1950s witnessed the rise of anticommunism and the national security state. Both developed at the same time and reinforced each other; the rise of anticommunism resulted in the growth of the national security state, and the development and expansion of the national security state reinforced the anticommunist fervor that permeated U.S. society. Rather than working as a constraint on U.S. intervention in the Third World, the politics of anticommunism and the national security state provided the foundation for—and, indeed, prompted—greater U.S. involvement and interventionism throughout the globe in order to contain communist aggression. This situation led directly to growing U.S. involvement in the Vietnam War.[9]

■ VIETNAM, THE COLLAPSE OF CONSENSUS, AND THE RISE OF FRAGMENTATION

The Vietnam War eventually became an agonizing experience for Americans, resulting in political challenges to the anticommunist consensus and the national security state. U.S. involvement, in support of the French effort to maintain its colonial empire in Indochina against Ho Chi Minh and the Vietnamese communists, began under the Truman administration and continued under Eisenhower. By 1954, the United States was paying 80 percent of the war's cost for the French. With the withdrawal of the French in 1954, following the battle of Dienbienphu and the signing of the Geneva Accords, the United States attempted unilaterally to support a stable and independent South Vietnam. However, under Presidents Kennedy and Johnson, the situation in the south deteriorated. The U.S. response was to Americanize the war—by 1967, over half a million U.S. soldiers were fighting a war in Vietnam at a cost of over $30 billion a year.

Throughout much of this period, the U.S. public—both elites and masses—tacitly supported increasing U.S. involvement in Southeast Asia. In reality, most Americans were unaware of where Vietnam was and what was happening there. They were not interested in foreign policy ventures so far from home. Yet, this was still a time of consensus. If the president of the United States, supported by the national security state, contended that Vietnam was being threatened by communism and that all the region's nations would fall if the threat were not contained, the American people stood behind him. Most Americans did not question the assumptions that led to the nation's involvement in Vietnam. They believed that the containment policy was necessary to defend U.S. national security and promote democracy, liberty, and justice throughout the world. It took U.S. involvement in the Vietnam quagmire to get people to ask questions again about the nature of the world and the proper U.S. foreign policy response.

What made Vietnam so traumatic for many Americans and so significant for U.S. society was that it was the first war in its history that the United States had lost. Americans were used to winning; they expected to succeed. Behind the anticommunism and containment policy of the consensus years was a common set of optimistic values that most Americans shared. As noted in Chapter 2, Americans were raised to believe that they were an innocent society, a benevolent society, an exceptional society.[10] Americans see themselves as a defensive people—not aggressive or imperialistic. When Americans do become involved in war, they become involved to help all people—"the war to end all wars." Furthermore, Americans typically see themselves in the forefront of civilization and progress in the modern world, a society that with "Yankee ingenuity" can accomplish anything it sets its mind to do.

The Vietnam War undermined many of these beliefs held by Americans. How could the most powerful country in the history of the world lose to a guerrilla insurgency? The war in Vietnam was a failure. Furthermore, Americans were dying for a lost cause—nearly 58,000 Americans died in Vietnam, with over 350,000 other Americans wounded. For what? The tragic loss of American lives led people to doubt the appropriateness of a foreign policy based on the global containment of monolithic communism. But there was more than just a questioning of the policy of global containment. The conduct of the war effort in Vietnam, such as the use of napalm and the My Lai massacre, also led many to question such deeply held values as American innocence and benevolence. In other words, not only did most Americans question the practicality of a policy of global containment, Vietnam also forced many Americans to question the morality of U.S. foreign policy and, with events at home such as the civil rights movement, the morality of its society. The result was that the consensus that had developed during the 1950s was politically challenged and shattered.

The events of the 1960s resulted in the rise of the political left in the United States and an alternative understanding of U.S. society.[11] Although the rise of anticommunism and, in particular, McCarthyism, had silenced most liberals and leftists during the early 1950s, the new left began to emerge on the political scene in the late 1950s with the rise of the civil rights movement and grew dramatically as the Vietnam War intensified. The hard-core political activists and members of the counterculture dissented and rebelled against mainstream society, the anticommunist consensus, and the national security state—all of which were perceived as being responsible for producing Vietnam. Members of the antiwar movement advocated U.S. withdrawal from the war. By the late 1960s, a substantial number of the American people had also turned against U.S. involvement in Vietnam— some wanted out via withdrawal, others wanted out through escalation.

For a while, the polarization between the antiwar movement and the executive branch, the counterculture and mainstream society, verged on civil war. But polarization gave way to fragmentation. Whereas once a consensus had been the basis of U.S. society and U.S. foreign policy, disagreement became the norm especially in the area of foreign policy. Since Vietnam, different general foreign policy orientations, representing different segments of society, have competed for ascendancy within U.S. society.[12]

Some people, especially those on the political right, continued to believe that the major global threat to the United States was communism directed by the Soviet Union. Proponents of such a "conservative internationalist" orientation argued that U.S. foreign policy needed to contain, if not roll back, Soviet communism. It should be pointed out that disagreement existed among conservatives concerning the severity of the communist threat and the appropriate foreign policy strategy. Those who tended to see a more monolithic communism tended also to favor a strategy of massive rearmament at home and rollback abroad. Those who focused more on the threat of the Soviet brand of communism emphasized a defense buildup and a more modest containment strategy.

Other people, especially from the liberal left, saw a much more complex and interdependent world, made up of many important countries and actors. Advocates of this "liberal internationalist" orientation argued that in such a complex global environment, the United States needed to deemphasize the role of force in addressing East-West issues (such as the U.S.-Soviet conflict), while West-West issues (such as U.S.-Japanese trade) and North-South issues (such as Third World debt) received greater attention. Although there was no consensus among the liberal left, the emphasis was on downplaying the Soviet threat and relying on preventive diplomacy to promote global peace and prosperity throughout the world.

Proponents of the third most popular position recognized the increasing complexity of the world while highlighting the difficulty the United States has in affecting it. They argued that the United States needed to limit its involvement to those few areas where it really has vital interests—especially Western Europe and Japan. Such a "noninternationalist" perspective traverses the traditional political spectrum and is particularly popular among segments of the mass public. Although other points of view exist beyond these three, they were the most popular vying for influence in the politics of U.S. foreign policy.

The fragmentation of public beliefs, especially at the pragmatic mass level, appeared to have contradictory implications for U.S. foreign policy in the Third World. Most Americans continued to be fearful and skeptical of communism; yet they also wanted more cooperative and peaceful relations with communist countries, including the Soviet Union. Likewise, most Americans continued to believe in a strong defense; yet they were reluctant to use force that would result in American soldiers dying abroad in a war. In other words, as a result of the Vietnam War, the "Munich appeasement syndrome," which dominated the thinking of the 1950s, was now joined by the "Vietnam syndrome." That is, most Americans during the 1970s and the 1980s did not want to appease communism, but they wanted to avoid another Vietnam.

The net result of the collapse of the anticommunist consensus for U.S. foreign policy was that U.S. interventionism in the Third World became more tentative and precarious. Short-term, small-scale interventions like

Grenada and Panama were palatable; long-term, large-scale, more costly interventions, as in Lebanon and Central America, were looked upon with great public skepticism. Thus, in the post-Vietnam domestic environment, presidents learned that, unlike in the consensus years, they did not come to office with automatic majorities behind their policies. No matter what presidents and their advisers believed, there was a substantial segment of U.S. society—among both elites and masses—that disagreed with presidential policy. This constraint was reinforced by the fact that much of the support that the president has initially, upon election, withers away over time.

The existence of fragmentation in public beliefs over U.S. foreign policy gave the president great opportunities but also great risks. Unlike in the 1950s, presidents were no longer driven to pursue only an anticommunist policy of containment. Yet, it was unclear how far the president could go in pursuing a policy before losing majority support. Most Americans expected presidents to fulfill the expectations that they generated before the public during the election, but the dissensus of the post-Vietnam years made it much more difficult for presidents to deliver.

■ VIETNAM, THE NATIONAL SECURITY STATE, AND THE RISE OF PLURALISM

The post-Vietnam domestic environment also resulted in the collapse of the foreign policy establishment, the reassertion of Congress, a more critical media, and the rise of divergent interest groups. Thus, presidents were not only confronted with greater diversity of thought, they were increasingly constrained by the existence of competing domestic actors and institutions on the foreign policy scene. Domestic politics, in other words, became much more complex and pluralistic. Moreover, these developments limited the power of the national security state, exacerbated the eclipse of presidential power, reinforced the constraints on Third World interventionism, and produced inconsistency in U.S. foreign policy with each change in administration.

The key to the U.S. foreign policy establishment's past ability to serve as the bridge between the different elements of the national security state was the existence of an informal network of like-minded individuals. But once the Vietnam War challenged the domestic consensus, members of the establishment differed over the war and proper U.S. foreign policy along the lines of the three different schools of thought previously discussed. So, as public beliefs fragmented, the consensus that held the foreign policy establishment together also dissolved, even more intensely given the establishment's level of individual interest and involvement in foreign policy.[13]

The Vietnam War also strained executive branch relations with the legislative branch. President Richard M. Nixon was elected in 1968 based on a secret plan to end the war. The secret plan consisted of a strategy simultaneously involving deescalation, escalation, and negotiations. Deescalation meant that the use of U.S. troops was slowly phased out through a process of "Vietnamization." Escalation entailed the stepped-up bombing of Indochina, as well as the invasion of guerrilla sanctuaries in Cambodia and Laos. Both deescalation and escalation were intended to produce a negotiated agreement with the North Vietnamese to end the war and buy South Vietnam a "decent interval" for survival. However, with escalation, the antiwar movement reached its height, calling for the immediate withdrawal of U.S. forces.

Much of the dissent reflected in the antiwar movement eventually surfaced in the U.S. Congress. The president was no longer seen to be doing what was necessary in the name of national security. Instead, more and more members of Congress saw an unresponsive and unaccountable "imperial presidency." Turnover in congressional membership—brought on as older, more conservative members retired or died—produced major battles between the legislative and executive branches over the conduct of foreign policy. Congress was clearly no longer willing to assume the acquiescent role it had played during the 1950s, when it rallied behind presidential policy. Many representatives and senators were now interested in directly affecting the conduct of foreign policy.

The president resisted congressional efforts to reassert its authority in foreign policy. Nevertheless, through its power to control appropriations, to investigate, and to pass legislation, Congress did reclaim some of its constitutional authority. For example, in 1973, it was able to regain part of its ability to be involved in decisions of war and peace by passing the War Powers Act. In 1975, it officially ended U.S. involvement in Vietnam by eliminating all funding. Congress also pressured the executive branch by exposing secret security commitments made by U.S. presidents to numerous countries throughout the world and publicizing CIA abuses abroad, including efforts to assassinate leaders and overthrow unfriendly regimes.[14]

Although Congress became more interested and active in the making of U.S. foreign policy, the president continued to exercise considerable power. Three general patterns emerged in the post-Vietnam era. For a few issues, such as human rights, Congress has often taken the lead in the making of foreign policy. For some other issues, like Central America, Congress has become a major participant and, in the mind of the president, a major obstacle to presidential management of U.S. foreign policy. For most issues, however, Congress continued to be on the sidelines, reacting to presidential initiatives. Therefore, the president remained powerful in foreign policy, with the knowledge, however, that presidential power would likely be constrained by congressional participation if an issue became politicized. Thus, President Gerald R. Ford's covert intervention in Angola in 1975, President Jimmy

Carter's efforts at SALT (Strategic Arms Limitation Talks) II ratification in 1979, and President Reagan's efforts to militarize Central American policy throughout the 1980s all met congressional opposition.

The turbulence of the 1960s, the Vietnam War, and the revelations of executive branch abuses in the name of national security shocked most Americans and made them very skeptical and critical of the presidency and the government. Whereas Americans once had great trust in their representatives and governmental institutions, lack of success in Vietnam and the revelations of Watergate prompted most of the public to lose faith in the honesty and integrity of the U.S. political system. This cynical attitude increasingly became reflected in the mass media. Journalists during the 1950s and early 1960s played a major role in communicating the perils of communism and the need for a global, interventionist foreign policy to contain the threat— they operated within the consensus. The end of consensus, however, meant that journalists also became divided in thought and much more partisan. More important, Vietnam and Watergate taught many members of the media that they could no longer trust public officials to tell the truth, that they had to look below the surface for the real story.

Thus, the media has become increasingly independent and potentially critical of government activities and public officials, including presidents. This is consequential for presidential power, as most people are heavily dependent on the media for telling them what to think about (that is, the media sets the political agenda) and for being the source of most of their information. It has thus played a critical role in making and breaking public personalities and affecting foreign policy. Both Presidents Carter and Reagan, for example, relied on media coverage in ascending to the presidency, and both were damaged politically by media coverage of the Iran hostage crisis and the Iran-contra affair, respectively.[15]

The breakdown of consensus also broadened and diversified the larger societal environment within which the government must operate. U.S. industry, labor, academia, and the intellectual community no longer stood united behind a global, interventionist U.S. foreign policy. As U.S. economic might declined relative to the growth of Japan, Western Europe, OPEC, and the newly industrializing countries, the paths of U.S. business and government no longer coincided as in the past. Some U.S. companies became increasingly global and free-trade oriented, whereas others became more protectionist. U.S. labor, in particular, became more protectionist over time. And in academia and among intellectuals, the diversity of thought that existed in society was even more pronounced. In other words, foreign policy beliefs became less uniform and more divisive throughout the institutional fabric of U.S. society.

The rise of a pluralistic environment clearly can be seen when examining interest-group activity in the area of foreign policy. Beginning in the 1960s, new national security and public interest groups arose from a variety of different ideological perspectives, many of them involving people who were once part of the old-boy network referred to as the foreign policy establishment—conservative groups such as the Heritage Foundation and the American Enterprise Institute and liberal groups like the Institute for Policy Studies and the Brookings Institution. The large number of interest groups and the variety of their foreign policy activity reflect the diversity of thought that followed Vietnam. These groups have been active in influencing Congress, the media, and the public to promote their interests (whether the goal is overthrowing the Sandinistas or imposing sanctions against South Africa). All this foreign policy activity made it that much more difficult for the president to control the agenda successfully and manage U.S. foreign policy in the post-Vietnam era.[16]

About the only patterns that continued in existence relatively unchanged were the national security bureaucracy and the military-industrial-scientific complex that developed throughout society during the Cold War years, both oriented around a large defense and the threat of force. The NSC, Defense Department, intelligence community, industrial defense contractors, and defense-oriented research community, as well as the individual networks that tie them together, have continued to exist and even prosper. However, they existed in a domestic environment that was much less supportive and occasionally more hostile than during the Cold War years of consensus.

■ CRISIS OF LEADERSHIP INTO THE POST–COLD WAR ERA

The domestic environment was marked by two trends during the post-Vietnam period that held important implications for U.S. interventionist practices in the Third World. First, the national security bureaucracy, the military-industrial-scientific infrastructure, and the conservative internationalist segment of society that emphasized the threat of Soviet communism all acted as a powerful force in promoting U.S. foreign policy in the direction of a large defense structure and reliance on the use of force. Second, the breakdown of consensus, the collapse of the foreign policy establishment, the rise of a reassertive Congress, a more critical media, and competing interest groups meant that no foreign policy orientation was able to maintain much public support over time.

In the past, given the rise of anticommunism and the national security state, the problem was that the president could lead the country, but only in the direction of fervent anticommunism, containment, and interventionism. In the 1970s and the 1980s, with the collapse of consensus and the changes in the national security state, the problem was that the president—and really, the political system—could not generate leadership in any direction for a sustained period of time. As Ole Holsti and James Rosenau have argued,

"Perhaps the only constancy in American foreign policy since Vietnam has been the conspicuous lack of constancy in its conduct."[17] In such an environment, all post-Vietnam presidents have failed. None has been able to generate a new consensus or sustain sufficient support behind his policies.

Presidents Nixon and Ford attempted to produce a more stable global order through a realpolitik policy based on détente with the Soviet Union. Yet their détente policies were attacked by both the liberal left and the conservative right. Ultimately, Nixon experienced a crisis of legitimacy over Watergate and was forced to resign, while Ford's lack of leadership resulted in his inability to win election to the presidency. President Carter tried to promote a global community in response to a complex world by emphasizing preventive diplomacy across a variety of issues. Yet Carter's stewardship was called into question by the political challenge posed by the conservative right over the Iran hostage crisis and the Soviet invasion of Afghanistan, issues that contributed to his failed reelection effort in 1980. President Reagan attempted to resurrect the containment policy of the past, given his view of communist expansionism, in order to deter Soviet power abroad. Reagan's leadership, the most politically successful in the post-Vietnam era, was nonetheless also challenged in foreign policy by first the liberal left, who opposed his hard-line policies against the Soviet "evil empire," and subsequently by the conservative right, who opposed Reagan's arms control efforts with Soviet leader Mikhail Gorbachev. Like Nixon with Watergate before him, President Reagan also experienced a crisis of legitimacy over the Iran-contra affair, although his popularity allowed him to survive the political storm.

What happened was that changes in the domestic environment after Vietnam produced a crisis of leadership for the presidency and the country. The president, the only person capable of providing national leadership, no longer was able to lead the country. The fragmented nature of U.S. beliefs, as well as competing domestic interests and institutions, constrained presidential action. No matter what presidents promised, domestically or in foreign policy, they were unable to fulfill expectations. The complexity of the domestic environment and the complexity of the global system simply no longer allowed much leeway for presidential success. Presidents could not lead and manage foreign policy for a sustained period of time, whether in an interventionist direction or not. The net result of this crisis of leadership has been that with each new administration, as well as over the course of the same administration, U.S. foreign policy has tended toward incoherency and inconsistency.

The waning of the Cold War raises obvious questions.[18] What national security threats does the United States face in the 1990s? What role should interventionism play in the future of U.S. foreign policy? How large should the military be in order to protect U.S. national security in the future? To what extent are covert paramilitary operations necessary? How much of a military-industrial-scientific infrastructure is necessary throughout society? With the end of the Cold War, it logically follows that the United States is less threatened by a now-fragmented Soviet Union, that its foreign policy can rely less on interventionism, and that the national security bureaucracy and military-industrial-scientific infrastructure could be scaled back considerably.[19] The end of the Cold War also would seem to suggest that the conservative internationalist beliefs, which formed the basis of the consensus during the Cold War years and have persisted since Vietnam, are likely to decline in a post–Cold War era, reinforcing the expansion in pluralist politics of the post-Vietnam era. All this points to a further weakening of the power of the presidency and a decline in the future of U.S. interventionism abroad.

However, a post–Cold War global environment will continue to hold considerable conflict, although on a smaller scale, in a world of great complexity. The most significant short-term development in this regard has been the Persian Gulf conflict, which is likely to reinforce concern with national security and strengthen those elements within government and society supporting strong presidential power and interventionism as features of U.S. foreign policy. In other words, although the end of the Cold War appears to reinforce the decline of the patterns of that era in the politics of U.S. interventionism that began following Vietnam, the Persian Gulf conflict has clearly given them a new lease on life. This reinforces the need for strong presidential power during periods of crisis and national emergency, a large military establishment and national security bureaucracy, and a sizable military-industrial-scientific infrastructure to support U.S. interventionism abroad. Hence, the outcome of the Persian Gulf war has strengthened the power of those political forces in U.S. society and government resistant to changes that seem warranted by the collapse of communism and the end of the Cold War. In fact, it could be argued that the Persian Gulf conflict, the collapse of communism, and the end of the Cold War have given the United States greater opportunity to exercise force abroad, at least in the short run. Now that the Soviet Union is no longer the major adversary, a primary constraint has been eliminated with respect to U.S. ability to intervene abroad.

Clearly, the end of the Cold War and the evolving post–Cold War global environment have contradictory implications for the future politics of U.S. interventionism. Although already forgotten, such tension for the future of interventionism was clearly evident during the Persian Gulf conflict. Initially after Iraq's invasion of Kuwait in August 1990, President Bush was able to dominate the policymaking process in sending a massive force of U.S. troops to the Persian Gulf to defend Saudi Arabia. The political response throughout the rest of the government and most of society—Congress, the public, and the media—was to rally around the flag. However, with President Bush's announcement in early November that U.S. forces would increase from 200,000 to over 400,000 personnel and take an offensive military posture to force Iraq out of Kuwait, the domestic political climate changed dramatically, reflecting its more fragmented and pluralist form. Dissent appeared in Congress, among former government officials, in group politics, and in public opinion, increasingly communicated by the mass media. Within a three-month period, President Bush went from exercising extraordinary power to intervene during a foreign policy crisis to experiencing a crisis of governance that could determine the fate of his presidency. Although the country rallied around the flag once again with President Bush's decision to go to war on January 16, 1991, the Persian Gulf crisis nevertheless highlighted the domestic tension and political instability that exist over U.S. interventionism abroad.

■ TOWARD THE FUTURE

The impact of the domestic environment on the future of U.S. interventionism cannot be predicted with any degree of certainty. The end of the Cold War has created increasing global complexity, posing both greater opportunities and constraints for the evolution and exercise of U.S. power. The collapse of communism and the fragmentation of the Soviet Union provide unique opportunities for more foreign policy change in a direction away from Cold War–era policies, a shift that would further weaken the president's ability to govern foreign policy and intervene abroad. Yet the continued existence of instability and conflict throughout the world, although on a smaller scale than a potential U.S.-Soviet war, reinforces continuity in presidential power and the demands of national security. Such contradictory patterns of global change suggest that the more fragmented and pluralist politics that have prevailed since the Vietnam War will likely continue in some form in the immediate future. Much will also depend on the foreign policy orientations of future presidents and their closest advisers. Ultimately, it is the dynamic interaction between global developments and the domestic environment that will determine the politics of foreign policy as U.S. society approaches the twenty-first century.

11

Government and the Military Establishment

Stephen Daggett

Shortly after Ronald Reagan was reelected president in 1984, a noteworthy debate broke out between Secretary of Defense Caspar Weinberger and Secretary of State George Shultz. "If we ever decide to commit forces to combat," Weinberger told the National Press Club in November 1984, "we must support those forces to the fullest extent of our national will for as long as it takes to win. We must have in mind objectives that are clearly defined and understood and supported by the widest possible number of our citizens. And those objectives must be vital to our survival as a free nation and to the fulfillment of our responsibilities as a world power."[1] The secretary's cautionary statement was, by all accounts, extremely popular inside the Pentagon, reflecting the sentiments of a senior military leadership still scarred by its experience in Vietnam, a trauma revived in some measure by the loss of 241 U.S. Marines in Lebanon in 1983.[2]

The speech was not so well received, however, elsewhere in the government. Secretary of State George Shultz, who opposed the withdrawal of U.S. forces from Lebanon after the marine barracks attack, responded two weeks later with a speech that pointedly challenged Weinberger's timorousness. "There is no such thing," said Shultz, "as guaranteed public support in advance. . . . Americans will always be reluctant to use force. . . . But a great power cannot free itself so easily from the burden of choice. It must bear responsibility for the consequences of its inaction as well as for the consequences of its action." The use of force is legitimate, said Shultz, "when it can further the cause of freedom and enhance international security. . . . And on such occasions we will be able to count on the full support of the American people."[3]

Though events in Lebanon motivated Weinberger's speech, and the military's experience of Vietnam shaped its content, the Weinberger-Shultz debate reflects a pattern of bureaucratic interests and conflicts that has characterized U.S. decisionmaking throughout the post–World War II era. This chapter considers the governmental-bureaucratic forces that influence the U.S. ability and willingness to intervene militarily in the Third World. It suggests that significant barriers to the effective application of force persist

in the U.S. government—especially within the military establishment—
despite efforts in the 1980s and the 1990s by some elements of the political
leadership and by parts of the military to prepare for armed responses to
conflict in the Third World.

■ BUREAUCRACY AND IDEOLOGY

The Weinberger-Shultz debate illustrates the institutional barriers to
interventionism within the U.S. military bureaucracy. In justifying the use
of force, Shultz's argument was primarily ideological, evoking U.S.
responsibility as a great power to preserve international security and stability
and citing a democratic nation's moral duty to advance the cause of freedom.
Weinberger's argument, in contrast, was shaped by the necessarily more
practical point of view of the military services. Weinberger listed six
conditions that should be fulfilled whenever U.S. military units are sent
into action: (1) An engagement must be vital to U.S. national interests
or those of its allies; (2) a commitment must be undertaken wholeheartedly,
with the clear intent of winning; (3) objectives must be clearly defined;
(4) the relationship between objectives and forces must be continually
reassessed and adjusted if necessary; (5) there must be a reasonable
assurance of public and congressional support; and (6) forces should be
committed to combat only as a last resort.[4] Weinberger generally has been
seen as one of the more intensely ideological officials in the Reagan
administration, but in this instance the secretary of defense was clearly
representing his agency. Although there was a moral dimension to his
analysis, the moral view was primarily that of senior officers in the military
services, insisting that if assigned a task, they should be given the tools to
carry out the job.

   This contrast between the pragmatic caution of the U.S. military
bureaucracy and the ideologically motivated activism of senior administration
political officials outside the Pentagon has recurred throughout the post–
World War II period. In most instances of direct U.S. military involvement
in distant conflicts, the decision to intervene has been initiated by the top
political leadership of a particular administration and acceded to with some
reluctance by the armed forces. As Morton Halperin wrote in his 1974 study
of the foreign policy bureaucracy:

> The attitude of the military services toward commitments and the use of
> force is surprising to observers who expect a bellicose outlook. . . . On
> the issue of American military intervention, the armed services have
> been in general quite cautious. At different times they have resisted
> proposals for intervention, remained neutral, or asked for authority to
> use all their existing forces to make the gamble of involvement less
> risky if taken at all. Professionally they prefer a conservative estimate

of the readiness of forces, and they are sensitive to the danger of using forces where they might be defeated or where they would be drawn away from the primary theater of operations.[5]

Halperin cited several examples, some of which dated back to the earliest days of the Cold War, to illustrate his point. During the Berlin Crisis of 1948, he noted, the JCS in Washington refused to endorse a proposal to confront the Soviets by sending an armed convoy down the road from the American zone to Berlin. The military, he said, did not recommend intervening at the outbreak of the Korean War in June 1950, nor were they the driving force in planning the Bay of Pigs invasion. The military opposed proposals to intervene in Laos in 1961 unless granted full authority to use all forces, including nuclear weapons. And the services did not ardently advocate U.S. involvement in Vietnam.[6] To this list, one must now add the Persian Gulf war. Two former chairmen of the Joint Chiefs of Staff warned against the early use of force in Senate testimony shortly after the president ordered a buildup of forces in the theater for offensive action. And according to an unrefuted account by journalist Bob Woodward, Chairman of the JCS General Colin Powell also felt it unwise to resort to force without first giving economic sanctions a longer time to work, though Powell never found occasion to voice his doubts directly to the president.[7]

The principles that Weinberger articulated in his Press Club speech, therefore, were not simply offspring of the post-Vietnam era. Rather, they reflect institutional interests and perspectives that are a persistent feature of the U.S. military establishment. In part, these interests are simply bureaucratic: Officials in bureaucracies typically are averse to risking the organizational damage that would result from failure. As such, military leaders prefer to avoid conflict except under conditions in which success is almost assured. Just as fundamentally, the historical roots of the current U.S. military structure make preparation for small wars into a kind of organizational afterthought.

■ THE PRIORITY OF LARGE WAR PLANNING

The defining characteristic of the U.S. defense posture in the post–World War II era has been that the U.S. military saw its primary job as deterrence of a major war with the Soviet Union and its allies in Europe. Only now, with the collapse of the Warsaw Pact and the fragmentation of the Soviet Union, is this perspective beginning to shift. From the start of the U.S. military remobilization at the time of the Korean War, Europe was the centerpiece of U.S. defense planning. Indeed, even in the midst of the Korean War, senior defense planners were preoccupied with the military situation in Europe, fearing that the North Korean attack on the South might be a diversion, presaging a Soviet offensive in Europe. As a result, once the initial buildup of forces for Korea was completed, the services substantially bolstered the strength of U.S. forces assigned to Europe.

After the Korean War and into the 1960s, the United States formally maintained a "two-and-a-half" war posture—that is, a requirement that it be able to carry on, simultaneously, two major wars, one in Europe and one in Asia, and a minor war somewhere else. But except during the administration of John F. Kennedy and the early years of the administration of Lyndon B. Johnson, planning for a major war in Asia and for Third World "half-wars" was a very low priority. During the administration of Richard Nixon, Secretary of Defense Melvin Laird explicitly renounced the two-and-a-half-war requirement, saying that the strategy was "overly ambitious" and that it had resulted in "an overdrawn military establishment." "Since then," Laird wrote later, "American ground forces have been postured according to the precept that forces sufficient for the defense of Europe are also capable of effectively responding to lesser threats elsewhere."[8] Even during the administration of Jimmy Carter, when the Persian Gulf became a preoccupation, and into the administration of Ronald Reagan, when officials laid out an expansive vision of the number of worldwide threats that might demand military responses, defense planning was, in fact, based predominantly on the requirements of a major war in Europe.

Indeed, although the Reagan administration widely bruited a strategy of preparing to meet several contingencies around the globe simultaneously, forces never grew sufficiently to meet the planning requirements, and the shift in doctrine only exacerbated what came to be called the "strategy-resources mismatch." When the JCS estimated the size of the force that would be necessary to provide a "reasonable assurance" of accomplishing the missions assigned to U.S. troops—an exercise carried out annually as part of the Planning, Programming, and Budgeting System (PPBS)—the result was very far from the force structure available. In 1982, the Joint Chiefs' "reasonable assurance" force called for twenty-two aircraft-carrier battle groups, rather than the fifteen projected to be available by the end of the decade, and thirty-three active divisions in the U.S. Army and Marine Corps, compared to the twenty-one actually planned.[9]

As it turned out, with defense budgets leveling off after 1985, the Reagan administration was unable to sustain even the relatively modest increases in the size of the force that it undertook during the president's first term. For example, in 1983 the army announced plans to grow from sixteen active divisions to eighteen. The two new units, along with three others in the active and reserve force, were organized as Light Infantry Divisions (LIDs), designed to be smaller and much more easily transportable than a full armored or mechanized division. These five divisions were intended for smaller conflicts, primarily outside of Europe.

The army's growth, however, was achieved not by adding personnel but by reorganizing to reduce the number of active-duty troops assigned to support functions. Thus, from the start, the growth to eighteen divisions was rather hollow. A full third of the army's forces intended for rapid deployment were in the reserves, and even the units that would be deployed first in a crisis depended heavily on the reserve component for critical support functions. Such forces would take a considerable amount of time to train and deploy, a posture that may be appropriate for European contingencies but not for crises that could develop rapidly and unexpectedly elsewhere.

Similarly, the expansion of the U.S. Navy toward 600 ships (with fifteen deployable aircraft-carrier battle groups and four battleships) was frequently taken as evidence of the Reagan administration's interest in adding forces for small wars in distant parts of the globe. But the main burden of the navy's argument for expanding to 600 ships—a clear impossibility in the budget-cutting atmosphere of the 1990s—was not to meet requirements for Third World contingencies. On the contrary, senior officials justified the navy's expansion on the basis of the contribution that the navy could make to winning a major war with the former Soviet Union. The central principle underlying the navy's new "maritime strategy" was that naval forces could be used in the event of a global conflict to take the offensive and carry the war directly to the Soviet homeland. Secretary of the Navy John Lehman explicitly insisted that the naval buildup was not to be justified in terms of peacetime deployments in the Persian Gulf or the possibility of minor wars there or elsewhere. "Every dollar" he said, "has to be justified by what it can do to defeat the Soviet maritime threat in time of war, and that is it and it only."[10]

■ ORGANIZATIONAL PRIORITIES

The fact that the U.S. military has been primarily organized to deter a major war with the now-fragmented Soviet Union and its former allies in Europe does not, of course, mean that smaller-scale military action is ruled out. On the contrary, the Persian Gulf war shows that U.S. military forces originally designed for a superpower confrontation in Europe can be highly effective when used against a far less challenging Third World foe. After the crumbling of the Berlin Wall and the collapse of the Warsaw Pact, U.S. military leaders saw little danger in drawing down forces oriented toward Europe and redeploying them against Iraq. In effect, the Persian Gulf war represented the victory of U.S. doctrine for a war in Europe in a non-European contingency. Moreover, the U.S. military in recent years has begun to think through more fully the unique requirements of low-intensity conflict. As noted in Chapter 3, proponents of planning for low-intensity conflict have identified several kinds of operations short of a major war to which U.S. forces might conceivably be committed—including proinsurgency, counterinsurgency, terrorism counteraction, peacetime contingency operations, peacekeeping, pacification of ethnic conflicts, humanitarian assistance, and military civic action.

The orientation of U.S. military forces toward a major war, however, makes it more difficult in important ways to prosecute such limited military actions. Although sufficient forces will always be available for actions like the invasion of Grenada or the bombing of Libya, and though some forces have always been specifically organized, trained, and equipped for small-scale operations, the bureaucratic structure of the U.S. military establishment has long been biased against a major focus on such minor, secondary conflicts; the U.S. ability to carry on small wars is, therefore, limited in significant ways. The military's focus on a major European conflict means that forces are trained, weapons are procured, and combat units are configured primarily for a large war. "The most substantial constraints on America's ability to conduct small wars," wrote Eliot Cohen, an academic expert on military policy, "result from the resistance of the American defense establishment to the very notion of engaging in such conflicts, and from the unsuitability of that establishment for fighting such wars."[11]

As the major counterinsurgency effort in which the United States was involved in the 1980s, the war in El Salvador forcefully illustrates how bureaucratic factors constrained prosecution of even a relatively limited intervention. Some of the constraints on U.S. military involvement in El Salvador were not per se bureaucratic and have been widely discussed. For example, rather than risk running afoul of the War Powers Act, which requires congressional approval to maintain the presence of U.S. troops in situations in which hostilities are imminent, the Reagan administration limited U.S. troop strength in El Salvador to 55 advisers and prohibited advisers from accompanying Salvadoran forces into the field. (In practice, the ceiling was stretched by the presence of temporary personnel, military attachés at the embassy, and other means, so that more than 150 U.S. military personnel were typically in El Salvador at a given time—but the ceiling nonetheless imposed a real constraint.)

In addition, in 1981 and 1982, as the Reagan administration was beginning to escalate its commitment to the government of El Salvador, the U.S. ambassador, Robert White, was often at odds with U.S. military officials in the region. Disputes involved how to deal with violations of human rights by the Salvadoran military and the extent of Salvadoran military involvement in civil administration. For their part, U.S. military officials have frequently expressed frustration with the extent of civilian control over U.S. policy in situations like that in El Salvador, where they perceived a military crisis. Even with a new, much more sympathetic ambassador in place, the military remained dissatisfied with legal requirements that separated administration of economic assistance from military aid and with a congressional prohibition on the training of foreign police agencies (though officials found some ways around this restriction).

Apart from such environmental factors limiting military freedom of action, however, constraints *within* the U.S. defense establishment also profoundly affect the ability of the military to engage in effective counterinsurgency. The most basic constraint remains the low priority accorded minor conflicts in Pentagon planning. In the case of El Salvador, the secondary status of the conflict was reflected, first of all, in the failure of military officials to pursue consistent long-term funding for military aid and otherwise to give priority to requirements of the action.

Funding for the war in El Salvador was always a contentious issue in the U.S. Congress and remained so into 1991. Beginning in 1981, the Reagan White House lobbied vigorously but rather inconsistently for assistance, frequently arguing that a tenuous military situation required aid on an emergency basis as a means of overcoming congressional resistance. As a result, military planning on the ground in El Salvador was disrupted by a process that U.S. military advisers there characterized as "living from one supplemental [appropriation] to the next."[12] Despite the complaints of in-country advisers, senior officials in the Defense Department reacted rather passively, reflecting the fact that El Salvador was not at the top of their agenda. Four army officers who extensively interviewed U.S. military and nonmilitary officials involved with the conflict reported that the military advisers complained that officials in Washington did not take the war seriously. "In the eyes of those serving in the theater," the officials noted, "support was grudging and suggested that overall 'peacetime' priorities survived intact despite the existence of their war. . . . Some changes occurred on the margins, but real priorities were unaffected." In short, serious consideration was reserved for the traditional "peacetime concerns" and the "big-ticket" theaters such as NATO.[13]

A former commander in chief of the U.S. Southern Command, the senior U.S. military official in the region, reportedly "concluded after numerous trips to Washington to present his case, that the Department of Defense viewed Central America primarily as a potential 'distraction' that could derail the Reagan military build-up by irritating the Congress."[14] The low priority accorded El Salvador by senior defense officials is also reflected in the Pentagon's failure to pursue development of a coherent, integrated, governmentwide policy that would unambiguously articulate U.S. goals and strategy.

The disinterest of senior Washington-based military leaders is not the only way in which the focus of U.S. military planning on big-ticket theaters affected conduct of the U.S. intervention in El Salvador. It also influenced the military equipment that the United States provided, the quality and skills of U.S. military personnel assigned to the war, and, most important, the military organization and strategy that U.S. advisers brought to the conflict.

□ Equipment

U.S. military equipment has been designed for fighting a major war against a sophisticated enemy in Central Europe. Indeed, even with the collapse of the Warsaw Pact and the disintegration of the Soviet Union, U.S. defense officials still put a premium on deploying new generations of weapons in order to ensure superiority in technology. U.S. forces are still being designed for intense conflict in which the ability to deliver massive firepower on selected targets is of decisive importance. Almost of necessity, such equipment, though sometimes offering advantages, is not optimal for counterinsurgency warfare. In El Salvador, the availability of large amounts of U.S. military assistance encouraged the military to "heavy up" infantry units with artillery and other equipment that slowed response time and extended logistics tails. Massive military assistance also led to an emphasis on airpower. The Salvador Air Force grew from about 20 aircraft to 135 by 1988, but this huge expansion created a shortage of pilots and maintenance personnel.[15] It also built into the Salvadoran military budget a large, permanent requirement for funds to operate and maintain the new equipment. Even during the 1980s when the war had settled into a protracted, classic guerrilla action, with few large battles, the firepower that infantry and air force units acquired was of little real use but continued to cost a great deal. As demonstrated by the case of El Salvador the natural U.S. reaction to a military confrontation will always be to put in more sophisticated equipment—a "rich man's approach to war."[16]

□ Personnel

Perhaps the most dramatic way in which the U.S. focus on large wars manifests itself is in policies governing the assignment of military personnel to counterinsurgency conflicts. The peacetime U.S. defense establishment is a huge, bureaucratic structure designed not to fight small wars but to prepare for a global conflagration. Promotion policies reflect this fact of life. The people who advance up to the general officer level are those with command experience in the major theaters of operation, with personal contact with senior officers in the Pentagon, and, in the 1980s, with experience in the weapons procurement system. Officers who serve in other areas for too long cannot develop the expertise that is most important to each of the military services and, just as important, do not develop ties with superiors willing to go to bat for smart young protégés. Indeed, each major arm within each of the services develops a subculture of its own and wants to promote its own in order to maintain its influence in inside decisionmaking; submariners, for example, compete with navy pilots for top slots, as the Strategic Air Command competes with the Tactical Air Command for predominance within the air force.

Dedicated low-intensity conflict forces are outside of the principal organizational structures of each of the services. Only within the army is there a very large special forces complement, and even there it is not of sufficient mass to significantly influence promotions, budgets, or weapons-system development. Indeed, within the army, special forces personnel are often rather derisively referred to as "snake-eaters," a term that reflects the fact that they remain alien to the professional values of the peacetime military.

In El Salvador, the priority of career paths other than special forces was acutely felt. Typically, the brightest, upwardly mobile officers in the army, which is the service principally responsible for counterinsurgency training, tried to avoid assignment to the war, preferring relatively short tours of duty in a number of slots that would advance their careers ("ticket punching," in the military vernacular). As a result, El Salvador received a group of military advisers that one army study group referred to as the "second team." The report noted that each of the services has a "first team," as determined by factors that make sense to that service. Yet, apart from the military group commander, the study group noted that "virtually none of the eligible Army officers assigned to El Salvador had commanded a battalion beforehand. Very few—only two by our count—went on to command subsequent to serving in El Salvador." Stressing that other indicators painted a similar picture, the report concluded that "the system has not exerted itself to supply the MILGROUP [military group] with only the best soldiers available. The personnel managers have not made winning in El Salvador a priority."[17]

□ *Military Organization and Strategy*

Because U.S. defense priorities have focused on a large, global war, U.S. command colleges trained officers in strategy and tactics for a major conflict, and the organization of U.S. military forces was designed for a major conflict in Europe. Counterinsurgency is taught at places like the Army War College, but it receives a secondary priority in the curriculum. More important, in the event of a major war, the role of the military would be, in a sense, relatively limited—its job is simply to fight the war. In a guerrilla conflict, however, the central task eventually is to reconstruct a functioning social order capable of winning the loyalty of the civilian population. But this requires accomplishing a set of tasks that are alien to the U.S. military tradition. Counterinsurgency theory recognizes the need for nonmilitary action as well as for military tactics appropriate for a guerrilla conflict. But, in practice, the U.S. military finds it difficult to implement an effective, coherent, multidimensional counterinsurgency program. It is good at fighting large military actions but not so good at organizing to combat an insurgency.

U.S. skill in organizing for large-scale combat was actually useful in the initial period of U.S. involvement in the Salvadoran war, from 1980 to 1984, when the guerrilla movement (the Faribundo Martí Front for National

Liberation, or FMLN) attempted a "final offensive" designed to achieve a military victory over the Salvadoran army. Between 1980 and 1984, with U.S. advice and funding, the Salvadoran military was transformed from essentially a constabulary into a much larger combat force organized into battalions with large numbers of trucks, helicopters, close air support aircraft, and artillery. When the FMLN was determined to battle the enemy directly, such large, firepower-reliant units were relatively effective, and the final offensive failed.[18]

After 1984, however, FMLN tactics changed, emphasizing hit-and-run attacks with small units, primarily directed against economic targets. But the Salvadoran military did not change its organization or tactics accordingly. Instead, it maintained its large-unit structure and adopted a primarily defensive posture to protect military garrisons, plantations, and the economic infrastructure. Efforts by U.S. advisers to wean the Salvadoran military away from the organization and strategy that originally proved successful (and that emulated the U.S. pattern) led nowhere.[19] In large part, the failure of the Salvadoran military to adopt small-unit tactics and related counterinsurgency strategies—including psychological operations, organization of village civil defense units, and military civic action programs—was not the result of any lack of encouragement by U.S. advisers. On the contrary, U.S. special forces advisers detailed to El Salvador were heavily indoctrinated in counterinsurgency theory, which they, in turn, attempted to convey to their in-country students.

These efforts, however, appear to have foundered, in part because of resistance by a Salvadoran military establishment with its own institutional culture and in part because of the plain inadequacy of U.S. advice to the task at hand. The U.S. doctrinal contribution amounted to little more than very good instruction in small-unit operations—what one official termed a "band-aid approach" to fighting the "other war"[20]—together with solemn affirmations that the outcome of the war would be determined by the ability of the Salvadoran military to appeal to the people's hearts and minds. In practice, the United States was unable to devise an adequate approach to winning the battle for popular support. To the extent that classical counterinsurgency was attempted, with a combination of psychological operations, formation of village defense units, and a targeted infusion of economic development projects, it ultimately foundered. As a result, the Salvadoran military grew frustrated with it, and Salvadoran officers fell back on techniques that at least did not fail dismally.

This problem may be unavoidable in the U.S. military. To the extent that Americans in El Salvador were aware of the need for a radical reorganization of the entire society, the U.S. military was not fully capable of defining, let alone imposing, the necessary changes. A few U.S. Green Berets could not bring about a revolution in Salvadoran class relations.

■ THE STRUCTURE OF COMMAND

The big-war orientation of the U.S. military not only affects its ability to carry on counterinsurgency operations that are inherently challenging; it also can interfere with the conduct of short military actions with clear objectives—the kinds of operations that obviously fulfill Weinberger's criteria for the use of force. Interservice rivalries and simple bureaucratic rigidity have repeatedly undermined the effectiveness of relatively minor, if demanding, military operations in the 1980s.

The abortive April 1980 Iran hostage rescue mission, for example, was a case in which poor planning, caused in part by the organization of the U.S. military, contributed to a disastrous failure. Part of the problem was that each of the military services insisted on getting a piece of the action, to the detriment of the operation. Air force C-130 transport aircraft flew army assault troops to "Desert One" where they were to meet with navy helicopters flown from an aircraft carrier by navy and marine pilots. The mission was aborted because six helicopters were required to carry on the mission, but only six of the eight assigned to the operation arrived at the desert rendezvous site, and one of those broke down. The failure of the operation was compounded into tragedy when a helicopter crashed into a C-130 after the mission was aborted, and eight members of the team were killed.

Though the mission was difficult and could very well have failed at a later point, it is not too much to expect that forces at least could have flown to the destination. A Pentagon investigative panel chaired by Admiral James Holloway concluded that the key problem with the operation probably involved the selection of helicopter pilots. Navy and marine pilots had far less experience in flying long distances over land than available air force pilots—but navy and marine pilots were assigned nonetheless.[21] Any pilot would have had difficulty flying through the sandstorms that the mission encountered, but pilots more experienced in similar operations might have had a better chance of getting to the rendezvous point.[22]

It has also been argued that the operation suffered from the lack of a single, overall commander. "There were," wrote one analyst, "no less than four commanders: the rescue force commander, the air group commander, the on-site commander, and the helicopter force commander," whereas the Joint Task Force commander was located aboard ship in the Persian Gulf. "The result," this writer claimed, "was an inability to improvise when things went wrong."[23]

Another case in which the lack of coordination among the services obviously interfered with the conduct of an operation occurred in the Grenada invasion of 1983. When the NSC, with the authority of the president, initially directed the military to prepare plans for evacuating U.S. citizens from the island, the task fell to the commander in chief of the U.S. Atlantic Command (CINCLANT), a navy admiral, as Grenada lies in his command's geographical area of responsibility. At first, the commander, Admiral Wesley McDonald, planned to employ a marine amphibious unit that was on its way to Lebanon but was still nearby. On reviewing the plan, the JCS concluded that army units should also be assigned to the operation. This has prompted speculation that the Joint Chiefs were merely ensuring, in classic fashion, that each service should have a piece of the action. But the JCS has unequivocally denied this. Instead, according to the JCS, the change was ordered because even McDonald had by then concluded that the mission exceeded the capability of a single marine battalion.[24]

Leaving aside the dispute over bureaucratic motives, it is clear that the operation suffered from a lack of coordination among the different service elements involved. It was decided that marine units would be responsible for taking the northern half of the island and army units the southern half, with overall command authority vested in Vice Admiral Joseph Metcalf, commander of the Second Fleet. But some army units initially could not communicate effectively with navy ships offshore to request and coordinate naval gunfire. Also, some messages failed to reach army forces on the ground, including one message concerning the existence of a second campus of the island's medical school where 224 American students were located.

The lack of communication was so serious that navy aircraft were initially prohibited from flying south of the marine sector without special permission. And even on the third and last day of heavy fighting, naval gunfire was not adequately coordinated with a major army assault. One underlying problem was that there was no unified commander on the ground—the army and Marine Corps commanders each reported separately back to Admiral Metcalf, who was aboard his command ship, the *Guam*, at sea.[25] To be sure, these problems were not enough to prevent the success of an operation in which U.S. forces possessed overwhelming military superiority (although the failure to locate the second campus in a timely fashion could have been a disaster had the Grenadians decided to retaliate by assaulting the unprotected American students). But the flaws in the operation do raise serious questions about the bureaucratic forces that determine the command structure in low-intensity conflict situations. As military theorist Edward Luttwak has pointed out, command was vested in naval officers Metcalf and McDonald, even though every aspect of the operation involved land warfare. If experienced army officers had planned the entire operation, Luttwak argued, a very different and more effective approach might have been employed—what Luttwak called a *coup de main*, in which forces simultaneously assault all key military targets in overwhelming force. Instead, the naval commanders elected to establish beachheads, in the style of the Normandy invasion, with subsequent, relatively slow advances.

One can, of course, dispute Luttwak's armchair strategy, and it is true that the naval commanders had advice from experienced Marine Corps officers attached to the navy and from army officers assigned to the operation as deputies. Nonetheless, Luttwak has a point in complaining that authority over the operation devolved on navy officers who were "expert in supervising the stately rotation of aircraft carriers between the Atlantic and Mediterranean, and in the planning of antisubmarine warfare and convoy escort," hardly the skills needed in directing a small-scale, short-term military action such as the invasion of Grenada.[26]

The Iran rescue mission and the invasion of Grenada illustrate the damage caused to small-scale military actions by the historic lack of coordination among the services. Each of the military services feels entitled to play a role at every level of military combat, making it difficult to assign sole responsibility for any one operation to any one service.

The most significant lesson of the Iran rescue mission and the invasion of Grenada is not about interservice rivalry, however, and many of these problems may have been overcome by the clarification of lines of command imposed by the Goldwater-Nichols Defense Reorganization Act. Rather, the underlying lesson is that the U.S. military is organized primarily to perform the peacetime mission of preparing to fight an all-out global war in order to deter that war. This peacetime function defines what Halperin would call the "organizational essence" of the contemporary U.S. military.[27] And this organizational structure is not designed for carrying on small-scale military action. Instead the operational control of U.S. forces is vested in commanders in chief of "unified commands," organized geographically, with support from "specified commands" that perform functions such as strategic airlift. The primary function of the commanders in chief, with the possible exception of the Southern Command in Panama and, in the past couple of years, the chief of the Central Command with responsibility for the Middle East, has been to prepare for a major conflict with the former Soviet Union. Nonetheless, the commanders in chief receive responsibility for the conduct of any small operation within their areas of authority and, indeed, will combat any effort to remove their control over such operations. Planning of the Grenada invasion, for example, bypassed the Joint Deployment Agency (JDA) that was established in 1979 to coordinate rapid deployment forces. Logistics were handled on an ad hoc basis and suffered severely from disorganization and delay.[28] And operational control of the ground campaign, as Luttwak noted, was vested in a navy commander.

During the 1980s the Defense Department was reorganized to establish an institutional base for low-intensity conflict. The department now has an assistant secretary of defense in charge of special operations, and a special operations command, headed by a four-star army general, has been set up at MacDill Air Force Base in Florida. It is instructive, however, that these organizational changes were imposed on the military by a few persistent members of Congress, over the opposition of an unhappy defense establishment. It took the Pentagon more than six months after Congress established the positions to appoint officials to the two new, senior special operations posts—and the appointment of an assistant secretary was tied up in haggling over the credentials of the administration's first choice. The navy's special operations forces have not been integrated into the new command—indeed, navy commanders have always viewed special operations as primarily a support function for larger-scale military action. Direct intervention by former Secretary of Defense Frank Carlucci was required to prevent the military services from cutting special-operations-related budgets substantially as part of their effort to trim the FY 1989 budget to meet spending targets. The resistance of senior military leaders to an elevated status for special operations forces speaks eloquently of the priority still accorded planning for a major war in the U.S. defense establishment.

■ GOVERNMENTAL-BUREAUCRATIC FORCES IN PERSPECTIVE

To point out that the big-war focus of U.S. military planning has interfered with the U.S. ability to fight small wars is not to suggest that the United States should fundamentally reorder its military priorities, although some low-intensity warfare experts might wish as much. Now that the prospect of a major war in Europe is shrinking virtually to the point of disappearing, European contingencies will no longer shape U.S. military force planning. Future forces will still, however, be determined on the basis of the most demanding contingencies that might be faced—such as the "mid-intensity" conflict with Iraq. Moreover, the institutional caution of the military in committing forces to low-intensity conflict may be useful to the extent that it helps to avoid future Vietnams or future Lebanons. Bureaucratic checks and balances are often of positive value. For example, the Iran-contra arms sales debacle would not have been possible if normal bureaucratic procedures had been followed.

To list all the bureaucratic limitations on the inclination and ability of the U.S. military to intervene in low-intensity conflict situations, however, is not to say that a resurgence of U.S. military activism is inconceivable. Though Weinberger's conditions on U.S. military involvement in minor conflicts appear restrictive, it also seems that they are being honored largely in the breach. The U.S. decision to escort reflagged Kuwaiti oil tankers in the Persian Gulf in 1987, for example, grew into an open-ended commitment in which the relationship between ends and military means was unclear. And in the wake of the Persian Gulf war, the United States may be taking on expanded responsibility for ensuring stability in the region. Whether Weinberger's conditions would prevent a major commitment of U.S. forces in the future is open to doubt. As former Senator William Fulbright commented, the Weinberger conditions "are so broad and subjective, so amenable to the widest variety of interpretation, that, had they been in place at the time, it is hardly likely they would have posed a serious obstacle to our involvement and escalation in Vietnam."[29] In the end, the decision to use military force is a political one—good choices, therefore, depend on the quality and vision of U.S. leaders.

■ 12

The Structure of the International System

Harry Piotrowski

When World War II came to an end, two "superpowers" emerged triumphant. The Soviet Union had pushed its frontiers, political influence, and military might into the center of Europe and the Far East. The United States, similarly, had advanced its own political, military, and economic power into the same regions. The former Europe-centric international system, which had been dominant since the sixteenth century and whose members had been devastated by war, had been replaced by an emerging bipolar system led by the two superpowers. In the process, military cooperation against Germany and Japan quickly gave way to a political deadlock (notably on the question of Poland's postwar government) and then to a confrontation that in 1947 became military in nature when President Harry S Truman intervened in Greece to suppress the uprising by communist insurgents.

This "turning point in American foreign policy," as Truman called it, rested on two premises. The first premise drew upon the lessons of history that the West had learned in dealing with Adolf Hitler: The aggressive aspirations of all dictators must be thwarted at the earliest moment possible; failure to intervene leads only to a wider conflict. Truman's second premise— that ideological compromise with the USSR was impossible—divided the world into two hostile camps: communism versus capitalism, totalitarianism versus the free world.

Truman's justification for intervention across the globe, however, contained two serious flaws. First, he assumed that Joseph Stalin's foreign policy was a carbon copy of Hitler's, that all dictators were driven by the same expansionist logic. Stalin, Truman explained in his memoirs, was out to conquer the world. But Truman would not appease Stalin; he would, instead, halt all manifestation of communist aggression. Yet Truman applied this lesson to Stalin at a time when Stalin was consolidating his position by withdrawing his troops from a host of countries: Albania, China, Czechoslovakia, Denmark, Iran, North Korea, Norway, and Yugoslavia. Khrushchev later completed what Isaac Deutscher called Stalin's policy of "self-containment" by withdrawing Soviet troops from Austria and Finland.[1]

The second flaw in Truman's argument consisted of his failure to recognize that communist movements often operated independently of Stalin, that the international stage contained actors other than those directed from Moscow and Washington. World War II had accelerated processes independent of Moscow. It had produced a civil war in Greece between the left and the right; in Vietnam, it had set into motion the resistance first against the Japanese and then against the French; it had revived anticolonial movements in Asia and Africa. In much of the world the war had produced a decisive shift to the left, a challenge to the status quo. Revolutionary movements tended to draw on Karl Marx's theory of the historical inevitability of revolutions and Vladimir Lenin's organizational program without, however, subordinating such movements to the will of Moscow. Much of the world was in flux at the time the United States set out to stem what the British premier Harold Macmillan later called "the winds of change."

The result was a foreign policy that treated any and all revolutionary activity as evidence of Stalin's evil machinations, the work of an international communist conspiracy. With such a narrow focus, Washington found it difficult to comprehend that other factors within the international system were at work: resurgent nationalism and anticolonialism, indigenous applications of Marxism-Leninism, communist polycentrism, the proliferation of both conventional and nuclear weapons, the rise of regional powers, and the relative decline of U.S. economic and military power. The international system was changing, but as long as the United States continued to base its foreign policy on Truman's original premises, intervention in the Third World became increasingly counterproductive, difficult, and costly in terms of political capital, money, and blood. An understanding of these trends—especially in the turbulent world of the 1990s—is necessary if policymakers wish to formulate constructive policies for the emerging post–Cold War era.

■ BIPOLAR VISION
CONFRONTS NATIONALISM

Truman's division of the world into two camps rested on the assumption that nations all too readily were willing to subordinate their interests to the grand ideal of supranationalism. But the proposition that nations were either part of the free world or of the communist bloc ignored the elemental force of nationalism. World War II had revealed European vulnerability, particularly in Asia, when the Japanese appeared, if only for a brief time, as liberators and drove out the Americans, British, Dutch, and French.

When the French sought to reassert themselves in Vietnam, they faced an organized resistance. The Vietminh leadership consisted of communists, but their leader Ho Chi Minh explained that it had been "patriotism not Communism that originally inspired me." "The reason for my joining the

French Socialist Party," Ho wrote, was that it expressed sympathy for "the struggle of oppressed people. But I understood [at the time] neither what was a party, a trade-union, nor what was Socialism or Communism."[2] Ho instead operated in the context of an ancient Vietnamese revolutionary tradition.[3] When the French, and later the Americans, focused on the communist content of the Vietnamese revolution, they ignored nationalism, the more potent element. In Vietnam, Ho grafted the national liberation movement onto communism, which gave him a vision of the future, the certainty of an historic process that promised victory, and an organizational blueprint.

During the early 1960s, the Vietnamese Buddhist monk Thich Nhat Hanh tried, without much success, to explain to U.S. readers that it was first and foremost Vietnamese nationalism that gave the National Liberation Front (NLF) its great popular support.[4] Communist ideology, the focus of U.S. obsession, scarcely played a role in motivating the resistance. The U.S. reporter, John Mecklin, wrote of a sixty-six-year-old headman of a village the communist-led Vietminh had controlled for thirteen years. This headman had never heard of the United States, the USSR, or even France. But he knew of "the big bird that spit fire [napalm] from the sky."[5] The Austrian reporter Bruno Knoebl described the interrogation of an NLF soldier who had no understanding of communism and could not understand the questions, let alone answer them. Of Karl Marx he knew nothing; but at the mention of Ho Chi Minh's name his face lit up. He recognized the name of the man who had driven out the French. Knoebl cited a U.S. official who explained that many prisoners "first learn what Communism really is from us during interrogation, in prison camps, and in reeducation courses."[6]

Indeed, U.S. involvement in the Vietnam War demonstrates the ignorance of U.S. officials concerning the potent force of nationalism and their inability to accommodate themselves to alien Third World cultures. U.S. officials envisioned the unfolding of a U.S. myth, the carrying forth of its own revolutionary heritage into the frontiers of emerging nations in the expectation that a distinctly American story would unfold. Instead, the United States ran head on into the ferocity of the Vietnamese revolutionary tradition.[7] Cold War rhetoric and propaganda repeatedly masked the reality in that country. The U.S. media, notably Henry Luce's *Time* and *Life*, heaped voluminous praise on the dictator Ngo Dinh Diem, referring to him as the "Churchill of Southeast Asia,"[8] ignoring the fact that he had just received 605,025 votes from 450,000 registered voters in Saigon[9] and was consolidating his dictatorship.

Frances FitzGerald was the first U.S. journalist to make a serious effort to put the revolution in South Vietnam into the context of Vietnamese history. She divided her book into two equal parts, the first dealing with the Vietnamese themselves, their history, revolutionary tradition, and culture. In her analysis of the NLF, she focused on the indigenous aspects of that organization, rather than treating it as something created and manipulated from the outside. Only in the second half of the book did she turn to the United States and its creation, the Saigon government.[10] As it was, her book appeared only in 1972, when domestic political considerations had already produced an irrevocable commitment to withdrawal.

In Algeria, a process of nationalist resistance similar to that in Vietnam took place. The French colonialists spoke of assimilating the Arabs into French society and culture without, however, offering them the opportunity to do so. More important, few Arabs sought to become French. The Arab rebellion, which manifested in the May Day and the V-E Day parades of 1945, underscored the warning by the Muslim scholar Abdelhamid Ben Badis that "the Algerian people are not French, do not wish to be and could not be even if they did wish."[11] When the French replied that Algeria was an integral part of France (a province no less), they were merely deluding themselves. The French subsequently killed 1 million Algerians between 1954 and 1962, yet they were unable to suppress the rebellion.

The immediate postwar years saw the success of several anticolonial, nationalist movements: in China, in 1949, under the communist Mao Zedong; in the Dutch East Indies, in 1949, under Achmed Sukarno; during 1947–1948, the British quit Burma, Ceylon, and India; the French abandoned Indochina in 1954. In Africa, the process of decolonization proceeded a bit slower. In the Gold Coast (today's Ghana), Kwame Nkrumah organized an effective political campaign while in a British prison, and in 1957 Ghana became the first African colony to gain its independence. The year 1960 saw a large number of African states follow suit, with Kenya and Tanzania, the former in a bloody uprising, gaining their independence in 1963. The Portuguese, the first Europeans to colonize Africa, were the last to leave (not counting the Dutch in South Africa), after they were beaten and finally withdrew from Angola and Mozambique in 1975.

Nationalist pressures and Washington's apparent inability to accommodate its role in a changing international system continued well into the 1970s and 1980s. During the three decades immediately preceding the Iranian revolution, the United States repeatedly underestimated the power of the religious mullahs, believing until the very end that the pro-U.S. Shah Mohammad Reza Pahlavi could ride out the storm. As is more fully discussed in Chapter 17, there was no appreciable understanding in Washington of the religious revival taking place and its links to fervent nationalism. The administration of Jimmy Carter was taken by surprise by the massive anti-U.S. demonstrations after it granted the shah permission to enter the United States for treatment of cancer. Many Iranians had not forgotten that in 1953 the CIA had returned the shah from his first journey into exile, and they now feared a repetition of history. The result was the hostage crisis from which the Carter administration never recovered.

In the Middle East, the United States has long been involved as a champion of Israel. This has produced a tendency to ignore the historical claims of the Arabs (see Chapter 20). The Palestinians became invisible, marginal people without a history and who, at best, played only a negative role as they stood in the path of the reconstitution of the historic state of Israel. It was only after the Palestinians began to take matters into their own hands, when they began to use terror to publicize their cause, culminating in the massive uprisings in the Israeli-controlled West Bank and Gaza Strip beginning in late 1987, that the United States began to take notice of Palestinian nationalism. As is discussed in Chapter 14, the United States similarly has been reluctant to embrace and recognize the legitimacy of black nationalist movements in South Africa.

Third World nationalism has repeatedly asserted itself since 1945. The Western response to it has been either to combat it—particularly when it was linked to communism—or to preempt it, to weld it to ideas of liberal capitalism with a resultant continued dependency on the West. But the revolutionary movements demanded a complete break with the Western heritage, its colonial control, economic exploitation, and racism. They sought instead the reconstitution of a national identity and the radical reconstitution of society; in short, a distinct break with the past tied to a view of the future. Revolutionary communism—and later militant Islam—offered such a solution to colonial dependency and humiliation.

■ MONOLITHIC COMMUNISM OR POLYCENTRISM?

A large number of Third World revolutionary movements were officially communist, but they were not necessarily controlled from Moscow—despite the rhetoric of "international communist solidarity." A national brand of communism is nothing new. Stalin always understood that among communist states, national interests would always predominate. From the outset, he was interested in developing the strength of his own state and relegating the interests of other communist parties to those of the Soviet Union. In 1948, a scant three years after the establishment of communist states other than the Soviet Union, the split between Stalin and the Yugoslav communist Joseph Tito took place over the elemental question of whose interests Tito should serve, those of the Soviet Union or those of Yugoslavia. The Italian communist Palmiro Togliatti later spoke of "polycentrism," of the existence of many communist centers. Polycentrism, however, is a euphemism for no center at all.

When U.S. officials took the view that there existed a monolithic communist bloc (that is, that communist movements were acting on Moscow's behest), they never properly understood that they would have had a relatively easy time neutralizing such a bloc if it had existed. When, during the 1930s, Stalin demanded and received absolute subordination to his authority from foreign communist parties, he also dealt them a mortal blow. These parties were now seen as agents of another power, brutal and uncivilized, more interested in defending the interests of the schemers in the Kremlin than those of their own working classes. The damage Stalin inflicted on these parties, however, has never been properly appreciated in the West.

Third World nationalist and communist movements have never suffered from this handicap. For one, they were always primarily nationalist—namely, anticolonialist—and only secondarily communist. Moreover, they had relatively little contact with Moscow. The Chinese communist revolution was on its own after 1927, after Stalin had told the communists to cooperate with the Nationalists led by Jiang Kaishek, who then turned on them. When the U.S. journalist Edgar Snow established contact with Mao Zedong in the late 1930s, Mao went to pains to explain his independence of Moscow. During World War II, U.S. agents of the OSS were unanimous in confirming this state of affairs. In Vietnam, Stalin played no role; only in 1952 did he even acknowledge the revolution's existence.

Yet, even when U.S. officials showed a measure of understanding and sympathy for the indigenous roots of revolution and upheaval, they all too often ran afoul of the official line, and their positions became untenable. During the McCarthy era, for example, a number of old China hands were accused of treason by the "China lobby," as attempts were made to place blame for "losing China" to communism. In 1949, Truman's State Department issued its famous White Paper on China—meant to stop criticism by the China lobby—to explain that it had done everything possible to save China from communism, that it had not lost China but that Jiang Kaishek had lost the support of his people. Truman's secretary of state, Dean Acheson, who had thought that the charges "flowed from ignorance of the facts" and believed "that the human mind could be moved by facts and reason,"[12] found out that facts and reason were irrelevant. The China lobby established a new set of facts: The Christian Jiang and his "democratic" government had been betrayed in Washington,[13] and woe to the administration that made another such mistake and suggested that a communist revolution enjoyed a measure of popular support.

The White Paper proved to be a disaster for the State Department. The critics reaffirmed the deeply ingrained view that what had transpired in China had not been a Chinese affair but had been orchestrated behind the walls of the Kremlin. They prevented an independent analysis of a world that was moving away from the official bipolar model toward a more multipolar international system (one with several political and military powers of varying strength). Not the least, they prevented a scholarly and independent analysis of events unfolding in Vietnam during the 1950s. The Democrats themselves quickly fell into line and began to repeat the arguments of the critics of the White Paper. Ignorance became an officially mandated policy, and the Truman administration made no use of individuals of differing views. George F. Kennan, who in 1947 had made his reputation by his analysis of Soviet behavior, was shortly eased out of the State Department.

After Stalin's death in 1953, the Communist Party of the Soviet Union (CPSU), at its 20th Congress in February 1956, sanctioned the legitimacy of Titoism when it acknowledged each party's right to an independent path to communism. Theoretically, polycentrism should have worked to the advantage of the United States, as it pointed to a fragmented communist camp. Instead, the United States now faced powerful independent nationalist movements whose communist content proved to be no handicap in organizing rebellions.

When the CPSU acknowledged the reality of a polycentric communist world, it did so only reluctantly and out of necessity. Between June 1953 (the uprisings in East Germany) and December 1979 (the Soviet invasion of Afghanistan), a major aim of Soviet foreign policy was to keep in power the fraternal communist parties along Soviet borders. In February 1956, at its 20th Congress, the CPSU recognized Yugoslavia's right to pursue its own road, and later that year, in October, it granted the Polish Communist party a measure of autonomy. But when the Communist party of Hungary gave up its leading political role and declared free elections and the country's neutrality (i.e., took it out of the Soviet Union's orbit), Moscow brought Hungary forcefully back into its military alliance, the Warsaw Pact. And when in 1968 the Communist party of Czechoslovakia appeared to have abandoned its political power, Leonid Brezhnev sent the Soviet armed forces to restore the party to its previous position. The result was the Brezhnev Doctrine by which the Soviet Union held that the Elbe River in the center of Europe had become its immutable Western defensive perimeter and that it had the right to intervene in the internal affairs of communist nations to perpetuate the status quo.

Nationalism, however, continued to pose a threat to the East European communist parties. In the eyes of the populations, the parties continued to be creations of a foreign power that—in the cases of Poland, Hungary, East Germany, and Romania—had long been a historical enemy. But as long as the Brezhnev Doctrine remained in force, the existence of "fraternal" communist parties in Eastern Europe remained assured.

The advent to power of Mikhail Gorbachev produced "new thinking" in Moscow. It led eventually to Gorbachev's announcement in November 1987 that the countries of Eastern Europe were free to determine their destinies without Soviet interference. It marked the beginning of the end of the Brezhnev Doctrine. When Gorbachev insisted that the East European communist parties must either learn from life or disappear, their days were numbered. Many in the West were skeptical of Gorbachev's pronouncements, finding it difficult to believe that the Soviet Union would not intervene to save its East European clients. The West German foreign minister, Hans-

Dietrich Genscher, however, thought that Gorbachev should be taken at his word.

The first test came in Poland where the head of the Polish Communist party, Wojciech Jaruzelski, the man who in 1981 had arrested the leaders of Solidarity, the anticommunist labor union, took a cautious step to bring Solidarity back into public life. The party and Solidarity worked out a power-sharing formula that led to free elections and ultimately to the demise of the Communist party. The contrast between Brezhnev and Gorbachev could not have been greater. In 1981, Brezhnev had made it abundantly clear that Solidarity could not conduct a popular referendum to replace the Communist party as the country's ruling body. But after Tadeusz Mazowiecki was elected Poland's prime minister in August 1989—the first noncommunist leader of Eastern Europe since shortly after World War II—Gorbachev welcomed this radical development. In Hungary, too, the Communist party acknowledged that it could no longer count on Moscow to interfere on its behalf and accepted the principle of free elections in which (in March and April 1990) it won 8 percent of the seats in parliament.

At first it appeared that the events in Poland and Hungary might be isolated instances taking place in countries in which the Communist parties had shown an occasional penchant for political experimentation. There was still the unresolved case of the hard-liners in power in East Germany, Czechoslovakia, Bulgaria, and Romania.

The government of East Germany understood its dilemma all too well. Shortly after Stalin died in March 1953, demonstrations in several cities took place. The East German authorities proved incapable of quelling the disturbances, and Soviet troops eventually had to move in. In sheer numbers, it was a minor affair, but it left an indelible imprint on the mentality of the East German leadership, which became increasingly fearful of its own population.

As late as October 1989, the East German communists still appeared to be in full control. Their dogmatic leader, Erich Honecker, had declared that he saw no need to follow the reformist example of Gorbachev. Just because his neighbor was putting up new wallpaper, he declared, was no reason to do the same. He refused to accept that the "new thinking" in Moscow meant the withdrawal from the Eastern rooms of what Gorbachev had called "our common European home." Gorbachev apparently warned the East German leadership against the use of force to counter mounting demonstrations. The party, no longer able to use force, sought to bring about a reconciliation with its population. But it was too little and too late. The new leader of the party, Egon Krenz, opened the Berlin Wall at a time when a large number of East Germans were already heading for West Germany through Hungary and Czechoslovakia. This dramatic breach of the wall, the supreme symbol of the postwar division of Europe, immediately put the question of German unification on the agenda. The discredited Communist party caved in to popular pressure, and less than a year later, by October 1990, East Germany ceased to exist. Immediately after Krenz opened the Berlin Wall, street demonstrations forced the Communist parties in Czechoslovakia, Bulgaria, and even Romania—where Nicolae Ceauşescu appeared to be solidly entrenched in power—to give up their political monopolies.

The central feature of Gorbachev's foreign policy was the elimination of the military confrontation in the heart of Europe. On December 7, 1988, he announced at the UN the unilateral and unconditional reduction of the Soviet Union's offensive military capability in Eastern Europe, notably its assault troops and their mobile bridges for crossing rivers. A year later, after the demise of Moscow's clients in Eastern Europe, the question of the withdrawal of Soviet troops took front and center. Gorbachev could not speak of a "common European home" while continuing to occupy its Eastern rooms. Czechoslovakia and Hungary, in particular, pressed the issue, which made the Warsaw Pact superfluous once the last Soviet troops left these countries. When Germany was formally unified on October 3, 1990, the Soviets (as well as the Western powers) ended the Allied control of Berlin. The process of Moscow's withdrawal from Eastern Europe was under way, to be completed by the final removal of Soviet troops from German soil by the end of 1994. The Cold War was for all intents and purposes over when the Warsaw Pact formally dissolved in 1991. The breakup of the Moscow-led political and military camp became a fait accompli, and the bipolar postwar world had become a historical relic.

The fragmentation of the communist world was but one side of the coin. The Western camp witnessed a similar process. For one, Western hegemony came to an end in many parts of the world where a Third World political movement was emerging. Leaders of newly independent nations, notably Jawaharlal Nehru of India and Gamal Abdel Nasser of Egypt, joined by Tito, took a third, neutral road and refused to become pawns in the great game of ideological conflict between Moscow and Washington. The Brahmin Hindu Nehru, the Muslim Arab Nasser, and the atheist communist Tito insisted on the superpowers' recognition of their national independence and dignity. They represented the bulk of the world's population as a counterweight to the imperial ambitions of politicians in Moscow and Washington.

Second, since the end of World War II, the Western European nations had experienced their own movement toward polycentrism. In the 1960s, Charles de Gaulle insisted that France carve out a diplomatic and military posture independent of Washington. France remained a member of NATO but decided to rely first and foremost on its own independent nuclear deterrent, the *force de frappe*. Since the 1960s, the partners of the United States have shown an increased tendency toward independence. Over the years, they have questioned the wisdom of a number of U.S. policies. Britain and France, for example, established diplomatic relations with Beijing at a time when U.S. politicians, such as Richard Nixon, were feverishly opposed to it. None of the NATO members drew the same dire conclusion from the Vietnamese insurrection (that is, that nations would fall like dominoes throughout Southeast Asia) as did the policymakers in Washington. When in April 1986, President Reagan sought to punish Libya's Muammar Qaddafi, France and Spain, both members of NATO, refused to cooperate. U.S. F-111 tactical fighter bombers stationed in Britain were forced to take a circuitous route around the Iberian peninsula that required midair refueling.[14] Finally, U.S. attempts to overthrow the Sandinista government in Nicaragua and the reluctance of Washington to deal effectively with the Palestinian question in the Middle East have not been supported by the majority of Washington's NATO allies.

■ THE RISE OF REGIONAL POWERS AND A MULTIPOLAR WORLD

The ferment in the international arena after 1945 produced several regional powers and continues to erode the bipolar structure World War II had created. The earliest and best example is the People's Republic of China. Shortly after its successful revolution in 1949, the PRC held the United States to a bloody draw in Korea when the United States sought to unite all of Korea under the aegis of the anticommunist Syngman Rhee. Mao Zedong gave notice that the PRC would not permit U.S. hegemony (nor that of the USSR, as it later turned out) along its borders. U.S. policymakers initially scoffed at the notion of Chinese military intervention against U.S. firepower only to suffer a rude awakening when the People's Liberation Army (PLA) drove U.S. forces back into South Korea. The PRC became the protector of North Korea and a regional force to be reckoned with. Subsequent talk in Washington of unleashing the Nationalist Jiang Kaishek of Taiwan proved to be at best political hot air, at worst dangerous nonsense. The Korean War showed that neither the United States nor Jiang could solve the problem of Red China.

More important, Mao cast China's long shadow into Vietnam. President Lyndon B. Johnson and his advisers repeatedly blamed Mao for the war in Vietnam, but the U.S. Joint Chiefs of Staff took seriously Mao's threats, as they had not during the Korean War, to intervene once the United States crossed the 17th parallel into North Vietnam. In the wake of the 1968 Tet offensive by the NLF and the North Vietnamese, it became clear that the United States did not have sufficient troops to win in Vietnam, let alone to take on the giant to the north with its unlimited human resources. Too many U.S. soldiers were already dying without directly taking on the PLA. The United States had reached a dead end in Vietnam.

Among earlier attempts to establish a regional presence, Egypt's Gamal Abdel Nasser sought to lead the Arab world from the beginning of the 1950s until his death in 1970. In short order, he freed himself from Western control, accepted Soviet military and economic aid, denied French and British control over the Suez Canal, and twice took the lead in failed wars to destroy the state of Israel. Nasser was unable to unite the fractious Arab world, but he gave notice that nations need not remain pawns in the great bipolar power struggle between East and West.

Iran emerged as a regional power in 1979. The shah had always dreamed of reconstituting the glories of ancient Persia, but in the arena of foreign affairs he proved to be quite cautious. He leaned toward the West, bought weapons largely from the United States, but was careful to maintain good relations with the USSR, which looked the other way as he chased down the Marxist Tudeh party. It was the shah's successor, however, the Ayatollah Ruhollah Khomeini, who sought to spread his revolution's influence far beyond Iran's borders. Khomeini, as the titular head of the Shia wing of Islam, began to attract followers throughout the Middle East. The Shias are, for the most part, the politically and economically dispossessed, who share a grievance against the status quo. They find their inspiration in the Prophet Mohammed's revolutionary activity in Mecca on behalf of the downtrodden. Their challenges to entrenched political power (Islamic or otherwise) have elevated political disobedience to a religious duty. They find comfort in Allah's will "to favor those who were oppressed . . . and give them power in the land."[15] When the United States intervened in the Lebanese civil war in 1983 on the side of the Maronite Christians, the U.S. Marines became the target of the full fury of a Shia suicide mission. Reagan quickly realized the limits of U.S. intervention, declared the mission a success, and then pulled out.

Khomeini's influence in the Middle East before his death was limited for the same reasons that have stayed the hand of the United States in other parts of the world—namely, the overbearing power of nationalism. Apart from the Shias in Iran, nearly all Shias in the Middle East are Arabs, and Khomeini proved incapable of bridging the ancient breach between Persians and Arabs. After Saddam Hussein of Iraq launched his invasion of Iran in 1980, Khomeini appealed to Iraq's majority Shia population, which, however, did not rally to his cause. They remained, their Shia affiliation notwithstanding, first and foremost Arabs. Still, Khomeini's revolution remained a force to be reckoned with. Despite U.S. military might, Iran humiliated the "Great Satan" during the hostage crisis of 1979–1981; its influence spread to Lebanon; it supported the mujahedin in Afghanistan who were fighting the lesser Satan, the officially atheistic Soviet state; and it appealed to the resurrection of Islam in an open challenge to the Western presence in the Middle East.

In Latin America, several nations have sought to play regional roles. The first was Fidel Castro's Cuba, which declared its economic and political independence from the United States in 1959. The United States initially responded with economic pressure by denying Castro the lucrative U.S.

market and, when that did not prevent Castro from turning to the Soviet Union, by organizing the ill-fated attempt to invade Cuba at the Bay of Pigs in April 1961. In the summer of 1962, Adlai Stevenson, the U.S. envoy to the United Nations, categorically rejected any acceptance of a communist government in the Western Hemisphere. But the Cuban missile crisis of October 1962 was resolved only after the United States acknowledged the sovereignty of Cuba and that the Monroe Doctrine (by which it reserved the unilateral right of intervention in Latin America) no longer applied to that nation. At first Cuba's influence remained restricted to the ideological sphere, as it was the first Latin American nation to have successfully repudiated its unequal relationship with the Colossus of the North. But in 1965, Ché Guevara, Castro's former comrade-in-arms in the struggle against Fulgencio Batista, launched his unsuccessful attempt to rouse the poverty-stricken peasants of Bolivia. And in 1975, Castro successfully intervened, with Soviet help, in the Angolan civil war by providing 50,000 troops to sustain that nation's Marxist government against rebel forces backed by the strange coalition of the PRC, South Africa, and the United States.

Mexico, despite its economic and political difficulties, has also sought to play a larger role to stay Washington's hand in Central America. The Reagan administration was stymied by a Central American consensus against U.S. intervention, despite Washington's persistent argument that the Sandinistas posed a common danger to the entire region. The last thing even the conservative government of Mexico wanted was to give the United States another opportunity to implement its self-appointed right to intervene. In many parts of Central America—Cuba, the Dominican Republic, Guatemala, Mexico, Nicaragua, Panama—the memory of U.S. intervention has been kept alive in histories, films, museums, and popular folklore. The leaders of these nations showed little desire to be seen as supporters of Yankee imperialism.

The Latin American nations understand that individually there is little they can do to oppose the United States but that there is power in unity. The Contadora Group (Colombia, Mexico, Panama, and Venezuela) called in 1983 for the withdrawal of all foreign advisers from Central America—U.S., Soviet, and Cuban—in short, for the political neutralization of the region. The president of Costa Rica, Oscar Arias, later proposed a similar solution, which earned him the prestigious Nobel Peace Prize in 1987. These proposals left the United States and its creation, the contras, diplomatically isolated. U.S. intervention in Nicaragua, à la Vietnam, would have to be in direct contravention of the wishes of Latin American nations, particularly after Cuba, Nicaragua, and the Soviet Union accepted Arias's plan.

In November 1987, the presidents of the Group of Eight—Argentina, Brazil, Colombia, Mexico, Peru, Panama, Uruguay, and Venezuela—met for the first time independently of the United States. In June 1988, seven of their foreign ministers met in Oaxaca, Mexico, where they issued a communiqué rejecting the frequent U.S. criticism of Latin America. Instead, they took the United States to task for doing little about the drug trade at home and rejected the notion that Latin America was solely responsible for the U.S. drug problem. They criticized the heavy-handed U.S. approach toward Nicaragua and Panama, while at the same time expressing little sympathy for Panamanian dictator Manuel Noriega (whose representative was not invited) and the Sandinista regime of Nicaragua. In the communiqué, they also complained about Latin America's economic dependence on the United States and urged, instead, closer economic ties with the Western European Community and Southeast Asia.[16]

Vietnam has become another regional power. It did so by virtue of its victory over the United States, the willing support of the Soviet Union, the inheritance of massive U.S.-weapons supplies, its political control of Laos, and its occupation of Cambodia. In 1979, Vietnam beat back the PLA when Beijing attempted to teach it a lesson in response to Vietnam's invasion of Cambodia in 1978. Beijing had no more luck than the United States, as Southeast Asia, a region the United States had once deemed vital to its security, remained in control of a communist regime loyal to the Soviet Union.

The exercise of U.S. political, military, and economic power in the Third World has become an increasingly difficult task. China has long been outside the U.S. sphere of influence, and its leadership bristled in the 1980s at the thought of the United States playing the "China hand" against the Soviet Union. In Southeast Asia, the United States has played an extremely limited role since 1975, with the exception of diplomatic support of the murderous Pol Pot regime in Kampuchea. Its pervasive influence in Iran came to an end in 1979. Similarly, the Nicaraguan revolution served notice that U.S. influence must come to an end now that the U.S.-organized and -financed election of Violeta Chamorro has brought the United States back in, but within limits. The February 1990 election, in which the National Opposition Union, a coalition of thirteen anti-Sandinista parties, won fifty-two of the National Assembly seats, was an attempt to reestablish U.S. influence in Managua. The Sandinistas, however, remained the single strongest party and in control of the army.

The trend toward regionalism has also made it increasingly difficult for the United States to control its clients. Israel has long rejected U.S. advice on how to deal with the West Bank and, in order to free itself of overbearing dependence on the United States, has developed not only its own nuclear arsenal but, in September 1988, launched its first reconnaissance satellite. West Germany, the post–World War II creation of the United States, has long ceased to be a ward of its creator. In the wake of the fatalities at the U.S.-sponsored air show in Ramstein in 1988, U.S. authorities were reminded that such displays—and the dangerous training exercises—could continue only at the pleasure of the host. The United States, after all, is but one member of NATO, an alliance of sovereign nations.

The sudden breakup of the Soviet Union's satellite empire had an additional impact on NATO. Its cement, the communality of interests in the face of the Soviet threat, began to weaken. The U.S. military umbrella was becoming superfluous. Moreover, Western Europe and Japan had emerged by the late 1980s as economic powers with wills of their own.

The events after 1989 underscored the fact that one of the post–World War II superpowers had dropped out of the race for preeminence. One superpower remained along with a host of secondary powers—such as Germany, Japan, the PRC, and Russia as the center of the constellation of states composing the former Soviet Union. This state of affairs suggested that the lesser powers would recognize a new unipolar reality, "the most striking feature of the post–Cold War world."[17] Yet the winding down of the Cold War has accelerated, rather than retarded, the trend toward a multilateral world because the same urgency for a country to align itself with a superpower no longer exists. That is particularly the case with Western Europe.

In March 1985, the twelve-member European Community (EC) announced its goal of a single unified economic market by the end of 1992. Completion of this economic integration will make the EC, with its population of 345 million, the world's most powerful economic market, outstripping the combined gross national product of the United States and Canada, which—in response to Western European economic integration—created their own free-trade zone in 1989. The new EC serves two main purposes: to create a more efficient economic system and to offer its members protection against outside competition, such as the United States and Japan. In addition, the EC is increasingly taking defense into its own hands with the creation of the Western European Union (WEU). The question is whether the WEU should supplement NATO or replace it.

The late 1980s were marked by a renewed self-confidence among West Europeans, particularly among the Germans, whose large population and economic power have made their country the leader among the nations of the EC.[18] The predicted demise of Western Europe, squeezed between the United States and the Soviet Union, became a thing of the past; Europe resembled no longer the "embers of a burned-out civilization."[19] The German government, which traditionally had deferred to the United States, began to carve out its own foreign policy initiatives within the context of the EC. It was but an inevitable reflection of the new reality of a multilateral world.

In the wake of the failed coup in Moscow in August 1991, the German government, in contrast to the Bush administration, wasted little time in extending diplomatic recognition to the Baltic states of Estonia, Latvia, and Lithuania. The move put Germany in the unusual posture of acting before Washington or any of its other European allies. At the same time, Germany called a meeting to renegotiate the status of NATO troops on its soil. The German government raised a point much discussed in West Germany over the past years, namely the extraterritorial status of foreign—notably British and U.S.—troops. Annual military exercises that churned up the countryside and low-level NATO aircraft training missions had all too frequently led to crashes taking a toll of civilian lives. In the eyes of the Germans, the time had come to scrap the extraterritorial concessions granted to foreign military forces at the outset of the Cold War. The time had come for Germany to reassert its full sovereignty.

It was Germany and the EC that sought to resolve the war of secession between Croatia and Serbia at a conference at The Hague, with Germany threatening to go it alone and recognize the independence of Croatia—a threat that became a reality in December 1991. And it was Germany's Chancellor Helmut Kohl who took the lead among Western leaders in urging massive economic aid to an unstable Soviet Union (and, as of 1992, famine-threatened Russia), prodding a reluctant Japan and United States into action.

In the late 1940s, the United States had been able to unite parts of the world in its effort to meet the Soviet threat. Two factors made the unquestioned U.S. role possible: (1) It was the only nation capable of meeting a potential Soviet military challenge, and (2) it had the financial clout to organize the postwar structure of the capitalist camp. But by the early 1990s, the Soviet threat and the preponderant economic power of the United States were no longer there. New financial centers—notably Tokyo and Frankfurt—have come into existence. Moreover, domestic pressure demands that the United States put its own house in order, especially its economic and educational infrastructure. It was Germany that since 1989 has provided the massive sum of over $50 billion to Eastern Europe to maintain stability there.[20] The Bush administration's reluctance to provide assistance to Russia and the other now-independent republics of the former Soviet Union masks the cold reality that the United States simply does not have the money to do so. A new world order will demand from the U.S. leadership the recognition of a complex and frequently messy multilateral world.

■ RELATIVE DECLINE OF U.S. POWER

The flip side of the rise of regional powers has been the relative decline of the economic and military power of the United States vis-à-vis the rest of the world. Four aspects of this relative decline—nuclear proliferation, spread of conventional weapons, alternative sources of external support, and rising economic costs of overseas commitments—pose additional constraints on the ability of the United States to bring its economic and military might to bear in the Third World.

Following the dismantling of U.S. conventional forces at the end of World War II, the United States was left in Europe with a nuclear deterrent but without enough troops to engage the Soviet Union in a land war. Although possessing the means to destroy the Soviet Union, the United States lacked the means to occupy that vast land and impose its political will.

If war, as Karl von Clausewitz said, is the continuation of politics and diplomacy by other means, nuclear weapons, although capable of destroying the enemy, cannot resolve the political issues. Moreover, in 1949 the Soviet Union broke the West's nuclear monopoly and by 1955 had built the long-range bombers that gave it the means to annihilate the United States. As early as 1950, during the Korean War, President Truman understood the risk of using nuclear weapons to obtain his political aim—the unification of Korea under U.S. auspices. A nuclear attack on the PRC could have put into motion the Soviet war machine, which at the time had the capability of overrunning Western Europe and delivering nuclear weapons against U.S. allies' installations in Europe and Asia.

During the Cuban missile crisis in 1962, the United States possessed a large advantage in nuclear warheads. But the crisis was resolved only after the United States granted the Soviet Union what it had been unwilling to concede earlier. It removed permanently its nuclear missiles from Turkey and offered a public pledge to respect the sovereignty of communist Cuba. The extraordinary nuclear power of the United States proved to be useless in resolving the political question of Cuba. In short order, the United States went from a rejection of diplomacy (namely, its refusal to recognize the Cuban revolution) to a consideration of military intervention (which would have meant war with the Soviet Union) to a diplomatic compromise (which removed the Soviet missiles from Cuba and those of the United States from Turkey and also eliminated the direct U.S. threat to Cuba). The Cuban missile crisis pointed to Khrushchev's proclivity toward "hare-brained schemes" (as his own party later charged), but it also underscored the limits of the U.S. ability to pursue the interventionist impulse to its logical and deadly conclusion in a world marked by increasing nuclear proliferation.

The missile crisis was resolved by the superpowers without Castro, who to his chagrin found out that he did not figure in the equation. In the 1990s, however, the world stands on the threshold of a nuclear proliferation whereby smaller nations will soon acquire nuclear capabilities. It is generally assumed that Israel and South Africa already have nuclear weapons. Both Iraq—long a vocal foe of Israel—and Pakistan—since its creation in 1947, on a war footing with India (a nuclear power since 1974)—seek to build the first "Islamic" bomb. The long slumbering territorial disputes among the lesser powers have the potential of escalating into nuclear confrontations the great powers will be unable to control.

The world also has become increasingly awash in conventional weapons.

Wars have traditionally ended with the belligerents drained of their capacity to continue the war. The productivity of the industrial nations, however, has put an end to this pattern. At the end of World War II, Germany and the Allies produced more war materiel than at the outset of the war. By the end of the conflict in Indochina, the NLF and the North Vietnamese army possessed a much greater store of weapons than at the beginning. Their chief supplier was the Soviet Union, but they also used Chinese and captured U.S. weapons.

One of the most notable trends of the post–World War II period is the increasing share of weapons acquisition by Third World countries and the growing proliferation of weapons producers. Whereas the chief arms exporters traditionally have been the United States, the Soviet Union, France, Britain, West Germany, and Italy, there has been a steady growth of second-tier producers in the Third World—most notably Brazil, the PRC, Egypt, India, Israel, Singapore, North Korea, and South Korea.[21]

According to Michael T. Klare, this has resulted in two major developments: First, Third World recipients have been able to diversify their sources of arms and subsequently weaken strong patron-client relationships with either of the two superpowers. "In many cases," Klare noted, "this has resulted in a greater degree of political autonomy on the part of Third World countries—often at the expense of the two superpowers, which have suffered dramatic political reversals in recent years." Second, diversification "has also made it easier for belligerents to obtain the arms and equipment needed to sustain high levels of combat—even in the face of an embargo imposed by the major suppliers." Klare concluded that this "is perhaps the outstanding lesson of the Iran-Iraq conflict, which has continued for seven grueling years despite the nominal efforts of both superpowers to limit arms transfers to the protagonists."[22] In a case of guerrilla warfare, the Algerian National Liberation Front received its arms mainly from West Germany but also from Argentina, Belgium, Czechoslovakia, Egypt, Ghana, Lebanon, Morocco, and the PRC.[23] With occasional exceptions, arms producers are willing to sell to anyone. The determinant is the bottom line of the ledger sheet.

The notable trend of U.S. decline is demonstrated by these alternative sources of military and economic support that both Third World governments and guerrilla movements can count on in the post–World War II period. When the United States intervened in Greece, it did so on the assumption that the world was organized around two poles. Had that in fact been the case, the United States would have had a much more difficult time in Greece. The world's communists would have stood solidly behind their comrades to deny a victory to the United States, the bastion of counterrevolutionary capitalism. But Stalin refused to enter the contest for Greece. He wrote off Greece in his meeting with the British Prime Minister Winston Churchill in October 1944; it now belonged to the Western sphere. Stalin wanted no part of the Greek communist revolution; he wanted it instead to "fold up . . . as quickly as possible," as he feared the projection of U.S. naval power into the eastern Mediterranean.[24] Moreover, Tito continued to support the Greek communists until his break with Stalin in 1948; then he too turned his back on the Greek communists, shut down the Yugoslav-Greek border, and denied them a place of refuge. In Greece, Truman had a free hand.

In short, between 1947 and 1955, the United States intervened in areas where the Soviet Union scarcely played a role. Stalin dug in behind his iron curtain and did not become involved in adventurous escapades abroad. After Stalin's death in March 1953, the CIA acknowledged that Stalin "did not allow his ambitions to lead him to reckless courses of action in his foreign policy." The CIA warned, however, that his successor might not be as cautious.[25] In 1955, Khrushchev overcame the opposition of the Stalinists, led by Foreign Minister Viacheslav Molotov, and began to commit the Soviet Union to a role outside Stalin's satellite empire. He would not tolerate Washington's policy of containment, which, he charged, was meant to encircle and strangle the Soviet Union. The first recipient of Soviet weapons and military advisers was Egypt's Nasser. The list of Soviet clients quickly grew: Angola, Cuba, Ethiopia, India, Indonesia, Iraq, Libya, Mozambique, Nicaragua, Peru, Syria. U.S. intervention henceforth would mean facing opponents who could count on a steady flow of weapons.[26] Toward the end of the 1980s, the Soviet Union under Gorbachev sharply curtailed its support of revolutionary movements, but continued to sell its weapons abroad for hard currency.

Finally, the relative decline of U.S. power has an economic side. In the thirty years between 1950 and 1980, the U.S. share of the world's GNP declined from approximately 40 percent to 20 percent. Between 1960 and 1980, U.S. military expenditures in relationship to the rest of the world dropped from 51 to 28 percent.[27] This economic slide has continued. The self-imposed burden of empire has become increasingly expensive. Allies often have to be bought at a high price. The Camp David agreement between Israel and Egypt was largely purchased with U.S. money. In 1992, for example, U.S. aid to these two countries totaled approximately $5.3 billion.

The presidents of the 1970s—Richard Nixon, Gerald Ford, and Jimmy Carter—adjusted their foreign policies in response to the relative decline of U.S. power. Nixon grudgingly ended the U.S. involvement in Vietnam and made peace with the PRC, in full contradiction of the original premise of U.S. involvement—namely, to halt Chinese communist expansion. Ford, who inherited Nixon's secretary of state, Henry Kissinger, offered no major departures and oversaw the helicopter evacuation of the U.S. Embassy in Saigon. Carter understood that there was little he could do as the Nicaraguan revolution unfolded in favor of the Sandinistas, who toppled the Somoza dynasty, long a loyal ally of the United States in the struggle against radicalism in Central America. Carter also made clear to the shah of Iran that the United States could not save his throne. All three presidents realized that the United States could not win an open-ended nuclear arms race with the Soviet Union and that the national interest demanded an agreement with the Kremlin to limit strategic weapons.

The Reagan administration, however, initially perceived these adjustments as the cause and not the consequence of the decline. The result was an ambitious and expensive armaments program to restore the strength and prestige of the United States. But this program came at an extraordinary price; U.S. society had to borrow against the future and, in the process, more than doubled the national debt. In the end, Reagan returned in part to the policies of the 1970s.[28] Indeed, negotiations over the settlement of regional conflicts and the conclusion of the INF Treaty (destroying an entire class of nuclear weapons) in the last year of Reagan's term in office harkened back to the détente era of the Nixon administration.

It is perhaps too early to assess the consequences of the unique U.S.-led war against Iraq in 1990–1991. The strong U.S. role suggested that a new unipolar world, centered around Washington, had come into existence. But what took place may not likely be repeated. Saddam Hussein, who had earlier used poison gas against his own people, stood virtually alone after he invaded and looted Kuwait, a major supplier of energy to the industrialized West. Gorbachev and his foreign minister, Eduard Shevardnadze, decided not to stand in the path of President Bush, who then had the luxury of gathering a massive coalition and preparing for six months to stage an assault against the demoralized Iraqi forces. Moreover, U.S. allies—such as Japan and Saudi Arabia—pledged to underwrite most of the costs of the war.

■ THE SYSTEM AND U.S. INTERVENTION IN PERSPECTIVE

In 1947, President Harry Truman designated the United States as the guardian at the gates of the free world. In practice, this meant that the United States would become the world's policeman against the revolutionary ferment World War II had put into motion. The moment of truth came when the United States had to decide whether or not to accommodate itself to a new order—to accept resurgent nationalism, the struggles against colonialism, the rise of regional powers, the proliferation of conventional and nuclear weapons, and the relative decline of U.S. power. In the U.S. political lexicon, however, accommodation with revolutionary movements smacked of appeasement. In the process, the interventionist impulse became one of the dominant factors in U.S. post–World War II foreign policy.

The Cold War has always been driven by the simplest of arguments, but these no longer suffice. Ho Chi Minh was never Hitler, and Nikita Khrushchev was not Lenin, let alone the firebrand Leon Trotsky. The greatest triumph of the presidency of the anticommunist Richard Nixon came when he took advantage of the Sino-Soviet split and sent his national security adviser, Henry Kissinger, to Beijing to sound out the PRC leadership. In a rare display of statesmanship, a U.S. president abandoned the official fiction that the PRC was but a puppet of Moscow. Nixon, a politician who had always seen the world in stark black-and-white colors, recognized that the world had become increasingly more complex since his red-baiting days as a young congressman and that the time had come to acknowledge a new reality. But Nixon's act was but a single step on a longer journey. The United States has not been able to shake itself of the impulse toward unilateralism and interventionism.

Conditions in the 1990s are more favorable for a reevaluation of U.S. foreign policy than at any time since World War II. President Reagan's dealings with Soviet leader Gorbachev constituted a significant positive step, as such meetings breathed life into the UN, which has begun the slow and painful process of resolving regional conflicts in Angola and in the Persian Gulf. For the first time since the creation of the UN in 1945, there exists a basic accord within the Security Council that makes possible the utilization of that international agency for its original purpose—to resolve the world's conflicts. Indeed, negotiations within the framework of the UN made it possible for the Soviet Union to end its bloody occupation of Afghanistan. In Angola, the U.S.-brokered Namibia and Angola Accords signified an important step in the process of negotiating the end to a long conflict. Most significant, perhaps, was recognition by Washington and Moscow—through negotiation of the INF Treaty—that it was pointless to pursue the quest of nuclear superiority.

Over the years, the United States has frittered away much moral capital that it may readily restore by learning to live in a complex and changing world, by abiding by the rules of international law, and by consulting with its allies rather than going it alone and against their wishes. Mikhail Gorbachev's "new thinking" in foreign affairs not only put the United States on the defensive, but it also forced the United States to reevaluate its Cold War policies. The United States has to free itself of many of the lessons learned in the past, lessons of dubious value for the future.

■ 13

International Law

Christopher C. Joyner

Save for very select, special circumstances, not all of which are universally accepted by international legal experts, intervention by one state into the affairs of another state for the express purpose of changing the latter's policies or conditions is flatly prohibited by international law. Despite this general prohibition, the United States has often intervened in the affairs of Third World countries, most notably in Central and South America. The primary legal justification for U.S. intervention in the post–World War II period has been "self-defense" against the intrusion of the former Soviet Union's ideological influence within a particular region. In Latin America, for example, this rationale has been cited for paramilitary aid given by the United States during the 1980s to the anti-Sandinista contras in Nicaragua and has been invoked to legitimize U.S. interventions in Guatemala (1954), Cuba (1962), the Dominican Republic (1965), Chile (1973), Grenada (1983), and, to a lesser degree, Panama (1989). Although this anticommunist ambition may appear clearly advantageous and laudable for U.S. national interests, it nevertheless skirts the fundamental issue of legal propriety: To what extent does such intervention, irrespective of its high-minded purposes, properly comport with the recognized tenets of international law governing the use of force between states? My fundamental aim in this chapter is to foster a better appreciation for international law's role as a constraint on every state's conduct of foreign policy. It becomes apparent that national governments—in this case, the government of the United States—sometimes adopt convenient legal license to interpret international law such that it serves their own interests as a supportive foreign policy instrument rather than as a force of restraint conducive to greater public world order.

■ THE NORM OF NONINTERVENTION

One of the oldest duties of states under international law is to refrain from intervention in the internal or external affairs of any other state or, for that matter, the relations between other states. During the twentieth century and, notably, in the Cold War era of superpower bloc politics and regional spheres of influence, this duty has been all too frequently ignored. As a result, the international law pertaining to intervention—particularly the universally recognized cardinal norm of nonintervention—has been clouded in the public mind and laid open to question.[1]

As a coercive act, intervention involves a conflict between two fundamental principles of international law: the right of self-defense by the intervening state and the right of independence on the part of the target state. International law does not furnish unrestricted license to any state to undertake a unilateral right of intervention that contravenes the right of another state's independence.[2]

The norm of nonintervention has been expressly set out and codified since World War I in several international instruments. The first modern international treaty designed to regulate state conduct in the use of force was the League of Nations Covenant. Article 10 of the Covenant declared that the "Members of the League undertake to respect and preserve as against external aggression the territorial integrity and existing political independence of all Members of the League."[3] Although the Covenant is no longer in force, its promulgation unmistakably indicated the direction in which international law was heading. The Covenant supplied an institutional framework for nonintervention, as it unequivocally advocated the protection of a state's territorial integrity and political independence. These two fundamental principles of international law represent the twin pillars upon which the very foundation of the contemporary legal concept of nonintervention rests.

With respect to the Americas, two regional treaties made early contributions to explicating the norm of nonintervention. In 1928, the Convention on the Duties and Rights of States in the Event of Civil Strife was signed in Havana, Cuba.[4] This treaty not only contained a general prohibition against intervention but also established a specific duty for governments to forbid intervention by their nationals into the affairs of other states. Likewise, in 1933 the Convention on Rights and Duties of States was signed in Montevideo, Uruguay. This multilateral accord tersely asserted in Article 8 that "[no] State has the right to intervene in the internal or external affairs of another." This rule was grounded in customary international law and articulated in Article 3, which maintained that "the State has the right to defend its integrity and independence . . . to organize as it sees fit, to legislate its interests [and to] administer its services."[5]

To complement these regional efforts exposing the impermissibility of intervention, an Additional Protocol Relative to Non-Intervention was concluded to the Convention on Rights and Duties in 1936 in Buenos Aires. Article 1 of the Protocol plainly affirms that the "High Contracting parties declare inadmissible the intervention of any one of them, directly or indirectly, and for whatever reason, in the internal or external affairs of any of the contracting parties."[6] In 1937 the emerging principle of nonintervention was again reinforced with the entry into force of the Convention on the Fulfillment of the Existing Treaties between the American States.[7] In reaffirming the Treaty of Non-Aggression and Conciliation concluded at Rio de Janiero in 1933,[8] the Americas Treaty Convention noted the prohibition against resorting to diplomatic or armed intervention, even in cases in which states are found to be in noncompliance with a treaty. Consequently, even if some state were to breach a treaty, other states party to the agreement would be bound to refrain from undertaking punitive intervention against the treaty violator.

The thrust of the contemporary norm of nonintervention is contained in Article 2, paragraph 4, of the United Nations Charter, which provides that "[all] Members shall refrain in their foreign relations from the threat or use of force against the territorial integrity or political independence of any State, or in any other manner inconsistent with the Purposes of the United Nations."[9] This statement entails a minimum condition for public order and has come to be regarded as the core provision of the Charter with respect to the use of force. The mandate clearly resides in contemporary international law that a state's violation of Article 2(4) through an act of intervention would constitute an act of aggression, unless legitimizing circumstances could be otherwise convincingly demonstrated.

The 1947 Inter-American Treaty of Reciprocal Assistance (Rio Treaty) reiterates the obligation of nonintervention set down in Article 2(4). Article 1 of the Rio Treaty mandates that states should not "resort to the threat or use of force in any manner inconsistent with the provisions of the Charter of the United Nations or of this Treaty."[10] Subsequent provisions reaffirm the inviolability of states' territoriality and political independence.

The Charter of the Organization of American States established a binding international legal regime particularly for those states in the Western Hemisphere. As such, it holds preeminent importance for any state's policy in the region that is thought to support or entail an act of intervention. The prohibition against intervention is clearly enunciated in Article 18:

> No State or group of States has the right to intervene, directly or indirectly, for any reason whatsoever, in the internal or external affairs of any other State. The foregoing principle prohibits not only armed force but also any other form of interference or attempted threat against the personality of the State or against its political, economic, and cultural elements.[11]

Article 20 of the OAS Charter serves specifically to substantiate this fiat. It tersely asserts that:

> The territory of a State is inviolable; it may not be the object, even temporarily, of military occupation or of other measures of force taken by another State, directly or indirectly, on any grounds whatsoever. No territorial acquisitions or special advantages obtained either by force or by other means of coercion shall be recognized.[12]

Other international legal documents underscore the unlawfulness of intervention. Foremost among them is the Declaration on the Inadmissibility of Intervention in the Domestic Affairs of States and the Protection of Their Independence and Sovereignty, adopted by the UN in 1965. This General Assembly statement unmistakably confirms the impermissibility of intervention in the modern international situation, and its first two provisions capture the essence of nonintervention in international law today:

> 1. No State has the right to intervene, directly or indirectly, for any reason whatever, in the affairs of any other State. Consequently, armed intervention and all other forms of interference or attempted threats against the personality of the State or against its political, economic and cultural elements, are condemned.
> 2. No State may encourage the use of economic, political or any other type of measures to coerce another State in order to obtain from it the subordination of the exercise of its sovereign rights or to secure from it advantages of any kind. Also, no State shall organize, assist, foment, finance, incite or tolerate subversive, terrorist or armed activities directed towards the violent overthrow of the regime of another State, or interfere in civil strife in another State.[13]

Thus, it is plainly prohibited for one state to intervene into the affairs of other states, irrespective of the reason and circumstance. Under contemporary international law, considerations affecting regional politics, spheres of influence, or bloc cohesion remain insufficient for legitimizing acts of intervention by one state against another. This cardinal rule of international law was reiterated by the UN General Assembly in 1970 in its Declaration on Principles of International Law Concerning Friendly Relations and Co-Operation Among States. The Declaration of Principles actually incorporated verbatim the two paragraphs cited from the Declaration on the Inadmissibility of Intervention in order to affirm the "principle concerning the duty not to intervene in matters within the domestic jurisdiction of any State, in accordance with the Charter [of the UN]."[14] Although these General Assembly resolutions do not carry the full weight of legally binding international commitments, they nevertheless do carry considerable moral suasion and evidence a consensus of international legal thought condemning the illicit use of intervention.

As with most rules, the historical experience of dealing with intervention in international law has prompted occasion for certain exceptions to be acknowledged. These exceptions, sometimes designated as "intervention by right," are actually intended to be applied toward constructive ends, in very selective circumstances, by being very restrictive in application. Under international law, these exceptions are not intended to supply unbridled licenses for intervention that governments may seize for their legal advantage when it is politically convenient to do so. In evaluating the contemporary legal attitude of the United States in its policy toward intervention, it remains important to consider whether U.S. actions fall within the scope of any or some of these exceptions to the nonintervention norm.

■ THE PERMISSIBILITY OF INTERVENTION

International law in this century has come to accept in varying degrees situations in which armed intervention may be permitted to occur. These include: (1) in certain circumstances, during civil conflict; (2) in cases involving humanitarian considerations; (3) in the exercise of rights of individual self-defense; (4) in instances of collective self-defense; (5) in response to an explicit, willful invitation by the legitimate government of a state; (6) in situations in which an existing treaty permits such intervention; and (7) in rare circumstances of abatement. In seeking to extract guidelines for regulating interventionist policies in international law, and to appreciate the relevance of U.S. policies in practice, it will be useful to examine each of these exceptions in more detail.

□ *Civil Conflict*

The legal norms governing civil conflict are complicated and contentious. The contemporary legal status of guerrillas, insurgents, and national liberation groups remains open to polemical debate. Even so, some rules involving intervention are plainly evident. First, the fundamental international legal principles of political independence and territorial integrity forbid states from operating to overthrow foreign governments. Indeed, international law supports the basic right of states to create their own government, constitution, and domestic laws without external coercion or suasion of any kind. It is, therefore, unlawful for any foreign government to assist civilians, either at home or abroad, in waging an internal war in some other state. Similarly, a general prohibition exists against states supplying aid to insurgent movements in other states. Unless explicitly invited by the legitimate government, outside states are legally obligated to remain estranged from internal conflict in other states. Yet, international law unquestionably upholds the right to give aid to a government when there exists little or no organized movement in that state. International law, moreover, generally sanctions recognized governments to receive assistance from other states during periods of internal conflict. The lawfulness of aid to the threatened government may be embellished further if foreign assistance is being rendered to insurgents by some outside power. Nonetheless, curbs must be placed on the level of assistance given.[15]

☐   *Humanitarian Intervention*

Situations with widespread atrocities or acute deprivation might present justifiable exceptions to the norm of nonintervention. Justification for armed intervention in these circumstances would rest upon the overwhelming need to act in the preeminent interest of humanitarian concerns. In the 1980s, the practice of states revealed two major instances in which humanitarian intervention might be permissible: (1) for the protection of nationals abroad; and (2) for the protection of human rights.

Traditionally, in international law, the right of a state to intervene may be permitted when another government mistreats the nationals of that state. A cardinal restriction on this right mandates that the intervening power must act solely to protect its nationals; no other interference is allowed. In addition, the risk to the threatened nationals must be genuine, imminent, and substantial. The military operation should be a limited-purpose rescue mission, not a formidable attack against the authority structure of a state.

Similar arguments have been marshaled to justify the use of intervention against a government committing large-scale atrocities against its own nationals. In order to safeguard the fundamental human rights of those citizens, the argument runs, a moral imperative exists that justifies intervention by another state or by a group of states. Although this reasoning may be morally attractive, it fails in political practice. The liability inherent in humanitarian intervention is that it might be used as a legal facade or policy rationale to disguise ideological, hegemonial, or aggressive motives. Another obvious problem is that selectivity often occurs in applying human-rights standards to various national situations. Governments whose foreign policies are generally compatible with some other state are not very likely to be condemned by the latter for their domestic human-rights conditions, much less invaded. Such political realities depreciate the legal vitality and significance of humanitarian intervention and have called into question its legitimacy as an instrument of international law.[16]

☐   *Individual Self-Defense*

A fundamental principle of international law gives states the legal right to use force in self-defense against an armed attack by another state. This principle is highlighted by Article 51 of the UN Charter, which provides in relevant part that "[n]othing in the present Charter shall impair the inherent right of self-defense if an armed attack occurs against a Member of the United Nations, until the Security Council has taken measures necessary to maintain international peace and security." However, this inherent right of self-defense does not automatically permit armed intervention into the territory or affairs of other states, as there are limitations and qualifications on the application of force in self-defense. Outstanding among these restrictions are, first, that the force used in self-defense must be actually necessary to defend the interest threatened and, second, that it must be reasonably proportionate to the danger to be averted.[17]

The notion of preemptive, or anticipatory, self-defense has been accorded legitimacy by some commentators but only in the event that a clear and present danger exists—that some armed attack is imminent and unavoidable. The situation involving a far-range anticipatory attack—that is, in which some perceived threat is foreseeable and conceivable but still remains a distant possibility that is more hypothetical than real—seems fraught with temptations for abuse. The interventionist practice of states in this century suggests that legalizing such a broad interpretation of anticipatory self-defense would be more likely to encourage acts of aggression than to deter them.[18]

☐ *Intervention as Collective Self-Defense*

International law permits collective intervention by member states of an international organization if done on behalf of the world community to maintain peace and to enforce rules and principles of international law. This type of intervention is meant to include both preventive and remedial measures undertaken by such bodies as the UN. To wit, Article 51 of the UN Charter codifies "the inherent right of individual or *collective* self-defense" (emphasis added) should an armed attack occur. Collective self-defense is actually military assistance given in concert to another state. What is important is that collective self-defense is still restricted in its application by the same bounds that limit states in their individual response to threats or use of force. That is, actions taken in collective self-defense must be necessary, immediate, and governed by the bounds of reasonableness and proportionality.[19]

☐ *Intervention by Invitation*

Intervention is permissible in international law when it comes at the genuine and explicit invitation of the legitimate government of a state. The legal merits of such invitational interventions will hinge on the particular circumstances of each individual situation. In this respect, the motives of the intervening state in taking the action, as well as the legitimacy of that government requesting the assistance, are critical for ascertaining the lawfulness of the case. To substantiate these criteria objectively remains difficult, and perceived permissibility may come down to political realities rather than neatly defined legal sureties.

Genuine invitations for outside intervention often have been made during civil conflicts, especially when the government in power wants to receive external assistance for quelling the insurrection. So long as the foreign aid and/or troops have been requested voluntarily by the host state's government, their interventionist status is sanctioned as permissible under international law.[20]

□ *Intervention by Treaty*

Under certain conditions, acts of intervention may be granted through treaty arrangements made by one state with another state. Some states have, in fact, concluded special bilateral treaties of "friendship and cooperation" specifying the possibility of intervention by the protector state in certain discretionary circumstances. Under these special, bilaterally negotiated conditions, the acceptability of treaty rights clearly is viewed in international law as a legitimate exception to the norm of nonintervention. The precondition here, of course, is that the treaty must still be in force and duly respected by both governments at the time an intervention occurs.[21]

□ *Intervention for Abatement*

International law recognizes the lawfulness of certain interventionist actions taken to abate an intolerable regional nuisance. Suppose that conditions in the territory of some state approach anarchy, and the constituted municipal authorities of that state are unable to restore domestic order. The abatement theory holds that neighboring states threatened by the chaotic situation may assume a legal duty to intervene, by armed force if necessary, in order to put down the disturbance. By that action, a neighboring state is entrusted with the responsibility to ensure that disruptive conditions do not spill over and upset its internal stability. As one recognized legal scholar has observed, "If no selfish aims are involved in the intervention in question, if no territorial aggrandizement or other gain is contemplated or realized, then it is difficult, in many instances, to deny a right, based on self-defense or self-preservation, to violate the ban on intervention for the sake of abating the nuisance at one's doorstep."[22]

In the case of intervention on grounds of abatement, the severity and magnitude of the turmoil in the afflicted state stand as critical determinants. External intervention is not permitted merely on the pretext of putting down insurrections next door. The turmoil in the affected state must be genuinely severe and sufficiently chaotic to pose a real threat to the territorial integrity and self-preservation of a neighboring state. Otherwise, the permissibility for intervention will be depreciated into an act of unlawful aggression.

■ **INTERVENTION AND U.S. PRACTICE**

The legal logic employed by the United States to support its use of intervention historically has been couched in the articulation of presidential doctrines. Accordingly, these dicta have significantly shaped the U.S. legal attitude toward the permissibility of intervention.

The foundation of U.S. interventionist policy in the Third World rests in the Monroe Doctrine and its Roosevelt Corollary. Enunciated on December 2, 1823, the doctrine asserted that: (1) no further European colonization should occur in the New World; (2) the United States should abstain from involvement in European affairs; and (3) European states must refrain from intervening in the affairs of governments in the Western Hemisphere.[23] Intended as a unilateral pronouncement of U.S. policy in dealing with the incursion or threat of incursion by European powers into the Western Hemisphere, the Monroe Doctrine came to be regarded as a defense doctrine, or what one commentator dubbed the "American doctrine of self-preservation."[24] Moreover, the Roosevelt Corollary, articulated by President Theodore Roosevelt in his Annual Message to Congress on December 6, 1904, expanded the scope of the doctrine by making the United States a self-appointed international policeman, providing a unilateral justification for increased intervention into the affairs of Latin American countries.

Important to realize is that neither doctrine drew its validity from any legislative pronouncement, nor from any international treaty instrument. Nor was the ambit of jurisdiction or application of either doctrine ever precisely defined by specific law or fiat. Indeed, both doctrines were applied historically on an ad hoc basis, in circumstances determined by the perception of U.S. policymakers, to explain the government's rationale for taking certain interventionist actions. In short, from the mid–nineteenth century through the early portion of the twentieth century, both doctrines were held out as pillars of U.S. foreign policy and, accordingly, were invoked periodically to justify unilateral interventions taken in the name of defending the Americas from European intrusions. For example, in the first three decades of the twentieth century, the United States intervened militarily on some sixty occasions in several smaller Caribbean and Central American states.[25] In all of these cases, little diplomatic consideration or formal concern was expressed by the United States about the international legal implications of these interventions or the critical attitude of other states.

Since World War II, the U.S. perception of aggression (that is, legally impermissible intervention) has been couched largely in terms of evaluating and containing radical, and particularly communist, intentions, capabilities, and strategies throughout the Third World in general and the Western Hemisphere in particular. Radical influence upon the domestic politics or governmental structure of a state may occur by friendly or hostile means. In either circumstance, an unstable situation in the region may intimate that a state is the victim of indirect communist aggression. Such a conclusion may be viewed as threatening to the U.S. security zone. This perception has historically produced reactions by the United States to provide military supplies to a receptive government (or political faction) in order to redress the radical threat. The temptation to engage in military intervention of one form or another has been more likely to rise as the perceived threat to U.S. security interests escalated. Important is that many of the fundamental principles embodied in the Monroe Doctrine have continued to influence U.S. interventionist policy in the Western Hemisphere. Indeed, the fundamental policy motive contained in the doctrine—intervention for self-defense—was resurrected and reactivated in post–World War II foreign policy doctrines.

The Johnson Doctrine derived from the episode in late April 1965 when the United States sent 21,000 troops to restore civil order in the Dominican Republic. The principal legal rationale for the action came to be self-defense—more accurately, anticipated national security considerations—against the perceived threat of communism being established in the Dominican Republic. The scope of the doctrine—the Western Hemisphere—was expanded in 1958 by the Eisenhower Doctrine and U.S. intervention in Lebanon to foster stability in that country. The Eisenhower Doctrine in effect authorized U.S. military action to prevent a communist takeover of Middle Eastern countries. As a consequence, both doctrines during the 1960s came to designate U.S. efforts to counter perceived communist threats in regions considered to be of significant foreign policy interest to the United States.[26]

During the 1980s, the administration of President Ronald Reagan articulated its own policy dictum to reinforce and expand this central theme of stifling communist intrusion into the Americas in particular and the Third World in general. Under the Reagan Doctrine, the United States indicated that it would aid and support paramilitary "freedom fighters" engaged in armed struggle against repressive totalitarian regimes of the left, including guerrilla movements in Angola, Afghanistan, Cambodia, and Nicaragua. Citing the legal rationale for the doctrine, President Reagan noted in his February 6, 1985 State of the Union Address:

> The Sandinista dictatorship of Nicaragua, with full Cuban Soviet-bloc support, not only persecutes its people, the church and denies a free press but arms and provides bases for communist terrorists attacking neighboring states. Support for freedom fighters is *self-defense and totally consistent with the OAS and U.N. Charters* [emphasis added].[27]

As Marxist encroachment was presumed in globalist fashion to be instigated by the Soviets in concert with its allies (such as Cuba in southern Africa and Nicaragua in Central America), the legal edict of self-defense was perceived by Washington policymakers as applicable. In the case of U.S. aid to the anti-Sandinista contras in Nicaragua, for example, the Reagan administration went to some lengths to justify its interventionist actions on legal grounds of self-defense, noting that Soviet-led communist intrusion was real, ongoing, illegal, and threatening to regional interests in general and U.S. interests in particular.[28]

The evolution of U.S. foreign policy doctrines—from the region-centric

Monroe Doctrine to the seemingly worldwide edict of the Reagan Doctrine—underscores a progression of U.S. legal logic justifying U.S. interventionist practices in the Third World. The common factors linking these various doctrines are several: First, each doctrine was issued unilaterally, leaving the United States as their only interpreter. Second, the United States insisted upon retaining the sole, exclusive right of interpretation for activating these doctrines—for determining when they were necessary, the dimensions of that need, and where they should be applied—as conceived in terms of U.S. diplomatic and security interests. Third, the unilateral character of these doctrines points up the guiding concept of the "free hand. " This refers to the notion that although the United States might be willing to act in concert with other states in the world, it reserves for itself the right to make the decision if, when, and under what circumstances any action would be undertaken. Finally, these doctrines explicitly have worked to fix a pervasive conviction in U.S. foreign policy during the twentieth century—namely, that the continued independence of states in the Third World from radical, and particularly communist, control is a diplomatic vital interest of the United States, a vital interest that the U.S. government should be prepared to protect with force and by military intervention if necessary.

Accordingly, these foreign policy doctrines have largely shaped the U.S. legal attitude toward the permissibility of intervention. Yet, the legal dimension of these doctrines is grounded in notions that are drawn neither from U.S. domestic law nor from international law. In fact, the U.S. public's historical view of presidential doctrines has been that they are special legal edicts bestowing upon the United States the singular right to take certain interventionist actions throughout the Third World. Such an attitude, however much it appears appropriate for U.S. national interests, falls short of keeping up with the international legal norm of nonintervention. These doctrines are not real tenets of international law; they are merely political instruments of self-defense, to be applied exclusively by the United States as that government alone defines and construes each case in the Third World.[29]

The most important common factor underpinning these presidential doctrines is that they are all couched in international realpolitik rather than in consensual international law. That is, although stated in terms of the legal justification of self-defense, these doctrines cannot perforce convey unilateral legal license to the United States to impinge upon the national sovereignty, territorial integrity, or political independence of any state in the Third World. To argue otherwise is to suggest the right of the United States to supersede the limits of self-defense and thereby mutate these doctrines into potential instruments for legitimizing the use of U.S. force throughout the Third World. The explicit view of international law clearly rejects the propriety of any such self-serving legal precepts. Yet, the lack of an overarching international enforcement mechanism (that is, reliance on voluntary adherence by individual states to international law) has ensured that states sometimes adopt legal license to interpret international law such that it serves their own interests.

The key legal facet of the Reagan Doctrine as implemented in Nicaragua, for example, centered around the rationale of U.S. self-defense and the related need to preempt Nicaraguan-sponsored armed aggression against El Salvador. However, serious questions surfaced over the applicability of Article 51 of the UN Charter to justify the U.S. interventionist role. In short, the legal notion of self-defense does not automatically include the unilateral right of an outside power to intervene against the territory of an aggressor state. Even if it were proven that the Sandinista government had been transporting significant amounts of aid to rebels in El Salvador—patently illegal under international law—responsive action by the United States nevertheless should not have been taken against the Sandinista government nor conducted in Nicaraguan territory. According to international law, the United States should instead have limited its actions to assisting the government of El Salvador in putting down the insurgency in its own state. Though this limitation may seem inherently unjust, providing opportunities for the instigating culprit, international law sanctions neither the notion that "might makes right" nor that "two wrongs make a right."

The Bush administration added a new dimension to the Reagan Doctrine with its massive intervention into Panama in December 1989. The objectives of the Panama incursion, dubbed Operation Just Cause by the Bush administration, were to (1) "protect American lives," (2) "support democracy" in Panama, (3) bring the indicted drug trafficker Manuel Noriega to justice, and (4) "protect the integrity of the Panama Canal Treaties."[30] Given these multiple and far-reaching goals, the action exceeded a mere rescue mission. It became a full-scale invasion of this small Central American state having 2 million inhabitants and a defense force of 12,500. The toll was high—23 U.S. soldiers killed and 300 wounded; 300 members of the Panamanian Defense Forces killed and 125 wounded; an estimated 500 Panamanian civilians killed and thousands wounded; and massive property damage amounting to more than $1 billion in the commercial sector alone.[31]

The United States justified its military action principally on the inherent right of self-defense. The killing of a U.S. military officer on December 16, the wounding of a second, and the beating of a third, accompanied by the sexual harassment of his wife, prompted President Bush to conclude that U.S. lives in Panama were at risk and that self-defense was warranted. Legal support for that action is found in Article 51 of the UN Charter, as well as Article 21 of the OAS Charter, which prohibits members from resorting to force "except in the case of self-defense in accordance with existing treaties."

The Bush administration also cited as legal justification the need to guarantee the security of the Panama Canal. Two chief treaty protocols control the U.S.-Panama relationship regarding the canal: the 1977 Panama Canal Treaty[32] and the 1977 Permanent Neutrality Treaty,[33] along with their respective implementing agreements and ratification documents. The 1977 canal treaty relinquished all U.S. rights to the waterway, but gives the United States the right to defend the canal,[34] with increasing Panamanian participation, until the year 2000, when the facility will pass to Panama. In tone and substance, the 1977 agreement establishes a new relationship to replace the patriarchal, colonial one contained in the 1903 treaty.

But neither treaty conferred any special right of intervention on the United States that would compromise Panama's political independence and sovereign integrity. In fact, the canal treaty was ratified with an appended joint communiqué of reservations and understandings that flatly renounced any right of the United States to intrude into the internal affairs of Panama.[35] At best the treaties permitted use of force in line with the UN Charter. Although the security of the canal was never at issue, international law could sanction reasonable use of force by the United States to safeguard the lives of its nationals, if indeed they were in danger. At worst the canal treaty imposed a more stringent additional primary-purpose test concerning the use of force by the United States. It is undeniable that U.S. nationals were under escalating threat from physical, political, and rhetorical abuse from members of the Panamanian Defense Force. To be lawful, however, the U.S. response should have been proportional to the threats encountered. One cannot help but wonder whether the murder of a U.S. soldier made it absolutely necessary for the United States to invade a sovereign country with 25,000 troops, install a new government, take captive the de facto head of the former government, and transport him back to the intervening state for arraignment on drug-smuggling charges.

The most recent episode of U.S. intervention occurred in January 1991 during the Persian Gulf war against Iraq. U.S. action did not come as a unilateral response, however. It was taken as part of a collective responsibility, formally approved by the UN Security Council, in order to force Saddam Hussein to cease the unlawful occupation of Kuwait that had persisted since Iraq's aggressive invasion of August 2, 1990.

The international reaction to Iraq's unlawful conquest was swift and telling. Led by the United States, the Security Council on August 2 adopted Resolution 660, which squarely condemned the invasion of Kuwait and demanded Iraq's unconditional and immediate withdrawal.[36] Over the next five months, sixteen additional Security Council resolutions were adopted, all carrying the force of obligatory international law on the UN membership. These resolutions imposed trade, financial, and transportation embargoes against Iraq; condemned its illicit annexation of Kuwait; affirmed protection of foreigners, diplomats, and Kuwaiti nationals held in Iraq and occupied Kuwait; and tightened and enforced the economic sanctions against Saddam Hussein. Clearly the most critical of these Security Council actions was Resolution 678, adopted on November 29, 1990. Sponsored by the United States, this resolution asserted that unless Iraq unconditionally withdrew from

Kuwait and released all foreigners by January 15, 1991, member states of the United Nations would be allowed to "use all necessary means to restore international peace and security in the area."[37] This measure unmistakably authorized the use of military force by states to repel Iraq's aggression. On January 16, UN efforts to deal with Iraq culminated in a U.S.-led coalition of twenty-eight countries instigating an intense air attack against Iraq and Kuwait. Then, on February 23, a massive ground assault was launched to forcibly eject Iraqi troops from Kuwait.

Taken through the UN Security Council, these actions imbued the U.S.-led coalition with international legitimacy. U.S. military intervention into Iraq was not action taken unilaterally; rather, it came as part of a collective self-defense effort dedicated to rescuing Kuwait from Iraqi aggression.

The Security Council had acted with unanimity to condemn Iraq's invasion. It had referred explicitly to Articles 39 and 40 of the Charter, thereby bringing the matter under Chapter VII and permitting the council to impose mandatory measures and, if necessary, economic and military sanctions. The council followed through with both.[38] True, the United States was a driving force behind these actions. It is also true that the United States upheld its own national interests in standing up to Iraqi aggression: The Bush administration was clearly concerned about maintaining secure access to oil resources in the Persian Gulf and about the political-economic implications of Saddam Hussein's possibly controlling nearly one-half of the world's known oil reserves. Especially salient were the implications that immense petro-revenues would have for building up Iraq's military machine, both in terms of conventional weapons and the acquisition of nuclear, chemical, and biological arsenals. No doubt, too, the Bush administration was seriously troubled that Iraq's aggression, by squarely challenging world peace, darkly tarnished the U.S. vision of an internationally cooperative post–Cold War world. In that connection, President Bush perceived Saddam Hussein's aggression in Kuwait as dragging the world community back into the Hitleresque 1930s. The mistakes learned from that tragic era, according to Bush administration officials, were not to be repeated in 1990: Only Iraq's complete withdrawal from Kuwait would be acceptable; "appeasement" with Saddam Hussein was not.

How did intervention by the United States into the situation with Iraq in Kuwait square with international law? A strong case can be made for the lawfulness of the procedures pursued, though serious questions do arise over the means implemented. Resort to the UN Security Council was essential. Even though the United States may have used political influence and economic incentives to secure the votes of council members on resolutions, those measures clearly were lawful within the realm of international diplomacy and negotiation. What remains problematic was the extreme level of destruction in Iraq, in particular the havoc wreaked by launching a bombing campaign so intense that the civilian economic infrastructure of Iraq may have been crippled for decades to come. Another troublesome episode occurred shortly after the 1991 Gulf war ended. As internal rebellion broke out in Iraq during March and early April, thousands of Kurds in the northwestern corner of the country were left trapped and vulnerable to attacks by troops loyal to Saddam Hussein. The Bush administration chose to wait and did not exercise immediate humanitarian intervention efforts aimed at protecting those refugees. Although U.S., British, and French relief assistance for the Kurds eventually was forthcoming through the good offices of Turkey, the credibility of the Bush administration's commitment to human rights and a "new world order" suffered conspicuously by its tragic month-long delay.

In the wake of a U.S.-prosecuted successful Gulf war, what can be said about intervention and the prospects for a U.S.-inspired "new world order"? Clearly there is a new configuration of global power relations. The collapse of communism in Eastern Europe, the disintegration of the Soviet Union as a viable state actor—never mind the role of superpower—and the conceivable breakup of Yugoslavia and Czechoslovakia, coupled with reconfigurations of borders in Africa, Asia, and the Middle East, all suggest shaky international stability. And Saddam Hussein remains in power, as do other radical regimes in Libya, North Korea, Cuba, and the People's Republic of China. But the United States has also learned that it is unable to play the role of world policeman, economically as well as politically. The United States cannot afford to pay all the bills anymore. Nor will future conflicts be as crystal clear or as morally neat as Saddam Hussein's aggression. The Iraq/Kuwait case was an easy one for the United States to gauge in terms of immediate stakes at risk. Conflicts in other parts of the world are not likely to be as politically, economically, legally, or morally certain.

■ THE BALANCE SHEET

Largely in reaction to U.S. interventionist policies between 1900 and 1930, the post–World War II attitude condemning the unlawfulness of intervention has become steadfast and staunch. Even so, the United States has persisted in legitimizing its interventionist policies on de facto grounds of preserving national security through self-proclaimed presidential doctrines. In the past decade, an upgraded effort has been made to fashion support for U.S. interventionist actions in international law, especially by suggesting that these actions fall within the context of permissible exceptions to the norm of nonintervention. The fact is, however, that U.S. interventionist policy remains motivated more by perceived national necessity and political expedition than by international responsibility and legal rectitude.

This observation does not mean that international law fails in its purposes, nor that U.S. interventionist practices are profound aberrations in contemporary international politics. Neither conclusion is accurate. What the historical attitude of the United States toward intervention in the Third World does signify is simply that governments tend to obey international law when it serves their national interests. For nearly all dealings in foreign relations, this remains the objective case. Yet, the reality is that in certain circumstances a state's respect for international law may be diminished when that government perceives its immediate interests to be better served by ignoring, circumventing, or violating specific international norms. This realization underscores the fact that states make international law, states apply international law, states enforce international law, and states break international law. The law is not wanting in its content or its practice or its enforcement; the governments of states are wanting in their willingness to respect the law on certain occasions.[39]

It is easy to make arguments based on absolutes at the cost of overlooking critical facts in an interventionist episode. It is also true that reliance upon absolutes for evaluating and appraising international events may be ill advised. Arriving at black-and-white legal answers rarely portrays the full accuracy of a situation in world politics. This realization is particularly apt with respect to intervention. International law is created by governments as they seek solutions for old problems and new crises. The history of regional and international efforts at cooperation is a record of pragmatic adjustments fashioned to reach objectives promoting general agreement. Acts of intervention tend to disrupt the entire international pattern of cooperation.

There is also the need to view international law from a practical vantage point and to realize that international law, as it is conceived, may take the form of practical idealism. Thus, the reality of interventionist practices suggests that international law should be seen as the deliberate, rational attempt to set order in the international community. To the extent that a state's policy comports with the norm of nonintervention, this attempt has succeeded. However, in cases in which a government opts to pursue its own policy priorities at the expense of intruding into the domestic affairs of some other state, serious questions must be raised about the propriety of such actions. Failure to do so not only shirks international responsibility; it also invites less respect for and greater abuse of the law. In this age of increasing political, economic, and sociocultural interdependence, such a disturbing trend hardly would be in the long-term interest of promoting world public order through legal recourse.

■ Part 5
CASE STUDIES

■ 14

South Africa

R. Hunt Davis, Jr. & Peter J. Schraeder*

The challenge presented to U.S. foreign policy by the situation in South Africa continues to be a deep and difficult one. South Africa is unique in that, unlike most other Third World countries, it is self-sufficient in food production; has a strong industrially based economy; boasts a highly developed infrastructure in terms of transportation, energy, education, and social services; and was a founding member of both the League of Nations and the United Nations. Yet these attributes of development are illusory because access to the country's economic wealth and political system historically has been highly skewed along racial lines under a system commonly known as apartheid. Whereas many black South Africans, especially those in the rural areas, suffer from acute poverty and malnutrition, nearly all whites are, at a minimum, relatively affluent in this racially segregated society. Moreover, despite the ongoing political dialogue at the beginning of 1992 between the Afrikaner government and the black majority that resulted in the Convention for a Democratic South Africa (CODESA) and the launching of the negotiating process leading to a new constitution, the fact that blacks still do not have the legal right to vote for national positions of power underscores the political side of the exclusionary equation.

The Afrikaner government's systematic exclusion of the majority black population from reaping the economic and political benefits of South Africa led to increasing domestic instability and the estrangement of the regime both regionally and within the international system during the post–World War II period. The majority of sub-Saharan African countries since independence consistently condemned the South African state for its treatment of the majority of the population and contributed toward making apartheid a major issue in the international arena. In the case of the United States, a combination of factors—heightened polarization and instability within South Africa and the region as a whole, pressures from African countries, and a

---

*Gwendolen M. Carter, who died in February 1991 after a long illness, was the co-author (with R. Hunt Davis, Jr.) of this chapter in the book's first edition. The present co-authors are deeply indebted to Gwen for the understanding and insights she provided on South African politics over her long career as a scholar. This chapter is dedicated to her memory.

highly vocal domestic antiapartheid movement—culminated in congressional passage of the Comprehensive Anti-Apartheid Act of 1986. By adopting a variety of sanctions designed to force the dismantling of apartheid and the creation of a nonracial, democratic government, Congress in the 1986 legislation created a watershed in U.S.–South African relations.

■ THE EVOLUTION OF THE U.S.–
SOUTH AFRICAN STRATEGIC RELATIONSHIP

U.S. policy in southern Africa historically has been relatively inert and passive on the issue of economic sanctions. One scholar, for example, has stated that "until the Carter administration, the United States took virtually no initiative in southern Africa, content at first to rely on the European imperial powers to maintain western supremacy there."[1] Of course, it should be kept in mind that much of the United States was still segregated into the 1960s (for example, the Selma, Alabama, march took place in 1965), and thus a racially stratified South Africa did not seem all that much out of step to U.S. policymakers. Furthermore, Washington's principal ally, Great Britain, had an enormous economic stake in South Africa, which was a much more important concern to the United States than was apartheid.

A variety of perceived strategic interests in South Africa led U.S. policymakers to seek closer ties with the apartheid regime from 1948 to 1960. The State Department led the way, responding favorably at the end of 1948 to a South African request to upgrade each country's respective diplomatic missions to embassy status and exchange ambassadors rather than ministers. Of primary interest to the State Department was South Africa's unswerving political and diplomatic support for U.S. containment policies in both Europe and Asia. For example, not only was South Africa one of the first countries to send an aircrew for the U.S.-led Berlin airlift in 1949, but its leaders also provided support for the U.S.-led military effort in the Korean War. Actions such as these were strongly rewarded, as evidenced by the State Department's handling of antiapartheid resolutions at the UN. Although the State Department supported the right of the UN General Assembly to "discuss" the issue of apartheid, U.S. representatives nonetheless were instructed to refuse to vote for specific resolutions. In a classic diplomatic balancing act, the State Department's primary objectives were to curry the favor of antiapartheid critics while at the same time avoiding any actions that would strain U.S.–South African ties.[2]

The Defense Department also lobbied for stronger U.S.–South African relations. In keeping with its primary bureaucratic mission of preparing for a global military conflict with the Soviet Union, the Defense Department argued that South Africa's strategic location, excellent port facilities, and experienced military forces ensured both "offensive and defensive roles" for that country in a major East-West military confrontation.³ As a result, military cooperation between the two countries took on many forms. In addition to routine exchange visits by ranking officers of both militaries, a 1951 military agreement authorized reimbursable U.S. military assistance under the Mutual Defense Assistance Act. Of even greater importance was routine access to South African ports, most notably the former British naval base at Simonstown. In exchange for this access, the Defense Department coordinated joint military maneuvers with the South African Navy. Finally, the Defense Department encouraged the sale of arms and, particularly, fighter aircraft to the South African Armed Forces. In 1952, for example, the United States agreed to sell over $112 million in arms to the South African military. The Joint Chiefs of Staff envisioned the fighters as being "immediately available for use in collective defense in the event of Communist aggression."⁴

The CIA constituted the third major proponent of closer U.S. ties with South Africa. Having begun under the Truman administration what one CIA officer described as a "long and cordial relationship" with the South African secret police, the CIA increasingly looked upon its South African counterpart as a natural ally in the global struggle against communist expansionism led by the Soviet Union.⁵ The primary reason for this outlook was the zealous anticommunist beliefs of the Afrikaner elite that equaled, if not surpassed, those of the most doctrinaire anticommunists within the U.S. government. For example, it is striking to note that the South African government adopted its Suppression of Communism Act at the same time that U.S. Senator Joseph McCarthy was leading a domestic witch-hunt against suspected U.S. communists and "fellow travelers." In the specific case of southern Africa, the CIA especially was interested in building up the counterintelligence capabilities of the South African security apparatus as a counterweight to potential revolutionary upheaval within the region. Indeed, as early as January 1949, the CIA was warning U.S. policymakers about the possibility for Soviet manipulation of African nationalism and the decolonization process to the detriment of U.S. interests on the African continent.⁶

Nuclear cooperation under the auspices of the U.S. Atomic Energy Commission constituted a final important element of the growing U.S.–South African security relationship. Because domestic reserves of uranium oxide (a crucial element in the development of nuclear devices) were insufficient to fuel the massive development of the U.S. nuclear arsenal during the 1950s, an agreement was signed with South Africa in November 1950. In return for U.S. scientific and technical collaboration as well as guarantees of any capital required to develop and expand production, the South African government agreed to provide the United States with its entire output of uranium oxide. The strategic importance of this link was underscored by U.S. purchases of over $1 billion worth of South African uranium production from 1952 to 1966.[7] As a result of this agreement, the national security bureaucracies began citing South Africa's willingness to accommodate the United States with respect to a vital strategic component of U.S.-Soviet nuclear rivalry as yet another rationale for strengthening U.S.–South African relations.

The virtually unquestioned nature of the growing U.S.–South African security relationship was not seriously challenged until 1960. On March 21 of that year, a large crowd of Africans (estimates of its size range from 3,000 to 20,000) gathered before the police station at Sharpeville to demonstrate against the pass laws. Nervous white police opened fire, killing 69 and wounding 180. A chain reaction of events spread throughout South Africa, ending with a declaration of a state of emergency and the outlawing of African political organizations.[8] The Sharpeville incident drew U.S. attention to the problems of apartheid in a dramatic manner and led to a gradual hardening of policy toward South Africa. In 1963, for example, President John F. Kennedy declared his administration's intention to terminate the sale of military equipment to South Africa. In 1965, President Lyndon B. Johnson ended the practice of U.S. warships calling at South African ports. Overall, though, the United States continued to adhere to a low-profile approach on South African issues—as well as for Africa as a whole—except when crises such as the Sharpeville incident brought African issues to the attention of the U.S. foreign-policy-making elite.

The administration of President Richard M. Nixon initiated a shift in policy toward South Africa, a shift that backed off from the cautious limits that previously had been placed on relations with that country. This change in policy was embodied in National Security Study Memorandum 39 (NSSM 39), one of eighty-five reviews ordered by the new administration in 1969. NSSM 39 set forth five options for a future U.S. foreign policy toward the southern African region: (1) closer association with the white regimes of the region; (2) broader ties with both white-ruled and black-ruled countries in order to foster moderation; (3) lessening ties with the white states and strengthening those with black states; (4) severing ties with the white states and establishing closer relations with the black states; and (5) withdrawal from the southern African region. The administration opted for the second option—dubbed "tar baby" by the option's opponents in the Department of State who felt that closer relations with the whites would become a quagmire for the United States—which in turn led to a relaxation of the political isolation and economic restrictions that had been placed on South Africa and the other white-ruled states in the region (Angola, Mozambique, and Rhodesia).

The basic premise of the new policy was that "the whites are here to stay" and that constructive change could come only through them; blacks could not hope to gain political rights through violence—this would only serve to open up opportunities to communists. The new policy thus sought to increase communications with the white minority governments of the region in order to induce them to modify their racial and colonial policies. It also provided more substantial economic assistance to the independent black states of the region in order to increase U.S. influence with them.[9] The mind-set behind this new policy was clearly a globalist one, for the real key to the situation in southern Africa, as far as Secretary of State Henry Kissinger and other U.S. policymakers were concerned, was the communist threat posed by guerrilla insurgencies supported by Moscow.

Events soon overtook the vital assumption of NSSM 39 that white rule would continue as a permanent feature of southern Africa. On April 25, 1974, a military coup d'état against the Marcello Caetano government in Portugal led to the demise of Portuguese colonial rule in Angola and Mozambique, facilitating the rise of black nationalist movements to power in both countries by 1975. Rather than accommodating the new political forces, however, Kissinger's fixation on the Soviet threat in the region resulted in U.S. covert intervention in Angola's 1975–1976 civil war, an action described by one author as one of "Washington's worst policy debacles" in Africa.[10] The result was just the opposite of what had been intended; rather than stemming Soviet influence, action led instead to stepped-up Soviet aid to the self-proclaimed Marxist government in Angola and, ultimately, to the massive Cuban military presence that bedeviled Washington for years afterward. In turn, U.S. intervention also led to a congressional break with the administration in 1976 with the passage of the Clark Amendment to the Defense Appropriations Bill, which prohibited all covert aid to any of the parties in Angola. It was not until April 1976 that Kissinger finally ventured into southern Africa and, in a speech in Lusaka, Zambia, promised a thorough reevaluation and basic revision of U.S. policy toward the region. Though there was a clear recognition that the situation had changed (some two years after the Portuguese coup, it might be added), the new policy varied little "beyond making the absolute minimum of concessions to African states (and critical Americans) who had to be kept in good humor."[11]

The election of Jimmy Carter to the presidency in 1976 seemed to herald a considerable change in U.S. policy toward Africa in general and a hardening of opposition to apartheid in particular. Gone was the low-profile approach toward South Africa. The issue of apartheid quickly moved into the foreign policy spotlight with the appointment of civil rights activist Andrew Young as ambassador to the United Nations and the heavy stress the new administration placed on human rights. One of the first steps was to secure congressional support for repealing the Byrd Amendment, legislation that had permitted the United States to import essential minerals from minority-ruled Rhodesia (Zimbabwe since 1980). Repeal put the United States back in compliance with UN sanctions on Rhodesia. Carter also moved well beyond his two predecessors and called for majority rule not only for Rhodesia and

Namibia but also for South Africa itself. In a May 1977 meeting with Prime Minister John Vorster of South Africa, Vice President Walter F. Mondale reiterated the administration's position on majority rule.

What on first appearance seemed to be a new direction in U.S. policy was revealed upon closer examination, however, to be a continuation of two of the mainstays of the Nixon-Ford years: opposition to the liberation movements and a search for moderate solutions. For example, although in the end refusing to recognize the April 20, 1979, elections in Rhodesia—which led to Bishop Abel Muzorewa becoming prime minister of a "new" Rhodesia-Zimbabwe—the Carter administration had been indecisive and ambiguous about the elections in the first place. Furthermore, in the previous year, the administration had strengthened the legitimacy of the Rhodesian government when it had acquiesced to the demand of twenty-seven U.S. senators that Prime Minister Ian Smith, Bishop Muzorewa, and several other leading white Rhodesians receive visas to visit the United States in order to generate support for their cause. What appeared to turn the administration away from looking at southern Africa on its own terms was the perceived increase of Soviet influence on the continent. In particular, the Angolan-based invasions of the Shaba province of Zaire in 1977 and 1978 and the massive Soviet and Cuban support of Ethiopia in its war with Somalia in late 1977 were critical events in this shift. As elsewhere on the continent, then, the seeming initial "success of the pro-Africa policy was merely apparent, never real, and it was soon eclipsed by the contrary influences of National Security Adviser Zbigniew Brzezinski and his globalist approach over the regionalist approach of Young."[12] Yet, critical as one may be of the failure of the Carter administration to move more aggressively on the question of South Africa, nonetheless the administration had abandoned the pro-white tilt of its predecessors.

The pro-white tilt of Washington returned in full and renewed force with the election of Ronald Reagan in 1980 and his appointment of Chester Crocker as assistant secretary of state for African affairs. Crocker was the theoretician behind the Reagan administration policy of "constructive engagement." The central argument of this policy was that "purposeful, evolutionary change toward a nonracial system" was a genuine possibility in South Africa and that U.S. interests lay in fostering such change. Pressure clearly would be necessary, but there also should be "a clear Western readiness to recognize and support positive movement, and to engage credibly in addressing a complex agenda of change."[13] The policy made reaching an accommodation with the white rulers of South Africa the key for securing U.S. economic and security interests in the area. Within South Africa, the Reagan administration pointed to the 1984 constitution, which extended a limited franchise to Colored and Indian voters, as proof that its policy was working; outside South Africa, it viewed the 1984 Nkomati Accord between South Africa and Mozambique, which committed the two countries to ending support of covert activities against each other, in a similar manner.

The true focus of the constructive engagement policy, however, was not the southern African region but the global arena. The key to policies directed by Crocker and his deputy, Frank Wisner, was their belief that Soviet military aggression in southern Africa would increase and, less convincing, that Cuban forces in Angola would be its focal point.[14] As a result of its globalist orientation, the Reagan administration reverted to the military option in two respects: (1) by engineering revocation of the 1976 Clark Amendment; and (2) by securing congressional backing under the auspices of the Reagan Doctrine for arming guerrilla forces led by Jonas Savimbi—the National Union for the Total Independence of Angola (UNITA)—that were attempting to overthrow the pro-Soviet Angolan regime headed by the Popular Movement for the Liberation of Angola (MPLA).

■ EXTENDED CRISIS AND PASSAGE OF THE 1986 COMPREHENSIVE ANTI-APARTHEID ACT

The underlying assumptions of constructive engagement were called into question by the most severe domestic crisis in South African political history. On September 3, 1984, a series of protests broke out in several black townships over the South African government's adoption of a tricameral parliament that extended limited political rights to Asians and Coloreds but continued to deny political franchise to the majority black population. Serving as a spark for the release of decades of pent-up hostility that to a lesser degree had surfaced at Sharpeville and in Soweto in earlier years, these protests turned into a popular rebellion that pitted blacks against the South African security and police forces over a period of two years. When the dust had settled, over 2,000 blacks had died and nearly 30,000 others had been detained for political reasons. Of particular concern to human-rights organizations was the detention of nearly 3,000 black children under the age of eighteen.[15]

The brutality of the South African government's response captured the attention of the world media and became a nightly staple of U.S. news broadcasts. Vivid footage of white police officers viciously attacking black protesters in black townships with whips and dogs offered a strong indictment of the horrors of apartheid and the shallowness of reforms undertaken by the Afrikaner government. Yet, in a hearing convened by the Senate Subcommittee on Africa less than three weeks after the outbreak of violence, Crocker stressed that it was still "premature" to dismiss the "new willingness" of the Afrikaner government to "support the concept of reform."[16] Capturing the mood of several congresspersons who had decided in 1981 to "keep quiet" and give Crocker "a chance to show what could be done with constructive engagement," Senator Paul Tsongas strongly criticized Crocker's continued support for a failed policy. "I really regret that in the 4 years and the opportunity that was had, that nothing has happened," explained Tsongas. "I think ultimately there is a moral responsibility to look back at one's stewardship and say, we made a difference, and the fact is, there has not been a difference."[17]

This clash between Crocker and Tsongas marked a turning point in the domestic debate over the proper course of U.S. foreign policy toward South Africa. As violence in South Africa continued to mount, apartheid became a domestic political issue for U.S. citizens increasingly prone to draw parallels between the legitimacy of the struggle by blacks in South Africa and the U.S. civil rights movement of the 1960s. In the absence of White House concern and given the arguments emanating from the executive branch that called for continuation of the status quo, rising popular demands for the United States to "do something" slowly captured the attention of vote-conscious members of Congress who previously had ignored the issue of apartheid. In short, the extended violence in South Africa served as a spark for the pro-sanctions viewpoint within the policymaking establishment in which Congress increasingly would assume the initiative in altering the direction of U.S.–South African relations.

The opening salvo of growing domestic concern over the violence in South Africa was launched by TransAfrica and its activist executive director Randall Robinson, who on November 21, 1984, staged a peaceful sit-in at the South African embassy in Washington, D.C., that led to his arrest. Accompanied by other notable African Americans, such as Walter Fauntroy, the District of Columbia's delegate to the House of Representatives, and Mary Frances Berry, an outspoken member of the U.S. Civil Rights Commission, this act captured the imagination of antiapartheid activists and led to the creation of the Free South Africa Movement, an umbrella organization of antiapartheid groups seeking to impose sanctions against South Africa. Rather than constituting a one-day media stunt, Robinson's arrest was duplicated nearly 6,000 times as antiapartheid activists staged similar sit-ins at the South African embassy and consulates around the United States during the twenty-three months that followed. The significance of these acts was further strengthened by the involvement and arrest of eighteen prominent members of Congress, the most notable being Senator Lowell Weicker and Representative Patricia Schroeder.

Congress soon responded to growing popular demands for punitive actions against South Africa. On June 4, 1985, the House of Representatives passed a sanctions bill (HR-1460) by a vote of 295 to 127 that called for bans on new U.S. corporate investment in South Africa, U.S. bank loans to the South African government, the importation of Kruggerands, computer sales to the South African government, and U.S.–South African nuclear cooperation.[18] The bill also included a clause that mandated consideration of new sanctions within twelve months.[19] Despite an unsuccessful filibuster attempt by Senator Helms, the Senate passed its version of sanctions legislation (S-995) on July 11 by a margin of 80 to 12.[20] The Senate version, however, was much weaker than its House counterpart. It included a ban on bank loans to the South African government, restrictions on the export of computer and nuclear products, mandatory adherence of U.S. corporations in South Africa to the Sullivan Principles (a set of guidelines for U.S. corporations doing business in South Africa drawn up by the Reverend Leon Sullivan, a member of the General Motors board of directors), and consideration of new sanctions after a period of two years. A joint House-Senate conference committee on July 31 adopted the more limited Senate bill with a ban on the import of Kruggerands and consideration of new sanctions legislation within twelve months being the only measures included from HR-1460.

The prospect of congressional passage of economic sanctions ensured the end of the parochial control the State Department's Africa Bureau wielded over U.S. foreign policy toward South Africa and placed the issue of apartheid squarely in the hands of the Reagan White House. In contemplating whether the administration could successfully veto the legislation and prevent a congressional override—the position favored by the State Department's Africa Bureau, the Defense Department, and the CIA—President Reagan and his advisers were faced with the Afrikaner government's "untimely" declaration of a state of emergency on July 25, 1985, and subsequent intensification of civil conflict in South Africa. Moreover, Republican senators, most notably Foreign Relations Committee Chairperson Richard Lugar, warned Reagan that unless some sanctions were adopted by the administration, there was a strong possibility that a White House veto would be overridden by both the House and the Senate.

Despite Reagan's inclination against any punitive actions toward South Africa, political pragmatism required taking the advice of Senator Lugar. In a successful tactical move designed to preempt Senate passage of the compromise sanctions legislation (the House already had passed the bill), Reagan issued Executive Order 12532 on September 9, 1985, which included bans on U.S. government loans to the South African government and the sale of computers to South African security agencies, placed limited restrictions on U.S.–South African nuclear cooperation, and ordered an investigation into the legality of banning U.S. imports of Kruggerands.[21] The biggest differences with the congressional bill were executive branch discretion as to when sanctions could be lifted and the omission of any clause requiring the automatic reconsideration of sanctions within a specific time.

The Reagan administration's attempt at co-opting the legislative process might have been successful had it been matched by decreasing levels of civil conflict in South Africa. However, growing levels of black rebellion were met by even stronger acts of suppression by the South African government, culminating in a second state of emergency being declared in June 1986 as part of a determination to crush all opposition. To make matters worse, on May 19, 1986, the South African government launched coordinated military strikes against suspected African National Congress (ANC) headquarters in Botswana, Zambia, and Zimbabwe. In the eyes of proponents of sanctions within the U.S. Congress, the combination of South Africa's internal and external policies completely discredited any arguments on the part of the Reagan administration that the Afrikaner elite was committed to reform.

The intensification of civil conflict in South Africa led to renewed congressional efforts in 1986 to pass antiapartheid sanctions legislation. A comprehensive sanctions bill (HR-4868) calling for a complete trade embargo and U.S. divestment of all economic holdings in South Africa passed by a voice vote in the House on June 12, 1986.[22] After sharp debate over several pieces of legislation and amendments, the Senate on August 14 passed its version of economic sanctions (S-2701) by a vote of 84 to 14.[23] Among the bill's most significant elements were the incorporation of the major provisions of the 1985 Executive Order, a ban on private bank loans to the South African government, and a prohibition on new investment in South Africa. A joint House-Senate conference committee in August 1986 voted to accept without amendment S-2701 as the conference report. As a result, both the Senate and the House passed that same month what has become known as the Comprehensive Anti-Apartheid Act of 1986. In addition to the major provisions already noted, the act included a ban on products produced or marketed by South African parastatals; a ban on U.S. imports of South African uranium, steel, and textiles; the withdrawal of U.S. landing rights for South African Airways; and the denial of visas for all South African officials except embassy and UN personnel.

Passage of the 1986 Anti-Apartheid Act once again placed the issue of sanctions squarely in the hands of the White House. Hoping to co-opt the legislative process as he effectively had done in 1985, Reagan predictably vetoed the sanctions bill and offered instead a milder version in the form of another Executive Order.[24] Convinced that if he could only take his case to the U.S. electorate, they would understand the logic of what the administration sought to accomplish in southern Africa, Reagan in a July 22, 1986, policy address broadcast live on network television rejected the imposition of further sanctions as "immoral" and "utterly repugnant."[25] In the eyes of opponents of constructive engagement, as well as of those sympathetic to the president's viewpoint, the halfhearted measures included in the speech and codified in the Executive Order were too little, too late. On September 29, 1985, the House voted 317 to 83 to override the President's veto. Four days later, the Senate followed suit by a 78-21 margin. In one of the greatest foreign policy defeats of the Reagan administration, these two votes constituted the official death of the policy of constructive engagement.

The reasons for this dramatic setback in administration policy were basically fourfold. First, the rising electoral strength of African Americans was translated into increasingly effective political organizations capable of bringing pressure to bear on Congress. The primary vehicle for this growing electoral voice outside of Congress was TransAfrica, the political lobby that effectively organized the dramatic protests at the South African embassy beginning in 1984. Within the halls of Congress, not only had the Congressional Black Caucus (CBC) grown in numbers (twenty-one members in 1986), but its members also had achieved greater seniority and positions of authority. It was precisely these leaders, such as Representatives Ronald Dellums and William H. Gray III, who were in the forefront of legislating sanctions against South Africa. A second reason for the setback in administration policy, which derived from the growing electoral strength of African Americans, was rising Republican concerns over the issue of race in U.S. foreign policy. This factor was especially important because it contributed to the divisiveness within the Republican Party in 1986 that was so crucial to the passage of sanctions legislation in the Republican-controlled Senate.

A third reason for the reversal of administration policy in South Africa was the steady growth of grassroots antiapartheid organizations. National leadership for hundreds of such groups was provided by the American Committee on Africa (ACOA) and its Washington counterpart, the Washington Committee on Africa (WCOA), the Interfaith Center on Corporate Responsibility (ICCR), and the American Friends Service Committee (AFSC). These groups, which had been growing slowly but steadily in strength since the 1970s, made slow but steady gains and increased significantly in influence after 1984. Extensive media coverage made the public more aware of the South African crisis.[26] Indeed, by 1986, nineteen state governments, sixty-eight cities and counties, and 131 colleges and universities had adopted various types of restrictions that affected nearly $220 billion of institutional assets related to pension and endowment funds.[27] In addition to promoting such divestment and disinvestment at the local and state levels, antiapartheid organizations provided invaluable organizational support when the sanctions movement became a national phenomenon in 1986. These groups cooperated with liberal congressional allies, particularly those on the House Subcommittee on Africa, to seek passage of antiapartheid legislation. Their contribution ranged from collecting data and providing witnesses crucial to congressional hearings to coordinating massive letter-writing campaigns to wavering congresspersons.

The fourth and most important factor contributing to passage of the 1986 sanctions legislation was the unfolding of what became perceived among the U.S. public as an extended crisis situation in South Africa. In the early stages of the crisis, President Reagan was able to hold the line on sanctions by issuing an Executive Order. However, as the violence in South Africa continued to intensify, U.S. policy toward South Africa increasingly became a domestic political issue for the U.S. electorate. Specifically, rising popular demands for the U.S. government to "do something" to stop the unfolding tragedy in South Africa galvanized the antiapartheid activities of African American lobbying groups, Republican splinter groups, and grassroots antiapartheid organizations. These groups, in turn, placed increasing pressure on vote-conscious congresspersons who recognized the popular political backlash that would accompany defeat of some sort of sanctions package. In hearings devoted to the question of sanctions, House Subcommittee on Africa Chairperson Howard Wolpe dramatized the crucial relationship between events in South Africa and the U.S. policymaking process: "Why are we so concerned with the passage [of sanctions legislation] at this point? The reason [is], very simply, because of the dramatic—very dramatic, I want to underscore that—deterioration of developments in South Africa."[28] The fact that these developments obviously were linked to the politicization of the apartheid issue within U.S. domestic politics was underscored by Republican Senate Majority Leader Robert Dole. "Let's face it, there's a lot of politics involved. . . . This has now become a civil rights issue."[29]

The override of Reagan's 1986 veto marked a historic turning point in U.S.–South African relations as Congress successfully reversed a policy strongly embraced by the executive branch. Although the resulting legislation was still too mild for numerous antiapartheid activists, passage of it was in sharp contrast to the historical U.S. tendency to rhetorically denounce South Africa's racial policies while simultaneously doing little to change the established status quo. The law now firmly matched U.S. words with actions. Most significant, perhaps, was that large numbers of Republicans—most notably in the Republican-controlled Senate—abandoned a popular president of their own party during an election year. As Senator Paul Simon, chairperson of the Senate Subcommittee on Africa, was to note: "Three years ago no one could have imagined that a Democratic House of Representatives and a Republican Senate would together repudiate the administration's policy, override a presidential veto, and forge a new direction for U.S. policy in South Africa." He continued: "Congress seized the mantle of leadership, took a moral stand, and rejected a policy that compromised our commitment to individual rights and equivocated on our moral stand against apartheid."[30]

■ THE SANCTIONS DEBATE IN A CHANGING REGIONAL ENVIRONMENT

The Bush administration entered office in February 1989 determined to avoid the bruising battles with Congress over South Africa so frequent during the Reagan years. For example, Secretary of State James A. Baker III indicated in his confirmation hearings that the administration was seeking a bipartisan approach built on close consultation with Congress. "No South African policy," explained Baker, "is going to work unless we're unified, unless we can coordinate well between the legislative and executive branches."[31] Bush sought to demonstrate his sympathy with the antiapartheid movement by personally meeting with South African activists and publicly expressing his abhorrence of apartheid.[32] "Reagan never succeeded in communicating his sympathy with the victims of apartheid," noted Herman Nickel, U.S. ambassador to South Africa from 1982 to 1986. "So the Congress doubted whether his heart was in the right place on the issue of racial justice generally and South Africa in particular."[33] In this regard, the Bush administration won the cautious praise of influential congressional opponents of apartheid, such as Representative Howard Wolpe. "I am encouraged by what seems to be a much more sensitive public posture toward the South African regime and what seems to be more interest and emphasis on this critical question," noted Wolpe. "But it remains to be seen," he cautioned, "whether this will really be followed up with the kind of measures that will make it clear to the South African regime that, absent an abandonment of apartheid and the onset of a negotiating process, there will be fundamental costs to the United States–South African relationship."[34]

Despite the willingness of Bush and his senior advisers to demonstrate that their "hearts were in the right places," U.S. foreign policy toward South Africa in the early months of the Bush administration differed little, if at all, from the later years of the Reagan administration. Because of the preoccupation with the dramatic sociopolitical changes in the Soviet Union and Eastern Europe, as well as the reunification of Germany and the future of the NATO alliance, U.S.–South African relations were relegated to the Africa specialists within the State Department. In congressional testimony strikingly reminiscent of Crocker's policy of constructive engagement, newly appointed Assistant Secretary of State for African Affairs Herman B. Cohen stressed that he perceived "new thinking" and a "new sense of realism" among the white Afrikaner elite. If supported by an active U.S. stance of "dialogue, negotiation and compromise," explained Cohen, "a democratic solution may be achievable."[35] Although willing to concede that economic sanctions had been successful in forcing the Afrikaner elite to consider negotiations with the black majority, Cohen nonetheless emphasized the State Department's continuing opposition to further sanctions against South Africa. This stance also enjoyed broad support within both the CIA and the Defense Department.

Executive branch opposition to further sanctions against South Africa stood in sharp contrast to the sentiments of congressional antiapartheid activists. Led by the House Subcommittee on Africa and the CBC, activists continued to favor the tightening of economic sanctions. At the very least, these members of Congress hoped that the Bush administration would support the "multilateralization" of sanctions. Specifically, antiapartheid activists were willing to concede the administration's unwillingness to advance beyond the sanctions legislation "currently on the books" in exchange for making that legislation the basis of a U.S.-supported resolution within the UN Security Council—a step the Reagan administration was unwilling to take.

As demonstrated by South Africa's successful refinancing in October 1989 of a significant portion of its outstanding international loans, however, an ongoing congressional-executive standoff favored continuation of the status quo. In this case, antiapartheid activists sought White House intervention to prevent international banks from extending the grace period for nearly $8 billion in South African loans scheduled to fall due in June 1990. Congressional activists had hoped to precipitate a major financial crisis in South Africa similar to the one in 1985 when banks recalled nearly $14 billion in debt, the idea being to undermine apartheid further and force the Afrikaners to negotiate with the black opposition. Yet in the face of executive branch opposition and the inability of Congress to muster enough interest to force the issue, Washington stood on the sidelines as South Africa reached agreement with its creditors. "This action represents an enormous boost for the defenders of apartheid," explained a disgusted Wolpe. "At the time that pressure is being mounted to bring about negotiations, this action is taken that substantially reduces that pressure."[36]

Unable to force the executive branch to adopt more stringent economic sanctions, congressional activists from mid-1989 on were faced with a growing movement within the executive branch to repeal certain portions of the 1986 Comprehensive Anti-Apartheid Act as a result of far-reaching changes in South Africa's political system. At the forefront of these political changes was Frederick W. de Klerk, the national chairperson of the ruling National party who in the September 1989 election emerged as the new president of South Africa. Adopting a reformist stance that in many respects paralleled the approach taken by Soviet leader Mikhail Gorbachev, de Klerk as early as June 1989 announced his intention to create a "new South Africa" in which the white minority would share power with the black majority.[37] In order to demonstrate his sincerity in seeking implementation of some type of power-sharing agreement, President de Klerk in the months that followed initiated a series of political reforms that began with the September 1989 legalization of peaceful antigovernment protests. In what surely will be recorded as one of the most significant moments in South African history, President de Klerk four months later announced the unconditional release of Nelson Mandela, the world-renowned ANC leader who had spent nearly twenty-eight years in South African prisons.

The evolving political events in South Africa contributed to a significant change in the sanctions debate within the U.S. policymaking establishment, which broke down essentially into four major groups. The first group, comprising those portions of the policymaking establishment that had never supported the imposition of economic sanctions—the State Department, the Defense Department, and the CIA—broached the idea of partially lifting some of those measures. One of the primary concerns of this group was that the growing polarization of South African politics could lead to the downfall of President de Klerk, a reformist leader who, like Gorbachev, was perceived as crucial to the reform process. Specifically, in order to forestall the rising electoral strength of right-wing forces in South Africa opposed to any changes in apartheid, this group argued that the judicious lifting of sanctions would strengthen the hand of President de Klerk. This viewpoint became increasingly debated after British Prime Minister Margaret Thatcher on February 21, 1990, announced her government's intention unilaterally to lift a self-imposed ban on new investment in South Africa.[38]

The second group consisted of those congressional activists who favored holding the line on sanctions until it became clear that the reform process in South Africa was irreversible. In September 1989, for example, members of this group were questioning whether President de Klerk represented "real change." Although he was perceived as much "smoother" than his predecessor and "better able to put a positive face on the tragedy of South Africa," congressional activists cautioned that this did not ensure a "fundamental change" in the structures of apartheid.[39] Even after a two-day fact-finding mission to South Africa in March 1990 in the aftermath of Mandela's release from prison, congressional activists, though hopeful, remained cautious. Describing the period as a "rare window of opportunity" for the creation of a nonracial democracy, congressional activists nonetheless noted that there remained significant obstacles to a lasting negotiated settlement.[40]

In addition to those groups favoring the partial lifting and maintenance of existing sanctions legislation—the dominant perspectives within the U.S. policymaking establishment during 1990—two other groups constituted fringe elements. Although having sharply declined in numbers as a result of the evolution of political events in South Africa, a third group continued to call for the strengthening of sanctions against it. The most prominent supporters of such an approach were Randall Robinson, executive director of TransAfrica, and other grassroots antiapartheid organizations. The final group included those conservative members of Congress, such as Senator Helms, who favored the complete lifting of economic sanctions. Whereas the number of proponents of further sanctions declined because of recognition that President de Klerk deserved to "be given a chance," proponents of completely lifting sanctions became isolated by the realization among some conservatives that the 1986 legislation did, in fact, contribute to political change in South Africa.

The primary issue in the growing congressional-executive sanctions debate was South African compliance with the legal requirements of the Comprehensive Anti-Apartheid Act of 1986. According to Section 311 of the act, President Bush was authorized to suspend or modify any of the sanctions measures if South Africa fulfilled the first and three out of the four remaining conditions listed here:

1. The release of Nelson Mandela, as well as all other persons persecuted for their political beliefs or detained unduly without trial;
2. Repeal of the state of emergency and release of all detainees held under such a state of emergency;
3. Unban all democratic political parties and permit the free exercise by South Africans of all races of the right to form political parties, express political opinions, and otherwise participate in the political process;
4. Repeal of the Group Areas Act and Population Registration Act and institution of no other measures with the same purposes; and
5. Agree to enter into good faith negotiations with truly representative members of the black majority without preconditions.

An Executive Order repealing sanctions would take effect thirty days after being issued unless Congress by a majority vote passed a joint resolution overturning the president's decision.

By June 1991, the reform process initiated by President de Klerk (measured in terms of South African compliance with the preceding five major conditions of the legislation) had reached the point that the White House could seriously entertain the lifting of sanctions.[41] First, the Afrikaner government demonstrated its willingness to enter into good-faith negotiations (condition 5) through ongoing talks with the black majority that had resolved several thorny political issues; most notable was the ANC's August 1990 agreement to suspend its guerrilla struggle in favor of peaceful negotiations.[42] A second requirement (condition 4) was met when the two primary legal foundations of the apartheid system—the Group Areas Act and the Population Registration Act—were repealed in June 1991.[43] Third, all previously banned political parties and organizations, most notable of them the ANC and the South African Communist Party (SACP), were legalized (condition 3) as of February 2, 1990.[44] A fourth requirement (condition 2) was met when, in the aftermath of similar actions in the Transvaal, Cape Province, and the Orange Free State in June 1990, the state of emergency was lifted in the remaining province of Natal in November 1990.[45]

The only really contested requirement (condition 1) revolved around the U.S. demand for the release of all political prisoners. In August 1990, the South African government agreed to the "phased release" of several categories of such prisoners by April 1991 as well as the return of more than 20,000 political exiles. This agreement, of course, followed on the heels of Mandela's dramatic release in February 1990, which was preceded by the release of seven prominent political prisoners in October 1989. A dispute arose, however, over who exactly constituted a political prisoner. Despite the amnesty granted to hundreds of individuals detained without trial or jailed for their political beliefs, the South African government refused to release prisoners who had committed "violent" crimes, even if those crimes were politically motivated. According to the Human Rights Commission, a monitoring group based in South Africa, approximately 800 such political prisoners were being held as of July 1991 in violation of the August 1990 agreement.[46] This interpretation was rejected by a State Department–sponsored fact-finding mission that concluded in July 1991 that all political prisoners jailed for nonviolent crimes—in essence an acceptance of the South African government's definition—had been released.

The State Department's certification of South African compliance with all five conditions of the 1986 antiapartheid legislation culminated a prorepeal trend within the national security bureaucracies that ultimately required an executive decision by the White House. Having never agreed with its advocates about the efficacy of the sanctions weapon in seeking an end to apartheid, President Bush on July 10, 1991, underscored the "irreversible" nature of political change in South Africa and announced the lifting of all punitive measures associated with the 1986 antiapartheid act.[47] "Since coming to office in 1989," he explained, "President de Klerk has repealed the legislative pillars of apartheid and opened up the political arena to prepare the way for constitutional negotiations, and as I've said on several occasions, I really firmly believe that this progress is irreversible."[48] As a result, bans were lifted on, among other things, the trade in various products, the provision of bank loans to the South African government, and new investments by U.S. companies.

The executive branch's decision to lift sanctions was not greeted warmly by those portions of the policymaking establishment that had been in the forefront of the sanctions campaign throughout the 1980s. Members of the House Subcommittee on Africa and the CBC favored the continuation of sanctions until a new constitution guaranteeing the right to vote for South African blacks was in place, despite the fact that this was not one of the conditions of the 1986 legislation. For these critics, lifting sanctions before the obtainment of some sort of power-sharing agreement only invited intransigence on the part of the minority white regime. "They will be removed, and it will be tragic," explained Representative Gray on the day Bush announced his decision to repeal sanctions. "If you lift them too soon, you lock in apartheid."[49]

The proponents of maintaining sanctions were severely hampered by the simple reality that South Africa largely had met the conditions originally laid down by Congress in 1986. As aptly noted by Representative Lugar, one of the original coauthors of the 1986 antiapartheid act who favored the lifting of sanctions, to change the conditions of the 1986 law to include some sort of power-sharing agreement was tantamount to changing the rules in the middle of a game.[50] Moreover, despite the continued existence of a broad constituency that at the very least wanted the Bush administration to hold off on immediately repealing sanctions, the lack of popular perceptions of an ongoing crisis in South Africa—indeed, the opposite was true—ensured that traditional ideological splits within Congress would hamper any efforts at achieving the number of votes necessary to stop the White House. "As long as there is continued, demonstrable progress in South Africa toward the removal of the obstacles," conceded Representative Wolpe, one of the congressional leaders who felt that the Bush administration's embrace of South Africa was premature, "I think Congress will adopt a wait-and-see attitude."[51]

The general movement toward reform in South Africa did not mean, however, that the Bush administration had a free hand in reestablishing the close U.S.–South African ties that existed before the mid-1970s. Despite such growing pressures within the executive branch, the antiapartheid coalition was sufficiently strong to maintain other forms of sanctions legislation unassociated with the 1986 antiapartheid act. In addition to a variety of legislation that will remain in place at the local, city, and state levels, continued restrictions at the federal level include legislation banning any exports to the South African military and police forces, as well as any form of intelligence sharing. Although Assistant Secretary of State for African Affairs Cohen indicated the possibility of seeking the prosecution of a "test case" in which local antiapartheid legislation failed to comply with new federal realities, this approach seemed highly unlikely given the continued political concerns of the antiapartheid movement. Whereas the lifting of sanctions in accordance with legislatively mandated conditions was one thing, to seek the reversal of other forms of legislation before actual constitutional changes in South Africa was quite another. It is for this reason, for example, that the State Department's Africa Bureau sought to soften the potential domestic firestorm that could have accompanied the lifting of sanctions by ensuring that the decision was announced in consultation with Mandela in the aftermath of a major ANC conference during the first week of July 1990, at the same time giving notice of a doubling in the levels of U.S. assistance (from $40 million to $80 million) devoted to housing, economic development, and education programs for black South Africans.[52]

■ TOWARD THE FUTURE

The United States long failed to recognize the legitimacy of African nationalism in South Africa, caught up as it was in a globalist approach to the region that shortsightedly emphasized anticommunism over racial equality. Yet once the Afrikaner regime began seriously to negotiate with the African National Congress, Washington also had to accord the ANC greater status. In addition, the organization's leader, Nelson Mandela, enjoys a high degree of popularity and respect in the United States, as his June 1990 visit so dramatically illustrated. The Bush administration duly recognized Mandela's status by inviting him to the White House, but it was Congress, in keeping with the policy momentum it had established on South Africa, that most enthusiastically received the ANC leader by inviting him to address a joint session. Mandela thus became one of only four private citizens ever to be accorded this honor.

On the surface the Bush administration has seemed to accept African nationalism in South Africa, but in actuality it is far from doing so. No longer driven by the exigencies of the Cold War, U.S. policy has focused on maintaining the existing economic system in as intact a state as possible. There are at least three components to this thrust. The first is to treat the issue of apartheid as strictly political and more specifically as a matter of eliminating racial discrimination. Thus, according to the State Department, "The United States seeks the elimination of apartheid and the establishment of a democratic nonracial South Africa through peaceful negotiations between the government and credible black leaders."[53] Or, as President Bush noted in his remarks following his repeal of sanctions: "Apartheid must be eliminated, and we've worked with the nations of the world to bring an end to this system of racial prejudice by every means possible."[54] By arguing that de Klerk is making irreversible progress toward this goal, the United States is also helping to restore the international legitimacy of the South African government and promote the legitimacy of the current economic system.

Second, U.S. policy has sought to open up the economic system to greater black participation without proposing basic restructuring. One example is the Assistance to Disadvantaged South Africans program, which focuses on education, human rights, black private enterprise, labor union training, and community development. Specifically, the program seeks "to broaden understanding of the free market system and prepare black business owners, managers, and employees for success in a postapartheid South Africa." Funding under the program has gone "to strengthen black business associations" and to "training black women to become leaders in the accounting and financial services field and providing credit to small businesses." Operated in conjunction with the African American Labor Center, the program "has helped black unions develop skills in organizing, collective bargaining, health and occupational safety, and grievance procedures."[55]

The third dimension of U.S. policy that seeks to check the growing influence of African nationalism is the promotion of "credible black leaders" (particularly Zulu Chief Gatsha Buthelezi). For instance, in speaking to reporters after lifting sanctions, President Bush placed the Zulu politician on a par with de Klerk and Mandela: "I've been impressed with the commitment by President de Klerk, by Nelson Mandela, by Chief Buthelezi, and many others to continue to build a constitutional democracy in South Africa."[56] Even though the Bush administration knows that it cannot ignore Mandela and the forces of African nationalism that he represents, Buthelezi nonetheless is the "credible black leader" that the White House would most like to see emerge out of the negotiating process with the government. The reason is easy to discern. Nelson Mandela speaks of removing racial oppression in the economic sphere as well as in the political sphere: "As far as the economic policy is concerned, our sole concern is that the inequalities which are to be found in the economy should be addressed." Continuing, he noted that "we are not looking at any particular model," although "we have mentioned state participation in certain specific areas of the economy, like mining, the financial institutions and monopoly industries."[57] This is in sharp contrast to Buthelezi's position: "We have been able to heed the lessons that Africa has taught us. Socialism, as it has been practised, hasn't worked on this continent. With the best will in the world in some countries, it has failed miserably. The fact is that the free enterprise system remains the only system in which wealth can be generated in such a way as to provide the jobs and infrastructure necessary for growth and stability."[58]

Events in South Africa continue as in the past to have a way of overtaking U.S. policy. The Bush administration had sought to ensure political continuity by promoting and assisting gradual reform, by strengthening the de Klerk government through lifting sanctions and other measures, and by helping build up Buthelezi and his Inkatha movement as a rival to Mandela and the ANC. Within less than a month of the lifting of U.S. sanctions, however, the "Inkathagate" scandal broke, with its revelations that South African police slush funds had been used to promote Inkatha activities and those of its trade union auxiliary. The effects of the affair were to undercut many of the hard-won political gains the government had garnered through its reform program, severely undermine the credibility of Buthelezi and Inkatha as a viable and independent alternative to the ANC, and advance significantly the standing of the ANC.[59] Indeed, this shift in political fortunes no doubt contributed significantly to the formal opening of official negotiations on South Africa's political future that got under way with the first meeting of the Convention for a Democratic South Africa (CODESA) in December 1991.

The launching of CODESA provides the Bush administration with the opportunity to revamp U.S. foreign policy toward South Africa. The globalist element stemming from the Cold War context has vanished, because the opposing side has disintegrated. The ideology of promoting the free enterprise system, however, very much continues, as does the belief that the white minority deserves consideration over any other segment of the South African population. This tendency was reinforced by de Klerk's willingness to hold a referendum in March 1992 on the issue of reform in South Africa in which whites overwhelmingly voted in favor (68.7 percent) of negotiating an end to apartheid. There thus remain strong continuities in U.S. policy toward South Africa, a policy that still has not undergone a fundamental restructuring to accommodate fully the forces of African nationalism and to accept unambiguously the proposition that destroying apartheid means transforming the economy as well as the politics of that racially divided country.

■ 15

The Philippines

Richard J. Kessler

The United States historically has been involved extensively in Philippine affairs, ranging from the colonization of that country in 1898 at the end of the Spanish-American War, through the patron-client relationship with Philippine President Ferdinand Marcos that spanned five U.S. administrations during the post–World War II period, to the ongoing close relationship between Washington and Philippine President Corazon Aquino. Yet, despite the intimacy of this relationship, U.S. policymakers have consistently been unclear or mistaken about the extent and character of U.S. leverage over the Philippine government and the ethical issue of intervening in internal Philippine affairs.

Some of the policy ambivalence was captured in a gaming exercise on the Philippines sponsored by the Pentagon in late 1984. One participating former State Department official, noting past U.S. experience with former client states such as Ethiopia, Iran, and Libya, asserted that the U.S. "capacity to manipulate the outcome of a political process in the state of disintegration, is very, very limited." The primary failing of U.S. foreign policy, which he noted was open to considerable debate, was that "we have failed quickly enough . . . to make clear our readiness to look at alternatives." More precisely, "we have failed to make clear our detachment from the sinking ship, and therefore have gone down with it."[1] As another member of the exercise stated, "there are points where we can misuse the tremendous leverage we have, and I think it would be a mistake to underestimate how much leverage we have."[2] Indeed, as the Philippines case will illustrate, the implementation of an interventionist foreign policy in the Third World is easier to discuss in theory than in practice.

■ EVOLUTION OF THE RELATIONSHIP

In 1898 President William McKinley prayed for God's guidance as to whether or not to colonize the Philippines after the Spanish forces in Manila had surrendered to U.S. Admiral George Dewey. According to McKinley, God approved and directed him "to educate the Filipinos, and uplift and Christianize them,"[3] conveniently ignoring three hundred years of the

Catholic Church's impact under the Spaniards. Little did McKinley know of the quagmire he was getting into. Others would soon learn.

Philippine independence fighters who had struggled against Spain now turned their cudgels on the Americans attempting to occupy their country in the aftermath of the Spanish-American War. The three-year U.S.-Philippine war cost at least 4,234 U.S. lives and the lives of more than 16,000 Filipinos. In one of the most famous encounters, thirty-six men of Company C of the U.S. Ninth Infantry were killed in Balangiga, Samar, on a Sunday morning in September 1901. A group of insurgents had infiltrated the village disguised as women, concealing their bolo knives in the coffins of supposed cholera victims. After the raid, the head of Company C's captain was found roasting over a fire. In revenge, General Jacob H. Smith, a veteran of the U.S. Civil War and Indian campaigns, ordered Samar Island to be pacified, telling his men to "kill and to burn! The more you kill and burn, the better you will please me."[4] Samar was to be transformed into a "howling wilderness" with no one older than ten surviving the attack. Thus, the Philippines was conquered once again.

McKinley promoted a policy of "benevolent assimilation," asserting that U.S. policy was to give Filipinos "good government and security in their personal rights."[5] He established a context for U.S. policy that has remained constant, a mixture of idealism and self-interest. At critical moments self-interest has won over idealism. The present U.S. involvement is rooted in the inability to escape this historical legacy.

The United States ruled the Philippines for almost half a century, finally granting it independence on July 4, 1946. In the aftermath of World War II, the United States provided $620 million in rehabilitation relief and compensation for war damage (after Dresden, Manila was the most devastated city), conditional upon the new Philippine government acceding to U.S. demands for special trade benefits and military bases. The aid had little impact on the country's economic and political dislocation from the war, and a communist-led, peasant-based insurgency known as the Hukbalahaps (Huks) grew in strength during the late 1940s and early 1950s. CIA agents intervened in the 1953 presidential campaign to promote the candidacy of populist Ramón Magsaysay, then defense secretary. After Magsaysay's election, U.S. military and economic advisers became more deeply involved in formulating social reforms and developing a counterinsurgency program to fight the Huks. Success in defeating the Huks in the early 1950s became a model for later U.S. support to the South Vietnamese government.

The Philippine Council on U.S. Aid (PHILCUSA) was formed to administer a new aid program that emphasized agricultural and rural development, including land reform, as well as technical training and education. The program did not produce all the changes hoped for, mainly because "attitudes and institutional rigidities inherited from the past . . . prevented more effective use of larger amounts of aid."[6] The U.S. problem was that aid given directly to individuals did not help economic restructuring and aid given to the government ended up in the hands of individuals. This situation only worsened under the leadership of President Ferdinand E. Marcos. Marcos's strategy was to gain as much U.S. unconditional aid as possible by using access to Philippine bases as leverage. Over time, this approach proved to be very successful.

Although Marcos was elected president in 1965 partly on the nationalist promise to keep the Philippines out of the Vietnam War, he almost immediately reversed himself after President Lyndon B. Johnson promised large amounts of U.S. aid. In 1969 Marcos won reelection to a second four-year term and, on September 21, 1972, he declared martial law when his foes were massing to gain control of the presidency at the end of his constitutionally mandated limit of two terms. As part of this declaration, Marcos suspended the constitution and imprisoned thousands of his opponents, including Senator Benigno Aquino.

The martial-law period was ambivalently perceived both in the Philippines and in the United States. Despite the arrests, many Filipinos welcomed the respite from the factionalized politics that seemed to impede Philippine progress: Specifically, the government received strong marks for its willingness to break up economic empires and confiscate weapons from private armies. The economy, too, grew as a result of improved commodity prices and heavy borrowing after the first oil price shock of 1973–1974, which forced the international banks to recycle large amounts of new petrodollars to the Third World. Although deeply suspicious of Marcos, the United States continued to supply substantial aid; renegotiating compensation for the U.S. bases in 1979 and 1983 led to even more assistance. Yet, even by 1978, as the second world oil price shock hit the Philippine economy, it had become apparent that Marcos's hold on the nation was slipping.

In response, Marcos made tentative efforts at appearing to democratize the country—allowing local elections in 1980, lifting martial law in 1981, and permitting elections to the National Assembly in 1984—but he still maintained firm control, ruling by executive decree. The assassination of his principal opponent, Senator Benigno Aquino, on August 21, 1983, just as Aquino returned from exile, provided the match that lit the smoldering fire of popular discontent.

Under increasing domestic and U.S. pressure, Marcos announced "snap" presidential elections for February 7, 1986. The opposition parties hurriedly organized behind the candidacy of Senator Aquino's widow, Corazon Cojuangco Aquino. The turnout in support of Aquino overwhelmed Marcos's efforts to cheat. Still, Marcos clung to power even as the nation took to the streets to protest his proclamation of victory. It is ironic that the coup de grace was accomplished by the Philippine military, which revolted against him, backed by a stunning display of people power (demonstrators formed a human wall around rebelling troops to protect them from those still loyal to Marcos). Marcos was ushered out of the country aboard a U.S. Air Force jet to exile in Honolulu as Corazon Aquino triumphantly took up residence at Malacañang Palace.

U.S. interest in aiding the transition to the post-Marcos era was considerable. At the end of 1986, U.S. bases in the Philippines included Subic Bay Naval Base, which covered 62,000 acres (25,000 hectares) and contained an air station, naval magazine, and repair facilities. U.S. Air Force facilities at Clark Air Base in Tarlac and Pampanga provinces similarly covered an enormous 130,000 acres. Both bases employed a total of 46,000 full-time Filipino workers. In addition, smaller communications, recreation, and air bases were spread throughout the archipelago, including the San Miguel Naval Communications Station, John Hay Air Station, Wallace Air Station, and a station in Mindanao that monitored Soviet atomic tests. Substantial, too, were U.S. economic interests in the country: Direct U.S. foreign investment exceeded $1 billion (nearly 50 percent of total foreign investment in the country); U.S. trade accounted for about one-third of the Philippines' total imports; and U.S. banks were owed about 60 percent of the Philippines' foreign commercial bank debt. Moreover, Filipino immigrants to the United States since 1972 had created a new bond between the two countries. Indeed, according to the U.S. Census Bureau, Filipinos will be the largest Asian ethnic group in the United States by the year 2000.

■ THE MARCOS ERA AND LOST OPPORTUNITIES TO INFLUENCE POLICY

During the twenty years that Marcos held onto power, U.S. policymakers consistently reiterated U.S. support for the Filipino people and democracy. In reality, the United States became concerned about Philippine democracy only when democracy became a security issue. Indeed, U.S. policymakers from Johnson to Reagan turned a blind eye toward corruption and the destruction of democracy under Marcos as long as U.S. access to the highly valued military bases was assured. As was the case in Nicaragua and Iran (see Chapters 16 and 17), the United States largely ignored the domestic nature of the regime until social instability began to threaten perceived U.S. interests. Although the outcome in the Philippines is a far cry from the anti-U.S. revolutionary regimes that took power in Iran and Nicaragua, serious problems remain, the most significant being the strong guerrilla insurgency active in all provinces of the nation.

U.S. policymakers, rather than accept the destruction of democracy in the Philippines and the subsequent risks this destruction entailed, had numerous opportunities to prevent this occurrence or, failing that, to distance the United States from the corrupt nature of the Marcos regime. The first incident, which set the tone of the U.S.-Marcos relationship, took place early in Marcos's first term, when President Johnson courted him to gain Philippine military participation in the Vietnam War. Although as a senator Marcos had opposed Philippine President Diosdado Macapagal's request to send units to Vietnam, once he became president he introduced legislation in February 1966 to send an engineer construction battalion. The United States paid for the unit, providing all allowances and equipment, although the Philippines paid salaries. U.S. funds were distributed in quarterly payments directly to Marcos with no accountability as to their use.[7] In a visit to the Philippines in October of that same year, Johnson expressed his appreciation by referring to Marcos as his "right arm in Asia."[8]

The troop agreement established a pattern to U.S.-Philippine relations under Marcos. Marcos used the agreement to obtain considerable increases in aid and placed President Johnson in a debt of gratitude, referred to in Filipino as *utang na loob*. Yet, the Philippines itself contributed little to the cause (the troops were not even combat soldiers). As one U.S. official commented, "The history of our relations was determined by our *utang na loob* to them."[9] In short, Marcos had Johnson at a disadvantage—and both knew it: Marcos was able to obtain more than what normally would be possible, whereas the United States was limited in what it could expect in return. Thus, when Johnson in late 1966 tried to get increases in Philippine troop commitments, he was turned down.

A second key incident involved the 1969 Philippine election, in which Marcos was fighting a tough reelection campaign with the Liberal party candidate, Senator Sergio Osmena, Jr. Prior to martial law, weak party lines in the Philippine Congress meant that the president was frequently attacked by members of his own party. Some critics could be partly muffled by the appearance of a U.S. blessing of the president's leadership. In this regard, Marcos sought to improve his election chances by successfully receiving the personal blessing of President Richard M. Nixon, the impact of which cannot be overestimated. On July 26, President Nixon stopped briefly in Manila for an official visit. Moreover, Marcos pressed for and received the appearance of the U.S. ambassador, Henry Byroade, at his side while campaigning. In the heat of the campaign, Marcos requested an official Washington envoy and, in a compromise move, received Ronald Reagan, then governor of California, for a visit in September.[10] Vice President Spiro Agnew also came to Manila, although after the election in December. (The United States may have also deliberately aided Marcos's campaign by covertly injecting several million dollars into the government banking system after Marcos threatened to search every U.S. naval vessel for contraband.[11])

A third incident occurred in the period leading up to Marcos's declaration of martial law on September 21, 1972. Marcos initially hesitated to declare martial law because he was uncertain of the U.S. reaction and was by nature risk-averse. The U.S. uncertainty posed a dilemma for him. Strong U.S.

disapproval could force him to reverse the decision. It was a moment, at least from Marcos's perspective, of great vulnerability to external factors. However, even tacit U.S. approval of his move would reverse the poles of dependence. Once the United States had sanctioned Marcos's dictatorship, it would be almost impossible to rescind approval.

Marcos thus worked to gain a U.S. endorsement. As it turned out, U.S concern over involvement in another Southeast Asian crisis, the Vietnam War, and the U.S. policy of lowering the profile of the U.S.-Philippine special relationship both worked in Marcos's favor. Martial law was perceived by the United States as an internal Philippine problem. It is surprising, too, that when Marcos met secretly with Ambassador Byroade in order to find out how the United States would respond if he had to take "stronger measures," Byroade obtained from the State Department a confidential message that "in the event of serious insurgency problems the United States would support the Office of the President." In essence the United States was expressing its support for Marcos.[12]

The immediate U.S. response to Philippine martial law was cautious. In fact, Byroade asked Washington to minimize its response, thus perhaps echoing Secretary of State Henry Kissinger's view that martial law was something U.S. policy could transcend. Neither Byroade nor any other prominent U.S. policymaker believed that Marcos would keep martial law in effect for as long as he did—until 1981. By not denouncing it, the United States gave it tacit approval.

This sequence of events taught Marcos another important lesson in his relations with the United States: When put to the test, the United States would forsake its principles or, at least, wash its hands of involvement. As long as Marcos played the game by not threatening U.S. interests, and as long as the internal situation did not get out of his control and threaten those interests, Washington would be happy to ignore his actions.

Yet, Marcos was still afraid of a diminished U.S. role in the Philippines. A great fear among Philippine policymakers was that the United States would withdraw from Clark and Subic. After 1972, U.S. aid became more vital if Marcos was going to have the means to expand his coercive power in the military and enforce his one-man rule while promoting economic growth; indeed, one of the things Marcos most feared was that the United States would favor another Philippine leader. Thus, Marcos's policy was to use any means short of provoking a rupture in relations to secure his flank from potential U.S. efforts to replace him while also always pursuing greater U.S. aid commitments.

The reopening of the base negotiations was another instance in which the United States could have distanced itself from Marcos. Talks that had been suspended in July 1974 until the U.S. political situation, then immured in the Watergate investigation, was "clarified"[13] were reopened after President Gerald R. Ford's visit in 1976. Marcos really did not want a new base agreement; he wanted more money, as Ambassador William Sullivan then recognized[14] and was simply using the threat of negotiations to attain his goal. That Marcos was concerned about U.S. intentions was indicated by reports from the Philippine embassy in Washington: "Provisions should now be made in anticipation of a possible phasing out or minimization of U.S. aid to the [Philippines] . . . both for military aid and non-military items, considering the evolving temper of the American Congress."[15] This prospect scared Marcos, and he proceeded to provoke U.S. attention by raising any number of objections, including doubts about the bases' military value and suggestions that the bases were a threat to regional peace and security.[16]

His tactic of holding the bases hostage for greater aid had some impact, especially on the local base commanders and the U.S. Pacific Command in Hawaii. In their view, Marcos had leverage, although the Pentagon, which had never been eager to reopen the subject, believed differently. Marcos impeded base operations by putting pressure on the base labor force, turning demonstrations on and off, and suggesting that he might use even more dramatic measures, such as blockading Subic Harbor or disrupting the fuel line to Clark. The local commander's first responsibility was to assure base operability, and U.S. field commanders could imagine any number of scenarios for disruption.

Perhaps Pentagon concerns drove the Carter administration to continue base negotiations after they broke down in the last weeks of the Ford administration. Moreover, completing the negotiations gave the clearest signal yet of U.S. support for the martial-law regime that Marcos would receive until the Reagan administration invited him to Washington for a state visit in 1982. There was no intrinsic reason for changing the terms of the agreement other than Marcos's demand for more aid: The 1947 Military Bases Agreement was not to expire until 1991. If Philippine nationalist sentiments needed to be assuaged, this could have been done unilaterally by permitting the Philippine flag to fly over the bases, reducing the bases' boundaries, or even appointing titular Filipino base commanders; a comprehensive new agreement was not needed. In addition, these actions would have signaled a willingness to put the Filipino people's interests above those of the United States and would not have been viewed as an endorsement of Marcos. Most important, nothing was gained by the base negotiations, but something was lost: an opportunity for the United States to distance itself from Marcos. The longer negotiations dragged on, the more important they became to Marcos. Failure to conclude the talks would have indicated a loss of U.S. support.

That Marcos tested the United States continually and found U.S. policy amenable is important, for he did it a fifth time in the dying days of his regime when General Fabian Ver was acquitted of conspiracy in Senator Aquino's assassination. Marcos chose to reinstate Ver as chief of staff despite numerous public and private U.S. statements to Marcos that such an action would trigger a "firestorm" of congressional protest and threaten U.S.-Philippine relations. When the firestorm did not occur in either Congress or the executive branch, this contributed to Marcos's decision to hold a snap presidential election in 1986 and use every available fraudulent method to win.

In the end, Marcos misjudged the United States, but not without cause. He had a sound basis for making his assessment of the U.S. character and U.S. policy interests in the Philippines. From 1972 to 1985, he had dealt with four U.S. presidents and found in all of them an essential unwillingness to rupture the U.S.-Philippine relationship even if basic U.S. values, such as respect for human life and freedom of speech, were at stake.

Perhaps this lack of attention to the Philippines was one of the additional costs of U.S. involvement in Vietnam. During their years in office following the U.S. withdrawal from Vietnam, Secretary of State Henry Kissinger and President Ford focused on shoring up U.S. Pacific allies through enhanced security assistance. Kissinger, emphasizing a point made by President Ford after his December 1975 trip to Asia, stated in July 1976 that "the linchpin of our Asian security effort must be a strong and balanced U.S. military posture in Asia."[17]

■ THE REAGAN ADMINISTRATION AND ATTEMPTS AT CHANGE

In the last year of Marcos's rule, U.S. policymakers tried to promote economic, political, and military reforms—acknowledging that it was unlikely that Marcos would agree to U.S. demands—all the while recognizing that if Marcos acceded to these changes, they would destroy his political power base. This decision to intervene more directly into Philippine affairs was only arrived at after a long internal debate. Some U.S. policymakers argued that the United States lacked the ability to influence Philippine affairs. Others argued that the United States had leverage but that using it would only worsen the situation. Finally, some believed that the United States should not intervene if U.S.-Philippine relations were to step beyond the confines established by the colonial experience. "This was a problem for Filipinos to resolve, not Americans," according to a senior State Department official.[18]

Senior U.S. policymakers finally had become convinced—in part, because of reports of Marcos's bad health—that his days were numbered and began focusing on protecting U.S. interests in a post-Marcos period. Thus, alternatives to Marcos's leadership became more important than retaining a close working relationship with him. In the 1984 National Assembly elections, the United States continually emphasized the importance of fair elections for restoring investor confidence and worked with the opposition to attempt to ensure a fair vote.[19] But even those policymakers who recognized that Marcos's term was ending hesitated to take forceful action, largely because of their belief that Marcos would hang onto power until his death. This explains the frustration expressed over the 1986 snap elections.

Early elections were not something the State Department desired, fearing that a disorganized opposition would be trounced easily by Marcos. Instead, the United States hoped that the basis for a democratic transition could be laid in the previously scheduled 1986 local elections and built upon with the then anticipated 1987 presidential elections. As one U.S. policymaker told me in November 1985, holding early elections had thrown off course the U.S. timetable, as this was the moment to be focusing on economic reforms.

With early presidential elections, U.S. policymakers tried to frame events in the best possible light, assuming Marcos would remain in power. With his reelection, the United States hoped that (1) there would be a vice president capable of taking over should Marcos become incapacitated; (2) Marcos would be in a position to undertake some difficult reforms, such as moving against his cronies (something he had previously feared doing); and (3) if his reelection was viewed as a "genuine mandate," then Filipinos would "feel better" and get on with addressing their social problems.[20] Yet, these desires depended on a scenario that was fundamentally at odds with Philippine realities; it presumed that Marcos retained majority support, that his political machine was intact, and that his coercive power was such that he could impose any settlement on the Filipino and U.S. peoples.

Through it all, Marcos was cognizant of the parameters of the U.S. relationship. He constantly sought to expand the boundaries of the relationship by pressing his policy objectives at multiple levels, pushing and prodding the United States to achieve his goals, using the back door to influence U.S. policy, always bargaining and manipulating. But his aims also knew limits. He was aware that the United States could change the Philippine policy environment almost overnight, although the Philippines could have no similar impact on the United States.

Marcos was particularly shrewd at exploiting U.S. security and economic interests in the Philippines, suggesting he could be trusted to safeguard U.S. interests while alternately issuing strong nationalist appeals and declaring that the Philippines could survive without U.S. support. As the rest of Asia stabilized and the Philippine domestic situation deteriorated, however, Marcos gradually began to enjoy less success in his endeavors. Only when the United States saw how crucial democracy in the Philippines was to U.S. security interests did the Marcos threat to break ties with the United States lose legitimacy. Much of the United States' problems in the Philippines may be traced to a lack of U.S. understanding and appreciation for the Philippine situation. Marcos understood the U.S. system; the United States did not understand his. Thus, the use of leverage by U.S. policymakers would have required more detailed knowledge of the dynamics of Philippine politics. Unfortunately, U.S. foreign policy tends to be driven by short-term pragmatism in four-year (or less) periods, with little strategic vision. As long as Marcos remained in control and the situation did not degenerate into crisis, there was little impetus to change policy.

What is striking about the 1977–1985 period was the slowness with which policymakers reacted to the gathering crisis and the failure of political appointees through successive administrations to pay attention to the concerns expressed by the professionals and then act accordingly. Low- and mid-level officials began documenting the problems long before Senator Aquino's assassination in August 1983. But even after Aquino's death, the reaction of policymakers at the highest level was minimal. As a senior NSC official observed in 1986, "The Philippines was going to be a crisis and we recognized it over two years ago." He further noted that "those of us involved in this policy who are Asianists, not politicos or pundits *knew* what we were doing."[21] Once a crisis was recognized, discussions focused on gaining agreement within the government as to the nature of the crisis and on developing a consensus on what actions the United States could and should take. A National Security Study Directive (NSSD) entitled "U.S. Policy Towards the Philippines," leaked in draft in early March 1985, concluded that Marcos was "part of the problem" but still "part of the solution" and suggested a range of actions the United States could take to encourage political, economic, and military reform, stating that "U.S. policies must be linked to progress" in all areas.[22] Yet, events overtook this carefully staged carrot-and-stick approach.

According to some views—that U.S. leverage is limited—it may be argued that the "people-power revolution" in February 1986 could not have occurred in any other way or at any other time. U.S. policy could help influence the direction of change in the Philippines but not direct its course or determine the outcome and, thus, could not be anything else but ad hoc— that is, reactive rather than anticipatory to events.[23]

The timing of policy initiatives and the use of leverage were also affected by factors in Washington. Washington's political climate, with a conservative president, made it difficult to obtain approval for forceful policy initiatives against authoritarian allies. As Senator Paul Laxalt noted, Reagan had a "soft spot" for Marcos.[24] A prominent Reagan appointee to the State Department explained in November 1985 that Reagan had "a very profound distaste for the treatment meted out to the Shah."[25] Reagan's attitude slowed further the already laborious process of developing a policy consensus among government agencies.

In short, the path of least resistance was followed. Only when the Philippines became a crisis were people willing to change policy direction and, in President Reagan's case, only at the last possible moment. The war of words could have begun much earlier. The need for economic, military, and political reforms could have been just as forcefully argued in the 1970s or in Reagan's first term as they were in 1986. Change might have occurred sooner. Yet, policymakers were driven by memories of the downfall of U.S. clients in South Vietnam and Iran, just as a previous generation of policymakers had been affected by the loss of China to Mao Zedong and the need to stop communist aggression in South Korea when they formulated policy toward Indochina. The failure to anticipate the need for change and to understand the Philippines' structural problems made more difficult the process of a democratic transition under President Corazon Aquino and, in addition, reduced U.S. leverage on the new government.

■ AQUINO AND THE U.S.-PHILIPPINE SPECIAL RELATIONSHIP

The events of February 1986 that ushered Corazon Aquino into power opened a new act in the U.S.-Philippine "special relationship." Aquino came to power with little direct U.S. support and with considerable international fanfare. The people-power revolution increased the Philippines' international stature and, in turn, limited U.S. influence when the political situation in Manila once again began to deteriorate.

Soon after President Aquino's accession to power, this reduced U.S. influence became apparent over the issue of how to handle an increasingly widespread communist-led guerrilla insurgency. Early on, U.S. policymakers became concerned about the Aquino government's failure to articulate and implement a comprehensive civilian-military counterinsurgency approach to reducing the threat of the 24,000-strong New People's Army (NPA). During Marcos's rule, the Communist Party of the Philippines (CPP) had grown from a handful of cadres in 1968 to a political presence in almost all of the country's seventy-three provinces. By 1988, it controlled an estimated 20 percent of the nation's *barangays* (districts) and had a mass base of several million supporters. It is ironic that although Marcos used the insurgency as his excuse for declaring martial law in 1972, it was then very limited in scope and personnel.

Upon coming to office, Aquino enunciated a policy of "national reconciliation," releasing political prisoners from jails, including the Communist party's founder, José Maria Sison, and the NPA's first chief, Bernabe Buscayno. A truce was even signed with the CPP in late 1986. Aquino believed that only by bringing the left into the established political process could a long-lasting resolution of the guerrilla insurgency be found. Yet, both the Philippine military and the U.S. government—most notably the Pentagon—were opposed to any deal that led to power-sharing with communists, and they therefore worked to undermine the truce that eventually broke down in early 1987. The key to the breakdown of the accord and the continuing guerrilla insurgency, however, is that Aquino's administration failed to address the root social causes of the rebellion, such as income inequalities and the lack of rural justice. The U.S. government had itself similarly failed to understand these problems and to design a program compatible with U.S. economic and military aid levels.

Land reform was the classic example. Although promising land reform during her presidential campaign, Aquino appeared to be interested less in developing and implementing a program upon becoming president. She did not want to rule by executive decree, as had her predecessor, desiring instead to leave major issues, such as land reform, to be resolved by a democratically elected congress. But the congress was not elected until May 1987 and did not take office until midsummer of the same year. By that time, it was evident that any land reform program would be half-hearted, given opposition by landowners who had begun organizing both politically and militarily, forming private armies, against any but the weakest initiative.

Although the United States recognized the importance of land reform as a means of reducing peasant grievances and improving incomes in rural areas, it too had done little to understand the dimensions of such a program. In fact, no one knew how much land was available for redistribution. No land surveys had been undertaken. The World Bank completed a land reform study by the summer of 1987, advocating redistribution of all farms above 7 hectares (approximately 17 acres). By the time that proposal was on the table, however, the political impetus for land reform had disappeared.

Another example of the limits of U.S. influence was the issue of military reform. Under both Marcos and Aquino, the United States advocated the need to "reprofessionalize" the Philippine military, providing it with better training, equipment, benefits, and leaders. Yet, although the military's revolt had been instrumental in bringing Aquino to power, she and many of her advisers remained suspicious of the military's intentions. Indeed, Defense Minister Juan Ponce Enrile—who had played an important role in the efforts that toppled Marcos—had presidential aspirations of his own and resisted Aquino's authority until he was fired in November 1987. Primarily because of the immediately perceived need to stem further dissension within the ranks, Aquino pursued a policy, not of reform, but of promoting officers who were loyal to her to key commands—a tactic that Marcos also had practiced, which eventually resulted in undermining his support among junior officers. Most important, Aquino's policy of national reconciliation—strongly resisted by the armed forces—in turn only made the military suspicious of her real intentions toward the communists. Only after an attempted military coup on August 28, 1987, did Aquino appear to recognize the need to win the military's support if she was to remain in office. Yet, when the United States pushed the importance of military reform and formulating a counterinsurgency campaign, it was accused by Philippine leaders of trying to undermine Aquino.

The difficulty of formulating a supportive but constructive policy limited U.S. influence. The desire to make clear complete U.S. support for President Aquino in order to dissuade potential usurpers from attacking her, to dispel the resentment of U.S. support for the Marcos regime, and to encourage foreign investment placed major constraints on U.S. policymakers. The "cobwebs of lingering doubt" about U.S. support for Aquino, as noted by her vice president Salvador Laurel in early 1986, were exploited by the Philippine government whenever the United States attempted to press issues such as economic and military reform.

U.S. influence was further limited by U.S. domestic budgetary constraints. Aid could not be increased to the levels necessary for the Philippine government to buy off the elites whose power base would be undermined if the government undertook the essential social reforms necessary to defeat the communist insurgency. But even more aid would not necessarily guarantee more effective programs if the government itself was not committed to reform. Indeed, Aquino's international stature had gained the Philippines major new commitments of bilateral and multilateral aid in her first two years in office, but efforts to use these funds were stymied by internal political disputes and her cabinet's inexperience at governing. By the end of 1987, aid amounting to $1.9 billion had backed up in the donor pipeline, leading many major donors to reduce their aid commitments for subsequent years.

In truth, many of the problems faced by the Aquino government were the creation of Ferdinand Marcos, but it would be false to blame Marcos for all the problems of the Philippines. With his absence, for example, communist rebels did not immediately come down from the hills, nor was corruption instantaneously eliminated from the society, nor did the military become at once professional and apolitical. The Marcos years had exacerbated existing social ills in the Philippines, but, despite his departure from the country to self-imposed exile in 1986, the oligarchy-dominated political and economic system remained.

These were problems long apparent to U.S. observers of the Philippines. Yet, U.S. policy did little to anticipate their impact on Philippine stability. Nor did U.S. policymakers attempt to assess the consequences of these enduring problems on the stability of a successor government. For example, even after Marcos was replaced by Aquino, U.S. policymakers still did not reassess their economic and security aid programs in light of Philippine problems to make them more effective. Two years after Aquino came to power, the U.S. Agency for International Development mission in Manila was still supporting essentially the same types of projects it had supported during the Marcos years, with little thought given to how these projects contributed to Philippine development. Rather than being prepared for change once Marcos was gone, U.S. policymakers continued along the lines previously prescribed, and policy continued to be reactive. No thought was given to long-range planning with the objective of sustaining Philippine democracy. Policy instead focused, as it had in the past, on demonstrating strong support for the government in power.

The Reagan administration's need to show its support for Aquino was understandable, given the considerable doubts raised about President Reagan's personal feelings toward the new Philippine leader. But, in so doing, the United States again fell into the traditional trap of tying U.S. policy to the legitimacy of a particular leader rather than to the people of the country. What is ironic is that this approach—as it restricted the flexibility of U.S. policy—suited the Aquino government just as well as it had suited the Marcos regime. Secretary of State George Shultz aggravated these constraints by stating publicly that the United States would have preferred to give the Aquino government more financial aid but was unable to do so because of domestic budgetary cutbacks. In response, the Aquino government demanded more demonstrations of U.S. personal support for Aquino. Thus, even as the Aquino government initiated policies that the United States privately raised doubts about—for example, support for anticommunist vigilante groups, demands for more helicopters to fight the insurgency, or failure to proceed with a land reform program—the United States, as in the past, was not in a position to criticize openly or to influence privately the direction of internal Philippine affairs.

Like the government under Marcos, the Aquino government had maneuvered the United States into a position in which U.S. policy was hostage to U.S. security interests. In 1988, negotiations were reopened over the amount of aid the United States would provide for access to military facilities over the three-year period remaining in the 1947 Military Bases Agreement—a treaty that expired in 1991 and that was not renewed by the Philippine Senate. U.S. policymakers felt constrained to keep any disagreement with the Aquino government as low-key as possible. Philippine policymakers recognized this constraint and exploited it almost as soon as the base negotiations began. By the fall of 1988, talks were briefly stalemated once again over the issue of money, with the Philippines requesting more than twice the amount the United States was willing to offer. The final agreement resulted in $481 million per year in economic and military assistance for 1990 and 1991—the last two years of the Military Bases Agreement. This sum was substantially less than the over $1 billion the Philippine government was requesting. But the protracted and often bitter negotiations also impeded progress on other issues, as rising nationalist sentiment in the Philippines became hostile to any sign of U.S. intervention. These issues included economic reforms and a deteriorating human-rights situation, as vigilante groups supported by the Philippine military carried out their own private war against the peasants. Thus, during a period of difficult democratic transition, U.S. influence was ironically at its lowest point, perhaps, in the history of the U.S.-Philippine special relationship, with the future of Philippine democracy in doubt.

■ INTERVENTION IN PERSPECTIVE

Six years after Corazon Aquino was swept into power by the Filipino people, she anointed Fidel Ramos as her successor. Whether the people would agree to that remained to be seen in the 1992 elections, but her endorsement of him symbolized the state of the Philippines. That Aquino, despite considerable pressure, had kept to her promise not to run for a second term and was prepared to transfer power by democratic means represented the positive change her presidential tenure had brought. That she endorsed a man who had for long loyally served Marcos and then stood by her side against numerous military coup attempts represented how much Philippine future was determined by its past.

Despite six years of extensive external support, both moral and financial, the legacy bequeathed by Corazon Aquino was at best a mixed one. Democratic political structures had been restored, but the style of politics was still oligarchic. Even Ferdinand Marcos's widow, Imelda, had returned to campaign for the presidency. Economic reforms had been initiated, but the style of the economy also was still oligarchic. Poorly implemented reforms coupled with continued corruption and exacerbated by natural disasters reduced the rate of economic growth below that of population growth.

In one area—the U.S.-Philippine "special relationship"—the past had been definitively sundered. Despite protracted and often bitter negotiations, the Philippine Senate refused in 1991 to approve the agreement to extend the 1947 Military Bases Agreement. At long last all U.S. military forces would be withdrawn by September 1992. Their withdrawal had been given impetus by the explosion of Mount Pinatubo in 1991, which forced the rapid evacuation of U.S. air forces from Clark Air Field and also caused considerable damage to Subic Bay. Ironically, after years of putting forth one strategic rationale after another for maintaining the U.S. military presence, the Pentagon ended up being more eager than any other portion of the U.S. policymaking establishment to withdraw. Among those factors contributing to the Pentagon's decision to support the withdrawal of U.S. forces were the reduction of a global military threat that accompanied the fragmentation of the Soviet Union, the necessity of reducing U.S. forces abroad as a result of budgetary considerations, and growing frustration over Filipino demands for exorbitant amounts of U.S. foreign aid in exchange for base rights.

The effect on the Philippines of the U.S. withdrawal remains to be determined, but it will likely be significant if slow to be perceived. For years, U.S. intervention, real or imagined, in Filipino affairs had been a major factor in determining Filipino political alignments. Even during the Aquino period, the helpful intervention of U.S. jets overflying an air base under attack from Filipino military coup plotters in 1989 had been instrumental in turning the tide against the coup as military fence sitters decided not to contest the power of the United States. Never again would such intervention be so easily accomplished.

At the same time, the end of the U.S. military presence would also likely translate into a decline in aid, particularly military assistance and Economic Support Funds. Congressional support for large amounts of development assistance, largely channeled through the Multilateral Assistance Initiative (MAI) for the Philippines, would also likely diminish. A diminishing amount of aid and interest in the Philippines meant a decline in U.S. influence in the Philippines. The use of aid to enhance policy dialogue with the Philippine government would no longer be an easy conversation to initiate.

The withdrawal of U.S. military forces and the potential decline in economic aid had its private-sector equivalent. The initial optimism expressed by foreign investors that the overthrow of Marcos would bring in its wake economic prosperity to the Philippines quickly wore off in the face of domestic political turmoil and the inability of the new leadership to deal decisively with the structural aspects of the country's severe economic problems. Nor was there much reason for scarce U.S. private capital to seek out the Philippines when there existed so many more opportunities with less risk in the newly industrializing economies in the rest of Southeast Asia.

The evolution of the relationship into one unencumbered by the thought of past slights or future necessities will likely take several generations to emerge. It took at least that long for Filipinos to develop such a relationship with Spain. Yet it is unlikely that Washington will be perceived with the same distance that Filipinos view Madrid. Unlike Spain, the United States remains both by geography and determination a Pacific power. Even as the United States was withdrawing from the Philippines, it was establishing a set of lower-profile but still important security ties with Singapore, Malaysia, and Thailand. From a Filipino perspective, the United States may not be in a position to intervene so directly in the affairs of the Philippines, but will be in a position to intervene in regional affairs. As a result, the love-hate relationship that has long characterized the relationship most likely will be transferred to the higher plane of regional politics.

The greatest argument against intervention is that it creates dependency. Dependency as a psychosis does not have to be real in order to have symptoms. In many ways, the real or imagined intervention by U.S. policymakers in the Philippines since independence has been used as an excuse by Filipino leaders to ignore domestic problems. The withdrawal of U.S. forces is not likely to change this state of affairs until Filipino politicians make a break with their own past by correcting the country's economic and social structures, which now ensure that many remain poor and few become rich.

16

Nicaragua

Peter Kornbluh

For over 135 years, U.S. policymakers have considered Nicaragua a test case of their power to dictate events in Central America and beyond. The long and tragic legacy of U.S. intervention in Nicaraguan affairs began in 1856 when a soldier of fortune named William Walker overthrew the Nicaraguan government, elected himself president, and sought to transform Nicaragua into a slave state. This legacy continued into the 1980s during the Reagan administration's multifaceted low-intensity warfare strategy to sponsor a counterrevolution against the Sandinista government.

Over the decades, the instruments of intervention have evolved from sending the U.S. Marines to sending the CIA. But the underlying foreign policy premises of such actions remain remarkably constant. Presidents from Theodore Roosevelt to George Bush have shared a hegemonic presumption about the role of the United States in the Western Hemisphere—the belief that the United States has both the right and the might to control internal events in Latin America regardless of international law and national sovereignty. "We do control the destinies of Central America and we do so for the simple reason that the national interest absolutely dictates such a course," as Under Secretary of State Robert Olds summed up this attitude in a January 1927 memorandum on Nicaragua; "it is difficult to see how we can afford to be defeated."[1] As international and domestic realities have changed, however, this policy of permanent engagement has become increasingly costly and counterproductive to the national interests U.S. policymakers claim to defend. And nowhere is this more dramatically demonstrated than in the past and current history of U.S. intervention in Nicaragua.

■ THE ERA OF HEGEMONY

Although Nicaragua gained its independence from Spain in 1821, due to geography it remained an object of empire. Situated in the middle of the Central American isthmus, the small nation of lakes, rivers, and volcanos was one of two potential sites for an interoceanic canal (the other, of course, was Panama). Hoping to reap the lucrative strategic and economic rewards of controlling a transisthmus waterway, the United States engaged in intense commercial and military competition with Great Britain for influence and control in Nicaragua in the mid-1800s. By the turn of the century, Nicaragua had become the principal staging ground for gunboat diplomacy, with U.S. Marines storming the shores in 1894, 1896, 1898, and 1910, occupying the country almost continuously between 1912 and 1933. U.S. officials handpicked Nicaragua's presidents, drafted electoral laws, trained the police, and authorized the national budget; and U.S. business interests—including lumber, mining, coffee, banana, shipping, and banking corporations—established virtually total domination over the Nicaraguan economy.

Pervasive U.S. control over all aspects of Nicaraguan society constituted nothing less than a U.S. version of colonialism. By 1927, as the noted columnist Walter Lippmann observed, it was clear that Nicaragua was "not an independent republic, that its government is the creature of the State Department, [and] that management of its finances and the direction of its domestic and foreign affairs are determined not in Nicaragua but on Wall Street."[2]

The national humiliation of total U.S. dominion over Nicaragua's affairs gave rise to what historians have called the United States' "first Vietnam"—a bloody five-year counterinsurgency war against the nationalist forces of Augusto Sandino. A diminutive-looking man who spent his early adulthood wandering through Central America, Sandino emerged from obscurity in the spring of 1927 when U.S. Marines once again intervened to impose political order in Nicaragua. Believing that bullets were the only defense of Nicaragua's sovereignty, Sandino and his motley army of miners and peasants vowed to take up arms until U.S. military forces withdrew from Nicaraguan territory. Although U.S. officials denounced him as a "common outlaw" and a "bandit," the *Washington Post* described Sandino as a "crude Bolívar of the Nicaraguan hills." His guerrilla campaign represented the first significant challenge to the exercise of U.S. hegemony in the Western Hemisphere.[3]

Between 1927 and 1933, the United States fought a running war of attrition with the first Sandinistas. At the height of the intervention, over 5,000 U.S. Marines were deployed in Nicaragua—a considerable show of force in an era when one U.S. warship on the horizon usually was sufficient to obtain Washington's foreign policy objectives in Central America and the Caribbean. The fighting was fierce. During the first year of combat with Sandino and his ragtag Army for the Defense of Nicaraguan National Sovereignty, the U.S. Navy reported eighty-five confrontations and sixty-six troop casualties. "The Naval forces ashore have encountered the most serious sustained guerrilla warfare that Central America records," the secretary of the navy reported to Congress in February 1928.[4]

Indeed, even in the heyday of gunboat diplomacy, the limits and costs of U.S. intervention were apparent. The U.S. Marines, with vastly superior firepower and numbers, found themselves confronting an enigmatic enemy whom they could neither physically eliminate nor politically contain. The continued military occupation and the inability of U.S. troops to quell Sandino's rebellion fostered extensive U.S. public dissent over the wisdom of the policy and sharp criticism from abroad about Washington's credibility. "We are being charged from one corner of the world to another with being the great threat to the peace . . . to have embarked upon an imperialistic program," U.S. Representative George Huddleston argued on behalf of a congressional resolution to withdraw the U.S. Marines from Nicaragua.[5] In a confidential memorandum to the U.S. military commander in Managua in March 1928, Secretary of State Frank Kellogg complained that "there is a great deal of criticism in the country about the way in which these operations are being dragged out, constant sacrifice of American lives, and without any concrete results. So far as anyone here can see what is now taking place can and will go on indefinitely."[6]

Unable to defeat Sandino, and under intense public pressure, President Herbert F. Hoover withdrew the marines in 1933. Before they departed, however, the United States implemented a policy of "Nicaraguanization"—creating and training a National Guard through which the United States would maintain preeminence in Nicaraguan affairs. Ostensibly, the Guardia was meant to be a nonpartisan police force that could enforce democratic stability and counter the expanding influence of Sandino. To be its commander, U.S. officials handpicked Anastacio Somoza, an English-speaking former latrine inspector. "I look upon him as the best man in the country for the position," U.S. diplomat Matthew Hanna stated in October 1932. "I know of no one who will labor as intelligently and conscientiously to maintain the nonpartisan character of the Guardia."[7]

Instead of remaining nonpartisan, however, the National Guard became Somoza's vehicle to dictatorial rule. On his orders, guardsmen assassinated Sandino in February 1934, eliminating the only man who had the military or political capacity to challenge Somoza's accession to power. In 1936, he overthrew President Juan Sacasa, the long-standing leader of Nicaragua's Liberal party (and Somoza's uncle by marriage), and had himself installed in the presidency.

From the start, the corrupt nature of the regime the United States had created was well known in Washington. Even before the marines departed, reports of widespread opposition to the Guardia's repression began to filter back to the State Department. Intelligence assessments of Somoza's rule were sharply worded. In one "strictly confidential" cable dated December 2, 1939, the U.S. Chargé Laverne Baldwin reported that Somoza's was a "purely military dictatorship" that was "ridden from top to bottom with graft, wasting the substance of a State which needs every centavo in the face of existing world conditions and the ever present extreme poverty of its lowest classes."[8] Somoza's excessive greed and his regime's endemic corruption had serious policy ramifications for the United States, Baldwin concluded:

> It seems that there are two possibilities for future action by the United
> States in the face of this trend of corruption which, if continued, must
> lead to the man's hanging himself by a noose placed by his own hands.
> We might let the man fall by lack of support from us. Such course . . .
> would necessarily mean an upheaval in the country and a period of
> revolutionary destruction. Presumably no serious thought will therefore
> be given it.

An alternative policy option, Baldwin wrote, would be "to assist the existing administration financially."[9]

With an extraordinary degree of prescience, Baldwin urged the administration of President Franklin D. Roosevelt to develop a long-range policy toward Nicaragua, noting that continuation of the military state and corruption under Somoza would "inevitably create strong and growing resistance to and criticism of the Government and its officers." Depending on what steps the United States took, Baldwin predicted "armed outbreaks" against Somoza's rule and noted that, because of Somoza's close ties to Washington, the government that succeeded him would prove much less hospitable to U.S. interests.[10]

■ CARTER AND NICARAGUA:
CONTAINING THE REVOLUTION

Four decades later, the administration of President Jimmy Carter confronted the Sandinista revolution. In the interim, Nicaragua had become the most important anticommunist client state in the Central American/Caribbean region, providing a staging ground for U.S. intervention in Guatemala (1954) and Cuba (1961). In return for his cooperation , one U.S. administration after another had looked the other way as Somoza created a family dynasty, with power passing first to his oldest son, Luis, in 1959, and then to Anastacio, Jr., in 1967. U.S. military and economic assistance to Nicaragua increased steadily between 1945 and 1975, even as Somoza's sons refined and expanded the repression and corruption that had characterized their father's rule. The elder Somoza's cruel joke—"Bucks for my friends, bullets for my enemies"—epitomized the nature of the dictatorship.[11] By 1978, when a spontaneous uprising led by the Frente Sandinista de Liberacion Nacional (FSLN—Sandinista National Liberation Front) began, the Somoza regime was internationally renowned, and repudiated, for its boundless greed and vicious human-rights violations.

Forty years of Somoza family rule left Nicaragua a corrupt, impoverished, and divided state. The dynasty's foundation of power finally began to crumble in the aftermath of a devastating earthquake that destroyed much of Managua in December 1972. For Nicaragua it was a disaster of major socioeconomic consequences; for Somoza it was a grand opportunity for self-aggrandizement. Taking advantage of his compatriots' suffering, he channeled millions of dollars of international relief assistance into his own coffers and those of his cronies. His greed not only undermined Nicaragua's economic redevelopment, it alienated the entrepreneurial and propertied classes, leaving the Somoza regime politically isolated and wholly reliant on National Guard force to stay in power. Somoza's escalating repression, however, only served to radicalize the situation, empowering the opposition to organize and unify and contributing to the growing popularity of the Sandinista guerrilla movement. In 1979, the broad dissatisfaction with Somoza's rule gave way to the revolutionary insurrection that Baldwin had foreseen almost forty years before.[12]

Although Jimmy Carter takes credit for a reformist interlude in U.S. interventionist history, his policy toward the Nicaraguan insurrection was based on the same presumptions of hegemony that dominated the approaches of his predecessors. Uncontrolled change in Central America remained anathema to U.S. officials wedded to the notion that Washington had a historical imperative to dictate events in its traditional sphere of influence. In language reminiscent of Under Secretary of State Robert Olds's imperial justification for U.S. intervention in 1927, Carter's NSC adviser, Zbigniew Brzezinski, argued that what was at stake in 1979 was "not just the formula for Nicaragua but a more basic matter, namely whether in the wake of our own decision not to intervene in Latin America politics, there will not develop a vacuum, which would be filled by Castro and others." "In other words," Brzezinski told Carter, "we have to demonstrate that we are still the decisive force in determining the political outcomes in Central America and that we will not permit others to intervene."[13]

The Carter administration's policy objectives during the Nicaraguan revolution were unambiguous: to prevent a Sandinista victory. Trapped by its own rhetoric on human rights and Somoza's unconcealed brutality, unilaterally sending the marines was not an option for the White House. Nevertheless, U.S. policymakers exercised every conceivable option of persuasion, short of brute force, to manipulate the course of Nicaragua's future.

Through diplomatic coercion, Washington applied its traditional influence over the Nicaraguan government. Having placed the first Somoza in power in 1933, in June of 1979 the United States informed his son that it was time to go. Carter officials recognized that Somoza had become a catalyst for radicalization and instability; the sooner he left, they reasoned, the easier it would be to block the ascendency of "radical" forces led by the heirs of Sandino—the FSLN—to power. Thus, on June 28, U.S. Ambassador Lawrence Pezzullo cabled Washington that he had met with Somoza and "suggested that we design a scenario for his resignation."[14]

The Carter administration's scenario for a transition of power in Nicaragua called for creating a provisional government of moderates that excluded the FSLN and preserving the National Guard, as Assistant Secretary of State Viron Vaky instructed Pezzullo "to avoid leaving the FSLN as the only organized military force."[15] Although the administration ruled out unilateral intervention to implement this strategy, it considered a U.S.-led multilateral military force to be a policy option. On June 15, Assistant Secretary of State Vaky sent a telex to all Latin American diplomatic posts stating that the United States wished "to explore selectively reactions and ideas regarding possible formation of an inter-American peace force to guarantee the transition process and facilitate pacification"—to halt the Sandinistas' push for power. U.S. embassies were told to inform their host governments that the United States feared the "potential for a Castroist takeover in Nicaragua" and sought a political solution involving the "preservation of existing institutions, *especially the National Guard*" (emphasis added).[16] Ten days later Secretary of State Cyrus Vance formally proposed this initiative to the Organization of American States. Representatives of the Latin American nations overwhelmingly rejected the initiative as a multilateral smokescreen for overt U.S. intervention.

During the final weeks of Somoza's rule, the Carter administration frantically attempted to alter the course of history in Nicaragua. The U.S. ambassador arranged for Somoza to step down, name an interim president who would call for a cease-fire, and appoint a new commander for the National Guard. The United States then delayed Somoza's departure, first allowing him to bomb civilian townships in order to halt the advance of FSLN troops and then using the date of his resignation as a bargaining chip to influence the membership of the transitional government selected by the Sandinistas.[17] In the end, however, these diplomatic schemes failed. On July 17, the day Somoza left for Miami, Florida, the National Guard disintegrated. Within forty-eight hours Washington's plan of succession collapsed, as Sandinista troops marched, unopposed, into Managua in triumph.

In the aftermath of the Carter administration's failure to deter the Sandinista's accession to power, U.S. officials shifted from a policy of hostility to cautious accommodation. Nevertheless, U.S. policymakers did not abandon hope of moderating the course of the new Nicaraguan government. "The real issue facing American foreign policy," Assistant Secretary of State Vaky stated, "is not how to preserve stability in the face of revolution, but how to create stability out of revolution."[18] Using the carrot of economic assistance, the White House advanced $15 million in emergency reconstruction aid to Nicaragua and pushed a $75-million assistance package through Congress. At the same time, however, President Carter authorized the CIA to covertly pass funds to anti-Sandinista labor, press, and political organizations—an operation resembling the CIA's destabilization campaign against the Chilean government of Salvador Allende a decade earlier.[19] Thus, when Ronald Reagan took office on January 20, 1981, he inherited a CIA covert operation against the Sandinistas already under way.

■ REAGAN AND NICARAGUA: LOW-INTENSITY WARFARE

The Reagan administration came into office predisposed to escalate U.S. intervention in Nicaragua. For the president and the conservative ideologues around him, Central America represented a symbol of Washington's loss of global preeminence in the aftermath of the Vietnam War. Yet, the new administration viewed Nicaragua more as a test of Reagan's campaign pledge to "project American power throughout the world" than as a serious threat to U.S. national security. Noting the long history of U.S. influence in Central America, former National Security Adviser Robert McFarlane later explained to Congress that the failure to intervene in Nicaragua would have jeopardized Washington's ability to dictate events elsewhere in the Third World. "If we could not muster an effective counter to the Cuban-Sandinista strategy in our own backyard, it was far less likely that we could do so in the years ahead in more distant locations. *We had to win this one*" (emphasis added).[20]

But, even an administration as committed to the use of force as Reagan's faced strict parameters on its instruments of intervention. Unlike the earlier era of gunboat diplomacy, in the 1980s a U.S. president could not cavalierly dispatch the marines to Central America. The Vietnam syndrome—a widespread public reluctance to see U.S. troops once again engaged in a distant Third World conflict—constrained Reagan's national security managers as they plotted U.S. strategy in Nicaragua. Ultimately, U.S. officials turned to an emerging doctrine known as low-intensity conflict (LIC) for post-Vietnam intervention in the Third World in general and Nicaragua in particular. In fact, reversing the Nicaraguan revolution became a test case for the Reagan Doctrine of supporting anticommunist insurgencies in an effort to roll back pro-Soviet regimes around the globe.

In "Covert Action Proposal for Central America," dated February 27, 1981, one of the earliest documents concerning the Reagan administration's plans to undermine the Nicaraguan government, McFarlane presented the case for a multifront assault short of direct military intervention: "The key point to be made now is that while we must move promptly, we must assure that our political, economic, diplomatic, propaganda, military, and covert actions are well coordinated." This approach reflected a new reliance on the LIC doctrine, which, according to Pentagon manuals, called for the "synergistic application of comprehensive political, social, economic and psychological efforts."[21] By combining various methods of pressure short of overt military deployment, the United States could engage in what one LIC proponent called "total war at the grassroots level," without the domestic and international political backlash that a conventional war would provoke.[22]

In Nicaragua, this "total-war" strategy called for four main fronts: (1) a paramilitary war; (2) a campaign of economic destabilization; (3) military psychological operations; and (4) a propaganda war directed not only at Nicaragua and Western allies, but also at the U.S. public.

□ The Paramilitary War

The Reagan administration's low-intensity warfare strategy depended on the creation of a proxy force of exiles such as the CIA had used to overthrow the Arbenz government in Guatemala in 1954 and in its failed effort against Fidel Castro at the Bay of Pigs in 1961. Thus, in 1981 a new generation of CIA-backed counterrevolutionaries emerged. The CIA organized disparate bands of former Nicaraguan National Guard officers and disaffected civilians into one group—the Nicaraguan Democratic Force (FDN). Although the contras, as they came to be known, subsequently went through several organizational reincarnations—the United Nicaraguan Opposition (UNO) and the Nicaraguan Resistance (RN)—the FDN remained the core of the anti-Sandinista forces.

The Reagan administration initially depicted the contras as an "interdiction force" meant to halt arms allegedly flowing from Nicaragua to guerrilla insurgents in El Salvador. When that justification for CIA paramilitary operations became politically untenable, Reagan officials presented the contras to the public as freedom fighters deserving of U.S. support. Privately, however, the administration was well aware of the character of its surrogates. Robert Owen, a key NSC liaison with the FDN, reported to Lieutenant Colonel Oliver North in March 1986 that the contra leaders were "liars and greed and power motivated" and that "this war has become a business for them." Owen concluded that the contras "are not the people to rebuild a new Nicaragua."[23]

For those in the Reagan administration wishing to "bleed" the Sandinista regime, nevertheless, the contras were perceived as the perfect instrument for a policy of punishment, enabling the United States to directly undercut Nicaragua's fragile postrevolutionary economic and social reconstruction. What U.S. officials depicted as a campaign to harass and pressure the Sandinistas into halting their alleged export of revolution into neighboring El Salvador, in practice translated into vicious attacks on small villages, state-owned agricultural cooperatives, rural health clinics, bridges, electrical generators, and, finally, civilian noncombatants. Indeed, CIA training manuals explicitly advised the contras on how to "neutralize carefully selected and planned targets," such as court judges, magistrates, police, and state security officials.[24]

Even with these ongoing attacks, senior U.S. policymakers demanded ever more dramatic and devastating paramilitary operations. "What [more] can we do about the economy to make these bastards sweat?" CIA director Casey repeatedly inquired of his subordinates running the Nicaragua project.[25] In response, the CIA launched its own direct attacks on Nicaraguan installations. In September 1983, CIA commandos launched a series of sabotage raids on Nicaraguan port facilities. In October, CIA operatives set ablaze Nicaragua's largest oil storage facility, destroying 3.4 million gallons of fuel and forcing the city of Corinto to be evacuated for two days.

This campaign of economic sabotage culminated in the first three months of 1984, when CIA "Unilaterally Controlled Latino Assets" (UCLAs)—the CIA term for their Latin American contract agents—mined Nicaragua's major harbors. "Our intention is to severely disrupt the flow of shipping essential to Nicaraguan trade during the peak export period," NSC officials Oliver North and Constantine Menges informed Robert McFarlane in a top secret memorandum on the minings. To advance "our overall goal of applying stringent economic pressure," North and Menges recommended expanding this program to include sinking a Mexican oil tanker in Nicaragua's port. Asserting that "our objective is to further impair the already critical fuel capacity in Nicaragua" and to increase Nicaraguan dependency on the Eastern bloc, North and Menges concluded: "It is entirely likely that once a ship has been sunk no insurers will cover ships calling in Nicaraguan ports. This will effectively limit their seaborne trade to that which can be carried on Cuban, Soviet Bloc, or their own [ships]."[26]

Although this plan never came to fruition, the United States continued direct paramilitary assaults on Nicaragua even after Congress terminated direct and indirect assistance to the contras in October 1984. In December of that year, for example, Oliver North contracted with a former member of the British Special Air Service, David Walker, to engage in "special operations" inside Nicaragua. Walker's saboteurs undertook a number of covert demolition activities in and around Managua—among them the March 6, 1985, bombing of a military complex that included a hospital.[27] Such "special operations attacks against highly visible military targets in Nicaragua," Oliver North indicated in a March 20, 1985, memorandum to NSC adviser Robert McFarlane, were "timed to influence the vote" in Congress to restore CIA assistance to the contras.[28]

□ *Economic Destabilization*

CIA/contra attacks on economic targets inside Nicaragua complemented the Reagan administration's efforts to destabilize the Nicaraguan economy from abroad. Much as the administration of President Richard M. Nixon had done against the socialist government of Salvador Allende in Chile, the Reagan White House successfully employed economic aid and sanctions as tools of intervention.

Whereas the Carter administration had used bilateral assistance as a carrot, the Reagan administration used it as a stick. Within weeks of taking office, the president terminated all U.S. economic aid programs to Nicaragua. Trade was similarly curtailed. A 1983 top secret CIA National Intelligence Estimate noted that "Nicaragua remains highly dependent on trade with the

United States."[29] In May of that year, the White House cut Nicaragua's quota of sugar exports to the United States. Two years later, President Reagan invoked the International Emergency Economic Powers Act to declare a full trade embargo with Nicaragua.

By necessity, the administration's economic war policy against the Sandinistas had international dimensions. To isolate Nicaragua economically, the United States pressured its allies in Latin America and Western Europe to curtail their own trade and aid to the Sandinistas. In 1983, according to an NSC action plan, Secretary of State Shultz was mandated to "press Western European governments at the highest level to cease financial support for the Sandinistas."[30] Mexico, Nicaragua's most important trading partner in Latin America, came under a concerted U.S. campaign of pressure to cut off Nicaragua. In National Security Decision Directive 124 (NSDD 124), signed in February 1984, the president authorized U.S. agencies to "intensify [their] diplomatic efforts with the Mexican government to reduce its . . . economic and diplomatic support for the Nicaraguan government."[31]

Moreover, the administration took its economic destabilization campaign into the boardrooms of the multilateral financial institutions, particularly the World Bank and the Inter-American Development Bank. There, U.S. representatives worked behind the scenes to build voting blocs against loans to Nicaragua, orchestrate negative project evaluations, or, if all else failed, block Nicaraguan grants from coming before the executive boards for final approval. Although the Sandinista government received rave reviews from internal bank assessments of the development projects they completed, Nicaragua received no loans from the World Bank after 1982 and no loans from the Inter-American Development Bank after 1983.

☐ *Military Psychological Warfare*

The third component of the Reagan administration's low-intensity war on Nicaragua was an unprecedented military buildup in Central America and continual joint U.S.-Honduran military war games in the region—part of an extensive psychological operation program to instill uncertainty in the Nicaraguan government about U.S. intentions. As one U.S. official noted, "One of the central purposes is to create fear of an invasion, to push very close to the border, deliberately, to set off all the alarms."[32] These operations also had an economic imperative. With government coffers already drained from the fight against the contras and the economic blockade, the constant threat of a direct U.S. military assault forced Nicaragua's leaders to divert personnel and resources from social programs into planning for the worst-case war scenario.

What LIC proponent Robert Kupperman called "the threat of force to achieve political objectives without the full-scale commitment of resources" proved an effective method of destabilizing the Sandinistas.[33] More than once, highly publicized U.S. military maneuvers with such names as Big Pine I and II, Grenadero 1, Ocean Venture, and Solid Shield provoked major war scares inside Nicaragua. Scores of citizens were sent home from work to dig air-raid shelters; thousands of Nicaraguans prepared for an invasion by taking militia training. In the meantime, economic production halted, cash crops went unharvested, and exports sat on docks. Without firing a shot, the Reagan administration managed to severely disrupt the normal political, economic, and social functions of an entire nation.

□ *The Propaganda War*

In the parlance of the Pentagon, these military psychological operations (psyops) against Nicaragua were called "perception management" programs. But the Reagan administration also conducted similar operations at home, against the U.S. public. This component of U.S. policy, known by the Orwellian term "public diplomacy," reflected the administration's understanding that the battle for the "hearts and minds" of the U.S. public was critical to its ability to wage even an unconventional war in Central America. "We continue to have serious difficulties with U.S. public and Congressional opinion which jeopardizes our ability to stay the course," one NSC Planning Group report on Central America noted as early as April 1982.[34]

The administration's obsession with shaping public opinion was manifested in President Reagan's January 1983 National Security Decision Directive 77 (NSDD 77), entitled "Management of Public Diplomacy Relative to National Security." NSDD 77 determined that "it is necessary to strengthen the organization, planning and coordination of the various aspects of public diplomacy of the United States Government."[35] This directive authorized the creation of a "public diplomacy" bureaucracy within the executive branch to facilitate propaganda on Central America. In a July 1, 1983, memorandum, NSC adviser William Clark advised other administration officials that "the President has underscored his concern that we must increase our efforts in the public diplomacy field to deepen the understanding of and support for our policies in Central America."[36] Clark authorized the creation of an Office of Public Diplomacy for Latin America and the Caribbean (S/LPD), to be housed in the State Department but run out of the NSC.

On the surface, the Office of Public Diplomacy operated as a ministry of information, producing and distributing vituperative anti-Sandinista and pro-contra White Papers, pamphlets, and briefing books for Congress, the press, and the public. Behind the scenes, however, the Office of Public Diplomacy conducted what one official called a "huge psychological operation, the kind the military conduct to influence the population in . . . enemy territory."[37] Indeed, the office drew on intelligence specialists for its staff, and the director of S/LPD, Ambassador Otto Reich, recruited psyops officials from the Department of Defense to assist the public diplomacy activities. "Current S/LPD projects of a priority nature require the expertise available from personnel of the 4th Psychological Operations Group, Fort Bragg, North Carolina," Reich wrote in a March 5, 1985, request to the Pentagon that resulted in the transfer of five military officials to Washington.[38]

The priority projects of the Office of Public Diplomacy included overt and covert propaganda, pressure on the media, and illegal lobbying tactics to manipulate public opinion against the Sandinista government and garner congressional votes for the contras. These operations went on until December 1987, when Congress closed the office pursuant to a General Accounting Office (GAO) investigation that revealed that the administration had engaged in "White Propaganda" operations—planting articles in the U.S. press. According to the GAO, the Office of Public Diplomacy "arranged for the publication of articles which purportedly had been prepared by, and reflected the views of, persons not associated with the government but which, in fact, had been prepared at the request of government officials and partially or wholly paid for with government funds." GAO investigators concluded that administration officials had "engaged in prohibited, covert propaganda activities designed to influence the media and the public to support the Administration's Latin American policies."[39]

The Reagan administration's public diplomacy operations played a significant role in achieving the president's preeminent foreign policy objective in 1986—restoration of official assistance to the contras. Whereas Congress had terminated monies for the contra program in October 1984, in August 1986 U.S. legislators approved $100 million in lethal and nonlethal assistance for the contras and lifted all restrictions concerning CIA and Department of Defense participation in the paramilitary war. The Office of Public Diplomacy "played a key role in setting out the parameters and defining the terms of the public discussion on Central America policy," Ambassador Reich noted in one May 1986 report to his superiors. "Despite the efforts of the formidable and well established Soviet/Cuban/Nicaraguan propaganda apparatus, the achievements of U.S. public diplomacy are clearly visible."[40]

Indeed, through the end of 1986, the architects of the administration's Nicaragua policy—CIA director William Casey, Robert McFarlane, John Poindexter, Oliver North, and Elliott Abrams—could count a number of successes. The public diplomacy apparatus had succeeded politically in "gluing black hats on the Sandinistas and the White Hats on the contras," as one secret NSC memorandum described the propaganda objective.[41] The contras had been secretly supplied for more than two years with arms and ammunition through a network of private intermediaries run out of the White House, enabling them to sustain their war of attrition until the U.S. Congress restored official funding. Moreover, that war had taken a heavy toll on human life and economic development in Nicaragua. In legal briefs filed at the International Court of Justice, the Sandinista government counted 2,961 military and 3,799 civilian deaths and over 10,900 persons wounded in the seven years of war. Material damage to property, according to Nicaraguan estimates, totaled $275,400,000, with production losses from contra and CIA sabotage valued at $1,280,700,000. Finally, Nicaraguan economists estimated losses to the gross domestic product (GDP) from contra violence, the mining of the harbors, and the trade embargo at $2,546,400,000, while asserting that the dire social consequences of the damage caused to Nicaragua's development potential "cannot be valued technically in monetary terms."[42]

■ THE IRAN-CONTRA SCANDAL

If a cargo plane from the NSC's illicit contra enterprise had not been shot down over southern Nicaragua on October 5, 1986, and a Lebanese journal had not published a month later an account of Robert McFarlane's secret trip to Iran, the Reagan administration might have successfully carried its policy of punishment against the Sandinistas to fruition. But former Attorney General Edwin Meese's November 25, 1986, admission that Reagan administration officials had diverted funds from covert arms sales to Iran to the covert war in Nicaragua intervened in U.S. politics. The revelations created what *Newsweek* called "instantly the worst scandal" in the Reagan presidency, paralyzing the executive branch, and prompting a massive congressional inquiry into the covert policies of the national security state.[43]

The Iran-contra investigation of the House and Senate Select Committees, and later the trials of Lieutenant Colonel Oliver North and Vice Admiral John Poindexter, revealed the intricate, and ugly, history of how the policy of rollback in Nicaragua had been made and implemented. Thousands of pages of top secret NSC, CIA, Pentagon, and State Department memoranda declassified during the investigations detailed far more than simply the diversion to the contras of $3.8 million of what North termed "residual funds" from Iranian arms sales. To comply with President Reagan's order to keep the contras together "body and soul" after Congress denied further official funding for the paramilitary war in 1984, the White House established an "off-the-shelf" arms resupply operation, complete with foreign funding, private-sector weapons procurement and logistics, mercenary trainers, and retired covert operatives running day-to-day contra activities.

The *Report of the Congressional Committees Investigating the Iran-Contra Affair* summarized this extraofficial covert program:

> Between June 1984 and the beginning of 1986, the President, his National Security Adviser, and the NSC staff secretly raised $34 million for the Contras from other countries. An additional $2.7 million was

provided for the Contras during 1985 and 1986 from private contributors who were addressed by North and occasionally granted photo opportunities with the President.

At the suggestion of Director Casey, North recruited Richard V. Secord, a retired Air Force Major General with experience in special operations. Secord set up Swiss bank accounts, and North steered future donations into these accounts. Using these funds, and funds later generated by the Iran arms sales, Secord and his associate, Albert Hakim, created what they called "the Enterprise," a private organization designed to engage in covert activities on behalf of the United States.

The Enterprise, functioning largely at North's direction, had its own airplanes, pilots, airfield, operatives, ship, secure communications devices, and secret Swiss bank accounts. For 16 months, it served as the secret arm of the NSC staff, carrying out with private and non-appropriated money, and without the accountability or restrictions imposed by law on the CIA, a covert Contra aid program that Congress thought it had prohibited.[44]

Although the operations of the Enterprise were known only to select national security managers in the White House, NSC, CIA, and State Department—several of whom later lied to Congress about this knowledge—numerous administration officials participated in other aspects of the illicit contra program.[45] Behind the scenes, U.S. officials created new civilian contra organizations designed to appeal to Congress.[46] The $27 million "humanitarian assistance" program, passed by Congress in 1985, became a front for airdrops of military equipment to rebel divisions inside Nicaragua.[47] With the approval of President Reagan, Vice President Bush, Secretary of State Shultz and others, quid pro quos were arranged with Honduras and Guatemala in return for their territorial support for ongoing contra operations. In September 1986, the Reagan administration even agreed to help General Manuel Noriega to "clean up" his drug-smuggling image, in return for his commitment to facilitate sabotage attacks inside Nicaragua.[48]

With a fresh infusion of $100 million and a congressional carte blanche to prosecute the paramilitary war against the Sandinistas, the CIA and the contras geared up for a final offensive in the fall of 1986. But the Justice Department's discovery of an April 4 memorandum in Oliver North's files stating that $12 million from the sale of arms to Iran "will be used to purchase critically needed supplies for the Nicaraguan Democratic Resistance Forces" provoked the scandal that led to the final unfolding of the secret contra war.[49] Facing overwhelming public repudiation of its illegal operations, the Reagan administration throughout 1987 repeatedly postponed returning to Capitol Hill for more contra assistance. In a vote on February 8, 1988, the House of Representatives narrowly rejected the White House request for $36.2 million in new war funds. Official military assistance came to a final halt, as did the administration's fanatical quest for a clear-cut Reagan Doctrine victory in Nicaragua.

■ THE BUSH ADMINISTRATION
AND THE NICARAGUAN ELECTIONS

Elected in the aftermath of the Iran-contra scandal, President George Bush understood that congressional opposition to aiding the contras was politically impossible to overcome. Pragmatically, the Bush administration shifted its focus to the more promising tactic of fostering an internal front against the Sandinistas for the elections on February 25, 1990. Nicaragua's electoral process—agreed to at the signing of the Oscar Arias peace plan in August 1987 and assured by the congressional cutoff of military aid to the contras in February 1988—provided a golden opportunity for President Bush to practice his own form of intervention. During the 1984 elections, the United States had pressured, and in some cases bribed, the Nicaraguan opposition to avoid participation, thus depriving the process of its legitimacy; toward that goal, the CIA paid off opposition candidates to withdraw from the race.[50] Given Nicaragua's dire economic conditions in 1989 and the distinct possibility that the opposition could win a fair election, Bush strategists took the opposite approach. Contra leaders were urged to return to Nicaragua and participate in the electoral process; as incentive, the State Department closed down the Nicaraguan Resistance offices in Washington and Miami.[51] U.S. advisers worked closely with the opposition's coalition, the National Opposition Union (UNO), fashioning a campaign strategy for presidential candidate Violeta Chamorro and her running mate, Virgilio Godoy.

In mid-1989, the CIA drew up a major plan for clandestine political operations to influence the election outcome, only to meet with stiff resistance from the House Permanent Select Committee on Intelligence. Nevertheless, and without informing Congress, the CIA instituted a covert operation known as the Nicaraguan Exile Relocation Program (NERP) through which over $600,000 was funneled to 100 contra exiles for political work inside Nicaragua between July 1989 and February 1990. More than $100,000 went to Alfredo Cesar, a former member of the contra directorate who had become Ms. Chamorro's key political adviser. Eleven contras who received NERP funding became candidates for the new Nicaraguan legislature.[52]

Overtly, Congress authorized $9 million in political assistance to Chamorro's coalition through the National Endowment for Democracy (NED). During the Reagan administration, the White House had used NED as a conduit for $5.6 million to pro-contra organizations, and to *La Prensa,* Nicaragua's opposition newspaper.[53] Because NED is prohibited from financing campaigns for public office, the Bush administration claimed the funds were intended to assist "political organizations, alliances, independent elements of the media, independent labor unions, and business, civic and professional groups . . . to ensure the conduct of free, fair and open elections."[54]

Washington's efforts to finalize through electoral intervention what the CIA had been unable to accomplish through paramilitary operations came to fruition on February 25, 1990. The upset victory of Violeta Chamorro and her UNO coalition, by a wide margin of 55 to 41 percent, was judged fair and free by international monitors, including former president Jimmy Carter. Given the catastrophic socioeconomic crisis wrought by a dark decade of U.S. low-intensity warfare against Nicaragua, and Mrs. Chamorro's promise that this war would end with her election, the outcome was hardly surprising. Indeed, although President Bush lauded the elections as a "victory for democracy"—and even complimented the Sandinistas on their electoral conduct—the vote represented the predictable culmination of Washington's lengthy and concerted campaign to roll back the Nicaraguan revolution.

■ **THE PRICE OF INTERVENTION**

After the electoral defeat of the Sandinistas, proponents of the decade-long war in Nicaragua claimed both credit and victory. "Our goal," Lieutenant Colonel Oliver North wrote in his memoir, *Under Fire,* was "to enable the contras to exert the kind of pressure on the Sandinistas that could ultimately lead to a free and democratic Nicaragua. Early in 1990, our efforts were vindicated."[55] In truth, the elections resulted from a Costa Rica–sponsored regional peace process that Washington repeatedly tried to sabotage, and were scheduled only after Congress finally terminated contra aid in the aftermath of the Iran-contra scandal, despite the Reagan administration's bitter objections. Still, the White House had demonstrated once again that it could wreak death and destruction upon a small Third World country and, through violence, reimpose its hegemony in Central America.

Although the United States had been unable to force the Sandinistas to "say uncle," the price of U.S. intervention for Nicaragua was high: thousands dead and tens of thousands wounded, orphaned, or homeless; an economy destroyed; a political environment violently polarized; a society rent with lost hope and dissension on all sides of the political spectrum; and no solution to these socioeconomic problems in sight. In order to "save" Nicaragua, U.S. policy had succeeded in virtually destroying it.

For the United States, however, the price also proved costly. The Iran-contra investigations revealed the extent to which the U.S. capacity to intervene abroad had been unleashed upon the very institutions of democracy at home that U.S. foreign policy is ostensibly designed to protect. National security managers perceived Congress and the U.S. people much the same way as they viewed the Sandinistas—as targets to be manipulated and coerced. The Iran-contra affair "was characterized by pervasive dishonesty and inordinate secrecy" as well as "a disdain for the law" that struck at the very heart of the basic checks and balances of the U.S. Constitution, according to the Congressional Select Committees.[56] The position of the president's advisers, such as National Security Adviser John Poindexter and NSC staffer Oliver North—that the executive branch had the right to circumvent Congress's power of the purse, run "off-the-shelf covert operations," organize private armies, and conduct independently financed wars—represented a bald effort to sabotage the U.S. constitutional system of governance. "That," concluded the *Report of the Congressional Committees Investigating the Iran-Contra Affair,* "is the path to dictatorship."[57]

In essence, the Iran-contra scandal and the contra-related scandals that preceded it represented the ultimate price to be paid for U.S. intervention in Nicaragua. The lessons of these scandals appeared obvious: Even a low-intensity war in Central America carried high costs for U.S. policy objectives abroad and high costs for the sanctity of U.S. democracy at home. Yet these lessons were forgotten as the "Nicaragua Decade" quickly faded from public memory and the Bush administration continued to turn to force as the principal foreign policy tool.

A historic opportunity was thus lost: the chance to address the longstanding presumption that the United States has the right to impose its will unilaterally on the countries of Latin America and elsewhere. Even as the Cold War came to an end as a catalyst for U.S. intervention in the Third World, this failure to reexamine the application of an imperial design in a postimperial world portended a repeat of such debilitating scandals in the future. Until U.S. policymakers understand that revolutions in countries like Nicaragua represent a test of the ability of the United States to coexist with its smaller neighbors, not of its ability to intervene successfully abroad, the specter of intervention will likely continue to haunt the U.S. people, in whose name such ill-advised policies are conducted.

17

Iran

Eric Hooglund

U.S. foreign policy toward Iran since the end of World War II has been dominated by the globalist perspective. Washington's preoccupation with keeping Iran free of Soviet influence has been reinforced by a perception that the country has a vital strategic significance: Iran shares a 1,200-mile border with the former Soviet Union in the north; its southern border is along the Persian Gulf; and it has been a major source of oil for the international market since the outbreak of World War I. The tendency to view Iran as a valuable pawn that could be won or lost in the game of international politics between the United States and the Soviet Union impeded official understanding of the strength of Iranian nationalism. This misunderstanding inevitably led to the formulation of U.S. policies that offended those Iranian political leaders popularly identified as patriots. The most spectacular of these policies was the covert intervention in 1953 to overthrow a popular prime minister and reinstate the power of a king perceived to be more amenable to Western interests. For the next twenty-five years, Iran, under the rule of Shah Mohammad Reza Pahlavi, remained a close ally of the United States.

Many Iranian nationalists never forgave the shah for using the support of the United States to create a royal dictatorship, and they resented the U.S. role in their country. The failure of the shah to achieve popular legitimacy and the widespread perception that he was subservient to the United States were important factors in the revolutionary turmoil of 1978–1979. That major political development, laden with anti-U.S. rhetoric and emotions, brought to power a new regime fearful of a repetition of the events of 1953 and determined to end the prospects for U.S. intervention in Iran's internal affairs. The protracted hostage crisis that bedeviled the last fourteen months of the administration of President Jimmy Carter dramatically symbolized Iran's assertion of independence from U.S. influence. Yet, U.S. policymakers seemed unwilling to accept that the altered relationship was permanent. Thus, efforts were initiated during the administration of President Ronald Reagan to woo Iran back into an anti-Soviet alliance. The clandestine arms sales to Iran during 1985–1986 represented striking evidence of the importance attached to Iran by those who viewed the country solely as a strategic asset or liability in the U.S. political rivalry with the Soviet Union.

■ WORLD WAR II AND THE 1953 COUP D'ÉTAT

U.S. involvement with Iran began during World War II when some 30,000 U.S. troops were sent there to join the allied British-Soviet forces that had occupied the then neutral country in 1941, ostensibly to purge it of German agents but, more practically, to utilize the railway from the Persian Gulf to the Soviet border for transporting military and other supplies to the Red Army. Cooperation between the United States and the Soviet Union did not long survive the war and as their alliance degenerated into a postwar competition for global influence, Iran emerged in early 1946 as a focus of their incipient Cold War confrontation. The United States supported Iran's protests before the new UN Security Council that Soviet troops, still in occupation of the northern provinces of Iran, had not withdrawn from the country in accordance with the 1942 Tripartite Agreement, which provided for the withdrawal of all foreign forces from Iran within six months of the end of hostilities in all theaters of the war. Although the Soviet forces eventually did withdraw, the crisis helped to shape official thinking in Washington that the Soviet Union wanted to occupy Iran in order to have access to the oil resources of the Persian Gulf.[1]

As the administration of President Harry S Truman developed a multifaceted containment policy toward the Soviet Union, Iran became an important element in the strategic concept of the Northern Tier, the string of nations along the Soviet Union's southern border that were to serve as a first line of defense against Soviet penetration into the Middle East. Accordingly, Iran was provided with modest amounts of military assistance intended to strengthen its defense forces. This assistance helped to develop the interest of Iran's shah in U.S. arms, an interest that would characterize the shah's relationship with successive U.S. administrations until he was overthrown in the 1978–1979 revolution.[2]

Economic and technical assistance programs also were used as part of an overall policy of keeping Iran a member of the U.S.-led bloc of anti-Soviet nations. In the early 1950s, these programs were popularly known as Point Four because President Truman had proposed economic aid initiatives for "less-developed countries" as the fourth point of his January 1949 inaugural address. Under the Point Four program, Iran received some $48 million for technical and developmental projects.[3]

Despite Washington's wooing of Iran, its full incorporation into an anti-Soviet defense alliance was delayed by the emergence of a strong nationalist movement that decried Iran's involvement in superpower rivalries and argued that true national independence meant neutralism in foreign policy and total sovereignty over all natural resources, especially oil (which, since 1908, had been controlled by the British). In 1949, the nationalists formed a National Front under the leadership of Mohammad Mosaddeq (1882–1967). The principal demand of the National Front was the nationalization of the British-owned Anglo-Iranian Oil Company (AIOC), which produced all of Iran's oil for domestic consumption and foreign export. When the National Front did come to power in 1951, it nationalized AIOC and thereby provoked a major crisis between Iran and Great Britain.[4]

The Truman administration was divided over how to deal with the nationalist challenge in Iran. Although Secretary of State Dean Acheson, Henry Grady, the U.S. ambassador to Iran, and other leading officials were fearful that the nationalist cause could be exploited by the Iranian Marxist party, the Tudeh, to bring Iran into the Soviet orbit, they believed that the nationalist demand for control over Iran's oil resources was basically a legitimate one. Consequently, they were reluctant to support the British, who were trying to get U.S. assistance for some form of military intervention, including even a coup d'état against Mosaddeq and the National Front.[5]

While Washington was trying to reach a consensus on a policy to keep Tehran from switching its allegiance from the Western superpower bloc to the Soviet-dominated Eastern bloc, political leaders within Iran were preoccupied with very different issues, such as the continuation of foreign influence on government, popular participation, and the distribution of power among competing interest groups. It was during this period that an irrevocable split occurred between the nationalists, who wanted a constitutional monarch or even a republic, and the royalists, who supported the concept of a strong monarchy for Iran. The shah (1919–1980) had acceded to the throne in 1941 after the British and Soviets had forced the abdication and exile of his father. Throughout the 1940s, the youthful shah generally had been unsuccessful in asserting his own authority over the parliament, or *majlis*. By 1951, when the shah was compelled to accept Mosaddeq as the prime minister chosen by the *majlis*, he had come to perceive the nationalists as the major threat to his own rule. In order to safeguard his position, the shah generally allied himself with those interests that were opposed to the National Front. Among the most powerful opponents of the National Front were foreign interests, in particular the AIOC and the British government.[6]

The stage for a coup d'état against the Mosaddeq government was set when the administration of President Dwight D. Eisenhower came to power in January 1953. Key officials, such as Director of Central Intelligence Allen Dulles and Secretary of State John Foster Dulles and the new U.S. ambassador to Tehran, Loy Henderson, perceived that the political situation in Iran made the country ripe to fall to the communists and uncritically embraced the British view that the nationalists were potential collaborators in turning Iran into a Soviet satellite. The United States consequently began to cooperate covertly with the British and royalist elements in Iran in planning and executing a coup d'état to remove Mosaddeq from office and to restore the authority of the shah.[7]

Although the U.S.-assisted military coup d'état of August 1953 was successful, it also ensured that Mosaddeq became a nationalist hero and left

the shah's popular image as that of a traitor, an image he never was able to
shake during the next twenty-five years of his reign. Even more significant,
in terms of U.S. interests, the coup made Iranian nationalists deeply
suspicious of the United States. The memory of the 1953 coup remained
forceful and played a significant role in the anti-U.S. sentiment that surfaced
periodically and in particular during the revolution of 1978–1979.[8]

But in 1953, officials in Washington regarded the coup against Mosaddeq
as a major triumph of covert action. In terms of U.S. strategic interests, they
perceived the results of the coup as positive: Iran became unambiguously a
client ally of the United States; in addition, the coup d'état not only restored
the power of a pro-Western shah but, more significant, restored control over
Iran's oil production to the West. Within one year of the coup, a new
consortium of Western oil interests was created to manage Iranian oil.
Although the fiction of Iranian ownership was maintained, actual production,
pricing, and export of oil was given contractually to this consortium. Iran
was required to compensate the AIOC—renamed British Petroleum—for the
loss of its concession, but the British also were pressured into ceding 60
percent of the share of the consortium to a group of major U.S. and European
petroleum companies. This agreement marked the beginning of U.S.
economic interests in Iran, interests that would intensify during the next
twenty-five years.[9]

■ STRENGTHENING OF THE U.S.-IRANIAN SECURITY RELATIONSHIP

After the 1953 coup, Iran was brought fully into the U.S. defense alliance
system against the Soviet Union. The Northern Tier concept was finally
realized through the creation in 1955 of the Baghdad Pact, a U.S.-sponsored
collective security arrangement that allied Iran with Great Britain, Iraq,
Pakistan, and Turkey. When a republican revolution toppled the pro-Western
monarchy in Iraq in 1958, the Baghdad Pact was transformed into the Central
Treaty Organization (CENTO). Although the United States never became a
formal member of CENTO, it played an active role in coordinating meetings
and providing military assistance and advice. Also, in order to counter the
perceived threat of internal subversion, the United States helped the shah in
1957 to create a secret police force, known by the Persian acronym SAVAK
(from its official name of Sazman-e Attelaat va Amniyat-e Keshvar, National
Security and Information Organization). Although intended to search out
those who advocated a violent overthrow of the government, SAVAK was
used primarily to silence those who criticized the regime or the person of the
shah. It acquired an unsavory reputation and was one more factor that helped
to tarnish the U.S. image.[10]

Iran also became one of the largest recipients of U.S. economic and military aid programs in the decade following 1953. The infusion of this assistance did not alleviate Iranian economic problems, however, which continued to be aggravated by widespread corruption at the highest echelons of the government. By 1960, there was a widespread feeling in Washington that the country was politically unstable. The administration of President John F. Kennedy, which shared the anticommunist views of its predecessors, believed that the principal threat to Iran (as well as to many other Third World countries) came not so much from external or internal subversion as from government incompetence and abuses that undermined its authority. The officials of the New Frontier were unimpressed with the shah's record and were determined to persuade him and leading Iranian officials that basic reforms were essential to keep the country from falling to Soviet influence. Thus, the Kennedy administration pushed ideas such as land reform, which it saw as a panacea to Iran's problems. In order to convince the shah that the United States meant business, Washington cut military grants and expanded economic assistance programs.[11]

The prodding from the United States fortuitously came just as oil revenues were increasing as a result of new production quota agreements and the establishment of OPEC. This combination of diplomatic pressure and larger budgets induced the shah to support numerous economic reforms that eventually ushered in a period of sustained economic growth. These reforms primarily benefited the industrial sector, as the state became the main promoter and protector of capitalist development. A limited land reform program redistributed approximately one-half of the arable land—then owned by large-scale, absentee owners—to about one-half of the peasants. Even though "the best and the brightest" of the Kennedy-era policymakers had assumed that the types of reforms instituted by the shah would lead eventually to broader political participation and thus to political stability, this did not happen. On the contrary, governmental control of opposition groups actually intensified after 1962. Nevertheless, the overall performance of Iran's economy and the positive perception of the shah's reforms created a surface impression of political stability that gradually became entrenched in Washington.[12]

Political discontent, which had been repressed since 1953, exploded in major urban demonstrations and riots in June 1963. The catalyst for the protests was the arrest of Ayatollah Ruhollah Khomeini, a senior clergyman who in 1962 had begun preaching sermons increasingly critical of the shah's foreign policy, especially his dependence upon the United States. The nationalist forces, however, were not unified at the time, an important factor that helped the U.S.-equipped security forces to suppress the demonstrators. Khomeini himself eventually was deported, and less prominent members of the clergy were sentenced to internal exile in remote towns. These events further tarnished the image of the United States, an image that was still blemished on account of the 1953 coup. The shah, meanwhile, argued inaccurately (but persuasively) that the turmoil had been instigated by elements opposed to his reforms. Leading Kennedy administration officials, who initially had urged reforms out of concern for Iran's stability, embraced the shah's explanation and interpreted the successful suppression of the "antireform" demonstrations as evidence of new political stability.[13]

After 1963, the nature of the relationship between Iran and the United States began to change, in part because of the increasing preoccupation of U.S. policymakers with the war in Vietnam. But equally important was the rise in Iran's oil revenues as a result of increased oil production. The newfound wealth freed Iran from dependence upon U.S. economic and military aid and enabled the shah to pay cash for the military hardware he desired. As early as 1965, an attitude began to emerge in Washington that the shah should not be discouraged from purchasing military equipment (as long as he was willing to pay) even if particular systems seemed extravagant in terms of Iran's defense needs. This attitude was reinforced by the 1967 decision to end all economic and military assistance programs to Iran because it was no longer perceived to be a less-developed country. The cessation of assistance symbolized the end of Iran's economic dependence on the United States. By the late 1960s, policymakers in Washington were interpreting Iran's prosperity, induced by oil revenues, as evidence of political stability and were perceiving the shah as a valuable ally in the Middle East region.[14]

In 1969, when President Richard M. Nixon proclaimed his doctrine that the United States would provide the means—weapons, not personnel—for friendly regimes to assume responsibility for the security of their own countries and regions, Iran under the shah was ready to take on its role as Washington's policeman in the Persian Gulf. The shah's longtime fascination with military equipment, especially aircraft, now had the opportunity to blossom fully. Indeed, during the administrations of Presidents Nixon and Gerald R. Ford, U.S.-Iranian relations were dominated by extensive sales of U.S. weapons. Iran's emergence as a major arms purchaser was legitimized by Nixon's instructions to the U.S. bureaucracy in 1972 to approve the sale of any weapons system requested by the shah no matter how sophisticated the system, with the notable exception of nuclear warheads. The shah's appetite for weapons proved almost insatiable as, beginning in 1974 as a result of the quadrupling of oil revenues, he had virtually limitless financial means with which to indulge his fancy. So important did the arms sales become for the U.S.-Iranian relationship that the Department of Defense sent a special sales representative to Iran to advise the government on what systems to purchase. Between 1970 and 1978, the shah ordered over $20 billion worth of U.S.-manufactured arms, making Iran the single largest foreign customer for U.S. military hardware (a striking transformation of the relationship that had existed only twenty years earlier).[15]

Under the mantle of the Nixon Doctrine, the shah actively sought to curb what both he and the United States perceived to be radical regimes and movements. Chief among these was the republican government in neighboring Iraq, which was viewed as a subversive threat to the conservative Arab monarchies of the Arabian Peninsula and as a client of the Soviet Union. As early as 1971, the shah sought to destabilize Iraq by providing covert support to various leaders of that country's disaffected Kurdish minority, concentrated in the mountainous area along the Iran-Iraq border. Iran's assistance intensified in 1974 after the major Kurdish leader rose up in open rebellion against Baghdad. Iran served as a conduit for the clandestine delivery of U.S. and Israeli military supplies to the Kurds and also provided logistical support and air cover for Kurdish military operations. Iran's increasingly overt intervention and the lack of effective support from the Soviet Union pressured the government of Iraq to seek a political accommodation with the shah. Known as the Algiers Agreement, this March 1975 accord essentially was an acknowledgment of Iran's preponderant influence in the Persian Gulf region.[16]

The shah also opposed the Marxist government of South Yemen, which had come to power following the former British colony's independence in 1967. He shared the U.S. view that Aden actively was supporting various guerrilla groups attempting to overthrow the Arabian Peninsula governments. Four of these countries (Bahrain, Oman, Qatar, and the United Arab Emirates) were small states that only became fully independent of Great Britain in 1971. Consequently, there was concern in both Tehran and Washington about the long-term stability of these pro-Western, hereditary-rule regimes. The shah was especially uneasy about Oman, where a long-simmering revolt against the sultan had succeeded in "liberating" considerable territory near the border with South Yemen. In 1973, he decided to dispatch a contingent of Iranian troops to Oman in order to help put down the rebellion. The intervention, which had the support of the United States, eventually achieved its objectives, although Iranian military advisers remained in Oman right up to the revolution.[17]

The massive arms sales to Iran had become controversial by 1976. A critical U.S. Senate report on the issue concluded that the arms sales program was "out of control" and warned of the possibility that the large numbers of Americans hired to maintain the weapons could be endangered if there were to be a change of regime in Iran.[18] Presidential candidate Jimmy Carter made arms sales in general one of his election campaign issues and specifically criticized the Ford administration for the sales to Iran. Nevertheless, when the Carter administration assumed power in early 1977, it was reluctant to reverse the arrangement with Iran. In fact, during the first year of the Carter administration, arms sales continued on the same scale as in previous years.[19]

Carter also had made human rights one of his campaign issues and, during the election debates, had singled out Iran as an example of a country in which human-rights abuses were widespread. Thus, the Carter administration came to office committed to a policy of promoting human rights in those dictatorships that were allied to the United States. In the case of Iran, however, administration policymakers concluded early that continuing the strategic relationship was more important than trying to pressure the shah to improve his government's human-rights record. In practice, this meant that officials would reassure the shah of the U.S. commitment while (sometimes) privately encouraging him to proceed toward his 1976 objective of liberalizing Iran's political system.[20]

■ THE REVOLUTION AND U.S. POLICY TOWARD THE ISLAMIC REPUBLIC

The revolution of 1978–1979 caught the Carter administration—and the shah—by surprise. The (mis)perception that the regime of the shah was stable was deeply engrained in official Washington. Nevertheless, the revolution against the shah was based on a broad coalition of secular and religious nationalists who shared similar views about the shah and his relations with the United States. The provisional government that initially replaced the shah in February 1979 was dominated by politicians who had opposed the shah since the early 1950s, and who remembered with bitterness the role of the United States in the coup against their hero, Mosaddeq. Both they and the religious leaders of the secretive Revolutionary Council had spent years in prison for opposition. Thus, they tended to be deeply suspicious of the United States and feared that Washington would try to reinstate the shah, whom they perceived as a U.S. puppet and as a traitor to his country. Their immediate foreign policy goals included the termination of the special relationship with the United States. Consequently, billions of dollars of ordered but not-yet-delivered arms were canceled, Iran's membership in CENTO was terminated, and Tehran announced that it would no longer serve as the policeman of the Persian Gulf region. In addition, relations with Israel and South Africa were broken in the belief that these had served U.S. and not Iranian interests.[21]

Although the leaders who composed the provisional government tended to suspect Washington's intentions toward their revolution, they believed Iran and the United States could maintain a relatively normal relationship once the former patron accepted the new political realities. More extreme revolutionaries, however, wanted to eradicate thoroughly U.S. influence from Iran. They viewed both the United States and the Soviet Union as equally malevolent powers in terms of their relations with the Third World but saw the United States as the greatest danger to Iran, underscoring the nature of the relationship between the two countries since the 1940s. These more extreme forces exploited the October 1979 admission of the shah into the United States for medical treatment to force a complete break in diplomatic relations.

Their vehicle was the hostage crisis, which developed in November 1979 after students invaded the U.S. embassy compound in downtown Tehran and captured its personnel to hold as hostages for the extradition of the shah.[22]

The hostage crisis continued for 444 days, and during this time it preoccupied the Carter administration to such an extent that attention to other issues was adversely affected. After initial efforts to resolve the crisis through diplomacy and economic pressures proved unsuccessful, the president authorized a covert operation in April 1980 to forcibly rescue the more than fifty hostages. This first major instance of clandestine intervention in Iran since 1953 failed in the Iranian desert, and the circumstances surrounding the failure added to the sense of humiliation that the protracted hostage crisis had engendered in the United States. Although covert planning for a second rescue attempt continued, the dispersal of the U.S. hostages to numerous secret locations throughout Iran made another attempt infeasible. The hostage crisis was not finally settled—through an Algerian-mediated agreement (the Algiers Accord)—until the very day that Carter left office as president.[23]

The administration of President Ronald Reagan took office in 1981 with an ideological view of the Soviet Union that had not evolved from that of the mid-1950s. That is, the ideologues believed that the Soviet Union was an "evil empire" bent on aggression against the interests of the West, and they were convinced that the Soviet invasion of Afghanistan in December 1979 demonstrated the hostile intentions of the USSR. Furthermore, Soviet aims in Afghanistan were perceived as part of a broader scheme to extend Moscow's influence into the Persian Gulf. Inevitably, this perception of a Soviet threat to the Persian Gulf region conditioned views of Iran. Nevertheless, the emotional impact of the protracted hostage crisis made the development of a coherent policy toward Iran difficult. Consequently, the Reagan administration's Iran policy evolved through three phases: (1) covert support for antiregime groups while overtly ignoring the country; (2) secret efforts to woo Iran through clandestine arms sales; and (3) a military containment policy that began in 1987.[24]

From the beginning, the Reagan administration faced a paradox with respect to Iran. The Islamic Republic was a government that was avowedly anticommunist; it had boldly and repeatedly condemned the Soviet Union's invasion of Afghanistan; it had criticized the USSR for behaving like an imperialist power; and Tehran generally had poor relations with its big neighbor to the north. At the same time, however, Iran was even more hostile toward the United States. The war between Iran and Iraq further complicated the situation. This war had begun in September 1980 when Iraq invaded Iran and subsequently occupied its oil-producing southwestern province for twenty months. Some Reagan administration officials were alarmed by the conflict because they were convinced it was potentially destabilizing for U.S. allies in the Persian Gulf. They also had believed for many years that Iraq, which had a treaty of friendship with the

Soviet Union, was one of Moscow's client states and argued that the anti-Soviet fervor of the regime in Tehran served overall U.S. interests. Other officials took the position that Iran's advocacy of exporting revolution was subversive of friendly regimes. Overlaying these contradictory political perceptions was a deep resentment of Iran because of the hostage crisis, an event that both conservatives and liberals believed had humiliated the United States.[25]

The different perspectives prevented the Reagan administration from formulating a coherent policy toward Iran. Throughout 1981, there did not appear to be any urgency to devise a specific policy, as Iraq seemed to have the upper hand in the Iran-Iraq war. In short, Iran was ignored. During the summer of 1982, however, the combined impact of Iran's successful offensives leading to an invasion of Iraq, the Israeli invasion of Lebanon, and the obvious worsening of relations between Iran and the Soviet Union compelled the administration to rethink its strategy. Achieving consensus was still not easy: Some officials began to fear "Islamic fundamentalism" nearly as much as communism, and advocated the containment of Iran; in contrast, other officials viewed Islamic fundamentalism as a potentially powerful ideological tool that could be used against the Soviet Union. The former group blamed Iran for a variety of Middle Eastern political developments that adversely affected U.S. interests in the region, in particular the incidents of terrorism in Lebanon. The latter group was less convinced of Iran's ability to direct anti-U.S. and anti-Western events in Lebanon and elsewhere and tended to believe in the possibility of reaching an understanding with Tehran based upon a shared interest in containing Soviet influence in the region.[26]

The lack of official consensus inevitably led to contradictory policies both within individual bureaucracies and between them. The CIA, for example, provided covert financial and material support as early as 1980 to various monarchist groups in exile that were advocating the overthrow of the regime in Tehran and the reestablishment of a pro-U.S. government. Yet, there was widespread disillusionment with these exile groups by 1984, and officials, such as CIA director William Casey, were ready to consider new approaches for regaining Iran. When some intelligence and national security officials became convinced that there were pro-and anti-Soviet factions within the Iranian government, the stage was set for devising a plan to cultivate the latter, who came to be referred to as the "moderates." The U.S. officials hoped to exploit the Iranian need for weapons in the war with Iraq to begin a process of assisting those Iranian factions who they believed were more sympathetic to the United States. The policy objective was to lay the groundwork for a new relationship with Iran, a relationship that could be developed after Khomeini died and an expected power struggle hopefully was won by the moderates. This rationale was used to justify arms sales to Iran; in return, the moderates were expected to use their presumed influence among the Arab groups holding U.S. hostages in Lebanon to seek the hostage's release.[27]

These views tended to dominate in the NSC and CIA during 1985 and 1986. They were not shared by officials in the State and Defense Departments who continued to perceive Iran as the principal threat to U.S. interests not only in the Persian Gulf but also in Lebanon. The inevitable result was contradictory policies toward Iran: Simultaneous with the covert policy of selling arms, the State Department was vigorously pursuing an overt policy—dubbed "Operation Staunch"—of trying to stop international arms sales to Iran. Operation Staunch was part of an undeclared but obvious U.S. tilt toward Iraq, a tilt prompted by a belief that Iraq could not win the war and a fear of the regional consequences if Iran were to win. The November 1986 revelations that former National Security Adviser Robert McFarlane had traveled secretly to Tehran for talks, and that arms sales agreements between the United States and Iran had been transacted even while Operation Staunch was in effect, demonstrated the deep divisions within the Reagan administration concerning the appropriate policy for dealing with Iran.[28]

The persistent fear of Soviet influence in the Persian Gulf served as the catalyst for the Reagan administration to unify around a consistent policy and extricate itself from the diplomatic scandal caused by the exposure of its secret arms deals with Iran. Soon after the initial revelations, the government of Kuwait renewed a request to both the United States and the USSR for protection of its oil tankers, frequently attacked by Iran in retaliation for Iraqi attacks upon Iranian shipping. When the Soviet Union agreed in February 1987 to lease three of its own tankers to Kuwait, the United States decided to respond by reflagging and escorting eleven Kuwaiti oil tankers while they transited the Persian Gulf. Although the United States proclaimed that its new policy of military intervention was to protect neutral international shipping, the bulk of commercial traffic in the waterway consisted of neutral ships carrying goods to or from Iran. Not only were these ships excluded from U.S. protection, but Iraq intensified its attacks upon them. The real aim, thus, was to protect from Iranian retaliatory strikes the shipping of the Arab states traditionally allied with the United States in order to discourage these countries from seeking Soviet protection for their commerce. The practical effect of the intervention was de facto support of Iraq against Iran.[29]

Though support of Iraq inevitably had the result of actually prolonging the war, Washington maintained that its true objective was to help end the conflict. In tandem with the military policy, the United States pursued diplomatic efforts through the UN to achieve a cease-fire. These initiatives, too, had the appearance of being pro-Iraqi and anti-Iranian. In particular, the United States cooperated with Baghdad to revise a draft cease-fire resolution that had Iran's support so that it favored the Iraqi position and included provisions for an international arms embargo against the party that rejected it. Under U.S. prodding, the Security Council in July 1987 reluctantly passed Resolution 598, calling for an immediate cease-fire in the war. Iran, however, frustrated the U.S. expectation of a subsequent UN vote on imposition of an embargo by neither accepting nor rejecting the resolution, and the United States ultimately failed to win support for further UN sanctions.[30]

The Iran-Iraq war continued for a full year beyond the passage of Resolution 598. It was the worst year to date in terms of the number of civilian casualties, the majority of whom were victims of Iraq's intensified use of chemical weapons and missiles against Iranian cities and towns. Tehran accused the United States of shielding Iraq and perceived the deployment of twenty-seven U.S. naval ships to the Persian Gulf as a direct provocation. Over time, a series of military confrontations occurred between U.S. and Iranian forces, such as the April 1988 retaliatory strike in which the United States destroyed two Iranian oil platforms and sank six ships (half of Iran's naval fleet), and the heightened tensions seemed to make a greater disaster inevitable. Such a disaster happened in early July, when the *U.S.S. Vincennes,* mistaking an Iranian civilian passenger airbus en route to Dubai in the United Arab Emirates for an attacking jet, shot it down over the Strait of Hormuz; all 290 aboard were killed.[31]

Even before the Iranian plane was shot down, the United States was concerned about the possibility that continued conflict with Iran would spiral out of control and lead to a general U.S.-Iran war. The international revulsion over Iraq's massive use of chemical weapons also made Washington uncomfortable with its policy of tilting toward Baghdad. Thus, when the airplane downing brought the United States and Iran to the brink of open war, the administration decided it was time to try to defuse the situation. The United States admitted that the shootdown was a "mistake" and offered to pay compensation to the families of the victims. Iran recognized the gesture as a signal and reciprocated by announcing its long-delayed acceptance of Resolution 598. In August, a cease-fire in the Iran-Iraq war was declared by the UN, which then dispatched observers to the area to monitor the front lines. The United States subsequently began to withdraw some of its vessels from the Persian Gulf. Ostensibly this was because neutral ships no longer needed military protection, but during the year the U.S. naval armada was in the Persian Gulf, more neutral ships had been attacked than in any previous year since the war began. The real aim of U.S. policy—to contain Iran and its revolution—could not be done simply by a show of force; the actual use of force to achieve this goal seemed too costly. Thus, it appeared by the end of 1988 that the United States was prepared to accept Iran, although officials in Washington were no closer to understanding the nature of Iranian—or Third World—nationalism than they had been before 1987.

■ ATTEMPTS AT FOSTERING A U.S.-IRANIAN RAPPROCHEMENT

The administration of George Bush was inaugurated in January 1989 determined to normalize relations with Iran. The new president emphasized in his inaugural address the importance his administration attached to restoring ties by implicitly promising Tehran that any gestures of goodwill would be reciprocated. In a subsequent interview, he called upon Iran to bury old enmities and rebuild relations.[32] Normalizing relations in the wake of nearly a decade of hostility, however, required more than an assertion of good intentions. The Iranians responded in their own media to U.S. overtures by stressing the need for concrete gestures to demonstrate that Washington's policy had changed. Senior U.S. officials recognized the need to adopt some positive steps that would defuse Tehran's suspicions. Before any concrete proposals could be developed, however, a new political crisis involving Iran and Britain erupted to sideline this effort.

The crisis in mid-February 1989 was prompted when Khomeini, acting in his capacity as supreme spiritual leader, issued an edict making it lawful for any Muslim to kill British author Salman Rushdie, whose novel *Satanic Verses* contained passages that many Muslims believed were blasphemous. Khomeini justified his decree on grounds that Rushdie had been born in India to Muslim parents; by writing such a religiously offensive book, he had renounced his Muslim heritage, a crime punishable by death under Islamic canon law. Khomeini's edict caused a public furor in Britain where Rushdie was a successful and acclaimed writer. The British government felt impelled to protect one of its citizens who was under threat of death by terrorists. Britain's partners in the European Community joined in condemning the decree and demanding that it be retracted. The incident resulted in the Europeans freezing their relations with Iran.

Because the United States had no ties with Iran, it was not directly affected by the Rushdie affair. Nevertheless, Khomeini's edict had a chilling effect on proposals for normalizing relations. Most officials attributed Iran's behavior to a presumed power struggle between the moderate and radical factions that intelligence experts had first identified in 1984–1985.[33] The administration concluded that saying as little as possible about the Rushdie affair would actually help the moderates to consolidate power because U.S. silence would deny the radicals anti-U.S. ammunition.[34] Hopes for ascendancy of the moderates increased in June 1989 when Khomeini died suddenly and Ali Akbar Hashemi Rafsanjani, whom policy analysts considered Iran's most influential moderate, announced his intentions to seek the presidency.

Despite the hopes placed in Rafsanjani, he did not conform to Washington's image of how a moderate should behave. Policy analysts were especially troubled by what they perceived as Rafsanjani's excessive friendliness toward the Soviet Union. Even though Moscow had cooperated with the United States in drafting UN Resolution 598, most senior officials of the Bush administration shared the Reagan view that the Soviet Union wanted to extend its influence over Iran. Consequently, they were alarmed when Rafsanjani, while on a state visit to the Soviet Union in June 1989, signed a $15 billion economic and military assistance agreement. Policymakers were concerned that this pact was a prelude to a major expansion of Soviet-Iranian ties. They recognized that the major source of contention between the two countries, Afghanistan, had been removed as a result of the February 1989 withdrawal of Soviet forces from that country, and they feared that the absence of relations between Tehran and Washington made it virtually impossible for the United States to counteract growing Soviet influence, a development seen as inimical to overall U.S. interests in the region.

In order to begin the process of restoring ties, the Bush administration eventually proposed to offer Iran gestures, such as setting aside a fund to compensate the families of those killed when the *U.S.S. Vincennes* accidentally shot down an Iranian passenger jet in 1988 and returning remaining frozen assets to the government. Washington was unwilling, however, to proceed unilaterally, but expected Tehran to reciprocate with its own goodwill gestures. Officials decided that Iranian assistance on two key issues would be construed as evidence that Tehran was serious about a rapprochement. These issues were a satisfactory resolution of the prolonged hostages episode in Lebanon and a reduction in incidents of international terrorism. The Bush administration believed that Iran exercised significant influence over Hizbollah and other Lebanese groups holding several U.S. and European citizens as hostages. Some officials were even convinced that radical Iranian political leaders actually controlled the Lebanese groups as well as terrorist hit squads operating in the Arabian Peninsula and elsewhere. Few officials were prepared to accept that the various Islamic political groups in Lebanon, the Persian Gulf, and the broader Middle East region were autonomous actors with agendas that might or might not coincide with Tehran's regional objectives.[35]

The issue of U.S. hostages in Lebanon became a major, albeit brief, foreign policy crisis during the summer of 1989. Israel's kidnapping of a prominent Shia clergyman from his home in south Lebanon provoked Lebanese groups holding hostages to kill one of their U.S. captives and to threaten the lives of others. Rafsanjani intervened with the Lebanese to prevent additional hostage killings. Washington appreciated his intercession, which helped to calm the crisis, but officials perceived Rafsanjani's inability or unwillingness to use his influence to get all the hostages freed as evidence of the continuing strength of Iran's radicals. The long ordeal of the hostages, which had begun with the initial kidnappings of U.S. citizens in Lebanon in 1984, would not finally be resolved until the end of 1991.

The lack of progress on hostages and the continuing suspicions that Iran was involved in the assassination of several regime opponents living in Europe disinclined the Bush administration to push ahead with normalization of relations. Ironically, Iran during the latter part of 1989 and the first half of 1990 strove to normalize its relations with most of Washington's allies, including the Arab states of the Persian Gulf and the countries of Western Europe. Tehran had just restored formal diplomatic ties with Kuwait when that country was invaded by Iraq, an incident that precipitated a major international crisis in the Persian Gulf. Iran denounced the Iraqi action but proclaimed its neutrality. Iraq was the only other country, besides the United States, with which Iran had not tried to normalize its relations. Indeed, in the two years since Tehran had accepted UN Resolution 598, Iran and Iraq, despite UN mediation, had made no progress toward implementing its clauses other than to accept and observe the cease-fire.

The United States was concerned about the Iranian reaction to its military intervention in the Persian Gulf. This concern was heightened when Saddam Hussein suddenly decided to offer Iran peace on its terms: that the contested international border of the two countries be down the middle of the Shatt al-Arab River. Tehran and Baghdad reestablished diplomatic relations and began the long-delayed exchange of prisoners of war. U.S. concerns that Iran would somehow try to sabotage the war effort against Iraq proved to be baseless. Although Tehran persistently condemned the U.S. military intervention, it just as persistently called for Iraq's withdrawal from Kuwait. In addition, Iran continued to honor the UN-mandated economic boycott of Iraq.

After the Persian Gulf war, the United States tended to suspect Iran of having fomented or at least assisted the Iraqi uprising against Saddam Hussein's government. Iran gave verbal support to the rebellion, especially in the south, and during the final days of fighting probably allowed Iran-based Iraqi dissidents and weapons to cross the border into Iraq. Nevertheless, Iran was as much caught by surprise as was the United States by the unexpected outbreak of a mass popular uprising in southern Iraq. After the Iraqi army had crushed the rebellion, thousands of Iraqis fled to Iran. A few weeks later when the Kurdish rebellion in northern Iraq also was suppressed, more than 1.2 million Kurds fled to Iran (1 million more fled toward Turkey, which permitted only half of them to cross the border), a situation that created an international humanitarian relief crisis.

After Iraq's defeat, Iran opposed the continued U.S. military presence in the Persian Gulf region and tried, unsuccessfully, to persuade Kuwait not to sign a military cooperation agreement with the United States. Iran's stated position was that outside powers should not intervene in the security affairs of the Persian Gulf but should accept the right of the local states to manage their own defense. Although Iran urged the countries of the Gulf Cooperation Council—Bahrain, Kuwait, Oman, Qatar, Saudi Arabia, and the United Arab

Emirates—to join in new collective security arrangements, it received only evasive responses about the desirability of greater cooperation. From a U.S. perspective, Iran's diplomatic efforts were not considered threatening. On the contrary, Tehran's cultivation of closer ties with the Arab countries of the Persian Gulf appeared to contribute to the political stability of the area, a very radical—but welcome—change from the role Iran had played throughout the 1980s.

■ LESSONS OF INTERVENTION

The history of the U.S.-Iran relationship demonstrates the problems for overall U.S. national interests of allying with a regime that does not have the popular support of its own people. For twenty-five years, the U.S. policy of unconditional support for the shah of Iran seemed to be paying off in terms of promoting U.S. interests in the Persian Gulf region. To policymakers in successive administrations between 1953 and 1978, Iran under the shah seemed like an excellent example of a country where Soviet influence had successfully been contained. The sudden and wholly unanticipated transformation of Iran from a dependable ally to an implacable foe during 1979 baffled Washington. More than ten years after the revolution, policymakers were still confused about how and why the relationship with Iran had collapsed, were generally unreconciled to accepting the new order, and were unable to formulate creative policies for dealing with Tehran.

The post-1979 problems between Washington and Tehran were the direct consequence of the nature of U.S. intervention in Iran during the regime of the last shah. By 1953, there had crystallized in Washington widespread concern that Iran might become part of the Soviet bloc. This concern had arisen out of the collective inability of officials to appreciate the significance of political developments in Iran. For example, during the late 1940s and early 1950s, when Iranian nationalists were trying to end the British government's control of Iran's oil industry and also were attempting to curtail the autocratic powers of the shah, U.S. policymakers erroneously perceived Iran's internal political conflicts as instability provoked by communist subversion. This perception led the United States to collaborate with Britain in carrying out the 1953 coup d'état against the popular, but neutralist, government of Prime Minister Mosaddeq. The reinstallation in power of the pro-Western, anti-Soviet shah proved to be a boon for U.S. interests. By 1970, Iran was perceived as a model of stability, and its ruler, the shah, as the U.S. policeman of the Persian Gulf.

The shah imposed short-term stability on Iran by repressing political dissent. It is ironic that the more dictatorial his regime became, the closer the U.S.-Iran relationship became. Thus, U.S. intervention in Iran after 1953 took the form of supporting the shah, initially through economic and military assistance (up to 1967) and then through massive transfers of sophisticated arms for which the shah paid cash. As the United States progressively became identified with the unpopular political and military policies of the shah, the Iranian perception of the United States as a country of positive, democratic values was seriously undermined. By the 1970s, the image of the United States that had taken hold among those Iranians disaffected with the royal dictatorship was that of a superpower exploiting Iran's resources and strategic position for its own benefit. The shah's diverse religious and secular opponents accused him of being little more than a U.S. puppet, a leader serving the interests of U.S. economic and military interests to the detriment of Iran.

U.S. policy toward Iran during this period was flawed by pervasive insensitivity to the nationalist feelings of the population. The preoccupation with having in Tehran a government that shared the U.S. aim of keeping Soviet influence checked in the Persian Gulf blinded successive administrations to the inherent contradictions of supporting a pro-U.S. leader who was perceived as unpatriotic by his own subjects. In essence, the thrust of U.S. policy was not Iran but rather the containment of the Soviet Union. This anti-Soviet objective helped to create an official mind-set whereby internal Iranian political challenges to the shah tended to be perceived as having been fomented by local communists at the instigation of the USSR.

Inevitably, the hated shah was toppled in a popular revolution. Because the shah had been widely perceived in Iran as a puppet of the United States, anti-U.S. sentiment tended to be closely intertwined with the anti-shah feelings. Officials in Washington, however, were no more ready after the revolution to acknowledge a legitimate basis for this animosity—a crucial first step in reaching a diplomatic reconciliation—than they had been to recognize it before the fall of the shah. During the nine-month tenure of the provisional government that replaced the monarchy, the United States refused to authorize any U.S. official to meet with Khomeini, the leader of the revolution. This aloofness tended to reinforce the worst fears of many Iranians: that the United States opposed the revolution and was planning to intervene to restore the shah to power. Although no evidence exists that this was Washington's intention in 1979, the admission of the shah into the United States for medical treatment confirmed in the minds of some revolutionaries that the United States was plotting a coup. The response to this episode—the seizure of the U.S. embassy in Tehran and the holding of hostages—ruptured completely what remained of a relationship that, prior to 1979, had been important to both countries.

The hostage crisis demonstrated the extremes to which Iranians were willing to resort to thwart any possible U.S. intervention. Policymakers in Washington, however, perceived this crisis as evidence of the fanaticism of the revolutionaries, a perception that persisted during the last year of the Carter administration and throughout the Reagan administration. Indeed, anti-

Iranian sentiment in Washington probably has become as strong as anti-U.S. sentiment in Tehran. The United States has provided covert support to groups opposed to the government in Tehran, but the focus of its intervention policies has been to contain, rather than to overthrow, the revolution. Although the NSC's secret initiative in 1985–1986 may seem to be an effort to adopt a more flexible policy toward Iran, it also was premised in part on a belief in the need to contain the revolution. In this case, the expectation was that arms sales would help pro-West moderates within the Iranian government eventually gain influence and adopt policies that would be less hostile to U.S. interests in the region.

In 1987, the United States undertook a more activist policy of trying to contain Iran with the threat of military force in the form of a naval armada in the waters off Iran's Persian Gulf coast. Washington assumed that a show of force would intimidate Iran into halting its retaliatory strikes against the shipping of Iraq and its Arab allies. This more strident containment policy not only failed to lessen Iran's attacks but actually brought Iran and the United States to the very brink of war. It also demonstrated how poorly policymakers had learned the primary lesson of U.S. intervention in Iran: that Iranian patriots, whether secular or religious, were determined that their country not be dependent on any foreign power and not be aligned with either the United States or the USSR in their superpower competition. The confrontations with Iran in the Persian Gulf exposed the limitations of military policies to achieve political objectives. The United States realized these limitations after the accidental downing of an Iranian civilian plane and began to find ways to defuse the tension between itself and Iran. Nevertheless, as long as the nature of Iranian nationalism remains misunderstood, it will not be easy for the United States to reach a mutually satisfactory accommodation with Iran.

■ 18

The Persian Gulf

Eric Hooglund

United States policy toward the Persian Gulf region since the end of World War II can be summed up in a single three-letter word: oil. From the Truman through the Bush administrations, the primary objective has been to prevent hostile powers from gaining control of the immense petroleum resources of Iran, Iraq, and the Arabian Peninsula. Before 1990, Washington perceived the Soviet Union as the principal threat to its economic interests in the Persian Gulf and devised policies that were aimed at containing the spread of Soviet influence in the region. Although U.S. strategy encompassed various responses to the possibility of a direct Soviet invasion of the region, the primary concern actually focused on the dangers posed by suspected Soviet subversion. Policymakers in successive administrations believed the Soviet Union instigated and/or infiltrated political movements that opposed local regimes friendly to the United States in hopes of replacing them with governments amenable to Moscow's direction. Containing Soviet subversive activities did not, in Washington's view, require direct military intervention. Instead, a major policy objective became the provision of sophisticated military equipment to the area's nondemocratic monarchies in order to enhance their capabilities to suppress dissident political groups inevitably described with adjectives such as communist, Marxist, radical, terrorist, and pro-Soviet.

Washington's preoccupation with containing perceived Soviet subversion had two serious consequences for U.S. policy in the Persian Gulf. First, by filtering political developments through Soviet lenses, policymakers were unable to appreciate the genuineness and depth of popular anger against repressive regimes and therefore failed to formulate creative strategies to deal with the unthinkable—the possible overthrow of friendly governments that lacked legitimacy. Thus, when two of the region's staunchest pro-Western monarchies were unexpectedly toppled, those of Iraq in 1958 and Iran in 1979, the United States had no effective policies for the political challenges posed by anti-U.S. rulers who behaved, contrary to official wisdom, independently of the Soviet Union. Second, the analytical focus on the Soviet Union seriously hindered the ability of policymakers to understand the significance of ideologies such as Islam and nationalism and of historical disputes over borders and resources. This lack of insight left the

United States ill-prepared for the emergence of local conflicts that threatened regional stability but had no apparent relationship to Cold War issues. Among the most explosive of these were Iraq's invasions of neighbors Iran (1980) and Kuwait (1990). The latter invasion led to the deployment of over 500,000 U.S. troops to the Persian Gulf region, the most massive U.S. intervention abroad since the Vietnam War.

■ *PAX BRITTANICA*

Even though the Persian Gulf became an arena of major U.S. military intervention in the early 1990s, during the initial two decades of the Cold War era the region rarely had been a central focus of U.S. foreign policy concerns. Washington generally was satisfied that its political arrangements with allies and local regimes provided appropriate protection for Western interests and therefore concentrated its attention elsewhere in the Middle East. From the end of World War II until 1968, Great Britain was the principal foreign power in the Persian Gulf, and the United States relied upon it to serve as the guardian of the region's security.

Britain's role in the area had long historical antecedents. By the nineteenth century, an imperialist Britain had consolidated its position as the most powerful external force in the Persian Gulf, a status it still retained during the early Cold War years. Among the territories on the Arabian Peninsula that constituted part of the British Empire were current-day Bahrain, Kuwait, Qatar, and the United Arab Emirates, all of which border on the Persian Gulf; Oman, which borders on the Persian Gulf, the adjacent Gulf of Oman, and the Arabian Sea; and the Gulf of Aden territory formerly known as the Aden Protectorate (the People's Democratic Republic of [South] Yemen, 1967–1990, now part of reunified Yemen). In addition, Britain had created Iraq as an independent state following World War I, and its monarchy, which the British had established in power, was loyal to Western interests until it was overthrown by nationalist military officers in 1958.[1]

Although the projection of British power and influence in the Persian Gulf proved sufficient to keep hostile foreign forces out of the region, the classic methods of nineteenth-century international politics proved inadequate to contain the tide of intense nationalism that swept the area, as well as the rest of Asia, in the aftermath of World War II. The first challenge to British dominance was on the northern side of the Persian Gulf where Iranian nationalists tried in 1951 to assert sovereignty over Iran's oil fields. At the time, the Anglo-Iranian Oil Company (later known as British Petroleum), which was 51 percent owned by the British government, held an exclusive concession for the production and marketing of Iranian petroleum. Britain and its allies, including the United States, failed to appreciate the depth of Iranian resentment over foreign control of their country's oil resources. On the contrary, they tended to view the ensuing oil nationalization crisis as part of a concerted effort by pro-Soviet forces to deny the West access to vital oil supplies. The crisis ended in 1953 when the United States, with British support, assisted a successful Iranian military coup d'état against the nationalists, an action that resulted in the restoration to power of the staunchly anti-Soviet shah. This intervention paved the way for the United States to replace Britain as the dominant foreign power in Iran, a development that would have major consequences for Persian Gulf policy in the 1970s.[2]

Resentment over foreign control of oil resources and a perception that the monarchy was subservient to British interests were also factors that inflamed nationalist sentiment in neighboring Iraq.[3] In addition, the predominantly Arab population of Iraq tended to blame Britain specifically, and the West in general, for the 1948–1949 conflict that had resulted in the creation of an independent Israel in most of the British-controlled Mandate of Palestine and had left 75 percent of the Palestinian Arabs as stateless refugees.[4] These attitudes made it inevitable that the Iraqi government's generally pro-Western policies, especially its 1955 decision to join Britain, Iran, Pakistan, and Turkey in a U.S.-sponsored collective security agreement (initially known as the Baghdad Pact but subsequently renamed the Central Treaty Organization), would be extremely unpopular. Britain's participation (with France and Israel) in the 1956 attack on Egypt, in retaliation for Cairo's nationalization of the Suez Canal, further inflamed anti-Western feelings.[5] Nevertheless, the Iraqi monarchy generally shared the British view that nationalist-inspired discontent was fomented by communists and responded with intensified political repression. Furthermore, Iraq was one of only two Arab countries to endorse the Eisenhower Doctrine, a 1957 unilateral commitment by the United States to assist any Middle Eastern country threatened by "international communism."[6]

The Iraqi monarchy was unexpectedly overthrown by a military coup d'état in 1958. Britain, preoccupied with political developments in neighboring Jordan, was unprepared for such a radical change in government and unable to prevent the establishment in Baghdad of a republican regime that was militantly anti-Western. Although Iraq experienced considerable political instability between 1958 and 1968, its successive governments persistently challenged British interests in the Persian Gulf. Iraqi oil production, which at the time was controlled by the joint British- and U.S.-owned Iraq Petroleum Company (IPC), was one of the most important issues in dispute. Baghdad's ruling military officers, aware of the recent fate of Iranians who had tried to nationalize their country's oil, initially avoided any direct confrontation by applying more subtle pressures on IPC, such as demanding for Iraq a larger share of the profits from oil sales and canceling concession areas that IPC had not explored or developed.

Oil also was the primary motive for Iraq's 1961 assertion of a claim to sovereignty over Kuwait, made after Britain announced that the sheikhdom, a British protectorate since 1899, would become fully independent. The available evidence is inconclusive as to whether Iraq, by then perceived in London and Washington as a Soviet puppet, was prepared to use force to annex Kuwait; Baghdad denied any such intention, but the implicit threat provoked an international crisis and prompted Britain to dispatch troops to the sheikhdom. Although a League of Arab States military contingent eventually replaced the British, the incident demonstrated the determination of the West to act decisively to confront a presumed threat to its oil interests. The episode also reinforced a perception among U.S. policymakers that Iraqi policies threatened all other countries in the region, and facilitated the involvement of the United States in covert activities aimed at destabilizing Iraq's government. Iraq did not recognize Kuwait's independence until a new military regime came to power in 1963. However, Baghdad never formally renounced its claim that the sheikhdom was an integral part of Iraq. This claim would be revived in 1990 to justify Iraq's occupation and annexation of Kuwait.[7]

Although the loss of Iraq was a psychological blow to the Western alliance system, it did not lessen Britain's ability to maintain its military position in the Persian Gulf. From London's perspective, the principal threat to the region was the anti-Western version of Arab nationalism popularized by Egypt's Gamal Abdel Nasser. Both the independent and dependent rulers on the Arabian Peninsula tended to share the British view and cooperated in efforts to suppress nationalist-inspired political movements in Aden, Bahrain, and Oman. Nevertheless, in the late 1950s and early 1960s, the British Empire was receding rapidly as former colonial possessions, first in West Africa, then in East Africa, became independent. This decolonization process made the retention of dependencies in the Arabian Peninsula appear anachronistic to many politically influential Britons. The cost of maintaining the large military base at Aden, especially in view of opposition to the British presence from a growing pro-independence movement, also raised questions about the continued need for imperial outposts.[8] The ruling Labor party was sensitive to public opinion on these issues and, after the defeat of Egypt in the June 1967 war, undertook a major review of British defense policy in the Middle East. In January 1968, London stunned the United States and its Arab allies by announcing that Britain would withdraw all its remaining military forces from east of Suez by the end of 1971 and grant full sovereignty to its remaining dependencies in the Persian Gulf.[9]

■ U.S. SURROGATES

The British decision to pull out of the Persian Gulf was an unwelcome surprise for the United States. Preoccupied with its increasingly unpopular intervention in Vietnam, Washington was not prepared to assume any new military obligations in 1968. Nevertheless, policy analysts were apprehensive about the implications of Britain's withdrawal and sought to devise a strategy that would preempt the creation of a political vacuum in this strategic and oil-rich region. Official concerns centered on the presumed inability of the small and underpopulated sheikhdoms to defend their impending independence. Their regimes were perceived as unstable and susceptible to overthrow by radical (that is, anti-U.S.) Arab nationalist forces. This view was reinforced by the recent experience of the Federation of South Arabia, which emerged as the Marxist state of South Yemen when Britain finally withdrew from Aden in 1967. Washington wanted to forestall similar political developments that could pave the way for Soviet influence to penetrate the region. The problem for officials, trying to formulate policy options in the shadow of Vietnam, was to find politically acceptable means of shoring up local regimes so that they would be capable of resisting any direct or indirect Soviet subversion.[10]

During 1968 the national security bureaucracy developed some initial ideas for finding a regional ally to take over Britain's role in the Persian Gulf. These ideas actually accorded with the policy outlook of the Nixon administration, inaugurated in January 1969. The basic premise of the new foreign policy philosophy, known as the Nixon Doctrine, was that individual countries should be responsible for their own security; the United States would provide them the military hardware, but not personnel, to defend against both internal subversion and external aggression. As applied to the Persian Gulf, the Nixon Doctrine meant that local governments would be the guardians of their own and, ipso facto, U.S. interests in the region. The two most obvious candidates to serve in the role as surrogates for the United States were Iran and Saudi Arabia. These were the largest countries in the area, they produced the greatest volume of oil, and they were close allies. By mid-1969, Washington had designated both Iran and Saudi Arabia as the twin pillars of its new security policy. To make sure these pro-Western monarchies would be capable of fulfilling their role, the United States proposed to sell them sophisticated weapons to combat any local insurgencies.[11]

As originally envisioned, Iran and Saudi Arabia were to share equally in keeping the peace in the Persian Gulf. Because the United States already had long-established security relations with both countries, officials assumed that adaptation to the new role would be relatively smooth for all parties. Confidence in the Saudi willingness to take on regional security responsibilities was especially high primarily due to continuous military ties dating back to World War II. Private U.S. oil interests had become involved in exploring and developing Saudi oil fields during the 1930s. The oil companies, which eventually consolidated as the Arab-American Oil Company (ARAMCO), constituted the principal lobby for U.S.-Saudi relations and in 1943 were instrumental in getting Washington to declare the defense of Saudi Arabia vital to the defense of the United States. This action paved the way for the provision of lend-lease assistance to Riyadh, the dispatching of a small U.S. military training mission, and the construction of a huge airbase at Dhahran.[12] The Dhahran facility, continuously maintained and improved as a military airfield, would prove its utility in 1990 when thousands of U.S. troops were airlifted to it, ostensibly to defend Saudi Arabia from an Iraqi attack.

Despite their deeply intertwined oil and security interests, Saudi Arabia did not serve as an effective regional surrogate for the United States. This failure stemmed not so much from any lack of enthusiasm in Riyadh as from the political exigencies of Washington's Middle East policies during the 1970s. Although the U.S. commitment to the security of Israel was a cornerstone of overall Middle East policy, there was considerable contention between the executive branch and Congress over what specific actions threatened Israel's security. The Nixon, Ford, and Carter administrations argued that the sale to Saudi Arabia of sophisticated weapons was necessary for the defense of the Persian Gulf and did not constitute any danger to Israel. Congressional leaders countered that Saudi Arabia was an Arab country hostile to Israel and might use the weapons in an Arab-Israeli conflict. Congress thus generally opposed the sale to Saudi Arabia of U.S. arms in the quantity and quality that the executive branch wanted. These periodic controversies did not prevent Saudi Arabian purchases of U.S. weapons. In fact, the kingdom was the second-largest buyer of arms—$12 billion worth between 1973 and 1977—after Iran. However, congressional intervention tended to embitter Saudi officials and to disincline them to assume a prominent role in regional security issues.[13]

In contrast to the Saudis, the shah of Iran (reigned 1941–1979) was eager to be recognized as the West's guardian of the Persian Gulf. Because Iran was not an Arab state and also maintained a multiplicity of discreet economic, cultural, and security ties with Israel, its arms purchases were not subjected to critical congressional review. Consequently, Iran emerged during the 1970s as the single largest purchaser of U.S. weapons—an average annual expenditure of $3.2 billion between 1973 and 1978—and the virtual gendarme of the region.[14] With Washington's approval, the shah intervened both covertly and openly to destabilize unfriendly regimes and suppress dissident political movements that threatened the stability of the newly independent sheikhdoms. On the eve of the British departure in late 1971, he dispatched Iranian troops and naval craft to occupy three small islands belonging to two of the sheikhdoms that were in the process of forming the United Arab Emirates. The United States and Britain excused this act of naked aggression on grounds that the islands lay astride the main shipping channel through the Strait of Hormuz, the waterway that connects the Persian Gulf and the Gulf of Oman.[15]

Iran's most serious intervention, however, was in Iraq. Baghdad and Tehran actually had not had good relations since the overthrow of the Iraqi monarchy in 1958. During the 1960s Iran had provided limited covert assistance to Iraq's Kurdish minority, who were fighting for autonomy in the predominantly Kurdish-populated northern provinces.[16] The shah did not have genuine sympathy for Kurdish aspirations—Iran had its own restive Kurdish minority—but hoped to pressure Iraq into accepting the middle of the Shatt al-Arab River as a common boundary. Ever since Britain, when establishing Iraq as an independent state in the 1930s, had imposed the low-tide shore on the Iranian side of the river as the international border, the riparian boundary had been an issue that rankled Iranian nationalists. Britain's withdrawal from the area, combined with U.S. support for Iran to assume regional police functions, provided an opportunity—peaceful or otherwise—to resolve this longstanding border grievance.[17]

U.S. relations with Iraq also had deteriorated since 1958. In the wake of the Egyptian-Jordanian-Syrian defeat in the June 1967 war against Israel, Baghdad had joined several other Arab capitals in severing diplomatic ties with Washington. By the time the Nixon Doctrine was being formulated, the official perception of Iraq was that its regime was a client, or even a puppet, of the Soviet Union. Iraq's subsequent nationalization of the IPC and signing of a friendship and cooperation treaty with the Soviet Union (both in 1972) reinforced these views. Containing Iraqi power in the region thus became synonymous with containing Soviet influence. Consequently, the United States backed Iran's policies aimed at destabilizing, or even overthrowing, Iraq's government. Initially this involved clandestine intelligence contacts with various Iraqi dissidents, including the Kurds who were disillusioned by the lack of progress on autonomy negotiations that had begun in 1970. Using Iranian agents as intermediaries, the CIA began supplying money and arms to the principal Kurdish leaders as early as 1972.[18] This tangible evidence of U.S. support induced the Kurds in 1974 to launch a full-scale military revolt against the Iraqi government. Iran's borders with the Kurdish region of northern Iraq remained open for relatively unhindered passage of military and other supplies, and on several occasions in late 1974 and early 1975, Iranian forces attacked Iraqi units pursuing the Kurds. Baghdad, realizing that the escalating fighting could lead to conflict with Iran and its patron, the United States, and that its own ally, the Soviet Union, could not be counted on for assistance, sought to neutralize Iran by offering the shah a resolution of the Shatt al-Arab boundary dispute. Under the terms of the 1975 Algiers Treaty, Iran and Iraq agreed to recognize the middle channel of the river as their international border. In an accompanying protocol pertaining to border security, each country promised not to support "subversive elements" in the other's territory.[19] Iran subsequently informed the stunned Kurds that all assistance would cease and the borders would be sealed. The United States acquiesced in the Iranian decision, in effect abandoning the Kurds, whose resistance was soon brutally crushed. Iraq avoided international censure for its treatment of the Kurds by adopting a virtual diplomatic volte face and cultivating good neighborly relations with Iran, Saudi Arabia, and the other Gulf countries.

Iranian intervention was directed not only at destabilizing unfriendly regimes but also at preserving friendly ones. In the early 1970s, Oman was the regional country most threatened by an internal armed opposition movement. The rebellion in Oman's western province of Dhofar had begun in 1965 as a protest against the repressive policies of the ruler of this British protectorate, Sultan Said bin Taimur Al Bu Said (reigned 1932–1970). Although Britain employed drastic measures to suppress the guerrilla movement, it was unwilling to commit a large military force in Oman, and the uprising gradually gathered momentum.[20] As they prepared to terminate their security role in 1970, the British deposed Sultan Said and installed in power his son, Qabus bin Said, in the hope that more enlightened policies would defuse the discontent. Oman retained its British-officered army at independence, but this force was unable to suppress the rebellion. Consequently, Sultan Qabus sought military assistance from his fellow monarchs, King Hussein of Jordan and the shah of Iran. The shah dispatched 30 helicopters with their crews in the summer of 1972 and a year later sent an estimated 4,000 troops, who conducted counterinsurgency operations from a base on an island off the Dhofar coast. By the end of 1975, the Dhofar rebellion had been effectively contained. However, the last Iranian contingents were not withdrawn from Oman until 1977.[21]

The shah's use of Iran's armed forces to help suppress the guerrilla movement in Oman paralleled his use of them to repress organized opposition at home. The shah's regime, similar to those of the Arabian Peninsula and even republican Iraq, was intolerant of political dissent. The facade of domestic tranquility that the military and security police maintained concealed widespread discontent. During 1977 and 1978, this popular discontent crystallized into a mass revolutionary movement demanding the removal of the shah, who was excoriated as a puppet of the United States. As the revolutionary mood gathered steam, military commanders, who had successfully crushed isolated guerrilla movements and protest demonstrations, realized that the armed forces had neither the training nor inclination to deal effectively with revolutionary urban crowds. Once the shah recognized that his domestic power—the security apparatus—was crumbling due to declining military morale and conscript desertions, and that he would not be able to obtain salvation through U.S. intervention, he voluntarily left the country. The monarchy was overthrown four weeks later; along with it went the policy of Iran serving as a surrogate to protect U.S. interests in the Persian Gulf.

■ THINGS FALL APART

The unanticipated loss of a major strategic ally left U.S. policy in the region temporarily adrift. The new republican regime in Tehran not only renounced Iran's former role as a regional gendarme but also called upon the Arabs of the Persian Gulf to rise up against their rulers. The Iranian rhetoric about Islamic revolution understandably caused consternation both in Washington and in the Middle East. The alarm of the Arabian Peninsula's hereditary rulers was not assuaged by their conviction that the United States had failed to intervene to save an ally as important as the shah. Nevertheless, because revolutionary Iran represented such an immediate ideological threat for their undemocratic systems of government, these monarchs perceived only two realistic alternatives for preserving their families in power: to permit greater citizen participation in the political processes or to maintain the political status quo by whatever means necessary, including force. The first choice generally was unacceptable not only because it would mean the erosion of privileges but also because many of the princes in decisionmaking positions believed that the shah's downfall had been precipitated by an assumed policy of political liberalization. The second choice, and the one that was adopted, involved even more dependence on the United States as a source of equipment to contain and/or suppress any antigovernment movements.

The concerns of the Persian Gulf monarchs during the first half of 1979 enabled the United States to persuade Saudi Arabia to adopt a more assertive role in regional security—in effect to take over the role that Iran had performed for nearly a decade. To enhance Saudi military capabilities, Washington provided Riyadh with assurances that previous political restrictions on Saudi purchases of sophisticated weapons would be circumvented (subsequent executive branch efforts to promote arms sales to Saudi Arabia would lead to major policy struggles with Congress). The Saudis welcomed an enhanced security relationship with the United States because they felt surrounded by political instability. In addition to the revolutionary chaos in Iran, North and South Yemen at the southern end of the Arabian Peninsula were involved in border clashes at the beginning of 1979, and across the Red Sea in the Horn of Africa, Ethiopia was threatening both Somalia and Sudan. Saudi Arabia shared the U.S. view that Ethiopia and South Yemen were Soviet clients pursuing subversive policies designed to advance Soviet interests and influence in the region. To counter the threat from pro-Soviet regimes, the Saudis agreed to subsidize purchases of U.S. weapons for North Yemen, Somalia, and Sudan.[22]

Despite Washington's hopes that an expanded Saudi security role would provide stability for the Persian Gulf, it soon became apparent that Saudi Arabia was not militarily capable of intervening in the unprecedented international crises that convulsed the region in the wake of the Iranian revolution. These crises included the fourteen-month U.S. hostage crisis

beginning in November 1979, the nine-year Soviet occupation of
Afghanistan beginning in December 1979, and the eight-year Iran-Iraq War
beginning in September 1980. In addition, Saudi Arabia itself was shaken by
a major but ultimately unsuccessful insurrection in late 1979. Inspired by a
vision of religious reform, several hundred Muslim zealots occupied Mecca's
Grand Mosque, Islam's holiest shrine, and battled for its control with security
forces for two weeks. The Saudi rulers felt compelled to seek assistance from
allies—including non-Muslim France, which dispatched a special antiterrorist
team—to help put down this potentially serious challenge to their
authority.[23] Even as the fighting was proceeding in the Grand Mosque,
members of Saudi Arabia's minority Shia Muslims living in towns along
the kingdom's oil-rich Persian Gulf coast staged violent demonstrations
against state-sanctioned policies that they alleged discriminated against non-
Sunni Muslims. The stationing of 20,000 National Guardsmen in the area
failed to prevent a second outbreak of Shia antistate violence in February
1980.[24]

For the Saudi ruling family, these religiously inspired disturbances as
well as similarly violent demonstrations in Bahrain and Kuwait were proof of
Iran's efforts to export its revolution. The kingdom's rulers remained
apprehensive about Iranian subversion throughout 1980. It is likely that they
welcomed Iraq's invasion of Iran in September and hoped that conflict would
end the ideological threat from Tehran. Although Saudi Arabia proclaimed its
neutrality, it refrained from any public criticism of Baghdad and even offered
generous loans and grants to help finance the Iraqi war effort. By the end of
the year, however, the Saudis realized that the disliked regime in Tehran was
not going to be defeated easily. Believing that Iranian subversion would
intensify as a means of pressuring the officially neutral but de facto pro-Iraq
regimes of the Persian Gulf, Saudi Arabia, with encouragement from the
United States, took the lead in persuading the five smaller states of Bahrain,
Kuwait, Oman, Qatar, and the United Arab Emirates to join with it in a new
collective security alliance, the Gulf Cooperation Council (GCC). Formally
inaugurated in February 1981, the GCC's most important activity was the
sharing of intelligence about suspected pro-Iranian groups in the region. Its
first major success was in December 1981 when GCC security forces
provided Bahrain's police with information that led to the arrest of more than
fifty Bahraini and eleven Saudi dissidents accused of plotting to overthrow the
government of Bahrain.[25]

The United States was as concerned as Saudi Arabia and the other
regional Arab states about the spread of Islamic revolution, but its primary
preoccupation remained the containment of Soviet influence. For twenty-five
years before the 1979 revolution, Iran, which shared a 1,200-mile border with
the Soviet Union, had been what national security experts called a strategic
asset in terms of overall anti-Soviet policy. Although the unexpected
overthrow of the shah forced Washington to accept the termination of its

special relationship with Tehran, policymakers perceived the Islamic Republic's coolness toward Moscow as a positive signal and believed it could cooperate with the new regime. Nine months after the revolution, however, all hopes of normalizing relations were firmly dashed by the hostage crisis, which symbolized in Iran the accession to power of political factions that were militant in their anti-U.S. stance and symbolized in the region the impotence of a superpower that had lost its principal client. Officials concerned about the impact of these events on U.S. prestige received yet another traumatic shock some fifty days into the hostage ordeal—it would last for 444 days—when the Soviet Union initiated an entirely new international crisis with its military invasion of Afghanistan, ostensibly at the invitation of that country's Marxist government. Even though Afghanistan was landlocked, its location—wedged between the Soviet Union, Iran, and Pakistan on the periphery of the Persian Gulf region—ensured that the United States would view the presence there of several thousand Soviet troops as a potentially serious threat to its interests.[26]

Although the Soviet intervention in Afghanistan had more to do with that country's internal problems than with international politics, from Washington's perspective it constituted an invasion that disturbed the regional balance of power even more fundamentally than had the Iranian revolution. Alarmists predicted that the Soviet action was the initial phase of a planned military drive to the Persian Gulf itself. According to this scenario, Iran, beset with revolutionary turmoil and embroiled in conflict with the United States over the hostages, would be the next target. Policymakers believed that the situation called for tangible evidence that the United States was committed to defending its interests in the region. Consequently, they formulated a new policy aimed at deterring further Soviet advances in the area. First announced by President Jimmy Carter in his January 1980 State of the Union address, this new policy became known as the Carter Doctrine. It boldly stated that "an attempt by an outside force to gain control of the Persian Gulf region will be regarded as an assault on the vital interests of the United States of America, and such an assault will be repelled by the use of any means necessary, including military force."[27]

Once the Persian Gulf had been explicitly defined as an area of vital U.S. interests, developing the military capability to protect these interests became an important policy objective. Officials recognized that the United States needed the means to intervene quickly in order to deter not only Soviet aggression but also subversion and other internal political threats to friendly regimes. The Pentagon promoted the concept of a Rapid Deployment Force (RDF) composed of U.S. troops who could be deployed rapidly to any trouble spot in the region. Under this force structure it was not necessary to maintain bases in the Persian Gulf. Rather, military units could train in the general Middle East area by conducting periodic joint exercises with the forces of regional allies. The first joint exercises actually were held with

Egypt in summer 1980, and in subsequent years Jordan, Oman, Somalia, and
Sudan agreed to participate.[28] In 1983 the Reagan administration expanded
and institutionalized the RDF by creating a new U.S. Central Command
(CENTCOM) with headquarters at McDill Air Force Base in Tampa, Florida,
and responsibility for military operations in the Persian Gulf region.
CENTCOM's experience in rapidly deploying air, ground, and naval units for
joint maneuvers, prepositioning supplies at overseas facilities, and creating
bases from scratch in a few hours all proved to be valuable training and
preparation for the real intervention in 1990.[29]

Despite U.S. concerns about the need to deter perceived Soviet
expansionism, a virtual policy preoccupation during the first six years of the
Reagan administration, the principal threat to the political stability of the
Persian Gulf during most of the 1980s did not come from Moscow but
originated out of indigenous problems that neither superpower understood or
could control. The most important of these crises was the Iran-Iraq War.
Saddam Hussein, who became president of Iraq in 1979, felt as much
threatened by the notion of Islamic revolution as did the monarchs of the
Arabian Peninsula and initiated the war primarily to contain the spread of this
idea.[30] At the time (September 1980), the United States was unprepared for a
regional conflict involving local states. Washington did not have formal
diplomatic relations with either Baghdad or Tehran, and informal relations
with both parties were strained. There was little sympathy for Iran because of
the bitter and protracted hostage ordeal that remained unresolved. Official
resentment of Iraq also was high because that country had taken a leading role
in 1979 in denouncing the U.S.-brokered peace treaty between Egypt and
Israel and generally had opposed U.S. policies throughout the 1970s. For
these reasons, the United States had neither the influence nor inclination to
affect the course of the war during its initial phase, approximately from
September 1980 to June 1982.

Washington had four main objectives during the initial phase of the Iran-
Iraq War: to prevent Soviet intervention, to contain the conflict from
spreading to its Gulf allies, to discourage arms sales to the belligerents, and
to secure a cease-fire. The United States was particularly concerned about
Soviet intentions despite the lack of evidence that Moscow perceived any
political advantages for itself as a result of the war. On the contrary, the
Soviet Union jeopardized its former friendly relations with Iraq by
terminating arms supplies to both parties and calling for a withdrawal of
military forces to international borders (Iraq occupied part of southwestern
Iran). Although Moscow maintained diplomatic ties with both Baghdad and
Tehran, its efforts to mediate the conflict were fruitless. In addition, the
Soviet Union was preoccupied with Afghanistan where resistance fighters,
called mujahedin, were conducting increasingly effective guerrilla warfare
with sophisticated weapons covertly supplied by the United States.[31]
Washington, however, generally was oblivious to the constraints on Soviet

policy and tended to focus on ways of minimizing the potential for Moscow to derive any benefits from the Iran-Iraq War. Consequently, other U.S. goals vis-à-vis this conflict received inadequate attention.

The United States could afford to ignore the war as long as the fighting between Iran and Iraq did not adversely affect its primary interests: the stability of regional allies and international oil supplies. Throughout 1981 the conflict appeared to be stalemated, a situation that caused policymakers to hope that the two disliked regimes would weaken each other to such an extent that neither would be able to pose a threat to regional allies for many years into the future. By August 1982, however, Iran had recovered from the initial shock of the invasion, forced Iraqi troops to withdraw from most of the territory they had captured at the outset of the war, launched its own invasion of Iraq, and successfully occupied land on the Iraqi side of the Shatt al-Arab River. For the next four years, Iran continued to make gradual advances. The reassertion of Iranian power and influence revived fears of Islamic revolution not only among the Persian Gulf's Arab rulers but also throughout the Middle East. With the assistance of its only ally, Syria, Iran was able to join the mélange of international actors who were intervening in Lebanon's civil war. The Iranians provided support for Lebanon's Shia militia, especially the Hizbollah, which in 1983 carried out several sensational car-bomb attacks, including on the U.S. embassy and Marine barracks, both in Beirut; these two incidents killed more than 300 people. In 1984 and 1985, Hizbollah groups kidnapped and held as hostages several U.S. citizens, including CIA Chief of Station William Buckley who subsequently died while in captivity. Iran also was suspected of involvement in terrorist incidents that occurred in the GCC countries in this same period. The most sensational attack was in Kuwait in December 1983 when dissident Arab Shias detonated bombs at the U.S. and French embassies and several Kuwaiti government installations.[32]

The revival of the threat of Islamic revolution compelled the United States to adopt more assertive policies to contain its spread. The most significant new policy was the rapprochement with Iraq, the principal enemy of Iran. The aim of this initiative, referred to as "tilting toward Iraq," was to pressure Iran into ending the war by accepting a cease-fire, a move Iraq had been calling for since June 1982. Policymakers believed that ending the conflict was central to containing the export of Islamic revolution because continuation of the war provided Tehran, which was generally isolated internationally, with incentives to support subversion and terrorism in the region. The rapprochement was inaugurated in 1983 with the dispatch of a high-level envoy to Baghdad to discuss matters of mutual interest, including diplomatic relations, which had been broken in 1967 (relations subsequently were reestablished in November 1984).[33]

The first signs of an official U.S. move away from neutrality came in 1984 when Washington effectively ignored internationally verified evidence that Iraq had used chemical weapons against Iranian troops and excluded Iraqi arms purchases from Operation Staunch, a State Department effort to persuade third countries to stop selling weapons to Iran. The tilt toward Iraq was welcomed by the GCC countries, especially Kuwait and Saudi Arabia, both of which had become the principal sources of financial assistance for the Iraqi war effort. The new U.S. policy failed, however, to achieve a cessation of hostilities. On the contrary, it emboldened Iraq to expand the war by attacking ships in the Persian Gulf carrying Iranian oil exports. Because Iraq's oil exports went overland via pipelines that were beyond range of Iranian bombers, Iran retaliated by attacking ships carrying oil from Iraq's de facto allies, Kuwait and Saudi Arabia. These raids and counterraids initiated the tanker war, a phase of the conflict that would last for four years.[34]

The tilt toward Iraq was not supported by all members of the Reagan administration. Officials who believed containment of the Soviet Union was a priority feared an obvious pro-Iraqi position could drive Iran into the Soviet camp. They were convinced that Tehran and Washington shared a common interest in keeping Moscow's influence in check; Baghdad, in contrast, historically had assisted Soviet penetration of the region.[35] Consequently, they obtained presidential authority to establish covert contacts with the Iranian government. During much of 1985 and 1986, the United States effectively pursued two simultaneous and contradictory policies in the Persian Gulf. Publicly, it opposed the continuation of the Iran-Iraq War, cultivated its new relationship with Iraq, and reassured its regional allies of its commitment to contain Islamic revolution. Clandestinely, however, the United States negotiated with Iran for the release of U.S. citizens being held as hostages in Lebanon, for the sale of U.S.-made weapons, and for the provision of intelligence about the Iraqi military. The unexpected revelation of these secret deals in November 1986 deeply embarrassed the United States. The GCC countries were especially shocked that Washington had sold Iran weapons that were being used to prolong the war.[36] For several weeks U.S. policy was in a state of disarray as the administration sought to find a means of reestablishing its tarnished reputation among its allies.[37]

■ PAX AMERICANA

The revelations about covert arms sales to Tehran ultimately had the effect of ending the ambiguity in U.S. policy toward the Iran-Iraq War. To reassure its shaken allies in the Persian Gulf, Washington decided in early 1987 to intervene in a decisive manner to bring about a cessation of hostilities and to contain Iranian subversion. One means for this intervention was a Kuwaiti request to have several of its oil tankers reflagged as U.S. ships, thereby entitling them to U.S. naval protection if attacked by hostile forces while engaged in peaceful commerce.[38] The reflagging operation was intended to deter Iran, which had been attacking Kuwait-owned tankers in retaliation for Iraq's aerial bombing of ships—most of which were from neutral countries—transporting cargo to and from Iranian ports.[39] Congress generally viewed the reflagging apprehensively because there was a potential for conflict with Iran if its forces attacked a tanker flying the Stars and Stripes. Ironically, it was Iraq that helped to resolve congressional and public doubts when it attacked, apparently in error, a U.S. naval ship patrolling off the coast of Bahrain. This May 1987 attack, which resulted in the death of thirty-seven U.S. soldiers, made freedom of navigation in the international waters of the Persian Gulf an issue that both Congress and the executive could rally around. By a twist of logic that did not appear to prick any consciences, Iran was blamed for the Iraqi attack on the *U.S.S. Stark*. With a virtual mandate for action, the president authorized U.S. naval convoys to accompany the newly "Americanized" tankers on their return to Kuwait and to defend them if necessary.

The sudden U.S. intervention in the Iran-Iraq War infuriated Tehran, which had been confident (perhaps unrealistically) of winning a decisive victory following a year of successful offensives. During June and July 1987, Iran tried to forestall the U.S. intervention by sowing mines in the Persian Gulf. This policy backfired as soon as the mines began damaging commercial ships, including some bound for Iran itself. Governments of countries that imported oil from the region were alarmed and echoed U.S. statements about the need to protect freedom of navigation. The United States not only increased its own naval presence in the area but also persuaded its European allies to dispatch minesweepers to help clear out the mines. By the end of 1987, the United States had forty-eight ships in the Persian Gulf and adjacent waters. This represented the largest number of U.S. ships assembled in one area since World War II. In addition, Belgium, Britain, France, Italy, and the Netherlands had dispatched a total of twenty-three vessels to protect ships flying their respective flags.[40]

The buildup of this armada in the Persian Gulf region was not done without concern for the Soviet reaction. In general, however, the Soviet Union tolerated the U.S. intervention. Mikhail Gorbachev had become the Soviet leader in 1985; both domestic and international policies were undergoing radical rethinking by 1987, although the Reagan administration did not recognize this at the time. As part of the new openness, Moscow had been holding regular consultations with Washington about the Iran-Iraq War.[41] Consequently, U.S. officials believed they and the Soviets shared a mutual interest in seeing the conflict end without a victor or vanquished. Nevertheless, they still were apprehensive that the war could serve as a vehicle for the Soviet Union to increase its influence in the area. This concern was momentarily rekindled in early 1987 when the Soviets agreed to provide protection for some Kuwaiti tankers, a decision that prompted Washington's hasty assent to the reflagging request. The United States, in effect, was still preoccupied with its rivalry with the Soviet Union and unprepared for any joint military efforts (although Washington subsequently did agree to cooperate diplomatically with Moscow in the drafting of the UN cease-fire resolution).[42] Later, when mines were discovered in Gulf waters, the Soviet Union sent a frigate and three minesweepers to the area to help defend the freedom-of-navigation principle. The United States had to accept what it considered an unwarranted intrusion because the Soviet naval presence was protecting Soviet commercial vessels in international waters. In actuality, the Soviet efforts complemented those of the United States and its European allies.

Iraq and the officially neutral GCC countries welcomed the U.S. intervention. Kuwait and Saudi Arabia in particular believed that the war threatened their economies, which were dependent on oil exports. The intensification of the tanker war during 1986 had demonstrated both their vulnerability to economic pressures and their impotence in protecting their vital resource. They consequently perceived the internationalization of the Iran-Iraq conflict as the most effective means of forcing Tehran to accept a cease-fire. Iraq also hoped that the U.S. and European presence would exert additional pressures on Iran. Saddam Hussein had concluded as early as 1982 that the war he had initiated no longer served Iraqi interests, and he blamed Iranian stubbornness and religious fanaticism for the continuation of hostilities. He recognized that his army would never be able to defeat the Iranians on the battlefield, but he also realized Iraq retained considerable air superiority over Iran. Once it became clear that neither the United States nor the European countries would interfere with Iraqi air strikes against Iranian targets, whether at sea or on land, he ordered a new round of attacks on Iran's shipping. In the last four months of 1987, Iraqi planes hit almost twice the number of ships that had been struck in all of 1986.[43]

Iraq's virtual impunity in attacking Iranian shipping encouraged it to make more extensive use of its missiles and chemical weapons. At the end of February 1988, Baghdad initiated a two-month campaign, referred to in the international media as "the war of the cities," during which more than 200 long-range missiles and more than sixty Soviet-made Scud missiles were fired at Tehran and other Iranian cities, causing considerable panic and terror among civilians. Although Iran responded in kind, its technically less-sophisticated missiles generally had shorter ranges, contained smaller amounts of explosives, and caused less damage. Iraq's most controversial tactic was its use of chemical weapons. Iraq had first used chemical weapons on the battlefield in early 1984 and had continued to use them sporadically and in small quantities thereafter. Many countries had expressed concern about their use, but the United States had adopted the position that both Iran and Iraq possessed chemical weapons and it was not possible to verify which country had used them in any specific battle. The United States maintained this stance even though Iran consistently denied possessing or ever using such weapons and all the documented victims of chemical attacks were Iranian military personnel.

Iraq apparently perceived the lack of U.S. censure for its earlier use of chemical weapons as an implicit acceptance of its right to employ whatever means necessary to defend its territory. Consequently, it used chemical weapons in greater quantities than previously during Iranian offensives in early 1988. Iraq's most widely publicized use of chemical weapons was on its own town of Halabja in the Kurdish region adjacent to the Iranian border. The area had changed hands several times since 1980. Iranian forces, who in March 1988 already occupied several Iraqi villages, launched a major offensive toward Halabja with the aim of capturing a nearby dam that supplied electricity for Baghdad. Kurdish guerrillas opposed to Saddam Hussein's government were operating in the area and cooperating with the Iranians. Iraqi troops evacuated Halabja to regroup around the dam, and Iraqi planes subsequently dropped poison gas bombs on the town. It remains unclear whether Iraq used chemical weapons in order to punish suspected Kurdish collaborators or on the belief that Halabja already had been captured by the Iranians. In any event, over 5,000 people, mostly women and children, were killed in the incident. Iranian forces and Kurdish guerrillas entered Halabja several hours later and invited the international press to bear witness to the atrocity.

Halabja had a major psychological impact on both Iraqi Kurds and Iranians. For the Iranians, who had the grim task of burying the dead, Halabja was a very demoralizing experience, and stories about the extent of the atrocity became increasingly exaggerated as they circulated along the war front and throughout the civilian population. Iran's soldiers never really fought effectively after Halabja, and during the final months of the war, they tended to withdraw from positions or surrender whenever the Iraqis initiated any offensives. The extensive use of chemical weapons probably played a crucial role in persuading Iran's leaders to accept a UN cease-fire resolution in July 1988.

Halabja also had an impact on policymakers in the United States.[44] It was no longer possible to ignore Iraqi use of chemical weapons. Nevertheless, because Washington had effectively sided with Iraq in its war with Iran, officials generally were reluctant to condemn Baghdad despite misgivings about the wisdom of its policies. In addition, ending the war had become a major aim of U.S. policy in the Persian Gulf. For that reason, both the State Department and the Pentagon agreed that the United States should avoid doing or saying anything that would permit Iran to benefit from its discovery of Halabja or contribute to lessening the pressure on Tehran to agree to a cease-fire. At the UN, where efforts got under way to pass a resolution demanding an end to the use of chemical weapons, U.S. representatives persuaded delegates to agree to generic language that did not cite Iraq as a violator of international conventions banning chemical weapons.

The pressures on Iran achieved their objective in July 1988 when Tehran finally agreed to a cease-fire. From Washington's perspective, this situation—a stalemate—was the most desirable outcome to the war. Neither country had achieved a victory or been defeated. It was expected that both states would be so preoccupied with their reconstruction efforts that they would proceed, albeit gradually, from cease-fire to peace negotiations without further resort to conflict. Even so, the United States planned to retain its naval presence in the area for an indefinite period as a deterrent to future hostilities. Officials also worried about possible Iranian attempts to export its revolution. They believed that the energies Iran formerly devoted to the war would now be focused on other adventures. Indeed, during the final year of the Iran-Iraq War, Tehran had broken diplomatic relations with Kuwait and Riyadh, and the prospects for any speedy resolution of their differences seemed remote. After the cease-fire came into effect, however, Iran did not try to intimidate its neighbors. On the contrary, it pursued a deliberate policy of cultivating good relations with the smaller states of Bahrain, Oman, Qatar, and the United Arab Emirates. Tehran also expressed interest in normalizing relations with Kuwait and Riyadh. In view of Kuwaiti and Saudi suspicions of Iranian intentions, this was a prolonged process. Nevertheless, Iran and Kuwait did reestablish formal ties in July 1990; diplomatic contacts between Iran and Saudi Arabia also had been initiated, but the reestablishment of relations was delayed by the Persian Gulf War.

Contrary to U.S. expectations, it was Iraq rather than Iran that challenged U.S. interests in the Gulf after July 1988. Although the Iran-Iraq War had ended in a stalemate, Saddam Hussein proclaimed an Iraqi victory and soon began to assert his country's right to be the region's dominant power. The two main constraints to his ambitions were economic and geographic. Economically, Iraq had emerged from the war with an estimated debt of $70 billion and needed substantial financial assistance for the reconstruction of war-damaged industry and infrastructure.[45] Baghdad's plans to overcome these difficulties depended on persuading the GCC states, especially Kuwait and Saudi Arabia, to agree to three demands: (1) cancel the loans they had extended to Iraq during the war; (2) give up part of their Organization of Petroleum Exporting Countries (OPEC) oil-production quotas to Iraq; and (3) adopt policies to maintain high prices for oil in the international market. Geographically, Iraq's limited shoreline along the Persian Gulf—less than 50 miles—seriously impeded the development of a credible naval force. Baghdad hoped to remedy this problem by obtaining long-term leases to two large Kuwaiti islands that controlled access to the Iraqi coast.

Not expecting Iraq to emerge as a major destabilizing force, during 1989 and early 1990 the United States was unsure how to interpret Iraqi pressures on the GCC countries, Kuwait in particular. One influential group of policy analysts believed Iraq was a potent ally against Iran, which they continued to view as the principal threat in the region. They cited sensational incidents, such as the 1989 religious decree calling for the death of a British author accused of insulting Islam (Salman Rushdie), as evidence of Tehran's continued support for terrorism and subversion. Compared with Iran, Iraq was a "moderate" country whose demands on its neighbors could be handled through skilled diplomacy. They used the adjective "moderate" to mean policies that did not conflict with U.S. regional objectives. Another group of analysts held an opposite view, namely that Baghdad's actions since the cease-fire demonstrated a return to the "radical" policies that had been followed before the war with Iran. They used "radical" to describe any policies that challenged the political and economic status quo in the Persian Gulf. These analysts feared Iraq would sponsor terrorism and subversion in Kuwait and other Arab states as a means of forcing the GCC countries to comply with its demands.

The issue that became a symbol of the sharp division among policy analysts was not U.S. interests but Iraq's use of chemical weapons. After the cease-fire with Iran, the Iraqi air force had dropped poison gas bombs on several Kurdish villages in northern Iraq, incidents that caused more than 75,000 Kurds to flee into Iran and Turkey. This new attack revived memories of Halabja and prompted the U.S. Senate to pass a resolution calling for economic sanctions against Iraq. For officials who distrusted Baghdad's intentions, the stockpiling of chemical weapons and the readiness to employ them constituted evidence that Saddam Hussein's regime would resort to any means, including the covert acquisition of nuclear weapons, to achieve its ambitions. In contrast, those analysts who believed the United States should maintain a cooperative relationship with Iraq tended to dismiss reports of Baghdad's use of chemical weapons as exaggerated or even as propaganda. Some of them actually authored a report in which they attempted to prove that it was Iran, not Iraq, that had fired chemical weapons into Halabja.[46] Ironically, this effort to exonerate Iraq was released in July 1990, less than one month before Iraq invaded Kuwait.

Although a policy consensus on dealing with Iraq had not been achieved when Saddam Hussein launched the invasion and occupation of Kuwait in 1990, that unexpected action precipitated an end to the debate. Kuwait symbolized the very essence of the economic and political order that U.S. policy had striven to maintain since Britain's withdrawal from the Persian Gulf. Policymakers recognized that Kuwait's disappearance as a sovereign entity was an unambiguous assault on the regional status quo. Within days, the Bush administration had formulated a coherent policy of military intervention aimed at restoring that status quo. This involved activating CENTCOM, which demonstrated the utility of years of rapid deployment and joint exercises training: Thousands of troops and their military equipment were airlifted to Saudi Arabia; these forces created bases in the desert literally overnight. By the end of 1990, over 400,000 U.S. military personnel were stationed in Saudi Arabia or on over sixty naval ships in the waters surrounding the Arabian Peninsula. Furthermore, Washington persuaded several of its key regional and European allies to contribute an additional 125,000 troops for an allied coalition. Even more significant, the United States obtained unprecedented Soviet support for its intervention, and this permitted Washington to acquire UN Security Council legitimization for its actions, first with an international boycott of Iraq and then with authorization for the use of force to end Iraq's occupation of Kuwait.

From the beginning of the Persian Gulf war in August 1990, the United States insisted that its only objectives were to compel Iraq's withdrawal from Kuwait and to restore the deposed government to power. Throughout the crisis, officials declined to meet with representatives from various Iraqi opposition groups. Policy analysts generally assumed that the Iraqi opposition leaders were either separatists (Kurds) or Islamic fundamentalists (Shias) and concluded that a government controlled by either group, or even a coalition, would be inimical to overall U.S. interests in the region.[47] After the humiliating Iraqi defeat at the end of February 1991, popular uprisings against Saddam Hussein's regime unexpectedly occurred in the south and the north of the country. Even though U.S. forces occupied part of southern Iraq, they did not interfere with the brutal repression of the uprising. In the north, however, more than 2 million refugees, mostly Kurds, fled their homes as the Iraqi army arrived to put down the rebellion. This mass exodus caused an international outcry that compelled the United States to intervene. With its European allies, the United States established a temporary security zone in northern Iraq to encourage the Kurds to return to their homes. After more than 1.5 million refugees did return, the United States and its allies left this security zone. Nonetheless, by the end of 1991, Kurdish forces exercised de facto control.[48]

■ LESSONS OF INTERVENTION

Whether the United States relied upon other countries or its own military might, its goals in the Persian Gulf were constant and limited: to protect its economic interests. This meant preserving in power local regimes that supported overall U.S. objectives. For forty years Washington perceived the principal threat as external to the region: that is, the Soviet Union. Successive administrations accepted a worldview that perceived Moscow as consistently trying to gain control over the area's oil resources, and they formulated strategies to keep Soviet influence in check. Indigenous political movements that challenged autocratic rule and/or criticized U.S. regional policies were branded subversive agents of the Soviet Union. The United States supported the efforts of friendly regimes to suppress such movements, believing (mistakenly) this to be the best way to ensure stability. When two repressive allies were overthrown in popular revolutions, the new governments remained deeply suspicious of Washington because of its past assistance to the deposed and disliked regimes.

After the 1979 Iranian revolution, the United States had to confront the reality of serious threats to its regional interests emanating from unfriendly local powers that were not under the influence of the Soviet Union. The most serious challenge to U.S. interests was posed by Iraq, a formerly hostile country that the United States had reluctantly befriended in an effort to contain perceived threats from Iran. Iraq saw the 1989–1990 collapse of the U.S.-Soviet Cold War rivalry as an opportunity to assert its role as the dominant power in the Persian Gulf. To achieve its ambitions, Iraq needed major concessions that would affect the security and economic autonomy of U.S. allies in the region. When one ally, Kuwait, refused the Iraqi demands, it was invaded, occupied, and proclaimed an integral part of Iraq. This stark challenge to the political status quo that the United States had striven for so long to maintain forced Washington into a dilemma. It could acquiesce in Iraq's forcible annexation of Kuwait, a policy that would send undesirable signals to other Arabian Peninsula monarchs, or it could adopt drastic measures aimed at trying to reverse Iraq's fait accompli. Washington chose the latter course and decided that military intervention was the most effective means of achieving its goal to liberate Kuwait.

Although military action was not initiated until January 1991, the military option actually had been chosen when the decision was made to deploy CENTCOM forces to Saudi Arabia. If the deployment failed to intimidate Saddam Hussein into evacuating Kuwait, then U.S. and allied forces would attack his army. The objective was not to defeat a brutal dictator, which Saddam Hussein was, but to cripple Iraqi military power to such an extent that it would be unable to threaten regional U.S. allies. Officials were not interested in changing Iraq's form of government, although they did hope that Saddam Hussein himself might be removed through an "orderly" military coup d'état. When it became obvious after the war that the Iraqi leader would probably remain in power indefinitely, the United States was prepared to tolerate this because a humiliated Saddam Hussein appeared more predictable than did the prospect of a less authoritarian regime subject to public pressures. The United States, in effect, feared the possibility of a popular government replacing Saddam Hussein because it did not have confidence that Arab democratic forces would adopt policies favorable to U.S. interests.

The primary result of the U.S. intervention was to preserve a generation of regimes in the Arabian Peninsula that are not representative of their respective peoples. The legitimacy of these regimes has yet to be tested, and few rulers appeared ready to permit this. The United States is comfortable with this situation because these rulers accommodate U.S. interests. It is a symbiotic relationship: The United States has access to oil, the ruling families retain power. From a U.S. perspective, this is politically safer than democratic regimes whose policies risk changing with every popular election. The fear of popular regimes is self-evident: Governments answerable to their publics might adopt policies hostile to U.S. interests. Nevertheless, U.S. efforts to maintain the political and economic status quo in the Persian Gulf actually may be sowing the seeds of an unstable future. That is, the rulers of the GCC countries may become for Washington what the governments of Eastern Europe were for Moscow before 1989: regimes that loyally carry out shared policy goals but whose interests have little in common with the majority of the peoples over whom they rule.

■ 19

Panama

Margaret E. Scranton

Historically, the relationship between Panama and the United States has been unusually close. As in Nicaragua (see Chapter 16), U.S. presidents throughout the twentieth century have shared a hegemonic presumption about Washington's right—indeed, destiny—to determine internal events in Central America and Panama. The absence of intervention has been the exception rather than the rule in U.S.-Panamanian relations.

Strategic access to the Panama Canal and stability in its environs have been, and remain, at the heart of Washington's interventionist practices. Toward these ends, U.S. policymakers confidently have claimed a right to intervene in Panama's internal affairs. Such a right was included in the 1903 Hay–Bunau-Varilla Treaty, by which the United States gained the right to construct, maintain, and defend the canal.[1] Panama's 1904 constitution gave the United States the right to intervene "anywhere" within the country to ensure "public peace and constitutional order."[2] Panama insisted on removing such language from the 1936 revision of the Panama Canal treaty,[3] and from the 1941 constitution. Nonetheless, U.S. policymakers from the 1940s to the 1990s, with some notable exceptions, continued to assert a right of intervention as if this were a self-evident and widely accepted legal precept. This presumption has transcended partisan control of the White House, both legislative and executive branches, and nine decades of history. Its latest manifestation was Operation Just Cause, the 1989 U.S. invasion designed to remove Panamanian strongman Manuel Antonio Noriega from power.

■ ORIGINS OF U.S. INVOLVEMENT

Washington's involvement in the politics and destiny of Panama predated the country's final separation from Colombia on November 3, 1903.[4] Between 1846 and 1902, the province of Panama attempted to secede or revolt on fifty-three occasions. According to an 1846 treaty, the United States responded to Colombia's requests to restore order on the isthmus, usually by dispatching war vessels but occasionally by landing U.S. troops.[5] These interventions occurred even while the United States was considering Nicaragua rather than Panama as the best site for a canal and reflected the priority the United States attached to maintaining stability in the region. Thus, the practice of intervening to restore stability began before canal construction and security became the forces driving U.S. policy toward Panama.

U.S. histories of Panama's independence focus on two foreigners whose daring, decisive actions provided the opportunity and necessary ingredients for Panama's independence: President Theodore Roosevelt and Philippe Bunau-Varilla. Bunau-Varilla was the Frenchman, motivated by financial and personal stakes in a failed French canal construction project, who brokered Panama's independence and wrote the immediately resultant 1903 canal treaty. Roosevelt later made the triumphant claim "I took the Canal Zone and left Congress to debate"; his determination to build a canal under U.S. control to bridge the seas set that project, and the Panamanian revolution, in motion.[6] Consequently, according to popular belief, the United States created Panama and then built the canal. Presidential candidate Ronald Reagan captured this sentiment in 1976: "We bought it, we paid for it, it's ours . . . and we're going to keep it."[7] While recognizing that U.S. gunboat diplomacy made the crucial difference between the 1903 independence movement and previous failed attempts, Panamanians attribute a more significant role to the shrewdness of the leaders who seized the moment to secede and Bunau-Varilla's betrayal of their cause.

Panama's independence, as popularly portrayed in both countries, entailed both a dependence on U.S. power and a willingness, among Panamanian leaders, to seek U.S. intervention to further their own aims. These characteristics set a pattern that both countries repeated, with few exceptions, during the next nine decades. In the United States, a hegemonic presumption became enshrined as an article of faith about its rights in Panama. For their part, Panamanian politicians of most persuasions often solicited U.S. intervention to resolve their own conflicts. Such actions occasionally generated intense anti-U.S. sentiment and violent protests. Antihegemonic sentiments alternated, and occasionally coexisted, with advocacy of close relations; most Panamanians have been, and continue to be, ambivalent about the United States.[8]

The 1903 treaty granted wide discretionary powers to the United States. Although this was quite typical of the concessionary grants great powers extracted from host governments at the turn of the century, Bunau-Varilla added an unusual element: perpetuity rather than a set duration of 99 or 100 years. Treaty provisions that explicitly derogated Panama's sovereignty made the perpetuity clause even more onerous. Article I bluntly characterized the power disparity: "The United States guarantees and will maintain the independence" of Panama. In Article II, Panama gave to the United States rights to use, occupy, and control a zone spanning five miles on each side of the canal and bisecting the country from the Atlantic to the Pacific coasts; additional islands, lands, and waters were also granted. Article III further clarified the scope of U.S. rights, granting "all the rights, power and authority . . . the United States would possess and exercise if it were the sovereign . . . to the entire exclusion of the exercise by the Republic of Panama of any such sovereign rights, power or authority."[9]

The 1903 treaty provided a clear and specific legal basis for U.S. control over a substantial amount of Panamanian territory as well as U.S. intervention in the event of disorder. Unlike the dozens of other U.S. interventions in the Western Hemisphere, in which Washington asserted a unilaterally claimed police power, such actions in Panama were also based on treaty rights. Panama's efforts to abrogate such language and regain its sovereignty over the Canal Zone became the focal point of U.S.-Panamanian relations for the next seventy-five years.

■ FROM CANAL CONSTRUCTION
TO NEGOTIATED WITHDRAWAL

Between 1904 and 1925, U.S. interventions to maintain stability frequently occurred in Panama City or Colón, the large cities at the canal's Pacific and Atlantic terminal points, and occasionally in outlying provinces.[10] In 1904, after a crisis caused by a showdown between the head of the army and civilian politicians, the United States recommended that the army be disbanded and replaced by a national police. It was. Thereafter, various civilian factions requested U.S. involvement in their struggles, including U.S. supervision of elections in 1906, 1908, 1912, 1916, and 1918. These events constituted precedents for U.S. policies during the 1980s and 1990s.

The major conflict in U.S.-Panamanian relations during the construction years arose over the steady expansion of U.S. control over Panamanian territory expropriated for construction, administration, maintenance, and defense of the canal. Controversy arose over differing interpretations of this right and the due process the United States was supposed to employ to obtain additional lands and waters.[11] The net result of U.S. pressures for expansion was a unique relationship for the United States: The U.S. Canal Zone became an extraterritorial enclave similar to foreign treaty ports in China and India.

The Canal Zone was presided over by a U.S. governor who was also a U.S. Army officer, reflecting a close relationship between canal administration and defense. This dual identity aptly captured the saliency of U.S. security concerns; these were later symbolized by the U.S. Army School of the Americas, which was used to train military forces from throughout the region.[12] Throughout these years, U.S. bases in Panama figured importantly in Washington's strategic thinking.

Washington's involvement with the Panamanian police and military was similar to U.S. practices in Central America, particularly Nicaragua. During the 1950s and 1960s, the U.S. Mutual Security Act guaranteed aid for the expansion of the National Police, an increasingly militarized institution that was transformed into a National Guard.[13] During the rise to power of José Antonio Remón from commandant of the National Police to president of the Republic, military and political power gradually were merged. Significantly, this process took place with the full knowledge and support of the United States. This internal power shift was further solidified when the military took power in 1968. Indeed, the United States settled into a pattern of increasing support for the military regime.

Several months after the October 1968 military coup, Colonel Omar Torrijos Herrera emerged as the strongman. He used a diplomatic strategy to pressure President Richard M. Nixon into revising U.S. canal policy. The result was a jointly agreed-upon formula, the 1974 Kissinger-Tack Agreement, for abrogating the 1903 treaty, abolishing the Canal Zone, and creating a partnership to manage and defend the canal until an unspecified date.[14] President Gerald R. Ford continued negotiations on this basis, as did President Jimmy Carter. Carter and Torrijos signed two new canal treaties in September 1977; both were ratified in 1978. One, the Panama Canal Treaty, abrogated the 1903 treaty and provided progressive increases in Panamanian participation in canal operation, administration, and defense until Panama assumes full control over the canal on December 31, 1999. At that time, the U.S. military presence in Panama will also end unless an agreement is negotiated to extend U.S. military base rights. Defense and security of the canal after the year 2000 will be guaranteed by the Treaty Concerning the Permanent Neutrality and Operation of the Panama Canal. This treaty, which took effect in 1979 along with the Panama Canal Treaty, gives both the United States and Panama the right to maintain and defend the neutrality of the Panama Canal.

Relinquishing the extraordinary rights the 1903 treaty entailed was very controversial in the United States. The 1978 treaties raised the question of U.S. rights to intervene in Panamanian affairs, before or after the year 2000, if some internal development threatened the security of the canal. After an acrimonious debate, a reservation named for Senator Dennis DeConcini reaffirmed Washington's classic hegemonic assumption: "In the event the canal is closed or its operations are interfered with," each country had "the right to take the steps it deemed necessary, including the use of military force in Panama, to reopen the Canal or to restore its operation." DeConcini's reservation proved to be so objectionable to Panama and some U.S. senators who favored the treaties that the Senate's Majority and Minority Leaders, Robert Byrd and Howard Baker, developed a countervailing reservation. This affirmed that U.S. efforts to reopen the canal would not be used as an excuse for intervention in Panama's internal affairs or to interfere with its political independence or sovereign integrity.

Panama's government was also a point of controversy in the ratification debate. One concession extracted by U.S. senators was a pledge by General

Torrijos to restore democracy. Torrijos, who viewed contemporaneous events in El Salvador and Nicaragua as outcomes to avoid in Panama, outlined a democratization schedule. Municipal elections were slated for 1980; a portion of the National Assembly would be elected in 1982; and presidential and full legislative elections would be held in 1984, culminating the restoration of civilian government. However, Torrijos's untimely death in 1981 paved the way for the rise to power of a new strongman, Noriega, who assumed command of the National Guard in 1983. General Noriega's policies further militarized Panamanian politics and society, actually reversing Torrijos's plan for the restoration of civilian government.

■ THE NORIEGA YEARS

Ratification of the 1978 canal treaties had ushered in a new era of U.S.-Panamanian relations characterized by Washington's acquiescence to military rule in Panama. This relationship became especially close during the early years of the Reagan administration, as policymakers sought to enhance ties with General Noriega. Noriega, in turn, was willing to facilitate various U.S. covert initiatives in the region, including the contra war, training Central American forces in Panama, and Panamanian cooperation in Israeli covert operations. In short, the Reagan administration actively used Panama as a strategic asset in its interventionist policies in Central America. This process was facilitated by Noriega's firm control over the expanded and renamed Panamanian Defense Forces (PDF).

During the period 1985–1987, several events caused the administration to consider Noriega a growing embarrassment and, ultimately, to remove him from power. Opposition to Noriega among U.S. officials had been growing since 1985, when Panamanian activist Hugo Spadafora was brutally murdered by the PDF and President Nicolás Ardito Barletta, who antagonized the PDF by calling for an investigation of the murder, was removed.[15] Of greater concern to the Reagan administration, however, was a growing scandal surrounding Noriega's involvement in the Iran-contra affair, particularly Panama's central role in international narcotics trafficking and money laundering. Once high-level officials agreed that Noriega's declining utility required his removal from office, a series of initiatives was implemented to achieve this goal.

An important aspect of these interventionist initiatives was a general consensus, expressed publicly and privately, that repudiated the use of force unless U.S. lives and property were threatened. Only one player, Assistant Secretary of State for Inter-American Affairs Elliott Abrams, advocated the use of force. The chairman of the Joint Chiefs of Staff, Admiral William Crowe, supported by Secretary of Defense Richard Cheney and National Security Adviser Colin Powell, strongly disagreed, because any military option would involve U.S. forces based in Panama. Such an action, Crowe believed, would jeopardize U.S. base rights around the world. As a result, numerous other strategies—adopted separately and sequentially, on an ad hoc basis—were employed in what eventually became a test of wills between Noriega and President George Bush. These strategies, which are addressed separately in the discussion that follows, overlapped during their implementation from June 1987 through October 1989, when the Bush administration reconsidered the use of force.[16]

□   *Popular Mobilization*

On June 6, 1987, Colonel Roberto Díaz Herrera publicly confessed to his own crimes on behalf of the regime and charged Noriega with numerous offenses: electoral fraud, drug trafficking, and Spadafora's murder. This constituted a split at the highest level of the PDF. More important, it ignited an unprecedented wave of public protest. In response, the U.S. government distanced itself from Noriega. In a clear protest, the Senate on June 26, 1987, passed by a vote of 84 to 2 Senate Resolution 239, which expressed support for the restoration of democracy and called on Noriega and others to step down during an investigation of Díaz Herrera's charges. The most significant implication of the resolution was that it united liberal and conservative wings of the Senate, symbolized by Edward Kennedy and Jesse Helms. In sharp contrast to congressional splits along party lines concerning conflicts in the Philippines and Nicaragua, the vote against Noriega was virtually unanimous.[17] President Ferdinand Marcos and the contras could count on blocs of congressional support, important foils in interagency policy debates; Noriega could not.

The executive branch also signaled that it was time for Noriega to exit. Leaks to the press conveying this message continued throughout the summer of 1987 while a rancorous bureaucratic debate was under way concerning options to effect Noriega's removal. The preferred option within some quarters was a PDF coup supported by "people's power" in the streets, modeled on the 1986 revolution against Marcos. Officials hoped that dissident PDF officers would conduct a coup, reform the military, and oversee a transition to civilian rule.[18] However, prospects for a PDF coup were uncertain; no other officers supported Díaz Herrera, and Noriega clearly threatened to punish the disloyal. The popular element of a Philippines scenario was also uncertain in Panama. A popular movement did mobilize in June, with *civilista* and party activists and a leadership group, the National Civic Crusade. The Reagan administration aided this movement through the National Endowment for Democracy and unofficial contacts with various leaders. According to U.S. officials, however, the civilian opposition was too weak and divided to incite and support a coup. The *civilista* movement continued its popular, nonviolent mobilization, particularly during the 1989 electoral campaign; meanwhile, the United States switched to another strategy.

□ Quiet Diplomacy

Unable to nudge Noriega out of power in June and July 1987 through popular mobilization, the Reagan administration turned to quiet diplomacy, using both private and official channels. A former official, Retired Admiral Daniel J. Murphy, undertook a private "back channel" mission in August and November 1987 to explain Washington's view of the situation.[19] This initiative ultimately failed; Murphy reported that Noriega and the opposition were too far apart to negotiate. An official mission sending the same "time to step back" message was undertaken in December 1987 by Assistant Secretary of Defense for International Security Affairs Richard Armitage. Armitage represented an institution that had supported Noriega in the past and in which Noriega presumably believed he still had allies. Armitage conveyed a unified position, strongly supporting Noriega's graceful departure from power. Noriega, however, manipulated the setting of Armitage's visit so that PDF officers got an impression of continued U.S. support.

The "step back" message was reiterated in Washington by Secretary of State George Shultz, but diplomacy failed to convince Noriega that he had to arrange an exit. The primary reason that quiet diplomacy failed was that the stakes, at this point, were not sufficiently high for Noriega to conclude that he had no choice. Signals about a graceful departure were not coercive; they appealed, instead, for Noriega to weigh the costs of remaining while his domestic base continued to erode versus the benefits of designing, while he still held power, reform of the military and an electoral transition. From June 1987 through October 1989, the United States was not demanding radical change in Panama; rather, U.S. policy sought "Noriegismo without Noriega." Policymakers were more interested in maintaining stability in Panama than in promoting genuine democratic reform.

□ Negotiations

Numerous initiatives were undertaken to negotiate Noriega's exit. Some were formal, involving State Department officials, particularly Assistant Secretary of State for Inter-American Affairs Michael Kozak; others were informal, such as discussions during late 1987 with a Panamanian official, José Blandón, and attempts in 1989 by former President Carter to broker a transition plan. In addition to these bilateral efforts, the Bush administration supported multilateral mediation by the Organization of American States (OAS) in late 1989. In all of these negotiations, the United States acted independently of the Panamanian opposition, using a style derived from the hegemonic presumption and decades of precedent. Opposition leaders justly complained about being treated as junior partners during various negotiations and diplomatic initiatives.

Initially, discussions among U.S. officials and opposition and government representatives about a plan for a transition from the military regime to an elected government seemed promising. Blandón was known as a close adviser to Noriega with a background in the Democratic Revolutionary Party (PRD), which was established by the military in 1978. Blandón was perceived as a direct link to Noriega, a status that signified his intention to strike a deal. Blandón's plan outlined a process for Noriega to retire, a phased return to the barracks, and elections. In January 1988, however, Noriega repudiated both Blandón and his plan. Either Blandón never truly represented Noriega, or Noriega decided, once he considered the details, that he would not accept this deal.

Kozak attempted to negotiate a similar transitional arrangement during April and May 1988. The unique element of this package was an offer to drop U.S. legal indictments that had been issued against Noriega in February 1988 in return for his voluntary departure. These discussions broke down on May 25, 1988, when a final agreement was almost concluded. Perhaps the White House would not explicitly agree to drop the indictments, for reasons related to the U.S. presidential campaign; or Noriega may have concluded that Washington could not be trusted to keep its end of the bargain. Alternatively, Noriega may never have intended to accept a deal; he simply may have been using negotiations to play for time. Nonetheless, this offer represented the maximum concessions the United States could offer. Once Noriega rejected it, bilateral negotiations ceased to be an option.

A year later, the United States supported multilateral negotiations. A mediation mission dispatched by the OAS in June and August 1989 also failed to achieve consensus among representatives of the Panamanian government, the military, and the opposition. Most observers cite the same reasons for this failure as were encountered in previous negotiations: Noriega simply was not interested in negotiating his withdrawal. Throughout 1988 and 1989, Noriega remained unconvinced that he must leave office. Neither U.S. officials, private emissaries, nor third-party mediators convinced him otherwise.

☐ *Legal Indictments*

Noriega and others involved in narcotics trafficking were indicted in February 1988 in two federal cases in Miami and Tampa, Florida. Neither indictment was initiated as a deliberate strategy to use the threat of legal proceedings to coerce Noriega into accepting an exit deal. Instead, district attorneys in Florida followed their own initiative, deliberately discounting Noriega's status as an official of a foreign government. They did not consult with foreign policy or national security officials; a high-level interdepartmental review of the pending indictments was not held until January 1988. The indictments did, however, have a direct impact on the negotiations strategy. Specifically, they created an impediment to arranging Noriega's exit, because he was unlikely to retire in a country from which he could be extradited to the United States. As discussed later, the indictments ultimately provided a dubious justification for Operation Just Cause and its goal of bringing Noriega "to justice" in the United States.

☐ *Economic Pressure and Sanctions*

A coalition of Panamanian opposition leaders and U.S. lawyers launched an economic pressure strategy designed to remove Noriega. They began when President Eric Arturo Delvalle was impeached after trying, unsuccessfully, to fire Noriega on February 25, 1988. Delvalle was an unlikely oppositionist: He had been handpicked by the military in 1984 to be vice president; he was elevated to the presidency, again by the military, when Noriega ordered the ouster of President Barletta. The coalition hoped to turn Delvalle's ouster into a political and economic crisis for Noriega. The Panamanians were led by former ambassador Gabriel Lewis Galindo, who recently had gone into exile, and Juan Sosa, Delvalle's ambassador to the United States; the lawyers, at the firm of Arnold and Porter, were led by William D. Rogers.[20] This unusual coalition kept in touch with the State Department and relied on its cooperation, but was neither created nor funded by U.S. officials.

The coalition hoped to create such a severe cash shortage in Panama (which uses the U.S. dollar as its currency) that the government would be forced to shut down and would fail to meet the payroll of Noriega's two main constituencies, the PDF and government workers. Two techniques were adopted: a general strike at home and a financial blockade from abroad. The latter was achieved by a "revolution by litigation" in which court orders froze Panamanian assets in U.S. banks and put payments owed by the U.S. government into escrow accounts. To succeed, the coalition needed the State Department to declare President Delvalle the official representative of Panama. Once this was accomplished, U.S. federal judges would rule favorably on restraining orders to prevent U.S. banks from transferring funds to Panama. This certification was made on March 2, 1988; Ambassador Sosa became the official custodian of Account #1, which provided operating expenses for the Delvalle "government."

The Reagan administration also increased economic pressure on Noriega's government. Panama was decertified under the Anti–Drug Abuse Act; this made mandatory an already existing suspension of economic and military aid. Decertification also required U.S. representatives at intergovernmental banks to vote against Panamanian loan requests, denying another potential source of cash. President Reagan ordered that all payments to Panama from U.S. government agencies, the largest being the Panama

Canal Commission, be put in escrow (Account #2). He also rescinded Panama's preferential status under the Generalized System of Preferences and the Caribbean Basin Initiative.[21] Congress called for even stiffer sanctions.

As designed, the economic pressure strategy seemed to be a potent weapon. It severely damaged the Panamanian economy,[22] but it did not dislodge Noriega. The strategy failed for several reasons. First, it inflicted more damage on the business community and populace than on Noriega and his inner circle; the people the United States was trying to support were damaged more quickly and severely than was Noriega. Although some demonstrations did result, economic hardship did not spark a dramatic escalation of public protest. Second, the financial embargo leaked; Noriega was able to obtain cash and access to resources from other countries. With this help, he was able to outlast the business community's strike, which ended in early April 1988. Finally, the U.S. government's economic pressures were not as forceful as possible. Exceptions were granted to U.S. businesses operating in Panama, which allowed funds to flow to the government. More important, implementation of the strongest economic sanctions, under the International Emergency Economic Powers Act (IEEPA), was deliberately delayed in April–May 1988 while Kozak was negotiating with Noriega. Critics suggested that if all possible forms of economic leverage had been brought to bear during early March—including strikes and demonstrations in Panama, a freeze on Panamanian assets in the United States, denial of U.S. payments and taxes due from U.S. businesses, and IEEPA sanctions—then a successful knockout blow could have been delivered. Instead, these pressures were applied sequentially, with the most significant measures not available until after Noriega had mobilized his own resources and the domestic opposition had been drained and exhausted. Sanctions remained in place until soon after the U.S. invasion.

☐ Electoral Pressures

In late 1988, when economic pressure seemed ineffective and after the Kozak agreement was rejected, the United States concluded that electoral pressures might both strengthen the opposition and convince Noriega that he could not remain in power much longer. Officials hoped the upcoming presidential election campaign would produce candidates capable of mobilizing domestic and international opposition. Toward this end, openly appropriated U.S. funds were granted to two electoral projects: (1) the Carter Center to investigate preparations for the election and conduct an observer mission and (2) the National Endowment for Democracy, which channeled aid to the National Civic Crusade. The National Democratic Institute for International Affairs, a subsidiary of the U.S. Democratic party, also supported an electoral project, and a Panamanian group supported an international observer mission.[23]

The aim of these electoral strategies was to achieve a victory of such proportions that Noriega had to accept defeat or use such blatant fraud that victory would be a hollow sham. This strategy worked even better than expected, given the negative assessments U.S. officials made of both traditional party leaders and the *civilista* movement. Reports on election day revealed a near nationwide trend of voting three-to-one against the government slate. Unable to manipulate a "victory," Noriega ordered the election annulled. More significant than the strength of their votes was the showing made by opposition candidates—Guillermo Endara, Ricardo Arias Calderón, and Guillermo "Billy" Ford—at a demonstration three days later. In the face of harassment by PDF and paramilitary forces called "Dignity Battalions," Billy Ford was spattered with the blood of his murdered bodyguard. A photograph later run as the cover of U.S. news magazines showed Ford, in his bloody shirt and with his arms outstretched, facing a tee-shirted man poised to swing an iron bar like a baseball bat. Video footage was even more dramatic, showing Ford yelling at the Dignity Batallions, "Not one more shot, damn it. Not one more shot." These images damaged Noriega's regime and enhanced the opposition's image in Panama and the United States. The candidates made a brave stand, but as a movement, the opposition still retreated when Noriega launched repressive crackdowns. Although the United States now had more credible leaders around whom to develop an anti-Noriega strategy, Panamanians preferred nonviolent conflict to the thousands of deaths "people's power" would exact.[24]

□   *Covert Operations*

Concluding that economic sanctions and electoral strategies, either alone or in tandem, could not remove Noriega, both the Reagan and Bush administrations approved covert operations. In all, five covert plans are known to have been authorized, code-named Panama 1 through Panama 5. Panama 1 and Panama 2 occurred before 1988. One apparently involved covert support for civilian opposition activity during late 1987; although no official comment has confirmed this operation, a subsequent effort (Panama 4) that channeled support and funds to opposition candidates is known to have had a precursor operation (either Panama 1 or 2). The other early operation probably involved efforts to encourage a military coup. No budget figures, personnel information, or other details have been reported for Panama 1 and 2. In marked contrast, Panama 3 became so controversial that this attempt to instigate a coup was described in the press. Panama 4 supported the opposition during the electoral campaign. Panama 5 was designed to incite and support another coup.

Neither Panama 3 nor Panama 5 achieved its desired result: Neither produced a military coup, and more important, the two coup attempts that did occur (March 1988 and October 1989) were not products of U.S. covert operations. Panama 3 involved a plan to identify a reformist officer who could overthrow Noriega, clean up the PDF, and resume the transition to democracy. The officer U.S. officials contacted was Colonel Eduardo Herrera Hassan, Panama's ambassador to Israel. He had been planning a coup since mid-1987; he merged his plan with U.S. objectives for Panama 3, which Reagan authorized in mid-July 1988 with a budget of $1 million. When members of congressional intelligence committees were informed, they expressed serious objections about the feasibility and legality of the plan. (In the event of Noriega's orchestrated death, for example, a long-standing executive branch ban on the assassination of foreign leaders would have been violated.) Congressional criticism prompted the Reagan administration to drop the operation despite the fact that the Herrera group received $1.3 million from escrow accounts.[25]

The March 1988 coup was led by four majors and a colonel, a group with a growing list of concerns: Spadafora's murder, the impeachment of Delvalle, Blandón's firing, and increasingly hostile relations with the United States. They concluded that Noriega was placing his interests above those of the PDF and that this situation would only worsen. These officers had grown concerned that Noriega was importing large weapons stocks from Cuba and caching them in the countryside, divorced from regular PDF channels. Two majors contacted the opposition to alert them to the coup's objectives: to promote a more professional PDF and to provide for a transition government and elections. In late February they, along with about twenty others, planned a traditional barracks coup.

The coup failed just as it was being initiated on March 16, 1988. Loyal officers, led by Captain Moisés Giroldi, surprised and defeated the participants. Within hours, Noriega reasserted control and purged those suspected of disloyalty. Noriega charged that the coup was a CIA operation, but several majors involved denied receiving any U.S. support. Instead, they acknowledged only making preventive contact with the U.S. military in Panama to avert a mistaken U.S. response.

Panama 4 provided covert support for opposition candidates during the 1989 election campaign. President Bush authorized this operation, budgeted at $10 million, in February 1989. Activities supported by Panama 4, which was implemented concurrently with noncovert U.S. electoral pressures, included money and material for printing, advertising, transportation, and communications. This covert operation had mixed results. It contributed to the success of the electoral strategy, but when the operation was exposed, radio equipment and its operator were featured on Panamanian news. The reason Noriega cited when he annulled the election was foreign interference.

The second PDF coup, also unrelated to U.S. covert operations, occurred on October 3, 1989. It was led by Major Giroldi, largely as a reaction against Noriega's actions since the first coup. At the last minute, Giroldi did ask for U.S. help, in the form of blocking two roads that loyal troops might use to rescue Noriega.[26] The Giroldi group, composed of officers slightly junior to those involved in the March coup, had no reported ties to civilian opposition leaders and intended to make only modest changes in the PDF. They were committed to retiring Noriega and his senior staff, not to power sharing or democratizing reforms. The rebel officers temporarily held Noriega, but he overwhelmed Giroldi, telephoned for help, and soon regained control. During the coup, U.S. forces blocked two roads, as they had been requested to do; they did not take further action when forces loyal to Noriega moved to rescue the general. Whereas the officers who rebelled in March were tortured and imprisoned, participants in the October coup were tortured and killed.

The last covert operation designed to encourage a coup, Panama 5, was approved by President Bush after the October 1989 coup failed. Although another attempt seemed unlikely, President Bush authorized this operation, budgeted at $3 million, under guidelines that included a more flexible interpretation of the assassination ban. Other details about Panama 5 remain sketchy. Apparently several alternative scenarios existed, including plans to apprehend Noriega and remove him to the United States as well as contingency plans for U.S. forces to support another coup. No known actions to implement Panama 5, except for rehearsals of maneuvers to support another coup, have been documented; in December 1989, this covert operation was overtaken by events.

□ *Operation Just Cause:*
   Invasion and Aftermath

Preparations to implement a major military operation designed to remove Noriega from power and bring him to trial in the United States, dismantle the PDF, and install a civilian government began in late October 1989.[27] After the October coup, the Bush administration concluded that nonmilitary intervention could not achieve these results. Panama 5 was authorized in case another coup were attempted or in the event that an opportunity to seize Noriega arose. But neither of these outcomes appeared likely to the three advisers who recommended preparations to use force: Secretary of Defense Cheney, Chairman of the Joint Chiefs of Staff Powell, and National Security Adviser Scowcroft. These three concluded that a coup would only yield minor changes in the PDF; Noriegismo without Noriega was reinterpreted to be a problem rather than a solution. They advised President Bush to revise contingency plans and begin readiness exercises for a major military operation. Noriega also authorized provocative actions against U.S. forces. Both sides were increasingly committed to push each other's limits.

The decision to launch Operation Just Cause was triggered by the one event both Presidents Reagan and Bush had said would put the option to use military force into play—threats to the lives of U.S. citizens. On the weekend of December 16–17, 1989, three such incidents occurred. On

December 16, First Lt. Robert Paz died from wounds he received when a car carrying four U.S. soldiers was fired upon as it ran a PDF roadblock near military headquarters. Two U.S. witnesses to that event, a Navy officer and his wife, were harassed and brutally interrogated by PDF. The next day, a U.S. Army lieutenant, thinking he was about to be fired upon, shot a Panamanian policeman, Corporal Cesar Tajada, in front of a laundry near U.S. military headquarters. These incidents were interpreted in Washington as a pattern of escalated threats to U.S. personnel that could quickly spiral out of control.[28] On December 17, President Bush decided "enough is enough" and gave the order to implement Operation Just Cause.

The military operation began late in the evening of December 19. The nighttime invasion added some 13,000 U.S. forces to the 13,000 already in Panama, yielding the largest (until the 1991 Persian Gulf war) military operation since Vietnam. U.S. forces were divided into four main task forces, each of which was responsible for specific geographical regions: (1) Task Force Atlantic (from the Atlantic coast to Gamboa and the Madden Dam), which included the 82nd Airborne and the 7th Infantry; (2) Task Force Bayonet (Panama City and central Panama Canal areas), comprising two Army battalions from Panama, one from Fort Polk, a Military Police (MP) battalion from Fort Meade, and an 82nd Airborne armored platoon; (3) Task Force Pacific (from the Pacific coast to midcountry) which included three battalions from the 82nd Airborne Division; and (4) Task Force Semper Fi (Bridge of the Americas and Howard Air Force Base), composed of a Marine rifle company and a light armored infantry company. A Special Forces task force also participated in operations to apprehend Noriega, subdue PDF Battalion 2000 at Río Hato, and secure the international airport.

The military invasion included three major components: a Special Forces operation designed to capture Noriega as the invasion began, a multitargeted attack on major PDF installations to destroy their capability to resist or restore the old regime, and operations to protect the Panama Canal.[29] Another objective cited by Bush, "to restore democracy," involved swearing in the civilians "elected" in May; this symbolic ceremony took place at a U.S. base as the invasion began. A U.S. officer asked whether the new Panamanian government would officially request U.S. military assistance; Endara, Arias Calderón, and Ford declined, on the grounds that the U.S. decision to invade had already been made without their consultation.

Efforts toward the first objective of the operation—apprehending Noriega—initially failed. As General Thomas Kelly later explained, "We thought we had a pretty good idea where he was last night. We went there, and he wasn't there."[30] The focus of this operation shifted to denying Noriega a safe haven, such as the Cuban or Nicaraguan embassy, and escape routes, such as the Paitilla Airport and sea launch points. Noriega remained in hiding until December 24, when he took refuge at the papal nunciature, the Catholic ambassadorial residence in Panama City. He remained there until January 4,

1990, when he surrendered to U.S. officials. Noriega was taken into custody, arrested, and flown to Miami for pretrial processing.

The second objective of Operation Just Cause focused on a wider array of targets: central and regional PDF command centers and facilities that could be used to resist U.S. forces. This element of the invasion was an operational success, with the use of heavy firepower for maximum effect—to gain the surrender of PDF combat personnel—and minimum collateral damage. The notable exception occurred at Noriega's headquarters, where the destruction of the Comandancia also caused fires in old wooden buildings across the street, which soon spread throughout several blocks of El Chorrillo. Fires in this neighborhood caused high civilian casualties and some of the most critical evaluations of Operation Just Cause. The worst fighting between PDF and U.S. forces was over within hours. In all, Panamanian military casualties were counted as 314 killed and 124 wounded; the best estimates of civilian deaths ranged from 400 to 750. Instead of the projected 70 U.S. casualties, only 23 military personnel died; 323 were wounded and three U.S. civilians also died.

Despite the lower than expected U.S. military casualties, two unexpected developments both prolonged U.S. military operations from an expected three to seven days and necessitated the deployment of 2,000 additional troops from the United States on December 23. Dignity Battalions, not regular PDF forces, resisted U.S. troops. Most of the combat involved sniper fire and small-scale skirmishes. Concurrently, looting and exchanges of fire among property owners, looters, and Dignity Battalions paralyzed several sections of Panama City and Colón. Surprised by the extent of the looting, U.S. forces slowly established law and order. A "cash for weapons" program helped decrease the street violence; in all, about 50,000 weapons were turned in for rewards averaging $150.

The final U.S. goal—securing areas and facilities adjacent to the Panama Canal—was an operational success. Ironically, security considerations led the United States to close the canal—the first closure in its history for such reasons—because part of its route passes near the Comandancia and other combat sites. The canal was reopened at 3:00 a.m. (Eastern Standard Time) on December 21, 1989.

In the immediate aftermath of the invasion, Panamanians took to the streets by the thousands, celebrating the end of twenty-one years of dictatorship. The jubilant reaction was vociferously pro–United States, and opinion polls in 1990 and 1991 continued to measure high levels of support for the U.S. military operation. Most observers attribute the popularity of the invasion to two factors. First, most Panamanians blamed the United States for keeping Noriega in power and then failing to remove him surgically, without damaging the country. Thus, they perceived the invasion as solving a problem Washington created rather than interfering in Panama's internal affairs. Second, many Panamanians concluded that they could not remove Noriega by themselves; the vast majority wanted him to step down and accepted U.S. force as necessary to achieve that outcome.

At home, Bush's popular approval rating skyrocketed, and the phrase "wimp factor" vanished from the press. In marked contrast, twenty Latin American countries voted for a strongly censorious OAS resolution,[31] which condemned the U.S. invasion as an illegal intervention.[32] In the UN Security Council, the United States vetoed a resolution that strongly "deplored" Washington's use of force. Later, the UN General Assembly passed a resolution condemning the invasion as a "flagrant violation" of international law. Nevertheless, negative diplomatic repercussions were transitory.

More durably detrimental were the effects in Panama, where popular expectations of the obligations the United States incurred during the invasion far exceeded what the Bush administration could deliver. The amount of U.S. aid—$42 million in emergency assistance and $420 appropriated for 1990–1991—was severely criticized, as was the new government's slow formulation of programs to which those funds could be committed. As of early 1992, less than 50 percent of these funds had actually been disbursed, although 100 percent was committed to officially approved projects.

Programmatically, U.S. postinvasion policy focused on immediate economic recovery projects and emergency needs, development assistance, and democratization initiatives designed to professionalize Panama's governmental institutions and the press. These are long-term projects the results of which will not be apparent for several years. Analysts are skeptical, however, about whether Panamanian leaders will demonstrate the political will and determination these initiatives require and whether U.S. policy, as an external influence, can promote meaningful democratization. In the short term, U.S. efforts during 1990 and 1991 to help restructure the PDF into a national police drew the sharpest criticism from citizens, policy analysts, and former PDF members. When disgruntled officers seized police headquarters in December 1990 to demonstrate their grievances, the Endara government called on U.S. troops rather than its own police to defuse the situation, indicating that the transition from postinvasion occupation to independent Panamanian governance was still incomplete.

■ **INTERVENTION IN PERSPECTIVE**

This most recent episode in a long history of U.S. intervention in Panama suggests several lessons and implications. One frequently cited lesson concerns the liability of close U.S. relations with dictators. In Panama, as in the Philippines, Nicaragua, and Iran, the United States was content for many years to subordinate concerns about democracy and human rights to national security interests. For reasons of state, the United States worked closely with Noriega, Marcos, Somoza, and the shah of Iran. Violent revolutions erupted in all but Panama, where the dictatorship was not as repressive and a nonviolent civilian movement was created. The Panama case confirms lessons learned elsewhere about working too long with dictators, the difficulties entailed in easing a dictator out of power before a crisis erupts, and the limits of U.S. influence over supposedly close friends.

As a military intervention, Operation Just Cause is best interpreted as a recent application of the rights the United States possessed under the 1903 treaty and of the Roosevelt "corollary." In 1904, President Roosevelt announced: "Chronic wrongdoing, or an impotence which results in a general loosening of the ties of civilized society, may . . . ultimately require intervention by some civilized nation," compelling the United States, "however reluctantly," to exercise "an international police power." This self-proclaimed responsibility, the familiar hegemonic presumption, constituted the main U.S. motive for Operation Just Cause. The fundamental reasons the United States invaded Panama were to remove an increasingly hostile and unpredictable dictatorship and to place in power a regime that might prove to be more stable as the year 2000 approaches.

Although it was an operational success, the U.S. invasion represented a strategic failure. All means short of force failed to dislodge Noriega; whether attributed to successful evasion by Noriega or to poor design or execution, all those initiatives failed. This placed the Bush administration in a situation with no apparently acceptable option except massive military force. As such, this failure was similar to other prolonged crises—in the Philippines, Nicaragua, and Iran—that received presidential attention only when they reached such a dangerous stage that restrained means were either exhausted or inappropriate.

Some analysts suggested that because Operation Just Cause was launched just before the February 1990 Nicaraguan election, the Panama invasion might portend other politically motivated U.S. military actions. They questioned whether this was the "Bush Doctrine"—namely, to use military intervention to correct flawed electoral outcomes. Panama, however, constitutes a very special case, with unique logistic and historic features. If a Bush Doctrine does emerge, the relevant parallel will be a policy of using force when a foreign leader goes too far and steps beyond tolerable conduct, but only after more moderate means, particularly diplomacy and economic pressure, have been judged to have failed.

Yet to be demonstrated and understood are the lasting effects of intervening, overtly and covertly, to support an opposition. Electoral pressures proved to be the most successful U.S. strategy in Panama, but those pressures alone could not install the victorious civilian slate. Whether that strategy, along with using an invasion to place a civilian government in office, will perpetuate Panamanian dependence and undermine current U.S. goals to promote democratic self-government is yet to be seen.

Panama's transition to democracy, planned in 1978, was derailed by

Noriega's determination to maintain a military regime and by the resulting pressure strategies and invasion. After such serious disruptions, particularly to the economy, the new regime faced monumental problems of reconstruction and development. However, one purpose of the invasion was to restore democracy; progress toward that goal thus will be a significant measure of the utility of direct military intervention. After two years, the civilians remain in office, although their coalition split and President Endara removed the Christian Democrats from ministerial posts. Public confidence in the government is very low, but many Panamanians support the idea of completing the full cycle of a presidential term of office, followed by national elections in 1994.

In the long run, the invasion reinforced the old pattern of depending on the United States to manage Panama's political problems. Once again, the United States finds itself intimately involved in funding and engineering institutional change to promote political stability. Washington's programs to democratize and professionalize Panama's political institutions have involved the United States much more closely in Panamanian politics than during the military regime. These programs are intended to develop self-governance, but the legacy of dependence and the fragility of Panama's civilian political sector may preclude their success.

The Arab-Israeli Conflict

Deborah J. Gerner

For the better part of the post–World War II period, the principal goals of the United States in the Middle East were to protect the supply of petroleum and the other natural resources for itself and its European allies, to prevent or minimize Soviet involvement in the region, and to support stable, viable, friendly governments.[1] The United States also desired the maintenance of secure, internationally recognized boundaries in the region to encourage stability. Decisions about the Arab-Israeli and Israeli-Palestinian conflicts were made in the context of these globalist-inspired objectives.[2] Successfully managing these disputes was important to the extent that the failure to do so could damage U.S. relations with the Arab world and Iran, thus making the states in the region susceptible to Soviet influence and risking the security of Middle Eastern oil resources. In addition, since 1967, U.S. support for Israel, as expressed through economic and military assistance and in the diplomatic arena, has become an increasingly important part of the equation. Conspicuously missing from the U.S. approach was a regionalist perspective that recognized the conflict over Israel/Palestine had to be viewed in its own historical, political, economic, cultural, and religious contexts rather than interpreted solely in a globalist, Cold War framework.

The beginning of the 1990s saw tremendous changes in the international system affecting U.S. perceptions of the Arab-Israeli conflict and the context within which it must be resolved. These changes include the dramatic improvement in East-West relations, the fragmentation of the Soviet Union, and the 1988 U.S. decision to hold discussions with the Palestine Liberation Organization (PLO). In the aftermath of the 1991 war that followed Iraq's invasion of Kuwait on August 2, 1990, Secretary of State James A. Baker III undertook a series of meetings with Arab and Israeli leaders to promote his ideas on resolving the Palestinian issue and the broader Arab-Israeli conflict. These culminated in a regional peace conference cosponsored by the United States and the former Soviet Union that began in Madrid in October 1991 and continued with four sessions in Washington, D.C. in 1991 and 1992, before moving to Rome, Italy. However, Arab-Israeli arguments over what constituted legitimate topics for discussion threatened to jeopardize the ongoing negotiations. U.S.-Israeli relations were also strained as a result of U.S. rejection of an Israeli request for $10 billion in loan guarantees and continued Jewish settlement in Arab territories occupied by Israel in the June 1967 war.

■ CREATION OF THE U.S. POLICY FRAMEWORK

As the major Western power at the end of World War II, the United States was expected by the international community to take a leading role in dealing with the Palestine question. The United States first became intimately involved in the controversy in the 1940s and in 1947 was instrumental in the passage of UN Resolution 181 on the partition of Palestine and the creation of the State of Israel.[3] At this point, however, the overall goals of the United States in the Middle East were still being formulated, and the country did not have a clear policy toward Israel, the Palestinians, or the Arab states. It fell to the administration of Dwight D. Eisenhower to develop what would become the U.S. foreign policy orientation toward the Arab-Israeli conflict for the next forty years.[4]

As originally formulated, there was nothing in the Eisenhower administration's approach that recognized the Palestinians as a distinct national group with political rights. In dramatic contrast to the positive, inspiring portrayal of the Jewish Israelis, the Palestinians were viewed exclusively as a refugee population that needed to be resettled, repatriated, rehabilitated, compensated, and otherwise seen to so that the Israeli-Palestinian dispute could be resolved and the United States could continue to forge political links with Iran, Israel, and conservative Arab states such as Jordan and Saudi Arabia.

This U.S. rejection of the political and national rights of Palestinians had a number of important implications. First, it meant the United States endorsed proposals that allowed Egypt to continue its military presence in the Gaza Strip while Jordan maintained control of the West Bank, including East Jerusalem. Both areas were originally intended by the United Nations to be part of an independent Palestinian state. Israel's annexation of other lands originally intended for this state—territories it captured during the Palestine War of 1948–1949 (also called Israel's War of Independence)—was accepted as a fait accompli.[5] As a result, policymakers made few if any efforts to identify Palestinian groups or individuals who had the authority to speak on behalf of the Palestinian community. U.S. officials in Washington long have met regularly with representatives of the Israeli government, but before the 1990s similar conversations with the Palestinian national leaders were all but nonexistent.

Furthermore, the U.S. decision to focus only on the states in the region ignored the fact that any proposed solution was useless unless it was acceptable to the Palestinians, even if it satisfied the leaders of Syria, Jordan,

Egypt, and other Arab states. Finally, the United States initially directed its attention to improving conditions for the Palestinian refugees through economic development activities such as the United Plan for Jordan Valley Development, rather than pushing strongly for repatriation, which was the preferred international solution for most other refugee populations. These factors partially explain why initial U.S. efforts at settling the dispute in the 1950s were unsuccessful: They were based on a series of false premises, including the assumption that if economic issues related to the Palestinian refugees could be addressed to the satisfaction of the Arab states, the political dimensions of the problem would be more easily resolved.[6]

Most significant was the U.S. belief that the vast majority of Palestinian refugees from the Palestine War should be settled as residents and citizens of the surrounding Arab states rather than be allowed to return to their homes within the new State of Israel. This was true despite public and private statements by U.S. officials indicating the United States would like to see Israel permit significant Palestinian repatriation and despite repeated U.S. cosponsorship of UN resolutions supporting such an approach.[7] Israel consistently refused to consider the possibility of significant repatriation, however, citing security concerns and economic constraints, and there is no evidence to suggest U.S. policymakers pressured Israeli leaders to change their position.

Compensation for property left in Israel by the Palestinian refugees was considered by the United States to be an essential element in any final peace agreement between Israel and the Arab states. At the same time, it was clear that the Israeli economy could not support such compensation and yet maintain the standard of living expected by its European immigrants. Therefore, in August 1955, Secretary of State John Foster Dulles indicated the United States would be willing to underwrite substantially an international loan to Israel to help cover the costs of compensation. Israel did not pursue this possibility, however, and no compensation occurred.[8] Officially, there has been no change in the U.S. policy regarding compensation, but the issue has been relegated to the back burner and is rarely mentioned.

Throughout this period, the United States stated repeatedly that it considered the 1949 armistice borders to be binding on all parties until permanent boundaries were negotiated. Policymakers also criticized Israeli border crossings and on several occasions cosponsored UN General Assembly or Security Council resolutions critical of Israel.[9] Israel consistently ignored these resolutions, causing increased tension between the two countries. The United States felt that the apparent inability of the UN to compel Israel to abide by its declarations damaged the UN's credibility in the eyes of the Arab countries; U.S. officials also judged Israel's actions to be counterproductive to regional stability and the prospects for peace. In addition, at least through the first half of the 1950s, the United States stressed that the armistice borders might require some minor adjustments in order to reunite Palestinian villages with their agricultural lands.[10]

The second Eisenhower administration began with the unresolved issue of complete Israeli withdrawal from Arab territories Israel captured in the 1956 Suez War (also known as the Sinai War). Among the various topics addressed within the voluminous amount of literature devoted to the war include the events leading to the Israeli attack of Egypt in the Sinai on October 29, the secret plan for the involvement of Britain and France (ostensibly to mediate but in fact as participants), U.S. anger at the actions of U.S. allies, and the actual course of the war.[11] The response of the United States to Israel's refusal to withdraw from the Gaza Strip after the cease-fire agreement is particularly important because it is one of the most direct cases of U.S. intervention in the Arab-Israeli conflict.

In the early days of the war, the United States worked intensely through the United Nations, sponsoring the initial cease-fire resolution on November 2, 1956, and calling for Israel to pull its troops behind the 1949 armistice line. A personal message from President Eisenhower to Israeli Prime Minister David Ben-Gurion on November 7 reinforced the U.S. position, and it appeared at first that Israel would acquiesce. Meanwhile, policymakers considered the methods available to convey U.S. dismay at Israel's attack and to put pressure on Israel. One suggestion was informally to hold up Israeli bank balances in the United States. However, this was judged impractical (as well as politically difficult) and was not pursued.[12]

Three months later, Israel still had not fully withdrawn its troops from all occupied areas, maintaining control of the town of Sharm al Sheikh, at the tip of the Sinai Peninsula overlooking the Strait of Tiran, and of the Gaza Strip. Eisenhower sent a blunt cable message to Ben-Gurion on February 3, 1957, urging that Israel withdraw its forces behind the armistice line, as called for by several UN resolutions, or risk damage to U.S.-Israeli relations. The following day, the United States voted in favor of two U.S.-sponsored UN resolutions: one calling on Israel to withdraw its troops behind the 1949 armistice line, the other calling on both Israel and Egypt to observe the armistice. Dulles then went public with administration criticisms of Israel in a press conference on February 5 and a week later sent a secret aide-mémoire to Ben-Gurion in which he warned that Israel risked angering members of the UN with its continuing "occupation in defiance of the overwhelming judgement of the world community."[13]

As was frequently the case with Middle East affairs during the Eisenhower administration, the issue took on an importance that transcended the immediate issue: How would policy on the Gaza Strip affect Arab perceptions of the United States? Would it provide an entrée for the Soviet Union? How would Israel's blatant refusal to follow UN resolutions affect that organization's credibility around the world? On February 16, Eisenhower met with several cabinet members to determine U.S. options and subsequently took several actions. He made public Dulles's aide-mémoire and contacted Ben-Gurion yet again by telegram. He and Dulles also met with a large group of congressional leaders from both parties who expressed great dismay over public criticism of Israel. In the meeting, Eisenhower spoke of his concern that there would be further interruptions in the supply of Middle East oil and that Soviet influence within the Arab world would increase if Israel continued to refuse to comply with UN demands. He was also convinced that if the United States failed to support the UN on this issue, "it would be a lethal blow to the principles of the world peace organization."[14] The same ideas were reiterated by Eisenhower in a radio and television address to the U.S. public that evening. The speech did not meet with universal approval. According to Representative Paul Findley, the public's reaction, as expressed in letters and telegrams to the White House, was 90 percent in support of Israel.[15] Still, Eisenhower held to his position that Israel had to withdraw its troops.

The issue finally came to a head on February 22, 1957, when Charles Malik, foreign minister of Lebanon, introduced a UN resolution calling for imposition of severe economic sanctions against Israel, including the termination of all military, economic, and financial assistance. Once it became clear that the United States would support this resolution, Israel gave in, albeit not before receiving repeated assurances from the Eisenhower administration regarding its support of free navigation through the Gulf of Aqaba. Israel completed its withdrawal of troops from Sharm al Sheikh and the Gaza Strip by March 7, 1957.

■ FORMATION AND STRENGTHENING OF A SPECIAL RELATIONSHIP

Once Israel's occupation of Gaza and Sharm al Sheikh ended, U.S. attention was pulled in other directions. Hungary, the arms race with the Soviet Union, the 1958 crisis in Lebanon, the Bay of Pigs, the Cuban missile crisis, and growing U.S. involvement in Southeast Asia preoccupied Presidents Eisenhower, John F. Kennedy, and Lyndon B. Johnson. One critical shift in U.S. policy did occur during this period, however: The United States began to develop a "special relationship" with Israel that continued into the 1990s. Between 1951 and 1960, for example, Israel received nearly $550 million in U.S. financial assistance.[16] Kennedy continued and increased this aid, pledging support for Israel's security (on nineteen separate occasions) if it was attacked by Arab states, and began to sell Israel advanced weapons such as the Hawk missile system, something Eisenhower had refused to consider.[17]

The trend of rising political, economic, and military assistance to Israel was strengthened after the June 1967 war—during which Israel captured the West Bank, including East Jerusalem, the Gaza Strip, the Syrian Golan

Heights, and the Sinai Peninsula (since returned to Egypt)—and Israel began to receive sophisticated offensive weapons from the United States. In the eyes of U.S. leaders, mired in the Vietnam War and increasingly isolated internationally, Israel's dramatic victories provided evidence that Israel could serve as a strategic asset in the Middle East.

The June 1967 war (sometimes referred to as the Six-Day War) also marked the initiation of significant mobilization of the U.S. Jewish population on behalf of Israel. Prior to this time, Zionists in the United States had intensely lobbied on behalf of Israel on only a few occasions, such as before the UN vote on the partition of Palestine and during the resolution of the 1956 Suez War. After 1967, Zionists among the U.S. Jewish community became far more involved in activities designed to strengthen political, military, and economic support for the expanded state and far more outspoken against elected leaders and appointed officials whose views differed from those of the supporters of Israel.[18] Zionists found a sympathetic audience for their views among the general U.S. population. There was an immediate and positive identification with the formerly European Israelis, whose culture, values, and religion were familiar to the U.S. public (unlike the predominantly Muslim Palestinians who appeared alien and therefore frightening). Furthermore, there remained continuing guilt feelings about the Holocaust and a recognition that U.S. immigration restrictions before World War II contributed to the deaths of European and Soviet Jews at the hands of the Nazis.

After the June 1967 war, the United States reiterated its commitment to the 1949 armistice lines, and has continued to do so through all subsequent presidential administrations. But although the United States verbally criticized Israel's gradual incorporation of the territories captured in the June 1967 war, it appeared implicitly to condone such actions through continually increasing bilateral assistance. Policy regarding the city of Jerusalem was particularly ambiguous. The United States frequently stated that the final status of Jerusalem should be determined by negotiation; however, the United States abstained on numerous UN Security Council resolutions condemning Israel's effort to extend its rule over all of Jerusalem. For this reason, many Israelis assumed that the United States was not serious when it said that *all* territories captured in the June 1967 war, including East Jerusalem, were considered occupied until a peace treaty determined their final status.

More generally, the United States became increasingly involved in Arab-Israeli affairs from the 1960s onward. This involvement largely took the form of providing or withholding military and economic assistance to Israel, Egypt, Jordan, and Saudi Arabia, but it also included mediating between Israel and various Arab states (such as in the 1978 Camp David meetings or the 1991–1992 regional peace conference) and, in 1982, sending U.S. Marines to Lebanon. During this period, the U.S. foreign policy community continued to express concern about regional stability, protection of petroleum resources, and, until the late 1980s, possible Soviet involvement in the

Middle East. Israel became part of the implementation of this policy along with Iran (before the Iranian revolution of 1979) and Saudi Arabia.

President Richard M. Nixon, like his predecessors, viewed the Middle East primarily in the context of continuing U.S.-Soviet rivalry; this remained the case even after the moves toward détente that characterized the latter years of his administration.[19] This view was shared by Nixon's foreign policy architect, National Security Adviser (and later Secretary of State) Henry Kissinger. Israel was important because it could serve as a surrogate for U.S. interests in the Middle East. In contrast, the Palestinians, particularly those who were refugees, were perceived as a potentially destabilizing influence. At the same time, Kissinger quickly concluded that the Palestinian issue was unsolvable in the short term, so he essentially ignored it in his step-by-step diplomatic approach in the region.

After the June 1967 war, there were sporadic air and land battles along the Suez Canal and in the Golan Heights in 1968 and 1969. This fighting, known as the "war of attrition," provided a new opportunity for the United States to attempt to mediate between Israel and its opponents. After months of quiet discussion and planning, including talks with Soviet leaders, Secretary of State William Rogers gave a major policy speech on December 9, 1969. Rogers reaffirmed the U.S. commitment to UN Resolution 242, including the principle of nonacquisition of territory by war and the call for Israel to withdraw from territories occupied in June 1967. He also proposed negotiations between Israelis and Egyptians, expressed concern for the Palestinian refugees of 1948 and 1967, and stated U.S. opposition to Israel's unilateral de facto annexation of Jerusalem.[20] Israeli leaders objected strongly to the speech because of its "land-for-peace" component and its criticism of Israel's policies toward Jerusalem. Although the first version of the Rogers Plan failed to gain approval (indeed, both Nixon and Kissinger actively worked to undercut it), over the next few months many of its points formed the basis of a new U.S. initiative to end the war of attrition. That plan was accepted by Egypt and Jordan in July and by Israel on August 4; a cease-fire went into effect the night of August 7.

The Rogers Plan did not represent a permanent solution to the Arab-Israeli conflict, however, particularly because Israel continued to occupy a significant amount of Arab territory. In October 1973, war broke out again when Egypt attacked Israel in order to regain control of the Sinai Peninsula and the Gaza Strip. In the midst of the hostilities—frequently called the Yom Kippur War or the Ramadan War—the Organization of Petroleum Exporting Countries (OPEC) unilaterally implemented an increase in the price of petroleum. In response to the U.S. decision during the war to resupply Israel with extensive military equipment (after the United States seemed to promise Arab leaders it would be more evenhanded toward the Arab-Israeli dispute than it had been in the past), Arab members of OPEC also imposed an oil embargo on the United States and several U.S. allies. The decision of Saudi

Arabia to support both actions should not have come as a shock to the U.S. policymaking establishment, although it did. For some time, King Faisal had been sending signals that if the United States expected to continue favorable relations with Saudi Arabia, it would need to indicate greater appreciation for Arab concerns regarding Palestinian rights and the return of the territories captured by Israel in the June 1967 war. These signals had been ignored.

The United States did not depend heavily on oil from the Arab countries. Still, the price increase and embargo were sufficient to disrupt the sensitive balance of U.S. energy supplies for several months. For perhaps the first time, events in the Middle East had a direct and obvious impact on the day-to-day lives of ordinary U.S. citizens. Although the embargo was lifted on March 18, 1974, petroleum prices did not return to their earlier levels, and in fact rose dramatically in the 1970s, in part because of the turmoil surrounding the Iranian revolution and the short-term Iranian decision to curtail oil production drastically. For the next ten years, international oil prices were controlled primarily by the decisions of OPEC acting as a producer cartel. Analysts differ on whether any changes in U.S. policy toward the Arab-Israeli conflict can be clearly attributed to the actions of OPEC. What does seem clear is that the high level of U.S. support for Israel was now recognized to have a potential economic cost, something that most U.S. citizens had not understood before this time.

Kissinger was intimately involved in obtaining a successful cease-fire to the October 1973 war. Once this was achieved, Kissinger focused on negotiations to bring about a partial Israeli withdrawal from the Egyptian Sinai and the creation of a UN buffer zone in the region. The first step was the Sinai I Accord, a preliminary disengagement agreement signed on January 18, 1974. After nearly two years of shuttle diplomacy, complicated by the disgrace and the eventual resignation of Nixon on August 9, 1974, and his replacement by President Gerald R. Ford, Kissinger's initial goals were achieved in September 1975 with the signing of the Sinai II Accord between Israel and Egypt.

■ CARTER AND THE CAMP DAVID ACCORDS

In his first two and a half years in office, Carter approached international politics very differently from most of his predecessors. He was a hands-on president whose ideology was as close to the political idealism of the 1918–1941 period as any president since Woodrow Wilson had been. Shortly after Carter took office in 1977, he began to address the Palestinian question, which he saw not only as a security concern but also as a human rights issue.[21] In a news conference on March 9, Carter indicated there were three elements needed for peace in the Middle East. Two of the points were standard

U.S. policy: "an ultimate commitment to complete peace in the Middle East," and the establishment of "permanent and recognized boundaries." Carter's third element, however, was new: "dealing with the Palestinian question."[22] In saying this, Carter began to address the crux of the problem that had been consistently ignored by previous U.S. presidents. A week later, Carter shook hands with a PLO observer at the United Nations. Although the symbolic action upset the Israelis, it gained Carter little with the Arab states or the Palestinians, who understood its limited significance.

In the months that followed, Carter attempted to convene an international conference to address the Middle East situation. His efforts were complicated by the results of the Israeli election in May 1977, which gave the conservative Likud party control of the Israeli parliament, the Knesset, for the first time in Israel's short history and made Menachem Begin the prime minister when the new government was formed in June. Israel officially accepted the idea of peace negotiations and an international conference, but Begin had little interest in either. The Arab states were more enthusiastic, recognizing that in such an arena the UN and the superpowers could be called upon to enforce international opinion (which generally favored the Palestinians). Although the PLO argued it should be included in the international conference, the United States felt constrained by Kissinger's pledge to Israeli Prime Minister Yitzhak Rabin that it would not recognize or negotiate with the PLO until the organization recognized Israel's "right to exist" and accepted UN Security Council Resolutions 242 and 338. The Soviet Union also indicated its support for an international conference in a joint U.S.-Soviet declaration made public on October 1. Israeli leaders were intensely upset by the joint statement, which among other points called for Israel's withdrawal from occupied Arab lands and referred to the "legitimate rights" of the Palestinians, and said they would refuse to participate in an international conference based on the document. Carter immediately backed away from the statement, placating Israel at the expense of angering the Soviet Union and the Palestinians.

Meanwhile, Jordan and Saudi Arabia were working to find a common ground between Egypt and Syria, which were unable to agree on the composition of the Arab delegations. The main problem was the high degree of mistrust between Egyptian President Anwar Sadat and Syrian leader Hafez Assad. Sadat feared that Assad would try to veto any Egyptian-Israeli accord reached at an international conference; Assad was afraid he would lose any ability to regain the Golan Heights if Sadat cut a separate deal with Israel. Neither leader placed the Palestinians high on his list of concerns. Ultimately, Sadat decided to attempt an initiative on his own. Against the advice of Egyptian Foreign Minister Ismail Fahmy—who resigned over the issue—Sadat announced to the Egyptian National Assembly on November 9, 1977, that he would go anywhere, even to Jerusalem, to meet with Prime Minister Begin. An invitation was forthcoming, and on November

20 Sadat addressed the Israeli Knesset and stated his desire for peace with Israel.

Sadat's visit was followed by months of fruitless discussions between Israel and Egypt. The bilateral talks broke off in July 1978. At this point, Carter stepped in and invited Sadat and Begin to meet with him for direct negotiations at the presidential retreat at Camp David, Maryland. For thirteen days, Carter attempted to discover common ground between the two leaders. The result was the Camp David Accords, signed on September 17, 1978. The first document, "A Framework for Peace in the Middle East," dealt with the West Bank and Gaza Strip. It called for the establishment of a Palestinian self-governing authority, to be followed by a five-year transition period, with the final status of the two territories to be negotiated. A second document, "Framework for the Conclusion of a Peace Treaty Between Egypt and Israel," outlined an understanding for an eventual Egyptian-Israeli peace treaty. Six months later, on March 26, 1979, Sadat and Begin met in Washington, D.C., to sign that treaty. Included with the treaty was an annex that set forth the details of Israeli withdrawal from Egyptian territory and another that specified the new relations that were to exist between the two states.[23]

Camp David provided something for each of the three leaders, although most analysts believe Israel came out ahead of Egypt. Sadat achieved a peace treaty with Israel, which allowed him to reduce Egypt's military expenditures. He also obtained increased economic and military assistance from the United States as well as the resumption of Egyptian control of the entire Sinai Peninsula. Egypt lost its influential position as a leader of the Arab world, however, and was ostracized for the next decade. Begin gained the neutralization of one of Israel's most powerful regional adversaries, a demilitarized zone between Israel and Egypt, an Israeli embassy in Cairo, and increased U.S. economic and military assistance. In exchange, Israel had to give up the Israeli settlements located in the oil-producing Sinai. Carter had a major foreign policy success, one of the few of his administration.

Many crucial details were left unspecified in order to achieve the agreement. For example, Jerusalem was not mentioned, although its political status is one of the most significant points of contention between Israelis and Arabs. The phrase used in the accords, "legitimate rights of the Palestinian people," had no legal meaning. It was later defined by Begin to refer only to Palestinian inhabitants of the Gaza Strip and the West Bank (excluding those in East Jerusalem) rather than to all Palestinians, and to mean much less than the self-determination intended by Sadat and Carter. There was nothing in writing to confirm Carter's conviction that Begin had promised to suspend Israeli settlements in the occupied territories indefinitely; instead, Israel put a three-month moratorium on settlement development, then returned to construction of them with renewed energy.

Finally, there was no way to compel Israel to move quickly on the proposed autonomy for the Palestinians. The Camp David framework had called for a "self-governing [Palestinian] authority . . . freely elected by the inhabitants of [the West Bank and Gaza] to replace the existing [Israeli] military government." The exact modalities for the establishment of this authority were to be agreed upon by Egypt, Jordan, and Israel, with no Palestinian involvement in the discussions. After a year of negotiations over the format of Palestinian autonomy, however, nothing had been accomplished. By then Carter's attention was focused on the overthrow of the shah of Iran and the subsequent hostage crisis in Tehran, and he was not in a position to put pressure on Israel.

If most people in Israel and the United States and some in Egypt cheered the Camp David Accords and the Egyptian-Israeli peace treaty, the majority of the Arab world was highly skeptical of what it perceived as a separate peace. On November 5, 1978, an Arab summit meeting held in Baghdad strongly condemned the Camp David Accords and warned Egypt against signing a peace treaty with Israel. At the same time, the Arab League voted to transfer its headquarters from Cairo to Tunis, where it remained for the next twelve years. The Arab states raised a number of concerns. First, Arab analysts pointed to the areas of ambiguity in the Camp David Accords and argued that Israel would find loopholes to avoid abiding by the spirit of the agreements. (Israelis similarly feared that Egypt would find such loopholes; they point to the lack of full normalization of relations as evidence that their concerns were legitimate.) Second, the Arab states believed Egypt sold out the Palestinians by not negotiating more specifically for complete Palestinian independence from Israeli control. Third, Arabs feared the treaty was a way of co-opting Egypt—then the militarily strongest of the Arab states in the region—so that Israel would be free to attack elsewhere. The 1982 invasion of Lebanon was seen as proof of this. Consequently, the position of the United States with most Arab states was not enhanced by its role in facilitating the Egyptian-Israeli rapprochement.

■ FROM MILITARY INTERVENTION TO DIPLOMACY IN THE REAGAN YEARS

President Ronald Reagan, who came to power in 1981, shared the globalist, anti-Soviet views of most of his predecessors.[24] It was this perspective that dominated the discussions during the tour Secretary of State Alexander M. Haig, Jr., made to the Middle East in April 1981. Among the items on Haig's agenda were a proposed U.S. arms deal with Saudi Arabia, the need for Egypt, Jordan, and Saudi Arabia to establish an informal military alliance with Israel to prevent Soviet encroachment in the region, and the continued fighting within Lebanon and between Israeli and PLO forces. Three weeks later, Syrian troops based in Lebanon moved missiles into Lebanon's Bekaa Valley in response to an Israeli attack against two Syrian helicopters in

Lebanon. The United States quickly sent special envoy Philip Habib to the Middle East to negotiate an agreement between Israel and Syria, but he was unable to gain the necessary concessions to have the missiles removed.

In this highly charged atmosphere, a successful Israeli bombing raid against an Iraqi nuclear reactor on June 7 resulted in strong condemnations by both the United States and the Soviet Union, leading to the temporary suspension of a previously negotiated delivery to Israel of four U.S.-made F-16 fighter planes. Meanwhile, Israeli and PLO raids and counterraids across the Israeli-Lebanese border became more frequent. In July, Israel bombed southern Lebanon steadily for a week, culminating the strike with an attack on Beirut on July 17 in which an estimated 300 people, mostly civilians, were killed. At this point, Habib was again sent to the region and, working with Saudi Arabia, was successful in arranging a cease-fire agreement between Israel and the PLO that went into effect July 24, 1981.

With the Israeli invasion of Lebanon on June 6 of the following year, the United States again found itself involved in the Israeli-Lebanese-Palestinian triangle.[25] In the wake of the attack, the U.S. representative at the UN supported repeated Security Council resolutions calling on Israel to withdraw. Throughout June and July, the United States attempted to mediate an end to Israel's assault on Lebanon. Finally, in August, the PLO agreed to withdraw from Beirut and redeploy its troops to several Arab countries willing to accept them, in exchange for an Israeli retreat. A week later Israel also acceded to the plan. A multinational peacekeeping force, including U.S., French, and Italian troops, was sent to Beirut to protect the civilian population during the PLO evacuation that began August 21. The U.S. Marines arrived on August 25, and the last of the PLO fighters left Beirut on September 1. The marines then withdrew from Lebanon on September 11, 1982.

In the midst of the PLO evacuation on September 1, President Reagan presented a peace initiative that called for "self-government by the Palestinians of the West Bank and Gaza Strip in association with Jordan" and a halt to the building of new Israeli settlements or the expansion of existing settlements. Reagan also said that the future of Jerusalem should be determined by negotiations and that "the question now is how to reconcile Israel's legitimate security concerns with the legitimate rights of the Palestinians."[26] The plan was immediately rejected by the Israeli cabinet. PLO leaders indicated they saw some positive elements in the speech, but they did not fully accept it either. Israel also rejected the eight-point Fez Summit peace plan presented by the Arab League on September 9. The plan called for a transition period culminating in an independent Palestinian state in the West Bank and Gaza Strip and UN Security Council guarantees for peace for all the states in the region. Israel's rejection disappointed the new secretary of state, George Shultz, who saw the Fez proposal as an opportunity for a breakthrough in the long stalemate between Israel and the Arab world because the plan accepted Israel within its pre-1967 borders.[27]

U.S. forces, again joined by French and Italian troops, returned to Lebanon on September 29 after the massacre by Israeli-allied Christian Phalangists of Palestinian and Shia Lebanese residents of the Sabra and Shatilla refugee camps outside Beirut. Their mandate was to help restore order and to train the Lebanese army. The multinational peacekeeping forces were not universally welcomed, and hostility toward their presence grew during the months that followed. On April 18, 1983, a suicide car-bomb attack on the U.S. embassy killed sixty-three persons; responsibility for the attack was claimed by Islamic Jihad, a pro-Iranian group. Six months later, on October 23, there was a truck-bomb attack against the U.S. military barracks that left 241 U.S. military personnel dead. A virtually simultaneous attack against French peacekeeping forces resulted in fifty-eight deaths. Although Reagan reaffirmed the U.S. commitment to remain in Lebanon as part of the peacekeeping mission, U.S. public opinion was outspoken against continuing the military presence. Finally, on February 7, 1984, Reagan announced U.S. troops would be redeployed to ships off the coast of Lebanon. On March 30, the U.S. ships left the area, ending a military action the goals of which were unclear from the beginning and the success of which was dubious at best by the end.

For more than four years, there was little U.S. involvement in the Arab-Israeli conflict. This changed on December 14, 1988, when the United States ended its policy of nonrecognition of the Palestine Liberation Organization. The United States had not spoken to the PLO officially for thirteen years, in accordance with Kissinger's 1975 pledge, and the Reagan administration's additional requirements that the PLO had to "renounce the use of terrorism" and revise the Palestinian National Charter that called for the abolition of the Zionist state before it could gain U.S. recognition. The events that led to this change reflect a modification in at least the outward appearance of both U.S. and PLO policies.

At the end of 1988, PLO leader Yasir Arafat was riding a wave of strong international support. The Palestinian uprising that began in December 1987 had increased global awareness of almost universal Palestinian anger and frustration with the continuing Israeli occupation of the West Bank (including East Jerusalem) and the Gaza Strip, and sympathy for the Palestinians was high.[28] Before the intifada, Israel had argued that its occupation was a purely benign "administration" accepted by Palestinians who might complain a bit but were basically content living under Israeli rule. After a year of mostly nonviolent Palestinian protests and harsh Israeli repression, this interpretation was no longer given much credence. Instead, it had become clear that the years of living under Israeli occupation had not diminished the Palestinians' sense of identity or their desire for national self-determination.

The Palestine National Council (PNC) meeting in November 1988 culminated in a Palestinian declaration of independence in the context of the original 1947 UN resolution on the partition of Palestine. Within two weeks, over sixty countries recognized the State of Palestine, and others expressed support for the principle of creating such a state. The United States was not in either group. Instead, Arafat's request for a U.S. visa to enable him to address the United Nations was rejected, which forced that body to take the unprecedented action of moving the entire General Assembly to Geneva, Switzerland, so that Arafat could speak during a special session.

In a series of public statements before, during, and after the UN meeting, Arafat pursued the elusive goal of U.S. recognition, indicating repeatedly that the PNC had rejected "terrorism in all its forms, including state terrorism." His carefully crafted speech to the United Nations included a critical sentence:

> The PLO will seek a comprehensive settlement among the parties concerned in the Arab-Israeli conflict, including the State of Palestine, Israel, and other neighbors, within the framework of the international conference for peace in the Middle East on the basis of Resolutions 242 and 338 and so as to guarantee equality and the balance of interests, especially our people's rights, in freedom, national independence, and respect the right to exist in peace and security for all.[29]

When the speech ended, many were convinced Arafat had satisfied the U.S. requirements for recognition, but Shultz disagreed. By this time Arafat had gone too far to turn back without gaining some political advantage for his concessions; similarly, U.S. allies quietly explained that the United States was damaging peace prospects and would look foolish in the eyes of the international community if it continued to deny recognition of the PLO despite Arafat's recent statements. Arafat decided to hold a press conference on December 14 and make one further attempt:

> In my speech also yesterday, it was clear that we mean our people's rights to freedom and national independence, according to Resolution 181, and the right of all parties concerned in the Middle East conflict to exist in peace and security, and, as I have mentioned, including the State of Palestine, Israel, and other neighbors, according to the Resolutions 242 and 338. As for terrorism, I renounced it yesterday [at the UN General Assembly] in no uncertain terms, and yet, I repeat for the record. I repeat for the record that we totally and absolutely renounce all forms of terrorism, including individual, group, and state terrorism.[30]

Late in the afternoon of December 14, 1988, Shultz announced that Arafat had met the longstanding U.S. conditions for negotiation and that the United States and the PLO were planning on opening a "substantive dialogue" immediately. On December 16, the first round of talks began in Tunis.

By making the decision to begin a dialogue with the PLO at the very end of the Reagan administration, Shultz handed the incoming administration of President George Bush a fait accompli. It would have been difficult for the new Secretary of State (James A. Baker III) to make such a radical move early on in the Bush presidency, whereas the political cost of maintaining an existing dialogue was much less. In fact, according to a Gallup poll conducted in October 1989, a majority of the U.S. public supported the U.S.-PLO dialogue.[31] In Congress, however, support for the ongoing discussions was tenuous. Under pressure from both houses of Congress, the Bush administration suspended talks with the PLO on June 20, 1990, three weeks after an unsuccessful attack on an Israeli beach by members of the tiny Palestine Liberation Front.[32] Israel praised the U.S. decision. For Palestinians, already embittered by the U.S. veto on May 31 of a UN Security Council resolution calling for an investigation of Israeli policies toward the Palestinians during the intifada, it was another sign that the United States held Palestinians and Israelis to different standards. After the veto, Palestinians called for an embargo on contact with U.S. officials, making the subsequent suspension of talks by the United States antclimactic.

There were few concrete results from the U.S.-PLO discussions, although the mere fact they occurred was judged by many to be a significant development in the U.S.-Palestinian relationship. The Arab-Israeli conflict did not appear to be a matter of great urgency for the Bush administration initially, but by the middle of 1990 it had gained a position of increased prominence and after the end of the 1991 Gulf war became a top priority. Throughout this period, the United States continued to reject the idea of an independent Palestinian state. Instead, it supported the possibility of a Palestinian-Jordanian federation or some other option left unspecified.[33]

■ THE CHANGED INTERNATIONAL ENVIRONMENT

The sweeping changes in the former Soviet Union and Eastern Europe that began in the late 1980s have several ramifications for U.S. policy toward the Arab-Israeli conflict. One interesting result of the improved East-West diplomatic climate is its potential effect on U.S. foreign aid priorities. For a number of years, Israel has been the largest recipient of U.S. military and economic assistance through the Foreign Military Sales Financing Program, the Economic Support Fund, and other aid programs. Although U.S. aid to Israel, in the early 1990s totaling more than $3 billion a year, will remain a major feature of the relationship for the foreseeable future, it will not necessarily be maintained at such a high level. There is continuing concern among U.S. policymakers as well as the general U.S. public about Israeli policies for dealing with the intifada and Israel's continuing human rights violations. This may translate into greater scrutiny being given to the aid allocated to Israel (at present, Israel is the only U.S. aid recipient that does not have to account for the money it receives) and resistance to maintaining the disproportionately high level of assistance. Reductions in Russian support for Syria, Libya, and other Arab opponents of Israel could provide an additional justification for a decrease in U.S. financial support of Israel.

Finally, the United States wants to provide increased foreign aid to Eastern Europe, Central America, and the newly independent countries of the former Soviet Union to encourage and support the political and economic transformations occurring there. Those resources have to come from somewhere: In a recessionary period, there is virtually no public support for an increase in overall foreign aid, so one possibility is to decrease the amount of assistance given to other major U.S. aid recipients, including Israel.

A second result of the new international political environment is growing Russian interest in constructive involvement in Middle East peace efforts.[34] The former Soviet Union frequently expressed its desire to have a role in the region, but these Soviet actions were assumed to be motivated primarily by superpower competition in the region, even as U.S. actions were. Russia now appears to be searching actively for positive, collaborative contributions it can make to increase stability in the Middle East. The idea of U.S.-Russian cooperation may not be as farfetched as it at first appears. Since World War II, the United States has wanted to limit Soviet influence in the Middle East because such influence was believed to be a destabilizing force that would jeopardize the U.S. political and military position and put the region's oil resources at risk. With the demise of the Soviet Union as a threat to U.S. goals, engaging in joint activities with its successor states— primarily the dominant Russian republic—becomes a serious possibility.

Of greatest significance, however, is the dramatic increase in the number of Jews allowed to leave the Soviet Union—more in 1990 and 1991 than at any point in the recent past—leading to the largest immigration to Israel since 1951. In previous years, a majority of Soviet Jews granted permission to emigrate chose to go to the United States. But new U.S. restrictions, established at the request of Israel, limit the number of Soviet Jews allowed to enter the United States annually. Consequently, the vast majority of these emigrants go to Israel: approximately 185,000 in 1990 (in addition to 15,000 emigrants from other countries) and 167,000 during 1991.[35] This massive influx put additional strains on an Israeli economy already burdened with heavy social welfare expenditures, inflation, rising poverty and unemployment, and the cost of maintaining the occupation over the West Bank and Gaza Strip, leading Israel to request additional financial assistance from the United States.

The Soviet immigration caused controversy between Israel and the United States because of Prime Minister Yitzhak Shamir's insistence that Soviet immigrants, like all Israelis, would be permitted to settle in any of the territories controlled by Israel, including the West Bank, the Golan Heights, and the Gaza Strip.[36] Most of those who moved to the occupied territories had no ideological commitment to living beyond the 1949 armistice lines, but were pushed out of Israel by the pressures on housing resulting from the latest wave of immigrants. In response to the increased settlement activities, Secretary of State Baker announced on March 1, 1990, that Israel must halt growth in new and existing Jewish settlements in the occupied territories before the United States would consider guaranteeing a $400 million loan Israel had requested to provide housing for Soviet immigrants. Baker explained that without such a halt, there was no way to assure that U.S.-guaranteed funds did not end up subsidizing housing in the occupied territories. Two days later, Bush responded to a question at a press conference by saying: "The foreign policy of the United States says we do not believe there should be new settlements in the West Bank or in East Jerusalem."[37]

Even though official U.S. policy since the June 1967 war had considered East Jerusalem, along with the rest of the West Bank, the Gaza Strip, and the Golan Heights, to be illegally occupied territory, this had not been stated so bluntly since 1980 when the Carter administration voted in favor of a UN Security Council resolution that condemned Israeli settlements in the occupied territories "including Jerusalem." There was a tremendous outcry in Israel protesting Bush's remarks. Although Bush later backed off slightly, saying that in his opinion "Jews and others can live where they want, East or West, and the city must remain undivided," he did not retract his previous statement on East Jerusalem.[38] As a result, Shamir moderated his public proclamations on the settlement of Soviet Jews for several months, but it rapidly became clear that even if Soviet Jews were not explicitly encouraged to live in the occupied territories, overall settlement activity was being escalated.[39]

Although the U.S. Congress passed the necessary legislation to guarantee the $400 million in housing loans on May 25, 1990, the State Department refused to provide the guarantees until it received clear assurance that no immigrants would be settled in any of the territories occupied by Israel in 1967. Each time the United States appeared ready to act, an Israeli government official would make a statement indicating that Israel had no intention of restricting settlement as required by the terms of the agreement.[40] Finally, on February 20, 1991, the United States released the loan guarantees as part of a one-year supplemental authorization package that also included $650 million in aid to reimburse Israel for economic losses sustained during the 1990–1991 Gulf war, $1.1 billion for defense-related equipment, and other military assistance.[41]

During the 1990–1991 Gulf war, Israeli leaders indicated that they would be requesting additional loan guarantees from the United States, but agreed to delay their official request until September 1991. At the same time, however, plans for expansion of existing Israeli settlements and establishment of new settlements were revealed in February 1991 in a report by Knesset members Dedi Zucker and Haim Oran. Quoting Housing Ministry figures, Zucker and Oran charged that the Shamir government had plans to construct 12,000 new housing units in the West Bank and Gaza Strip by the end of 1993. Such construction could lead to a 50 percent increase in the Jewish population in the occupied territories (excluding East Jerusalem), although these areas would remain heavily Palestinian.[42] Consistent with these plans, several new

West Bank and Golan Heights settlements were established in the spring and summer of 1991.

In testimony before the U.S. House Appropriations Foreign Operations Subcommittee, Baker was highly critical of the Israeli settlement boom: "Nothing has made my job of trying to find Arab and Palestinian partners for [peace negotiations with] Israel more difficult than being greeted by a new settlement every time I arrive. I don't think there is any bigger obstacle to peace than the settlement activity that continues not only unabated but at an enhanced pace."[43] Bush, too, was blunt. When Baker came under criticism from some members of Congress for his remarks, Bush backed him up: "Secretary Baker was speaking for this Administration and I strongly support what he said and what he is trying to do. Our policy is well known, and it would make a big contribution to peace if these settlements would stop."[44]

Shamir insistently discounted these remarks, however: "Settlement in every part of the country continues and will continue. . . . [U.S. leaders] try to link the two things, but no one said aid will end. I don't think it will happen. . . . It is inconceivable that our great friend the United States will change its ways."[45] His optimism proved misplaced. When Israel officially requested the $10 billion in loan guarantees at the beginning of September 1991, the Bush administration promptly called on Congress to put off any discussion of the issue for 120 days so it would be dealt with after the proposed Arab-Israeli peace conference had begun. Bush also indicated that before the loan guarantees were granted, he wanted a pledge from Israel that it would halt further settlements in the occupied territories. The result was a nasty series of exchanges between U.S. and Israeli leaders, including an accusation of anti-Semitism against Bush by one Israeli cabinet member that was promptly disavowed by other Israeli leaders.

Many members of Congress expressed dismay over the delay and the linkage between the aid and Israeli settlement policy, but ultimately concluded they lacked the votes to overturn the promised presidential veto of any loan guarantee legislation passed in the fall. In the months that followed, U.S. supporters of Israel lobbied hard for the loan guarantees and a variety of plans were proposed. Ultimately, however, none of the compromises offered were acceptable to Israel, and the loan guarantees were not granted. Bush's strong stand was the first time since the 1950s that a U.S. president had used economic pressure against Israel and the first time ever that a president had explicitly told Israel that unless settlements in the occupied territories were halted, the United States would limit its economic assistance.

During the Gulf crisis, the Bush administration said repeatedly that once Iraq had withdrawn from Kuwait, the next priority for the United States was to address the Arab-Israeli conflict. Speaking before a joint session of Congress on March 6, 1991, Bush reaffirmed this position, stating that "a comprehensive peace must be grounded in UN Security Council resolutions 242 and 338 and the principle of territory for peace. This principle must be elaborated to provide for Israel's security and recognition, and at the same time for legitimate Palestinian political rights."[46]

Two days later, Baker began the first of more than a half dozen trips to the Middle East. Before Baker's arrival, Egyptian leaders indicated their interest in an Arab-Israeli peace conference, although Egyptian Foreign Minister Esmat Abdel Meguid indicated they would prefer an international conference under the sponsorship of the UN Security Council to a more limited regional conference under U.S. and Soviet sponsorship. After their discussions with Baker, Israeli leaders indicated that Israel too would be willing, under certain conditions, to attend a regional peace conference sponsored by the United States and the Soviet Union. Among Israel's caveats were that the regional meeting would last for one day only, to be followed by bilateral talks, and that there would be no participation of the PLO, Palestinians from East Jerusalem, or expelled Palestinians.[47]

While in Jerusalem, Baker also met with ten Palestinians from the occupied territories on March 12. The meeting was viewed as significant because it represented the end of the Palestinian boycott on contact with U.S. officials that was instituted after the U.S. veto of the May 1990 UN resolution calling for an investigation of Israel's policies toward the Palestinians. In an eleven-point document given to Baker, the Palestinian delegation affirmed that the PLO was their sole representative; called for an end to Israel's occupation of the West Bank, Gaza Strip, and East Jerusalem and the establishment of an "independent Palestinian state on the national soil of Palestine, next to the state of Israel" and said that any transitional arrangements must be "structured within a comprehensive, interconnected, and coherent plan with a specified time frame for implementation and leading to Palestinian statehood."[48]

In subsequent meetings throughout the region, Baker developed a compromise plan that called for a regional conference, cosponsored by the United States and the Soviet Union and based on UN Security Council Resolutions 242 and 338, that would begin with a joint ceremonial opening before breaking up into bilateral talks between Israel, the Arab states bordering Israel, and the Palestinians. Palestinians would participate as part of a Palestinian-Jordanian delegation; the role of the United Nations would be limited to that of silent observer to the negotiations.[49]

The proposal was initially rejected by both Israel and Syria. Bush then intervened directly in the negotiations, sending personal letters to Arab and Israeli leaders that presented what he considered a reasonable proposal, given each country's concerns and conditions. Shamir responded quickly and publicly, rejecting Bush's request that Israel make at least some symbolic concessions to get the peace process moving.[50] Frustrated, Bush indicated he might simply issue invitations for a peace conference under conditions he and Baker believed represented a reasonable compromise and see who showed up. This, Bush and Baker believed, might put pressure on Israel in particular and, to a lesser extent, Syria to prove they were seriously interested in peace negotiations. Eventually, Syria and then Israel signed on to the proposal, and the twentieth session of the PNC, held in September, also endorsed the conference and approved Palestinian participation.

The U.S.- and Soviet-sponsored Madrid Conference opened on October 30, 1991, with negotiators from Egypt, Israel, Lebanon, Syria, Jordan, and the Palestinians in attendance, along with representatives from the European Community and silent observers from the Gulf Cooperation Council. It was a breakthrough for the Palestinians, who for the first time were able to represent themselves in peace negotiations. Technically, the Palestinians were part of a joint delegation with the Jordanians (one of Israel's numerous requirements), but they were treated as autonomous actors by other representatives, including the United States, and the media. Having once included the Palestinians—who were widely regarded as articulate, intelligent, and flexible spokespersons for their position—in direct bilateral and multilateral talks, participants will find it difficult to exclude them in the future.

The initial bargaining positions presented by Israel and Syria were tough and inflexible, as each side hurled accusations of terrorism against the other. The Palestinians were more conciliatory, making proposals for a transition to self-rule; the Lebanese were somewhat constrained by their close relationship with Syria. After three days, the opening phase of the negotiations ended, followed by a single day of bilateral discussions on November 3. Then everything ground to a halt. Israel argued the talks should be moved to the Middle East; the Arabs wanted to remain in Madrid. Israeli and Arab delegates left Madrid with no agreement about when or where further talks would occur.

Although the Madrid Conference had not been a failure, neither could it be judged a success. In particular, Baker expressed his disappointment at the reluctance of the parties to pursue preliminary confidence-building measures, such as Israel ending its settlements in exchange for Arabs suspending their economic boycott of Israel and the Palestinians halting the intifada.[51] In the weeks that followed, the Israelis took steps to emphasize their position that they would not make territorial compromises with the Palestinians or other Arabs. The Knesset passed a resolution declaring that Israel's control of the Golan Heights was not negotiable (while the Madrid Conference was under way, Israel had established a new settlement there), and Shamir made a number of public statements intended to emphasize that the lands currently under Israeli control represented "an essential minimum of territory."[52]

In an attempt to get the peace process moving again, the United States issued invitations to all those in attendance at the Madrid Conference inviting them to Washington, D.C., to continue bilateral discussions beginning on December 4, 1991. All the Arab delegations accepted and arrived in Washington in time for the opening of the second round of negotiations, but Israel balked, insisting it could not possibly be ready until December 9. The Arabs then announced they would not meet on December 9, the anniversary of the beginning of the intifada. Substantive negotiations between Israel and Syria and between Israel and Lebanon finally began on December 10 and continued through December 18, although little progress was made. The talks involving Israel, Jordan, and the Palestinians never advanced beyond procedural matters.

Bilateral negotiations continued throughout the spring in Washington, D.C., with sessions in January, February, and April 1992. Israelis and Palestinians exchanged proposals for some type of interim self-governing Palestinian authority in the occupied territories, but there was no agreement on the areas of responsibility that would be granted this entity. The Israelis offered to give Palestinians greater control over civil services and regulatory agencies such as local transportation, culture, health, industry, and religious affairs, but refused to consider any transfer of control over land, water, or security from Israel to the Palestinians and ignored the Palestinian proposal for elections. Palestinian proposals called for an almost total Israeli withdrawal from the occupied territories and elections for legislative and judicial branches of a new Palestinian government. The result was a stalemate in the Israeli-Palestinian bilateral talks. Israel and all the Arab states did agree to move subsequent negotiations to Rome, Italy, in response to Israel's desire that the discussions occur closer to the Middle East.

■ INTERVENTION IN PERSPECTIVE

For much of the past fifty years, the United States has been involved in the Arab-Israeli and Israeli-Palestinian conflicts. Its actions were determined primarily by a series of broad foreign policy goals that included assuring access to petroleum resources, minimizing Soviet influence among the Arab states, and maintaining regional stability, even at the expense of supporting authoritarian or corrupt regimes. Under Eisenhower, these globalist goals led the United States to take a relatively evenhanded approach toward the countries involved in the Arab-Israeli conflict. At the same time, Eisenhower put into place a U.S. policy toward the Palestinians that effectively denied them national self-determination through U.S. acceptance of Israeli, Jordanian, and Egyptian control of former Palestinian territories and a lack of U.S. support for Palestinian repatriation.

From the 1950s onward, therefore, the United States pursued policies in direct opposition to Palestinian national autonomy. This approach was consistent with the generally hostile attitude of the United States toward other African, Asian, and Arab national liberation movements in the post–World War II period, particularly those that incorporated "armed struggle" or held revolutionary ideas. In addition, in the mid-1960s, the United States began to establish an unusually close relationship with Israel that continues into the 1990s. These three policies—the globalist agenda, extensive diplomatic, economic, and military support for Israel, and opposition to Palestinian self-determination—have influenced U.S. actions for nearly thirty years. They have led the United States to become a major arms supplier in the region, selling or giving weapons to a dozen Middle Eastern countries, and to serve as a frequent mediator between Israel and its Arab protagonists. On several occasions, such as during the 1956 and 1973 Arab-Israeli wars, after the 1982 Israeli invasion of Lebanon, and in 1991 and 1992 with the debate over loan guarantees and Israeli settlements, the United States has intervened more actively to attempt to mold policies and outcomes in ways more to its liking. The United States has also used its position as a permanent member of the UN Security Council to veto numerous resolutions critical of Israel and its long-standing occupation of Arab territories, alienating European and Third World allies.

Throughout this period, the United States operated from the flawed assumption that what was best for U.S. global interests, in the context of the Cold War, was also best for the Middle East. Or, perhaps it would be more accurate to say, the United States chose policies that would enhance its global hegemonic position without particular regard for how they would affect the peoples of the Middle East. At no point were the Israeli-Palestinian and Arab-Israeli conflicts addressed by the United States from a perspective that emphasizes the regional context, with its unique history and culture, and the rights of all people to self-determination. Perhaps it is not surprising, therefore, that U.S. intervention has not brought either peace or stability to Israel and its Arab neighbors.

Ironically, even from a realist perspective, the utility of U.S. Middle East policy can be called into question. Over the years, it has led to the disruptive effects of the Arab oil embargo, the use in the 1980s of over 50 percent of an already limited U.S. foreign aid budget in support of the Camp David Accords (and the resulting inability to respond to pressing Third World development needs), and the loss of U.S. lives in Lebanon. The Israeli-Palestinian dispute concerns the fate of perhaps 5 million people in a land virtually devoid of natural resources or strategic location, yet it has had a disproportionate influence on the overall foreign policy priorities of the United States for at least twenty-five years.

Even from a Cold War perspective, this emphasis was unnecessary, given that the Arab world, with its strong Islamic tradition and persistently independent states, has always been an unlikely venue for the successful export of Soviet-style communism. With the end of the Cold War and the opening of regional peace negotiations at the end of 1991, it is possible that this pattern will be broken. The continued international dominance of the United States, however, makes it more likely that it will persist in intervening in the Middle East in support of its perceived national interests, regardless of how these correspond to the needs and desires of the people of the region.

■ Part 6
CONCLUSION

◼ 21

U.S. Intervention in Perspective

Peter J. Schraeder

The rise of the Cold War was a critical driving force in the spread of U.S. interventionist practices in the Third World during the post–World War II era. In sharp contrast to the relatively constrained geographical focus of the Monroe Doctrine (the Western Hemisphere) during the nineteenth century, the Cold War era was marked by a variety of presidential doctrines— beginning with the Truman Doctrine of 1947 and culminating in the Reagan Doctrine of the 1980s—declaring the self-appointed right of the United States to intervene throughout the globe. Whereas an expansionist Europe was the target of President James Monroe, various strategies of containment of the Soviet Union and communism became the cornerstone of post–World War II administrations from Presidents Harry S Truman to Ronald Reagan.[1] Several instruments of intervention were brought to bear on this Cold War struggle with the Soviet Union. Foreign economic and military aid, for example, totaled nearly $825 billion from the 1940s to the 1980s. At the other end of the coercive spectrum, direct U.S. military intervention, after a lull in the early post-Vietnam period, witnessed a resurgence under the guise of low-intensity conflict doctrine. By the end of the 1980s, one could also point to a significant expansion of covert action led by a rejuvenated CIA, the application of a formal doctrine of paramilitary intervention to such diverse countries as Afghanistan, Angola, Cambodia, and Nicaragua, and the existence of over thirty cases of economic sanctions imposed against a variety of Third World regimes. In short, the Third World served as a proxy Cold War battlefield for U.S. policymakers who sought to avoid direct military confrontation with the Soviet Union.

The decline of the Cold War at the beginning of the 1990s dramatically called into question an interventionist foreign policy built upon the twin themes of anticommunism and containment. The primary perceived adversary of the United States in the Third World had followed in the footsteps of other great empires throughout history, fragmenting into a host of smaller, independent, and, most important of all, noncommunist countries. In a noteworthy example of how perceptions had dramatically changed since as recently as the mid-1980s when President Reagan spoke of the former Soviet

Union as the "evil empire," the Bush administration announced on January 22, 1992, that it intended to seek approximately $645 million in aid for its former enemy.[2] As demonstrated by the Bush administration's handling of the Persian Gulf war, however, the decline of the communist threat did not necessarily mean a concomitant decline in U.S. interventionist practices in the Third World. Rather, it appears that the Bush administration's desire to build a "new world order" in the post–Cold War era is predicated on a highly interventionist foreign policy designed to deter a variety of perceived threats within the Third World. Among these are rising ethnic conflict, Islamic fundamentalism, nuclear proliferation, chemical weapons production, and the spread of international drug cartels.

Despite this trend toward greater interventionism during both the Cold War and post–Cold War eras, two parallel trends—one domestic and one international—have placed more constraints on the successful application of U.S. power in the Third World. In the domestic realm, a fragmented political culture is no longer content, as it was during the 1950s and the 1960s, to follow the lead of the executive branch in support of an interventionist foreign policy. Similarly, growing pluralism within the international arena, as the bipolar system of the 1950s evolves toward an emerging multipolar system, has unleashed new forces not necessarily willing to follow the lead of the United States. The net result of these trends is that U.S. interventionist practices may become increasingly counterproductive and costly if policymakers fail to formulate policies that reflect domestic and international realities. "As the greatest power of the postwar era, we acquired a tendency to think that we had a responsibility to intervene and keep order, and to promote and carry out worldwide programs of development and democratization," cautions J. William Fulbright, former U.S. senator (1945–1974) and well-known commentator on U.S. foreign policy. "Only through costly experience have we begun to realize that, more often than not, intervention has been against our own best interests—and in many if not most cases, too, it has not served a useful purpose in the countries involved."[3]

My purpose in this chapter is to offer a set of guidelines for U.S. foreign policy in the emerging post–Cold War era that build upon both past successes and past failures. These guidelines are not intended to be steadfast rules regardless of history or context, but rather to serve as the basis for reassessing nearly fifty years of U.S. interventionist practices in the Third World. In this sense, my primary purpose in this chapter is to contribute to the ongoing debate over what should constitute a proper U.S. foreign policy, yet I recognize that there will forever be differences of opinion and interpretation among individuals of integrity. It is only by presenting these points for subsequent discussion that a policy consensus—the basis for an effective foreign policy in a democracy—can be achieved.

■ NATIONAL SECURITY VERSUS DEMOCRACY

One of the most significant dilemmas facing U.S. policymakers in the post–World War II period, especially in the wake of Vietnam, has been the balancing of perceived national security interests with the need for openness and public debate required by democracy in the formulation of foreign policy. As noted in several chapters, inherent in this balancing act is the growing conflict between the executive branch and Congress over the role that each should play in the foreign-policy-making process. In the words of one observer, there exists a "chronic tension" between the U.S. democratic domestic political system and its nondemocratic national security system.[4]

In the wake of perceived executive branch excesses related to the foreign conduct of the Vietnam War, the domestic abuses of Watergate, and illegal covert activities in the Third World, Congress attempted during the 1970s to strengthen its oversight capabilities by adopting the War Powers Act and creating intelligence oversight committees. The explicit goal of these initiatives was to avoid future Vietnams by requiring that proposed interventions be submitted to reasoned debate apart from that within the limited circle of presidents and their immediate staffs. The implicit goal was to check what was perceived to be overly powerful national security bureaucracy elites—headed by an imperial president—who "circumvented the authority of Congress and the courts, viewed themselves as being above the law, particularly in foreign policy matters, and used secrecy and distortion to deceive Congress and the public in order to accomplish their policy objectives."[5]

The White House steadfastly has resisted congressional attempts at enhanced oversight, with every president of the post–World War II period declaring the constitutional preeminence of the executive branch in the making of foreign policy.[6] In the case of the Persian Gulf war, for example, the Bush administration moved nearly 400,000 troops to the Persian Gulf region and imposed a complete air and naval blockade on Iraq before seeking a congressional resolution authorizing the use of force. Seeking a congressional resolution of support only on the eve of a UN Security Council–imposed deadline for Iraq's withdrawal from Kuwait (after which military force was justified by the UN), the Bush administration clearly sought to provide Congress with a fait accompli. Although the Bush administration's authorization of Operation Desert Storm against Iraq in January 1991 ultimately was preceded by a congressional resolution supporting the use of force and, from the positive vantage point of domestic politics, resulted in extremely light U.S. casualties, the White House tendency to resist congressional attempts at oversight has often had tragic results. Refusing to recognize the constitutionality of the War Powers Act, for example, and subsequently failing to submit policy to the scrutiny of public debate, President Ronald Reagan unilaterally acted to send the U.S.

Marines to Lebanon as part of a "peacekeeping" force, changing course only after their tragic deaths. The Reagan administration similarly refused to submit to congressional scrutiny its Persian Gulf policy of escorting neutral ships, which inevitably led to hostile confrontations with Iran.

More significant is when questionable executive branch actions have impinged directly upon the domestic democratic rights of the U.S. population. In the case of the administration of President Richard M. Nixon, the Federal Bureau of Investigation (FBI) employed wiretaps and informants to monitor, harass, and suppress political dissent against the growing war in Indochina, eventually applying these covert activities against the Democratic party. An April 1976 Senate select committee report noted that these tactics were "unworthy of a democracy and occasionally reminiscent of the tactics of totalitarian regimes."[7]

As discussed in Chapter 16, the Reagan administration resorted to similar illegal tactics against the U.S. public to further its paramilitary goals in Nicaragua. These various tactics, declared illegal in the *Report of the Congressional Committees Investigating the Iran-Contra Affair*, included pressure on the U.S. media not to print stories; lobbying tactics to manipulate U.S. public opinion against the Sandinistas and, therefore, to achieve congressional support for the contras; and "white propaganda" operations—the planting of false articles in the U.S. press. Indeed, one of the most damaging aspects of the administration's secret war was the Iran "arms-for-hostages" deal and the subsequent illegal diversion of profits from these sales to the contras in violation of the Boland Amendment. As Harry Howe Ransom perceptively concludes in Chapter 7, the Iran-contra episode revealed "the corruptive impact of secrecy, which invites serious violations of law and moral standards. . . . Invisible government, based upon a doctrine of ends justifying means, had become a reality."

The question remains how to ensure accountability and legitimacy within the foreign-policy-making process. Noting the damaging effects of past policies, it is hard to accept the view espoused by some proponents of the national security bureaucracy that "saving constitutional democracy may require partially sacrificing it."[8] Taking a completely different view, Morton A. Halperin has convincingly argued that a successful national security policy, especially as it pertains to major episodes of military and covert intervention, requires public and congressional approval.[9]

Halperin's solution for restoring accountability and fostering a foreign policy partnership revolves around amending the War Powers Act in three aspects and making it inclusive of both military and covert intervention. The first amendment would delete the "60–90" statute that requires the president to withdraw U.S. forces from the combat zone within ninety days if, after sixty days, the action has not been approved by Congress. Not only has the executive branch considered the statute unconstitutional (citing it as its reason for not complying with the reporting and consultative provisions of the War Powers Act), but reformers have viewed it as unnecessarily tying the hands of the president.[10]

A second amendment would create a "permanent consultative body" comprising the majority and minority leaders of both houses, the speaker of the house, and the president pro tempore of the Senate, with whom the president would have to consult before initiating any military or covert actions. An expanded consultative body—including the individuals already mentioned as well as the chairperson and ranking minority members of the House and Senate Armed Services, Foreign Affairs, and Intelligence Committees—"would join in consultation with the president and discuss among themselves an appropriate legislative response to the situation at hand." And a third amendment would require advance congressional approval of any military or covert action save for three specific exceptions: to repel attacks against U.S. armed forces located outside U.S. territory; to repel direct attacks against U.S. territory; and to rescue U.S. citizens being held hostage in foreign countries.[11]

Halperin has argued that these amendments ensure a balance between the war-power prerogative of Congress and the necessity for the president to be able to take "immediate action to defend the United States and its citizens" when time is of the essence. Moreover, the proposed policy partnership ensures that (1) questionable or otherwise risky policy would receive a much-needed "second opinion," as the "potential for making mistakes or abusing power increases when the number of alternative views declines"; (2) advance congressional approval would legitimize U.S. intervention once initiated, fostering bipartisanship and a united front to both allies and adversaries; and (3) prior approval would aid in preventing "the backlash from Congress that inevitably follows a foreign policy failure."[12] In short, these reforms would contribute to relieving the "chronic tension" between justified national security concerns and the requirements of democratic society, as well as helping to resolve what Jerel A. Rosati refers to in Chapter 10 as the "crisis of leadership" of the executive branch. With policies built upon the solid foundations of congressional and public support, the president could lead with confidence, charting a consistent and coherent foreign policy in the Third World.

■ THE REGIONALIST-GLOBALIST DEBATE

The most important guideline of any future foreign policy is that policymakers must discard the ill-conceived globalist notion that external forces—whether a communist Soviet Union of the 1980s, a noncommunist Russia of the 1990s, or a radical leader, such as Libya's Muammar Qaddafi— are the chief provocateurs of conflict and instability in the Third World. As Harry Piotrowski explains in Chapter 12, one of the primary flaws of the administration of President Truman was the failure to recognize that communist movements often acted independently of Soviet leader Joseph Stalin, an oversight that contributed to the ill-founded conception of a monolithic and expansionistic communist bloc controlled by Moscow. Indeed, the Cold War era witnessed the growing polycentrism of communism in the Third World and the growth of highly nationalist leaders, such as China's Mao Zedong and Yugoslavia's Joseph Tito, quite independent of Moscow's wishes. Yet official tunnel vision, seemingly only capable of viewing social change through East-West lenses, ensured a highly reactive policy constrained by the blinders of anticommunism.

In a manifestation of this tunnel vision, the United States assumed the right to overthrow even democratically elected Third World regimes that were perceived in Washington as being led by radical nationalist or leftist leaders. Documented examples of countries where such regimes were targeted for destabilization include Iran (1953), Guatemala (1954), British Guiana (1953–1964), Indonesia (1957), Ecuador (1960–1963), Brazil (1964), the Dominican Republic (1965), Costa Rica (mid-1950s), and Chile (1970–1973).[13] The case studies of Iran and Guatemala are especially instructive in that U.S. intervention ultimately contributed to long-term results that were quite sobering: The CIA-installed shah of Iran was ultimately overthrown in a revolution that gave rise to the extremely anti-U.S. Islamic fundamentalist regime headed by the Ayatollah Khomeini, and Guatemala continues to suffer from a legacy of military dictatorships and guerrilla insurgencies. The crisis generated by U.S. intervention in Iran and the potential for future U.S. foreign policy crises in Guatemala suggest that perhaps the United States would have been better off (or at the least no worse off) siding with each country's democratic, albeit leftist, regime.

Another significant outcome of U.S. success in these two initial attempts at overthrowing leftist regimes was that it gave subsequent administrations a false sense of power and ability to control the nature of other Third World regimes. As Ransom notes in Chapter 7 concerning U.S. intervention in Iran, "the political leadership in Washington drew more about the efficacy of covert action than was warranted from this example. The heady wine of success led them to believe that this was a foreign policy tool that could be applied with equal success in other problem areas of the world." Similarly, it was the so-called Guatemala model of paramilitary intervention that led U.S. policymakers to assume wrongly that the Bay of Pigs invasion would ignite nationalist uprisings throughout Cuba and lead to the ouster of Cuban dictator Fidel Castro. What policymakers of the time failed to understand was that both the Iranian and the Guatemalan regimes represented fragile democratic coalitions with powerful domestic enemies— most notably, disenchanted militaries—that were all too happy to take control in exchange for U.S. economic and military support. As discussed later, Washington was soon to learn that unstable democratic regimes are much easier to destabilize than regimes governed by revolutionary nationalist movements.

Although it is important to recognize, as the globalists do, the contributing role that external powers can play in a particular conflict, a regionalist perspective should constitute the core of U.S. foreign policy in the Third World during the post–Cold War era. According to the regionalist perspective, local issues and concerns, not adherence to the ideology of some foreign power, are the primary reasons for conflict and revolution in the Third World. Specifically, regionalists argue that one must deemphasize the external dimension of conflict in favor of its internal economic, cultural, and political roots. In this fashion, the conflict becomes legitimate in its own right and lends itself to resolution based on internal reform.

The administrations of Presidents John F. Kennedy and Jimmy Carter were somewhat representative of this regionalist emphasis. Both deviated from the dominant Cold War viewpoint that revolutions were caused primarily by external communist aggression by centering on the internal causes of upheaval and the need for structural reform to alleviate them. Despite these reformist interludes, both administrations' attempts at resolving the internal conditions that breed insurgency failed because, like their predecessors and contemporaries, Kennedy and Carter still favored excluding leftist groups from political participation. As aptly noted by a distinguished group of specialists concerned with the resolution of guerrilla conflict in Central America, genuine structural reform, and hence any defusing of the guerrilla threat, remains "highly unlikely as long as the left is automatically to be excluded from political participation."[14]

The case of El Salvador may be instructive. A reform-minded junta took power there in October 1979, aspiring to initiate reformist changes that had the potential of alleviating the country's growing guerrilla insurgency.[15] The junta accepted leaders from the centrist opposition and was willing to carry out a dialogue with the radical left with the idea of including them in a future reconciliation government, but they were soon stymied by rightist elements within the military. Although politically willing to move against the rightist elements (a group whose power had to be broken before genuine reform could take place), the junta hesitated for lack of support from the Carter administration. Despite its advocacy of social reform, Washington "balked at the October junta's willingness to bring the popular organizations into the government and to seek an accord with the guerrillas," inevitably leading to a continuing stalemate in the guerrilla war.[16] When successor governments in the 1980s attempted to initiate agrarian reform—one of the key problems fueling the conflict—the net result was failure: A still powerful right resisted, and the left, still disenfranchised politically, responded with increasing guerrilla attacks. Although favoring social reform, Carter's reliance on the Cold War precept of limiting leftist participation mitigated its potential benefits. This trend was exacerbated by the Reagan administration's overwhelming commitment to a military, as opposed to a negotiated, settlement of the conflict.

As noted in Chapter 1, one case during the Cold War era stood out as the exception to the traditional U.S. reflex to limit leftist participation: the transition from white minority to black majority rule in Zimbabwe (formerly Rhodesia), even though this ensured a regime dominated by the Marxist Patriotic Front (PF). The case is significant for three reasons: (1) A more ideological approach would have eschewed supporting the PF because of its obvious communist links and outspoken preference of its leaders for Marxism; (2) the United States recognized the legitimacy of the guerrilla struggle and that its resolution depended on internal political and economic reforms; and (3) the United States recognized the positive role to be played by the radical left in the reform equation. Indeed, despite the Marxist rhetoric of Zimbabwe's Prime Minister Robert Mugabe, he clearly has followed a pragmatic policy of socioeconomic reform and maintenance of ties with the West—underscoring that ideology should not be the yardstick by which the United States determines enemies or allies in the Third World. Most important, U.S. willingness to involve the left in meaningful political participation where it previously had been denied a role demonstrated that such participation could be the key to alleviating long-term guerrilla insurgency.

These lessons provide the basis for reassessing traditional U.S. responses to left-wing guerrilla insurgencies in the emerging post–Cold War era. In the case of El Salvador, for example, the Bush administration's support for a negotiated settlement reflected the growing recognition among policymakers (particularly those in Congress) that the guerrilla insurgency was driven by lack of social reform (i.e., legitimate, unfulfilled popular needs) and not by external forces, such as the former Soviet Union and Cuba. Although massive U.S. economic and military aid (approximately $4 billion during the 1980s) was able to prevent a short-term victory by the guerrillas, in the long run it merely strengthened those forces in the government opposed to reform and contributed to a military stalemate. As demonstrated by the peace accord signed between the Cristiani government of El Salvador and the FMLN guerrilla forces on January 16, 1992, the proper approach of the United States during the 1980s should have been to emphasize its belief in the negotiated resolution of the conflict based on the twin principles of national reconciliation and socioeconomic reform. According to the treaty, the guerrillas agreed to lay down their arms and take part in the democratic process in return for a government commitment to grant an amnesty to guerrilla combatants and to oversee a variety of socioeconomic reforms, such as the government purchase of lands for distribution to peasants.[17] Although the primary determinant of the peace process was a recognition by both the government and guerrilla leaderships that neither could militarily prevail in the conflict, a regionalist perspective on the part of the U.S. government at a much earlier stage could have helped shorten the twelve-year conflict and avoid many of the over 75,000 largely civilian casualties that resulted.

■ REVOLUTIONARY NATIONALISM AND SOCIAL CHANGE

A historical distrust of even democratically elected leftist regimes and consistent efforts to suppress leftist insurgencies constituted part of a greater dilemma of U.S. foreign policy during the Cold War era: Washington's inability to formulate an effective policy for dealing constructively with revolutionary nationalism and social change. Especially at the height of the Cold War, U.S. policy was excessively driven by ideology: Whereas leftist insurgencies were perceived negatively and were to be suppressed, antileftist insurgencies fighting revolutionary nationalist regimes were perceived positively and were to be supported. The Reagan Doctrine, with its commitment to aiding anticommunist guerrilla insurgencies fighting pro-Soviet Third World regimes, was a manifestation of this point of view.

The primary fault with this ideological focus is that opposing ideologies do not in and of themselves preclude a mutually beneficial relationship. For example, despite conservative demands to the contrary, the Reagan administration under the guidance of Secretary of State George Shultz and Assistant Secretary of State for African Affairs Chester Crocker provided extensive economic and military aid to the Marxist government of Mozambique, a policy continued under the Bush administration that ultimately led to that government's abandonment of Marxism as the guiding principle for economic and political organization. As demonstrated by this case, policymakers should not automatically dismiss positive relations with a revolutionary regime simply because of the stated ideological goals of its leaders. Concrete actions rather than the ideological makeup of the regime, whether monarchist, socialist, Marxist, democratic, or some variant thereof, should be the basis for any future relationship. Positive steps by any given revolutionary regime should be met with equal enthusiasm on the U.S. side.

Rather than emulate the example of Mozambique, the United States generally has sought a confrontational policy with revolutionary nationalist regimes, especially when they have overthrown former pro-U.S. regimes. Often the relationship between the United States and the revolutionary regime in this context is at first strained. In the case of Nicaragua, the Sandinista leadership was suspicious of U.S. attitudes toward the revolution, primarily because of past U.S. support for a string of Somoza dictatorships and previous intervention in Latin America, whereas the United States feared that the Sandinista regime would become "another Cuba," providing forward bases for Soviet forces and attempting to expand its revolution throughout Central

America by force. Yet, fears should not become the basis for foreign policy; when they do, they create a self-fulfilling prophecy.

The parallels between the counterproductive U.S. efforts to overthrow both the Cuban and Nicaraguan revolutions are especially instructive. As was noted in several chapters, the United States, fearful that the revolutionary leaders of both countries would become the tools of Soviet intervention in the Western Hemisphere, employed various instruments of coercion—ranging from diplomatic isolation, to the adoption of economic sanctions, to the support of paramilitary guerrillas—in an effort to derail their revolutions. In the case of Nicaragua, the primary problem with the interventionist approach was that it underestimated the popular support of the Sandinista regime and the legitimacy of the 1979 revolution. The same mistake was made with Castro's Cuba, and over thirty years of confrontation with that regime has achieved little if any benefit for U.S. foreign policy. Most important, continued U.S. intervention, coupled with the very real fear of a direct U.S. invasion, provided both regimes with little recourse other than to seek a closer security relationship with the Soviet Union—the exact opposite of what Washington said it was trying to achieve. In the Cuban case, for example, Soviet Premier Nikita Khrushchev ridiculed as "stupid" U.S. efforts to "drive Castro to the wall," nonetheless relishing the expected results: "Castro will have to gravitate to us like iron filing to a magnet."[18]

The paradox of U.S. intervention against radical revolutionary regimes, according to Anthony Lake, former director of policy planning in the U.S. State Department, is that "polls have generally shown that while the [U.S.] public wants success (the defeat of these regimes), it must come at little cost to the United States (that is, involve no great losses through intervention, grain embargoes, or other actions)."[19] Cognizant of this fact, the Reagan and Bush administrations resorted to the lower-cost strategy of paramilitary intervention. Yet, as discussed in Chapter 8, although this type of intervention exhibited the ability to disrupt severely the target country's economic and political system, it is inadequate if the goal is to overthrow the revolutionary regime by force. Rather than folding in the face of external pressure, both Cuba and Nicaragua were able to exploit the tension to whip up popular support. Moreover, U.S. intervention allowed both revolutionary regimes to more easily silence domestic opponents, concentrate power, and blame Washington for failed domestic economic policies.

A more desirable way of dealing with radical social change in the Third World during the emerging post–Cold War era was nicely demonstrated in 1991 by Washington's response to the revolutionary overthrow of Mengistu Haile Mariam, a self-proclaimed Marxist dictator who ruled Ethiopia from 1974 to 1991.[20] As guerrilla advances during the first four months of 1991 made it increasingly clear that Mengistu's days were numbered, the United States intensified its involvement in negotiations between the Ethiopian government and the guerrilla opposition by sending a high-level delegation to the Ethiopian capital that included Irving Hicks, deputy assistant secretary of state for African affairs; Robert C. Frasure, a member of the NSC; and Rudy Boschwitz, a former Republican senator from Minnesota who acted as President Bush's personal envoy. In addition to meeting with Mengistu, both Hicks and Frasure traveled to Khartoum, the capital of Sudan, to meet with the leaders of the Tigrean People's Liberation Front (TPLF) and the Eritrean People's Liberation Front (EPLF), the two major guerrilla armies seeking the overthrow of the Mengistu regime. The level of U.S. involvement in these negotiations intensified when, in the aftermath of Mengistu's departure from power on May 21, 1991, for political exile in Zimbabwe, Assistant Secretary of State for African Affairs Cohen flew to London to mediate personally between the guerrilla factions and a rapidly collapsing Ethiopian government led by Mengistu's vice-president, Lieutenant General Tesfaye Gebre-Kidan.

The net result of U.S. involvement was a significant contribution to an orderly transfer of power in Ethiopia that largely avoided the bloodshed associated with U.S. policy disasters in Somalia and Liberia. (In both of these cases, U.S.-supported leaders were driven from power by coalitions of guerrilla forces that, after achieving initial victories, presided over the escalation of ethnically or clan-based violence in 1991.) As part of the agreement that received the personal blessing of the United States in the form of a public announcement by Cohen on May 28, 1991, the TPLF took control of Addis Ababa and began putting together a broad coalition government that largely was in place by the beginning of July. The most critical element of the U.S.-sponsored agreement was Washington's support for a UN-supervised referendum in Eritrea—a northern territory militarily controlled by the EPLF and that had been fighting for independence since the 1960s—within a period of roughly two years to determine if the people of the territory truly desired independence. The decision to support regional self-determination through the ballot box, when officials were fully cognizant of the fact that the outcome most assuredly would be an independent Eritrea, represented a significant change in U.S. foreign policy from its almost unquestioned support from the 1950s to the 1980s for the territorial integrity of Ethiopia. Regardless of the referendum's outcome, the Africa Bureau made it clear that further U.S. involvement and, most important, the establishment of a foreign aid relationship that went beyond humanitarian relief were dependent on the establishment of some type of representative democracy in Ethiopia.

■ THE LEGITIMACY OF FORCE

The problems associated with using force to overthrow revolutionary regimes in Cuba and Nicaragua, short of a direct U.S. invasion, are indicative of what should constitute an important guideline of U.S. foreign policy during the emerging post–Cold War era: a deemphasis on the role of military force when pursuing long-term goals in the Third World. This should not be taken to the other extreme, however, to mean that the United States must adopt a strict policy of nonintervention. As Ted Galen Carpenter correctly concludes in Chapter 9, "no great power can eschew the use of military force in all circumstances." Rather, the challenge lies in establishing those circumstances in which the use of force is both a legitimate and useful tool of intervention. A brief comparison of U.S. efforts in Afghanistan and Nicaragua provides several tentative guidelines:

1. *Majority support within the target country.* The popular or unpopular nature of the target Third World regime is especially crucial to successful U.S. intervention. In Afghanistan, popular feelings were almost unanimous in desiring a Soviet withdrawal from their country, and traditional Afghani nationalism ensured a steady stream of recruits to carry out a jihad (holy war) against what were perceived as atheistic invaders. In Nicaragua, however, the Sandinistas were ushered into power on the back of a popularly based revolutionary movement, whereas the contras, primarily because of the great number of Somoza sympathizers among their ranks, were rejected by the majority of the population as an artificial creation of Washington.

2. *Majority regional and international support.* A second gauge of the legitimacy and the probable success of an interventionist policy is its level of regional and international support. In Afghanistan, the mujahedin enjoyed overwhelming regional and international support. U.S. efforts not only were supported by traditional regional allies, such as Pakistan and Saudi Arabia, but also by communist China and revolutionary Iran. A 1987 vote in the UN General Assembly that overwhelmingly called for a Soviet withdrawal (123 voted in favor, 19 were opposed, and 11 abstained) clearly indicated the substantial level of support enjoyed by the mujahedin.[21] U.S. efforts in Nicaragua, to the contrary, were opposed by the majority of nations within the region as well as within the international system, most notably U.S. allies in Europe.[22] Most significant were Latin American denunciations of U.S. military efforts to overthrow the Sandinistas. Rather, the Contadora nations, led by Mexico, and the Central American nations, led by President Oscar Arias of Costa Rica, preferred to pursue a nonmilitary solution to reaching an accommodation with Nicaragua.

3. *International law.* Although international law prohibiting intervention may be ignored with relative impunity by nations pursuing self-interested policies, as Christopher C. Joyner underscores in Chapter 13, there is no denying its importance as a legitimizing factor (as to what goals and actions are acceptable within the consensual framework of law). In the case of Afghanistan, accepted precepts of international law clearly branded as illegal the Soviet invasion and occupation of that country, legitimizing aid to

insurgents seeking to force a Soviet withdrawal. In the case of Nicaragua, however, the International Court of Justice ruled that U.S. support of the contras violated international legal norms and subsequently ordered the immediate termination of such activities—an edict the Reagan administration chose to ignore by claiming that the court had no jurisdiction to rule in the matter. "When seen retrospectively," explains Joyner, "it becomes clear that by turning away from the court, the United States lost legal credibility, appeared diplomatically disingenuous, and allowed Nicaragua to gain a propaganda advantage in view of its lawful appeal to the international legal forum."[23]

Although the combination of these three guidelines cannot, of course, guarantee a successful interventionist episode—indeed, success depends on a host of factors, including the goal pursued—they at least enhance the possibility for success and most certainly ensure that U.S. policies foster a legitimacy that will allow it to lead both regionally and within the international system. If we apply these three guidelines to the Bush administration's handling of the Persian Gulf war, for example, it quickly becomes clear why the ultimate U.S. decision to use military force to restore the independence of Kuwait was both successful and legitimate in the eyes of most international commentators: (1) According to accepted precepts of international law, Iraq illegally invaded, occupied, and annexed Kuwait; (2) the vast majority of the Kuwaiti people desired an Iraqi withdrawal; and (3) the use of force was overwhelmingly supported both regionally and within the international system, most notably in terms of a UN Security Council resolution demanding Iraq's unconditional withdrawal from Kuwait. An important key to the success of U.S. intervention in the Persian Gulf was the Bush administration's willingness to act in a multilateral framework in coordination with other nations and not according to some ideological litmus test. Although critics can rightfully question the Bush administration's motives—the protection of oil interests as opposed to the more dubious goal of "restoring" democracy in Kuwait—and its hasty resort to the use of military force rather than giving sanctions a longer time to work, U.S. efforts nonetheless were based on an extremely well-crafted coalition of regional and international forces that transcended both ideological and religious lines.

The Persian Gulf war was also significant in terms of its impact on the so-called Vietnam syndrome—a clear and pervasive reluctance on the part of the U.S. public no longer automatically to accept arguments promoting U.S. military intervention (and thus U.S. casualties) in Third World lands. The dramatic levels of popular support for Operation Desert Storm seemed to indicate that the beginnings of a new interventionist consensus has emerged that shows the public increasingly is willing to perceive the United States as the guarantor of peace and stability throughout the world. Indeed, in a shift that began with popular support for the 1983 invasion of Grenada (a small island state with almost no military forces in the Caribbean) that was similarly forthcoming for the 1989 military invasion of Panama (a larger country with a medium-sized military force in Central America), the massive U.S.-led military operation against Iraq indicated the reemergence of a trend that during the Cold War era had led to U.S. involvement in the highly costly and divisive Vietnam War. It is important to remember, however, that each of these three military operations conformed to the central dictum of the Vietnam syndrome that is still very prevalent in the popular psyche as well as strictly observed by military planners: The military intervention must be short in duration and low in the numbers of U.S. casualties. It is precisely for this reason that the Bush administration accepted the recommendations of the Joint Chiefs of Staff and opted for a quick and massive buildup of forces that could assure a quick victory over the Iraqi forces. The true test of what may be an emerging interventionist consensus will occur if and when policymakers err and commit the United States to a military conflict lasting months rather than days or weeks.

Despite the successful outcome of Operation Desert Storm in restoring Kuwait's independence, U.S. policymakers do not perceive such large-scale military operations against powerful Third World armies—dubbed "mid-intensity conflict" (MIC)—as constituting the primary role of the Defense Department during the emerging post–Cold War era. Rather, as Michael T. Klare succinctly discusses in Chapter 3, the military is instead preparing for a host of military contingencies that fall under the rubric of low-intensity conflict doctrine. Among the most controversial of these, most notably in terms of potentially embroiling U.S. military forces in an extended military engagement abroad, is the growing involvement of the U.S. military in the so-called war on drugs. Specifically, despite initial reservations over becoming involved in what many military planners consider to be police work, the Pentagon's budget devoted to antinarcotics efforts abroad has risen from $440 million in 1989 to a projected total of approximately $1.2 billion in 1992. "With the close of the Cold War and the shrinking military budgets," noted one observer of the changing international arena, "the war on drugs is one of the few growth areas the Pentagon has left."[24]

Growing U.S. military involvement in the Andean region offers an excellent example of the potential pitfalls of a militarily based solution to the war on drugs. Despite the commitment of approximately $2.2 billion in aid (including military equipment and U.S. advisers) to combat cocaine production in the Andean countries of Bolivia, Colombia, and Peru (the so-called Andean Initiative), cocaine production in the region is said to have "skyrocketed" from roughly 397 tons in 1988 to 990 tons two years later.[25] Similarly, a congressional report explained in 1990 that coca cultivation was "approaching 200,000 tons of coca leaf a year, enough to satisfy four times the annual estimated U.S. cocaine market."[26]

Apart from the debate over whether one can really stop the drugs at the "source" as long as demand within the United States remains constant or continues to grow (and thus for every drug-producing lab destroyed in a given region or country, two more crop up in another place), critics point to two major problems. First, just as U.S. support for the strengthening of Latin American militaries from the 1950s to the 1980s often contributed to the dismantling of democracy in these countries, so too can support for the militarization of the drug war potentially lead to new forms of authoritarianism in the region. Of even greater concern to critics, however, is the possibility of involving the United States in a protracted civil war within the region. For example, the United States increasingly has become involved in the Peruvian government's counterinsurgency efforts against a growing guerrilla insurgency known as the Sendero Luminoso (Shining Path), all under the auspices of eradicating the coca trade that is largely controlled by the insurgents in guerrilla-held territories. The costs of U.S. involvement were clearly demonstrated in January 1992 when three U.S. citizens associated with a State Department–sponsored eradication program were killed by Shining Path guerrilla forces.[27]

■ DEMOCRACIES AND DICTATORSHIPS

Just as ideology historically has led U.S. policymakers to oppose leftist regimes blindly, so too has it led these same individuals to support right-wing dictatorships whose leaders joined the United States in its anticommunist crusade. Examples include Fulgencio Batista of Cuba, Ferdinand Marcos of the Philippines, Mobutu Sese Seko of Zaire, Jean-Claude Duvalier of Haiti, and the Somoza family dynasty in Nicaragua. The often disregarded long-term problem with this anticommunist strategy was that the elites who became the "bastions for democracy" and, therefore, staunch U.S. allies have usually been traditional dictators who lack popular support, concern themselves primarily with personal aggrandizement, and therefore demonstrate a general disregard for social reform or broadly shared development policies. The core of the problem is that these dictators (whether of the right or the left) seek legitimacy in the form of external economic and military aid in the international arena rather than attempt to build a popular basis for support among their own people. When the United States has been willing to fill the role of patron by dispensing generous amounts of aid, the dictator's need to foster popular domestic legitimacy is sorely circumscribed. Likewise, as dissent against the regime grows, the tendency is toward greater repression than reform.

The negative result of backing authoritarian rulers more willing to repress than reform has been a long string of revolutions that have vented an accompanying anti-U.S. rage, including the case studies of Nicaragua and

Iran, as described in Chapters 16 and 17. This result should not be surprising, as the United States has generally been perceived by the disaffected portion of the population in such countries as both the midwife and primary prop of the hated regime. Although the United States may be able to buy stability in the short term, such successful actions as defeating the nationalists in Iran in 1953 or suppressing Sandino's forces in Nicaragua during the 1930s often bode ill for stability and U.S. interests in the long term.

Distinguished experts on Central America have formulated a set of straightforward, yet stringent, guidelines for stemming the cycle of repression and resultant anti-U.S. revolutions in that region that are similarly applicable to the entire Third World.[28] First, apart from humanitarian assistance, which should be distributed "strictly on the basis of need," economic aid should be withheld from regimes "determined to maintain deep social inequality or that are gross and consistent violators of internationally recognized human rights." The authors have warned that when dealing with such regimes, the United States "must guard against the temptation to reward minimum changes that are no more than cosmetic efforts to influence U.S. aid policy." Yet, when countries show a genuine commitment to broadly shared development programs that attack the root causes of social inequality—such as land reform, literacy, and rural health care—the United States should be willing to lend a helping hand.[29]

The guidelines for military assistance are even more stringent. This type of aid, according to the experts, "should be limited to governments that enjoy some popular basis of legitimacy so that U.S. aid will not be used for the repression of popular dissent—a more restrictive criterion than the simple absence of gross and consistent human rights violations." In this regard, the authors noted only two legitimate needs for military equipment that the United States should be willing to meet: "the need for adequate forces to defend a nation against external aggression, and the need to defend democratic institutions against internal violence by a small, well-armed minority."[30] The necessity for a popular basis of legitimacy (not necessarily a multiparty system) is extremely important. In instances in which this attribute is missing, U.S. military support becomes the basis for internal repression and control, again working counter to long-term U.S. interests in the Third World.

The key to this restructured foreign aid program, which inevitably would require the reduction of special relationships currently held with authoritarian governments, does not mean that the United States should adopt an isolationist foreign policy. Rather, it underscores the necessity of committing valuable resources only to those nations sharing an interest in promoting and maintaining societies built on popular consent and broadly shared development. In this sense, the United States actively should cultivate close relationships with regimes carrying out these programs, assisting financially when the need arises. In sum, a regime committed to the principles of broadly shared development and respectful of the human rights of its people inevitably enhances its domestic support and represents a positive, long-term investment for the United States.

U.S. policymakers will inevitably find themselves confronted by a situation in which a close ally's democratic institutions and processes are subverted by a leader or faction desirous of assuming personal control and power. Richard J. Kessler, in Chapter 15, describes in detail how this occurred from 1965 to 1986 in the Philippines under the administration of President Ferdinand Marcos. In cases like this, the United States should utilize its economic and military influence (gradually curtailing both types of aid, beginning with military) with the country in question to foster a return to democratic practices. Kessler notes that the United States lost several opportunities to influence policy, the most notable being when Marcos broached the possibility of declaring martial law and suspending the constitution to illegally remain in office. As Kessler concludes, strong U.S. disapproval could have forced him to reverse the decision. "It was a moment, at least from Marcos's perspective, of great vulnerability to external factors."

The most important aspect of the Philippine case study is that five U.S. administrations ignored the dismantling of Philippine democracy because of strategic concerns over continued U.S. access to bases in the country; as Kessler notes, the United States became concerned about democracy in the Philippines "only when democracy became a security issue." Even the Carter administration's human rights program, which questioned the utility of identifying the United States with inherently unstable dictatorships, was compromised by strategic exceptions; when the pursuit of human rights clashed with perceived national security interests, especially in proven allies of strategic importance (such as Iran, the Philippines, South Korea, and Zaire), national security interests prevailed.[31] Putting aside the debate over whether or not the United States actually requires bases in the Third World now that the Cold War has come to an end, long-term U.S. interests logically demand that the United States not turn a blind eye while democracy is destroyed in order to maintain these security interests. As the United States learned the hard way in Ethiopia, Iran, and Nicaragua (that is, in other nations of so-called strategic concern, past or present), ignoring the repressive nature of regimes that lack popular support is a surefire way to lose these strategic assets in the long run, as well as to foster the emergence of a government potentially hostile to the United States.

A further reality of the international system of the emerging post–Cold War era is that there exists a whole host of authoritarian governments of both the right and the left that systematically abuse the rights of their people, but which are not reliant upon the United States for either economic and military aid. As the United States cannot and should not be the guardian of all the countries of the world, it should maintain no more and no less than proper relations with these countries, withhold any type of military and economic aid, and make its abhorrence of their human rights transgressions known within the international system. In extreme cases, however, when the international system is confronted with a regime that grossly violates accepted international standards of human rights, the United States should join other nations in adopting multilateral sanctions to change the nature of that regime. As the United States should not casually be in the business of dictating the structure of Third World regimes, sanctions should adhere to the same rigorous formula of legitimacy as was earlier applied to the use of military force: (1) The action should comply with internationally accepted standards of international law; (2) the sanctions should be supported by the majority of the target nation's population; and (3) the sanctions should be supported overwhelmingly both regionally and within the international system. Again, the key to this type of policy is that the United States act in a multilateral framework in coordination with other nations and not according to some self-prescribed ideological litmus test.

The case study of the apartheid regime of South Africa clearly serves as a useful example of when sanctions should be adopted. Embracing a political system in which minority white ethnic groups composing roughly 15 percent of the population historically have denied political franchise to a largely black majority composing 73 percent of the population (Asians and people of mixed race make up the remainder), South Africa became the target of increasing international condemnation and isolation from the 1950s to the 1980s. In the case of the United States, condemnation of the racially based apartheid system culminated in congressional passage of the Comprehensive Anti-Apartheid Act of 1986, legislation that was repealed in 1991 when it became clear that the white minority had initiated an irreversible process designed to enfranchise politically all ethnic and racial groups within the country. The 1986 legislation clearly corresponded with the three previously noted criteria for intervention: Not only were the sanctions within the bounds of the international legal tenet of humanitarian intervention (see Chapter 13), but they were supported by a significant portion of South Africa's black population, as well as regionally and internationally in a diplomatic coalition that transcended ideological lines.

■ UNILATERALISM VERSUS MULTILATERALISM

An extremely fruitful initial outcome of the end of the Cold War was the lessening of superpower tensions throughout the various regions of the Third World and the intensification of superpower negotiations to resolve regional conflicts. An early example of what such cooperation could yield was demonstrated by the 1988 U.S.-brokered accords that linked South Africa's withdrawal from Namibia and independence for that country in exchange for the withdrawal of Cuban troops from Angola—a country that served as a proxy East-West battlefield in which over 341,000 people (mostly civilians) died during the 1970s and the 1980s. In an event of historic proportions, Namibia on March 21, 1990, achieved independence under the leadership of African nationalist Sam Nujoma as one of the few multiracial, multiparty democracies on the African continent. Two important ingredients that facilitated the resolution of this long-festering regional conflict were Assistant Secretary of State for African Affairs Chester Crocker's tireless efforts to make the U.S. a peace broker in the negotiating process, as well as the Soviet Union's willingness to pressure its Angolan and Cuban allies to accept a negotiated settlement. Both of these ingredients—which built upon the crucial willingness of regional African participants to seek a negotiated settlement—obviously were by-products of a decline in Cold War tensions beginning in the late 1980s.

The example of Namibia is not unique. Rather, it is indicative of the benefits to be derived in the emerging post–Cold War era from the peaceful pursuit of conflict resolution based on multilateral diplomacy. In addition to the peaceful settlement of disputes in southern Africa, one can point to relevant examples in other regions of the Third World: the September 1991 superpower accord prohibiting any further U.S. and Soviet (now Russian) aid to military factions in Afghanistan; the October 1991 Cambodian peace agreement in preparation for multiparty elections in 1993; and the January 1992 treaty ending the twelve-year civil war in El Salvador. As demonstrated in these and other cases, the lessening of Cold War tensions has ushered in a new international environment of compromise that can facilitate the ending of bloody conflicts.

The fragmentation of the Soviet Union into several independent countries has led to a debate over the evolving nature of the international system with serious implications for U.S. interventionist practices. In a celebrated article by Charles Krauthammer, for example, the decline of the Soviet Union is described as having contributed to the creation of a "unipolar" international system in which the United States—the "unchallenged superpower"—can freely lay down the rules of world order.[32] Critics of the unilateral approach instead focus on the domestic and international constraints still faced by U.S. policymakers in the post–Cold War era. "Even if Krauthammer is correct that at present the international system is unipolar—and he is far too quick to dismiss the significance of other players—there is little in the history of international relations to suggest that such a phenomenon could be sustained for a significant length of time," explains Ted Galen Carpenter in a critique of Krauthammer's thesis. "Attempting to specify and execute its own definition of a new world order would seem to be precisely the kind of conduct that would accelerate the efforts of other countries to balance Washington's power." "Predictably," Carpenter concludes, "such pretensions have already provoked apprehension and hostility among political and intellectual elites in nations as diverse as France, India, and Japan."[33]

The most effective course for the United States to follow in the emerging post–Cold War era is that of building a regional and international consensus for its interventionist policies in the Third World. A critical element of this approach should be the recognition of the valuable role to be played by the various organs of the UN or by regional organizations, such as the Organization of American States (OAS), particularly in terms of facilitating the end of regional conflicts. Specifically, U.S. policymakers should take advantage of the consensus-building functions achievable through multilateral negotiations within the context of the UN or regional organizations. In the case of Cambodia, for example, the UN served as an indispensable forum for securing the October 1991 peace agreement in preparation for UN-supervised elections in 1993. Similarly, approval from the UN Security Council was extremely influential in securing a truly international coalition against Iraq. And UN peacekeeping operations have dramatically expanded during the post–Cold War era (eight new operations since 1988 out of a total of twenty-one for the post–World War II era), with forces being deployed as of 1992 in seven regional hotspots: Angola, Central America and El Salvador, the Israeli-annexed Golan Heights, Kuwait, Lebanon, and the Western Sahara.[34] In short, interventionist practices based upon international law and the creation of an international consensus not only enhance the possibility for success but also foster a legitimacy that will allow the United States to lead within the international system in an emerging post–Cold War world.

■ LEADING WITH CONFIDENCE IN THE POST–COLD WAR ERA

The last half century of U.S. interventionist practices in the Third World literally has guaranteed the extension of U.S. power to virtually all corners of the globe. For better or for worse, the United States rose out of the ashes of World War II to become the most powerful nation the world had ever seen. U.S. economic and military power reached its height in the decade immediately following the war, but the twin trends of the fragmentation of U.S. political culture and the rising pluralism within the international system have since seriously changed the parameters within which U.S. policies must be formulated. Yet, as Joseph S. Nye, Jr., perceptively noted, "Although the United States must adjust to a new era of multipolarity and interdependence in world politics, Americans should not underestimate U.S. strength." Indeed, "with more than one-fifth of world military and economic product, the U.S. remains the most powerful state in the world and will very likely remain that way far into the future."[35]

For the United States to lead with confidence well into the twenty-first century requires the basic redesigning of U.S. interventionist practices, as outlined here. In the domestic realm, the president should establish a greater partnership with Congress, formulating policies built upon the strong foundations of congressional and public support. Secure in this support, the president could lead with confidence, charting a consistent and coherent foreign policy in the Third World. In the international realm, interventionist practices should attempt to build upon both a multilateral regional and international consensus, with the United States taking the lead in utilizing the forum of the UN and accepted precepts of international law in garnering support. Although adherence to the guidelines put forth in this chapter may not always guarantee the success of U.S. foreign policy in the Third World, they raise the possibility for success substantially and most certainly ensure the legitimacy that is necessary for leadership both regionally and within the international system.

Acronyms

ACOA	American Committee on Africa
AFL-CIO	American Federation of Labor-Congress for Industrial Organization
AFSC	American Friends Service Committee
AID	Agency for International Development
AIOC	Anglo-Iranian Oil Company
ANC	African National Congress (South Africa)
ANS	Armée Nationale Sihanoukienne (Cambodia)
ARAMCO	Arab-American Oil Company
ARENA	Nationalist Republican Alliance (El Salvador)
ASEAN	Association of Southeast Asian Nations
CARICOM	Caribbean Community
CBC	Congressional Black Caucus
CDB	Caribbean Development Bank
CENTCOM	Central Command
CENTO	Central Treaty Organization
CGDK	Coalition Government of Democratic Kampuchea (Cambodia)
CIA	Central Intelligence Agency
CINCLANT	commander in chief of the U.S. Atlantic Command
CIS	Commonwealth of Independent States
CNN	Cable News Network
CODESA	Convention for a Democratic South Africa
COSATU	Congress of South African Trade Unions
CPP	Communist Party of the Philippines
CPSU	Communist Party of the Soviet Union
DCI	director of central intelligence
DDP	deputy director for plans
DIA	Defense Intelligence Agency
EC	European Community
EPLF	Eritrean People's Liberation Front (Ethiopia)
ESF	Economic Support Fund
FBI	Federal Bureau of Investigation
FDN	Nicaraguan Democratic Force

FMLN	Faribundo Martí Front for National Liberation (El Salvador)
FNLA	National Front for the Liberation of Angola
FSLN	Sandinista National Liberation Front (Frente Sandinista de Liberacion National) (Nicaragua)
FY	fiscal year
GAO	General Accounting Office
GCC	Gulf Cooperation Council
GDP	gross domestic product
GNP	gross national product
GPO	Government Printing Office
ICCR	Interfaith Center on Corporate Responsibility
ICJ	International Court of Justice
IEEPA	International Emergency Economic Powers Act
IFDP	Institute for Food and Development Policy
IMF	International Monetary Fund
INF	intermediate-range nuclear forces
IPC	Iraq Petroleum Company
ITT	International Telephone and Telegraph
JCS	Joint Chiefs of Staff
JDA	Joint Deployment Agency
KPNLF	Khmer People's National Liberation Front (Cambodia)
LIC	low-intensity conflict
LIDs	Light Infantry Divisions
MAI	Multilateral Assistance Initiative
MBA	Military Bases Agreement (Philippines)
MFN	most-favored-nation states
MIC	mid-intensity conflict
MILGROUP	military group
MP	Military Police
MPLA	Popular Movement for the Liberation of Angola
NAM	Non-Aligned Movement
NATO	North Atlantic Treaty Organization
NDU	National Defense University
NED	National Endowment for Democracy
NERP	Nicaraguan Exile Relocation Program
NICs	Newly Industrializing Countries
NIEO	New International Economic Order
NJM	New Jewel Movement (Grenada)
NLF	National Liberation Front (Vietnam)
NNPA	Nuclear Non-Proliferation Act
NP	National Party (South Africa)
NPA	New People's Army (Philippines)
NPT	Non-Proliferation Treaty

NRP	New Republic Party (South Africa)
NSA	National Security Agency
NSAM	National Security Action Memorandum
NSC	National Security Council
NSDD	National Security Decision Directive
NSSD	National Security Study Directive
NSSM	National Security Study Memorandum
OAS	Organization of American States
OECS	Organization of Eastern Caribbean States
OIDP	Overseas Internal Defense Policy
OPC	Office of Policy Coordination
OPEC	Organization of Petroleum Exporting Countries
OSO	Office of Special Operations
OSS	Office of Strategic Services
PDF	Panamanian Defense Forces
PF	Patriotic Front (Zimbabwe)
PFP	Progressive Federal Party (South Africa)
PHILCUSA	Philippine Council on U.S. Aid
P.L. 480	Public Law 480
PLA	People's Liberation Army (PRC)
PLO	Palestine Liberation Organization
PNC	Palestine National Council
PPBS	Planning, Programming, and Budgeting System
PRA	People's Revolutionary Army (Grenada)
PRC	People's Republic of China
PRD	Democratic Revolutionary Party (Panama)
psyops	psychological operations
RDF	Rapid Deployment Force
RENAMO	Mozambique National Resistance
RN	Nicaraguan Resistance
SACP	South African Communist Party
SALT	Strategic Arms Limitation Talks
SAVAK	National Security and Information Organization (Sazman-e Attelaat va Amniyat-e Keshvar) (Iran)
SEALs	sea-air-land commandos
SEATO	Southeast Asian Treaty Organization
S/LPD	Office of Public Diplomacy for Latin America and the Caribbean
SWAPO	South West African People's Organization (Namibia)
TPLF	Tigrean People's Liberation Front (Ethiopia)
UCLAs	Unilaterally Controlled Latino Assets
UDF	United Democratic Front (South Africa)
UN	United Nations
UNITA	National Union for the Total Independence of Angola

UNO	National Opposition Union (Nicaragua)
UNO	United Nicaraguan Opposition
USIA	United States Information Agency
USSR	Union of Soviet Socialist Republics
WCOA	Washington Committee on Africa
WEU	Western European Union

Notes

■ **CHAPTER 1: STUDYING U.S.**
INTERVENTION IN THE THIRD WORLD

1. Tim Shorrock, "The Struggle for Democracy in South Korea in the Rise of Anti-Americanism," *Third World Quarterly* 8,4 (October 1986): 1203–4.

2. Third World countries have also been referred to as "undeveloped," "underdeveloped," "developing," "less-developed," and "nondeveloped." For an examination of the nonaligned movement and the NIEO, see Richard L. Jackson, *The Non-Aligned, the U.N. and the Superpowers* (New York: Praeger, 1986).

3. For a more in-depth discussion of these characteristics, see Joseph Weatherby, Jr., et al., eds., *The Other World: Issues and Politics in the Third World* (New York: Macmillan, 1987), esp. ch. 1.

4. For an early application of these concepts, see Walter W. Rodney, *How Europe Underdeveloped Africa* (Washington, D.C.: Howard University Press, 1982); and Andre Gunder Frank, *Capitalism and Underdevelopment in Latin America: Historical Studies of Chile and Brazil* (New York: Monthly Review Press, 1967). For a good overview, see Ronald H. Chilcote, *Theories of Development and Underdevelopment* (Boulder: Westview, 1984).

5. For further discussion, see Peter Worsley, *Three Worlds: Culture and World Development* (Chicago: University of Chicago Press, 1984), esp. pp. 306–44.

6. See the following series of articles in *Third World Quarterly* that offer a good overview of the evolution of the debate over usage of the term "Third World": Leslie Wolf-Phillips, "Why Third World?" 1, 1 (1979): 105–14; Peter Worsley, "How Many Worlds?" 1, 2 (1979): 100–8; S. D. Muni, "The Third World: Concept and Controversy," 2, 2 (1980): 315–18; Grant McCall, "Four Worlds of Experience and Action," 2, 2 (1980): 536–54; Leslie Wolf-Phillips, "Why 'Third World'? Origin, Definition and Usage," 9, 4 (1987): 1311–27.

7. The statistics in this section are derived from U.S. Department of Commerce, Bureau of the Census, *Statistical Abstract of the United States 1987* (Washington, D.C.: Department of Commerce, 1990), pp. 797–801, 856.

8. See Bernard Wysocki, Jr., "Returning to the Third World: Emerging Nations Revive as Investment Hot Spots, But the Risks Are Hard to Assess," *Wall Street Journal,* September 9, 1991, pp. R1, R2.

9. Michael T. Klare, "Deadly Convergence: The Arms Trade, Nuclear/Chemical Missile Proliferation, and Regional Conflict in the 1990s," in Michael T. Klare and Daniel C. Thomas, eds., *World Security: Trends and Challenges at Century's End* (New York: St. Martin's, 1991), pp. 170–96.

10. Richard F. Grimmett, *Trends in Conventional Arms Transfers to the Third World by Major Supplier, 1981–1988* (Washington, D.C.: Congressional Research Service, 1988), pp. 34, 57. Quoted in ibid., p. 170.

11. For discussion, see Peter A. Clausen, "Nuclear Proliferation in the 1980s and the 1990s," in Klare and Thomas, *World Security,* pp. 144–69.

12. See Klare, "Deadly Convergence."

13. Quoted in Michael T. Klare and Peter Kornbluh, "The New Interventionism: Low-Intensity Warfare in the 1980s and Beyond," in Klare and

Kornbluh, eds., *Low-Intensity Warfare: Counterinsurgency, Proinsurgency, and Antiterrorism in the Eighties* (New York: Pantheon, 1988), p. 4.

14. For a discussion on the foreign policy impact of the Committee on the Present Danger, see Jerry W. Sanders, *Peddlers of Crisis: The Committee on the Present Danger* (Boston: South End, 1983). For Cato Institute analyses, see Sheldon L. Richman, "The United States and the Persian Gulf," Cato Institute Policy Analysis no. 46, January 10, 1985; Ted G. Carpenter, "U.S. Aid to Anti-Communist Rebels: The 'Reagan Doctrine' and Its Pitfalls," Cato Institute Policy Analysis no. 74, June 24, 1986; and Leon T. Hadar, "Extricating America from its Middle Eastern Entanglement," Cato Institute Policy Analysis no. 154, June 12, 1991. For a detailed discussion of how U.S. stakes and threats have been exaggerated in the Third World, see Robert H. Johnson, "Exaggerating America's Stakes in Third World Conflicts," *International Security* 10, 3 (Winter 1985–86): 32–68.

15. William Shawcross, *Sideshow: Kissinger, Nixon and the Destruction of Cambodia* (New York: Pocket, 1979), esp. pp. 19–35.

16. Figures are derived from *The World Almanac and Book of Facts 1988* (New York: Pharos, 1987), pp. 338–39.

17. See, for example, Luigi Sensi, "Superpower Interventions in Civil Wars, 1945–1987," paper prepared for the 29th Annual Meeting of the International Studies Association, St. Louis, Mo., March 30–April 2, 1988; and Herbert K. Tillema, "Escalation and International War in the Nuclear Age: Foreign Overt Military Interventions, 1945–1988," paper prepared for the 32nd Annual Meeting of the International Studies Association, Vancouver, British Columbia, Canada, March 19–23, 1991.

18. Quoted in Arthur Schlesinger, Jr., "Foreign Policy and the American Character," *Foreign Affairs* 62, 1 (Fall 1983): 5.

19. Richard J. Barnet, *Intervention and Revolution: America's Confrontation with Insurgent Movements Around the World* (New York: World Publishing, 1968), p. 56.

20. William M. Leogrande, "Cuba," in Morris J. Blachman, William M. Leogrande, and Kenneth E. Sharpe, eds., *Confronting Revolution: Security Through Diplomacy in Central America* (New York: Pantheon, 1986), pp. 232–33.

21. Morris J. Blachman et al., "The Failure of the Hegemonic Strategic Vision," in Blachman, Leogrande, and Sharpe, *Confronting Revolution*, p. 391.

22. For a good discussion of these factors, see Barry Rubin, *Modern Dictators, Third World Coup Makers, Strongmen, and Populist Tyrants* (New York: McGraw Hill, 1987), esp. pp. 76–108.

23. This does not mean, however, that the United States always supported such a program nor that U.S. influence was the key in determining the process. For instructive accounts, see Anthony Lake, *The "Tar Baby" Option: American Policy Toward Southern Rhodesia* (New York: Columbia University Press, 1976); and Henry F. Jackson, *From the Congo to Soweto: U.S. Foreign Policy Toward Africa Since 1960* (New York: Quill, 1984).

24. See Blachman, Leogrande, and Sharpe, *Confronting Revolution*, chs. 3, 12–14.

25. Gary L. Guertner, "Global Strategy and Regional Pragmatism in U.S. Foreign Policy," *International Studies Notes* 12,1 (Fall 1985):17.

26. Robert O. Keohane and Joseph S. Nye, *Power and Interdependence: World Politics in Transition* (Boston: Little, Brown, 1977), pp. 27–28.

27. Richard E. Feinberg, *The Intemperate Zone: The Third World Challenge to U.S. Foreign Policy* (New York: W. W. Norton, 1983), p. 34.

28. For a discussion of conflicting lessons, see Richard A. Melanson, *Writing History and Making Policy: The Cold War, Vietnam, and Revisionism* (Lanham, Md.: University Press of America, 1983).

29. Melvin Gurtov and Ray Maghroori, *Roots of Failure: United States Foreign Policy in the Third World* (Westport, Conn.: Greenwood, 1984), p. 173.

30. See Charles F. Doran, George Modelski, and Cal Clark, eds., *North/South Relations: Studies in Dependency Reversal* (New York: Praeger, 1983).

31. Rubin, *Modern Dictators*, p. 315.

32. Walter LaFeber, *Inevitable Revolutions: The United States in Central America* (New York: W. W. Norton, 1983), p. 15.

33. See Benjamin Hart, "Rhetoric vs. Reality: How the State Department Betrays the Reagan Vision," Heritage Foundation Backgrounder no. 484, 1986. For a brief discussion of the conflict between U.S. conservatives who favor support and State Department rejection of those demands, see James Brooke, "Visiting U.S. Aide Condemns Mozambique Rebels," *New York Times*, April 27, 1988, p. A6.

■ **CHAPTER 2: THE EVOLUTION OF THE INTERVENTIONIST IMPULSE**

1. See Albert Weinberg, *Manifest Destiny: A Study of Nationalist Expansionism in American History* (Baltimore: Johns Hopkins Press, 1935).

2. "Memorandum of a Conversation, July 6, 1945," in U. S. Department of State, *Foreign Relations of the United States: The Conference at Berlin*, vol. 1 (Washington, D.C.: Government Printing Office), pp. 997–98.

3. "Secretary's Exposition of American History at the Kraft Dinner, November 13, 1952" (by an unknown notetaker), *The Papers of Dean Acheson*, Harry S Truman Library, Independence, Mo.

4. Quoted in Lloyd C. Gardner and William L. O'Neill, *Looking Backward: A Reintroduction to American History* (New York: McGraw-Hill, 1974), p. 54.

5. The complicated process by which social tensions, especially in the major port cities, combined with the aspirations of colonial elites to produce the American Revolution (then turned outward against external enemies) is discussed in Gary B. Nash, *The Urban Crucible: Social Change, Political Consciousness, and the Origins of the American Revolution* (Cambridge: Harvard University Press, 1979). The roots of James Madison's famous prescription for preserving republicanism by enlarging the sphere, as outlined in *Federalist Papers* no. 10 and no. 51, so as to diversify and separate factions, may be seen clearly in the prerevolution decade.

6. Francis Wharton, ed., *The Revolutionary Correspondence of the United States*, vol. 6 (Washington, D.C.: Government Printing Office, 1889), p. 132.

7. William Appleman Williams, *The Contours of American History* (New York: World Publishing, 1961), p. 179.

8. Jefferson to James Madison, August 16, 1807, in Paul Leicester Ford, ed., *The Writings of Thomas Jefferson*, vol. 9 (New York: G. P. Putnam's, 1896), pp. 124–25.

9. Patricia Nelson Limerick, *The Legacy of Conquest: The Unbroken Past of the American West* (New York: W. W. Norton, 1987), pp. 18–19.

10. The Big Three met at the Potsdam Conference in 1945 to begin discussion of postwar problems. Frustrated by the delays and the wrangling,

President Truman exclaimed to an aide: "Jimmy, do you realize that we have been here seventeen whole days? Why, in seventeen days you can decide anything!" Robert Murphy, *Diplomat Among Warriors* (New York: Pyramid, 1965), pp. 278–79.

11. Limerick, *Legacy of Conquest*, p. 324.

12. Quoted in Richard W. Van Alstyne, "Empire in Midpassage, 1845–1867," in William Appleman Williams, ed., *From Colony to Empire: Essays in the History of American Foreign Relations* (New York: Wiley, 1972), p. 111.

13. See Walter LaFeber, "The 'Lion in the Path': The U.S. Emergence as a World Power," *Political Science Quarterly* 101, 5 (1986): 705–18.

14. Ibid.

15. Frederic Bancroft, *The Life of William H. Seward*, vol. 2 (Gloucester, Mass.: Peter Smith, 1967), p. 13.

16. Ibid.

17. The fullest discussion is Ernest Paolino, *The Foundations of the American Empire: William H. Seward and U.S. Foreign Policy* (Ithaca, N.Y.: Cornell University Press, 1973), p. 28.

18. Bancroft, *The Life of William H. Seward*, p. 68.

19. See William O. Scroggs, *Filibusters and Financiers: The Story of William Walker and His Associates* (New York: Macmillan, 1916).

20. Wood to Root, January 13, 1900, *The Papers of Elihu Root*, Library of Congress, Washington, D.C.

21. Bryan to Thomas Bailly-Blanchard, December 19, 1914, U.S. Department of State, *Foreign Relations of the United States, 1914* (Washington, D.C.: Government Printing Office, 1922), pp. 370–71.

22. "Present Nature and Extent of the Monroe Doctrine and Its Need of Restatement," June 11, 1914, Records of the Department of State, National Archives, Washington, D.C., File No. 710.11/185 1/2.

23. LaFeber, "The 'Lion in the Path,'" p. 714.

24. Quoted in Roy Flint, "The United States Army on the Pacific Frontier, 1899–1939," in Joe C. Dixon, ed., *The American Military and the Far East* (Washington, D.C.: Government Printing Office, 1980), p. 151.

25. Ray Stannard Baker and William E. Dodd, eds., *The Public Papers of Woodrow Wilson,* vol. 5 (New York: Harper and Brothers, 1972), pp. 223–38.

26. See, for example, Carl P. Parrini, *Heir to Empire: United States Economic Diplomacy, 1916–1923* (Pittsburgh: University of Pittsburgh Press, 1969); and Joan Hoff Wilson, *American Business and Foreign Policy, 1920–1933* (Lexington: University of Kentucky Press, 1971).

27. See William C. McNeil, *American Money and the Weimar Republic: Economics and Politics on the Eve of the Great Depression* (New York: Columbia University Press, 1986).

28. Quoted in Lloyd C. Gardner, *A Covenant with Power: America and World Order from Wilson to Reagan* (New York: Oxford University Press, 1984), p. 45.

29. Quoted in Ronald J. Stupak, *American Foreign Policy: Assumptions, Processes and Projections* (New York: Harper and Row, 1976), p. 188.

30. U.S. Congress, Senate, Committee on Foreign Relations, *Hearings Held in Executive Session: Legislative Origins of the Truman Doctrine,* 80th Cong., 1st Sess., 1973, p. 197.

31. Quoted in Lloyd C. Gardner, Walter F. LaFeber, and Thomas J. McCormick, *Creation of the American Empire: U.S. Diplomatic History* (Chicago: Rand-McNally, 1973), p. 458.

32. NSC–68, April 14, 1950, printed in U.S. Department of State, *Foreign*

Relations of the United States, 1950, vol. 1 (Washington, D.C.: Government Printing Office, 1977), pp. 234–92.

33. Seymour Hersh, "The Price of Power: Kissinger, Nixon and Chile," *Atlantic Monthly* (December 1982): 31–58.

34. "Memorandum for Record," June 23, 1954, *The Dwight D. Eisenhower Papers,* Eisenhower Library, Abilene, Kans., Whitman File, Legislative Meetings.

■ CHAPTER 3: THE DEVELOPMENT OF LOW-INTENSITY CONFLICT DOCTRINE

1. U.S. Commission on Integrated Long-Term Strategy, *Discriminate Deterrence* (Washington, D.C.: Government Printing Office, 1988), pp. 13–14.

2. For discussion of this phenomenon, see Michael T. Klare and Peter Kornbluh, eds., *Low-Intensity Warfare: Counterinsurgency, Proinsurgency, and Antiterrorism in the Eighties* (New York: Pantheon, 1988), ch. 1. See also U. S. Department of Defense, *Proceedings of the Low-Intensity Warfare Conference* (Washington, D.C.: Government Printing Office, 1986) (hereinafter, *LIC Proceedings*).

3. Frank C. Carlucci, *Annual Report to the Congress,* U.S. Department of Defense, Fiscal Year 1989 (Washington, D.C.: Government Printing Office, 1988) (hereinafter, *DOD Report FY 89*), p. 24.

4. *DOD Report FY 89,* p. 63; see also pp. 58–62, 225–30.

5. Address at the U.S. Coast Guard Academy, New London, Conn., May 24, 1989 (White House Press Office transcript).

6. Dick Cheney, *Report of the Secretary of Defense to the President and the Congress,* January 1990, pp. iii, v.

7. For discussion, see Stephen E. Ambrose, *Rise to Globalism,* 4th rev. ed. (New York: Penguin, 1985), pp. 58–79; Richard J. Barnet, *Intervention and Revolution: The United States in the Third World,* rev. ed. (New York: New American Library, 1980), pp. 119–56.

8. See Ambrose, *Rise to Globalism,* pp. 79–98.

9. Ibid., pp. 99–115. For the text of NSC-68, see U.S. Department of State, *Foreign Relations of the United States, 1950,* vol. 1 (Washington, D.C.: Government Printing Office, 1977), pp. 234–92.

10. For discussion, see Richard M. Freeland, *The Truman Doctrine and the Origins of McCarthyism* (New York: Knopf, 1972).

11. See Ambrose, *Rise to Globalism,* pp. 132–79.

12. Maxwell D. Taylor, *The Uncertain Trumpet* (New York: Harper and Row, 1960), pp. 5–6.

13. For summary and analysis of NSAM 124 and NSAM 182, see Klare and Kornbluh, *Low-Intensity Warfare,* pp. 27–30. On Kennedy and counterinsurgency, see Richard J. Walton, *Cold War and Counter-Revolution: The Foreign Policy of John F. Kennedy* (New York: Viking, 1972). On counterinsurgency doctrine, see Douglas S. Blaufarb, *The Counterinsurgency Era* (New York: Free Press, 1977).

14. U.S. Congress, House, Committee on Appropriations, Subcommittee, *Department of Defense Appropriations for 1964,* Hearings, 88th Cong., 1st Sess., Pt. 1, 1963, pp. 483–84.

15. Taylor memorandum to Robert S. McNamara, January 22, 1964, as reprinted in the *New York Times,* June 13, 1971, p. A35.

16. On Vietnam, see George McT. Kahin, *Intervention: How America Became Involved in Vietnam* (New York: Knopf, 1986), pp. 146–235; Stanley Karnow, *Vietnam: A History* (New York: Penguin, 1984), pp. 312–473; and Gabriel Kolko, *Anatomy of a War* (New York: Pantheon, 1985).

17. For discussion, see Michael T. Klare, *Beyond the "Vietnam Syndrome"* (Washington, D.C.: Institute for Policy Studies, 1981), pp. 1–8.

18. Elmo R. Zumwalt, Jr., "Heritage of Weakness: An Assessment of the 1970s," in W. Scott Thompson, ed., *From Weakness to Strength* (San Francisco: Institute for Contemporary Studies, 1980), pp. 34, 39.

19. Interview in *U.S. News and World Report,* April 16, 1979, pp. 49–50.

20. See *Washington Post,* June 22, 1979, and *New York Times,* June 28, 1979.

21. Cited in the *New York Times,* January 24, 1980.

22. See Reagan's remarks at West Point on May 27, 1981, as reported in the *New York Times,* May 28, 1981.

23. See Klare and Kornbluh, *Low-Intensity Warfare,* ch. 4.

24. Remarks before the American Newspaper Publishers Association, Chicago, Ill., May 5, 1981 (U.S. Department of Defense transcript).

25. Richard Halloran, "Reagan as Military Commander," *New York Times Magazine,* January 15, 1984, pp. 24–25.

26. For discussion, see Klare and Kornbluh, *Low-Intensity Warfare,* ch. 1. For a compendium of Pentagon views, see *LIC Proceedings.* The landscape of LIC is further spelled out in U.S. Army Command and General Staff College, *Low-Intensity Conflict,* Field Circular 100-20 (Ft. Leavenworth, Kans., 1986) (hereinafter, USACGSC, FC 100–20).

27. *Taking the Stand: The Testimony of Lt. Col. Oliver L. North* (New York: Pocket Books, 1987), p. 12.

28. Neil C. Livingstone, "Fighting Terrorism and 'Dirty Little Wars,'" in William A. Buckingham, Jr., ed., *Defense Planning for the 1980s* (Washington, D. C.: National Defense University Press, 1984), pp. 166–67, 186.

29. Ibid., pp. 186–87.

30. *LIC Proceedings,* p. 10.

31. On current U. S. counterinsurgency doctrine, see USACGSC, FC 100-20, chs. 3–5. See also Klare and Kornbluh, *Low-Intensity Warfare,* pp. 56–62 and chs. 5 (on El Salvador) and 7 (on the Philippines).

32. See USACGSC, FC 100–20, chs. 8 and 9. See also Klare and Kornbluh, *Low-Intensity Warfare,* pp. 66–69.

33. Robert C. McFarlane, "Deterring Terrorism," *Journal of Defense and Diplomacy* (June 1985), p. 8. See also U.S. Army Training and Doctrine Command, *U.S. Army Operational Concept for Terrorism Counteraction,* Pamphlet No. 525–37 (Ft. Monroe, Va., 1984). On NSDD 138, see *Los Angeles Times,* April 15, 1984, and *Washington Post,* April 18, 1984.

34. See David C. Morrison, "The Pentagon's Drug Wars, " *National Journal,* September 6, 1986, pp. 2105–7. On "Operation Blast Furnace," see *New York Times,* July 16–18 and September 24, 1986.

35. A. M. Gray, "Defense Policy for the 1990s," *Marine Corps Gazette* (May 1990): 18.

36. Steven Metz, "U.S. Strategy and the Changing LIC Threat," *Military Review* (June 1991): 23.

37. Statement of the Secretary of Defense before the House Foreign Affairs Committee, Washington, D.C., March 19, 1991 (Department of Defense transcript), p. 7.

38. For information on these operations, see James L. Jones, "Operation

PROVIDE COMFORT," *Marine Corps Gazette* (November 1991): 99–107; Floyd D. Kennedy, Jr., "Operation SHARP EDGE," *National Defense* (December 1990): 88; T. W. Parker, "Operation SHARP EDGE," *U.S. Naval Institute Proceedings* (May 1991): 102–106; Glen R. Sachtleben, "Operation SHARP EDGE," *Marine Corps Gazette* (November 1991): 77–85; and "Somalia Evacuation—Eastern Exit," *Marine Corps Gazette* (February 1991): 3.

39. For discussion of the MIC paradigm, see Michael T. Klare, "Beyond Desert Storm: The New Military Paradigm," *Technology Review* (May/June 1991): 28–36.

40. Statement before the House Foreign Affairs Committee, March 19, 1991.

41. James R. Locher III, "Low Intensity Conflict—Challenge of the 1990s," *Defense/91* (July–August 1991): 19.

42. "As we seek to build a new world order in the aftermath of the Cold War, we will likely discover that the enemy we face is less an expansionist communism than it is instability itself," *National Security Strategy of the United States*, The White House, August 1991, p. 25.

43. Address at the Air University, Maxwell Air Force Base, Alabama, April 13, 1991 (White House Press Office transcript).

44. Locher III, "Low-Intensity Conflict," p. 18.

45. See Jones, "Operation PROVIDE COMFORT."

46. For discussion of the political and military implications of humanitarian relief operations, see David Morrison, "Operation Kinder and Gentler," *National Journal* (May 25, 1991): 1260.

47. Locher III, "Low-Intensity Conflict," p. 19.

■ CHAPTER 4:
THE GLOBALIST-REGIONALIST DEBATE

1. See, for example, among proffered forms of change, Barrington Moore, Jr., *Injustice: The Social Bases of Obedience and Revolt* (White Plains, N.Y.: M. E. Sharpe, 1978), pp. 500–5; and Leon Trotsky, "Revolution and the Proletariat," in John G. Wright, *The Permanent Revolution and Results and Prospects* (New York: Pathfinder, 1970), pp. 62–68.

2. Kenneth Waltz, *Theory of International Politics* (Reading, Mass.: Addison-Wesley, 1979), pp. 170–76.

3. "It is no accident that between the Berlin Crisis and the invasion of Czechoslovakia, the principal threats to peace came from the emerging areas. The temptation to deflect domestic dissatisfactions into foreign adventures is ever present." Henry A. Kissinger, *American Foreign Policy* (New York: W. W. Norton, 1974), p. 80.

4. "The international system would be more stable and less conflictual if the North and the South had less to do with each other." Stephen D. Krasner, *Structural Conflict: The Third World Against Global Liberalism* (Berkeley: University of California Press, 1985), p. 30.

5. Roger D. Hansen, *Beyond the North-South Stalemate* (New York: McGraw Hill, 1979), p. 284.

6. Robert O. Keohane, *After Hegemony: Cooperation and Discord in the World Political Economy* (Princeton: Princeton University Press, 1984).

7. Edward N. Luttwak, *The Great Strategy of the Soviet Union* (New York: St. Martin's, 1983).

8. Speculation that Gorbachev was stressing "a defensive nature of military preparedness" in East-West matters did not extend to "wars of national liberation." Andrew Borowiec, "Are Soviets Giving up Dogma That War with the West Is Inevitable?" *Washington Times,* November 12, 1987, pp. A1, A9.

9. Alexander Dollin, "Policy-Making and Foreign Affairs," in James Cracraft, ed., *The Soviet Union Today: An Interpretive Guide* (Chicago: Educational Foundation for Nuclear Science, 1983), p. 55.

10. Jean-Pierre Cot, "Winning East-West in North-South," *Foreign Policy,* no. 46 (Spring 1982): 3–18.

11. Jorge I. Dominguez, "U.S., Soviet, and Cuban Policies Toward Latin America," in Marshall D. Shulman, ed., *East-West Tensions in the Third World* (New York: W. W. Norton, 1986), pp. 44–77.

12. Said Amir Arjomand, "Iran's Islamic Revolution in Comparative Perspective," *Comparative Politics* 38, 3 (April 1986): 384–414; and Kathleen M. Christenson, "Myths About Palestinians," *Foreign Policy,* no. 66 (Spring 1987): 109–27.

13. Paul Bairoch, *The Economic Development of the Third World Since 1900* (Berkeley: University of California Press, 1975), p. 195.

14. Georges Lefebvre, *The Coming of the French Revolution* (Princeton: Princeton University Press, 1970), pp. xv–xvi.

15. Benjamin Ward, *The Ideal Worlds of Economics: Liberal, Radical, and Conservative Economic World Views* (New York: Basic Books, 1979), pp. 77–78.

16. Abraham F. Lowenthal, "Ronald Reagan and Latin America: Coping with Hegemony in Decline," in Kenneth A. Oye, Robert J. Lieber, and Donald Rothchild, eds., *Eagle Defiant: United States Foreign Policy in the 1980s* (Boston: Little, Brown, 1983), pp. 311–36.

17. For the record among the advanced industrial countries on some of these indexes, see Geoffrey Garett and Peter Lange, "Performance in a Hostile World: Economic Growth in Capitalist Democracies, 1974–1980," *World Politics* 38, 4 (July 1986): 517–45.

18. Stephan Haggard, "The Newly Industrializing Countries in the International System," *World Politics* 33, 2 (January 1986): 343–70; and Bela Belassa, *The Newly Industrializing Countries in the World Economy* (New York: Pergamon, 1981).

19. Sylvia Ann Hewlett, *The Cruel Dilemmas of Development: Twentieth Century Brazil* (New York: Basic Books, 1980), pp. 233–43.

20. See Robert W. Tucker, *The Inequality of Nations* (New York: Basic Books, 1977).

21. Richard E. Feinberg, "Reaganomics and the Third World," in Oye, Lieber, and Rothchild, *Eagle Defiant,* pp. 132–66.

22. David A. Lake, "Power and the Realist World: Towards a Realist Political Economy of North-South Relations," *International Studies Quarterly* 31, 2 (June 1987): 217–34.

23. Samuel P. Huntington, "Renewed Hostility," in Joseph S. Nye, Jr., ed., *The Making of America's Soviet Policy* (New Haven: Yale University Press, 1984), pp. 265–90.

24. Barry M. Blechman, Janne E. Nolan, and Alan Plan, "Pushing Arms," *Foreign Policy,* no. 46 (Spring 1982): 138–54.

25. Richard Rosecrance, *The Rise of the Trading State: Commerce and Conquest in the Modern World* (New York: Basic Books, 1986), pp. 119–33.

26. Roger Errera, "Democracies and Human Rights: The Heritage and the Challenge," *Atlantic Community Quarterly* 25, 2 (Summer 1987): 189–200, esp.

196–97; and John F. McCamant, "Social Science and Human Rights," *International Organization* 35, 3 (Summer 1981): 531–52, esp. 543–47.

27. Christopher H. Pyle, "Defining Terrorism," *Foreign Policy,* no. 64 (Fall 1986): 63–78.

28. Philip Windsor, "Terrorism and International Law," *Atlantic Community Quarterly* 25, 2 (Summer 1987): 201–9.

29. Stanley Hoffman, "Requiem," *Foreign Policy,* no. 42 (Spring 1981): 3–26, esp. 3–4.

30. Ole R. Holsti and James N. Rosenau, "Consensus Lost, Consensus Regained? Foreign Policy Beliefs of American Leaders, 1976–1980," *International Studies Quarterly* 30, 4 (December 1986): 375–410, esp. 407–8.

31. Stephen J. Solarz, "When To Intervene," *Foreign Policy,* no. 63 (Summer 1986): 20–39.

32. Bruce Russett and Elizabeth C. Hanson, *Interest and Ideology: The Foreign Policy Beliefs of American Businessmen* (San Francisco: W. H. Freeman, 1975); pp. 220–43.

33. Francis Fukuyama, "Military Aspects of U.S.-Soviet Competition in the Third World," in Shulman, *East-West Tensions,* pp. 181–211.

34. Janice Gross Stein, "Extended Deterrence in the Middle East: American Strategy Reconsidered," *World Politics* 39, 3 (April 1987): 326–52.

35. Robert M. Cutler, Laure Despres, and Aaron Karp, "The Political Economy of East-South Military Transfers," *International Studies Quarterly* 31, 3 (September 1987): 273–99, esp. 294–95.

36. Bruce R. Kuniholm, *The Origins of the Cold War in the Near East* (Princeton: Princeton University Press, 1980), pp. 383–431.

37. William R. Cline, "Resource Transfers to the Developing Countries: Issues and Trends," in William R. Cline, ed., *Policy Alternatives for a New International Economic Order: An Economic Analysis* (New York: Praeger, 1979).

38. Patrick J. McGowan and Dale L. Smith, "Economic Dependency in Black Africa: An Analysis of Competing Theories," *International Organization* 32, 1 (Winter 1978): 179–236.

39. Jorge Castaneda, "Latin America and the End of the Cold War," *World Policy Journal* (Summer 1990): 469–93.

40. Charles Maechling, Jr., "Washington's Illegal Invasion," *Foreign Policy,* no. 79 (Summer 1990): 113–31.

41. Robert A. Pastor, "Preempting Revolutions: The Boundaries of U.S. Influence," *International Security* 15, 4 (Spring 1991): 55.

42. H. W. Brands, Jr., "Decisions on American Armed Intervention: Lebanon, Dominican Republic, and Grenada," *Political Science Quarterly* 102, 4 (Winter 1987): 624.

■ CHAPTER 5:
ECONOMIC AND MILITARY AID

1. The figures used throughout this section, for regional distributions and program types, are in constant FY 1987 dollars. A detailed analysis of the changing priorities of the foreign assistance program is provided by Stanley Heginbotham, "Foreign Aid: The Evolution of U.S. Programs," Congressional Research Service Report no. 86–86 F, April 16, 1986.

2. Peter McPherson, "Security Benefits of Foreign Assistance to U.S." (Speech, U.S. AID, Washington, D.C., May 1984), p. 3.

3. *Commission on Security and Economic Assistance: A Report* (Washington, D.C.: Department of State, 1983), p. 3 (hereinafter, *Report*).

4. Ibid., p. 31.

5. Cited in James Bovard, "Free Food Bankrupts Foreign Farmers," *Wall Street Journal,* July 2, 1984, p. A18.

6. Sudhir Sen, "Farewell to Foreign Aid," *World View* 25, 7 (July 1982): 8.

7. Francis Moore Lappé, Joseph Collins, and David Kinley, *Aid as Obstacle: Twenty Questions about our Aid and the Hungry* (San Francisco: Institute for Food and Development Policy, 1981), pp. 95–96.

8. Ibid., p. 116.

9. Ibid., p. 118.

10. The reflexive response of many presidential panels and independent analysts to the problem of underdevelopment abroad is to propose another Marshall Plan—for Central America, the Philippines, or wherever. But the Marshall Plan's effect on Europe's recovery may have been less than has been traditionally assumed. See Tyler Cowen, "The Marshall Plan: Myths and Realities," in Doug Bandow, ed., *U.S. Aid to the Developing World: A Free Market Agenda* (Washington, D.C.: Heritage Foundation, 1985), pp. 61–74. In any case, Europe had developed and only needed to be "reconstructed," whereas Third World states lack the basic legal institutions and economic infrastructure necessary to prosper.

11. Development is more complex than just a rising GNP, but economic growth is one of the easiest surrogate variables to measure. Most important, it is usually the variable employed by U.S. policymakers.

12. Alan Rufus Waters, forthcoming Heritage Foundation Backgrounder, 1989.

13. Thomas Sowell, *The Economics and Politics of Race* (New York: William Morrow, 1983), p. 240.

14. Stephen Hellinger, Douglas Hellinger, and Fred M. O'Regan, *Aid for Just Development: Report on the Future of Foreign Assistance* (Boulder: Lynne Rienner Publishers, 1988), p. 5.

15. Ibid., pp. 30–31.

16. See, for example, Doug Bandow, "The U.S. Role in Promoting Third World Development," in Bandow, ed., *U.S. Aid to the Developing World,* pp. xviii–xvi; and James Bovard, "The Continuing Failure of Foreign Aid," Cato Institute Policy Analysis no. 65, January 31, 1986. This is not to suggest that no foreign aid program has ever worked. Creation and distribution of oral rehydration packets, for example, which treat victims of diarrhea, certainly have saved lives abroad. But even well-intended health programs suffer from a variety of problems, some of which are detailed in Carol Adelman et al., "A New Rx Is Needed for World Health Care," Heritage Foundation Backgrounder no. 592, July 9, 1987.

17. Karl Maier, "Zimbabwe Creates an 'Agricultural Miracle' in Africa—But Can the Continent's Newest Nation Survive It?" *Christian Science Monitor,* September 27, 1988, p. 14.

18. *Report,* p. 33.

19. For a generally excellent overview of the civil war and the role of the United States therein, see Brook Larmer's five-part series in the *Christian Science Monitor,* October 19–21, and October 24–25, 1988. The titles of the articles in order of date are "Backsliding to the Bad Old Days" (pp. 14–15); "The Shifting Battlefront" (pp. 16–17); "Papering over the Economic Divide" (pp. 16–17);

"The Politics of Polarization" (pp. 16–17); and "Hard Lessons for the U.S. and the Region" (pp. 14–15).

20. For a discussion of the agricultural program, see Bovard, "The Continuing Failure," pp. 6–8. Also see U.S. Agency for International Development (AID), *Agrarian Reform in El Salvador: A Report on Its Status,* Audit report no. 1-519-84-2 (Washington, D.C.: AID, 1988).

21. Larmer, "Backsliding," p. 15.

22. This is true despite the fact that, as noted earlier, enhancing the military's power in an undemocratic state is likely to increase repression. Moreover, to the extent that U. S. military aid encourages a country to devote more of its resources to defense, it is likely to grow more slowly economically. For example, one UN study found that higher military spending consistently lowered economic growth rates and that every additional dollar spent on military outlays cuts agricultural production twenty cents. Cited in Doug Bandow, "Aid That Just Buys Guns," *Wall Street Journal,* June 14, 1988, p. A34.

23. Ibid., pp. 32–33.

24. Stephen Kinzer, "U.S. Fails to Win Tough Statement Against Nicaragua," *New York Times,* August 2, 1988, p. 4.

25. Linda Feldmann, "Critics Charge US Policy Fuels Conflict in Somalia," *Christian Science Monitor,* August 10, 1988, p. 4.

26. U. S. Congress, Senate, Committee on Foreign Relations, *Report of the Senate Committee on Foreign Relations on S. 1274, No. 100-60,* 100th Cong., 1st Sess., May 22, 1987, pp. 143–66. Ironically, the Reagan administration has, however, used a country's UN voting record as one factor in determining the recommended level of aid.

■ CHAPTER 6: ECONOMIC SANCTIONS

1. The recent OAS embargo of Haiti, due to the recent application of sanctions, is not included in the statistics used throughout this chapter.

2. See Gary Clyde Hufbauer, Jeffrey J. Schott, and Kimberly Ann Elliott, *Economic Sanctions Reconsidered,* 2 vols., rev. (Washington, D.C.: Institute for International Economics, 1990).

3. Quoted in Stephen B. Cohen, "Conditioning U.S. Security Assistance on Human Rights Practices," *American Journal of International Law* 76 (April 1982): 265.

4. Ibid.

5. *Economic Sanctions Reconsidered,* vol. 2, pp. 336–39. See also Cohen, "Conditioning U.S. Security Assistance," pp. 246–79.

6. Although opposition to apartheid was a factor in the imposition of sanctions, this case is considered separately from the broader U.S./UN sanctions campaign against South Africa.

7. David A. Flores, "Export Controls and the U.S. Effort to Combat International Terrorism," *Law and Policy in International Business* 13 (1981): 550. See also *Economic Sanctions Reconsidered,* vol. 2, pp. 327–29.

8. Unlike David A. Baldwin's study, *Economic Statecraft: Theory and Practice* (Princeton: Princeton University Press, 1985), there was no attempt to assess the role of symbolism—for both domestic and international audiences—in the use or effectiveness of sanctions. Nor is there an appraisal of the usefulness of sanctions in deterring future "bad" behavior.

9. Some cases may have more than one objective, as shown in Table 6.1.

For purposes of the statistical analysis, however, such cases were classified only by the most difficult objective.

10. These results are very similar to those found in *Economic Sanctions Reconsidered*. Looking at all 116 cases, we found that sanctions contributed to a successful outcome in 52 percent of the destabilization cases, 33 percent of the modest-goal cases, a third of the military-disruption cases, and less than a quarter of other major cases.

11. Baldwin, *Economic Statecraft,* passim.

12. This does not contradict the earlier conclusion that modest goals will be relatively easier to achieve. If a modest objective is also very low priority, the political will to sustain and vigorously pursue it may be lacking, especially if it is relatively more important to the target country. A similar conclusion is reported by Albert E. Hirschman, *National Power and the Structure of Foreign Trade* (Berkeley: University of California Press, 1980).

■ CHAPTER 7: COVERT INTERVENTION

1. *Intelligence: The Acme of Skills* (Washington, D.C.: Office of Public Affairs, Central Intelligence Agency, 1982), p. 28.

2. *The CIA's Secret Operations* (New York: Reader's Digest Press, 1977), p. 13.

3. Quoted in U.S. Congress, Senate, Church Committee, Final Report, no. 94–755, vol. 4, 94th Cong., 2nd Sess., 1976, p. 53 (hereinafter, *Church Committee Report*).

4. Commission on CIA Activities Within the United States, Nelson Rockefeller, Chairman, *Report to the President* (Washington, D.C.: Government Printing Office, 1975), p. 5.

5. *Church Committee Report,* vol. 1, pp. 159–61.

6. See "The Pike Papers," *Village Voice,* February 16, 1976.

7. Harry Rositzke, "America's Secret Operations: A Perspective," *Foreign Affairs* 53, 2 (January 1975): 344–51.

8. Loch K. Johnson, *A Season of Inquiry: The Senate Intelligence Investigation* (Lexington: University Press of Kentucky, 1985), esp. chs. 22 and 23.

9. *The Iran-Contra Report* (Washington, D.C.: Government Printing Office, 1987). See also Bob Woodward, *Veil: The Secret Wars of the CIA, 1981–1987* (New York: Simon and Schuster, 1987).

10. *Church Committee Report,* vol. 1, passim.

11. U.S. Congress, Senate, Church Committee, "Alleged Assassination Plots Involving Foreign Leaders," *An Interim Report,* no. 94-465, 94th Cong., 1st Sess., 1975. See also Warren Hinckle and William W. Turner, *The Fish Is Red: The Story of the Secret War Against Castro* (New York: Harper and Row, 1981).

12. Kermit Roosevelt, *Countercoup: The Struggle for the Control of Iran* (New York: McGraw-Hill, 1979).

13. U.S. Congress, Senate, Church Committee, "Coven Action," *Hearings,* vol. 7, appendix A, "Covert Action in Chile, 1963–1973," 94th Cong., 1st Sess., 1975, pp. 144–209 (hereinafter, *Hearings*).

14. William Colby, *Honorable Men: My Life in the CIA* (New York: Simon and Schuster, 1978), p. 109.

15. Ibid.

16. Ibid., ch. 4. For a description of various episodes of election intervention, see William Blum, *The CIA: A Forgotten History* (London: Zed Books, 1987).

17. *Hearings,* p. 95.

18. Terrence Smith, "Secret CIA Propaganda Overseas" (three-part survey), *New York Times,* December 25–27, 1977.

19. In addition to Woodward, *Veil,* see also Jay Peterzell, *Reagan's Secret Wars* (Washington, D.C.: Center for National Security Studies, 1984); Thomas Powers, *The Man Who Kept the Secrets* (New York: Knopf, 1979); John Prados, *Presidents' Secret Wars: CIA and Pentagon Covert Operations Since World War II* (New York: William Morrow, 1986); John Ranelagh, *The Agency: The Rise and Decline of the CIA* (New York: Simon and Schuster, 1986); and Gregory F. Treverton, *Covert Action: The Limits of Intervention in the Postwar World* (New York: Basic Books, 1987).

20. Woodward, *Veil,* pp. 396–97.

21. The following five paragraphs are derived from Harry Howe Ransom, "The Intelligence Function and the Constitution," *Armed Forces and Society* 14, 1 (Fall 1987): 43–63.

22. See Stephen Engelberg, "C.I.A. Seeks Looser Rules on Killings During Coups," *New York Times,* October 8, 1989, p. A1.

23. Daniel Patrick Moynihan, "Assassinations: Can't We Learn?" *New York Times,* October 20, 1989, p. A27.

24. *New York Times,* December 22, 1991, p. A6.

25. David Ignatius, *The Washington Post National Weekly Edition,* October 6, 1991.

26. President's Special Review Board, John Tower, Chairman, *The Tower Commission Report* (New York: Bantam and Times Books, 1987), p. 63.

■ CHAPTER 8: PARAMILITARY INTERVENTION

1. Although most writers refer to the Guatemalan case as a coup d'état, it is treated in this chapter as a paramilitary intervention because it involved the use of an assembled exile invasion force, which later would serve as a model for future U.S. intervention in the Third World. For an overview of this case, see Richard H. Immerman, *The CIA in Guatemala: The Foreign Policy of Intervention* (Austin: University of Texas Press, 1982).

2. See Peter Wyden, *Bay of Pigs: The Untold Story* (New York: Simon and Schuster, 1979).

3. For a debate on this point, see John Ranelagh, *The Agency: The Rise and Decline of the CIA* (New York: Simon and Schuster, 1987), pp. 362–64.

4. Quoted in Ted Galen Carpenter, "The United States and Third World Dictatorships: A Case for Benign Detachment," Cato Institute Policy Analysis no. 58, August 15, 1985, p. 7.

5. For an overview of this case, see John Prados, *Presidents' Secret Wars: CIA and Pentagon Covert Operations Since World War II* (New York: William Morrow, 1986), pp. 128–48.

6. Prados, *Presidents' Secret Wars,* p. 161. The Tibetan campaign was part of an overall destabilization program of the PRC. For a more complete description, see ibid., pp. 61–78.

7. For a discussion of these two examples, consult Prados, *Presidents' Secret Wars,* pp. 239–60 (Vietnam) and pp. 261–96 (Laos).

8. For a brief discussion of this case, see William Blum, *The CIA: A Forgotten History* (London: Zed Books, 1987), pp. 275–78.

9. John Stockwell, *In Search of Enemies: A CIA Story* (New York: W. W. Norton, 1978), p. 68.

10. Wayne S. Smith, "A Trap in Angola," *Foreign Policy,* no. 62 (Spring 1986): 73.

11. The Reagan administration did not dogmatically follow ideological criteria, as it refused to support anticommunist guerrilla insurgencies in Ethiopia and Mozambique. For a sympathetic analysis of the Reagan Doctrine, see Jeane Kirkpatrick, *The Reagan Doctrine and U.S. Foreign Policy* (Washington, D.C.: Heritage Foundation, 1985). For a critical view, see Ted G. Carpenter, "U.S. Aid to Anti-Communist Rebels: The 'Reagan Doctrine' and Its Pitfalls," Cato Institute Policy Analysis no. 74, June 24, 1986.

12. Quoted in Carpenter, "U. S. Aid to Anti-Communist Rebels," p. 1.

13. For a good overview of early U.S. involvement, see Selig S. Harrison, "Afghanistan: Soviet Intervention, Afghan Resistance, and the American Role," in Michael T. Klare and Peter Kornbluh, eds., *Low-Intensity Warfare: Counterinsurgency, Proinsurgency, and Antiterrorism in the Eighties* (New York: Pantheon, 1988), pp. 183–206.

14. Thomas L. Friedman, "U.S. and Soviets to End Arms Sales to Afghan Rivals," *New York Times,* September 14, 1991, pp. A1, A4.

15. Quoted in Clifford Krauss, "Afghanistan: The Place Where the Cold War Didn't Go Out of Style," *Washington Post,* February 17, 1991, sec. 4, p. 4.

16. For example, see Edward Giardet, "U.S. Afghan Policy: Mired in Success," *Christian Science Monitor,* July 12, 1988, pp. 7, 9.

17. See Edward A. Gargan, "In a Despairing Afghanistan, There Is Caviar for the Few," *New York Times,* September 24, 1991, p. A9.

18. Quoted in Barbara Crossette, "Pact Clears Way for Kabul Shift: Deadline for Ending Military Aid to Afghan Rivals Met by U.S. and Moscow," *New York Times,* January 2, 1992, p. A4.

19. Ibid.

20. Ibid.

21. Ibid.

22. Giardet, "U.S. Afghan Policy."

23. Stephen Van Evera, "American Intervention in the Third World: Less Would Be Better," in Charles W. Kegley, Jr. and Eugene R. Wittkopf, eds., *The Future of American Foreign Policy* (New York: St. Martin's, 1992), pp. 285–300.

24. "3 Cambodian Factions Sign a UN-Enforced Peace Pact; Khmer Rouge Shares Rule," *New York Times,* October 24, 1991, pp. A1, A6.

25. Alan Riding, "350,000 to Return: Vietnam, China, Soviets and U.S. Broker End to a Nightmare," *New York Times,* October 24, 1991, pp. A1, A6.

26. Confidential interview, January 10, 1992.

27. Quoted in Philip Shenon, "Khmer Rouge Said to Conceal a Future Force," *New York Times,* November 11, 1991, p. A1.

28. Ibid., p. A5.

29. Philip Shenon, "A Khmer Rouge Suffers Beating By Cambodians," *New York Times,* November 28, 1991, p. A1.

30. Philip Shenon, "In a Surprise, Cambodia Appoints Sihanouk as the President," *New York Times,* November 21, 1991, p. A4.

31. See Andrew Meldrum, "At War with South Africa," *Africa Report* 32, 1 (January–February 1987): 28.

32. For text of the accords, see *New York Times,* December 23, 1988, p. A5. See also James Brooke, "Accord for a 2-Year Angola Pullout Reported," *New York Times,* September 30, 1988, p. A6.

33. See, for example, Paul Lewis, "With Angry Exchanges, Accords Are Signed on Angola," *New York Times,* December 23, 1988, p. A5.

34. See Clifford Krauss, "U.S. and Soviets Offer to Oversee a Truce and Vote in Angola," *New York Times,* October 2, 1990, p. A5.

35. Alan Riding, "Angola and Rebels Sign Pact Ending 16-Year War," *New York Times,* June 1, 1991, p. A2.

36. "Angola's Old Foes Struggle to Unite: Effort to Forge a Single Army Is Slowed by Aid Problem," *New York Times,* December 16, 1991, p. A4.

37. Quoted in Riding, "Angola and Rebels Sign Pact."

38. Christopher S. Wren, "Ex-Rebel Leader Returns to Luanda," *New York Times,* September 30, 1991, p. A3.

39. Smith, "A Trap in Angola," p. 64; John D. Battersby, "South Africa's Foreign Minister Sees Talks at a Critical Junction," *New York Times,* July 7, 1988, p. A8; and John D. Battersby, "South Africa Agrees to Peace Accord," *New York Times,* November 23, 1988, p. A5.

40. Forrest D. Colburn, "Embattled Nicaragua," *Current History* 86, 524 (December 1987): 406. See also Stephen Kinzer, "Sandinista Says Colonel's Election Shows Contras' True Character," *New York Times,* July 22, 1988, p. A3.

41. Van Evera, "American Intervention in the Third World," pp. 291–2.

■ CHAPTER 9: DIRECT MILITARY INTERVENTION

1. For an examination of the militarization of the drug war in Latin America, see Ted Galen Carpenter and R. Channing Rouse, "Perilous Panacea: The Military in the Drug War," Cato Institute Policy Analysis no. 128, February 15, 1990. The use of the drug war as a cover for U.S. military assistance to "friendly" regimes that are confronting left-wing insurgencies is discussed in Jonathan Marshall, *Drug Wars: Corruption, Counterinsurgency, and Covert Operations in the Third World* (San Francisco: Cohan and Cohen, 1991).

2. For examples of this reasoning, see Lyndon B. Johnson, *The Vantage Point: Perspectives on the Presidency, 1963–1969* (New York: Holt, Rinehart, and Winston, 1971), pp. 232–69, 422–24, 528–31; and Richard M. Nixon, *No More Vietnams* (New York: Arbor House, 1985), passim.

3. For critiques of the president's hyperbole, see Ted Galen Carpenter, "Bush Jumped the Gun in the Gulf," *New York Times,* August 18, 1990; Christopher Layne and Ted Galen Carpenter, "Arabian Nightmares: Washington's Persian Gulf Entanglement," Cato Institute Policy Analysis no. 142, November 9, 1990; and Christopher Layne, "Why the Gulf War Was Not in the National Interest," *Atlantic Monthly* (July 1991): 54, 65–81.

4. Arthur M. Schlesinger, Jr., *The Imperial Presidency* (Boston: Houghton Mifflin, 1973), pp. 127–208; and Ted Galen Carpenter, "Global Interventionism and a New Imperial Presidency," Cato Institute Policy Analysis no. 71, May 6, 1986.

5. Doug Bandow, "The Persian Gulf: Restoring the Congressional War Power," in Ted Galen Carpenter, ed., *America Entangled: The Persian Gulf Crisis and Its Consequences* (Washington: Cato Institute, 1991), pp. 97–104.

6. Walter LaFeber, *Inevitable Revolutions: The United States in Central America* (New York: W. W. Norton, 1984), pp. 34–69; and Dana G. Munro,

Intervention and Dollar Diplomacy in the Caribbean 1900–1921 (Princeton: Princeton University Press, 1964), passim.

7. For discussions of the domestic debate surrounding the advent of explicit U.S. imperialism, see Robert L. Beisner, *Twelve Against Empire: The Anti-Imperialists, 1898–1900* (Chicago: University of Chicago Press, 1968); and Walter Karp, *The Politics of War* (New York: Harper and Row, 1979), pp. 3–116.

8. *New York Times,* November 29, 1984, p. A5.

9. Carpenter, "Global Interventionism," pp. 6–7.

10. "Memorandum: Meeting at Blair House, July 3, 1950," Dean Acheson Papers, box 65, Harry S Truman Library.

11. For an example of Truman's awareness of the subterfuge, see Joseph C. Goulden, *Korea: The Untold Story of the War* (New York: McGraw-Hill, 1982), pp. 105–6.

12. Callum MacDonald, *Korea: The War Before Vietnam* (New York: Free Press, 1986), pp. 13–14, 41, 60.

13. Stephen E. Ambrose, *Eisenhower: The President* (New York: Simon and Schuster, 1984), p. 466.

14. For Eisenhower's statements and message to Congress on July 15, 1958, see "United States Dispatches Troops to Lebanon," *Department of State Bulletin* 39, 997 (August 1958): 181–86.

15. Ambrose, *Eisenhower,* p. 465.

16. Johnson, *The Vantage Point,* p. 202.

17. Stephen E. Ambrose, *Rise to Globalism,* 4th rev. ed. (New York: Penguin, 1985), p. 220.

18. Discussions of the motives for the U.S. intervention include Abraham F. Lowenthal, *The Dominican Intervention* (Cambridge: Harvard University Press, 1972); and Jerome N. Slater, *Intervention and Negotiation: The United States and the Dominican Revolution* (New York: Harper and Row, 1970).

19. See the November 4, 1983, speech by State Department spokesman Kenneth Dam, reprinted in Hugh O'Shaughnessy, *Grenada* (New York: Dodd and Mead, 1984), pp. 246–54.

20. Jonathan Kwitny, *Endless Enemies: The Making of an Unfriendly World* (New York: Congdon and Weed, 1984), pp. 410–11; O'Shaughnessy, *Grenada,* pp. 150–51.

21. See David J. Scheffer, "Use of Force After the Cold War: Panama, Iraq, and the New World Order," in Louis Henkin, et al., *Right v. Might: International Law and the Use of Force,* 2d ed. (New York: Council on Foreign Relations Press, 1991): 109–172.

22. Ted Galen Carpenter, "Panama Smacks of Search for a New U.S. Enemy," *Army Times,* January 15, 1990. The removal of the Noriega regime appears to have had little lasting effect on Panama's role in the drug trade. See Michael Isikoff, "Drug Activity in Panama Has Increased, GAO Says," *Washington Post,* July 23, 1991, p. A3.

23. Schlesinger, *The Imperial Presidency,* pp. 177–96. For an example of similar State Department views on the scope of presidential power, see Leonard C. Meeker, "The Legality of United States Participation in the Defense of Vietnam," *Department of State Bulletin* 54, 1396 (March 1966): 484–85.

24. Quoted in "Tough Duty," *New Republic,* December 10, 1990. For critiques of the various justifications offered by the administration and its political allies, see Layne and Carpenter, "Arabian Nightmares"; and Layne, "Why the Gulf War Was Not in the National Interest."

25. Some perceptive observers questioned the alleged military prowess of Iraqi forces long before the war erupted in January 1991. See, for example, Tom Marks, "Iraq's Not-So-Tough Army," *Wall Street Journal,* August 21, 1991, p. A14. Marks was an analyst who had studied Iraq's military for U.S. intelligence agencies.

26. Clifford Krauss, "Dependence and Sovereignty Pull at Panama's Equilibrium," *New York Times,* February 11, 1991, p. A1.

27. For an example of two "experts" who egregiously failed to understand the consequences of Washington's tilt toward Baghdad during the Iran-Iraq War, see Daniel Pipes and Laurie Mylroie, "Back Iraq," *New Republic,* April 27, 1987, pp. 14–15. Pipes and Mylroie asserted that the defeat of Iraq would "endanger the supply of oil, threaten pro-American regimes throughout the area and upset the Arab-Israeli balance." Three and a half years later, they used virtually identical arguments to justify going to war against Iraq.

28. The preeminent example of that thinking can be found in Charles Krauthammer, "The Unipolar Moment," *Foreign Affairs* 70 (America and the World 1990–91): 23–33. For a critique of Krauthammer's thesis and other aspects of the new world order, see Ted Galen Carpenter, "The New World Disorder," *Foreign Policy* 84 (Fall 1991): 24–39.

■ CHAPTER 10: THE DOMESTIC ENVIRONMENT

1. See Eric F. Goldman, *The Crucial Decade—and After: America, 1945– 1960* (New York: Random House, 1961); Richard A. Melanson, *Writing History and Making Policy: The Cold War, Vietnam, and Revisionism* (Lanham, Md.: University Press of America, 1983); and Daniel Yergin, *Shattered Peace: The Origins of the Cold War and the National Security State* (New York: Houghton Mifflin, 1978).

2. See Robert Griffith, *The Politics of Fear: Joseph R. McCarthy and the Senate* (NewYork: Hayden, 1970); William Manchester, *The Glory and the Dream: A Narrative History of America, 1933–1972* (New York: Wiley, 1972); and Richard H. Rovere, *Senator Joe McCarthy* (New York: World Publishing, 1970).

3. See Godfrey Hodgson, *America in Our Time* (New York: Vintage, 1976).

4. See Hodgson, *America in Our Time;* Richard E. Neustadt, *Presidential Power: The Politics of Leadership* (New York: Wiley, 1976); and Arthur Schlesinger, Jr., *The Imperial Presidency* (Boston: Houghton Mifflin, 1973).

5. See James A. Nathan and James K. Oliver, *Foreign Policy Making and the American Political System* (Boston: Little, Brown, 1987); and Jerel A. Rosati, *The Politics of United States Foreign Policy* (Dallas, Tex.: Harcourt Brace Jovanovich, forthcoming 1993).

6. See Rosati, *The Politics of United States Foreign Policy.*

7. See Richard Barnet, *Roots of War: The Men and Institutions Behind U.S. Foreign Policy* (Baltimore: Penguin, 1972); David Halberstam, *The Best and the Brightest* (New York: Random House, 1971); Godfrey Hodgson, "The Foreign Policy Establishment," *Foreign Policy,* no. 10 (Spring 1973): 3–40; and Walter Isaacson and Evan Thomas, *The Wise Men: Six Friends and the World They Made* (New York: Simon and Schuster, 1986).

8. See Barnet, *Roots of War;* Hodgson, *America in Our Time;* Fred Kaplan, *The Wizards of Armageddon* (New York: Touchstone, 1983); and Nick Kotz, *Wild Blue Yonder and the B-1 Bomber* (Princeton, N.J.: Princeton University Press, 1988).

9. See Leslie H. Gelb with Richard K. Betts, *The Irony of Vietnam: The System Worked* (Washington, D.C.: Brookings, 1979).

10. See Loren Baritz, *Backfire: A History of How American Culture Led Us into Vietnam and Made Us Fight the Way We Did* (NewYork: Morrow, 1985); Hodgson, *America in Our Time*; and Tamil R. Davis and Sean M. Lynn-Jones, "City upon a Hill," *Foreign Policy,* no. 66 (Spring 1987): 3–19.

11. See Todd Gitlin, *The Sixties: Years of Hope, Days of Rage* (New York: Bantam, 1988); Hodgson, *America in Our Time*; and Rosati, *The Politics of United States Foreign Policy.*

12. See I. M. Destler, Leslie H. Gelb, and Anthony Lake, *Our Own Worst Enemy: The Unmaking of American Foreign Policy* (New York: Simon and Schuster, 1984); Ole R. Holsti and James N. Rosenau, *American Leadership in World Affairs: Vietnam and the Breakdown of Consensus* (Boston: Allen and Unwin, 1984); Jerel A. Rosati and John Creed, "Extending the Three-Headed and Four-Headed Eagles: Elite Beliefs in U.S. Foreign Policy," paper presented at the annual meeting of the International Studies Association, Atlanta, 1992; and William Schneider, "Public Opinion," in Joseph S. Nye, Jr., ed., *The Making of America's Soviet Policy* (New Haven: Yale University Press, 1984), pp. 11–35.

13. See Rosati, *The Politics of United States Foreign Policy.*

14. See Thomas M. Franck and Edward Weisband, *Foreign Policy by Congress* (New York: Oxford University Press, 1979); Thomas Mann, ed., *A Question of Balance: The President, the Congress, and Foreign Policy* (Washington, D.C.: Brookings, 1990); Jerel A. Rosati, "Congressional Influence in American Foreign Policy: Addressing the Controversy," *Journal of Political and Military Sociology* 12 (Fall 1984): 311–33; and Schlesinger, *The Imperial Presidency.*

15. See Doris A. Graber, *Mass Media and American Politics* (Washington, D.C.: Congressional Quarterly Press, 1984); and Daniel C. Hallin, *The Uncensored War: The Media and Vietnam* (Berkeley: University of California Press, 1986).

16. See Destler, Gelb, and Lake, *Our Own Worst Enemy;* and Nathan and Oliver, *Foreign Policy Making.*

17. Holsti and Rosenau, *American Leadership in World Affairs,* p. 1.

18. See Rosati, *The Politics of United States Foreign Policy.*

19. See, for example, Morton H. Halperin and Jeanne M. Woods, "Ending the Cold War at Home," *Foreign Policy,* no. 81 (Winter 1990–91): 128–43.

■ **CHAPTER 11: GOVERNMENT AND THE MILITARY ESTABLISHMENT**

1. Caspar W. Weinberger, "The Uses of Military Power," Remarks prepared for delivery to the National Press Club, Washington, D.C., November 28, 1984.

2. Weinberger's speech may be read as almost a summary of conclusions of official military summaries of the lessons of Vietnam. See Colonel Harry Summers, *On Strategy: A Critical Analysis of the Vietnam War* (New York: Dell Publishing, 1982). This work is the result of Summers' study of the war for the U.S. Army War College and was reviewed by senior army officers and other officials.

3. George Shultz, "The Ethics of Power," Address at Yeshiva University, New York, December 9, 1984.

4. Weinberger, "The Uses of Military Power."

5. Morton H. Halperin, *Bureaucratic Politics and Foreign Policy* (Washington, D.C.: Brookings, 1974), pp. 60–61.

6. Ibid.

7. Bob Woodward, *The Commanders* (New York: Simon and Schuster, 1991).

8. Melvin R. Laird, "A Strong Start in a Difficult Decade: Defense Policy in the Nixon-Ford Years," *International Security* 10, 2 (Fall 1985): 16.

9. Pat Towell, "Reagan Defense Plan Stresses Deterring the 'Soviet Threat,'" *Congressional Quarterly Weekly Report,* April 10, 1982, pp. 795–96.

10. Quoted in Michael R. Gordon, "John Lehman: The Hard Liner Behind Reagan's Navy Buildup," *National Journal,* October 3, 1981, p. 1765. For a discussion, see John J. Mearsheimer, "A Strategic Misstep: The Maritime Strategy and Deterrence in Europe," *International Security* 11, 2 (Fall 1986): 3–57.

11. Eliot A. Cohen, "Constraints on America's Conduct of Small Wars," *International Security* 9, 2 (Fall 1984): 165.

12. Lt. Col. A. J. Bacevich, Lt. Col. James D. Hallums, Lt. Col. Richard H. White, and Lt. Col. Thomas F. Young (all U.S. Army), "American Military Policy in Small Wars: The Case of El Salvador," Paper presented at the John F. Kennedy School of Government, Harvard University, March 22, 1988, p. 22.

13. Ibid., pp. 14–15.

14. Ibid., p. 15.

15. Ibid., pp. 57–58.

16. Ibid., p. 56.

17. Ibid., pp. 29–30.

18. Ibid., pp. 67–68.

19. Ibid., pp. 69–70.

20. Ibid., p. 84. For a discussion, see pp. 79–84.

21. See Morton H. Halperin and David Halperin, "The Key West Key," *Foreign Policy,* no. 53 (Winter 1983–84): 124.

22. For a further discussion that emphasizes this point, see U. S. Congress, Senate, *Defense Organization: The Need for Change,* Staff Report to the Committee on Armed Services, 99th Cong., 1st Sess, October 16, 1985, p. 362.

23. Steven Smith, "Policy Preferences and Bureaucratic Positions: The Case of the American Hostage Rescue Mission," in David C. Kozak and James M. Keagle, eds., *Bureaucratic Politics and National Security: Theory and Practice* (Boulder, Colo.: Lynne Rienner, 1988), p. 137.

24. *Defense Organization,* p. 364.

25. This discussion draws heavily on ibid., pp. 363–68.

26. Edward Luttwak, *The Pentagon and the Art of War* (New York: Simon and Schuster, 1985), pp. 55–57.

27. Halperin, *Bureaucratic Politics,* p. 28.

28. *Defense Organization,* pp. 368–70.

29. J. William Fulbright and Seth P. Tillman, "Schultz-Weinberger Nondifferences," *New York Times,* December 9, 1984, p. E21.

■ CHAPTER 12: THE STRUCTURE OF THE INTERNATIONAL SYSTEM

1. Isaac Deutscher, *What Next?* (New York: Oxford University Press, 1953), pp. 96–112.

2. Bernard B. Fall, ed., *Ho Chi Minh on Revolution: Selected Writings, 1920–1966* (New York: Praeger, 1967), p. 5. Ho's writings stress atrocities that robbed the Vietnamese of their humanity rather than abstract ideology. See esp. pp. 3–47.

3. The 1,500-year-long struggle against Chinese domination ended in 1287 when the Vietnamese routed 300,000 Mongol troops. In 1954, General Vo Nguyen Giap evoked the memory of this battle when he defeated the French at Dienbienphu. Communism was of secondary importance. Stanley Karnow, *Vietnam: A History* (New York: Viking, 1983), ch. 3.

4. Thich Nhat Hanh, *Vietnam: Lotus in a Sea of Fire* (New York: Hill and Wang, 1967), p. 71.

5. John Mecklin, *Mission in Torment: An Intimate Account of the U.S. Role in Vietnam* (Garden City, N.Y.: Doubleday, 1965), pp. 36, 77.

6. Bruno Knoebl, *Victor Charlie: The Face of the War in Vietnam* (New York: Praeger, 1967), pp. 126, 114.

7. John Hellmann, *American Myth and the Legacy of Vietnam* (New York: Columbia University Press, 1986), p. 221.

8. John Osborne, "The Tough Miracle Man of Vietnam: Diem, America's Newly Arrived Visitor, Has Roused His Country and Routed the Reds," *Life,* May 13, 1957, pp. 156–176.

9. Bernard B. Fall, *Last Reflections on a War* (Garden City, N.Y.: Doubleday, 1967), p. 167.

10. Frances FitzGerald, *Fire in the Lake: The Vietnamese and the Americans in Vietnam* (Boston: Little, Brown, 1972).

11. Tanya Matthews, *War in Algeria: Background for Crisis* (New York: Fordham University Press, 1961), p. 20. Official French figures put Algerian fatalities of May 1945 at 1,165 ; the official Algerian figure is 45,000; the U. S. OSS estimates 6,000. See OSS, "Moslem Uprisings in Algeria, May 1945," *OSS Research and Analysis Report,* no. 3135, May 30, 1945, National Archives, Washington, D.C.

12. Dean Acheson, *Present at the Creation: My Years in the State Department* (New York: W. W. Norton, 1969), p. 302.

13. Robert P. Newman, "The Self-Inflicted Wound: The China White Paper of 1949," *Prologue* (Fall 1982): 141–56.

14. Among the European allies, only British Prime Minister Margaret Thatcher supported the raid on Libya, largely because of the "Falkland factor," the recognition that Britain could not have won the war against Argentina without U.S. Logistic support. Joseph Lelyveld, "Intense Talks Led to Thatcher Ruling," *New York Times,* April 16, 1986, p. A14.

15. N. J. Dawood, *The Koran,* 4th ed. (New York: Penguin, 1974), Surah 28: 5, p. 75.

16. "Ganging up on Uncle Sam," *The Economist,* July 16, 1988, pp. 36–37.

17. Charles Krauthammer, "The Unipolar Moment," *Foreign Affairs,* vol. 70, no. 1 (1991), pp. 23–24.

18. The leading economic powers in the EC are Germany, France, Italy, and the United Kingdom. Other members are Denmark, Ireland, the Netherlands, Belgium, Luxembourg, Portugal, Spain, and Greece. The population of the unified German state is 84 million; in 1988 and 1989, West Germany was the world's leading exporting country.

19. Hagen Schulze, *Die Wiederkehr Europas* (Berlin: Wolf Jobst Siedler, 1990), p. 7.

20. German aid also amounted to 56 percent of all Western assistance to the

Soviet Union; *The Week in Germany: A Weekly Publication of the German Information Center,* September 13, 1991, p. 2.

21. See Michael T. Klare, "The Arms Trade: Changing Patterns in the 1980s," *Third World Quarterly* 9, 4 (October 1987): 1257–81.

22. Ibid., pp. 1278–79.

23. George Thayer, *The War Business: The International Trade in Armaments* (New York: Simon and Schuster, 1969), pp. 340, 138–41.

24. Stalin told Yugoslav Vice President Milovan Djilas: "Do you think . . . the United States, the most powerful state in the world, will permit you to break their lines of communication in the Mediterranean Sea?" Quoted in Milovan Djilas, *Conversations with Stalin* (New York: Harcourt, Brace, and World, 1962), pp. 181–82.

25. CIA special estimate, advance copy for National Security Council, March 10, 1953, "Probable Consequences of the Death of Stalin and the Elevation of Malenkov to Leadership in the USSR," p. 4, in Paul Kesaris, ed., *CIA Research Reports: The Soviet Union, 1946–1976* (Frederick, Md.: University Publications of America, 1982), reel II, frames 637–48.

26. See Uri Ra'anan, *The USSR Arms the Third World: Case Studies in Soviet Foreign Policy* (Cambridge: Massachusetts Institute of Technology Press, 1969).

27. Kenneth A. Oye, "Constrained Confidence and the Evolution of Reagan Foreign Policy," in Kenneth Oye, Robert J. Lieber, and Donald Rothchild, eds., *Eagle Resurgent? The Reagan Era in American Foreign Policy* (Boston: Little, Brown, 1987), pp. 10–11.

28. Ibid., pp. 5–8.

■ CHAPTER 13: INTERNATIONAL LAW

1. See R. J. Vincent, *Nonintervention and International Order* (Princeton: Princeton University Press, 1974).

2. See Derick W. Bowett, "The Interrelation of Theories of Intervention and Self-Defense," in John Norton Moore, ed., *Law and Civil War in the Modern World* (Baltimore: Johns Hopkins University Press, 1974), pp. 38–50; and J. L. Brierly, *The Law of Nations,* 6th ed., edited by Sir Humphrey Waldock (London: Oxford University Press, 1963), p. 402.

3. Covenant of the League of Nations (Treaty of Versailles, Part 1, Articles 1–26), done June 28, 1919, Great Britain Treaty Series No. 4 (Command No. 153).

4. Done February 20, 1928, 46 Statutes 2749, United States Treaty Series No. 814, 134 League of Nations Treaty Series 45.

5. Done December 26, 1933, 49 Statutes 3097, United States Treaty Series No. 881, 165 League of Nations Treaty Series 19.

6. Done December 23, 1936, 51 Statutes 41, United States Treaty Series No. 923, 188 League of Nations Treaty Series 31 (amending the Convention on Rights and Duties of States in note 5 supra).

7. Done December 23, 1936, 51 Statutes 116, United States Treaty Series No. 926, League of Nations Treaty Series No. 4548.

8. Done October 10, 1933, 49 Statutes 3363, United States Treaty Series No. 906, League of Nations Treaty Series No. 3781.

9. Done at San Francisco, June 26, 1945, 59 Statutes 1031, United States Treaty Series No. 933, 3 Bevans 1153.

10. Done September 2, 1947, 62 Statutes 1681, Treaties and Other International Acts Series No. 1838, 21 United Nations Treaty Series 77.

11. Done April 30, 1948, 2 United States Treaties 2394, Treaties and Other International Acts Series No. 2361, 119 United Nations Treaty Series 3, as amended by Protocol of Buenos Aires, February 27, 1967, 21 United States Treaties 607, Treaties and Other International Acts Series No. 6847, 789 United Nations Treaty Series 287, at Article 18.

12. Ibid., Article 20.

13. General Assembly Resolution 2131, 20 United Nations General Assembly Official Records, Supplement No. 14, p. 11, United Nations Doc. A/6014 (1966).

14. General Assembly Resolution 2625, 25 General Assembly Official Records, Supplement No. 28, p. 121, United Nations Doc. A/8028 (1971).

15. See the works contained in Moore, *Law and Civil War,* and Marjorie M. Whiteman, *Digest of International Law,* vol. 5 (Washington, D.C.: Government Printing Office, 1965), pp. 250–57, 276–81, 522–34.

16. See Roger Clark, "Humanitarian Intervention: Help to Your Friends and State Practice," *Georgia Journal of International and Comparative Law* 13 (1983): 211–13.

17. See L. F. L. Oppenheim, *International Law: A Treatise,* vol. 1, *Peace,* 8th ed., edited by Hersch Lauterpacht (London: Longmans, 1955), pp. 298–99.

18. Compare the views of Myres McDougal, "The Soviet-Cuban Quarantine and Self-Defense," *American Journal of International Law* 57 (1963): 597–600; and Ian Brownlie, "The Use of Force in Self-Defense," *British Year Book of International Law* 37 (1962): 266–89.

19. Oppenheim, *International Law,* pp. 310, 319–20; and Whiteman, *Digest of International Law,* pp. 1080–87.

20. See Ian Brownlie, *International Law and the Use of Force by States* (Oxford: Clarendon, 1963), pp. 321–27.

21. Oppenheim, *International Law,* pp. 307–10; and Brownlie, *International Law,* pp. 318–320.

22. Gerhard von Glahn, *Law Among Nations: An Introduction to Public International Law,* 6th ed. (New York: Macmillan, 1992), pp. 165–66.

23. The text of the Monroe Doctrine is reprinted as "Monroe's Seventh Annual Message to Congress," in James D. Richardson, ed., *A Compilation of the Messages and Papers of the Presidents, 1789–1897,* vol. 2 (Washington, D.C.: Government Printing Office, 1896), pp. 207–20.

24. Donald M. Dozer, ed., *The Monroe Doctrine: Its Modern Significance* (New York: Knopf, 1965), p. 4.

25. John Gerassi, *The Great Fear in Latin America* (New York: Collier Books, 1965), p. 231.

26. For elaboration, see Abraham F. Lowenthal, *The Dominican Intervention* (Cambridge: Harvard University Press, 1972).

27. "State of the Union Address," *Washington Post,* February 7, 1985, p. A16.

28. An articulate view of self-defense as a justification for U.S. actions in Nicaragua is John Norton Moore, "The Secret War in Central America and the Future of World Order," *American Journal of International Law* 80 (1986): 43–127. For my view, see Christopher C. Joyner and Michael A. Grimaldi, "The United States and Nicaragua: Reflections on the Lawfulness of Contemporary Intervention," *Virginia Journal of International Law* 25 (1985): 621–89.

29. The U.S. invasion of Grenada stands as a recent example of this predominant unilateral proclivity. See Christopher C. Joyner, "The United States

Action in Grenada: Reflections on the Lawfulness of Invasion," *American Journal of International Law* 78 (1984): 131–44. For the Reagan administration's legal view, see John Norton Moore, "Grenada and the International Double Standard," in ibid., pp. 145–68.

30. "Statement by Press Secretary Fitzwater on United States Military Action in Panama," *Weekly Compilation of Presidential Documents* 25, December 25, 1989, p. 1975.

31. *Congressional Record,* S12, January 23, 1990 (address by Senator Kennedy).

32. Agreed to September 7, 1977, United States–Panama, 33 Statutes 39, Treaties and Other International Acts Series No. 10030.

33. Agreed to September 7, 1977, United States–Panama, 33 Statutes 1, Treaties and Other International Acts Series No. 10029.

34. Panama Canal Treaty, Article IV.

35. See "Panama–United States: The Panama Canal Treaties and Related Documents," reprinted in *International Legal Materials* 16 (1977), pp. 1021–98.

36. Security Council Resolution 660, August 2, 1990, U.N. Doc. S/RES/660 (1990).

37. Security Council Resolution 678, November 29, 1990, U.N. Doc. S/RES/678 (1990).

38. For discussion, see Christopher C. Joyner, "Sanctions, Compliance and International Law: Reflections on the United Nations' Experience against Iraq," *Virginia Journal of International Law* 32 (Fall 1991), pp. 1–46.

39. For elaboration, see Christopher C. Joyner, "The Reality and Relevance of International Law," in Charles Kegley and Eugene Wittkopf, eds., *The Global Agenda,* 3rd ed. (New York: McGraw-Hill, 1992), pp. 202–15.

■ CHAPTER 14: SOUTH AFRICA

1. Sam C. Nolutshungu, "South African Policy and United States Options in Southern Africa," in Gerald J. Bender, James S. Coleman, and Richard L. Sklar, eds., *African Crisis Areas and U.S. Foreign Policy* (Berkeley: University of California Press, 1985), p. 56.

2. For discussion, see Thomas J. Noer, *Cold War and Black Liberation: The United States and White Rule in Africa, 1948–1968* (Columbia: University of Missouri Press, 1985), pp. 38–40.

3. Assessment of the JCS on November 15, 1950, as quoted in Kevin Danaher, *The Political Economy of U.S. Policy Toward South Africa* (Boulder and London: Westview, 1985), p. 68.

4. JCS, "Memorandum for the Secretary of Defense, Subject: Fighter Planes for South Africa," December 11, 1956. Quoted in Danaher, *The Political Economy,* p. 69.

5. Interview quoted in Danaher, *The Political Economy,* p. 68.

6. CIA Memorandum, "The Political Situation in the Union of South Africa," January 31, 1949, President's Secretary's Files, box 256, Truman Library. Quoted in Noer, *Cold War,* pp. 24–25.

7. For discussion, see Danaher, *The Political Economy,* p. 68. See also U.S. House, Committee on Foreign Affairs, Subcommittee on Africa, *U.S. Business Involvement in Southern Africa* (Part II) (Hearings, May–December 1971), 92d Cong., 1st Sess., Washington, D.C.: GPO, pp. 40–76.

8. African political organizations outlawed included the African National Congress and the Pan Africanist Congress.

9. For a full discussion of NSSM 39, see Mohamed A. el-Khawas and Barry Cohen, eds., *The Kissinger Study of Southern Africa: National Security Study Memorandum 39* (Nottingham: Spokesman Books, 1975).

10. Kevin Danaher, *In Whose Interest?* (Washington, D.C.: Institute for Policy Studies, 1984), p. 79.

11. Nolutshungu, "South African Policy," p. 57.

12. Henry F. Jackson, *From the Congo to Soweto: U.S. Foreign Policy Toward Africa Since 1960* (New York: Quill, 1984), pp. 157–58.

13. Chester A. Crocker, "South Africa: Strategy for Change," *Foreign Affairs* 59, 2 (1980–81): 324–25.

14. For further discussion, see Gwendolen M. Carter, *Continuity and Change in Southern Africa* (Los Angeles: Crossroads, 1985), p. 35.

15. For an overview of the early stages of the political violence, see U.S. House, Committee on Foreign Affairs, Subcommittee on Africa, *The Current Crisis in South Africa* (Hearing, December 4, 1984), 98th Cong., 2nd Sess., Washington, D.C.: GPO, 1985.

16. Quoted in U.S. House, Committee on Foreign Relations, Subcommittee on Africa, *U.S. Policy on South Africa* (Hearing, September 26, 1984), 98th Cong., 2nd Sess., Washington, D.C.: GPO, 1985, p. 9.

17. Ibid., p. 27.

18. "Sanctions: The Time Has Come!" *The Washington Notes on Africa* (Summer 1985).

19. A more comprehensive sanctions bill was proposed by Representative Dellums. Dellums unsuccessfully sought to attach an amendment to HR-1460 that would have banned all U.S. trade with and mandated complete corporate divestment from South Africa. This amendment failed by a vote of 340–80.

20. Two other sanctions bills introduced into the Senate were S–1235 and S–1020. Introduced by Senators Edward Kennedy (D-MA) and Lowell Weicker (R-CT), S–1235 was the Senate equivalent of HR–1460. Introduced by Senators William Roth (R-DE) and Mitchell McConnell (R-KY), S–1020 included provisions that were amended onto S–995 (ban on bank loans to South Africa and restrictions on the export of computer and nuclear products to South Africa).

21. For a copy of this order and the president's remarks prior to its signing, see "South Africa: Presidential Actions," *Department of State Bulletin* 85, 2103 (October 1985): 1–8.

22. The final bill reflected adoption of the Dellums amendment that had been defeated in 1985. This amendment replaced sanctions legislation originally submitted by Representative Gray. Among the components of the Dellums bill were bans on new investment, bank loans to the South African government, and coal, steel, and uranium imports from South Africa; divestment from the South African computer market; and withdrawal of U.S. landing rights for South African Airways. See Ronald V. Dellums, "The Need for Comprehensive Sanctions," *Washington Notes on Africa* (Summer 1986).

23. S–2701 was originally proposed by Senator Lugar, chairperson of the Senate Foreign Relations Committee. Three other major bills were introduced into the Senate for consideration. Senator Nancy Kassebaum (R-KS), chairperson of the Senate Subcommittee on Africa, introduced S–2636, which included a ban on new U.S. investment in South Africa. Senator Alan Cranston (D-CA) introduced the Senate equivalent of the final version of HR–4868. Senator Edward Kennedy (D-MA) introduced S–2498, which was the Senate equivalent of the original, milder version of HR–4868.

24. For various statements of President Reagan concerning this veto, see "Economic Sanctions Against South Africa," *Department of State Bulletin* 86, 2117 (December 1986): 35–37.

25. President Ronald Reagan, "Ending Apartheid in South Africa," address reproduced in Pauline H. Baker, *The United States and South Africa: The Reagan Years* (New York: Foreign Policy Association, 1989).

26. Ibid., p. 31.

27. Ibid.

28. Quoted in U.S. House, Committee on Foreign Affairs, Subcommittees on International Economic Policy and Trade, and on Africa, *Legislative Options and United States Policy Toward South Africa* (Hearings and Markup, April 9, 16; June 4, 5, 1986), 99th Cong., 2nd Sess., Washington, D.C.: GPO, 1987, p. 246.

29. Quoted in Pauline H. Baker, "The Sanctions Vote: A G.O.P. Milestone," *New York Times,* August 26, 1986.

30. Paul Simon, "The Senate's New African Agenda," *Africa Report* 32, 3 (May–June 1987): 14.

31. Quoted in Robert Pear, "U.S. Putting Hope in South Africa," *New York Times,* September 6, 1989, p. A3.

32. For example, Bush met with Albertina "Mama" Sisulu, the copresident of the United Democratic Front and wife of Walter Sisulu, one of the most prominent leaders of the ANC, in June 1989. One month earlier, Bush met with South African Archbishop Desmond Tutu, who noted that the president had a "warm openness" to taking the "moral leadership" in the dismantling of apartheid. See Bernard Weinraub, "Bush Meets Tutu and Vows to Press Pretoria," *New York Times,* May 19, 1989, p. A8.

33. Quoted in ibid.

34. Ibid.

35. Quoted in David B. Ottaway, "State Nominee Stresses Peace in Africa," *Washington Post,* May 4, 1989, p. A21.

36. Quoted in Christopher S. Wren, "Pretoria and Banks Reach Pact," *New York Times,* October 20, 1989, p. A5.

37. William Claiborne, "Pretoria's Power-Sharing Plan Modeled on Swiss Federal System," *New York Times,* June 30, 1989, p. A5.

38. See "Britain Breaks European Ranks to Ease South Africa Sanctions," *New York Times,* February 21, 1990, pp. A1, A4.

39. The quotations are those of Howard Wolpe, quoted in Pear, "U.S. Putting Hope," p. A3.

40. See David B. Ottaway, "U.S. Panel Hails S. African 'Dynamic,'" *Washington Post,* March 5, 1990.

41. For a brief summary, see "South African Sanctions: Go Slow," *New York Times,* July 5, 1991, p. A10. For an earlier discussion of South Africa's compliance with the conditions of the 1986 act, see Robert Pear, "Bush Invites Mandela to the White House," *New York Times,* February 12, 1990, p. A12. For the administration's interpretation of South African compliance, see the annual "Report of the Congress Pursuant to Section 501 of the Comprehensive Anti-Apartheid Act of 1986."

42. See Christopher S. Wren, "De Klerk Announces New Round of Talks with Mandela Aides," *New York Times,* July 21, 1990, p. A3; Alan Cowell, "African National Congress Suspends Its Guerrilla War," *New York Times,* August 7, 1990, p. A2.

43. See Christopher S. Wren, "South Africa Scraps Law Defining People by Race: The Legal Foundation of Apartheid System Is Eliminated," *New York Times,* June 19, 1991, p. A1.

44. See the numerous articles contained in the February 3, 1990, edition of the *New York Times* that carried the headline: "South Africa's President Ends 30-year Ban on Mandela Group; Says It Is Time for Negotiation."

45. See Christopher S. Wren, "De Klerk Lifts Emergency Rule in Natal Province," *New York Times*, Ocotber 19, 1990, p. A3; "South Africa Lifting State of Emergency," *Chicago Tribune*, June 8, 1990, sec. 1, pp. 1, 24; Cowell, "African National Congress Suspends Its Guerrilla War"; and "In South Africa: The Nightmare Ends," *New York Times*, August 8, 1990, p. A14.

46. See Christopher Wren, "Dispute on Pretoria's Stance on Prisoners Persists," *New York Times*, July 13, 1991, p. A3.

47. Thomas L. Friedman, "Bush Lifts Ban on Economic Ties to South Africa: Calls Apartheid's End 'Irreversible' and Cites Prisoner Releases," *New York Times*, July 11, 1991, p. A1, A6.

48. "Excerpts from Bush's Remarks on Sanctions: 'This Progress is Irreversible,'" *New York Times*, July 11, 1991, p. A6.

49. Keith Bradsher, "Support for Pretoria Sanctions Weak," *New York Times*, July 10, 1991, p. A3.

50. Neil A. Lewis, "Administration Hoping to Lift U.S. Sanctions," *New York Times*, June 18, 1991, p. A6.

51. Bradsher, "Support for Pretoria Sanctions Weak."

52. Freidman, "Bush Lifts Ban on Economic Ties to South Africa," p. A6.

53. Bureau of Public Affairs, U.S. Department of State, "South Africa: U.S. Policy," *Gist* (March 1990).

54. "Excerpts from Bush's Remarks on Sanctions."

55. Bureau of Public Affairs, U.S. Department of State, "U.S. Support for a Postapartheid South Africa," *Gist* (March 1990).

56. "Excerpts from Bush's Remarks."

57. "Excerpts from Remarks by Mandela to Newspaper Editors and Writers," *New York Times*, June 22, 1990, p. A12.

58. Mangosuthu G. Buthelezi, *South Africa: My Vision of the Future* (New York: St. Martin's, 1990), p. 28.

59. For further details on Inkathagate, see Patrick Laurence, "The Credibility Gap," *Africa Report* 36, 5 (September–October 1991): 44–48.

■ CHAPTER 15: THE PHILIPPINES

1. Quoted from a recording of the meeting made available to me and confirmed by a participant.

2. Ibid.

3. See Joseph L. Schott, *The Ordeal of Samar* (New York: Bobbs-Merrill, 1964), p. 62.

4. Ibid.

5. Quoted in Richard J. Kessler, "U.S. Policy Toward the Philippines," Stanley Foundation Policy Paper no. 37, June 1986.

6. U.S. Congress, House, Committee on Foreign Affairs, *Hearings on Mutual Security Act of 1958*, 85th Cong., 2nd Sess., Pt. 4, 1958, p. 566.

7. U.S. Congress, Senate, Committee on Foreign Relations, *United States Security Agreements and Commitments Abroad, the Republic of the Philippines, Hearings Before the Subcommittee on United States Security Agreements and Commitments Abroad*, 91st Cong., 1st Sess., Pt. 1, September 20, October 1–3,

1969, p. 37. Also see Raymond Bonner, *Waltzing with a Dictator* (New York: Times Books, 1987), p. 75.

8. See Scott W. Thompson, *Unequal Partners: Philippine and Thai Relations with the United States, 1965–75* (Lexington, Mass.: Lexington Books, 1975).

9. Thompson, *Unequal Partners,* p. 82.

10. Richard J. Kessler, "Marcos and the Americans," *Foreign Policy,* no. 63 (Summer 1986): 50.

11. See Thompson, *Unequal Partners,* pp. 66–67, 142; and W. Scott Thompson, "How to Intervene in the Philippines," *Washington Post,* January 14, 1986, p. A19.

12. Interview, former senior State Department official, July 10, 1985, Washington, D.C.

13. William E. Berry, "American Military Bases in the Philippines," Ph.D. dissertation, Cornell University, 1981, p. 276.

14. Interview, former senior State Department official, November 1984, Washington, D.C. Berry, "American Military Bases," p. 301, also agrees.

15. Embassy of the Philippines, *Annual Report* (FY 1975/76), Washington, D.C., pp. 22–23.

16. Interview, U.S. State Department officials, Washington, D.C., November 1986.

17. Henry Kissinger, "America and Asia," *Department of State Bulletin* 75, 1938 (August 16, 1976): 20.

18. Handwritten note passed to me in 1986. See also Kessler, "Marcos," pp. 40–57.

19. Richard J. Kessler, "Politics Philippine Style—Circa 1984," *Asian Survey* 24, 12 (December 1984): 1209–28.

20. Interview, U.S. State Department official, November 14, 1985.

21. Written communication to me, undated, but received March 11, 1986.

22. National Security Study Directive, "U.S. Policy Towards the Philippines. Executive Summary." This document was leaked to the press by a Filipino opponent of Marcos.

23. See Richard Holbrooke, "Removal of Marcos Was a Triumph for Reagan's Ad-Hocism," *Washington Post,* March 2, 1986, p. C1.

24. Personal conversation with me on November 3, 1985.

25. Interview, November 14, 1985, Washington, D.C.

■ CHAPTER 16: NICARAGUA

1. "Nicaragua has become a test case," Olds wrote in his January 2, 1927, memorandum, which advocated U.S. intervention to counter purported Mexican influence in Nicaragua's internal instability. Quoted in Richard Millett, *Guardians of the Dynasty: A History of the U.S.-Created Guardia Nacional de Nicaragua* (Maryknoll, N.Y.: Orbis Books, 1977), p. 52.

2. Quoted in Ronald Steel, *Walter Lippmann and the American Century* (Boston: Little, Brown, 1980), p. 237.

3. For U.S. efforts to portray Sandino as a common criminal as opposed to a nationalist leader, see *New York Times,* July 19, 1927, p. A10.

4. For figures on the costs of the war against Sandino, see Lejeune Cummins, *Quijote on a Burro: Sandino and the Marines, a Study in the Formulation of Foreign Policy* (Mexico: n.p., 1958), p. 68.

5. For a broader discussion of domestic reaction to the war against Sandino, see Peter Kornbluh, "U.S. Involvement in Central America: A Historical Lesson," *U.S.A. Today,* September 1983, pp. 45–47.

6. Kellogg's cable, "Strictly Personal and Confidential for General McCoy from the Secretary of State," is found in the McCoy Papers, Manuscript Division, Library of Congress. See also Millen, *Guardians of the Dynasty,* p. 88.

7. Hanna is quoted in a cable to the State Department, October 28, 1932, National Archive Record Group 59 817.1051/707 1/2.

8. See Laverne Baldwin to Secretary of State Cordell Hull, December 2, 1939, National Archive Record Group 817.00/8736, p. 13.

9. Ibid., p. 14.

10. Ibid., p. 13.

11. Somoza is quoted in John Booth, *The End and the Beginning: The Nicaraguan Revolution* (Boulder, Colo.: Westview Press, 1982), p. 61.

12. For a discussion of how opposition to the Somoza dynasty evolved, see ibid., pp. 71–180.

13. Brzezinski's argument with Carter is taken from his diaries and is recorded in Robert Pastor, *Condemned to Repetition: The United States and Nicaragua* (Princeton: Princeton University Press, 1987), p. 162.

14. See U.S. Department of State, Pezzullo to secretary of state, Cable no. 857, "First Visit to Somoza," June 28, 1978.

15. See U.S. Department of State, Vaky to Pezzullo, Cable no. 168715, "Nicaraguan Scenario," June 30, 1979.

16. U.S. Department of State, Viron Vaky to all American Republic diplomatic posts, Cable no. 153522, June 15, 1979.

17. See Peter Kornbluh, *Nicaragua: The Price of Intervention* (Washington D.C.: Institute for Policy Studies, 1987), pp. 15–19.

18. Quoted in ibid., p. 19.

19. See Robert C. Toth and Doyle McManus, "Contras and CIA: A Plan Gone Awry," *Los Angeles Times,* March 3, 1985.

20. See McFarlane's testimony before the Iran-Contra Select Committees, May 11 and 13, 1987.

21. See U.S. Army, Training and Doctrine Command (TRADOC), "U.S. Army Operational Concept for Low Intensity Conflict," February 1986, p. 2.

22. Colonel John Waghelstein, *Military Review* 65, 2 (February 1985): 87.

23. Owen to North, "Overall Perspective," March 17, 1986. Document released during Iran-contra hearings as exhibit no. 13.

24. For quotations from the CIA's contra manual, see *The CIA's Nicaragua Manual: Psychological Operations in Guerrilla Warfare* (New York: Vintage Books, 1985).

25. Casey is quoted in Bob Woodward, *Veil: The Secret Wars of the CIA, 1981–1987* (New York: Simon and Schuster, 1987), p. 282.

26. Memorandum for Robert C. McFarlane, March 2, 1984, from Oliver L. North and Constantine Menges, "Special Activities in Nicaragua." Released as Oliver North exhibit no. 177 during the Iran-contra hearings.

27. For North's discussions with Walker, see Peter Kornbluh, "What North Might Have Wrought," *The Nation,* June 26, 1987, p. 887.

28. NSC, North to McFarlane, "Timing and the Nicaraguan Resistance Vote," March 20, 1985.

29. CIA, National Intelligence Estimate, "Nicaragua: The Outlook for the Insurgency," June 30, 1983, p. 17.

30. NSC, "Strategy on Central America," July 6, 1983.

31. Cited in Kornbluh, *Nicaragua: The Price of Intervention,* p. 116.

32. Quoted in Joel Brinkley, "Nicaraguan Army: 'War Machine' or Defender of a Besieged Nation," *New York Times,* March 30, 1985, p. A16.

33. Quoted in Michael T. Klare and Peter Kornbluh, eds., *Low-Intensity Warfare: Counterinsurgency, Proinsurgency and Antiterrorism in the Eighties* (New York: Pantheon, 1988), p. 147.

34. The NSC Planning Group report was reprinted in full. See "National Security Council Document on Policy in Central America and Cuba," *New York Times,* April 28, 1983, p. A1.

35. See NSDD 77, Management of Public Diplomacy Relative to National Security, January 14, 1983, p. 1.

36. Clark's July 1, 1983, memorandum, entitled "Public Diplomacy (Central America)," was released during the Iran-contra hearings.

37. Alfonso Chardy, "NSC Oversaw Campaign to Sway Contra Aid Vote," *Miami Herald,* July 19, 1987, p. A1.

38. See U.S. Department of State, Reich to Department of Defense, Ray Warren, "Subject: TDY Personnel for S/LPD," March 5, 1985, p. 1. This document is on file at the National Security Archive in Washington, D.C.

39. See GAO letter to Rep. Dante Fascell and Rep. Jack Brooks, September 30, 1987.

40. Quoted in Robert Parry and Peter Kornbluh, "Iran-Contra's Untold Story," *Foreign Policy,* no. 71 (Fall 1988): 27.

41. Ibid., p. 6.

42. Figures are quoted from Nicaragua memorial presented to the International Court of Justice, March 29, 1988, p. 2.

43. See coverage of Iran-contra in *Newsweek,* December 8, 1986, p. 33.

44. See the *Report of the Congressional Committees Investigating the Iran-Contra Affair,* 100th Cong., 1st sess. (Washington, D.C.: GPO, November 1987), p. 4.

45. National Security Adviser Robert McFarlane, Assistant Secretary of State for Inter-American Affairs Elliott Abrams, and CIA Central American Task Force Chief Alan Fiers eventually pled guilty to charges of misleading Congress. Lt. Col. Oliver North and Vice Admiral John Poindexter were convicted on similar charges although their cases were overturned on appeal.

46. See Owen to North, "Overall Perspective," March 17, 1986.

47. *Report of the Congressional Committees Investigating the Iran-Contra Affair,* pp. 63–64.

48. For a comprehensive treatment of the Reagan administration's quid pro quo deals with Honduras, Guatemala, Panama, and numerous other countries, see the U.S. government stipulation released during the Oliver North trial, April 6, 1989.

49. The "diversion memo" is titled "Status of American Hostages in Beirut" and dated April 4, 1986.

50. CIA involvement in the 1984 elections is cited in the Report of the Latin American Studies Association Delegation to Observe the Nicaraguan General Election of November 4, 1984, *The Electoral Process in Nicaragua: Domestic and International Influences,* November 19, 1984.

51. *Newsday,* July 15, 1989.

52. See *Newsweek,* October 21, 1991.

53. For a discussion of NED grants and *La Prensa,* see John Spicer Nichols, "La Prensa: The CIA Connection," *Columbia Journalism Review* (July/August 1988).

54. See U.S. Agency for International Development, *Report to Congress*

(PL. 101–119), "AID Grant to the National Endowment for Democracy (NED) and Summary of NED's Intended Subgrants," December 4, 1989.

55. Oliver L. North and William Novak, *Under Fire: An American Story* (New York: HarperCollins, 1991), p. 406.

56. For these quotes, see the Executive Summary of the *Report of the Congressional Committees Investigating the Iran-Contra Affair,* pp. 13, 18.

57. Ibid., p. 390.

■ CHAPTER 17: IRAN

1. For an analysis of U.S. involvement with Iran during World War II, see James A. Bill, *The Eagle and the Lion: The Tragedy of American-Iranian Relations* (New Haven: Yale University Press, 1988), pp. 18–26, 31–39.

2. For more details, see Barry Rubin, *Paved with Good Intentions: The American Experience in Iran* (New York: Oxford University Press, 1980), pp. 36–39.

3. For a generally positive, but frank, evaluation of the Point Four program in Iran written by its first director, see William Warne, *Mission for Peace: Point 4 in Iran* (Indianapolis: Bobbs-Merrill, 1956).

4. The most detailed study of this conflict is Richard Cottam, *Nationalism in Iran* (Pittsburgh: University of Pittsburgh Press, 1979).

5. The United States seems to have tried to dissuade Great Britain from undertaking coup attempts in 1951 and 1952. This interpretation is supported by an analysis of the various memoranda of conversations between Secretary Acheson and the British ambassador to the United States, Sir Oliver Franks. For the Acheson-Franks conversations, see *Iran White Paper,* National Security Archive, Washington, D.C., documents numbered 709–32 of Department of State typed list.

6. See Nikki Keddie, *Roots of Revolution: An Interpretive History of Modern Iran* (New Haven: Yale University Press, 1981), pp. 134–35.

7. For a detailed analysis of U.S. involvement, see Mark J. Gasiorowski, "The 1953 Coup d'Etat in Iran," *International Journal of Middle East Studies* 19, 3 (August 1987): 261–86.

8. See Richard Cottam, "American Foreign Policy and the Iranian Crisis," *Iranian Studies* 13, 1–4 (1980): 281–83.

9. Keddie, *Roots of Revolution,* p. 142.

10. For more detail on the development of U.S.-Iran relations from 1953 to 1961, see Bill, *The Eagle and the Lion,* pp. 113–27.

11. Bill, *The Eagle and the Lion,* pp. 131–51.

12. For an analysis of the shah's economic policies, see Fred Halliday, *Iran: Dictatorship and Development* (New York: Penguin Books, 1979), pp. 138–72. The land reform program is examined in Eric Hooglund, *Land and Revolution in Iran, 1960–1980* (Austin: University of Texas Press, 1982), pp. 47–99.

13. Khomeini's role during the 1963 demonstrations is described in detail in Keddie, *Roots of Revolution,* pp. 158–60. Also see Richard Cottam, *Iran and the United States: A Cold War Case Study* (Pittsburgh: University of Pittsburgh Press, 1988), pp. 130–31.

14. U.S.-Iran relations during the Johnson administration are examined in Bill, *The Eagle and the Lion,* pp. 154–80.

15. For a detailed account of arms sales to the shah during this period, see

Michael T. Klare, *American Arms Supermarket* (Austin: University of Texas Press, 1984), pp. 112–23.

16. See Phebe Marr, *The Modern History of Iraq* (Boulder, Colo.: Westview Press, 1985), pp. 112–21; and Bill, *The Eagle and the Lion,* pp. 204–7.

17. The shah's intervention in Oman is described in Richard Cottam, "Arms Sales and Human Rights: The Case of Iran," in Peter Brown and Douglas Maclean, eds., *Human Rights and U.S. Foreign Policy* (Lexington, Mass.: Heath, 1979), pp. 289–90.

18. U.S. Congress, Senate, Subcommittee on Foreign Assistance, Committee on Foreign Affairs, *U.S. Military Sales to Iran* (Washington, D.C.: Government Printing Office, 1976), pp. xiii, 1–2.

19. Gary Sick, *All Fall Down: America's Tragic Encounter with Iran* (New York: Random House, 1985), pp. 25–27.

20. Sick, *All Fall Down,* pp. 22–24; and Bill, *The Eagle and the Lion,* pp. 219–44.

21. Eric Hooglund, "Government and Politics," in Helen Metz, ed., *Iran: A Country Study* (Washington, D.C.: Library of Congress, 1989), pp. 438–44; and Shaul Bakhash, *The Reign of Ayatollahs* (New York: Basic Books, 1984), pp. 69–70.

22. See Bill, *The Eagle and the Lion,* pp. 276–86, 293–96.

23. The most complete description of the efforts to resolve the hostage crisis, written from the perspective of a Carter administration official, is Sick, *All Fall Down,* pp. 195–342.

24. For more detail, see Eric Hooglund, "Reagan's Iran: Factions Behind U.S. Policy in the Gulf," *Middle East Report* 151 (March–April 1988): 29–31.

25. The Reagan administration's difficulties in trying to fit Iran into a Cold War perspective are analyzed by Richard Cottam, "Iran and Soviet-American Relations," in Nikki Keddie and Eric Hooglund, eds., *The Iranian Revolution and the Islamic Republic* (Syracuse: Syracuse University Press, 1986), pp. 229–32.

26. Hooglund, "Reagan's Iran," p. 30; Cottam, *Iran and the United States,* pp. 237–42.

27. For the change in CIA Director Casey's views on Iran and the subsequent change in covert policy, see Bob Woodward, *Veil: The Secret Wars of the CIA, 1981–1987* (New York: Simon and Schuster, 1987), pp. 111–12, 407–8. For an evaluation of the presumed pro-U.S. (moderate) and pro-Soviet factions in the Iranian government, see Eric Hooglund, "The Search for Iran's 'Moderates,'" *Middle East Report* 144 (January–February 1987): 5–6.

28. For analyses of the contradictory U.S. policies toward Iran during 1985–1987, see Nikki Keddie, "Iranian Imbroglios: Who's Irrational?" *World Policy Journal* (Winter 1987–1988): 29–54; and Cottam, *Iran and the United States,* 243–45.

29. Keddie, "Iranian Imbroglios," pp. 4–47.

30. Gary Sick, "The Internationalization of the Iran-Iraq War: The Events of 1987," in Mike Gasiorowski and Nikki Keddie, eds., *Iran, the U.S. and the U.S.S.R.* (New Haven: Yale University Press, 1989).

31. For details of these incidents see the *Washington Post,* April 19 and July 4, 1988.

32. *Washington Post,* January 21, 1989.

33. Washington's penchant for classifying Iranians as moderate or radical politicians is analyzed in Hooglund, "The Search for Iran's 'Moderates,'" pp. 5–6.

34. Academics as well as bureaucrats see the Iranian political elite as divided into two contending factions and advocate Washington's rapprochement with the

moderates, who are also referred to as pragmatists or realists; radicals are sometimes referred to as idealists or militants. See, for example, R. K. Ramazani, "Iran's Foreign Policy: Contending Orientations," *Middle East Journal* 43, 2 (Spring 1989): 215–17.

35. For a fuller discussion of Bush administration views on Iran's role in the Lebanon hostage ordeal, see Eric Hooglund, "U.S. Policy Toward the Persian Gulf in the 1990s," in Charles Davies, ed., *After the War: Iraq, Iran, and the Arab Gulf* (Chichester: Carden Publications, 1990), pp. 405–6.

■ CHAPTER 18: THE PERSIAN GULF

1. For an authoritative account of the establishment of British hegemony along the Persian Gulf coast of the Arabian Peninsula, see Briton Cooper Busch, *Britain and the Persian Gulf, 1894–1914* (Berkeley and Los Angeles: University of California Press, 1967). British policy from 1914 to 1960 is discussed in John Marlowe, *The Persian Gulf in the Twentieth Century* (London: Cresset, 1962).

2. A good summary of the British role during the Iranian oil nationalization crisis is Anthony Sampson, *The Seven Sisters: The Great Oil Companies and the World They Shaped* (New York: Bantam, 1978), pp. 135–53. The U.S. role is discussed in Chapter 17 of this book. For more comprehensive examinations of the U.S., British, and Iranian roles, see James A. Bill and William Roger Louis, eds., *Musaddiq, Iranian Nationalism, and Oil* (Austin: University of Texas Press, 1988).

3. For a comprehensive analysis of the interplay of British policy and Iraqi politics see Majid Khadduri, *Independent Iraq, 1932–1958,* 2nd ed. (London: Oxford University Press, 1970).

4. Tareq Ismael discusses the impact of the loss of Palestine on Arab nationalism in *The Arab Left* (Syracuse, N.Y.: Syracuse University Press, 1976), pp. 6–19.

5. The impact of the 1956 Suez War on Iraq is discussed in George Lenczowski, *The Middle East in World Affairs,* 4th ed. (Ithaca, N.Y.: Cornell University Press, 1980), pp. 287–88.

6. The regional impacts of the Baghdad Pact and the Eisenhower Doctrine are evaluated in Harry N. Howard, "The Regional Pacts and the Eisenhower Doctrine," in Parker T. Hart, special ed., *America and the Middle East, Special Issue of The Annals of the American Academy of Political and Social Science,* vol. 401 (May 1972): 85–94.

7. The most complete analysis of Iraq in the early years following the 1958 overthrow of the monarchy is Majid Khadduri, *Republican Iraq: A Study in Iraqi Politics Since the Revolution of 1958* (London: Oxford University Press, 1969). See especially pp. 166–172 for a discussion of the 1961 crisis over Kuwait's independence.

8. The best account of the nationalist struggles against British rule and British-supported rulers in the Arabian Peninsula is Fred Halliday, *Arabia Without Sultans* (Harmonsworth: Penguin, 1974).

9. Halliday analyzes the motives for Britain's decision to withdraw its military presence from the Persian Gulf in ibid., pp. 453–56.

10. For a summary of how experts viewed the likely consequences of British withdrawal from the Persian Gulf, see The Center for Strategic and International Studies, *The Gulf: Implications of British Withdrawal,* Special Report Series no. 8 (Washington, D.C.: Georgetown University, February 1969). Also see J. C.

Hurewitz, "The Persian Gulf: British Withdrawal and Western Security," *Annals* 401 (May 1972): 106–15.

11. Michael Klare examines the evolution of the twin pillars policy in *American Arms Supermarket* (Austin: University of Texas Press, 1984), pp. 112–15.

12. Halliday, *Arabia Without Sultans*, pp. 50–51.

13. For statistics on Saudi arms purchases during the 1970s, see Klare, *American Arms Supermarket*, pp. 129–133; and Congressional Quarterly, *The Middle East: U.S. Policy, Israel, Oil, and the Arabs*, 4th ed. (Washington, D.C.: Congressional Quarterly, 1979), pp. 45–52.

14. Klare, *American Arms Supermarket*, p. 127.

15. On the Iranian occupation of the three UAE islands, see Rouhollah K. Ramazani, *The Persian Gulf: Iran's Role* (Charlottesville: University Press of Virginia, 1972), pp. 56–68; and *MERIP Reports*, "US Strategy in the Gulf," no. 36 (April 1975): 19–20.

16. Iran's relations with Iraqi Kurds during the 1960s are described in Chris Kutschera, *Le Mouvement National Kurde* (Paris: Flammarion, 1979), pp. 255–58 and 263–73.

17. For a history of the Iran-Iraq border dispute, see Kaiyan Homi Kaikobad, *The Shatt-al-Arab Boundary Question: A Legal Reappraisal* (Oxford: Clarendon, 1988).

18. Revelations about CIA involvement with Iraq's Kurds were detailed in a secret report prepared by a U.S. House of Representatives subcommittee chaired by Representative Otis Pike. The Pike Report was leaked to the media and published by *The Village Voice*, February 16, 1976.

19. Complete texts of the Algiers Communiqué, subsequent treaty, and its protocols are in Kaikobad, *The Shatt-al-Arab Boundary Question*, Annexe 5, pp. 134–35; Annexe 6, pp. 136–38; and Annexe 7, pp. 139–42.

20. The best account of the Dhofar rebellion is Halliday, *Arabia Without Sultans*, pp. 304–54.

21. On Iranian military intervention in Oman, see Fred Halliday, *Mercenaries: Counter-Insurgency in the Gulf* (London: Spokesman, 1977), p. 32; and *MERIP Reports*, "Neo-Piracy in Oman and the Gulf," no. 36 (April 1975): 20–22.

22. U.S. prodding of Saudi Arabia to assume a more activist military role is examined in Klare, *American Arms Supermarket*, pp. 136–38.

23. The rebels finally were subdued following a series of assaults that left over 200 persons dead. For a detailed account of the Grand Mosque incident, see Jim Paul, "Insurrection at Mecca," *MERIP Reports*, No. 91 (October 1980): 3–4.

24. For more on the Shia demonstrations in Saudi Arabia, see R. K. Ramazani, *Revolutionary Iran: Challenge and Response in the Middle East* (Baltimore: Johns Hopkins University Press, 1986), pp. 39–40.

25. On the attempted coup in Bahrain, see Fred Lawson, *Bahrain: The Modernization of Autocracy* (Boulder: Westview, 1989), pp. 124–25; and Ramazani, *Revolutionary Iran,* pp. 48–53.

26. On U.S. attitudes toward the Soviet role in Afghanistan, see Steven Galster, "The Spynest Documents: Destabilizing Afghanistan," *Covert Action,* no. 30 (Summer 1988): 52–4.

27. The complete text of Carter's State of the Union address is in the *New York Times*, January 23, 1980.

28. On the early development of the RDF, see Joe Stork, "The Carter Doctrine and US Bases in the Middle East," *MERIP Reports*, no. 90 (September 1980): 3–14.

29. For more on the early development of CENTCOM, see Martha Wenger, "The Central Command: Getting to the War on Time," *MERIP Reports,* no. 128 (November–December 1984): 19–26.

30. Phebe Marr, "The Iran-Iraq War: The View from Iraq," in Christopher C. Joyner, ed., *The Persian Gulf War* (Westport, Conn.: Greenwood, 1990), p. 60.

31. On U.S. military assistance to the Afghan resistance forces in the early 1980s, see Steven Galster, "Never-Ending Flow: The Afghan Pipeline," *Covert Action,* no. 30 (Summer 1988): 55–8.

32. For further details on the terrorist incidents in Lebanon and Kuwait in 1983 see Robin Wright, *In the Name of God: The Khomeini Decade* (New York: Simon and Schuster, 1989), pp. 116–23.

33. For further discussion, see Eric Hooglund, "The Policy of the Reagan Administration Toward Iran," in Nikki Keddie and Mark Gasiorowski, eds., *Neither East nor West: Iran, the Soviet Union, and the United States* (New Haven: Yale University Press, 1990), pp. 191–92.

34. For further discussion, see Elizabeth Gamlen, "U.S. Responses to the 'Tanker War' and the Implications of Its Intervention," in Charles Davies, ed., *After the War: Iraq, Iran, and the Arab Gulf* (Chichester: Carden Publications, 1990), pp. 318–21.

35. These officials also believed that an internal power struggle was inevitable following the death of the aged leader Ayatollah Khomeini, and that the Soviet Union would benefit unless the United States took measures to establish some influence among Iranian leaders. See further Eric Hooglund, "The Policy of the Reagan Administration Toward Iran," in Keddie and Gasiorowski, eds., *Neither East nor West,* p. 184.

36. Joseph Kechichian, "The Gulf Cooperation Council and the Gulf War," in Joyner, ed., *The Persian Gulf War,* p. 103.

37. Gary Sick, "Slouching Toward Settlement: The Internationalization of the Iran-Iraq War, 1987–1988," in Keddie and Gasiorowski, eds., *Neither East nor West,* p. 223.

38. David Caron, "Choice and Duty in Foreign Affairs: The Reflagging of the Kuwaiti Tankers," in Joyner, ed., *The Persian Gulf War,* pp. 156–57.

39. An equally important motivation was U.S. concern that the Soviet Union would agree to reflag Kuwaiti ships and thereby gain a new foothold in the region. For further discussion, see Gamlen, "U.S. Responses to the 'Tanker War,'" pp. 322–24.

40. For more on the international "peacekeeping" armada see Jochen Hippler, "NATO Goes to the Persian Gulf," *Middle East Report,* no. 155 (November–December 1988): 18–21.

41. Roderic Pitty, "Soviet Perceptions of Iraq," *Middle East Report,* no. 151 (March–April 1988), p. 27.

42. Fred Halliday, "The USSR and the Gulf War: Moscow's Growing Concern," *Middle East Report,* no. 148 (September–October 1987), p. 11.

43. See Tables 10.1 and 10.2 in Gary Sick, "Slouching Toward Settlement," in Keddie and Gasiorowski, eds., *Neither East nor West,* pp. 222, 231.

44. See further Eric Hooglund, "U.S. Policy Toward the Persian Gulf in the 1990s," in Davies, ed., *After the War,* p. 403.

45. Iraq's economic problems in the 1988–1990 period are examined in Kiren Aziz Chaudhry, "On the Way to Market: Economic Liberalization and Iraq's Invasion of Kuwait," *Middle East Report,* no. 170 (May–June 1991): 14–23.

46. See the U.S. Army report by Stephen Pelletiere, Douglas Johnson, and Lief Rosenberger, *Iraqi Power and U.S. Security in the Middle East* (Calisle Barracks, Penn.: U.S. Army War College, 1990).

47. Eric Hooglund, "The Uprisings' Fundamentals Aren't Religious," *Newsday,* March 17, 1991, pp. 43, 46.

48. On the repression of the Iraqi rebellions, see Eric Hooglund, "The Other Face of War," *Middle East Report,* no. 171 (July–August 1991), pp. 7–10.

■ CHAPTER 19: PANAMA

1. Article VII states: "The same right and authority [to act as if it were sovereign] are granted to the United States for the maintenance of public order in the cities of Panama and Colón and the territories and harbors adjacent thereto in case the Republic of Panama should not be, in the judgement of the United States, able to maintain such order." A Convention Between the United States and Panama for the Construction of a Ship Canal (Hay–Bunau-Varilla Treaty), November 18, 1903, 33 Stat. 2234, Treaty Series 431.

2. Humberto E. Ricord, *Las Constituciones Panameñas del Siglo XX* (Panama City: Editora Perez y Perez, 1987), p. 8.

3. A Treaty of Friendship and Cooperation Between Panama and the United States (Hull-Alfaro Treaty), March 2, 1936, 53 Stat. 1807, Treaty Series 945.

4. Initially administered as part of the vice royalty of New Granada, Panama declared its independence from Spain in 1821; Panama then joined the Republic of New Granada; in 1841 it seceded and was independent for thirteen months, after which Colombia reasserted its sovereignty over the isthmus.

5. Such interventions occurred in 1850, 1851, 1853, 1854, 1856, 1860, 1873, 1885, 1901, and 1902. Article XXXV of this treaty (A General Treaty of Peace, Amity, Navigation and Commerce Between the United States of America and the Republic of New Granada [Bidlack-Mallarino Treaty], December 12, 1846; 9 Stat. 881, Treaty Series 54) granted to U.S. personnel, vehicles, and goods the same access and privileges for transit across the Isthmus of Panama as Grenadine citizens and goods. Then U.S. rights were specified: "In order to secure to themselves the tranquil and constant enjoyment of these advantages" the United States would "guarantee positively and efficaciously to New Granada, by the present stipulation, the perfect neutrality of the before mentioned Isthmus, with the view that the free transit from the one to the other sea, may not be interrupted or embarrassed in any future time while this Treaty exists; and in consequence, the United States also guarantee, in the same manner, the rights of sovereignty and property which New Granada has and possesses over the said territory."

6. David McCullough's *The Path Between the Seas* (New York: Simon and Schuster, 1977) is the best account of these events.

7. *New York Times,* February 29, 1976, p. A42.

8. For example, public opinion surveys conducted during March and from May 29 to June 2, 1991, found Panamanians responding to a question about closing all U.S. bases by the year 2000 with 58.4 percent and 63.5 percent, respectively, in favor of retaining U.S. bases; the results of the Dichter & Neira survey were reported in *La Prensa,* July 4, 1991. These surveys also asked if Panamanians considered themselves to be fundamentally anti-Yanqui (anti-American); in May/June, only 33.0 percent responded affirmatively, but this was up from 26.9 percent in March 1991.

9. The 1936 Hull-Alfaro Treaty abrogated this provision.

10. The provincial exceptions were significant because they demonstrated

that U.S. rights to restore order and maintain stability extended beyond the terminal canal areas to include Panamanian territory too.

11. G. A. Anguizola provides the best chronicle of these events. Typical is the case he relates concerning Taboga Island, which the United States proposed seizing for defense purposes in November 1918, after World War I. Taboga, in the Pacific near Panama City, was used as a resort by wealthy Panamanians. The foreign minister suggested several other small islands as alternative defense sites, but a U.S. military legation landed and demanded that the Tabogans depart. After vigorous protests broke out in Panama City, the United States reduced its claim to 1160 hectares and agreed not to dispossess the Tabogans without time to pack their belongings. Panamanian protests continued, and finally, in April 1920, the United States demanded 14 hectares and Panama acquiesced. See "Fifty Years of Isthmian-American Relations: An Analysis of the Causes Jeopardizing Isthmian-American Friendship," unpublished doctoral disseration, Indiana University, Bloomington, Indiana, 1954.

12. The School of the Americas was closed and transferred to Panama in compliance with the 1978 Carter-Torrijos treaties; its functions were relocated to a U.S. base, Ft. Benning, in Georgia.

13. The best source on this progression is Steve C. Ropp, *Panamanian Politics: From National Guard to Guarded Nation* (New York: Praeger, 1982).

14. This formula, in turn, was a direct descendant of an earlier statement of principles announced in 1965 by President Lyndon B. Johnson and President Marco A. Robles. The 1965 statement marked the first time the United States agreed to make significant revisions in the rights and powers it exercised according to the 1903 treaty. For a summary of these events and an analysis of the evolution of U.S. canal policy objectives, see William L. Furlong and Margaret E. Scranton, *The Dynamics of Foreign Policymaking: The President, the Congress, and the Panama Canal Treaties* (Boulder: Westview, 1984).

15. Barletta was already vulnerable, however, because of his economic austerity policies and his style, which antagonized political leaders.

16. These strategies are discussed in detail in Margaret E. Scranton, *The Noriega Years: United States–Panamanian Relations, 1981–1990* (Boulder: Lynne Rienner, 1991).

17. One of the no votes was cast by Senator Christopher Dodd (D-CT), who opposed Noriega, on the grounds that a harsh public stand would stiffen Noriega's resistance rather than encourage his voluntary exit.

18. In May 1987, coincidentally, a U.S. program funded Panamanian participation in a multinational delegation that visited the Philippines to study the NAMFREL experience and its application for upcoming elections in delegates' countries. Two of the three Panamanian delegates became immediately involved in a civilian movement and later applied their experience to preparations for the 1989 presidential election. At the U.S. embassy in Panama, the deputy chief of mission during the events of 1987 was John Maisto, who had been posted in the Philippines during Marcos's ouster crisis.

19. Whether Murphy's mission was officially initiated by the administration is not known; substantial evidence exists to suggest that his mission was welcomed and appreciated by the administration. Murphy told a congressional committee that he instigated his mission as a private businessman hoping to restore a good investment climate to Panama. Murphy did, however, meet with executive branch officials before and after his trips to Panama. Murphy was a credible messenger, having been chief of staff to Vice President Bush and the deputy director of intelligence while Bush was CIA director.

20. Rogers discussed his actions and expectations in an interview with

Marjorie Williams, "The Panama File: A D.C. Attorney's 'Revolution by Litigation,'" *Washington Post,* March 22, 1988, p. D2.

21. This affected some $96 million worth of goods annually; the denial of Canal Commission payments amounted to $6.5 million per month.

22. A Panamanian economist reported the following conditions as of late April 1988: industrial production down 40 percent, gasoline sales down 50 percent, supermarket sales down 30 percent, and business in the Colón free zone down 50 percent. In addition, Guillermo Chapman reported that more than 75,000 employees were laid off, more than 150,000 government employees received only partial paychecks, sales of consumer goods almost ceased, and hundreds of businesses, including many banks, were forced to close (*USA Today,* April 25, 1988).

23. This group issued a report; see Comité de Apoyo a los Observadores Internacionales, *Panamá: Testimonio de un Proceso Electoral* (n.p., 1989).

24. Opposition leaders, including Billy Ford and the first vice-presidential candidate, Ricardo Arias Calderón, repeatedly stated that they refused to lead their people to be slaughtered by Noriega.

25. The $1.3 million figure was reported by William Scott Malone, "The Panama Debacle—Uncle Sam Wimps Out," *Washington Post,* April 23, 1989, p. C4. He also reported a figure "substantially less than $1 million" cited by another source.

26. Controversy persists about the amount and type of help that Giroldi requested. Most analysts have concluded that some confusion existed at the time, and that the situation unfolded so quickly that reactions from Washington would have to have been much more timely than they were for new instructions, to take whatever measures might have been necessary to save the coup, to have been issued in time to act effectively.

27. For analyses of the decision to invade, see Scranton, *The Noriega Years* (ch. 7); Michael Conniff, *Panama and the United States: The Forced Alliance* (Athens: The University of Georgia, 1992), ch. 9; and Thomas Donnelly, Margaret Roth, Caleb Baker, *Operation Just Cause: The Storming of Panama* (New York: Lexington, 1991), chs. 2–6.

28. This interpretation was reinforced by a political power play Noriega had executed on December 15, 1989. He not only obtained a grant of additional powers from the legislative body, he also obtained passage of a resolution declaring Panama to be "in a state of war so long as the United States continues its policy of aggression." This language had been used before, but it was interpreted as a direct threat and a "declaration of war" by Panama on the United States in the context of the three incidents that subsequently occurred.

29. For an analysis of the operation, see Bruce W. Watson and Peter G. Tsouras, eds., *Operation Just Cause: The U.S. Intervention in Panama* (Boulder: Westview, 1991); and Malcolm McConnell, *Just Cause* (New York: St. Martin's, 1991).

30. Cable News Network, "Daily Pentagon Briefing," December 21, 1989.

31. The English version used the phrase "deeply regret" the invasion; the Spanish version was stronger, using the words "deeply deplore." This was the first time, however, that the United States had not been able to prevent such a resolution from coming to the floor, which it had accomplished after the Dominican and Grenada interventions.

32. Charles Maechling, Jr., discusses legal aspects of U.S. policy and the invasion in "Washington's Illegal Invasion," *Foreign Policy* 79 (Summer 1990): 113–131.

■ CHAPTER 20: THE ARAB-ISRAELI CONFLICT

1. Portions of this chapter originally appeared in *One Land, Two Peoples: The Conflict over Palestine,* 1991. Reprinted with permission of Westview Press, Boulder, Colorado. Research assistance was provided by Julia C. Pitner.

2. These priorities are clear not only from public previously classified policy documents of the period but also from memoirs and interviews by and biographies about the main individuals involved in creating those policies. See, for example, Dwight D. Eisenhower, *The White House Years: Waging Peace, 1956–61* (Garden City, N.Y.: Doubleday, 1965); Stephen E. Ambrose, *Eisenhower: The President* (New York: Simon and Schuster, 1984); John Emmet Hughes, *The Ordeal of Power: A Political Memoir of the Eisenhower Years* (New York: Atheneum, 1963); and Robert H. Ferrell, ed., *The Eisenhower Diaries* (New York: Norton, 1981).

3. An extended discussion on the factors that motivated President Harry S Truman's policy toward Israel can be found in Michael J. Cohen, *Truman and Israel* (Berkeley: University of California Press, 1990).

4. A useful overview of Eisenhower's foreign policy orientation can be found in Richard A. Melanson, "The Foundations of Eisenhower's Foreign Policy: Continuity, Community, and Consensus," in Richard A. Melanson and David Mayers, eds., *Reevaluating Eisenhower: America's Foreign Policy in the 1950s* (Urbana: University of Illinois Press, 1987). Also see Deborah J. Gerner, "Missed Opportunities and Roads Not Taken: The Eisenhower Administration and the Palestinians," *Arab Studies Quarterly* 12, 1–2 (Winter-Spring 1990): 67–100.

5. [Acting Secretary of State] Robert A. Lovett to [U.S. Representative on the Palestine Conciliation Commission] Mark F. Ethridge, Washington, D.C., January 19, 1949, *Foreign Relations of the United States,* vol. 6 *The Near East, South Asia and Africa* (Washington, D.C.: U.S. Government Printing Office, 1977), pp. 681–83. See also Avi Shlaim, *Collusion Across the Divide* (New York: Columbia University Press 1988); and Mary Wilson, *King Abdullah, Britain and the Making of Jordan* (New York: Cambridge University Press, 1987).

6. James Baster, "Economic Aspects of the Settlement of the Palestine Refugees," *Middle East Journal* 8, 1 (Winter 1954): 66.

7. Edward H. Buehrig, *The UN and the Palestinian Refugees: A Study in Nonterritorial Administration* (Bloomington: Indiana University Press, 1971), p. 15.

8. John Foster Dulles, "The Middle East," address made before the Council on Foreign Relations, New York, August 26, 1955, *Department of State Bulletin* 33 (September 5, 1955): 378–80.

9. James J. Wasworth, "Security Council Censure of Action at Qibiya," statement made in the UN Security Council, November 20, 1953, *Department of State Bulletin* 29 (December 14, 1953): 839–41; Henry Cabot Lodge, "Egyptian-Israeli Dispute Before the Security Council Condemns Israel for Action Against Syria," statement made in the UN Security Council, January 12, 1956, *Department of State Bulletin* 345 (January 30, 1956): 182–184.

10. Parker T. Hunter, Director, Near East Section, Department of State, to William A. Eddy, Arabian American Oil Company, January 29, 1954, U.S. State Department Confidential File, Palestine-Israel, 1950–54, p. 2.

11. See, for example, Stephen Green, *Taking Sides: America's Secret Relations with a Militant Israel* (New York: Morrow, 1984); and Donald Neff, *Warriors at Suez: Eisenhower Takes America into the Middle East* (New York: Linden Press/Simon and Schuster, 1981).

12. Memorandum of Conversation, President with Dulles, Undersecretary

Hoover, Goodpaster, and others, October 30, 1956, File: October 1956, Staff Notes, Box 19, Diary Series, Dwight D. Eisenhower Library.

13. Henry Cabot Lodge, "Question of Withdrawal of Israeli Forces from Egypt," statements to the UN General Assembly, January 27 and 23, 1957, *Department of State Bulletin* 36 (February 18, 1957): 325–28; Aide-mémoire of U.S. Secretary of State Dulles handed to Israeli Ambassador Abba Eban, February 11, 1957, reprinted in Milton Viost, *Sands of Sorrow: Israel's Journey from Independence* (New York: Harper & Row, 1987), p. 288.

14. Sherman Adams, *Firsthand Report: The Story of the Eisenhower Administration* (New York: Harper & Brothers, 1971), pp. 281–82.

15. Paul Findley, *They Dare to Speak Out: People and Institutions Confront Israel's Lobby* (Westport, Conn.: Lawrence Hill, 1985), p. 119.

16. *The Link,* December 1982, p. 3; cited in Cheryl A. Rubenberg, *Israel and the American National Interest: A Critical Examination* (Chicago: University of Illinois Press, 1986), pp. 67, 96. This figure does not include loans through the Export-Import Bank.

17. Lewis J. Paper, *The Promise and the Performance: The Leadership of John F. Kennedy* (New York: Crown, 1975), p. 334. See also Mordechai Gazit, *President Kennedy's Policy Toward the Arab States and Israel* (Tel Aviv: Shiloah Center for Middle Eastern and African Studies, 1983); and George Lenczowski, *American Presidents and the Middle East* (Durham, N.C.: Duke University Press, 1990).

18. Differing perspectives on pro-Israel lobbying efforts can be found in Mitchell Geoffrey Bard, "The Water's Edge and Beyond: Defining the Limits to Domestic Influence on U.S. Middle East Policy" (Ph.D. dissertation, University of California-Los Angeles, 1987); David Howard Goldberg, *Foreign Policy and Ethnic Interest Groups: American and Canadian Jews Lobby for Israel* (Westport, Conn.: Greenwood Press, 1990); Lee O'Brien, *American Jewish Organizations and Israel* (Washington, D.C.: Institute for Palestine Studies, 1986); and Edward Tivnan, *The Lobby: Jewish Political Power and American Foreign Policy* (New York: Simon and Schuster, 1987).

19. Nixon's comments during the October 1973 war make this quite clear: "No one is more keenly aware of the stakes: oil and our strategic position. . . . Some of [the Arab countries] are desperately afraid of being left at the mercy of the Soviet Union. . . . The other aspect is our relations with the Soviet Union. . . . We can't allow a Soviet-supported operation to succeed against an American-supported operation. If it does, our credibility everywhere is severely shaken." Quoted in Henry Kissinger, *Years of Upheaval* (Boston: Little, Brown, 1982), p. 536. A number of scholars have argued that after 1973, the United States had as its goal "the complete eradication of Soviet influence from the region." See Maya Chadda, *Paradox of Power: The United States in Southwest Asia, 1973–1984* (Santa Barbara, Calif.: ABC Clio, 1986), p. 4.

20. "Text of Speech by Secretary Rogers on U.S. Policy in the Middle East," *New York Times,* December 10, 1969.

21. Jimmy Carter, *Keeping Faith: Memoirs of a President* (New York: Bantam, 1982), pp. 269–429; William B. Quandt, *Camp David: Peacemaking and Politics* (Washington, D.C.: The Brookings Institution, 1986); Cyrus Vance, *Hard Choices: Critical Years in American Foreign Policy* (New York: Simon and Schuster, 1983).

22. "Transcript of the President's News Conference," *New York Times,* March 10, 1977, p. 26.

23. Quandt, *Camp David,* Appendixes G and I.

24. Kenneth A. Oye, Robert J. Lieber, and Donald Rothchild, eds., *Eagle*

Resurgent? The Reagan Era in American Foreign Policy (Boston: Little, Brown, 1983); Naseer Aruri, Fouad Moughrabi, and Joe Stork, *Reagan and the Middle East* (Belmont, Mass.: Association of Arab-American University Graduates, 1983).

25. Several contemporary accounts of the 1982 Lebanon war, primarily from the perspective of Palestinians, are contained in Ibrahim Abu-Lughod and Eqbal Ahmad, eds., *The Invasion of Lebanon: Special Issue of Race and Class* 24, 4 (Spring 1983). A quite different view is expressed in Chaim Herzog, *The Arab-Israeli Wars* (New York: Random House, 1982).

26. "Transcript of the President's Address to the Nation on the West Bank and Palestinians," *New York Times,* September 2, 1982.

27. "Resolutions of the Twelfth Arab League Summit, Fez, Morocco, September 9, 1982," in William B. Quandt, ed., *The Middle East: Ten Years After Camp David* (Washington, D.C.: The Brookings Institution, 1988), pp. 471–72.

28. A superb collection of pieces on the intifada can be found in Jamal R. Nassar and Roger Heacock, eds., *Intifada: Palestine at the Crossroads* (New York: Praeger, 1990). F. Robert Hunter, *The Palestinian Uprising: A War by Other Means* (Berkeley: University of California Press, 1991) provides a history of the intifada's first two years, based heavily on oral histories Hunter collected in 1988 and 1989. See also Don Peretz, *Intifada: The Palestinian Uprising* (Boulder, Colo.: Westview Press, 1990); Deborah J. Gerner, "Evolution of the Palestinian Uprising," *International Journal of Group Tensions* 20, 3 (Fall 1990): 233–65; and Gerner "Palestinians, Israelis, and the Intifada: The Third Year and Beyond," *Arab Studies Quarterly* 13, 3–4 (Fall–Winter 1991): 19–60.

29. "Arafat's Statement on Plans for Peace in the Middle East," *New York Times,* December 15, 1988.

30. "Yasir Arafat, text of press conference statement, Geneva, 14 December 1988," reprinted in *Journal of Palestine Studies* 18, 3 (Spring 1989): 181.

31. "A Gallup/IPS Survey Regarding the Conflict Between Israel and the Palestinians," *Journal of Palestine Studies* 19, 2 (Winter 1990): 75–86.

32. On September 28, 1991, during the twentieth meeting of the PNC, the leader of the Palestine Liberation Front, Abu Abbas, was removed from the PNC Executive Committee. At the time, Arafat expressed hope this would pave the way for a resumption of the U.S.-PLO dialogue. See Chris Hedges, "P.L.O. Drops Abu Abbas from Top Policy Council," *New York Times,* September 29, 1991, p. A10.

33. The political communiqué of the nineteenth PNC did call for a confederal relationship between the states of Palestine and Jordan, but only after Palestine had established itself as a fully independent state.

34. As of early 1992, it appeared that most of the diplomatic initiatives undertaken by the Soviet Union before December 1991 would be taken over by Russia.

35. *New Outlook* (December 1990–January 1991): 25; Joel Brinkley, "Rush of Soviet Immigrants to Israel," *New York Times,* July 2, 1991; and *Washington Report on Middle East Affairs* 10, 9 (April/May 1992): 2.

36. Joost R. Hiltermann, "Settling for War: Soviet Immigration and Israel's Settlement Policy in East Jerusalem," *Journal of Palestine Studies* 20, 2 (Winter 1991): 77.

37. "Baker Is Pressing Israelis on Peace," *New York Times,* March 2, 1990; *Washington Post,* March 6, 1990. A chronology of U.S. settlement policy is provided in Donald Neff, "Settlements and Guarantees: The U.S. Threatens Linkage, *Middle East International* 409 (September 27, 1991): 3–4.

38. "Baker's Tone on Jerusalem Softens," *New York Times,* March 31, 1990.

39. Nadav Shragai, "They Call It Expansion," *Ha'aretz,* July 13, 1990,

translated and reprinted in Israel Shahak, ed., *From the Hebrew Press: Monthly Translations and Commentaries from Israel* 2, 9 (September 1990): 28–32; Lily Galilee, "No Choice Housing," *Ha'aretz,* July 13, 1990, translated and reprinted in Shahak, ed., *From the Hebrew Press* 2, 10 (October 1990): 3–8.

40. See, for example, Shamir's comment that the Israeli pledge not to settle Jewish immigrants across the green line did not include East Jerusalem (*Jerusalem Post,* October 8, 1990) and his statement to Likud leaders that the ideal of Likud remained "a State of Israel between the sea and the Jordan River . . . for future generations and for the mass aliya" (*New York Times,* October 19, 1990; *Jerusalem Post,* November 18, 1990).

41. Richard H. Curtiss, "After Baker's Fourth Shuttle, Next Move Is Up to Bush," *Washington Report on Middle East Affairs* 10, 1 (May/June 1991): 89. This allocation was in addition to the more than $3 billion in economic and military aid that Israel receives from the United States each year.

42. Palestine Human Rights Information Center (Chicago/Jerusalem), *Human Rights Update: March 1991,* p. 36; Anat Tal-Shir and Ariela Ringel-Hoffman, "The Return of the Bulldozer," *Yediot Ahronot Friday Supplement,* April 19, 1991, translated and reprinted in *Al Fajir English Weekly,* April 22, 1991.

43. Thomas L. Friedman, "Baker Chides Israel on New Settlements," *New York Times,* May 23, 1991, p. A4.

44. Thomas L. Friedman, "Bush Backs Baker's Criticism of Israeli Settlements," *New York Times,* May 24, 1991, p. A4.

45. Richard H. Curtiss, "It's Lift-Off or Abort as Bush-Baker Initiative Nears Point of No Return," *Washington Report on Middle East Affairs* 10, 2 (July 1991): 7.

46. Donald Neff, "The Empty Ring to Bush's 'New World Order,'" *Middle East International* 396 (March 22, 1991): 3.

47. Thomas L. Friedman, "Israel Backs Plan for Single Session on Mideast Peace," *New York Times,* April 10, 1991.

48. "Palestinians Nationalists from the Occupied Territories, Memorandum to Secretary Baker, Jerusalem, 12 March 1991," reprinted in *Journal of Palestine Studies* 20, 4 (Summer 1991): 163–164.

49. Thomas L. Friedman, "Baker Going to Mideast Again with Compromise Proposals," *New York Times,* May 10, 1991.

50. Joel Brinkley, "Shamir, in Letter, Rejects Bush Plea," *New York Times,* June 8, 1991; and Joel Brinkley, "Israel Sets New Condition for Joining Peace Talks," *New York Times,* June 11, 1991.

51. Thomas L. Friedman, "Mideast Session Adjourns, with Prospects Uncertain for Second Phase of Talks," *New York Times,* November 2, 1991, p. A1.

52. Clyde Haberman, "Israel Re-Emphasizes Hard-Line Stance on Talks," *New York Times,* November 14, 1991, p. A4.

■ CHAPTER 21: U.S. INTERVENTION IN PERSPECTIVE

1. For an excellent discussion of containment, see John Lewis Gaddis, *Strategies of Containment: A Critical Appraisal of Post-War American National Security Policy* (New York: Oxford University Press, 1982).

2. See Thomas L. Friedman, "Bush to Press Congress to Approve $645 Million for Ex-Soviet Lands," *New York Times,* January 23, 1992, p. A1.

3. J. William Fulbright (with Seth P. Tillman), *The Price of Empire* (New York: Pantheon, 1989).

4. Kenneth E. Sharpe, "The Real Cause of Iran-Gate," *Foreign Policy,* no. 68 (Fall 1987): 19.

5. Morris J. Blachman and Kenneth E. Sharpe, "De-Democratizing American Foreign Policy: Dismantling the Post-Vietnam Formula," *Third World Quarterly* 8, 4 (October 1986): 1271.

6. For a good overview of the debate, see Francis D. Wormuth and Edwin B. Firmage, *To Chain the Dog of War: The War Power of Congress in History and Law* (Dallas, Tex.: Southern Methodist University Press, 1986).

7. Cited in Sharpe, "The Real Cause," p. 28. Sharpe notes, however, that Nixon's domestic covert activities had roots in previous administrations. See Frank J. Donner, *The Age of Surveillance* (New York: Vintage, 1981).

8. Sharpe, "The Real Cause," p. 35, summarizes nicely several of these views.

9. Morton H. Halperin, "Lawful Wars," *Foreign Policy,* no. 72 (Fall 1988): 173–91.

10. See ibid., pp. 187–91.

11. Ibid., pp. 193–95, 176.

12. Ibid., pp. 193–95.

13. For discussion, see Stephen Van Evera, "American Intervention in the Third World: Less Would Be Better," in Charles W. Kegley, Jr., and Eugene R. Wittkopf, eds., *The Future of American Foreign Policy* (New York: St. Martin's, 1992), pp. 290–1.

14. This is one of the major themes of Morris J. Blachman, William M. Leogrande, and Kenneth E. Sharpe, eds., *Confronting Revolution: Security Through Diplomacy in Central America* (New York: Pantheon, 1986). Quote from p. 304.

15. The discussion of El Salvador is drawn from ibid., esp. ch. 3.

16. Ibid., p. 304.

17. See Tim Golden, "Salvadorans Sign Treaty to End the War," *New York Times,* January 17, 1992, pp. A1, A5. See also Shirley Christian, "Salvadoran Chief and Rebels Reach Broad Agreement," *New York Times,* September 26, 1991, pp. A1, A8.

18. Quoted in Ted G. Carpenter, "The United States and Third World Dictatorships: A Case for Benign Detachment," Cato Institute Policy Analysis no. 58, August 15, 1987, p. 7.

19. Anthony Lake, "Wrestling with Radical Third World Regimes: Theory and Practice," in John W. Sewell, Richard E. Feinberg, and Valeriana Kallab, eds., *U.S. Foreign Policy and the Third World: Agenda 1985–86* (New Brunswick, N.J.: Transaction, 1985), p. 144.

20. The information contained in the following two paragraphs is part of a larger manuscript devoted to analyzing the evolution of U.S. foreign policy toward Africa. See Peter J. Schraeder, "Speaking with Many Voices: Continuity and Change in U.S. Foreign Policy Toward Africa During the Post–World War II Period," unpublished Ph.D. dissertation, University of South Carolina, Columbia, South Carolina, 1990.

21. See Paul Lewis, "U.N. Urges Soviet Pullout in Afghanistan," *New York Times,* November 11, 1987, p. A8.

22. For the various European positions concerning the Reagan Doctrine, see Evan Luard, "Western Europe and the Reagan Doctrine," *International Affairs* 63, 4 (Autumn 1987): 563–74.

23. See Christopher C. Joyner, "International Law," in Peter J. Schraeder,

ed., *Intervention in the 1980s: U.S. Foreign Policy in the Third World* (Boulder: Lynne Rienner, 1989), p. 203.

24. Clifford Krauss, "U.S. Plans to Aid Army in Peru to Fight Cocaine," *New York Times,* January 25, 1992, p. A4.

25. See Peter R. Andreas, Eva C. Bertran, Morris J. Blachman, and Kenneth E. Sharpe, "Dead-End Drug Wars," *Foreign Policy,* no. 85 (Winter 1991–92): 108.

26. House of Representatives, Committee on Government Operations, *U.S. Anti-Narcotics Activities in the Andean Region,* 101st Cong., 2nd Sess. (Washington, D.C.: Government Printing Office, 1990) (House Report 101–991, 18), cited in ibid. See also Elaine Sciolino, "World Drug Crop Up Sharply in 1989 Despite U.S. Effort," *New York Times,* March 2, 1990, pp. A1, A2.

27. Krauss, "U.S. Plans to Aid Army in Peru," p. A4.

28. This discussion of economic and military aid is taken from Blachman, Leogrande, and Sharpe, *Confronting Revolution,* ch. 14.

29. Ibid.

30. Ibid.

31. Michael T. Klare and Cynthia Arnson, *Supplying Repression: U.S. Support for Authoritarian Regimes Abroad* (Washington, D.C.: Institute for Policy Studies, 1981), p. 15.

32. See Charles Krauthammer, "The Unipolar Moment," *Foreign Affairs* 70 (1990–1991): 23–33.

33. Ted Galen Carpenter, "The New World Disorder," *Foreign Policy,* no. 84 (Fall 1991): 27–28.

34. For a good summary, see United Nations, *The Blue Helmets: A Review of United Nations Peace-Keeping* (New York: United Nations, 1991). See also Paul Lewis, "U.N.'s Fund Crisis Worsens as Role in Security Rises," *New York Times,* January 27, 1992, pp. A1, A5.

35. Joseph S. Nye, Jr., "Understanding U.S. Strength," *Foreign Policy,* no. 72 (Fall 1988): 106, 108.

Selected Bibliography

■ **CHAPTER 1: STUDYING U.S. INTERVENTION IN THE THIRD WORLD**

Barnet, Richard J. *Intervention and Revolution: The United States in the Third World,* rev. ed. New York: New American Library, 1980.

Berg, Robert J., and David F. Gordon, eds. *Cooperation for International Development: The United States and the Third World in the 1990s.* Boulder and London: Lynne Rienner, 1989.

Feinberg, Richard E. *The Intemperate Zone: The Third World Challenge to U.S. Foreign Policy.* New York: W. W. Norton, 1983.

Girling, John L. S. *America and the Third World: Revolution and Intervention.* London: Routledge and Kegan Paul, 1980.

Gurtov, Melvin, and Ray Maghroori. *Roots of Failure: United States Policy in the Third World.* Westport, Conn.: Greenwood, 1984.

Kegley, Charles W., Jr., and Eugene R. Wittkopf, eds. *The Future of American Foreign Policy.* New York: St. Martin's, 1992.

Kolko, Gabriel. *Confronting the Third World: United States Foreign Policy, 1945–1980.* New York: Pantheon, 1988.

Kwitny, Jonathan. *Endless Enemies: The Making of an Unfriendly World.* New York: Congdon and Weed, 1984.

Oye, Kenneth A., Richard J. Lieber, and Donald Rothchild, eds. *Eagle in a New World: American Grand Strategy in the Post–Cold War Era.* New York: Harper Collins, 1992.

Staniland, Martin, ed. *Falling Friends: The United States and Regime Change Abroad.* Boulder, Colo.: Westview, 1991.

■ **CHAPTER 2: THE EVOLUTION OF THE INTERVENTIONIST IMPULSE**

Beale, Howard K. *Theodore Roosevelt and the Rise of America to World Power.* Baltimore, Md.: Johns Hopkins University Press, 1956.

Gardner, Lloyd C. *A Covenant With Power: America and World Order from Wilson to Reagan.* New York: Oxford University Press, 1984.

Kahin, George. *Intervention: How America Became Involved in Vietnam.* New York: Knopf, 1986.

LaFeber, Walter F. *Inevitable Revolutions: The United States in Central America.* New York: W. W. Norton, 1986.

Limerick, Patricia Nelson. *The Legacy of Conquest: The Unbroken Past of the American West.* New York: W. W. Norton, 1987.

Mead, Walter Russell. *Mortal Splendor: The American Empire in Transition.* Boston: Houghton Mifflin, 1987.

Nash, Gary B. *The Urban Crucible: Social Change, Political Consciousness, and the Origins of the American Revolution.* Cambridge: Harvard University Press, 1979.

Schmidt, Hans. *Maverick Marine: General Smedley D. Butler and the*

Contradictions of American Military History. Lexington: University of Kentucky Press, 1987.

Van Alstyne, Richard W. *The Rising American Empire.* Chicago: Quadrangle Books, 1965.

Williams, William Appleman. *The Tragedy of American Diplomacy.* New York: World Publishing, 1959.

■ CHAPTER 3: THE DEVELOPMENT OF LOW-INTENSITY CONFLICT DOCTRINE

Barnett, Frank R., et al., eds. *Special Operations in U.S. Strategy.* Washington, D.C.: National Defense University Press, 1984.

Blaufarb, Douglas. *The Counterinsurgency Era: U.S. Doctrine and Performance.* New York: Free Press, 1977.

Kitson, Frank. *Low-Intensity Operations: Subversion, Insurgency, Peace-Keeping.* London: Faber, 1971.

Klare, Michael T. *War Without End: American Planning for the Next Vietnams.* New York: Knopf, 1972.

Klare, Michael T., and Peter Kornbluh, eds. *Low-Intensity Warfare: Counterinsurgency, Proinsurgency, and Antiterrorism in the Eighties.* New York: Pantheon, 1988.

Livingstone, Neil C. "Fighting Terrorism and 'Dirty Little Wars,'" in William A. Buckingham, Jr., ed., *Defense Planning for the 1980s.* Washington, D.C.: National Defense University Press, 1984.

Osgood, Robert E. *Limited War Revisited.* Boulder, Colo.: Westview Press, 1979.

Paschall, Rod. *LIC 2010: Special Operations and Unconventional Warfare in the Next Century* (final report of the CSIS Conventional Combat 2002 Project). Washington, D.C.: Brassey's, 1990.

Sarkesian, Sam C., and William L. Scully, eds. *U.S. Policy and Low-Intensity Conflict.* New Brunswick, N.J.: Transaction, 1987.

U.S. Department of Defense. *Proceedings of the Low-Intensity Warfare Conference.* National Defense University, Fort Lesley McNair, Washington, D.C., January 14–15, 1986. Washington, D.C.: Government Printing Office, 1986.

■ CHAPTER 4: THE GLOBALIST-REGIONALIST DEBATE

Bairoch, Paul. *The Economic Development of the Third World Since 1900.* Translated by Lady Cynthia Postan. Berkeley: University of California Press, 1975.

Doran, Charles F. *Domestic Conflict in State Relations: The American Sphere of Influence.* Beverly Hills, Calif.: Sage, 1976.

Doran, Charles F., George Modelski, and Cal Clark, eds. *North/South Relations: Studies in Dependency Reversal.* New York: Basic Books, 1975.

Gilpin, Robert. *U.S. Power and the Multinational Corporation: The Political Economy of Foreign Direct Investment.* New York: Basic Books, 1975.

Hansen, Roger D. *Beyond the North-South Stalemate.* New York: McGraw-Hill, 1979.

Hoffman, Stanley. *Primacy or World Order: American Foreign Policy Since the Cold War*. New York: McGraw-Hill, 1978.

Krasner, Stephen D. *Structural Conflict: The Third World Against Global Liberalism*. Berkeley: University of California Press, 1985.

Meier, Gerald M. *Leading Issues in Economic Development*. 4th ed. New York: Oxford University Press, 1984.

Rosecrance, Richard. *The Rise of the Trading State: Commerce and Conquest in the Modern World*. New York: Basic Books, 1986.

Shulman, Marshall D., ed. *East-West Tensions in the Third World*. New York: W. W. Norton, 1986.

■ CHAPTER 5: ECONOMIC AND MILITARY AID

Bandow, Doug, ed. *U.S. Aid to the Developing World: A Free Market Agenda*. Washington, D.C.: Heritage Foundation, 1985.

Bauer, P. T. *Equality, the Third World, and Economic Delusion*. Cambridge: Harvard University Press, 1981.

————. *Dissent on Development*. Cambridge: Harvard University Press, 1976.

Bovard, James. "The Continuing Failure of Foreign Aid." Cato Institute Policy Analysis no. 65, January 31, 1986.

Guess, George. *The Politics of United States Foreign Aid*. New York: St. Martin's, 1987.

Harberger, Arnold, ed. *World Economic Growth: Case Studies of Developed and Developing Nations*. San Francisco: Institute for Contemporary Studies, 1984.

Krauss, Melvyn. *Development Without Aid: Growth, Poverty and Government*. New York: McGraw-Hill, 1983.

Lal, Deepak. *The Poverty of "Development Economics."* London: The Institute of Economic Affairs, 1983.

Lappé, Frances, et al. *Betraying the National Interest*. New York: Grove Press, 1987.

Powelson, John, and Richard Stock. *The Peasant Betrayed: Agriculture and Land Reform in the Third World*. Boston: Oelgeschlager, Bunn, and Hain, 1987.

■ CHAPTER 6: ECONOMIC SANCTIONS

Adler-Karlsson, Gunnar. *Western Economic Warfare, 1947–67: A Case Study in Foreign Economic Policy*. Stockholm: Almqvist and Wiksell, 1966.

Baldwin, David A. *Economic Statecraft: Theory and Practice*. Princeton: Princeton University Press, 1985.

Barber, James. "Economic Sanctions as a Policy Instrument." *International Affairs* 55 (1979): 367–84.

Doxey, Margaret P. *International Sanctions in Contemporary Perspective*. New York: St. Martin's, 1987.

Hufbauer, Gary Clyde, Jeffrey J. Schott, and Kimberly Ann Elliott. *Economic Sanctions Reconsidered*, 2 vols. rev. Washington, D.C.: Institute for International Economics, 1990.

Knorr, Klaus. "International Economic Leverage and Its Uses." In Klaus Knorr and Frank Traeger, eds., *Economic Issues and National Security*. Lawrence, Kans.: Regents Press, 1977.

Leyton-Brown, David, ed. *The Utility of Economic Sanctions.* London: Croom Helm, 1987.

Losman, Donald L. *International Economic Sanctions: The Cases of Cuba, Israel, and Rhodesia.* Albuquerque: University of New Mexico Press, 1979.

Olson, Richard Stuart. "Economic Coercion in World Politics: With a Focus on North-South Relations." *World Politics* 31 (July 1979): 471–94.

Wallensteen, Peter. "Characteristics of Economic Sanctions." *Journal of Peace Research* 5, 3 (1968): 248–67.

■ CHAPTER 7: COVERT INTERVENTION

Constantinides, George C. *Intelligence and Espionage: An Annotated Bibliography.* Boulder, Colo.: Westview Press, 1983.

Draper, Theodore. *A Very Thin Line: The Iran-Contra Affair.* New York: Hill and Wang, 1991.

Dulles, Allen. *The Craft of Intelligence.* New York: Harper and Row, 1963.

Godson, Roy, ed. *Intelligence Requirements for the 1980s.* 7 vols. Washington, D.C.: National Strategy Information Center (vols. 1–5) and Lexington, Mass.: Lexington Books (vols. 6–7), 1979–1986.

Marchetti, Victor, and John D. Marks. *The CIA and the Cult of Intelligence.* New York: Dell Books, 1980.

Phillips, David Atlee. *The Night Watch: Twenty-Five Years of Peculiar Service.* New York: Atheneum, 1977.

Shulsky, Abram N. *Silent Warfare: Understanding the World of Intelligence.* Washington, D.C.: Brassey's, 1991.

Smith, Bradley F. *The Shadow Warriors: OSS and the Origins of the CIA.* New York: Basic Books, 1983.

Treverton, Gregory F. *Covert Action: The Limits of Intervention in the Postwar World.* New York: Basic Books, 1987.

Turner, Admiral Stansfield. *Secrecy and Democracy: The CIA in Transition.* Boston: Houghton Mifflin, 1985.

■ CHAPTER 8: PARAMILITARY INTERVENTION

Elliott, David, ed. *The Third Indochina Conflict.* Boulder, Colo.: Westview Press, 1986.

Harrison, Selig S. "Afghanistan: Soviet Intervention, Afghan Resistance, and the American Role." In Michael T. Klare and Peter Kornbluh, eds., *Low-Intensity Warfare: Counterinsurgency, Proinsurgency, and Antiterrorism in the Eighties.* New York: Pantheon, 1988.

Immerman, Richard H. *The CIA in Guatemala: The Foreign Policy of Intervention.* Austin: University of Texas Press, 1982.

Kirkpatrick, Jeane. *The Reagan Doctrine and U.S. Foreign Policy.* Washington, D.C.: Heritage Foundation, 1985.

Lake, Anthony, ed. *After the Wars: Reconstruction in Afghanistan, Indochina, Central America, Southern Africa, and the Horn of Africa.* Washington, D.C.: Overseas Development Council, 1990.

Luard, Evan. "Western Europe and the Reagan Doctrine." *International Affairs* 63, 4 (Autumn 1987): 563–74.

Peterzell, Jay. *Reagan's Secret Wars*. Washington, D.C.: Center for National Security Studies, 1984.

Prados, John. *Presidents' Secret Wars: CIA and Pentagon Covert Operations Since World War II*. New York: William Morrow, 1986.

Stockwell, John. *In Search of Enemies: A CIA Story*. New York: W. W. Norton, 1978.

Wyden, Peter. *Bay of Pigs: The Untold Story*. New York: Simon and Schuster, 1979.

■ CHAPTER 9:
DIRECT MILITARY INTERVENTION

Blechman, Barry M., and Stephen S. Kaplan, eds. *Force Without War: U.S. Armed Forces as a Political Instrument*. Washington, D.C.: Brookings, 1978.

Carpenter, Ted Galen, ed. *America Entangled: The Persian Gulf Crisis and Its Consequences*. Washington: Cato Institute, 1991.

Kahin, George M. *Intervention: How America Became Involved in Vietnam*. New York: Knopf, 1986.

Layne, Christopher. "Why the Gulf War Was Not in the National Interest." *Atlantic Monthly* (July 1991): 54, 65–81.

Lowenthal, Abraham F. *The Dominican Intervention*. Cambridge: Harvard University Press, 1972.

MacDonald, Callum. *Korea: The War Before Vietnam*. New York: Free Press, 1986.

Munro, Dana G. *Intervention and Dollar Diplomacy in the Caribbean, 1900–1921*. Princeton: Princeton University Press, 1964.

Quandt, William B. "Reagan's Lebanon Policy: Trial and Error." *Middle East Journal* 38 (Spring 1984): 237–54.

Rubner, Michael. "The Reagan Administration, the 1973 War Powers Resolution, and the Invasion of Grenada," *Political Science Quarterly* 100 (Winter 1985): 627–47.

Scheffer, David J. "Use of Force After the Cold War: Panama, Iraq, and the New World Order." In Louis Henkin, et al., *Right v. Might: International Law and the Use of Force*. 2d ed. New York: Council on Foreign Relations Press, 1991.

■ CHAPTER 10: THE DOMESTIC ENVIRONMENT

Barnet, Richard. *Roots of War: The Men and Institutions Behind U.S. Foreign Policy*. Baltimore: Penguin, 1972.

Destler, I. M., Leslie H. Gelb, and Anthony Lake. *Our Own Worst Enemy: The Unmaking of American Foreign Policy*. New York: Simon and Schuster, 1984.

Gelb, Leslie H., with Richard K. Betts. *The Irony of Vietnam: The System Worked*. Washington, D.C.: Brookings, 1979.

Halberstam, David. *The Best and the Brightest*. New York: Random House, 1971.

Hodgson, Godfrey. *America in Our Time*. New York: Vintage, 1976.

Holsti, Ole R., and James N. Rosenau. *American Leadership in World Affairs: Vietnam and the Breakdown of Consensus*. Boston: Allen and Unwin, 1984.

Melanson, Richard A. *Writing History and Making Policy: The Cold War, Vietnam, and Revisionism*. Lanham, Md.: University Press of America, 1983.

Rosati, Jerel A. *The Politics of United States Foreign Policy*. Dallas, Tex.: Harcourt Brace Jovanovich, 1993.

Schlesinger, Arthur, Jr. *The Imperial Presidency*. Boston: Houghton Mifflin, 1973.

Yergin, Daniel. *Shattered Peace: The Origins of the Cold War and the National Security State*. New York: Houghton Mifflin, 1978.

■ **CHAPTER 11: GOVERNMENT AND THE MILITARY ESTABLISHMENT**

Betts, Richard K. *Soldiers, Statesmen, and Cold War Crises*. Cambridge: Harvard University Press, 1977.

Cohen, Eliot A. "Constraints on America's Conduct of Small Wars." *International Security* 9, 2 (Fall 1984): 151–81.

Halperin, Morton H. *Bureaucratic Politics and Foreign Policy*. Washington, D.C.: Brookings, 1974.

Komer, Robert. *Bureaucracy Does Its Thing: Institutional Constraints on U.S.-G.V.N. Performance in Vietnam*. R-967-ARPA 1972. Santa Monica: Rand Corporation, 1973.

Kozak, David C., and James M. Keagle, eds. *Bureaucratic Politics and National Security: Theory and Practice*. Boulder, Colo.: Lynne Rienner, 1988.

Laird, Melvin R. "A Strong Start in a Difficult Decade: Defense Policy in the Nixon-Ford Years." *International Security* 10, 2 (Fall 1985): 5–26.

Luttwak, Edward. *The Pentagon and the Art of War*. New York: Simon and Schuster, 1985.

Ryan, Paul B. *The Iranian Rescue Mission*. Annapolis, Md.: Annapolis Naval Institute Press, 1985.

Summers, Colonel Harry. *On Strategy: A Critical Analysis of the Vietnam War*. New York: Dell Publishing, 1982.

Woodward, Bob. *The Commanders*. New York: Simon and Schuster, 1991.

■ **CHAPTER 12: THE STRUCTURE OF THE INTERNATIONAL SYSTEM**

FitzGerald, Frances. *Fire in the Lake: The Vietnamese and the Americans in Vietnam*. Boston: Little, Brown, 1972.

Garthoff, Raymond. *Detente and Confrontation: American-Soviet Relations From Nixon to Reagan*. Washington, D.C.: Brookings, 1985.

Griffith, William E. *Peking, Moscow, and Beyond: The Sino-Soviet Triangle*. Washington, D.C.: Center for Strategic Studies, 1973.

Kedourie, Elie. *Islam in the Modern World*. New York: Holt, Rinehart, and Winston, 1980.

Kennedy, Paul. *The Rise and Fall of the Great Powers: Economic Change and Military Conflict from 1500 to 2000*. New York: Random House, 1987.

Keohane, Robert O. *After Hegemony: Cooperation and Discord in the World Political Economy*. Princeton: Princeton University Press, 1984.

Klare, Michael T., and Daniel C. Thomas, eds. *World Security: Trends and Challenges at Century's End.* New York: St. Martin's, 1991.

Linder, S. B. *The Pacific Century.* Stanford: Stanford University Press, 1986.

Mazrui, Ali A., and Michael Tidy. *Nationalism and New States in Africa from About 1935 to the Present.* London: Heinemann, 1985.

Oye, Kenneth A. "International Systems Structure and American Foreign Policy." In Kenneth A. Oye, Robert J. Lieber, and Donald Rothchild, eds., *Eagle Defiant: United States Foreign Policy in the 1980s.* Boston: Little, Brown, 1983.

■ CHAPTER 13: INTERNATIONAL LAW

Bemis, Samuel F. *The Latin American Policy of the United States: An Historical Interpretation.* New York: Harcourt Brace, 1943.

Dinerstein, Herbert S. *Intervention Against Communism.* Baltimore: Johns Hopkins University Press, 1967.

Falk, Richard A., ed. *The Vietnam War and International Law.* Princeton: Princeton University Press, vol. 1, 1968; vol. 2, 1969; vol. 3, 1972; vol. 4, 1976.

Hart, Albert A. *The Monroe Doctrine: An Interpretation.* Boston: Little, Brown, 1916.

Lillich, Richard B., ed. *Humanitarian Intervention and the United Nations.* Charlottesville: University of Virginia Press, 1973.

Miller, Linda B. *World Order and Local Disorder: The United Nations and Local Conflicts.* Princeton: Princeton University Press, 1967.

Moore, John Norton, ed. *Law and Civil War in the Modern World.* Baltimore: Johns Hopkins University Press, 1974.

Perkins, Dexter. *A History of the Monroe Doctrine.* Boston: Little, Brown, 1955.

Thomas, A. J., and Ann Thomas. *Non-Intervention: The Law and Its Import in the Americas.* Dallas: Southern Methodist University Press, 1956.

Vincent, R. J. *Nonintervention and International Order.* Princeton: Princeton University Press, 1974.

■ CHAPTER 14: SOUTH AFRICA

Baker, Pauline H. *The United States and South Africa: The Reagan Years.* New York: Foreign Policy Association, 1989.

Carter, Gwendolen M. *Continuity and Change in Southern Africa.* Los Angeles: Crossroads, 1985.

Davis, R. Hunt, Jr., ed. *Apartheid Unravels.* Gainesville: University of Florida Press, 1991.

Davis, Stephen M. *Apartheid's Rebels: Inside South Africa's Hidden War.* New Haven: Yale University Press, 1987.

Fatton, Robert. *Black Consciousness in South Africa.* Albany: State University of New York Press, 1986.

Hanlon, Joseph. *Beggar Your Neighbours: Apartheid Power in South Africa.* Bloomington: Indiana University Press, 1986.

Jackson, Henry F. *From the Congo to Soweto: U.S. Foreign Policy Toward Africa Since 1960.* New York: Quill, 1984.

Johns, Sheridan, and R. Hunt Davis, Jr., eds. *Mandela, Tambo, and the African*

National Congress: The Struggle Against Apartheid, 1948–1990. New York and Oxford: Oxford University Press, 1991.

Study Commission on U.S. Policy Toward South Africa. *South Africa: Time Running Out.* Berkeley: University of California Press, 1981.

Wilson, Francis, and Mamphela Ramphele. *Uprooting Poverty: The South African Challenge.* New York: W. W. Norton, 1989.

■ CHAPTER 15: THE PHILIPPINES

Bain, David Howard. *Sitting in Darkness: Americans in the Philippines.* Boston: Houghton Mifflin, 1984.

Bonner, Raymond. *Waltzing with a Dictator: The Marcoses and the Making of American Policy.* New York: Times Books, 1987.

Johnson, Bryan. *The Four Days of Courage: The Untold Story of the People Who Brought Marcos Down.* New York: Free Press, 1987.

Karnow, Stanley. *In Our Image: America's Empire in the Philippines.* New York: Ballantine, 1989.

Lande, Carl H., ed. *Rebuilding a Nation, Philippine Challenges and American Policy.* Washington, D.C.: Washington Institute Press, 1987.

Miller, Stuart Creighton. *"Benevolent Assimilation": The American Conquest of the Philippines, 1899–1903.* New Haven: Yale University Press, 1982.

Pringle, Robert. *Indonesia and the Philippines: American Interests in Island Southeast Asia.* New York: Columbia University Press, 1980.

Rosenberg, David A., ed. *Marcos and Martial Law in the Philippines.* Ithaca: Cornell University Press, 1979.

Shalom, Stephen R. *The United States and the Philippines, A Study of Neocolonialism.* Philadelphia: Institute for the Study of Human Issues, 1981.

Thompson, W. Scott, *Unequal Partners: Philippine and Thai Relations with the United States, 1965–75.* Lexington, Mass.: Lexington Books, 1975.

■ CHAPTER 16: NICARAGUA

Bermann, Karl. *Under the Big Stick: Nicaragua and the United States Since 1848.* Boston: South End Press, 1987.

Blachman, Morris J., William M. Leogrande, and Kenneth E. Sharpe, eds. *Confronting Revolution: Security Through Diplomacy in Central America.* New York: Pantheon, 1986.

Booth, John. *The End and the Beginning: The Nicaraguan Revolution.* Boulder, Colo.: Westview Press, 1982.

Dickey, Christopher. *With the Contras.* New York: Simon and Schuster, 1985.

Gutman, Roy. *Banana Diplomacy: The Making of U.S. Policy in Nicaragua, 1981–1987.* New York: Simon and Schuster, 1988.

Kornbluh, Peter, and Malcolm Byne, eds. *The Iran-Contra Affair: The Making of a Scandal, 1983–1988.* Washington, D.C.: National Security Archive, Chadwyck-Healey, 1990.

———. *Nicaragua: The Making of U.S. Policy, 1978–1990.* Washington, D.C.: National Security Archive, Chadwyck-Healey, 1991.

Millett, Richard. *Guardians of the Dynasty: A History of the U.S.-Created Guardia Nacional and the Somoza Family.* Maryknoll, N.Y.: Orbis Books, 1977.

Pastor, Robert. *Condemned to Repetition: The United States and Nicaragua.* Princeton: Princeton University Press, 1987.
Walker, Thomas, ed. *Reagan vs. the Sandinistas: The Undeclared War on Nicaragua.* Boulder, Colo.: Westview Press, 1987.

■ CHAPTER 17: IRAN

Abrahamian, Ervand. *Iran Between Two Revolutions.* Princeton: Princeton University Press, 1982.
Bill, James A. *The Eagle and the Lion: The Tragedy of American-Iranian Relations.* New Haven: Yale University Press, 1988.
Cottam, Richard. *Iran and the United States: A Cold War Case Study.* Pittsburgh: University of Pittsburgh Press, 1988.
Gasiorowski, Mark J. *U.S. Foreign Policy and the Shah: Building a Client State in Iran.* Ithaca, N.Y.: Cornell University Press, 1991.
Halliday, Fred. *Iran: Dictatorship and Development.* New York: Penguin Books, 1979.
Hooglund, Eric. *Land and Revolution in Iran, 1960–1980.* Austin: University of Texas Press, 1982.
Ioannides, Christos. *America's Iran: Injury and Catharsis.* Lanham, Md.: University Press of America, 1984.
Keddie, Nikki, and Eric Hooglund, eds. *The Iranian Revolution and the Islamic Republic.* Syracuse: Syracuse University Press, 1986.
Ramazani, R. K. *Revolutionary Iran: Challenge and Response in the Middle East.* Baltimore: Johns Hopkins University Press, 1987.
Sick, Gary. *All Fall Down: America's Tragic Encounter with Iran.* New York: Random House, 1985.

■ CHAPTER 18: THE PERSIAN GULF

Acharya, Amitav. *U.S. Military Strategy in the Gulf.* London: Routledge, 1989.
Davies, Charles, ed. *After The War: Iran, Iraq, and the Arab Gulf.* Chichester: Carden Publications, 1990.
Farouk-Sluglett, Marion, and Peter Sluglett. *Iraq Since 1958.* London: I. B. Tauris, 1990.
Joyner, Christopher C., ed. *The Persian Gulf War: Lessons for Strategy, Law, and Diplomacy.* Westport, Conn.: Greenwood, 1990.
Keddie, Nikki, and Mark Gasiorowski, eds. *Neither East nor West: Iran, the Soviet Union, and the United States.* New Haven: Yale University Press, 1990.
McNaugher, Thomas. *Arms and Oil: U.S. Military Strategy and the Persian Gulf.* Washington: The Brookings Institution, 1985.
Mofid, Kamran. *The Economic Consequences of the Gulf War.* London: Routledge, 1990.
Quandt, William B. *Saudi Arabia in the 1980s: Foreign Policy, Security, and Oil.* Washington, D.C.: The Brookings Institution, 1981.
Schofield, Richard. *Kuwait and Iraq: Historical Claims and Territorial Disputes.* London: Royal Institute of International Affairs, 1991.
Stork, Joe. *Middle East Oil and the Energy Crisis.* New York: Monthly Review, 1975.

■ CHAPTER 19: PANAMA

Conniff, Michael. *Panama and the United States: The Forced Alliance*. Athens: University of Georgia Press, 1992.
Dinges, John. *Our Man in Panama: How General Noriega Used the United States—and Made Millions in Drugs and Arms*. Rev. ed. New York: Random House, 1991.
Furlong, William L., and Margaret E. Scranton. *The Dynamics of Foreign Policymaking: The President, the Congress, and the Panama Canal Treaties*. Boulder, Colo.: Westview, 1984.
LaFeber, Walter. *The Panama Canal: The Crisis in Historical Perspective*. Rev. ed. New York: Oxford University Press, 1990.
McCullough, David. *The Path Between the Seas*. New York: Simon and Schuster, 1977.
Pippin, Larry LaRae. *The Remón Era: An Analysis of a Decade of Events in Panama*. Stanford, Calif.: Institute of Hispanic American and Luso Brazilian Studies, 1964.
Ropp, Steve C. *Panamanian Politics: From Guarded Nation to National Guard*. New York: Praeger, 1982.
Sánchez, Guillermo, and Richard Koster. *In the Time of the Tyrants*. New York: Norton, 1990.
Scranton, Margaret E. *The Noriega Years: U.S.-Panamanian Relations, 1981–1990*. Boulder, Colo.: Lynne Rienner, 1991.
U.S. Senate. Committee on Foreign Relations. *Background Documents Relating to the Panama Canal*. Committee Print, 95th Congress, 1st session, November 1977. Washington, D.C.: Government Printing Office, 1977.

■ CHAPTER 20: THE ARAB-ISRAELI CONFLICT

Curtiss, Richard H. *A Changing Image: American Perceptions of the Arab-Israeli Dispute*. 2nd ed. Washington, D.C.: American Educational Trust, 1986.
Green, Stephen. *Living by the Sword: America and Israel in the Middle East*. Brattleboro, Vt: Amana Books, 1988.
Khouri, Fred J. *The Arab-Israeli Dilemma*. 3rd ed. Syracuse, N.Y.: Syracuse University Press, 1985.
Lenczowski, George. *American Presidents and the Middle East*. Durham, N.C.: Duke University Press, 1990.
Lukacs, Yehuda, ed. *The Israeli-Palestinian Conflict: A Documentary Record*. New York: Cambridge University Press, 1992.
Quandt, William B. *Camp David: Peacemaking and Politics*. Washington, D.C.: The Brookings Institution, 1986.
———. *Decade of Decisions: American Policy Toward the Arab-Israeli Conflict, 1967–1976*. Berkeley and Los Angeles: University of California Press, 1977.
Rubenberg, Cheryl A. *Israel and the American National Interest: A Critical Examination*. Chicago: University of Illinois Press, 1986.
Suleiman, Michael W., ed. *America and the Palestinians: A Special Issue of Arab Studies Quarterly* 12, 1–2 (Winter–Spring 1990).
Tschirgi, Dan. *The American Search for Mideast Peace*. New York and London: Praeger, 1989.

■ CHAPTER 21: U.S. INTERVENTION IN PERSPECTIVE

Andreas, Peter R., Eva C. Bertram, Morris J. Blachman, and Kenneth E. Sharpe. "Dead-End Drug Wars." *Foreign Policy*, no. 85 (Winter 1991–92): 106–28.

Blachman, Morris J., and Kenneth E. Sharpe. "De-Democratizing American Foreign Policy: Dismantling the Post-Vietnam Formula." *Third World Quarterly* 8, 4 (October 1986): 1271–1308.

Carpenter, Ted Galen. "The New World Disorder." *Foreign Policy*, no. 84 (Fall 1991): 24–39.

Fulbright, J. William (with Seth P. Tillman). *The Price of Empire.* New York: Pantheon, 1989.

Krauthammer, Charles. "The Unipolar Moment." *Foreign Affairs* 70 (1990–1991): 23–33.

Lake, Anthony. "Wrestling with Third World Radical Regimes: Theory and Practice." In John W. Sewell, Richard E. Feinberg, and Valeriana Kallab, eds., *U.S. Foreign Policy and the Third World: Agenda 1985–86.* New Brunswick, N.J.: Transaction, 1985.

Parry, Robert, and Peter Kornbluh. "Iran-Contra's Untold Story." *Foreign Policy*, no. 72 (Fall 1988): 3–30.

Rubin, Barry. *Modern Dictators: Third World Coup Makers, Strongmen, and Populist Tyrants.* New York: McGraw-Hill, 1987.

Sharpe, Kenneth E., et al. "Security Through Diplomacy: A Policy of Principled Realism." In Morris J. Blachman, William M. Leogrande, and Kenneth E. Sharpe, eds., *Confronting Revolution: Security Through Diplomacy in Central America.* New York: Pantheon, 1986.

United Nations, *The Blue Helmets: A Review of United Nations Peace-Keeping.* New York: United Nations, 1991.

About the Contributors

DOUG BANDOW is a nationally syndicated columnist for the Copley News Service and a senior fellow at the Cato Institute. He served from 1981 to 1982 as a special assistant to President Reagan, where he handled military manpower and international development issues. The author and coeditor of several books, including *U.S. Aid to the Developing World: A Free Market Agenda* (1985), he is currently writing a book on the U.S. defense commitment to South Korea. He has written for *Foreign Policy, National Interest, Orbis*, and many other publications.

TED GALEN CARPENTER is director of foreign policy studies at the Cato Institute. An expert on defense and foreign policy issues, his work has appeared in the *Wall Street Journal*, the *New York Times, Harper's, Foreign Policy, The National Interest*, and other publications. His most recent book, *A Search for Enemies: America's Alliances After the Cold War* (forthcoming 1992), examines the evolution of alliance patterns in the post–Cold War era.

STEPHEN DAGGETT is a specialist in national defense at the Congressional Research Service of the Library of Congress. He has written extensively on the U.S. military budget and defense policy planning process. His work has appeared in *Foreign Policy, Arms Control Today*, and the *American Defense Annual*, as well as in various military publications.

R. HUNT DAVIS, JR., is professor of history and former director of the Center for African Studies at the University of Florida. From 1980 until 1988 he served as editor of the *African Studies Review*. He is author of *Bantu Education and the Education of South Africans in South Africa* (1972), editor of *Apartheid Unravels* (1991), and coeditor of *Mandela, Tambo, and the African National Congress: The Struggle Against Apartheid, 1948–1990* (1991).

CHARLES F. DORAN is Andrew W. Mellon Professor of International Relations at the Johns Hopkins School of Advanced International Studies and the author of more than sixty scholarly articles and books on international politics and political economy. His research

467

encompasses security policy; domestic and interstate conflict; and commercial, environmental, and energy resource questions. His most recent books include *Systems in Crisis: New Imperatives of High Politics at Century's End* (1991) and *The Gulf, Energy, and Global Security: Political and Economic Issues* (1991).

KIMBERLY A. ELLIOTT is research associate for the Institute for International Economics in Washington, D.C. She has coauthored several studies on the roles of trade and sanctions in U.S. foreign policy, including *Trade Protection in the United States: 31 Case Studies* (1986) and *Economic Sanctions Reconsidered* (1990).

LLOYD C. GARDNER is Charles and Mary Beard Professor of History at Rutgers University, where he specializes in the history of U.S. foreign policy. His most recent books include *A Covenant with Power: America and the World from Wilson to Reagan* (1984), *Safe for Democracy: The Anglo-American Response to Revolution 1913 to 1923* (1984), and *Approaching Vietnam: From World War II Through Dienbienphu* (1988).

DEBORAH J. GERNER is associate professor of political science at the University of Kansas, specializing in international relations, foreign policy decisionmaking, and Middle East politics. Her research is informed by frequent trips to the region, particularly to Israel and Palestine. She is the author of *One Land, Two Peoples: The Conflict over Palestine* (1991) and numerous articles on the Arab-Israeli conflict, the Palestinian intifada, and U.S. foreign policy toward the Middle East.

ERIC HOOGLUND is senior editor of *Middle East Journal* and a research associate at the Center for Middle Eastern Studies at the University of California, Berkeley. He has taught Middle East politics and U.S. foreign policy at several universities. His major works include *Land and Revolution in Iran, 1960–1980* (1982), *The Iranian Revolution and the Islamic Republic* (1986), and *Crossing the Waters: Arabic-Speaking Immigrants to the United States Before 1940* (1987).

CHRISTOPHER C. JOYNER is professor in the department of political science at the George Washington University. Specializing in international law and world politics, he is the author of numerous articles on the international legal implications of U.S. intervention in the Third World. His works also include *The Antarctic Legal Regime* (1988), *The Persian Gulf War* (1990), and the upcoming *Antarctica and the Law of the Sea*.

RICHARD J. KESSLER is a professional staff member of the Senate Committee on Foreign Relations. He has made numerous trips to the Philippines, has served as a visiting research fellow at the University of the Philippines, and has published numerous articles on U.S. foreign policy toward Asia and the Philippines.

MICHAEL T. KLARE is director and associate professor of the Five College Program in Peace and World Security Studies based at Hampshire College. He is the defense correspondent of *The Nation* and author of numerous articles on U.S. military policy. His books include *Beyond the "Vietnam Syndrome"* (1981), *American Arms Supermarket* (1985), and the coedited *Low-Intensity Warfare: Counterinsurgency, Proinsurgency, and Antiterrorism in the Eighties* (1988).

PETER KORNBLUH is a senior analyst at the National Security Archive in Washington, D.C. where he specializes in U.S. policy toward Latin America. He is the author of *Nicaragua: The Price of Intervention* (1987), coeditor of *Low-Intensity Warfare: Counterinsurgency, Proinsurgency, and Antiterrorism in the Eighties* (1988) and *The Iran-Contra Affair: The Making of a Scandal, 1983–1988* (1990), and editor of *Nicaragua: The Making of U.S. Policy, 1978–1990* (1991).

HARRY PIOTROWSKI is professor in the History Department at Towson State University. His specialty is the history of U.S.-Soviet foreign policy, especially as it pertains to the Third World. His most recent work is the coauthored *The World Since 1945: A History of International Relations* (1990). He is currently working on a study of the origins of the Cold War.

HARRY HOWE RANSON is professor emeritus of political science at Vanderbilt University. A noted scholar of foreign and defense policymaking and strategic intelligence, he has written numerous articles and books, including *The Intelligence Establishment* (1970), *Can American Democracy Survive Cold War?* (1963), and *Central Intelligence and National Security* (1958).

JEREL A. ROSATI is associate professor in the Department of Government and International Studies at the University of South Carolina. His area of specialization is the theory and practice of foreign policy, with an emphasis on the study of U.S. foreign policy. He is the author of *The Carter Administration's Quest for Global Community: Beliefs and Their Impact on Behavior* (1987) and *The Politics of United States Foreign Policy* (forthcoming 1993). He is currently working on *Foreign Policy Restructuring: How Countries Respond to Change*.

PETER J. SCHRAEDER, the editor of this volume, is assistant professor in the Department of Political Science at Loyola University of Chicago, where he specializes in international relations theory, comparative politics of the developing areas, and U.S. foreign policy, especially as all three relate to Africa. He has lectured and carried out research in Benin, Burundi, Djibouti, Ghana, Kenya, Mozambique, Rwanda, Sierra Leone, and Somalia. He is the author or coauthor of several books and articles, including *Djibouti* (1991), *Intervention in the 1980s: U.S. Foreign Policy in the Third World* (1989), *Somalia* (1988), and *Cameroon* (1986). His most recent work, *Speaking with Many Voices: Continuity and Change in U.S. Foreign Policy Toward Africa During the Post–World War II Period,* offers a historically informed theoretical analysis of U.S. Africa policies.

MARGARET E. SCRANTON is associate professor of political science at the University of Arkansas at Little Rock, where she specializes in international politics and U.S.-Panamanian relations. In 1981 she received the American Political Science Association's Helen Dwight Reid Award for the best doctoral dissertation in the field of international relations law and politics. Her publications include *The Noriega Years: U.S.-Panamanian Relations, 1981–1990* (1991) and the coauthored *The Dynamics of Foreign Policymaking: The President, the Congress, and the Panama Canal Treaties* (1984). Her current research focuses on Panama's National Civic Crusade and the *civilista* opposition movement.

Index

abatement theory, 236
Acheson, Dean, 24, 32–34, 214, 305
Abrams, Elliott, 296, 347
Adams, Henry, 28
Aden, 324
Aden Protectorate, 322
Additional Protocol Relative to Non-Intervention, 230; Article 1, 230
Afghanistan, 70, 215, 219; Bush administration and, 140; civil war, 6, 403; compared to Cambodia, 143; Reagan administration and, 122, 131, 140, 238; Soviet Union and, 44, 45, 116, 137, 141, 150, 189, 228, 331, 332; U.S. paramilitary intervention and, 48, 137–41, 146, 149, 150, 151, 238, 385, 396
African American Labor Center, 265
African National Congress (ANC), 256, 260, 262, 264, 266
Afrikaner, 247, 249, 253, 256, 259, 262, 264
Agency for International Development (AID), 76, 84, 86, 89, 180, 281
Agnew, Spiro, 273
Aguinaldo, Emiliano, 31
Air War College, 50
Akhunzada, Nasim, 140
Alamo, 27
Alaska Purchase, 28–29
Albania, 60, 209; U.S. paramilitary intervention and, 132
Algeria, 212
Algerian National Liberation Front, 225
Algiers Agreement, 309
Algiers Treaty, 311, 327
Allende, Salvador, 43, 98, 100, 119, 290, 293
Alliance for Progress, 77
Allied Pacific Printing, 121
Alvor Agreement, 135, 147
American Civil War, 28–29
American Colonies, 55, 57
American Committee on Africa (ACOA), 257
American-Cuban Treaty, 30

American Enterprise Institute, 188
American Federation of Labor-Congress for Industrial Organization (AFL-CIO), 181
American Friends Service Committee (AFSC), 257
American Indians, 24, 29,
American Revolution, 23, 25, 28, 34
Amin, Idi, 107
Amnesty International, 64
Andean Initiative, 153, 398
Andes, 398
Anglo-Iranian Oil Company (AIOC), 305, 322
Angola, 212, 226, 228, 252, 404; Bush administration and, 144, 145, 146, 147; civil war, 6, 10, 44, 136, 220, 403; colonialism and, 251; Cuba and, 44; Ford administration and, 131, 137, 147, 186, 258; Reagan administration and, 144, 145, 146, 147; U.S. paramilitary intervention and, 48, 122, 131, 135, 144–47, 149, 150, 151, 238, 385; U.S. sanctions and, 97, 106, 250
Angola Accord, 145, 228
Annapolis, 23
Antarctic Circle, 31
Anti-Drug Abuse Act, 351
apartheid, 106, 147, 247–267, 402
appeasement, 177, 227, 242
Aquino, Benigno, 271, 275, 278
Aquino, Corazon Cojuangco, 269, 271, 272, 279–82, 283
Arab-American Oil Company (ARAMCO), 325
Arabian Sea, 322
Arab-Israeli conflict, 362–82. *See also* Israel *and* Palestine.
Arafat, Yasir, 373, 374
Arab League, 371, 372
Arbenz Guzman, Jacobo, 292
Argentina, 111, 225; potential nuclear capability, 7; U.S. sanctions and, 98, 100, 101, 104, 105
Arias, Oscar, 220, 396
Arias plan, 220, 299
Armas, Castillo, 132

471

About the Book

The geographical realm of U.S. intervention in the Third World has evolved from the Western Hemisphere focus of the Monroe Doctrine during the nineteenth century to the worldwide embrace of the Bush administration's "new world order" as the twentieth century draws to a close. As U.S. policymakers continue to grapple with the necessity of formulating Third World policies to successfully guide the United States into the emerging post–Cold War era, the time seems ripe for a critical assessment of past U.S. interventionist practices in the countries of Latin America, Asia, the Middle East, and Africa.

This volume provides a comprehensive overview and analysis of the origins, tools, and constraints of U.S. policy in the Third World. Five themes serve as the guiding principles of the book: the overemphasis in U.S. foreign policy on what has been called the "globalist" perspective; the desirability of greater emphasis on the "regionalist" perspective; the increasing nonviability of military force in achieving long-term U.S. foreign policy objectives; the inability of the United States to control Third World nationalism; and the need for greater U.S. tolerance of social change in the Third World.

This revised edition of *Intervention in the 1980s* includes new material on:

- Bush administration policy
- The impact of the end of the Cold War
- U.S. military intervention in Panama and Iraq
- Events in Iran, the Philippines, Nicaragua, and South Africa
- Additional case studies covering Panama, the Persian Gulf, and the Arab-Israeli conflict